SCIENCE INSTRUCTION IN THE MIDDLE AND SECONDARY SCHOOLS

Fourth Edition

EUGENE L. CHIAPPETTA
University of Houston

THOMAS R. KOBALLA, JR.
University of Georgia

ALFRED T. COLLETTE
Syracuse University

Merrill,
an imprint of Prentice Hall
Upper Saddle River, New Jersey   *Columbus, Ohio*

Library of Congress Cataloging-in-Publication Data
Chiappetta, Eugene L.
    Science instruction in the middle and secondary schools/
Eugene L. Chiappetta, Thomas R. Koballa, Jr., Alfred T. Collette.
—4th ed.
      p. cm.
    Collette's name appears first on the earlier edition;
Koballa's name does not appear on earlier edition.
    Includes bibliographical references and index.
    ISBN 0-13-651118-X (alk. paper)
    1. Science—Study and teaching (Secondary)—United
States. I. Koballa, Thomas R. II. Collette, Alfred T. III Title.
    Q183.3.A1C637 1998
    507'.1'273—dc21   97-14717
                                         CIP

Cover photo: © David Young-Wolff/Photo Edit
Editor: Bradley J. Potthoff
Production Editor: Alexandrina Benedicto Wolf
Design Coordinator: Julia Zonneveld Van Hook
Text Designer: Mia Saunders
Cover Designer: Thomas Mack
Production Manager: Pamela D. Bennett
Electronic Text Management: Marilyn Wilson Phelps, Matthew
    Williams, Karen L. Bretz, Tracey B. Ward
Director of Marketing: Kevin Flanagan
Marketing Manager: Suzanne Stanton
Advertising/Marketing Coordinator: Julie Shough

This book was set in Berkeley Old Style and Zapf Humanist by
Prentice Hall and was printed and bound by Courier/Kendall-
ville, Inc. The cover was printed by Phoenix Color Corp.

Earlier editions, © 1994 by Macmillan Publishing; 1989, 1986
by Merrill Publishing Company.

Photo credits: pp. 2, 17, 22, 31, 44, 56, 60, 74, 93, 100, 110,
120, 134, 138, 151, 160, 182, 196, 199, 208, 216, 217, 223,
236, 245, 258, 262, 267, 286, 296, 312, 318, 319, 330, 350,
351, 356, 366, and 372 by the Authors; p. 13 Courtesy of
Lyndon B. Johnson Space Center; and p. 164 Courtesy of
National Aeronautic and Space Administration.

Printed in the United States of America

10 9 8 7 6 5 4 3 2 1

ISBN: 0-13-651118-X

Prentice-Hall International (UK) Limited, *London*
Prentice-Hall of Australia Pty. Limited, *Sydney*
Prentice-Hall of Canada, Inc., *Toronto*
Prentice-Hall Hispanoamericana, S. A., *Mexico*
Prentice-Hall of India Private Limited, *New Delhi*
Prentice-Hall of Japan, Inc., *Tokyo*
Simon & Schuster Asia Pte. Ltd., *Singapore*
Editora Prentice-Hall do Brasil, Ltda., *Rio de Janeiro*

To the science educators who made significant contributions to this text through their research, scholarship, and suggestions and to the members of the science teaching profession who are graduates of our respective science education programs

■

PREFACE

Science Instruction in the Middle and Secondary Schools is intended to help science teachers prepare students to become scientifically and technologically literate in order for them to lead a productive life in a sophisticated biotechnological, electronic, and communication era. This goal presents a tremendous challenge for science teachers because of the fundamental understanding that students must acquire concerning science, mathematics, and technology, and because of the dynamic nature of the American society with its cultural diversity and ongoing social changes. In addition, there are too many students reporting that science courses are difficult and uninteresting. It is also the case that some segments of our society are not only underrepresented in science and engineering professions but are receiving a less than adequate science education.

In response to the present situation in science education, a national science education reform movement is underway in America. Two foci of the reform emphasize that science is for all students and that learning science is an active process. Another focus is the teacher. We believe that science teachers must consider many facets of science teaching in order to provide science courses that meet students' needs and help them to appreciate science and technology. Teachers must understand the nature of science and technology and possess a strong content background. They must also understand how students learn and be able to ascertain what knowledge and skills students possess when they enter the classroom. Teachers must be able to use a variety of instructional strategies to help students represent knowledge and find meaning in it. Furthermore, science teachers

must be able to develop alternative and authentic assessment programs that address many learning outcomes in order to determine student achievement. Finally, science teachers should become active in local, state, and national professional organizations so that they continue to stay up-to-date and grow professionally.

New features have been added to the fourth edition. Open cases can be found near the beginning of many chapters. "Stop and Reflect" exercises have been placed at the end of certain sections within each chapter. "Resources to Examine" are at the end of each chapter. Little science puzzlers, science demonstrations, and science laboratory activities can be found in the appendixes. These features are described below.

Use of This Text

Those who use this methods textbook should use it interactively. Exactly how it will be used must be in accord with the instructor's own background and expertise in science and science teaching. In some instances the book may be used to introduce concepts or ideas that are later expanded upon through class discussion, teacher demonstration, or laboratory activities. Here the book serves as the students' first contact with understandings critical to their success as future teachers. At other times the book may be used to provide students with additional information regarding an important idea or teaching practice after it is introduced in class. Here the book functions to reinforce and strengthen the understandings introduced by the instructor. By no means should this book be viewed as the sole and definitive source on science teaching and learning.

Features of the Text

Science Instruction in the Middle and Secondary Schools has many unique and useful features. Of particular interest are vignettes and open cases that highlight particular teaching situations. These offer wonderful opportunities for students to critique and reflect on real-life classroom experiences. A feature called "Stop and Reflect" appears frequently in most chapters to help students review and construct meaningful understandings from what they have read. These segments in the textbook will further assist methods course instructors to use the text interactively.

Many activities are described in the text to highlight important teaching methods and aspects of science learning. In addition, many science activities are described in the appendixes for methods course instructors and their students to use. These activities are grouped as science puzzlers (Appendix A), science demonstrations (Appendix B), and science laboratory exercises (Appendix C). At the end of each chapter, an "Assessing and Reviewing" section includes activities and questions that may be used during class or assigned for homework. A section new to this fourth edition called "Resources to Examine" provides information about additional readings, activities, and science teaching materials that we believe all science teachers should have for their professional development.

This methods textbook is the result of more than forty-five years of science education experience. During these years, many changes have occurred in the profession. Nevertheless, other aspects have remained the same. Science teachers who are knowledgeable and enthusiastic about their work and who make science rel-evant and interesting seem to produce positive results through their teaching. We have tried to emphasize in this textbook what effective science teachers have always displayed in their teaching as well as to incorporate new research findings.

ACKNOWLEDGMENTS

Many people contributed to this textbook, both to this edition and to past editions. We very much appreciate them. We would especially like to thank the following individuals for their contributions to the fourth edition: April Adams, Spring Woods High School; Jill Bailer, Jane Long Middle School; Steve Fleming, Pasadena High School; Sara McNeil, University of Houston; Virginia Tucker, Spring Woods High School; Robert Wright, Chevron Corporation; Eric Pyle, West Virginia University; David Butts, University of Georgia; and Robert Shrigley, Pennsylvania State University.

The invaluable feedback of the following reviewers are also greatly appreciated: Michael Odell, University of Idaho; Samuel A. Spiegel, Florida State University; and Robert E. Yager, The University of Iowa.

Finally, with deep gratitude, we would like to thank our families for their support and encouragement during the preparation of this book.

Eugene L. Chiappetta
Thomas R. Koballa, Jr.
Alfred T. Collette

BRIEF CONTENTS

■

CONTENTS

PART THREE

PLANNING FOR INSTRUCTION   285

CHAPTER 12
PLANNING AND TEACHING
SCIENCE LESSONS   286

CHAPTER 13
PLANNING A SCIENCE UNIT   312

PART FOUR

ASSESSMENT IN SCIENCE TEACHING   329

CHAPTER 14
ASSESSING LEARNING OUTCOMES   330

PART ONE

BACKGROUND FOR TEACHING SCIENCE

CHAPTER 1

THE NATURE OF SCIENCE

Science can be thought of as the study of nature in an attempt to understand it and to create knowledge.

Science instruction must reflect valid views of the nature of science. Teachers' lectures, classroom discussions, laboratory activities, assigned readings, long-term investigations, and examination questions should correspond to what are generally accepted as science content and processes. Erroneous beliefs about how scientists go about their work must be eliminated, as must highly simplistic approaches to problem solving and overly simplistic examples of concepts, laws, and principles that distort this scientific knowledge. Science teachers, curriculum developers, and science educators must possess a broad understanding of the nature of science so that they make accurate interpretations and presentations of this discipline. Further, their understanding must lead to helping students appreciate the worth of science and how it can benefit their lives. Science teaching must be in line with relevant and authentic science information in order to improve the scientific literacy of all Americans.

OBJECTIVES

This chapter is designed to help the reader meet the following objectives:

- Arrive at a definition of science that represents what scientists do in their work.
- Reflect upon the extent to which science teaching situations exhibit "authentic science" after examining many facets of the scientific enterprise that are associated with the history and philosophy of science.
- Analyze science teaching situations and instructional materials to determine the extent to which they reflect four dimensions or themes of scientific literacy that are central to science teaching.

WHAT IS SCIENCE?

Arriving at a Definition of Science

Science is a broad-based human enterprise that is defined differently depending on the individuals who view it. The layperson might define science as a body of scientific information; the scientist might view it as a set of procedures by which hypotheses are tested; a philosopher might regard science as a way of questioning the truthfulness of what we know. All of these views are valid, but each presents just a partial definition of science; only collectively do they begin to define the comprehensive nature of science. Science is an enterprise that has changed over the centuries. Further, it encompasses many fields, such as physics, chemistry, biology, and the geosciences, which sometimes employ different approaches to the study of reality. Let's examine what scientists attempt to do in their work to assist in arriving at a definition of science.

Science can be thought of as the study of nature in an attempt to understand it and to create new knowledge that provides predictive power and application. This description is implied in the following statement by Edward Teller (1991), an eminent nuclear physicist:

> A scientist has three responsibilities: one is to understand, two is to explain that understanding and three is to apply the results of that understanding. A scientist should have no other limitations. A scientist isn't responsible for that which he has discovered (pp. 1, 15).

The notion that scientists try to **understand, explain,** and **apply** offers science teachers a simple and clear idea of the scientific enterprise. Scientists strive to understand the phenomena that make up our universe—from the pulsating beats of our hearts to the migration of birds to the explosion of stars. Their aim is to describe the internal and external structure of objects, the mechanisms of forces, and the occurrence of events to the point where their descriptions can be used to predict future events with great precision. Scientific understanding goes beyond description to the deeper level of explanation that coalesces many observations, facts, laws, and generalizations into coherent theories that connect ideas with reality, not only specifying what is occurring, but how and why it is occurring.

Scientists **make public** their understanding through carefully prepared papers. Often their manuscripts are presented at professional meetings and published in professional journals. In both instances, and especially the latter, the work is carefully reviewed by colleagues who make critical comments and suggestions, thereby recommending the work for publication or rejection. Published works are open to additional examination by the scientific community where the **logic and reasoning** can be evaluated and procedures and results can be tested by additional observation and experimentation. Further, the work is open to scrutiny by colleagues in order to determine if **ethical principles** have been violated, such as presenting erroneous data or taking credit for discoveries that others have claimed. Scientific ideas must be articulated in a manner that permits other scientists to **confirm** them, to determine their validity, and to translate the knowledge into useful products.

In addition to understanding and explaining phenomena, scientists strive to apply the knowledge that they construct about the world. Many scientists, along with engineers and technologists, spend much of their time designing and producing **useful products** for society. Most of these products hold the potential to improve the quality of life, such as manufactured drugs, genetically engineered hormones, electronic communications, superconducting devices, and the like. It's impossible to calculate the number of ways in which science and engineering have added to our quality of life, but the fact that they have done so has earned them high esteem in our society.

The earlier statement that we quoted by Edward Teller that scientists are not responsible for their work is open to debate, because many would argue that science is a human activity and those involved must be responsible for their actions and products. There is a significant relationship between science and society, in which the society keeps watch over and influences the scientific enterprise.

■ STOP AND REFLECT! ■

Before reading further, do the following:

■ Answer the question, What is science? Include in your answer what scientists do in their work.

■ Use your definition of science to examine the activity "Investigating Animals' Reactions to Light" in Box 1.1 and indicate the extent to which Mr. Pearl's instruction reflects authentic science.

Many Facets of Science

There is more to science than the definition of science and the activities of scientists presented so far. Science encompasses many diverse ideas and has evolved over many thousands of years. Further, various aspects of science are viewed differently by scientists, philosophers,

BOX 1.1

■

INVESTIGATING ANIMALS' RESPONSES TO LIGHT

Mr. Pearl initiated the study of ecology with a set of investigations concerning animals' responses to light. The inquiry took place over several weeks and paralleled many other instructional activities on the topic. The following is an overview of how Mr. Pearl directed this activity. He began by introducing the project and outlining the procedures to be followed.

MR. PEARL: Over the next three weeks I want the class to study the responses of various animals to light. You will begin by working independently and then with your laboratory group. To start, I want you to do the following:

■ Make a list of five to ten animals and describe how you believe they react to light. Consider when the animals seek food, eat, and sleep. Remember that humans are classified as animals just as insects, birds, and mammals are.

■ For each animal, explain its response to light by specifying how the behavior is beneficial to the organism.

■ Identify two or three animals that you wish to study because it is possible to either observe them in their natural environment or to maintain them in our classroom/laboratory.

After the students thought and wrote for ten minutes, Mr. Pearl led a discussion regarding the animals they listed and their respective reactions to light. The discussion was lively and brought forth many ideas. The students mentioned the nocturnal behavior of bats, owls, and moths. Some students talked about fishing and how certain fish seem to be more active during various times of the day. Others focused on the habits of ants, termites, and worms. One student mentioned reading about the psychological effects that winter has on some people due to the lack of sunshine.

The students were placed into groups to discuss which animals they might study. Then Mr. Pearl worked with each group to select an animal that was feasible for the group to study. The animals identified for this inquiry were brine shrimp, tadpoles, meal worms, and ants. Most of these organisms could be studied in the biology classroom/laboratory. However, one group indicated that they wanted to use a pond in a wooded area of their neighborhood where tadpoles could be observed.

At this point the teacher provided these additional directions to the students:

1. In your laboratory notebook, name the animal you are studying.

2. Write a paragraph describing how your organism might react to light.

3. List five to eight questions that you will attempt to answer from your investigation. Below are a few questions to consider.

■ How does the intensity of the light affect the animal?

■ Does heat play a role in the response to light?

I'll stop here because I want *you* to generate the questions. When you have a list of questions, discuss them with your lab partners and together decide on the questions you will attempt to answer. Then show the questions to me so that we can determine their suitability for guiding your inquiry.

4. Design procedures to answer your questions regarding light and animal behavior. On a sheet of paper, list a question and outline the procedure that will provide an answer to it. I will discuss the procedure with you and offer suggestions. After

our discussion I will direct you to put this information in your laboratory note-book.

5. Carry out the investigation and record the results in your lab notebook.

6. After you have carried out your experiment, go to several sources to gather information about your organism's behavior toward light, as well as that of at least two other animals. Use the references provided on the side shelf, go to the library, talk with people who are knowledgeable about this area of biology, and use the World Wide Web. Seek information about the habitat in which your animal lives in order to get an idea about its interaction with light. Do the same for one other animal. Write at least one paragraph regarding light reaction for your animal and one other. Be sure to identify and use the biological terms that are used by scientists to explain the concepts and principles that we are studying concerning light.

7. Compare in writing the findings from your investigation with what you first believed about the behavior of your animal and light, and do the same with the information that you gathered from written and human sources. If you need to conduct additional experiments and make additional observations to resolve any discrepancies, please do so.

8. Write at least three paragraphs discussing what you found in your investigation of animals' behavior to light. Indicate how your organism may have adapted to light over many millions of years of evolution, relating this investigation to what we studied previously concerning diversity, adaptation, and survival.

and historians. Martin, Kass, and Brouwer (1990) reinforce this position and stress that science is a broad-based discipline with many faces, and in order to make school science more authentic, educators must become knowledgeable about "the history of science, science, technology, and reflection on the nature of scientific knowledge" (p. 542). In addition, they advise that even these aspects of science are incomplete, recommending that science educators and science teachers consider the following facets to broaden their conceptions of the scientific enterprise.

1. **The formation of scientific knowledge—epistemological considerations.** Science must be considered in light of how people acquire and construct knowledge. In essence, the mind forms knowledge by attempting to make sense out of reality—creating ideas from one's personal point of view. The mind does not acquire knowledge as one would fill a bucket with water, but constructs it from personal experience, thinking about what others have produced and discussing ideas with others.

Philosophers of science have long been interested in the nature of knowledge and how it is developed over time. This branch of philosophy is called **epistemology.** Epistemologists ask fundamental questions about the principles, laws, and theories of science as well as the methods. They examine the truthfulness of scientific knowledge and the extent to which it reflects reality.

Ideas like empiricism, instrumentalism, objectivism, realism, and relativism can influence the way we think about scientific knowledge and teach about it (Rorty, 1991; Duschl, 1994; Matthews, 1994). For example, if one views scientific knowledge in a relativistic sense, it can take on various meanings, depending upon the individual or society. If one views knowledge as realistic, then it will be anchored in objects and events of the world, strongly linked to reality rather than to the perceptions and thinking of individuals.

2. **The methods of science—methodological fidelity.** It is crucial that science teachers recognize the many methods used to gain knowledge and that no one method is accepted as the only method of science. Percy Bridgman's (1950) comment reinforces this idea: "The scientific method, as far as it is a method, is nothing more than doing one's damndest with one's mind, no holds barred." Alan Chalmers (1982, p. 169) stresses that "there is no timeless and universal conception of science or scientific method" that can distinguish science from other forms of knowing or make science superior to other human enterprises.

3. **What we can assume about science—presuppositionalist point of view.** The new philosophy of science often uses the term **presupposition** to refer to ideas and methods that scientists assume or take for granted. For example, space-time exists, matter exists,

and Newton's laws generally hold. When a scientist studies a phenomenon, he or she assumes that certain ideas hold and that they can be used to guide inquiry. These ideas or presuppositions are important for scientific progress. Most important, they are known and accepted by members of a scientific community.

Thomas Kuhn (1970) explains that a set of beliefs, methods, and understandings held by a group of scientists provides guidance to those engaging in this line of work. He calls these paradigms or conceptual frameworks and stresses their importance for understanding how science is conducted. Kuhn points out that within each paradigm there are three types of problems that consume scientists: (1) refining the facts, (2) aligning theory with reality, and (3) providing greater articulation of a paradigm theory. Much of science, or normal science as Kuhn refers to it, is "mop-up work" that engages the thinking and problem solving of scientists in these three tasks. Very little normal science addresses the formation of new paradigms and the exploration of novelties. Only occasionally are insights made that lead to the formation of new theories. Further, this process usually occurs over decades and the discoveries are often not recognized immediately.

Doing science and creating knowledge are highly passionate activities that are difficult to express in words. Polanyi (1958) indicates that although the contents of science can be articulated and passed on through textbooks and instruction, the art of scientific research cannot. Doing science is best developed through mentor/apprenticeship arrangements. Knowing **how** leads to knowing **what**. The ideas that science is a highly passionate enterprise and that it relies upon assumptions and presuppositions have come under attack by religious fundamentalists as well as philosophers of science as being very subjective and weak (Strahler, 1992).

4. Striving to reject theories—the falsificationists. The work of Karl Popper (1972) provides a starkly different view of science than that expressed by Thomas Kuhn. Popper stresses that the scientist's ultimate purpose is to attempt to falsify theories by constructing hypotheses that have the potential to be shown to be false. For Popper (1963), confirming a theory is easy, especially if that is what one is attempting to accomplish. Humans possess the propensity to find what they are seeking, but the real test of a useful explanation is to set up conditions in an attempt to discredit it. Popper (1963) states that if we wish to seek truth, we must begin by "criticizing our most cherished beliefs" (p. 6).

5. Anything goes—the hedonists. Paul Feyerabend (1981) recommends to individuals pursuing knowledge that they do so by producing many ideas that explain nature. The search for knowledge and understanding is one that requires opening up the mind and following one's intuition. He believes that those who conduct science must attempt to find answers and explanations rather than attempt to discredit explanations.

A considerable amount of skepticism toward science can be found in the philosophy of science literature. Feyerabend has voiced some of the most scathing remarks. Although he claims not to be opposed to science, his rhetoric removes the uniqueness and shine that the scientific enterprise holds for many in Western society. Feyerabend indicates that scientists put forth theories that are subjective and even irrational. Further, "science provides fascinating stories about the universe. . . . In fact . . . modern scientists are every bit the equal of such ancient entertainers as myth-tellers, troubadours and court jesters" (cited in Horgan, p. 31).

6. Public and personal side of science. The private side of science offers a different picture of the scientific enterprise than that which is often presented in textbooks and in research journals. Although the public side of science is often portrayed as objective and precise, the private side can be quite different. Scientists are passionate about their ideas and often cling to them in the face of conflicting facts (Mitroff, 1974). Scientists can often search for explanations in idiosyncratic ways, using their own personal language and symbols. The work of the scientist can be learned only by doing this type of activity, which is difficult to describe.

7. Historical importance of science. Science has a definite place in the history of humankind, and presenting its evolution can reveal a great deal about its nature. For example, the study of the development of theories over many hundreds of years can bring out themes and principles that are central to understanding important ideas. This evolutionary process is illustrated well by the case of astronomy. Long ago the earth was thought to be at the center of the universe, and then the Sun was considered the center of the solar system with planets moving in circular orbits about it. We have progressed to the present view where the planets follow elliptical paths around the Sun. Further, the history of science illustrates the tentative nature of theories and the importance of confirmation of ideas to the establishment of scientific knowledge. Consequently, if we desire to produce scientifically literate people, we must not only convey what is known, but how that knowledge was derived (Duschl, 1990).

8. Societal influence on science. Science is not isolated from society. In fact, its popularity and funding is highly influenced by the religious, ideological, economic, ethical, and cultural values of societies. Early science grew out of myth and religious ideas. Many of the useful discoveries that modern societies enjoy were the result of scientists working together on weapons and defense systems. Both large and small scientific projects are funded by governmental grants, reflecting the values that the government and society place on the acquisition of certain types of knowledge.

One obvious reason for the many facets of science is that the scientific enterprise has evolved over the centuries and continues to evolve, changing constantly. The nature of science can be viewed at many levels of complexity and abstraction. During the first century B.C., early science was highly descriptive. Greek philosophers attempted to describe natural phenomena by drawing upon myth and religion. Their science was not empirical. Many of the theories put forth by these early scientists were erroneous, which is also true of today's scientists. Aristotle, for example, believed that objects of unequal size fell to the ground at different rates of speed. Ptolemy believed that the earth was the center of the solar system.

The sixteenth and seventeenth centuries ushered in modern science in that visible phenomena were described more accurately using logic and mathematics. The movement toward accuracy for explaining nature is evident in the work of Galileo, who presented his ideas in the form of simple mathematical formulas to show the distance traveled by a falling body over a given period of time. Similarly, Newton used a simple formula to relate the attractive force between two bodies, which he stated as being directly related to their masses and inversely proportional to the distance separating them squared.

At the turn of the twentieth century, the scientific community probed deeper into the structure of matter, the nature of space and time, and the chemical basis of life. For example, quantum mechanics attempts to explain matter at the atomic and subatomic levels, while relativity addresses space and time in frames of reference that approach the speed of light and where large gravitational fields exist. Cosmology endeavors to explain the origin of the universe back to a time represented by the blink of an eyelid before its inception. Molecular biology analyzes living systems at the level of the gene.

As the twentieth century draws to a close, a "new science" called **chaos** has emerged. "Where chaos begins, classical science stops" (Gleick, 1987, p. 3). This new paradigm addresses complex phenomena that until now have drawn little attention from the scientific community. It focuses upon very complex phenomena that appear random and chaotic and attempts to find their inherent order. Chaos concerns itself with phenomena more on the human scale than does quantum mechanics, such as changes in wildlife populations, disorder in the atmosphere, irregularity in heartbeats, the patterns in

rising columns of smoke, the clustering of automobiles on expressways, the winding of rivers, and so on. This new direction in science is made possible by computer technology that can present graphic and pictorial images to highlight subtle patterns embedded in seemingly random events.

In some instances, determining what something "is not" helps to better understand what that something "is." At first thought, this idea appears so useful and simple for distinguishing science from nonscience. For example, would not most scientists be quick to say that science is much different from astrology or parapsychology? Identifying a single criterion (or several for that matter) to distinguish scientific theories from crackpot ideas, however, is a formidable exercise. Most criteria that have been proposed meet with criticism.

Morris (1991) presents the example of distinguishing between superstring theory and the claims given by astrologers. He points out that if subjecting one's theory to empirical testing is used as the criterion for being scientific, then astrologers fare even better than the superstring theorists. Most physicists would agree that it is virtually impossible to observe a superstring, because this fundamental entity is hypothesized to be many millions of times smaller than a quark, for whose existence superstrings are theoretically responsible. On the other hand, one can set up tests to determine the apparent influences that heavenly bodies exert on human affairs, even if the results may provide little data to confirm these relationships. Morris points out that both scientific and nonscientific theories seem to be the result of thought, imagination, speculation, and problem solving. Both enterprises put forth bizarre ideas. In the final analysis, however, scientific theories generally offer clear, logical, and simple explanations of phenomena that provide useful insights into nature.

To say that science is a way of knowing implies that science is only one of many ways to establish knowledge about the world and that it competes with other ways humankind establishes knowledge. We must be mindful that other cultures—African, Asian, Hispanic, and Native American—have a world view that differs from the Western view of science (Stanley & Brickhouse, 1994). Among these cultures there may be alternative views, say of medicine, that have value. To many people, these alternative views and practices do not seem to offer a serious challenge to the contemporary scientific establishment when it comes to understanding and explaining nature (Loving, 1995). We want to affirm, however, that science is a useful enterprise that contributes significantly to society.

All the sciences, in spite of manifold differences, have in common that they are devoted to the endeavor to understand the world. Science wants to explain, it wants to generalize, and it wants to determine the causation of things, events, and processes. To that extent, at least, there is a unity of science. (Mayr, 1982, p. 32)

In closing this section, it is important to emphasize that science is a broad-based enterprise that has changed over the years. To characterize science as understanding, explaining, and applying knowledge presents a very simple definition. However, in order for science teachers to understand science, they must study the manner in which knowledge is constructed over time as well as the methods that are used to validate knowledge, the creative and personal side of science, and the place of science in society.

■ STOP AND REFLECT! ■

Keep in mind the many facets of science that were presented in this section as you answer the following questions.

- Revisit Box 1.1. To what extent do Mr. Pearl's instructions reflect authentic science?
- What was stated in the section regarding the many facets of science that might help science teachers or laypersons realize that science is neither an absolute form of knowledge nor a meaningless enterprise?

THEMES OF SCIENTIFIC LITERACY AS THEY RELATE TO INSTRUCTION

Sometimes reading about the philosophy of science can become confusing and leave one with the impression that science is not much different than mysticism or religion. Further, this literature presents many discussions on what science is not, obscuring the intent of science education, which is to promote an appreciation for science and help people to learn more about this enterprise. Fortunately, there are dimensions of science that scientists and science educators readily recognize and accept as useful. These dimensions or themes can be used to plan, carry out, and analyze science instruction.

We will refer to these dimensions as **themes of scientific literacy** and state them as follows: (1) science as a way of thinking, (2) science as a way of investigating, (3) science as a body of knowledge, and (4) science and its interactions with technology and society. These major areas of science can be used to analyze what is being emphasized in a teaching session, laboratory exercise, textbook chapter, and so on. Their presentation in Figure 1.1 emphasizes that science content is often given more consideration than the other dimensions.

Before reading further, recall your experiences as a student in a college science class. What stands out in your mind regarding these experiences? Did the instructors get you to think about the topic under discussion? Did they spend time explaining to you how ideas were invented and their related phenomena discovered? Were major investigations or experiments discussed, illustrating how they contributed to the establishment of the laws and theories under study? Was lecture time spent on the applications of the subject matter or their relevance to society? The chances are high that many of the science classes in which you enrolled in college or took in high school were comprised mostly of lectures that presented a large body of information.

We believe strongly that science lectures at the middle school, high school, and college levels must go beyond the presentation of technical information. These sessions should be more balanced, showing how scientists go about their work and how their results impact the work of other scientists, as well as that of society. Science textbooks must also convey a more balanced view of science than they have in the past. If the presentation of science content comprises 80% or 85% of a given textbook, little text is left to help students understand how ideas were formed (Lumpe & Beck, 1996). The four themes we will discuss here—thinking, investigation, knowledge, and science/technology/society—can help science teachers to become more sensitive to the importance of balance in the curriculum (Chiappetta, Sethna, & Fillman, 1991).

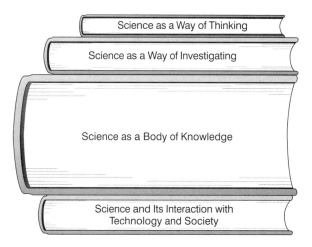

FIGURE 1.1   Four Themes or Dimensions of Science That May Be Evident in Science Instruction to Various Degrees

Science as a Way of Thinking

Science is a human activity that can be characterized by the thinking that occurs in the minds of people who participate in it. The mental work of scientists illustrates curiosity and desire to understand phenomena. These individuals possess attitudes, beliefs, and values that motivate them to ask questions and find solutions. Scientists are curious and imaginative and they apply reasoning in their quest to figure out and explain natural phenomena. Their work, as viewed by many philosophers of science and cognitive psychologists, constitutes creative activity whereby ideas and explanations are constructed in the mind. This thinking and reasoning offer important clues regarding the nature of science and how science makes progress.

Beliefs.   The tendency for scientists to find out seems to be motivated by their belief that nature is understandable and predictable and that they can construct laws and theories to explain nature. Scientists are deeply involved emotionally and personally in their work, constantly striving to better understand the natural and physical world (Roe, 1961). They believe that useful explanations of phenomena can be pieced together by the scientific community. In addition, scientists also dispel ideas and beliefs they perceive to be erroneous.

The early scientific thinkers relied on thought and logic to explain what they saw in the skies, for example. They attempted to break away from certain myths and tales to explain objects that changed position in the skies overhead (de Santillana, 1961). Although the beliefs and reasoning of early scientists seem faulty in retrospect, their methods were quite revolutionary at the time and they provided a foundation for studying important ideas. Aristotle, for example, believed that the planets moved in circular orbits around the earth. His work caused others to examine planetary motion. A later example of a scientific belief that prompted further study by others comes from Paul Ehrlich, a famous bacteriologist:

> Ehrlich's search for substances, which are selectively absorbed by pathogenic organisms, was inspired by his firm belief that drugs cannot act unless fixed to the organism, but today many effective chemotherapeutic drugs are known not to be selectively fixed to the ineffective agents. (Beveridge, 1957, p. 61)

Curiosity.   Scientists as a group seem to be uncontrollably curious. They constantly explore their environment and frequently ask the question, Why? This curiosity is often manifested in their having many interests, even beyond that of unraveling the mysteries of natural phenomena. Nicholas Copernicus, for instance, who caused a scientific revolution by placing the Sun at the center of our solar system, pursued many vocations. "Copernicus was a churchman, a painter, a poet, a physician, an economist, a statesmen, a soldier, and a scientist" (Hummel, 1986, p. 55). Benjamin Franklin likewise demonstrated his many interests as a printer, publisher, inventor, statesman, and scientist.

Imagination.   In addition to being curious, scientists rely heavily on imagination. The early Greek philosophers and scientists tried to visualize a harmonious universe with heavenly bodies moving in a particular manner. Clerk Maxwell formed mental pictures of the abstract problems that he attempted to solve, especially electromagnetic fields. Many in a college organic chemistry course have listened to the story of how August Kekule came to visualize the benzene ring during a dream:

> The atoms flitted before my eyes. Long rows, variously, more closely, united; all in movement wriggling and turning like snakes. And see, what was that? One of the snakes seized its own tail and the image whirled scornfully before my eyes. (cited in Beveridge, 1957, p. 76).

Reasoning.   Associated with imagination is reasoning. The history of science provides many examples of how those who participate in the scientific enterprise study phenomena with considerable reliance on their own thinking as well as that of others. According to Albert Einstein, science is a refinement of everyday thinking, a belief that becomes evident when one studies the work of scientists in their attempt to construct ideas that explain how nature works. Science teaching can benefit greatly from the inclusion of narratives about the development of the major theories of the natural and physical world, illustrating how these explanations evolved and changed over time (Duschl, 1990). Examples of science courses that focus on the nature of scientific thinking can be found among the national curriculum projects produced during the 1960s. Harvard Project Physics, in particular, centered its textbook and supplemental reading on historical accounts of how scientific principles and theories were put forth by various individuals. A classic example of how a scientist used a thought experiment to illustrate correct and incorrect reasoning about the motion of celestial bodies is given in Galileo's *Two New Sciences,* where he presents a conversation between three characters: Simplicio, who represents the Aristotelian view of mechanics; Salviati, who represents the new view of Galileo; and Sagredo, who represents a man with an open mind and eager to learn. This short excerpt taken from the dialogue illustrates how Galileo attempted to reason that two bodies, regardless of their mass, will fall to the ground at the same rate.

SIMPLICIO: There can be no doubt that one and the same body moving in a single medium has a fixed velocity which is determined by nature and which cannot be increased except by addition of impetus or diminished except by resistance which retards it.

SALVIATI: If we take two bodies whose natural speeds are different, it is clear that on uniting the two, the more rapid one will be partly retarded by the slower, and the slower will be somewhat hastened by the swifter. Do you not agree with me in this opinion?

SIMPLICIO: You are unquestionably right.

SALVIATI: But if this is true and if a larger stone moves with a speed of, say, eight, while a smaller moves with a speed of four, then when they are united, the system will move with a speed of less than eight; but the two stones when tied together make a stone larger than that which before moved with a speed of eight. Hence the heavier body moves with less speed than the lighter one; an effect which is contrary to your supposition. Thus you see how, from your assumption that the heavier body moves more rapidly than the lighter one, I infer that the heavier body moves more slowly.

SIMPLICIO: I am all at sea. . . . This is, indeed, quite beyond my comprehension.

Simplicio retreats in confusion when Salviati shows that the Aristotelian theory of fall contradicts itself. But whereas Simplicio cannot refute Galileo's logic, his own eyes tell him that a heavy object does fall faster that a light object. (Project Physics Course, 1975, pp. 43–45)

If educators turn to the history of science, they will find many examples of thought experiments that illustrate creativity, imagination, and reasoning. The writings of Ernst Mach contain numerous examples of puzzles that were contrived to cause one to think deeply about physical phenomena. Mach (1838–1916), a great scientist and philosopher, presented thought experiments for his readers to perform in each edition of his Zeitschrift. One such mind teaser asks, "What happens when a stoppered bottle with a fly on its base is in equilibrium on a balance and the fly takes off" (cited in Matthews, 1991, p. 15).

Scientists engage in a variety of reasoning behaviors to elucidate patterns in nature. Sometimes they use inductive thinking; at other times they use deductive thinking. Through inductive reasoning, one arrives at explanations and theories by piecing together facts and principles. Although Sir Francis Bacon did not originate the inductive method, he did a great deal to promote this approach. Bacon argued strongly that the laws of science are formed from data collected through observation and experimentation (Bruno, 1989). In doing so, he stressed empiricism over deductive logic. Nevertheless, deductive thinking is no less important in the thinking process.

Deductive thinking involves the application of general principles to other instances. The deductive process makes inferences about specific situations from known or tentative generalizations. This form of reasoning is often used to test hypotheses, either confirming or disproving them. Deduction is frequently used in astronomy to predict events from existing theories. It has also been used extensively in the area of theoretical physics to predict the existence of certain subatomic particles, many of which have been discovered years after their announcements. The hypothetical-deductive approach is also a suggested strategy to use for instructing students in biological sciences to help them better understand these disciplines (Moore, 1984).

Cause-and-effect relationships.   Scientists often seek to establish cause-and-effect relationships to advance their understanding of the world. The search for cause and effect is central to experimentation and to modern science. Further, this conceptual relationship helps to explain the mechanism by which cause **produces** effect. Many events can stimulate cause-and-effect reasoning, from the very common to less frequent, such as:

- Why do cats give birth only to kittens?
- Why do some people who smoke develop lung cancer?
- Why do tornadoes form?
- Why do comets reappear every so many years?

In concept, the logic of the cause-and-effect relationship is simple:

Here A is shown to cause B. A common example of this simple relationship can be observed by plucking a guitar string. If you shorten the string and pluck it, the string produces a high pitched sound. Consider human respiration. If you cut off all oxygen to the human body, the person will die. Cells need oxygen to carry out important processes, which in humans enters the body by way of the lungs. Thus the phrase, Oxygen supports life.

The cause of an event must provide the antecedent conditions that are **necessary** and **sufficient** for the event to occur. For example, we often hear the comment that cigarette smoking causes lung cancer. Some scientists, as well as tobacco company representatives, object to that statement. Not every person who smokes gets lung cancer. Some people smoke for 50, 60, 70, or 80 years and never contract lung cancer. Smoking may more correctly be termed a risk factor for lung cancer, because we cannot say that tobacco is the sole agent for causing this disease or that smoking tobacco will always result in lung cancer.

With living organisms cause-and-effect relationships are very difficult to establish. The problems involved in the search for causes in living organisms are formidable. Ernst Mayr (1961) posits the cause for a single bird's migration from New Hampshire in late August:

> There is an immediate set of causes for the migration, consisting of the physiological conditions of the bird interacting with the photoperiodicity and drop in temperature. We might call these the proximate causes of migration. The other two causes, the lack of food during the winter and the genetic disposition of the bird, are the ultimate causes. . . . There is always a proximate set of causes and an ultimate set of causes; both have to be explained and interpreted for a complete understanding of the given phenomenon. (p. 1503)

Do not assume that physical scientists have an easier task determining causation than biological scientists. Consider investigations into the nature of subatomic particles. Physicists have turned to probability and complex mathematical formulas to explain the behavior of electrons and dozens of other subatomic particles, rather than determining the exact nature of a given particle. Further, those in the historical sciences (evolutionary biology and geology) are very hard pressed to establish cause-and-effect relationships in their work.

Self-examination.   Scientific thinking is more than an attempt to understand nature. It is also an attempt to understand itself, to look into the ways by which people arrive at their conclusions about nature. To paraphrase Poincare, an intelligent person cannot believe everything or believe nothing. What then can intelligent persons believe and what must they reject, and what can they accept with varying degrees of reservation?

Scientists have always concerned themselves with these questions; indeed, physics was once called "natural philosophy." But never have scientists spent more effort than today in examining their processes of reasoning. Investigations into the particulate nature of matter, quantum mechanics, and acceptance of the principle of indeterminacy have undermined our earlier notions of the predictability and well-behaved order of nature that once were never questioned. Even the more reluctant scientists have been forced to look closely at their ways of thinking.

Many other ideas besides those just mentioned can be assigned to science as a way of thinking. For example, objectivity, open-mindedness, and skepticism are often ascribed to the scientific attitude. Although these images of scientists are put forth in textbooks, and we would like them to be true, they may not necessarily represent the manner in which all scientists conduct their work. Holton (1952) reminds us about the distinction between public and private science that challenges the empiricist stereotype of the detached, objective researcher, who the public sees in the final edited version of the scientist's work. Gauld (1982) cautions science educators about their beliefs regarding the empiricist conception of the scientific attitude and suggests perhaps eliminating it from science education. "Teaching that scientists possess these characteristics is bad enough but it is abhorrent that science educators should actually attempt to mold children in the same false image" (Gauld, 1982, p. 118).

Science as a Way of Investigating

Those who desire to understand nature and to discover its laws must study objects and events. The clues to nature's "clockwork" are imbedded in reality. They must be uncovered through experimentation and observation, and reasoned out through the human thought process. Some people go so far as to say that "understanding the process—the way scientific information is obtained, tested, and validated—is more important than knowledge of any specific product of science" (Hetherington, Miller, Sperling, & Reich, 1989).

Science as a way of investigating utilizes many approaches to constructing knowledge. Science has many methods, which demonstrates humankind's inventiveness for seeking solutions to problems. Some of the approaches used by scientists rely heavily on observation and prediction as in astronomy and ecology. Other approaches rely on laboratory experiments that focus on cause-and-effect relationships such as those used in microbiology. Among the many processes often associated with science and inquiry are observing, inferring, hypothesizing, predicting, measuring, manipulating variables, experimenting, and calculating. A realistic idea of the many aspects that are related to inquiry and research are offered by Franz (1990):

experimentation	strategy
reason	intuition
chance	overcoming difficulties
observation	serendipity
hypotheses	

In spite of what is sometimes reported about scientific investigations, especially in science textbooks, inquiry is often idiosyncratic. Furthermore, there is no "scientific method." **The notion that there is a scientific method should be dispelled from science teaching.** For example, the work of Karl Pearson (1937) and

Investigating reality is necessary to confirm science understanding.

Courtesy Lyndon B. Johnson Space Center. Houston, Texas.

others who believed that they could capture the scientific method in the following five steps is still taught in some science courses and it often appears in the introductory chapter of many middle and senior high school science textbooks.

1. Observing
2. Collecting data
3. Developing a hypothesis
4. Experimenting
5. Concluding

Researchers do not necessarily follow this set of procedures or any other set, in spite of the fact that these steps might be evident in the polished, edited research reports that appear in scientific journals.

Hypothesis.   A hypothesis is an investigative tool that helps the inquirer to clarify ideas and state relationships so they can be tested. It is an untested condition to be examined. A hypothesis is a concise statement that attempts to explain a pattern or predict an outcome. Hypotheses stem from questions that a scientist asks concerning a problem under study. They are tentative

ideas that must be tested by additional observation, experimentation, or prediction. Hypotheses set the stage for challenging an idea to determine if it merits at least a temporary place in the fabric of scientific knowledge. All descriptions of scientific methods agree on the need for good research hypotheses to carry out meaningful investigations.

Even though a situation can be set up that could disprove a hypothesis, contrary evidence may not necessarily lead to the complete rejection of a hypothesis.

> If the generalization has any reasonable body of supporting data, the finding of new facts which do not fit usually leads to the refinement or elaboration of the original hypothesis. . . . On the other hand, if the original basis for the hypothesis was slender, the unfavorable instances may so outweigh the favorable ones as to make it reasonable to believe that the earlier agreement was a matter of pure chance. Also, a new hypothesis may be developed which fits the original data as well. (Wilson, 1952, p. 28)

People who engage in experimentation probably do so from a more optimistic point of view than attempting to discredit their ideas, as suggested by Popper (1963). In reality, they are betting on their hypotheses, hoping their experiments will confirm their predictions. What generally occurs is an unexpected result, however, which can be difficult to explain. Chamberlin (1965) urges researchers to propose not just one hypothesis but as many as the mind can invent, thus freeing the mind from bias that might result from excessive love of one's intellectual child. With many hypotheses, the researcher can be somewhat more objective and increase the probability for identifying several causes, knowing that some of the hypotheses will not survive. Nature is complex; attempting to explain it by limiting ourselves to one hypothesis is too narrow and self-defeating.

Observation.   Observation is certainly one cornerstone of science. Although most observations are carried out through the sense of sight, other senses like hearing, feeling, smelling, and tasting can also be part of the observation process. Through observation, data and information are gathered and organized in order to make sense out of reality. This is how facts are established so that hypotheses can be tested to arrive at theories. The body of knowledge formed by scientists is the result of extensive observations that eventually coalesce into concepts, principles, and theories.

The list of individuals who have made significant contributions to science as the result of their keen observations is long. Among those worth mentioning is Tycho Brahe, who amassed the most important observations regarding the motion of stars and planets during the Middle Ages. These observations, in turn, were used by Kepler to produce the now accepted idea that planets move in elliptical orbits around the Sun. Tycho used his eyes as well as a few simple devices to study the movement of celestial bodies.

> Tycho made his observations with scrupulous regularity, repeating them, combining them, and trying to allow for the imperfection of his instruments. As a result he reduced his margin of error to a fraction of a minute of an arc, and provided the sharpest precision achieved by anyone before the telescope. (Boorstin, 1985, p. 307)

Although observation plays a central role in scientific investigation, this skill is tied closely to the knowledge, thinking, and motivation of the observer. As Goethe said, "We see only what we know." Thus the scientist as well as the layperson sees with the mind. Beveridge (1957) points out that what people observe in a situation depends upon their interests. Furthermore, he claims that false observations occur when the senses provide the wrong information to the mind or when the mind plays tricks on the observer by filling in information from past experiences. Often the observer focuses attention on what is expected, thus missing unexpected

occurrences and valuable facts. Although observation seems to be the most basic and fundamental of the inquiry skills, it is a complex activity that merits careful study in and of itself.

Experimentation.   Along with observation, experimentation is central to the scientific enterprise and the development of modern science. Through experimentation, ideas can be confirmed or supported and erroneous beliefs that have been passed down by authority can be discarded. Experimentation permits us to probe nature's secrets, which seem to be tightly guarded and often disguised. The controlled experimentation offers the scientist an opportunity to test ideas and determine cause-and-effect relationships. Experimental activities range from using a match to burn a peanut to using a particle accelerator to smash a proton.

Modern science came into being in the sixteenth century when individuals like Galileo and Copernicus turned away from Greek science, which was dominated by the philosophers who distrusted experimentation. Greek philosophers relied primarily on reasoning to develop their ideas. Some of these individuals placed little value upon practical activities that could reveal the obvious. They shunned the technologies of the craftsperson, such as mechanical and optical devices that could provide accurate observations (Aicken, 1984).

When one experiments, events are introduced producing relationships that can be studied carefully. The conditions of these interventions are known and controlled. In this manner, the procedure is documented and thus can be reproduced by others. The controlled experiment is often used to test a hypothesis concerning cause-and-effect relationships. Condition A, for example, is altered to determine its effects on condition B. The situation that is manipulated by the researcher is called the independent variable, and the resultant variable is called the dependent variable. Other variables are held constant and their conditions noted. In situations where living organisms are under study, randomization of organisms or subjects into experimental and control groups is most desirable.

We must guard against placing ultimate trust in experimentation for evidence. Beveridge (1957) warns not to put excessive faith in experimentation because the possibility of error in technique always exists, which can result in misleading outcomes.

> It is not at all rare for scientists in different parts of the world to obtain contradictory results with similar biological material. Sometimes these can be traced to unsuspected factors, for instance, a great difference in the reactions of guinea pigs to diphtheria toxin was traced to a

difference in diets of the animals. In other instances it has not been possible to discover the cause of the disagreement despite a thorough investigation. (p. 34)

Mathematics.   Roger Bacon expressed it well when he said, "Mathematics is the door and the key to science." His quote suggests that mathematics is necessary to the understanding of nature's clockworks and without it we cannot get inside to find out what is taking place. The formulas and symbols assist us to identify relationships that represent laws and patterns in nature. At a very deep level, mathematics helps us to express models of situations that we cannot possibly observe. The atom, for example, is so small that we cannot see it or the electrons and protons that form its structure. The simple planetary models that we often see in textbooks or the packet-of-pulsating wave models may be inaccurate visualizations of the atom. According to scientists who study atoms and subatomic particles, the atom may be an entity that we cannot visualize. Nevertheless, mathematical models have been devised that predict with great accuracy the behavior of groups of atoms and subatomic particles. Mathematics has been used successfully to provide useful representations of nature that are out of our perceptual reach.

The power of numbers and the intimate association between mathematics and the evolution of science is evident throughout recorded history (de Santillana, 1961). For example, Pythagoras, in his studies of nature, mingled astronomy, geometry, music, and arithmetic. He indicated that numbers were special and that the universe produced melody and is put together with harmony. He described the motion of the stars in terms of rhythm and melody. Pythagoras's one physical discovery had to do with the patterns of sound produced by changing the length of a plucked string. He noted that moving a bridge to different locations or intervals on the string changed the sound. The ratios 1:2, 4:3, and 3:4 were important numerical relationships that resulted in distinct sounds. He further discovered that the numbers 1, 2, 3, and 4, which formed these ratios, added up to 10, the "perfect number."

Galileo, it is often said, made significant contributions to modern science because he attempted to explain phenomena with evidence, using mathematical relationships. Many connect Galileo with the falling stone controversy. Those who subscribed to Aristotle's notion of falling bodies believed that a heavier object falls at a faster rate than a lighter object. Galileo said, Wait a minute. If you try this out, you will find that they both fall at the same rate, provided that air resistance is ignored. His work on this problem resulted in the celebrated formula,

$$s = 16t^2$$

which states that a falling body has traveled a certain distance s after falling t seconds. Galileo also showed that the trajectory of a ball thrown in the air follows the parabolic path.

Science as a Body of Knowledge

The body of knowledge produced from many scientific fields represents the creative products of human invention that have occurred over the centuries. The enormous collection of ideas pertaining to the natural and physical world is organized into astronomy, biology, chemistry, geology, physics, and so on. The result is a compilation of carefully catalogued information, containing many types of knowledge, each of which makes its own unique contribution to science. The facts, concepts, principles, laws, hypotheses, theories, and models form the content of science. These ideas possess their own specific meaning, which cannot be understood apart from the processes of inquiry that produced them. Therefore, the content and methods of science are tied together, and teaching one without the other distorts the learner's conception and appreciation for the nature of science.

Facts.   The facts of science serve as the foundation for concepts, principles, and theories. A fact is often thought of as truth and the state of things. Facts represent what we can perceive through our senses and they are usually regarded as reliable data. Often two criteria are used to identify a scientific fact: (1) it is directly observable and (2) it can be demonstrated at any time. Consequently, facts are open to all who wish to observe them. We must remember, however, that these criteria do not always hold, because factual information regarding a one-time event, such as a volcanic eruption, may not be repeatable. In addition, there is uncertainty and limitation in measurement that accompanies facts. Therefore, data can never be considered absolutely pure and unequivocally true, because they contain a probability of error.

The presentation of facts alone in a science course is not enough, because the receiver of the information should know how the facts were established. For example, it is widely known that food can spoil in the presence of microorganisms, causing whoever eats it to become very sick or die. This fact becomes intelligible and meaningful when students learn how various types of food poisoning have been established. For example, one of the most deadly food poisonings is botulism, which is caused by the anaerobic bacteria *Clostridium botulinum*. A tiny amount of toxin produced by this organism is deadly. A lethal dose of the *botulinum* toxin is approximately .0000001—one ten-millionth of a gram (Black, 1994). Therefore, one gram of this compound is enough to kill about 10,000,000 people. The toxin acts by paralyzing muscles, blocking the neurotransmitter acetylcholine, thus stopping breathing. Canned foods, such as beans, corn, and beets, must be heat-treated to prevent this bacterium from multiplying while in an air-tight container.

The historical accounts of food poisoning from bacteria and fungi are numerous. Microbial contamination of milk, cereal, and bread, for example, provide a meaningful context for explaining the mechanisms that have established the causal factors of food poisoning. Therefore it is a **fact** that microorganisms can impart toxins to food, causing sickness or death. Perhaps not all of the facts given in a science course can be taught within a context of how they were arrived at, but many can and should be.

Concepts.   Facts have little meaning by themselves. They are raw material in a sense and must be examined to form meaningful ideas and relationships. Thinking and reasoning are required to identify patterns and make connections between the data, thus forming relationships we call concepts. A concept is an abstraction of events, objects, or phenomena that seem to have certain properties or attributes in common. Fish, for example, possess certain characteristics that set them apart from reptiles and mammals. Most bony fish have scales, fins, and gills. According to Bruner, Goodnow, and Austin (1956), a concept has five important elements: (1) name, (2) definition, (3) attributes, (4) values, and (5) examples. The process of concept formation and attainment is an active process and requires more than simply conveying these elements to the learner. The students must establish some of the attributes and discover some of the patterns between data if the concepts are to become linked to other meaningful ideas in their minds. In addition, concepts can be affective as well as cognitive.

Many of the terms associated with scientific fields represent concepts. They are ideas used to form categories. In biology, for example, tree, grass, insect, ape, gene, and enzyme each represent a class of entities that share common characteristics. In chemistry, element, molecule, compound, mixture, acid, base, and isotope can be considered concepts. There are physics concepts, such as electron, proton, neutron, wave, solid, and x-ray. Concepts become meaningful to learners when they have had many opportunities to experience examples or

instances of them. For example, we form the class of animals called fish by observing a variety of fish and noting that they live in water, take in water through their mouths, have fins, and so on. Categorizing phenomena aids scientists and the public at large to form knowledge about the world in which we live.

Principles and laws.   Principles and laws also fall into the general category of a concept. Although they can be considered broader than a simple concept, principles and laws are often used synonymously. These higher order ideas are used to describe what exists. They are often accepted as facts; nevertheless, their distinction and empirical basis must be remembered. Principles and laws are composed of concepts and facts. They are more general than facts but are also related to observable phenomena. Gas laws and laws of motion, for example, specify what can be observed under certain conditions. The principles that regulate growth and reproduction provide reliable information regarding changes that take place in living systems.

Theories.   Science goes beyond the classification and description of phenomena to the level of explanation. Scientists use theories to explain patterns and forces. Theories are ambitious intellectual endeavors, because they deal with the complexities of reality—that which is obscure and hidden from direct observation. This idea becomes evident when one considers the theory of the atom, which states that all matter is made up of tiny particles called atoms, many millions of which would be required to cover the period at the end of this sentence. This visual conception becomes even harder to grasp when we consider the aspect of the theory that suggests an atom is mostly empty space with a small dense center and charged particles moving in certain regions of space far out from the center.

Theories have a different purpose than to organize facts, concepts, and laws. They incorporate this type of knowledge to explanations of why phenomena occur as they do. Theories are of a different nature; they never become fact or law, but remain tentative until disproved or revised.

Any physical theory is always provisional, in the sense that it is only a hypothesis: you can never prove it. No matter how many times the results of experiments agree with some theory, you can never be sure that the next time the results will not contradict the theory. On the other hand, you can disprove a theory by finding even a single observation that disagrees with the predictions of the theory. As philosopher of science Karl Popper has emphasized, a good theory is characterized by the fact that it makes a number of predictions that could be disproved or falsified by observation. Each time new experi-

ments are observed to agree with the predictions the theory survives, and our confidence in it is increased; but if
ever new observation is found to disagree, we have to
abandon or modify the theory. At least that is what is supposed to happen, but you can always question the competence of the person who carried out the observation.
(Hawking, 1988, p. 10)

Theories are of great importance to science. They
represent some of the most monumental and creative
works of humankind, which are evident in the theory of
the atom, special and general relativity, plate tectonics,
and natural selection, to name a few. These inventions of
the mind incorporate a great deal of thinking, imagination, writing, and modeling. Consider natural selection,
for example. Darwin used domestic breeding as a model
for selection and used Malthus's notion of struggle for
the existence for survival of the fittest (Harre, 1970).
Recall the four postulates of natural selection: (1) all
organisms produce more offspring than can survive, (2)
overproduction occurs that leads to a struggle for survival, (3) individuals within a species vary, and (4) those
organisms best adapted tend to survive. Overproduction, competition, variation, mutation, struggle for existence, and adaptation are just some of the concepts and
principles that are used in Darwin's theory for explaining
the evolution of life on this planet, which has been
changing for some three billion years. Science educators
have the responsibility to help others to comprehend the
nature of theories by showing how they attempt to
explain complex phenomena that cannot be observed
directly.

Models.   The term model is often used in the scientific
literature. A scientific model is the representation of
something that we cannot see. These models become
mental images or constructs that are used to represent
phenomena and other abstract ideas. They include the
most salient features of the idea or theory that the scientist is attempting to make comprehensible and to
explain. The Bohr model of the atom, the planetary
model of the solar system, the wave and particle models
of light, and the double helix model of DNA are all concrete representations of phenomena that we cannot perceive directly. Generally, models are deduced from
abstract ideas, and sometimes there are no sharp distinctions between models, hypotheses, and theories. Textbooks are the major referent for most of our notions
about scientific models. They are useful to help us
become familiar with important ideas. Unfortunately,
many come to believe that the models presented in science textbooks are the real thing, forgetting that a model
is used only to help one conceptualize the salient features of a principle or theory, and that the mental picture is not what exists in reality.

Science and Its Interactions
with Technology and Society

Science is intimately related to technology and society.
In some instances, science produces knowledge that
results in useful applications through devices and systems. We have evidence of this all around us, from
microwave ovens to compact disc players to computers.
In other instances, technology helps to further scientific
investigation. Consider how the light microscope has
contributed to our understanding of bacteria and how
the electron microscope has enhanced our understanding of viruses. Computers are advancing scientific knowledge daily.

Just as scientific knowledge impacts society, society
impacts science. Most scientific work is funded through
government grants and private business. The money is
generally targeted for projects that study important societal problems, such as cardiovascular disease, cancer,
and weapon systems. Today's research is carried out by
teams of scientists working cooperatively to solve societal problems. More than ever before science is rooted in
society and connected with technology. This topic will
be taken up in greater detail in Chapter 7 on science,
technology, and society, but serves here to reinforce the
idea that this themes is an integral part of the nature of
science.

*School science should include the study of technologi-
cal devices along with basic science.*

■

ASSESSING AND REVIEWING

1. Identify the ideas that you will use in planning and teaching science to help students understand and appreciate this enterprise. Construct a visual representation of major terms that presents your conception of science. You might begin by placing "The Nature of Science" at or near the center of your graphic organizer and connecting it with lines to the key terms.

        (The Nature of Science)

2. Let's examine a science teacher's approach to experimentation to determine the extent to which it reflects authentic science to the students.

   TEACHER: Today, class, you are going to conduct an investigation to determine how many paper clips you can hang on the end of a magnet before the force gives way and the clips fall off. I want you to follow the scientific method that we use to guide our laboratory work. Remember the steps of this method listed on the poster.

> **The Scientific Method**
>
> 1. Problem
> 2. Hypothesis
> 3. Procedure
> 4. Results
> 5. Conclusion

  a. Evaluate this approach to teaching science by writing one sentence indicating the extent to which it reflects the way scientists go about their work.

  b. In one or two paragraphs, substantiate your evaluation of this teaching episode from what you read in this chapter.

3. How would you distinguish science from other ways of knowing, such as myth and religion?

4. Analyze a teaching situation or instruction materials to determine which dimension(s) or theme(s) of science discussed in this chapter is emphasized. Make an outline of the major terms associated with (1) science as a way of thinking, (2) science as a way of investigating, (3) science as a body of knowledge, and (4) science and its interactions with technology and society. Use these categories to determine the science curricular emphasis in the following paragraphs that you might find in a science textbook.

  a. Heat, temperature, and energy are related. Consider, for example, what happens when you vigorously rub your hands together. The rapid motion of skin moving across skin causes the molecules in these layers of polymers to vibrate faster, producing heat. While working in a cannon factory, Benjamin Tompson noticed that drilling into brass caused the metal to get hot, but the heat went away when he stopped drilling. This led Tompson to relate motion to heat and energy.

  b. There is a global debate taking place concerning the rain forests that are being cut down in South America. The people of that region believe it is their right to clear the trees so that they can cultivate the land and grow crops to feed themselves. People in other parts of the world are distressed to learn of the rain forest destruction; they want the trees to take in carbon dioxide from the atmosphere and give off oxygen. Further, they fear that many species of plants and insects will become extinct with the disappearance of the rain forest habitat.

■

RESOURCES TO EXAMINE

Science for All Americans. 1994. American Association for the Advancement of Science, New York: Oxford University Press.

Read the first chapter, "The Nature of Science." This important document offers a very clear presentation on what is science. All science teachers should have a copy of this book in their professional library and refer to it for guiding their understanding of science teaching.

What Is This Thing Called Science? 1982. Alan Chalmers, Portland, OR: International Specialized Book Services. Distributed in the United States and Canada by International Specialized Book Services, 5804 NE Hassalo Street, Portland, OR 97213-3640.

Chalmers contrasts what we know about the nature of science with the philosophy of science and the history of science. In this easy-to-read paperback of 170 pages, he provides numerous examples to help the reader understand the many facets of science, such as inductivism, falsificationism, theories, objectivism, realism, instrumentalism, and truth.

Ten myths of science: Reexamining what we think we know about the nature of science. 1996. William McComas, *School Science and Mathematics, 96,* 10–16.

McComas's six-page article will help science teachers to examine their views of science. He discusses hypotheses, scientific method, objectivity, and experimentation.

REFERENCES

Aicken, F. (1984). *The nature of science.* London: Heinemann Educational Books.

Beveridge, W. I. B. (1957). *The art of scientific investigation.* New York: Vintage Books.

Boorstin, D. J. (1985). *The discoverers.* New York: Vintage Books.

Black, H. (1994, December) Poison that heals. *Chem Matters,* 7–9.

Bridgman, P. W. (1950). *The reflections of a physicist.* New York: Philosophical Library.

Bruner, J. S., Goodnow, J. J., & Austin, G. A. (1956). *A study of thinking.* New York: John Wiley.

Bruno, L. C. (1989). *The landmarks of science.* New York: Facts on File.

Chalmers, A. F. (1982). *What is this thing called science?* Portland, OR: International Specialized Book Service.

Chamberlin, T. C. (1965). The method of multiple working hypotheses. *Science, 148,* 754.

Chiappetta, E. L., Sethna, G. H., & Fillman, D. A. (1991). A quantitative analysis of high school chemistry textbooks for scientific literacy themes and expository learning aids. *Journal of Research in Science Teaching, 28,* 939–951.

de Santillana, G. (1961). *The origins of scientific thought.* New York: New American Library of World Literature.

Duschl, R. A. (1990). *Restructuring science education.* New York: Teachers College Press.

Duschl, R. A. (1994). Research on the history and philosophy of science. In D. L. Gabel (Ed.), *Handbook of research on science teaching and learning* (pp. 443–465). New York: Macmillan.

Feyerabend, P. K. (1981). *Philosophical papers.* Cambridge: Cambridge University Press.

Franz, J. E. (1990). The art of research. *ChemTech, 20*(3), 133–135.

Gauld, C. (1982). The scientific attitude and science education: A critical reappraisal. *Science Education, 66,* 109–121.

Gleick, J. (1987). *Chaos.* New York: Penguin Books.

Harre, R. (1970). *The principles of scientific thinking.* Chicago: University of Chicago Press.

Hawking, S. W. (1988). *A brief history of time.* New York: Bantam Books.

Hetherington, N., Miller, M., Sperling, N., and Reich, P. (1989). Liberal education and the sciences. *Journal of College Science Teaching, 19*(2), 91.

Hodson, D. (1988). Toward a philosophically more valid science curriculum. *Science Education, 77,* 19–40.

Holton, G. 1952. *Introduction to concepts and theories in physical science.* Reading, MA: Addison-Wesley.

Horgan, J. (1993). The worst enemy of science. *Scientific American, 268*(5), 36–37.

Hummel, C. E. (1986). *The Galileo connection.* Downers Grove, IL: InterVarsity Press.

Kuhn, T. S. (1970). *The structure of scientific revolutions.* Chicago: University of Chicago Press.

Loving, C. C. (1995). Comments on multiculturalism, universalism, and science education. *Journal of Research in Science Teaching, 79,* 341–348.

Lumpe, A. T., & Beck, J. (1996). A profile of high school biology textbooks using scientific literacy recommendations. *The American Biology Teacher, 58,* 147–153.

Martin, B., Kass, H., & Brouwer, W. (1990). Authentic science: A diversity of meanings. *Science Education, 74,* 541–554.

Matthews, M. R. (1991). Ernst Mach and contemporary science education reforms. In M. R. Mathews (Ed.), *History, Philosophy, and Science Teaching* (pp. 9–18). New York: Teachers College Press.

Matthews, M. R. (1994). *Science teaching*. New York: Routledge.

Mayr, E. (1961). Cause and effect in biology. *Science, 134,* 1503.

Mayr, E. (1982). *The growth of biological thought*. Cambridge: Belknap Press of Harvard University Press.

Mitroff, I. (1974). *The subjective side of science*. Amsterdam: Elsevier Scientific Publishing.

Moore, J. A. (1984). Science as a way of knowing. *American Zoologist, 24,* 467-534.

Morris, R. (1991). How to tell what is science from what isn't. In J. Brockman (Ed.), *Doing science*. New York: Prentice Hall.

Pearson, K. (1937). *The grammar of science*. London: Dutton.

Polanyi, M. 1958. *Personal knowledge*. Chicago: University of Chicago Press.

Popper, K. (1963). *Conjectures and refutations: The growth of scientific knowledge*. New York: Harper & Row.

Popper, K. (1972). *The logic of scientific discovery*. London: Hutchinson of London.

Project Physics Course. (1975). *Project physics*. New York: Holt, Rinehart and Winston.

Roe, A. (1961). The psychology of the scientists. *Science, 134,* 456–459.

Rorty, R. (1991). *Objectivity, relativism, and truth. Philosophical papers: Volume I*. Cambridge: Cambridge University Press.

Stanley, W. B., & Brickhouse, N. W. (1994). Multiculturalism, universalism, and science education. *Journal of Research in Science Teaching, 78,* 387–398.

Strahler, A. N. (1992). *Understanding science*. Buffalo, NY: Prometheus Books.

Teller, E. (1991, March 12). Teller talks. *The Daily Cougar, 57*(83), pp. 1, 15. Houston: University of Houston.

Wilson, E. B., Jr. (1952). *An introduction to scientific research*. New York: McGraw-Hill.

■

NATIONAL STANDARDS AND
INNOVATIVE PROGRAMS

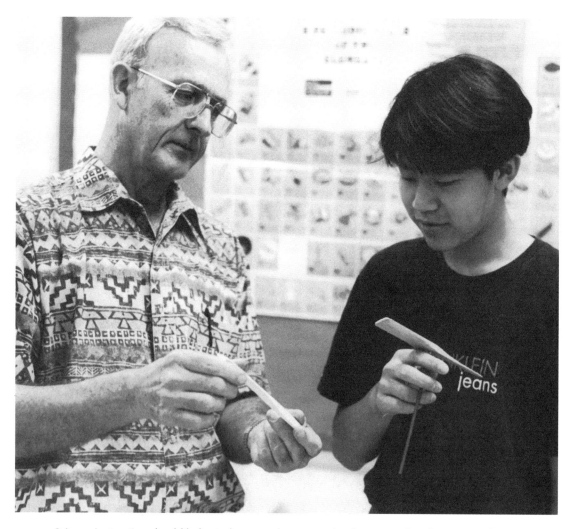

Science instruction should help students see the connection between what they are taught in the classroom and the world around them.

A nation as large and diverse as the United States of America can benefit from a set of standards to guide its education system. School districts and teachers need some guidelines from which to formulate goals and directions for their educational programs. The national standards that have been put forth for science in the 1990s provide science teachers, science coordinators, school district administrators, and state directors of science with useful ideas that have been prepared by national committees. In science education there are several standards, each produced by a nationally recognized group of professionals who have carefully formulated their recommendations for carrying out a science education reform to produce a nation that is more scientifically literate. In addition, there are many new science programs and curriculum materials to support the reform movement. These materials have the potential to make science more relevant for students, giving them a useful science education.

OBJECTIVES

This chapter is designed to help the reader meet the following objectives:

- Examine a brief history of science education in the United States over the past two hundred years.
- Become familiar with the intent of national committees who have produced guidelines and standards for the science education reform movement.
- Identify innovative curriculum materials that can make science comprehensible and relevant to students at the middle and high school levels.

INTRODUCTION

A reformation is occurring in science education across the nation. Major events are taking place to change science teaching in grades K–12 in order for students to become better educated in science, technology, and mathematics and to appreciate these enterprises. Many professional organizations have put forth recommendations and developed national science education standards to guide science education. A large variety of instructional materials is being produced to help students learn fundamental ideas and to find relevance in science and technology. Teacher institutes, workshops, and courses are being offered to educate science teachers to meet the challenge of helping students who live in a diverse multicultural society to become more scientifically literate. Money is being provided at the state and national levels and by business and industry to fund the reform. Importantly, there appears to be a consensus among many educators, professional groups, governmental organizations, and the business community regarding the outcomes that should be realized from this movement.

Science education in America has experienced other reforms and changes during the past two centuries. Each of these periods of reform provided new goals and directions for science education, just as the current reform does. Further, they brought renewed interest and desire to improve what takes place in schools. The intent of those making the recommendations is often to emphasize neglected goals in order to produce courses that better serve students and society. Although the recommendations of committees and individuals appear to emphasize balance in the curriculum, they often either omit or de-emphasize important aspects of science teaching. We hope that this will not be the situation for the present reform.

If you examine the goals of science education over the past two hundred years, you will see that there are many recurrent themes, such as science for all students, updating the content, learning about the nature of science, and the inclusion of technology in the curriculum. These themes are made prominent by the social, economic, and political forces of a given period. Science teachers should attend to these forces, because they are ever present and important.

The social, political, economic, and cultural forces that drove the reform movement in science education during the 1950s and 1960s are much different than those driving the reform movement today (Fensham, 1988). The cold war period between the United States and the Soviet Union and the launching of Sputnik placed national security and the need for a scientific work force high on the nation's political agenda. The government found it necessary to lead the star wars era with scientists and engineers who could meet the challenge of protecting the country against Soviet aggression. The 1970s brought disillusionment with science, and attention on science education was greatly reduced while the country was trying to get over the Vietnam conflict. In the 1980s science education became the focus of a great deal of criticism. Now the nation realizes that it must educate its citizens to become scientifically and technologically literate in order to be a productive society. The emphasis today is on science for everyone. Minorities and women are encouraged to participate in careers in science and engineering. The reform movement this time is being stimulated by the competition from countries in many parts of the world that threatens to diminish the economic leadership of the United States.

Science teachers want to take part in a movement that will help them to be successful in their work. Of particular interest to them are the national standards and the curriculum materials that have been developed for their classrooms. Before we present the recommendations and standards from national committees and a description of innovative instructional materials that have been produced, however, science education over the past two hundred years is reviewed briefly to highlight the themes and trends that have dominated the past and can be found in the present.

A BRIEF HISTORY OF SCIENCE EDUCATION

The Period between 1800 and 1910

During the early part of the 1800s, very little took place regarding science education. The nation was primarily an agricultural society and the cities were just beginning to take form. Children spent more time working on the farm than attending school. Whatever took place in the elementary school under the name of science was didactic in nature, requiring students to memorize facts to support religious doctrines (Underhill, 1941).

Between 1860 and 1880 there was a movement to promote "object teaching," which was based upon the teaching of Pestalozzi, a Swiss educator. Object teaching was an attempt to make instruction more concrete and student centered. The intent was to give children real objects with which to experiment and make observations rather than lecturing to them. The object teaching movement sought to develop student thinking and to de-emphasize the memorization of facts.

Around 1890 the nature study movement was begun in New York State by Liberty Hyde Bailey, who was a professor at Cornell University. Bailey observed the migration of people into the cities and was concerned that children would grow up knowing very little about nature and the environment. He wanted to stimulate interest in living things and he wanted students to study the natural environment. Bailey promoted his ideas through the Cornell School Leaflets. The early editions of the leaflets centered on the study of birds, flowers, insects, and trees.

Science teaching in the secondary schools began in academies around the late 1700s and early 1800s. Academies were private schools that prepared students of means for college and professional life. During their early period religious instruction dominated, but gradually other subjects were added to the curriculum. Astronomy, physics, chemistry, botany, geology, geography, navigation, and surveying were some of the subjects included in the science curriculum.

In the mid-1800s high schools came into being. In 1872 the Kalamazoo Decision to support high schools through a tax opened up high school education to many. This tax bill was important because many people were migrating to the city and the industrialization of the country was dependent upon a work force that possessed the ability to read and communicate. The industrialization of cities created a need for practical science courses that included technology. In the sciences, these courses included zoology, botany, astronomy, surveying, mensuration, mechanics, engineering, geology, and mineralogy. The courses emphasized the practical arts and citizenship (Lacey, 1966).

Science education before 1910 is enlightening to study because it shows the beginning of science instruction in this country. The very fact that science became part of the curriculum indicates that it was perceived to be an important aspect of schooling. As primitive as the schools and curricula might seem, they illustrate some of the same trends and raise some of the same issues that are under discussion today. For example, in the elementary school, the object teaching lessons and nature study movement stressed the importance for children to study real objects and de-emphasized the memorization of facts. Some of these very ideas survive in the science education literature today, urging elementary school teachers to involve students in hands-on activities and to center the teaching of science on concrete learning experiences rather than basing these experiences on textbook reading and completing work sheets.

College science teaching, an approach that included lecture with some laboratory work, influenced science in the high schools before 1910. High school science courses that modeled college and university science teaching were viewed as very specialized and only appropriate for those going on to college, which excluded most students. When the Committee of Ten (Committee

on Secondary School Studies, 1893) set out to standardize high school curricula, it emphasized that the secondary schools in the United States did not exist for the sole purpose of preparing boys and girls for college. This report, along with others, promoted articulation between elementary and secondary school programs. It also caused colleges to have less influence over high school science offerings.

The Period between 1910 and 1955

During the first half of the twentieth century, the United States grew rapidly and became a modern nation. The country also went through a severe depression and took part in two world wars. The modernization and growth of the country influenced the structure of public schooling whereby the 6-3-3 organizational pattern of grades, elementary through high school, was put in place. Science in the elementary school was influenced by the work of science educator Gerald Craig. The elementary curriculum that Craig developed centered on generalizations and concepts from the various science disciplines. This influence resulted in readers that taught children science content, but the curriculum was lacking in inquiry and hands-on activities.

The junior high schools flourished during this period of population growth. General science became a ninth grade subject at first, but later was taught in grades 7 and 8. Biology was generally taught in tenth grade, chemistry in eleventh grade, and physics in twelfth grade. General science and biology stressed the practical aspects of science and environment and were more popular courses than chemistry or physics. In fact, advanced general science was proposed for grades 11 and 12.

During the periods after the two world wars, national committees attempted to influence science teaching and promote a general education for all students. These ideas are reflected in the *Thirty-First Yearbook, Part 1* (National Society for the Study of Education, 1932) and the *Forty-Sixth Yearbook, Part 1* (National Society for the Study of Education, 1947). The recommended objectives for science teaching in the latter book are (1) functional information of facts, (2) functional concepts, (3) functional understanding of principles, (4) instrumental skills, (5) attitudes, (7) appreciations, and (8) interests. These objectives stress a working knowledge and appreciation of science and the applications of science in society. Although stated in somewhat broader terms, these ideas are similar to the list of thirteen descriptors for a scientifically and technologically literate person put forth by the National Science Teachers Association in 1982.

The influences of the times are often reflected in school science programs. For example, the technology of

World War II, such as radio, photography, and aviation, was evident in general science and physics courses. However, the advances made in the pure sciences during this period of time were not known to the public and therefore they did not influence public school science education. The making of the atomic bomb advanced physical science many years in a very short period of time (Rhodes, 1986). The Manhattan Project brought together many of the most capable scientists, whose work on the atom created new knowledge in the areas of physics and chemistry. Much of this new knowledge did not reach high school or college chemistry and physics textbooks until ten or fifteen years after the end of World War II.

The Period between 1955 and 1970

After World War II the country was rebuilding its economy and the population began to grow. The number of students in the schools increased, and science course enrollment in the elementary and secondary schools increased as well. At the same time, it was realized that few young people were choosing careers in science and mathematics, which caused scientists and mathematicians to examine the contents of secondary school science courses even before Sputnik was launched in 1957. Science textbooks and science teaching practices were criticized severely. The mathematicians and scientists claimed that the courses lacked rigor, were taught dogmatically, were content oriented, lacked conceptual unity, were outdated, and had little bearing on what was really happening in the scientific disciplines.

When Sputnik was launched in 1957, the concerns of scientists, mathematicians, and politicians brought about a massive reform in science and mathematics education never before witnessed in public education. Many millions of dollars were spent on the development of curriculum projects that were unique to education at all levels, from the elementary school through senior high school. Programs were offered across the nation at colleges and universities to update science teachers' content knowledge. Some of these teacher training programs included familiarization with the new curriculum projects, whereas other programs were offered specifically to train teachers to implement a given curriculum project. Unfortunately, most of the money spent on the reform movement in science education was on the development of new programs, as opposed to training teachers to understand and use the programs. As a result, only a small percentage of the teachers who used these innovative materials had adequate knowledge of the content and understanding of the philosophy behind the programs and the instructional approaches recommended by the authors.

A distinguishing characteristic of the nationally recognized curriculum projects was the emphasis upon the nature of science and teaching inquiry-based courses. The scientists who developed the programs wanted students to learn that science is a dynamic enterprise where knowledge is constructed through observation and the examination of data. Consequently, laboratory work was a central activity in these courses. Some of the courses consisted almost entirely of laboratory work; others placed laboratory work before classroom discussion and textbook reading. The textbooks written for these programs illustrate how scientists discovered certain principles and laws. They de-emphasized memorization of facts and vocabulary, often pointing out to the reader that this is what is known and how it was arrived at.

The Period between 1970 and 1980

The intent of the program developers of the curriculum projects of the late 1950s and 1960s was to interest more students in science and give them a greater appreciation for this enterprise—its contents and processes. Little time elapsed after the implementation of these courses of study, however, before dissatisfaction with them was voiced. The programs did not seem to be living up to expectation. Hurd (1969) pointed out that the programs had weaknesses as well as omissions. The following are some of the weaknesses of these innovative courses cited by science educators:

- The courses were too specialized and discipline centered.
- The topics were too classically oriented, and more relevant topics that related to society were omitted.
- There was too much theory and concept orientation in the programs.
- The courses were too difficult for the average student.
- There was a lack of humanistic, social, and historical aspects that are necessary for a general education in science.
- Teachers found it difficult to teach these courses.

We must remember that these programs were very different from the traditional textbook-based science courses used in most science classrooms. Perhaps the biggest difference between the curriculum projects and traditional courses was the instructional approach. The alphabet programs (BSCS, PSSC, ESCP, etc.), as they were sometimes referred to, stressed an inquiry-based approach to instruction. Inquiry and discovery seem to be foreign ideas to many science teachers, however. The experience of these individuals as students in science courses was one of spending most of their time in class listening to lectures about science with some verification laboratory exercises. Forming concepts and discovering laws through inductive laboratory activities was either not part of their science education, or, if it was, it made little impression and was quickly forgotten. Even today, teaching science as inquiry is not visible in most classrooms across the nation because teachers are not prepared to use this approach and schools do not value it (Stake & Easley, 1978). In the back-to-the-basics movement of the past decades, science teachers have been encouraged to teach and test for factual information, a force that has driven inquiry out of the curriculum.

The discontent with the post-Sputnik curriculum projects was evidenced in new programs that began in the mid-1960s and were implemented in schools during the 1970s. The first of these programs was the Intermediate Science Curriculum Study (ISCS). This junior high school program had three levels. Levels 1 and 2 pertained to physics and chemistry, respectively. They consisted entirely of laboratory work and stressed self-paced learning. Level 3 was composed of many modules for studying earth and life sciences. These individualized materials provided a large variety of activities for students to choose from to study science. Similarly, the Individualized Science Instructional Systems (ISIS) materials were meant to promote self-paced, individualized learning among high school science students. The instructional materials were composed of a large number of minicourses that related science to the lives of people.

During the 1970s, educators had an enormous array of science curriculum materials and ideas from which to choose. Hundreds of programs were available, many of which were the result of national curriculum project writing teams. Nevertheless, the nation's youth were not turning toward science and engineering, nor were they performing well on national assessments to determine knowledge and understanding of these fields. How could so much money and effort from our best scientists and educators produce so little in terms of science education?

The Period between 1980 and 1990

A great deal of criticism and controversy occurred during the 1980s regarding the status of science education. *A Nation at Risk* (National Commission of Excellence in Education, 1983) states clearly that "our educational system has fallen behind and this is reflected in our leadership in commerce, industry, science and technological innovations which is being taken over by competitors throughout the world" (p. 5). Many of the reports and discussions that appeared in the literature were drawn

from a multitude of studies conducted in the 1970s. For example, the National Science Foundation funded three contracts in 1976 to analyze science education in grades K–12. Helgeson, Blosser, and Howe (1977) at Ohio State University summarized studies during the period from 1955 to 1975. Weiss (1979) of the Research Triangle Institute conducted surveys of teachers, administrators, and other school personnel. Stake and Easley (1978) from the University of Illinois coordinated eleven indepth case studies of schools across the nation. The National Science Foundation also funded contracts to nine professional organizations to read these studies and report on their implications to their respective memberships. The more than two thousand pages of reports from the professional groups were synthesized and interpreted by Norris Harms and other science educators in Project Synthesis (Yager, 1982).

Project Synthesis produced four goal clusters that attempted to convey the goals of science education in operational terms. The four clusters are as follows:

> Goal Cluster 1: Personal Needs
>
> Goal Cluster 2: Societal Issues
>
> Goal Cluster 3: Academic Preparation
>
> Goal Cluster 4: Career Education

These broadly stated goals were used to analyze science education as it existed and to project what it ought to be. Out of Project Synthesis and many other studies came a movement that has directed science education beyond its discipline base. Note the importance in considering the needs of students and their careers. Further, note the prominence of societal issues as an important goal, which stresses the interaction of science and technology with society.

In the last decade of the twentieth century, the United States is again experiencing a school science reform. The reform is in reaction to political forces that desire the nation to be strong economically, necessitating a scientifically literate populace. The electronic-, communication-, and information-age society in which we live requires citizens who can develop these technologies as well as live with them. Science teachers have been given the challenge of educating the youth of America to participate in a highly technologically based world in which they must gather information using computers and electronic devices. However, in order to profit from these activities, students must possess a knowledge base that will permit them to assimilate information from printed and electronic sources and to make sense out of it. There is a great deal of fundamental knowledge that students must construct in the areas of biology, chemistry, earth science, and physics in order to use it in their daily lives and in the workplace. Science teachers must understand the reasons, recommendations, and implications of this reform, because political forces are powerful factors that greatly affect what takes place in education (Dow, 1991). Let's examine the national standards and guidelines to determine what is recommended to be learned in science by students who will be living in the twenty-first century.

NATIONAL GUIDELINES AND STANDARDS

Project 2061

In the mid 1980s, the American Association for the Advancement of Science (AAAS) spearheaded the science reform movement by initiating Project 2061. The central theme of their reform effort is to produce a scientifically literate society by the year 2061 when Halley's comet can again be observed from Earth. The AAAS is taking the long view in its reform effort, because it believes that important societal changes may take a great deal of time to achieve. One of the first documents it produced is titled *Science for All Americans* (AAAS, 1989). As the name implies, the intent is for "all" students to receive an education in science.

The AAAS reform project stresses the critical need to produce a scientifically literate society so that individuals can deal with the problems they will face in the new millennium. Many of the problems that U.S. citizens must concern themselves with are global, such as population growth, destruction of tropical rain forests, extinction of plant and animal species, scarce natural resources, and nuclear war. Science can provide knowledge and understanding about natural phenomena and social behavior that can benefit society. However, it will take an educated society, versed in science and technology, to comprehend societal problems and to deal effectively with them. "The life-enhancing potential of science and technology cannot be realized unless the general public can understand science, mathematics, and technology, and acquires scientific habits of mind. Without a science-literate population, the outlook for a better world is not promising" (AAAS, 1990, pp. xiv–xv).

Science for All Americans identifies serious shortcomings of our educational system, which science teachers must address in order for a serious science reform to take place. It reminds us that a great deal of instruction that takes place in science classrooms centers around learning answers rather than exploring questions. Memorization is emphasized at the expense of critical thinking.

Often reading about science takes the place of doing science. Students are not encouraged to work together on problems and to discuss their findings with others.

> The present curricula in science and mathematics are overstuffed and undernourished. . . . Some topics are taught over and over again in needless detail; some that are of equal or greater importance to science literacy— often from the physical and social sciences and from technology—are absent from the curriculum or are reserved for only a few students. (AAAS, 1990, p. xvi)

The idea that science courses cover too much material is a serious problem. This situation must be changed by focusing on less material and studying it in greater depth, which will actually result in students learning more. The "less-is-more" idea has become a slogan in the reform and it should be taken seriously by all science teachers.

The recommendations in the *Science for All Americans* document are clear about the education that a student must receive in order to be scientifically literate. Indeed, it is a comprehensive and interdisciplinary education that is proposed. Students must come to understand the nature of science, mathematics, and technology, and how these enterprises function separately and together. They must be versed in the physical, life, and social sciences from which they gain fundamental knowledge and understanding of reality. Students must study the designed world that has been shaped by human action to further the progress of society. Great importance should be placed upon providing students with a historical perspective of how the fundamental science ideas have evolved, such as the place of the earth in the solar system, matter and energy, fire, the atom, germs, and the diversity of life. Importantly, the reform project places a premium on the development of habits of mind that stress useful values, attitudes, and skills that students must acquire as they become versed in science, mathematics, and technology.

In addition to *Science for All Americans*, Project 2061 has produced another important document titled *Benchmarks for Science Literacy* (AAAS, 1993). *Benchmarks* specifies a common core of learning for students at specific points in their K–12 education. The document lists learning outcomes that all students should know or be able to do in science, mathematics, and technology by the end of grades 2, 5, 8, and 12. These objectives identify fundamental ideas that **all** children can attain. However, the document reminds us that many students are capable of going beyond these outcomes. Further, science teaching can use many methods and approaches to help students achieve these literacy goals. Examine Box 2.1 for a sample of learning outcomes in the *Benchmarks* pertaining to cells.

BOX 2.1

■

CELLS

A Sample of Learning Outcomes from the *Benchmarks*

The Living Environment

KINDERGARTEN THROUGH GRADE 2

By the end of the second grade, students should know that:

■ Magnifiers help people see things they could not see without them.

■ Most living things need water, food, and air.

GRADES 3 THROUGH 5

By the end of the fifth grade, students should know that:

■ Some living things consist of a single cell. Like familiar organisms, they need food, water, and air; a way to dispose of waste; and an environment they can live in.

■ Microscopes make it possible to see that living things are made mostly of cells. Some organisms are made of a collection of similar cells that benefit from cooperating; some organisms' cells vary greatly in appearance and perform very different roles in the organism.

GRADES 6 THROUGH 8

By the end of the eighth grade, students should know that:

■ All living things are composed of cells, from just one to many millions, whose details usually are visible only through a microscope. Different body tissues and organs are made up of different kinds of cells. The cells in similar tissues and organs in other animals are similar to those in human beings but differ somewhat from cells found in plants.

■ Cells continually divide to make more cells for growth and repair. Various organs and tissues function to serve the needs of cells for food, air, and waste removal.

■ Within cells, many of the basic functions of organisms—such as extracting energy from food and getting rid of waste—are carried out. The way in which cells function is similar in all living organisms.

■ About two-thirds of the weight of cells is accounted for by water, which gives cells many of their properties.

GRADES 9 THROUGH 12

By the end of the twelfth grade, students should know that:

■ Every cell is covered by a membrane that controls what can enter and leave the cell. In all but quite primitive cells, a complex network of proteins provides organization and shape and, for animal cells, movement.

- Within the cell are specialized parts for the transport of materials, energy capture and release, protein building, waste disposal, information feedback, and even movement. In addition to these basic cellular functions common to all cells, most cells in multicellular organisms perform some special functions that others do not.

- The work of the cell is carried out by many different types of molecules it assembles, mostly proteins. Protein molecules are long, usually folded chains made from twenty different kinds of amino-acid molecules. The function of each protein molecule depends on its specific sequence of amino acids, and the shape the chain takes is a consequence of attractions between the chain's parts.

- The genetic information in DNA molecules provides instruction for assembling protein molecules. The code used is virtually the same for all life forms.

- Complex interactions among the different kinds of molecules in the cells cause distinct cycles of activities, such as growth and division. Cell behavior can also be affected by molecules from other parts of the organism or even other organisms.

- Gene mutation in a cell can result in uncontrolled cell division, called cancer. Exposure of cells to certain chemicals and radiation increases mutations and thus increases the chance of cancer.

- Most cells function best within a narrow range of temperature and acidity. At very low temperatures, reaction rates are too slow. High temperatures and/or extremes of acidity can irreversibly change the structure of most protein molecules. Even small changes in acidity can alter the molecules and how they interact. Both single cells and multicellular organisms have molecules that help to keep the cell's acidity within a narrow range.

- A living cell is composed of a small number of chemical elements, mainly carbon, hydrogen, nitrogen, oxygen, phosphorous, and sulfur. Carbon, because of its small size and four available bonding electrons, can join to other carbon atoms in chains and rings to form large and complex molecules.

From *Benchmarks for Science Literacy* (pp. 111–114). Copyright © 1994 by the American Association for the Advancement of Science. Used by permission of Oxford University Press, Inc.

National Science Education Standards

The National Research Council (NRC) has produced a publication titled *National Science Education Standards* (NRC, 1996). This document stresses the importance for every citizen to become scientifically literate. Our society requires that we examine and use scientific information. We need a background in science in order to analyze this information and to make informed decisions. We need to be able to reason logically and to think scientifically about problems that confront us in our daily lives. The knowledge and skills that are central to science are also necessary for many jobs and careers whether or not they are in scientific fields. The following quote by the National Research Council (1996) reflects the intent of the *Standards*:

The *National Science Education Standards* are designed to guide our nation toward a scientifically literate society. Founded in exemplary practice and research, the *Standards* describe a vision of the scientifically literate person and present criteria for science education that will allow that vision to become a reality. (p. 1)

The *Standards* make it clear that scientific literacy is at the center of the reform movement. A scientifically literate person is identified as one who is curious about the world and desires to ask questions and find answers to those questions. These individuals can describe and explain natural phenomena as well as predict their behavior. They can also deal with science and societal issues by expressing them from an informed point of view, using their knowledge to evaluate the issues.

Knowledge and understanding of science are important guidelines for the realization of a scientifically liter-

Science courses should incorporate more investigations in order to develop the ability to understand knowledge and to value inquiry.

ate society. Students must learn fundamental scientific facts, concepts, principles, laws, theories, and models. These ideas must be integrated into students' cognitive structures so that they can be recalled and applied in their decision-making activities. Further, students must be able to use this understanding to distinguish between scientific information that is valid and that which is unsubstantiated.

Inquiry is a theme that runs through the *Standards*. This concept is defined relative to scientific inquiry, which centers around humankind's probing the natural world in search of explanations, based on evidence, leading toward an understanding of reality. Scientific inquiry includes both the ideas under study as well as the way in which those ideas come to be known. The *Standards* make it clear that there are many ways to inquire and to find out, from conducting firsthand investigations to reading about what others have found. Further, "conducting hands-on science activities does not guarantee inquiry, nor is reading about science incompatible with inquiry" (NRC, 1996, p. 23). Box 2.2 presents the changing emphases that are recommended in the science reforms regarding how to teach science **as** inquiry.

Science and technology are seen as compatible and necessary to the development of scientific literacy. They are closely tied together and should be part of reform science programs. However, they are different enterprises. The major aim of science is to understand nature,

whereas the major aim of technology is to create devices and systems to assist society.

The *National Science Education Standards* provide science teachers as well as the entire profession with important guidelines that they can use to plan, organize, develop, implement, and evaluate science programs, which will make a difference in reforming science education. There are many dimensions to science teaching and they must be considered in the development of effective science programs that will produce scientifically literate citizens.

Scope, Sequence, and Coordination

In the late 1980s, the National Science Teachers Association initiated a science reform project for grades 6–12. The project is called Scope, Sequence, and Coordination (SS&C) and its aim is to change the structure of science curricula in the middle and senior high schools. The rationale for altering the content structure that exists is a belief that teaching the separate disciplines—biology, chemistry, earth/space science, and physics—each year is inefficient and does not integrate the sciences so that they make sense to the students. With the "layer cake" curriculum that has been in existence for over a century, students take earth science for one year, biology for one year, and perhaps chemistry one year. This year-long concentrated approach does not lend itself to building upon what the students have studied in previous science courses. Further, the one-year science courses that are traditionally taught are usually textbook-based experiences, which are heavy on content and learning large numbers of facts. The one-discipline-based science course often results in students memorizing many terms, taking factually oriented paper-and-pencil tests, and remembering very little fundamental science.

Scope, Sequence, and Coordination's recommendation for reforming middle and senior high school science is to teach all four of the major science disciplines—biology, chemistry, earth/space science, and physics—each year in grades 6–12. In this manner, students would be able to connect the sciences and learn through a coordinated sequence the fundamental principles of the four major disciplines of science. Further, if the curriculum adheres to the less-is-more notion that covering fewer topics can help students learn more about a given area, students will develop a deeper understanding of a given set of important ideas.

The term **scope** refers to the coherence of the curriculum that can be achieved by studying a set of fundamental ideas over six or seven years of school science.

The term **sequence** addresses student learning with the belief that students should be taught beginning with concrete ideas and moving toward the abstract as they advance through the grade levels. In addition, science programs should space the learning so that fundamental ideas are studied over many years rather than many days or weeks. Also, the curriculum should provide application of knowledge so that it is relevant to students' lives. The term **coordination** refers to studying the four basic disciplines each year and ensuring for continuity.

Science teachers should examine the publication *Scope, Sequence, and Coordination of Secondary School Science, Volume 1: The Content Core* for a thorough description of the recommendations that the National Science Teachers Association (1992) has put forth to change the way science is organized in the secondary schools. More recently, this project has coordinated their efforts with the *National Science Education Standards*, producing a curriculum framework called *Scope, Sequence, and Coordination: A Framework for High School Science Education* (Aldridge, 1996), which lists content standards and implementation guidelines for reforming science education.

BOX 2.2

■

RECOMMENDATIONS FOR TEACHING SCIENCE FROM *NATIONAL SCIENCE EDUCATION STANDARDS*

Changing Emphases

The *National Science Education Standards* envision change throughout the system. The science content standards encompass the following changes in emphases:

Less Emphasis on	*More Emphasis on*
Knowing scientific facts and information	Understanding scientific concepts and developing abilities of inquiry
Studying subject matter disciplines (physical, life, earth sciences) for their own sake	Learning subject matter disciplines in the context of inquiry, technology, science in personal and social perspectives, and history and nature of science
Separating science knowledge and science process	Integrating all aspects of science content
Covering many science topics	Studying a few fundamental science concepts
Implementing inquiry as a set of processes	Implementing inquiry as instructional strategies, abilities, and ideas to be learned

Changing Emphases to Promote Inquiry

Less Emphasis on	More Emphasis on
Activities that demonstrate and verify science content	Activities that investigate and analyze science questions
Investigations confined to one class period	Investigations over extended periods of time
Process skills out of context	Process skills in context
Emphasis on individual process skills such as observation or inference	Using multiple process skills—manipulation, cognitive, procedural
Getting an answer	Using evidence and strategies for developing or revising an explanation
Science as exploration and experiment	Science as argument and explanation
Providing answers to questions about science content	Communicating science explanations
Individuals and groups of students analyzing and synthesizing data without defending a conclusion	Groups of students often analyzing and synthesizing data after defending conclusions
Doing few investigations in order to leave time to cover large amounts of content	Doing more investigations in order to develop understanding, ability, values of inquiry, and knowledge of science content
Concluding inquiries with the result of the experiment	Applying the results of experiments to scientific arguments and explanations
Management of materials and equipment	Management of ideas and information
Private communication of student ideas and conclusions to teacher	Public communication of student ideas and work to classmates

Reprinted with permission from NATIONAL SCIENCE EDUCATION STANDARDS. Copyright 1996 by the National Academy of Science. Courtesy of the National Academy Press. Washington, DC.

■ STOP AND REFLECT! ■

Think about the national guidelines and standards that have been presented and respond to the following questions:

■ What is the major intent of each of the science reform documents: *Science for All Americans, Benchmarks for Science Literacy, National Science Education Standards,* and *Scope, Sequence, and Coordination?*

■ Do any of the national guidelines make recommendations that would change significantly how science is taught in grades 6–12 if they were followed?

■ What major themes do the national guidelines have in common?

INNOVATIVE MIDDLE SCHOOL SCIENCE PROGRAMS

Great Explorations in Math and Science

The Lawrence Hall of Science at the University of California at Berkeley has a long history of producing materials for science instruction that have been used in many schools across the nation. One of the programs, Great Explorations in Math and Science (GEMS), has resulted in a large variety of teaching modules that addresses many aspects of science for students at many grade levels. The instruction is activity oriented, engaging students in the process of finding out about many phenomena. Often students inquire by taking the role of an investigator.

Over the past few decades, many teacher's guides for this program have been produced. The following is a list of some of the GEMS booklets (Lawrence Hall of Science, 1985), along with the recommended grade levels.

Acid Rain (6–10)

Animals in Action (5–9)

Color (5–9)

Crime Lab (4–8)

Earthworms (5–9)

Fingerprinting (4–8)

Height-O-Meters (6–10)

Hot Water & Warm Homes from Sunlight (4–8)

The Magic of Electricity (3–6)

Mapping Animal Movements (4–8)

Of Cabbage & Chemistry (4–8)

Oobleck: What do Scientists Do? (4–8)

Paper Towel Testing (5–9)

River Cutter (6–9)

Sunlight (4–8)

Vitamin C Testing (4–8)

From this sample of teacher's guide titles, you can visualize the interest that might be generated from students who are learning science from an effective science teacher using these materials.

The teacher's guide is the primary teaching aid. It provides a great deal of guidance regarding how to plan and implement lessons as well as what to anticipate from students. An introduction is given that describes the flow of activities. A time frame indicates the approximate duration of each instructional component. Most of the materials are available in the home, grocery store, and pet shop. Sometimes a key instructional material is provided with the teacher's guide. The major skills, concepts, and themes of the module are listed to guide instruction and assessment.

Project WILD

The Western Association of Fish and Wildlife Agencies and the Western Regional Environmental Education Council (1993) have cosponsored the development of a program called Project WILD. They, along with many other agencies and organizations in the United States and in other countries have developed a large compendium of interdisciplinary, supplemental conservation and environmental education programs for educators of students in grades K–12. These materials emphasize wildlife from the microscopic to the very large. The philosophy of the program is that young people and their teachers have an interest in learning about the earth and the wildlife for which it provides a home. Further, humans need to become responsible members of the ecosystem and provide an environment that supports all forms of life.

> The goal of Project WILD is to assist learners of any age in developing awareness, knowledge, skills, and the commitment to result in informed decisions, responsible behavior, and constructive actions concerning wildlife and the environment upon which all life depends. (Western Regional Environmental Education Council, 1992, vi)

The Project WILD activities are of high interest to students because they engage students in classroom discussions, role-playing, gathering information from people, collecting data from the environment, taking photographs, deciding on issues, reflecting on their lives, solving problems, communicating with others, and so on. Further, the content of the lessons are inherently interesting to them. Most students like to observe and study nature. The nearly one hundred activities are organized into seven areas: (1) awareness and appreciation; (2) diversity of wildlife values; (3) ecological principles; (4) management and conservation; (5) people, culture, and wildlife; (6) trends, issues, and consequences; and (7) responsible human action. The following are some of the titles of Project WILD activities:

What's Wild?	Museum Search for Wildlife
Grasshopper Gravity!	Who Pays for What?
Habitat Lap Sit	Does Wildlife Sell Cigarettes?
Animal Poetry	Wildlife Issues: Community Attitude Survey
The Hunter	Cabin Conflict

Wild Edible Plants

Forest in a Jar

Owl Pellets

Which Niche?

Fire Ecologies

No Water off a Duck's Back

When a Whale is Right

Playing Lightly on the Earth

What Did Your Lunch Cost Wildlife?

Improving Wildlife Habitat in the Community

Project WILD's activity guide contains a very large number of instructional activities that focus upon many creatures living in a variety of environmental settings. Each activity provides the teacher with objectives, methods of instruction, background information, materials that will be needed, procedures, and evaluation. In addition, each activity indicates the age group for whom the activity is appropriate, the school subjects in which it might be used, the skills that students will use in participating in the instruction, the duration of the activity, and key vocabulary terms. These activities can be infused into many science classes in middle and high schools. They are especially appropriate for life science, integrated science, and biology courses.

Science Education for Public Understanding Program

There is another curriculum project from Lawrence Hall of Science (1992). Now called Science Education for Public Understanding Program (SEPUP), it was originally called Chemical Education for Public Understanding (CEPUP). The program is intended for the middle grades, but it can be used in high school as well. The aim of the program is to highlight chemicals and their role in our lives and to do so in a manner that promotes decision making. The program does not teach students which decisions to make, but it helps them to acquire the knowledge and understanding in order for them to engage in critical reasoning and to participate in a democratic society.

The SEPUP project has produced a large number of instructional modules to help middle school teachers instruct students in many areas that relate to science, chemistry, the environment, and everyday living. A list of most of the SEPUP modules follows:

Chemical Survey & Solutions and Pollution

Chemicals in Foods: Additives

Determining Threshold Limits

Environmental Health Risks

Household Chemicals

Investigating Chemical Processes: Your Island Factory

Investigating Ground Water: The Fruitvale Story

Investigating Hazardous Materials

Plastics in Our Lives

Risk Comparison

Understanding Health Risks

Toxic Waste: A Teaching Simulation

The Waste Hierarchy: Where Is "Away"

Each of the SEPUP modules includes a teacher's guide and a kit of materials for hands-on activities. The teacher's guide is informative and facilitates active student learning. The instruction is designed to promote concept acquisition, process skill development, and societal issue discussion. The teacher's guide provides the teacher with an overview of the important ideas to be addressed in these areas. Note how the conceptual overview of one of the modules, *Household Chemicals*, is presented for the teacher (Lawrence Hall of Science, 1995, x).

Teacher's Manual

Household Chemicals

Science Concepts	**Science Processes**	**Societal Issues**
Chemicals interact in specific proportions. Concentrations of a chemical in solution affect its behavior.	Make quantitative comparison of bleach solutions. Predict outcomes of experiments.	How do we make decisions regarding amounts of chemicals? Is more necessarily better?
Chemicals can be unsafe if used incorrectly.	Collect, process, and analyze survey data.	What does the public need to know about the use of household chemicals?

If you examine the conceptual understandings that are shown in this sample of learning outcomes, you note the emphasis placed on important dimensions of science education, namely, concepts, processes, and societal issues. If you examine the instructional activities, you will note how the program engages students in activities that make science, technology, and their interaction with society meaningful.

Integrated Science

The Center for Communication and Educational Technology (1996) at the University of Alabama has developed a middle school science program called Integrated Science, which is supported by a public and private partnership. The program was designed to reflect the national standards and recommendations that appear in *Science for All Americans*, *Benchmarks for Science Literacy*, and *Scope, Sequence, and Coordination*. Integrated Science is a three-year continuum of study for students beginning in grade 6 and advancing to grade 8 where they study only a small group of topics from the perspective of biology, earth/space science, chemistry, and physics. The goal for this program is to interest students in science and keep them enrolled for many years.

Science teachers who use the program are given many resources and considerable support. Each week there are three 20-minute prerecorded telecasts with a lead instructor, along with visiting scientists, students, and teachers, introducing the major topics and concepts. New teachers to the program can attend a week-long workshop at the university in the summer. Each participating school system provides their teachers with a computer, modem, and phone line so that they can receive e-mail and interact with others in the project by asking questions and receiving information.

The classroom activities center around observing familiar phenomena through hands-on activities. The activities are intended to develop critical thinking and to relate science to everyday life. Lessons and demonstrations are coordinated to the telecasts. Further, some of the instruction takes place in cooperative group learning. A student handbook is provided for each block, which gives additional background material and homework assignments.

The contents of the *Integrated Science Program* are reflected in the following example, showing that only four blocks of content are taught each year.

	Grade 6	Grade 7	Grade 8
Block I	Clues	Patterns	Waves
Block II	Machines	Matter	Energy
Block III	Cycles	Change	Stages
Block IV	Environment	Environment	Environment

Further examination of the contents reveals that each block is supported by a theme and several topics.

INNOVATIVE HIGH SCHOOL SCIENCE PROGRAMS

BSCS Biology: A Human Approach

The Biological Sciences Curriculum Study (BSCS) is a nonprofit science education research group that has been developing innovative instructional materials for four decades. One of their most recent course developments is called *BSCS Biology: A Human Approach* (BSCS, 1997), which is targeted for high school biology. As the name implies, the course gives special emphasis to studying biology from a human perspective within a context that will be relevant to students' lifelong learning. The instructional materials are designed to help high school students distinguish *Homo sapiens* from other living systems as well as identify the characteristics they share with other living systems. Further, the course is designed to help students learn more about the role of humans and their place in the biosphere.

BSCS Biology: A Human Approach embodies other goals beyond the human focus. The course stresses the recommendations of the *National Science Education Standards*. For example, the course aims to help students master the processes of scientific inquiry, problem solving, and ethical analyses. It addresses personal, social, and ethical implications of biology and biotechnology in society. In addition, a major goal of the entire course is to ensure that students understand the major concepts of biology.

The textbook for the course is different from the traditional, commercially prepared biology textbook. For example, the BSCS text contains sixteen chapters as opposed to the forty or fifty chapters that can be found in traditional high school biology textbooks. A sample of chapter headings is listed here:

Chapter 1: The Human Animal

Chapter 3: Products of Evolution: Unity and Diversity

Chapter 5: Human Homeostasis: Health and Disease

Chapter 7: Performance and Fitness

Within the student text are labs, hands-on investigations, and essays. The program also has multimedia components, a teacher's guide, a teacher's resource book, an implementation guide, and an assessment package.

Biology: A Community Context

Through funding from the National Science Foundation, a new high school biology course was developed at Clemson University called *Biology: A Community Context* and is intended to be used in heterogeneously mixed classrooms. The intent of *Biology: A Community Context* is not to attempt to cover all or most of the topics found in a traditional high school biology textbook. Instead, the course places major content emphasis on ecology, evolution, and genetics. The pedagogical emphasis is on engaging students in inquiry-based activities.

The *Biology: A Community Context* (Leonard & Penick, 1998) textbook is organized into eight units as follows:

1. Matter and Energy for Life
2. Ecosystems
3. Populations
4. Homeostasis: The Body in Balance
5. Inheritance
6. Behavior and the Nervous Systems
7. Biodiversity
8. The Biosphere

Examination of these units reflects the aim to make biology a highly relevant course for students by focusing on environmental issues and ecological principles.

Biology: A Community Context is structured to be inquiry oriented and constructivistic in nature. This approach to biology requires teachers to engage students in exploring and finding out rather than dispensing knowledge. The text is composed of a variety of activities to promote student interaction. For example, a unit may begin with what is called the "Opening Scenario," which is a compelling visual or video. These activities provide a setting for real issues and problems to be addressed. The scenario may be followed by brainstorming and discussion. The teacher is provided questions to guide discussion. Students keep a journal in which they write throughout the school year.

"Structured Inquiries" follow the "Opening Scenarios" and extend over many days. Some of these activities are designed to develop specific skills, whereas others provide basic concept information that is necessary for resolving issues. "The Science Conference" is used to clarify and present ideas, which may lead to another instructional type of activity called "Individual Inquiries." These inquiries may involve small cooperative group investigations or individual work. "The Science Congress" is also used for instructional purposes in *Biology: A Community Context*. It is more formal than the conference and seeks closure on a particular issue. Finally, there is "The Forum," where students play various roles to debate issues and exchange points of view. This results in students making decisions and taking action.

Insights in Biology

The Education Development Center (EDC) has long been a developer of innovative curriculum materials. The EDC (1997) has produced a high school biology course called *Insights in Biology*. This course is designed to make biology an interesting subject to learn. The developers have organized the program into a modular format that centers around fundamental principles of biology within a context that is relevant for students to learn. This approach differs from the traditional textbook-based biology course that contains a large compilation of factual information.

The topics for each of the modules were selected with the high school student in mind. They are used to serve as a "hook" to grab students' attention and to help them focus on fundamental principles of biology. The topics help to integrate information and experiences into a coherent set of learning outcomes. The titles of the modules are:

Matter of Life

Traits and Fates

Different Stages through the Ages

What on Earth?

The Blueprints of Infection

The modules that comprise the *Insights in Biology* program can be used to form an entire course, or a teacher can incorporate one or more of them into an existing course of study. Each module consists of an extensive set of learning activities. The teacher's guide for one module can contain up to three hundred pages and the student's manual up to two hundred pages. The activities vary widely, from reading a newspaper clipping to solving a biological problem. Take, for example, the module called The Blueprints of Infection. Some titles of the activities in this module designed for students are "Disease Detective," "Epidemic!," "Search for the Cause," "Language of the Cell," "The Cholera Connection," "Viral Hitchhiker," "I Opened the Window and In-flew-enza," and "Immune System to the Rescue."

Chemistry in the Community

The American Chemical Society has developed a high school chemistry course to support the reform movement in the high school. The course is called *Chemistry in the Community (ChemCom)* and its major aim is to promote scientific literacy among students in chemistry by emphasizing the impact of chemistry on society. *ChemCom* is designed to help students

- Realize the important role that chemistry will play in their personal and professional lives

- Use chemistry knowledge to think through and make informed decisions about issues involving science and technology

- Develop a lifelong awareness of both the potential and the limitations of science and technology. (American Chemical Association, 1993, xi)

The course and textbook are organized into eight topics that relate chemistry to everyday life. The topics serve as the context for problem solving. The chemistry involved is used to analyze and understand situations in our homes and communities. Note the relevance of the themes that are evident in the following eight topics that form this innovative course of study.

Supplying Our Water Needs

Nuclear Chemistry in Our World

Conserving Chemical Resources

Chemistry, Air, and Climate

Petroleum to Build? to Burn?

Health: Your Risks and Choices

Understanding Food

The Chemical Industry: Promise and Challenge

In addition to providing a different content focus for each unit from that of the traditional chemistry textbook, the *ChemCom* instructional approach is different. The text contains a large variety of student-oriented activities. Often the unit begins with a vignette that describes a situation of public concern, for example, a fish kill in a nearby waterway. There are laboratory, problem-solving, decision-making, and discussion activities. The text also contains short informative readings, along with crossword puzzles and situations to analyze. Students are active participants in this chemistry program. Although it may not seem evident at first glance, the units contain a great deal of fundamental chemistry for students to learn within a meaningful context.

Conceptual Physics

A small percentage of high school students enroll in a full year of physics. Most students avoid physics because it is too difficult. Physics courses are usually mathematics-based and require students to solve word problems that involve algebraic and trigonometric formulas. Paul Hewitt has developed a conceptual approach to physics that focuses upon comprehension of fundamental ideas, using very little mathematics. He uses simple English rather than mathematics to explain physics concepts. Hewitt has a talent for explaining ideas and believes if you get students to comprehend physics principles in everyday language, they will be better able to use mathematics in future courses to further their understanding of this abstract field.

Hewitt (1992, 1993) has authored conceptual physics textbooks for both college and high school levels. His textbooks contain many examples to illustrate physics principles and laws, which are accompanied by photographs and diagrams. Hewitt creates his own illustrations, often in cartoon form, to help the reader visualize concepts. The combination of written explanations and visuals seems to enhance comprehension and stimulate interest in physics. The high school program is accompanied by a teacher's guide and laboratory manual. In addition, Hewitt has prepared a booklet called *Next Time Questions*. This teaching aid contains a large number of questions (with answers) to stimulate thinking about physics concepts. Figure 2.1 is one of the examples from the booklet regarding the transmission of heat.

FIGURE 2.1   An Example of a
Thought Question Concerning
the Transmission of Heat

Conceptual **PHYSICS**

SUPPOSE IN A RESTAURANT YOUR
COFFEE IS SERVED ABOUT 5 OR 10 MINUTES
BEFORE YOU ARE READY FOR IT. IN ORDER
THAT IT BE AS HOT AS POSSIBLE WHEN YOU
DRINK IT, SHOULD YOU POUR IN THE
ROOM-TEMPERATURE CREAM RIGHT AWAY
OR WHEN YOU ARE READY TO DRINK
THE COFFEE?

ASSESSING AND REVIEWING

1. Consider *Benchmarks for Science Literacy*, a major
reform document produced by the American Association for the Advancement of Science that was discussed in this chapter. Examine the generalizations
pertaining to the cell (see Box 2.1), stating what all
students should know by the time they complete
high school. Then note the last statement under
grades 9–12:

   A living cell is composed of a small number of
   chemical elements, mainly carbon, hydrogen, nitrogen, oxygen, phosphorous, and sulfur. Carbon,
   because of its small size and four available bonding
   electrons, can join to other carbon atoms in chains
   and rings to form large and complex molecules.

Think about a middle and high school science program for grades 6–12 and indicate when and where
students should learn these concepts. Give the grade
levels, courses, and experiences that would develop
this knowledge so that it has meaning for students.

2. The *National Science Education Standards* is an
important document that discusses the many
changes that must occur throughout the educational system in order for a successful science education reform to occur. Box 2.2 summarizes some of
the changes in emphasis that are recommended by
the *Standards*. The following is a sample of these
ideas upon which to reflect:

Less Emphasis on	More Emphasis on
Studying subject matter disciplines (physical, life, earth sciences) for their own sake	Learning subject matter disciplines in the context of inquiry, technology, science in personal and social perspectives, and history and nature of science
Covering many science topics	Studying a few fundamental science concepts
Activities that demonstrate and verify science content	Activities that investigate and analyze science questions
Process skills out of context	Process skills in context
Getting an answer	Using evidence and strategies for developing or revising an explanation
Science as exploration and experiment	Science as argument and explanation
Concluding inquiries with the result of the experiment	Applying the results of experiments to scientific arguments and explanations

Discuss the implications for teaching science in the middle and senior high school if teachers change the way science is often taught and the way it is recommended.

3. Examine the Scope, Sequence, and Coordination (SS&C) project described in this chapter that was developed by the National Science Teachers Association. Consider the program's intent to change middle through high school science from teaching the major fields of science (biology, chemistry, earth/space science, and physics) in separate years to teaching all four in the same year, in each of grades 6–12.

a. How much of a change will this require in order for most school districts to adopt the SS&C approach?

b. What would a 6–11 or a 6–12 SS&C curriculum be like?

4. You will be greatly advantaged by assembling a large number of resources that can be used to teach science. Examine the innovative programs described within and the resources given at the end of this chapter. From these resources select information, modules, and books that will help you to become more effective in your teaching and do what is necessary to obtain them.

■

RESOURCES TO EXAMINE

Benchmarks for Science Literacy. 1993. American Association for the Advancement of Science, New York: Oxford University Press. Address for ordering: 2001 Evans Road, Cary, NC 27513-2010. Phone: (800)451-7556.

All school science departments should have a copy of this book, which contains general statements of learning for twelve areas of science education, such as the nature of science, the physical setting, the living environment, the human organism, the designed world, historical perspective, habits of mind, and more. The generalizations are arranged into what students should know by the end of grades K–2, 3–5, 6–8, and 9–12. Science teachers can compare what they expect students to learn at the end of their course with these standards.

National Science Education Standards. 1996. National Academy Press. 2101 Constitution Ave., NW, Box 285, Washington, DC 20055. Phone: (800)624-6242 or (202)334-3313 (in the Washington area).

This is a 243-page booklet that gives an overview of what should take place to achieve a successful science education reform. It gives science standards for teaching, professional development, assessment, science content, and science programs. All science teachers should have a copy of this booklet for frequent reference.

Project WILD. 1992. Project WILD national office: 5430 Grosvenor Lane, Bethesda, MD 20814. Phone: (301)493-5447. E-mail: natpwild@igc.apc.org. Or Western Regional Environmental Educational Council at

4014 Chatham Lane, Houston, TX 77027. Phone: (713)520-1936.

Every middle and high school science teacher interested in life science, biology, and environmental education should become familiar with Project WILD. The organization provides workshops for teachers and a 380-page activity guide. As described in this chapter, the K–12 activity guide is a compendium of activities that will interest students in studying the living world as it relates to the environment.

Lawrence Hall of Science. Registration Office, University of California at Berkeley, Berkeley, CA 94720. Phone: (510)642-5134.

The Lawrence Hall of Science has produced a large number of innovative instructional materials for the science classroom. Descriptions of Great Explorations for Math and Science (GEMS) and Science Education for Public Understanding (SEPUP) were given in this chapter. In addition, the Lawrence Hall of Science has many other instructional materials to examine for use in improving the scientific and mathematics literacy of students.

Biology: A Community Context. 1998. Authored by William Leonard and John Penick, published by South-Western Educational Publishing, Cincinnati, OH 44227-9985.

This biology course has a different content coverage than traditional high school biology courses. It focuses on a limited number of biology units (eight) that stress ecology, genetics, and the environment. Furthermore, the textbook's instructional approach is inquiry-oriented, which means that students are active learners who interact a great deal with the instruction. The authors have included a variety of instructional strategies to help students construct their knowledge of biological principles.

Chemistry in the Community (ChemCom). 1993. Produced by the American Chemical Society and published by Kendall/Hunt Publishing Company, Dubuque, Iowa 52004-1840. Phone: (800)258-5622.

This course is designed to help students realize the important role that chemistry will play in their personal lives and perhaps in their work. Knowledge of chemistry is used during instruction to assist students in making informed decisions about science and technology. The textbook topics are relevant to everyday living. The instructional activities and laboratory exercises can be used in other science courses in addition to chemistry. Because of the useful activities and information it contains, the *ChemCom* textbook is one that all middle and high school science teachers should have in their professional library.

REFERENCES

Aldridge, B. G. (Ed.). (1996). *Scope, sequence, and coordination: A framework for high school science education.* Arlington, VA: National Science Teachers Association.

American Association for the Advancement of Science. (1989). *Science for all Americans.* New York: Oxford University Press.

American Association for the Advancement of Science. (1990). *Science for all Americans.* New York: Oxford University Press.

American Association for the Advancement of Science. (1993). *Benchmarks for science literacy.* New York: Oxford University Press.

American Chemical Society. (1993). *Chemistry in the community.* Dubuque, IA: Kendall/Hunt.

Biological Sciences Curriculum Study. (1997). *BSCS biology: A human approach.* Dubuque, IA: Kendall/Hunt.

Center for Communication and Educational Technology. (1996). *Integrated science program.* Tuscaloosa: University of Alabama.

Committee on Secondary School Studies. (1893). *Report of the Committee of Ten on secondary school studies.* Washington, DC: National Education Association.

Dow, P. B. (1991). *Schoolhouse politics: Lessons from the Sputnik era.* Cambridge: Harvard University Press.

Education Development Center (EDC). (1997). *Insights in biology.* Dubuque, IA: Kendall/Hunt.

Fensham, P. J. (1988). Familiar but different: Some dilemmas and new directions in science education. In Peter J. Fensham (Ed.), *Development and dilemmas in science education.* London: Falmer Press.

Helgeson, S. L., Blosser, P. E., Howe, R. W. (1977). *The status of pre-college science, mathematics, and social science education: 1955–75. Vol. 1: Science education.* Columbus, OH: ERIC Center for Science and Mathematics Education at Ohio State University.

Hewitt, P. G. (1992). *Conceptual physics: The high school program.* Menlo Park, CA: Addison-Wesley.

Hewitt, P. G. (1993). *Conceptual physics*. New York: Harper-Collins College Publishers.

Hurd, P. D. (1969). *New directions in teaching secondary school science*. Chicago: Rand McNally.

Lacey, A. (1966). *A guide to science teaching in the secondary schools*. Belmont, CA: Wadsworth.

Lawrence Hall of Science. (1985). *Great Explorations in Math and Science Project*. Berkeley: University of California at Berkeley, The Regents of the University of California.

Lawrence Hall of Science. (1992). *Science Education for Public Understanding*. Berkeley: University of California at Berkeley, The Regents of the University of California.

Lawrence Hall of Science. (1995). *Household chemicals*. Menlo Park, CA: Addison-Wesley.

Leonard, W., & Penick, J. (1998). *Biology: A community context*. Cincinnati, OH: South-Western.

National Commission of Excellence in Education. (1983). *A nation at risk: The imperative for education reform* (Stock No. 065-000-001772). Washington, DC: U.S. Government Printing Office.

National Research Council. (1996). *National science education standards*. Washington, DC: National Academy Press.

National Society for the Study of Education. (1932). A program for science teaching. In *Thirty-first yearbook, part 1*. Bloomington, IL: Public School Publishing.

National Society for the Study of Education. (1947). In *Forty-sixth yearbook, part 1*. Chicago: University of Chicago Press.

National Science Teachers Association. (1992). *Scope, sequence, and coordination of secondary school science. Volume 1: The content core*. Arlington, VA: Author.

Rhodes, R. (1986). *The making of the atomic bomb*. New York: Simon and Schuster.

Stake, R. E., & Easley, J. A. (1978). *Case studies in science education*. Urbana: University of Illinois Center for Instructional Research and Curriculum Evaluation.

Underhill, O. E. (1941). *The origin and development of elementary school science*. New York: Scott Foresman.

Weiss, I. R. (1978). *Report of the 1977 national survey of science, mathematics, and social studies education*. Research Triangle Park, NC: Center for Educational Research and Evaluation.

Western Regional Environmental Education Council. (1992). *Project WILD*. Bethesda, MD: Author.

Yager, R. E. (1982). The current situation in science education. In J. R. Staver (Ed.), *1982 AETS yearbook*. Columbus, OH: ERIC Center for Science, Mathematics and Environmental Education at Ohio State University.

CHAPTER 3

THE NATURE OF ADOLESCENT LEARNERS AND THEIR SCHOOLS

All students should be encouraged to take an active part in science.

The American educational system is facing a great challenge today to provide an equitable education for all students. The diversity among students is causing considerable concern among science teachers. They must rethink the entire curriculum for this changing population of learners. To meet the challenge, teachers must address cultural background, ethnicity, gender, disabilities, and adolescent development in their decisions about the science education of students in a pluralistic society. Schools must also change to prepare this new generation of learners for the information age of the next century. Restructuring and reform are the true constants in today's middle and secondary schools. So it is that science education occurs in a context that is bound by the nature of the learners and their schools. An understanding of middle and secondary learners and their schools is needed to meet the demands of science teaching.

OBJECTIVES

This chapter is designed to help the reader meet the following objectives:

- Formulate a picture of the diversity of today's middle and secondary school population.

- Analyze science teaching situations and instructional materials to determine the extent to which they reflect equity in science education.

- Determine how to meet the needs of exceptional students who are enrolled in science classes—especially the learning disabled, physically disabled, and gifted and talented.

- Reflect upon the extent to which science teaching situations and instructional materials should be responsive to the physical, cognitive, personal, and social developmental levels of adolescent learners.

- Describe the distinguishing features of today's middle and secondary schools and the nature of the restructuring efforts ongoing in these schools.

STUDENT DIVERSITY

If you are reading this book, the probability is quite high that you are in your mid-twenties or slightly older, white, and come from a rather comfortable middle-class family. It is also very likely that you lived in a household with two parents who both worked and that you had no encounters with law enforcement, except, perhaps, for a traffic ticket. You likely went to school with people like you, enjoyed school, and did rather well in science classes. As an adult you may recall your adolescent years as a relatively enjoyable time. If this description comes close to matching you and you expect to encounter students who are similar to you in today's middle and secondary science classrooms, you are in for a surprise. Who are the students in American middle school and secondary science classrooms?

Demographics

Even as educational leaders have searched for new ways to enhance excellence in science teaching and learning, the demographic context of the middle and secondary science classroom has changed. Several of the changes that have occurred in recent years directly impact the success experienced by students in science and their continued participation in science classes. In the mid-1980s, the school age population began to increase after nearly fifteen years of decline. Along with this increase has come a tremendous growth in the diversity of the student population. Factors responsible for this growth in diversity include immigration and higher birth rates among some ethnic groups.

The *Indicators of Science and Mathematics Education-1995* (Suter, 1996) describes the nature of this growth. In 1993, the white K–12 school age population was estimated at about thirty-five million students. Although this number seems large, it reflects a 16 percent decrease from 1970. During this same twenty-three-year period, the population of black students increased from 14 percent to 16 percent. This increase brings the total school age population of Black Americans to over seven million. The population of other groups, mostly Asian Americans but also including Native Americans, has increased to about two million, or about 5 percent of the total school age population. The largest increase has occurred in the Hispanic population. From when it was first measured in 1975 to 1993, the Hispanic K–12 population has increased by 7–12 percent. Hispanics comprise the fastest growing segment of the school age population and now number over five million students.

Other statistics tell more about the students in today's science classrooms:

- One in five children 6–17 years old lives in a family whose income is below the poverty level. (Suter, 1996)

- A language other than English is spoken at home by 14 percent of all students. (Suter, 1996)

- Thirty percent of families have only one parent, and among Black American families it is 63 percent. (Suter, 1996)

- Almost five million students have a disabling condition, but only 1 percent are physical impairments. The rest are cognitive, social-personal, or intellectual disabilities. (Lynch et al., 1997)

- High school dropout rates exceed 30 percent among Hispanics and Native Americans. (Snyder & Hoffman, 1995; Lynch et al., 1997)

- Forty-five percent of high school seniors have used illicit drugs. (Snyder & Hoffman, 1995)

- Thirty-seven percent of all students in our nation's schools are persons of color. (National Center for Educational Statistics, 1996)

Factors Affecting Success in Science

Diversity by itself does not affect students' success in science, but factors often related to diversity do. For instance, socioeconomic status is viewed as the "single most powerful factor" that affects science performance and motivation (Lynch et al., 1997, p. 13). Students from poor families who attend schools that are inadequately funded do less well in science than their contemporaries (Kozol, 1991). A disproportionate number of Black Americans, Hispanics, and Native Americans are poor and attend poor schools. There is little doubt that poverty contributes to the poor science performance and lack of motivation among students from these ethnic groups. Children of the poor lack many of the experiences that help other students succeed in school, and inadequately funded schools are ill prepared to help these children catch up. Many Asian Americans seem to have escaped the conditions of poverty through their educational achievements, but among recent Asian American immigrants, particularly those from Southeast Asia, the problems of poverty are very evident (United States Commission on Civil Rights, 1992).

Many recent immigrants, particularly young Asians and Hispanics, come from homes in which English is not spoken (Suter, 1996). This situation places excessive demands on students to learn English at the same time they are trying to learn science. Poor science performance among these students is due to the high vocabulary demands and the abstract understandings associated with science learning (Lee, Fradd, & Sutman, 1995).

Some Asian Americans seem to compensate for their limited English proficiency by excelling in school subjects that make low demands on their language skills (Lynch et al., 1997). Students from rural areas, regardless of ethnicity, are also disadvantaged when their science experiences and curricular choices are compared with those students at schools in larger communities. The lack of opportunity negatively impacts the science opportunities and performance of these students.

The factors of socioeconomic status, immigration status, proficiency in English language, and geographic location are among those used to identify students at-risk. At-risk students are those students who past trends indicate have a greater than average chance of not succeeding in school and dropping out. U.S. Department of Education statistics reveal that most at-risk students have one or more of the following risk factors (cited in Rothman, 1990):

- Are from single parent families
- Live in families with incomes below the poverty level
- Are at home alone more than three hours
- Have limited English proficiency
- Have a sibling who dropped out of school
- Have parents who are not high school graduates

As Muth and Alvermann (1990) acknowledge, however, "it is not only the underachieving minority students who drop out of high school" (p. 50). Students from all population groups drop out when they become disillusioned with the school experience. Science classes can either contribute to feelings of disillusionment or make school an exciting and enjoyable place to be.

The previous discussion highlights the characteristics of a rapidly changing, diverse student population

---

■ STOP AND REFLECT! ■

Before going further, do the following:

- Write a description for a class of students that reflects the diversity of today's student population. Then pick one student from the class description. What factors are likely to affect this student's success in science?

- Read the entry from Ms. Kendall's journal in Box 3.1. What ideas does Ms. Kendall have for helping her new Chinese student? What else might she consider?

---

that will no doubt challenge the teaching skills of even the best prepared science teachers. Such student diversity will make traditional teaching practices such as lecture obsolete. Teaching practices that take into account the heterogeneity of the students in terms of background, knowledge, motivation, and language will be required for the twenty-first century.

EQUITY IN SCIENCE EDUCATION

Equity in science education means that all students regardless of cultural background, ethnicity, gender, or special needs have the same opportunity to learn quality science (Atwater, Crockett, & Kilpatrick, 1996). The outcome of this quality science experience is citizens able to make use of science in their daily lives and to pursue science and science-related jobs of the highest caliber. Echoed in the saying Science for All is the ultimate goal of equity in science education, that is, to ensure that no group is underrepresented in science. The discussion in the previous section suggests that we are a long way from realizing this goal.

Lynch and her colleagues (1997) offer two compelling reasons for advancing equity in science education. The first is economic. Equity in science education will result in a work force better prepared for the science- and technology-related jobs of the twenty-first century. This highly skilled work force will benefit the nation's economy as high-tech jobs are filled by U.S. citizens and not lost to companies overseas. The second reason is based in social justice. We have the obligation to prepare all students to function in our modern science-based society. Additionally, these authors advance the argument that equity in science education should be about educating students in the culture of power that permits access to scientific knowledge. Central to this argument is the idea that the more you know, the more powerful you are. And as our previous discussion of demographics clearly indicates, science knowledge is not equally distributed among all groups in American society. According to Atwater et al. (1996), teachers maintain power in science classrooms through their selective silence and by the ways in which they present information and interact with students. Empowered science classrooms, where teachers and students function as a community of learners, are the desirable state.

Culturally Based Deficiencies

Schools must respond to the needs of today's diverse student population by addressing the issue of equity. But, how should this occur? In the past it was believed

BOX 3.1

■

MS. KENDALL'S JOURNAL

Ms. Kendall is a veteran teacher at Riverview High School. Her teaching assignment consists of three sections of chemistry and two of physical science. She keeps a daily journal. The following is her journal entry for April 6.

■

Today was an average day. Nothing outstanding happened and nothing terrible happened. I was glad that all three of the students who were scheduled to make up the last test at 8:00 A.M. came, although one student did not appear until 8:20. This was the third morning that I had scheduled for that one test. In the advanced class, we finished our discussion of solids and reviewed for the test tomorrow. Even with a test imminent, some students were still not interested in listening to a review of the material. I had to stop twice and wait for them to stop talking before I continued.

On the administrative side of teaching, I received notification to attend the disciplinary hearing for Anthony. He was the student that I smelled alcohol on during class last Friday. I didn't see him drinking but the odor was unmistakable. My guess is that he will be suspended for at least two weeks and then placed in In-School Suspension for awhile. I plan to recommend counseling on drug abuse during the hearing. He is a good kid. I also need to talk with Julie's parents about her drop in performance. She is very active in extracurricular activities and thinks science is a male thing. I wonder if these factors are responsible for her decline in class work. She made 32% on the last test, but is capable of much better work. She acts in class as if everything is so much effort. A parent conference is definitely needed. I'll speak to Julie about it tomorrow, before contacting her parents.

I was assigned a new student today. She is Chinese and speaks very little English. Her father is a consultant to the plant here and she will be attending school here for the next two years. I have scheduled a meeting with the ESL [English as a Second Language] teacher for tomorrow morning at 8:00 A.M. to discuss how to help her in my class. There is one other Chinese student who might be willing to assist her.

My average classes are working well. I don't like being so strict with them, but if I relax one minute the entire class is in chaos. I still have several students in each class who are completely unmotivated. I can't believe that they don't find some of the material that we are covering interesting, since the program that we are using is an STS approach. There is one problem that I have to work on with them. I cannot start class on time because I have four or five students who hover around me asking questions about grades, absences, homework, missed work, work that is due, and just about anything else. I really need to find a way to be responsive to them and begin class in an organized fashion. Each student has a right to my time, if I could find the time to give them. What a dilemma.

■

Captured in Ms. Kendall's journal entry are her reflections of the day's events. Her thoughts are of students, her interactions with them as she tries to help them learn, and the milieu in which they interact–the school. Through her personal thoughts we can begin to get a sense of the students and their school.

that equity in science education could be achieved by overcoming the deficiencies that are brought to school by culturally diverse students. The lack of success experienced by these students was assumed to be due to their home culture being less advanced than that of students from the cultural mainstream. Remediation designed to compensate for their lack of knowledge, skills, and attitudes in science was considered the solution to increasing science participation and performance in school and, ultimately, the number of culturally diverse persons who pursued science and technical careers.

Today most people reject this deficit model. Instead, the focus is on the incompatibilities between the students' background and culture and the expectations of the science classroom. As a microcosm of the school culture, science classes tend to promote the values ascribed to by the mainstream white, male-dominated, middle-class culture (Hodson, 1993; Stanley & Brickhouse, 1994). Competition, fast work, and respect for the teacher are valued; rigid time schedules are followed; and students are expected to graduate from high school and go to college or seek work. In attempting to achieve equity in science education, teachers must recognize that these values are not shared by all students. Fairness and impartiality on the part of the science teacher are key to an equitable science education for all.

Multicultural Science Education

An alternative to the notion of cultural assimilation in science is multicultural science education. Nested within the larger framework of multicultural education, it is a concept not without ambiguity. Multicultural science education "can mean many things to many people" (Hodson, 1993, p. 688). According to Ogawa (1995), "awareness of cultural diversity in science education seems to be at the crux of multicultural science education" (p. 584). Atwater (1991) extends the work of James Banks to define it as "a construct, a process, and an educational reform movement with the goal of providing equitable opportunities for culturally diverse student populations to learn quality science in schools, colleges, and universities" (in Atwater & Riley, 1993, p. 664). Hodson (1993) warns about defining multicultural education too narrowly and contends that what constitutes multicultural science education will vary depending on the region, community, school, and classroom in which it is practiced. Further, that which constitutes multicultural science education in a class of mostly Black or Hispanic students will be different from that in a class of mostly white students (Hodson, 1993).

Two themes central to multicultural science education, regardless of context, are cultural pluralism and antiracism. A pluralistic society is one in which all groups of people are of equal standing. Promoting cultural pluralism means "that members of the dominant community learn to appreciate, understand, and value the different conventions and cultural norms of other and smaller groups of citizens, and that members of racial and ethnic minority communities reinforce and perpetuate their own cultural identities, thereby developing more positive self-images" (Hodson, 1993, p. 688). Antiracist science education, according to Reiss (1993), "aims to counteract and combat attitudes and behaviours which can lead to prejudice, discrimination and injustice . . . through science teaching" (p. 14).

Most multiculturists agree that promoting cultural pluralism without addressing racism is not sufficient (Banks, 1994; Reiss, 1993). They also warn that expecting antiracism to result from a cultural diversity approach that presents racism as a vestige of ignorance is unrealistic (Troyna, 1987; Troyna & Hatcher, 1992). Antiracism education in science must be "built on the premise that it is necessary to recognize, confront, challenge, and oppose racist beliefs and practices directly" (Hodson, 1995, p. 689). Before addressing ways in which school science can be presented to make it attractive and accessible to students from all cultures, we will first turn our attention to the nature of science and how science is perceived from the perspective of different cultures. In Chapter 1, we talked about science as a way of knowing and the need to be mindful of the world view of other cultures. In the next section that conversation will be extended with greater attention given to how world view influences what one considers science to be.

Nature of Science

At the center of the push for multicultural science education is the issue of what counts as science. A world view is one's belief system about the universe and the ways in which humans interact with nature. School science has traditionally asked students to adopt a Eurocentric world view. This is the world view commonly shared by white males of European decent, who have historically dominated modern science. World views vary from one culture to another. For example, most Native Americans strive to live in harmony with nature, whereas most westerners try to control it.

The multiculturalist position is that science is a human construction and therefore notions about what science is have changed over time and are influenced by culture (Stanley & Brickhouse, 1994). For example, early Islamic science included such topics as logic, grammar, music, and rhetoric (Reiss, 1993). Science in African culture is inextricably linked to religion (Jegede, 1994). What is called science today is actually a recent invention and can be traced to seventeenth century England.

The influence of culture on science is no less evident today than it has been in the past. Scientists choose what they want to investigate. Of course their choices are based on personal interests, but often they are greatly influenced by the culture in which they live. Government and private funds available to find a cure for AIDS and to map the human genome have encouraged scientists to take up these challenges in large numbers. In contrast, when funds were pulled from the Texas Super Conductor Super Collider project in the early 1990s, interest in research related to particle acceleration waned. Moreover, the mood and mind-set of society often affects the value given to scientific advancements. People of the seventeenth century were inclined to accept William Harvey's explanation of blood circulation because of their familiarity with industrial pumping systems of the day, even though the role of the heart in blood circulation was described centuries before. Today the use of acupuncture to stop pain and cure ailments is viewed with some skepticism in the United States, but perhaps this will change as more is learned about it. Even society's image of a scientist is affected by culture. Scientists are typically portrayed in children's drawings as nerdy white males wearing eyeglasses and white lab coats (Chambers, 1983).

Taking this discussion a step further, Ogawa (1995) argues that rather than multicultural science education, we should really be considering science education from a multiscience perspective. He says that science exists at the personal level and cultural level, which he calls indigenous science. Both the personal theories that one holds about the natural world and those shared by members of a cultural group must be considered when teaching modern Western science. Whether called multicultural science education or multiscience education, the focus is squarely on providing the best science education possible for a culturally diverse student population.

Others who write about the nature of science take issue with the multiculturalist position and claim that science is universal. What is meant by this claim is that there is a universal form of knowledge that transcends cultural interpretations (Matthews, 1994). That is to say that scientific knowledge has no national, political, or cultural boundaries. An important tenet of the universalist tradition is that the efficacy of humans' explanations of the natural world are grounded in reality. An example may help clarify this idea. Consider a violent thunderstorm. Those outdoors during the storm will likely get wet or even struck by lightning. According to the universalist position, it is the character of the storm, not the meteorologists' rules of evidence and justification, that ultimately judges the efficacy of the science of meteorology (Matthews, 1994).

The universalist position has been challenged by multiculturalists on the grounds that it presents a biased interpretation of the nature of science. The universalist position is considered biased primarily because it fails to consider knowledge systems developed by non-Western and ancient cultures as science (Stanley & Brickhouse, 1994). Multiculturalists claim that the universalist position is only one among many possible scientific frameworks for investigating the natural world (Loving, 1995). By considering modern Western science as the only knowledge system, Stanley and Brickhouse (1994) warn that we run the risk of limiting our ability to generate new knowledge by destroying knowledge systems viewed as inferior.

Despite their differences, multiculturalists and universalists do agree on several points. One is that not all knowledge systems developed by different cultures and called science are equally sound. A second is that students in the United States must come to understand modern Western science. The final point is that a shift from universal science, which is taught in most science classes today, to multicultural science education has significant implications for the science classroom.

Multicultural Science Classrooms

Suggestions are plentiful about how to alter science curriculum and instruction to make them better reflect the vision of multicultural science education. Textbook publishers are very cognizant of the need to provide teachers with information about the contributions of other cultures to modern science and ideas for addressing the needs of culturally diverse students. As each day passes, more research attention is given to issues of multicultural science education. Few curricula exist that address multicultural science education head-on, however, and most science teachers are not sure how to transfer the research findings into practice. What can you do to make your science classroom a better place for all students, especially those who are culturally diverse? Here are some recommendations.

Content Integration.   Content integration in science education involves "using examples and content from a variety of cultures and groups to illustrate key concepts, principles, generalizations, and theories" in science (Banks, 1994, p. 5). Atwater et al. (1996) acknowledge that incorporating examples and content from different cultures enhances the excitement and relevance of lessons and is likely to promote science learning as students connect the lessons to their personal lives. But as Baptiste points out, all content integration is not the same (in Baptiste & Key, 1996). He has delineated three levels of content integration. Level one focuses on awareness and involves adding multicultural experiences to the curriculum. Celebrating the Nobel-Prize-winning accomplishments of Har Gobind Khorana (elucidation of the genetic code) on his birthday, and teaching about the scientific discoveries of Black Americans like Charles Drew (blood groups) or Percy Julian (isolating sterols for soybeans) during Black History Month are but two examples of content integration at level one.

Baptiste's second and third levels involve more than add-ons to the curriculum. The second level involves integrating the contributions of many cultures and peoples into the curriculum. One example of this level is found in the *ChemCom* (American Chemical Society, 1993) unit "Understanding Foods." The culminating experience for this unit asks students to compare the nutritional value of meals from several cultures, including Mexican and Japanese, in terms of food energy, protein, iron, and vitamin B1. At Baptist's third level, cultural and social issues become the centerpiece of the curriculum. Farming practices, medicines used to treat diseases and other ailments, saltmaking, tools for making calculations, and chemical dyes are just a few examples of topics that provide ideas for a science curriculum that integrates information about ancient and modern cultures and may lead students to take socially responsible actions. According to Atwater and her colleagues (1996), teachers function as social activists at Baptiste's third level.

> They help their science students promote equitable opportunities, have respect for those who are members of oppressed groups, and practice power equity in the school and community. Furthermore, they help students to use their science knowledge to change the world around them. (p. 170)

Unless you have studied the history of science from the perspective of different cultures, you are probably not well prepared to engage students in learning experiences that reflect either Baptiste's second or third levels. It will take time to develop lessons and units that integrate content that reflects different cultural perspectives.

Cultural Harmony.   It is agreed that science learning occurs in a cultural context. Unfortunately for many culturally diverse students, the culture of the science classroom is an unfamiliar one. For these students to be successful, school science must be related to their home culture. In *Science in the Multicultural Classroom* (1995), Barba writes about "culturally harmonious variables as those culture-of-origin beliefs, attitudes, and practices which influence (both positively and negatively, functionally and dysfunctional) the teaching/learning process" (p. 14). These variables, Barba notes, affect students' interactions with teachers and classmates and how they go about constructing knowledge in the science classroom. Culturally diverse students develop

meaningful science understandings when they see their culture facilitating learning rather than as an impediment to it.

Six culturally harmonious variables described by Barba (1995, pp. 14–18) that affect science learning are (1) format of print materials, (2) instructional language, (3) level of peer interactivity, (4) role models, (5) elaboration of context, and (6) interactivity with manipulative materials. Culturally diverse students, particularly those who are learning English, benefit from printed materials that are highly visual and tell a story, much like a comic book. Students can construct meaning from following along with the pictures or by reading the "ballooned" captions, with or without assistance. For these same students, learning science in their home language can aid concept acquisition, help them learn English, and improve their feelings toward themselves and science class. Use of a home language facilitates the assimilation and accommodation of new knowledge within an existing schema.

Culturally diverse students, according to Barba (1995), also benefit from and enjoy peer tutoring in small-group settings. Science concept acquisition and attitudes toward science are improved when students participate in same-age or cross-age cooperative groups. Another boost to learning and self-esteem is the presence of culturally familiar role models, in person, videos, or books. These role models may range from the likes of the famous physicist Luis Alverez to the high school graduate who tells about her first semester as a college chemistry major. Acquisition of declarative knowledge is further enhanced when the presentation of new science content is coupled with culturally familiar objects, examples, and analogies, and when students are provided with regular opportunities to interact directly with the material being learned. When culturally diverse students work with laboratory equipment and manipulative materials, they learn faster and what is learned is not quickly forgotten.

The results of Rakow's (in Rakow & Bermudez, 1993, p. 676–677) survey of teachers who work with Hispanic American students provides additional suggestions for working with all culturally diverse students.

- Help students develop self-esteem by showing them that they can succeed.
- Describe the relationship between that which students are learning in science class and future careers.
- Use praise frequently to reinforce and encourage.
- Hold high expectations for all students.

Countering Racism.   Today, most science textbooks published in the United States are checked by multicultural content reviewers for racist language, stereotyping, the inclusion of ethnic minorities in pictures, and the like. Also, most teachers are careful of their language so as not to offend or make any student feel uncomfortable. As Hodson (1993) points out, however, there are other aspects of science instruction that teachers need to consider when intending to counter racism. Teachers of biology need to realize that when teaching anatomy and physiology, the use of animal parts from cows may be offensive to Hindu students and those of pigs offensive to Jewish and Muslim students. Further, the teaching of evolution and sex education are incompatible with some Islamic and fundamentalist Christian beliefs.

Addressing racism in science classes also means establishing more democratic procedures and attacking scientific racism (Hodson, 1993). Although it is essential that classroom leadership be provided by the teacher, it is equally important that students be able to make some decisions about their own learning. Making allowance for students' preferred learning styles is one way to extend the ideas of democracy into the science classroom. It is well documented that culturally diverse students tend to possess the characteristics of field-sensitive learners. These students prefer collaborative work and working one-on-one with teachers. They also like to interact with teachers on a personal basis, desire careful explanations of all assignments and learning expectations, and are more highly motivated when science concepts are related to their personal lives (Atwater et al., 1996). In contrast, most students of the dominant white culture tend to be field-independent learners with learning preferences that are just the opposite of culturally diverse students. Designing lessons that address different learning styles sends the message that all students are valued and respected. Democracy in the classroom can also extend to content and assessment methods by using learning contracts, portfolios, and group activities.

Scientific racism involves the misuse of scientific information to support the notion that one human group is superior to others (Hodson, 1993). It is often the practice of hate groups and should not be tolerated by science teachers. To combat scientific racism, Hodson (1993) recommends a critical approach to science that may include the following components:

- study of the concept of race
- consideration of the ways in which the notion of race has been misused by certain groups to perpetuate stereotypes and institutionalize injustice
- discussion of other examples of the misuse of science for sociopolitical motives (p. 697)

Case studies are ideal for combating scientific racism. Suitable topics range from the continued misuse of Charles Darwin's principle of natural selection to claims of the intellectual superiority of whites based on IQ and SAT scores.

Gender and Science Education

Equity in science education extends to issues of gender. Many of the same claims that support multicultural science education can also be used to argue for gender-inclusive science education. Trying to identify gender-based deficiencies and correct them in hopes that more females will be attracted to science is no more an option here than it is for culturally diverse populations. Recasting science as socially constructed, subjective, passionate, and accessible is central to gender-inclusive science education.

Gender Identity.   From a very young age "children begin to form gender schemas, or organized networks of knowledge about what it means to be male or female" (Woolfolk, 1995, p. 172). Interactions with parents, peers, and teachers contribute to the development of these gender schemas. For example, parents tend to play more roughly with their sons than with their daughters, and girls generally are given gifts of cuddly stuffed animals and dolls whereas boys receive toy tool sets and model airplanes. By early adolescence, these schemas are quite well developed and greatly influence students' science-related interests and preferences.

Gender schemas developed by both males and females indicate that science has a masculine image. Through participating in science, particularly advanced physical science classes, a boy's masculinity tends to be reinforced, whereas a girl's femininity is diminished (Kahle, 1996). Such factors as the sheer number of male scientists as compared to female, the classroom practices of science teachers, and the ways in which school science materials have traditionally presented science to students have all contributed to science's masculine image (Kelley, 1985).

Girls' participation and interest in science are also dependent on whether the biological science or physical sciences are considered. Girls are usually, but not always, more interested in the biological sciences and less interested in the physical sciences than boys (Harvey & Edwards, 1980; Rennie, Parker, & Kahle, 1996). Kelly (1987) suggests that girls are more turned off by the physical sciences because of a lack of self-confidence and a fear of failure associated with the difficult nature of most physical science classes. She also sees the lack of relevance between physical science topics and girls' everyday concerns as another reason for girls to shy away from the physical sciences.

It is too often said that girls are less able science students than boys because of mental abilities. Only on tests of spacial ability, however, are any apparently gender-based differences noted (Mathur, 1991; Woolfolk, 1995). Test results show that girls are slower than boys at mentally rotating three-dimensional objects in space. These differences are not due to mental deficiencies, however, but are a result of differential experiences. Boys, more so than girls, tend to participate in activities that involve the mental rotation of objects, such as playing video games and sports including football and basketball (Linn & Hyde, 1989).

Women's Ways of Knowing.   Women come to know and perceive reality in ways different from men. Viewing knowledge from the perspective of women is helpful to an understanding of girls' beliefs and decisions regarding science. Belenky, Clinhy, Goldberger, and Tarule (1986) group women's ways of knowing into the following stages:

> silence—no voice in what constitutes knowledge and subject to the whims of outside authority
>
> received knower—recipient of knowledge, but incapable of creating knowledge
>
> subjective knower—creator of personal knowledge perceived as intuitive and subjective
>
> procedural knower–creator of knowledge by objective, systematic analysis
>
> constructed knower—creator of contextualized knowledge through the use of both subjective and objective procedures (p. 15)

These stages should be viewed as a developmental pathway beginning with silence and leading to constructed knower. The challenge for science teachers is to help girls move along this pathway.

This challenge can be met, according to Belenky and her colleagues (1986), by engaging in connected teaching. Connected teaching in the science classroom involves helping students realize that science is a human construction, that all that is written in textbooks and recorded on videotape is not to be accepted as truth, and that conversations in science classes are usually not about facts but about models and theories. In the connected classroom, students are comfortable with uncertainty, and knowledge is constructed through consensus. The connected teacher is not the voice of scientific authority, but one who, much like the students, struggles to make sense of the world. Belenky et al. (1986) clarify the teacher's role in a connected classroom by comparing the metaphors of teacher as midwife and teacher as banker. "While the bankers deposit knowledge in the learner's head, the midwives draw it out. They assist the students by giving birth to their own ideas, in making their own tacit knowledge explicit and

elaborating on it" (p. 217). It is this connected learning experience that women prefer.

Feminist Science Education.   If credence is given to women's ways of knowing, then fundamental changes are needed in the way in which science is presented in schools. Bentley and Watts (1986) offer three approaches to consider: girl-friendly science, feminine science, and feminist science. Girl-friendly science advocates making traditional science more attractive to girls by changing the image of science presented in science classes. Challenging stereotypes, emphasizing the aesthetic appeal of science, and framing science curricula in a social context are all examples of ways to make science girl friendly. Feminine science emphasizes changing the atmosphere of science classes to better suit girls. Changes to foster feminine science include attending to the social and moral issues of science and emphasizing cooperation and caring rather than competition in all school science activities.

Feminist science steps beyond the other two approaches to challenge the universalist assumptions about the nature of science. Feminist science, according to Bentley and Watts (1986), is based on a philosophy of wisdom rather than knowledge. This philosophy of wisdom takes into account the personal, social, and creative aims of the individual and is reflected in investigative approaches that embrace subjectivity. A science class based on this feminist approach would allow for considerable learner autonomy, explore multiple views of science, and emphasize personal feelings and intuition as important to developing science understandings. It is the feminist science approach that most closely aligns with the connected learning experience suggested by Belenky and her colleagues (1986).

Teachers concerned with gender-inclusiveness in science education should, according to Reiss (1993), view Bentley and Watts's approaches as three different answers to the question, What should science education for girls be like? Although feminist science might be the final answer, feminine science is seen as an acceptable answer and girl-friendly science is better than doing nothing at all. Effective models for changing to a more gender-inclusive science education include the Career Oriented Modules for Exploring Topics in Science (COMETS), the Computer Equity Expert Project, and the mid-West states' Center for Sex Equity in Schools (Harding & Parker, 1995). Additionally, there are many strategies a teacher can use to move along the continuum from doing nothing to a feminist school science. Several suggestions by Bentley and Watts (1986), Kahle (1996), and Parkinson (1994) for doing so are listed here. Their suggestions are not unlike excellent teaching strategies appropriate for use with all students regardless of gender.

- Choose textbooks that show both males and females doing science and that present the scientific contributions of women.

- Choose science materials, such as case studies and life histories, that portray science as the subjective and passionate study of the natural world.

- Involve students in activities that focus on visual-spacial skills, such as constructing molecular models, graphing data, making mobiles, and working with tangram puzzles.

- Use learning tasks with many approaches and more than one right answer.

- Present information about science and science-related careers and the educational requirements for the careers.

- Incorporate frequent laboratory work to increase both interest in science and experience in problem-solving and scientific investigation.

- Be on the lookout for unintended biases in your classroom, such as calling on boys more than girls and allowing boys to dominate discussions and laboratory groups.

- Teach the skills of listening, supporting, and negotiating along with the more traditional skills of science.

- Use gender-free language.

- Invite female scientists and female college students who have gone on to major in science to visit your classroom.

- Celebrate the contributions of women in science and other human endeavors.

- Assess student progress often using a variety of assessment forms.

- Use assessment as an opportunity to encourage and support students.

As powerful as these suggestions are, Tobin (1996) points out that teachers are unlikely to be successful in achieving gender-inclusiveness in the classroom without the direct involvement of students. He recommends that students be taught to recognize gender inequities in the science classroom and be empowered to create equal opportunities for all.

■ STOP AND REFLECT! ■

Before going further, do the following:

- Reread Box 1.1, "Investigating Animals' Reactions to Light," in Chapter 1. How could Mr. Pearl's instructions be rewritten to reflect the nature of science from a multicultural science education perspective?

- Refer to Ms. Kendall's journal entry presented earlier in this chapter in Box 3.1 where she writes about Julie's declining performance and her belief that science is a male thing. What could Ms. Kendall do in her science classes to convey to Julie and other students that science is socially constructed, subjective, passionate, and accessible to women?

EXCEPTIONAL STUDENTS

Although all students should be considered exceptional, there are some students who perform much differently than the "average." They are often not well served by regular classroom instruction, but deserve the same opportunities afforded all other students to learn quality science. For these students, equity in science education requires accommodating their exceptionality.

The list of special needs is extensive, and therefore our discussion will focus on those special needs students who are usually found in regular science classes. These include the learning disabled (LD), physically disabled, and the gifted and talented. Special assistance is sometimes provided by special education or resource teachers to help the science teacher address the special needs of these students. The purpose of discussing the characteristics and needs of these students is to make teachers more sensitive to the individual differences found in the student population and to better prepare them to work with all types of students. Before turning our attention to the different types of special needs, we will first discuss the legal reasons for addressing the needs of special students in regular science classes.

Inclusion and the Law

Three federal laws directly impact the teaching of students with special needs in regular science classes. The first one, passed by Congress in 1975, is Public Law 94-142, the Education for All Handicapped Children Act. This law requires that all schools must place students who are mentally or physically handicapped in the "least restrictive environment." Least restrictive environment is usually interpreted to mean the regular classroom. The other two laws were passed in 1990. The Individuals with Disabilities Education Act (PL 101-476) substituted the word "disabled" for "handi-capped" and expanded the educational programs for these students, and the Americans with Disabilities Act (PL 101-336) ensures the full civil rights of all disabled persons.

Practically speaking, these laws have resulted in the full inclusion of exceptional students in all school programs. Thus, the likelihood is great that students with special needs will be found in all science classes. Full inclusion has presented the science teacher with unique instructional problems. What should the science teacher do when confronted with the special needs student in the regular classroom? Where can the teacher obtain information about the instructional needs of such a student? According to PL 94-142, an Individualized Education Program (IEP) must be written for every special needs student, regardless of exceptionality, who is placed in a regular classroom. The IEP is developed by a team of individuals including specialists, teachers, and administrators and must be approved by the parents or guardians of the student as well as appropriate school personnel. The IEP for each student includes goals, instructional activities, and the evaluation procedures, which can guide the teachers as well as the student. Any information may be included with the IEP that will assist teachers, such as records relating to testing and placement. PL 101-336 guarantees that the IEP and other records be maintained in confidence and be available to parents or guardians at their request. It also gives parents or guardians the right to challenge the IEP and to bring counsel, legal or otherwise, to meetings where the IEP is developed and discussed.

Once the IEP is crystallized and approved by appropriate parties, it becomes mandatory and must be followed as well as possible. Such plans include information such as the following:

- The results of an assessment battery given to the student
- The interpersonal relationships of the special needs student with other students
- Behavioral problems and recommendations as to how to handle the problems
- The goals that have been set for the student
- The services that have been provided to help the student achieve his or her educational goals
- Procedures for evaluating goals and the timetable for evaluating them
- A statement regarding the general health of the student as well as the exceptionality or exceptionalities exhibited by the student
- Recommended instructional activities for various subject areas

When dealing with the special needs students in the regular classroom, teachers should refer to IEPs for assistance. The IEP is the best source to obtain direction and guidance for instructing the special needs student.

Learning Disabilities

The term **learning disabilities** is used to describe students of average or above average intelligence with learning problems that result from some type of dysfunction of the central nervous system. The dysfunction affects the person's ability to take in information through the senses and make use of it. According to Mastropieri and Scruggs (1993), LD students have difficulty attending to learning tasks; remembering directions, factual information, and new vocabulary; and applying what has been learned. At times, LD students may engage in unacceptable social behavior due to misreading social cues, feelings of pending failure, or hyperactivity disorders. But as Hofman (1994) points out, "being learning disabled does not imply impairment in learning ability, only a different ability to receive information and experience science" (p. 76).

It is very likely that one or more LD students will be found in every science class. As a teacher of LD students, there are a few things to consider. First, it is important to learn as much as possible about LD students' abilities and disabilities. But rather than trying to accommodate a student's needs based solely on your own coursework and reading or conversations with others, ask the student for help to devise individual learning accommodations. LD students are the best sources of information about their learning problems and should be consulted regularly about what they can and cannot do (Hofman, 1994). Second, discrimination is too often associated with the LD label. Too many teachers and counselors hold low expectations for LD students and discourage them from enrolling in advanced science classes and pursuing science careers. The consequences of pull-out programs and tracking can be particularly devastating to LD students. Pull-out programs often deprive LD students of science opportunities, and low expectations are likely to become self-fulfilling prophecies when LD students' access to challenging science experiences is limited by placement in the general track. Third, the science strategies that work for LD students are generally the same ones that work with all types of students. This enables LD students to participate in most regular classroom activities.

The following list includes examples of the modifications and accommodations recommended by Mastropieri and Scruggs (1995) and Patton (1995) for teaching science to LD students:

- Choose approaches to teaching that are activity-oriented.
- Use teaching strategies that emphasize structure, clarity, redundancy, enthusiasm, appropriate pace, and maximum engagement.
- Partner regular students with LD students.
- Help LD students monitor their own behavior by using checklists.
- Adapt science activities by reducing the level of abstraction or breaking them into smaller parts.
- Use performance assessment to assess science understandings.

Physical Disabilities

Most teachers will encounter physically disabled students in their science classes because they make up over 1% of the school age population (Mastropieri & Scruggs, 1993). Students with auditory, mobility, and visual disabilities are being aggressively integrated into regular science classes. Participating in regular classes ensures that these youngsters have the opportunity to develop useful science skills and understandings that will assist them in living fulfilling and productive lives. Many national science organizations, including the National Science Teachers Association, the American Association for the Advancement of Science, and the American Chemical Society, have affirmed the importance of science for the

physically disabled by supporting the development of materials on this topic.

Visually Impaired Students.   The category **visually impaired** comprises a wide range of vision problems. Some individuals are totally blind, whereas others can see outlines of objects to various degrees. Some individuals can see only objects and print that are within a few inches or feet of their eyes and then only with corrective aids. There are also individuals who are limited to a narrow field of vision of 20 degrees or less, as opposed to the 180 degrees that people with normal vision experience.

Mastropieri and Scruggs (1993, p. 48) point out that words and phrases such as "here/there," "nearly/almost," "this/that," and "over there" are meaningless to the visually impaired. These authors recommend that teachers use explicit language when providing verbal descriptions or directions to these students. For example, say "index and ring fingers" rather than "those body parts" and "from pH 4.3 to pH 7.1" not "from this pH to that." These suggestions for modifying science learning experiences along with others are found in the Science Activities for the Visually Impaired (SAVI) materials. Very appropriate for middle school students, SAVI modules address topics ranging from mixtures and solutions to structures of life and scientific reasoning. SAVI materials may be obtained from the Lawrence Hall of Science, University of California at Berkeley.

Students with low vision can benefit from good overhead lighting, a seating position that allows for maxi-

Provisions must be made for those students with special needs.

mum visibility of the chalkboard and demonstration areas, enlarged printed materials, and extra time for reading and viewing (Weigerber, 1993). Thoughtful adaptation of many science activities can make them usable with low-vision students. For example, microscope-generated images can be enlarged with the use of microprojectors and large-screen videos, and a stethoscope can be used to allow students to hear the movement of leaf-cutter ants in search of food. Additionally, the use of olfactory indicators can make it possible for both low-vision and blind students to perform acid-base titrations in chemistry (Flair & Setzer, 1990).

Safety is an added concern when working with visually impaired students in science. All activities must be carefully considered for possible dangers to the visually impaired student and others in the class. Visually impaired students need to become familiar with the classroom layout, especially the location of exits, fire extinguishers, and other safety equipment. Chemicals should be supplied for laboratory activities in small quantities, and, if possible, in plastic containers. All containers should be labeled with large letters, and visually impaired students should be encouraged to wear rubber gloves, in addition to aprons and goggles, when using chemicals (Kucera, 1993). Among low-vision students, visual fatigue from long periods of work may lead to accidents. The possibility of accidents can be reduced by marking materials and equipment with high visibility tape (e.g., optic orange) and organizing them for easy access.

Hearing-Impaired Students.   Deaf and hard-of-hearing students present special challenges to the science teacher. Deaf people are disabled to the extent that they cannot understand speech through their ears, with or without the use of a hearing aid. Hard-of-hearing people are disabled to the extent that they have difficulty understanding speech with or without a hearing aid. Deaf and hard-of-hearing students are generally not as advanced in their cognitive development as those who have normal hearing due primarily to problems with reading (Mertens, 1991). Moreover, hearing impairments tend to function as a social barrier because they impede communication with other students (Kucera, 1993).

Hearing-impaired students very much need science course experiences. They are often given a great deal of language and speech instruction, to the exclusion of experiences in the content areas of mathematics, science, and social studies. Science, especially, can help these students develop and attain concepts through hands-on experiences (Mastropieri & Scruggs, 1992). One approach to ensure access to science for hearing-impaired students is to adapt existing science programs to meet their needs. The Science Education for Public Understanding Program (SEPUP), Full Option Science System (FOSS), and Project Wild are among the programs that have been adapted for use with hearing-impaired students at the middle school level.

In addition to suitable instructional materials, role models are needed to inform hearing-impaired students that they too can succeed in science, according to Harry Lang (1994). His study of the history of science brought to light the contributions of many scientists with hearing impairments, including Leo Lasquereux, founder of North American paleobiology; Thomas Meehan, the father of American horticulture; and Guillaume Amontons, who conceived the idea of absolute temperature.

Hearing loss is an invisible impairment because there are no outward characteristics that can be observed to indicate the impairment (Keller, Pauley, Starcher, Ellsworth, & Proctor, 1983; Kucera, 1993). Teachers and fellow classmates tend to forget that these individuals cannot hear because they compensate for their hearing loss by carefully attending to visual cues. In addition, students who are hard-of-hearing sometimes fake comprehension as a way to hide their impairment. Consequently, these students are not instructed properly and miss a great deal in the educational process.

There is much that science teachers can do to accommodate the needs of learning-impaired students in regular science classes. The following list includes some recommendations from persons who have worked to make science education barrier-free for these students (Anderson, 1982; Kucera, 1993; Mertens, 1991):

- During lectures and discussions, face the student when speaking, repeat questions asked by other students, and summarize class discussions. Also, use visual aids, including diagrams, models, and pictures, to augment presentation.

- Make provisions for closed-captioning of videos shown in class.

- Arrange for the student to get class notes from other students, because watching the teacher or interpreter and taking notes at the same time is difficult for a hearing-impaired person.

- Interpretation in science classes is difficult for both the interpreter and hearing-impaired students because many scientific terms do not have signs in sign language. Therefore, write new scientific terms on the chalkboard during class or provide them in advance.

- Insist that hearing-impaired students adhere to the same behavioral standards required of other students.

Motor/Orthopedically Impaired Students.   The range of conditions that represent motor/orthopedically impaired students is enormous. These conditions affect the spinal column (spina bifida), brain functioning (epilepsy), muscular system (muscular dystrophy), limbs (amputation), joints (arthritis), respiratory system (asthma), and heart (heart disease). These students have special needs according to their health, mobility, communication, social, and cognitive status (Keller, 1994). In some cases, there are minimal assistive needs, whereas in other cases the assistive needs are extensive and obvious because of the conditions.

Students with motor or orthopedic disabilities often lack the science experiences and understandings common to nondisabled students, because science has traditionally not been a part of the early schooling provided for these students (Keller, 1994). If this is found to be the case, opportunities to involve students in these missed learning experiences will need to be built into the curriculum. Modules or activities from such multisensory curriculum programs as Science Enrichment for Learners with Physical Handicaps (SELPH), Parallel Science Materials (PSM), and Elementary Science Study (ESS) can be used for this purpose. SELPH modules are appropriate for disabled middle school students and address topics ranging from magnetism and electricity to environmental energy. The fourteen PSM life and earth science units and the twenty-eight ESS activities are well suited for motor/orthopedically disabled middle school and secondary students.

Many of the accommodations and modifications recommended for other types of disabilities are also appropriate for motor/orthopedically disabled students. First, teachers must believe that the motor/orthopedically disabled student is capable of performing well in science. Also, teachers must develop an understanding of the student's disability and the implication of the disability for science instruction. Most importantly, teachers must actively solicit from the motor/orthopedically disabled student ways to address his or her special needs.

Gifted and Talented Students

Often overlooked in science classes are the special needs of bright and highly motivated students. These so-called gifted and talented students are not only the high academic achievers, but those who exhibit high levels of creativity, persistence, and motivation to achieve (Renzulli & Reis, 1991). "Students who are gifted and talented combine superior cognitive abilities with an advanced ability to learn and use the methodology of production" (Kirschenbaum, 1988, p. 55).

The abilities of gifted and talented adolescents are often first noticed in the areas of oral and written language, mathematics, music, and problem solving. They are also evident in psychomotor ability and leadership. A survey of young people identified as gifted revealed the following characteristics:

Inquisitiveness	Varied interests
Energetic outlook	Keen observer
Humorous demeanor	Sensitive to self and others
Avid reader	Sense of timing
Physical prowess	Product excellence
Intellectual curiosity	Sense of appreciation
Conversational	Interest in one or more subjects
Acute listener	

Young people who tend to exhibit any combination of the above characteristics will need the curricular and instructional flexibility to demonstrate their unique skills. There is a growing group of gifted educators that advocates the early identification of these characteristics so that they become traits of behavior by the time these individuals become teenagers (Bireley & Genshaft, 1991). For example, the characteristic described as inquisitiveness must be recognized by the teacher and allowed expression. If this is stifled, the student will not develop other characteristics such as intellectual curiosity, a sense of verbal timing, or the ability to react and interact with a sense of humor. These characteristics are seen as interactive and geometric if they are first identified and then supported for each student.

Two strategies used to address the special needs of gifted and talented students are acceleration and enrichment. An accelerated curriculum is one in which students move through the courses and subject matter at a faster rate than their same age peers. In middle school this practice could involve sixth graders joining a seventh grade class for science instruction. In high school it might involve students passing a science course by examination or taking courses on a part-time basis at local colleges and universities. Acceleration is sometimes scorned for interfering with students' social development; however, research indicates that acceleration does not impede social development. Acceleration does produce achievement gains beyond those possible when no special provisions are made for gifted students (Jones & Southern, 1991).

Enrichment programs permit gifted students to have new experiences in addition to what the other students are experiencing. Enrichment can be provided through field trips, science bowls, academic decathlons, and opportunities to study about the work of Rosalin Franklin (DNA), Barbara McClintock (jumping gene), John Goodricke (binary stars), and other gifted historical figures in science. Mentor or apprenticeship programs, where students spend time working with scientists in the field or their laboratories, are another form of enrichment. Advanced Placement (AP) programs, which allow students to study college-level courses while still in high school, provide both acceleration and enrichment.

In heterogeneous classes, gifted and talented students should carry out the regular class work as well as special assignments. They can participate in introductory phases of units, field work, and group work. Gifted students particularly benefit from student-centered instruction and the opportunity to investigate real problems. While other students are doing individual work such as reading, reviewing, and writing, gifted students can engage in activities that are more suited to their superior abilities.

The greatest help that can be given to gifted and talented students is the opportunity to do original research. They prefer to investigate problems that have undisclosed outcomes. Their investigations may begin as an outgrowth of regular class work, but they should be encouraged to carry out their investigations in and out of school. Many of these students are very willing to work in the evenings and on weekends with help and encouragement from science teachers, parents, or guardians. These efforts at original research may lead to participation in local, regional, and state science fair competitions.

Special provisions are often made for teaching science to gifted and talented students. AP courses are taught by highly qualified teachers and often in specially equipped high school laboratories. Science instruction for gifted middle school students may be provided by a special "gifted teacher." Additionally, district-wide science magnet schools and special state schools exist to meet the needs of gifted and talented adolescents.

Both complexity and controversy surround the challenge of identifying gifted and talented youth. An IQ of 120 or more is a criterion sometimes used to classify a person as gifted. Other criteria that are applied include one's ability to:

learn easily and quickly

remember what is heard

comprehend meanings

make use of practical knowledge

make use of a large vocabulary

manipulate symbols and systems made up of symbols (Reynolds & Birch, 1977; Woolfolk, 1995)

Identifying gifted and talented students from among groups traditionally underrepresented in science may require the use of additional considerations. For exam-

ple, among Native-Americans strong problem-solving skills, artistic creativity, knowledge of tribal traditions and ceremonies, and active listening are considered important characteristics of gifted and talented adolescents (Kirschenbaum, 1988). Additionally, many students who rejoice at the status of "gifted and talented" in the elementary grades may choose to reject this label as adolescents due to peer pressures or family expectations. The more information that one gathers, the better one's chances are for identifying students who need a curriculum to enhance their talents.

■ STOP AND REFLECT! ■

Before going further, do the following:

■ Explain the purpose of an IEP. What information included in an IEP would be of use to the science teacher?

■ Identify adaptions that would make a science learning experience more suitable for a visually impaired student. Do the same for an LD student.

■ Distinguish between accelerated and enrichment programs for gifted and talented students. How does each program type contribute to the intellectual growth of these students?

ADOLESCENT DEVELOPMENT

An important characteristic of adolescence is the pronounced physical change in youngsters that accompanies puberty. Equally dramatic are the cognitive changes that mark the adolescent years. These fundamental physical and cognitive changes lead to the many personal and social challenges that adolescents face. In this section, the physical and cognitive changes of adolescents are considered first, followed by some of the characteristic changes in personal and social reasoning exhibited by adolescents. Finally, implications of adolescent development for science teaching and learning are discussed.

Physical Development

Adolescents experience extraordinary physical growth and change. They grow taller, gain weight, experience changes in motor performance, and develop secondary sex characteristics. These gradual biological changes, which occur over a period of several years, lead to reproductive maturity. Puberty is the term often used to describe this series of biological changes (Rowe & Rodgers, 1989). On average, girls experience the onset of these biological changes around age 10.5, whereas boys experience them about 2 years later at age 12.5 (Santrock, 1995). Genetic factors and nutrition affect the onset of puberty and contribute to the great variability in physical characteristics often witnessed among middle school and secondary students.

It would not be at all surprising to see differences in height of a foot or more in any middle school science class. These differences in height, and also in weight, are a result of the adolescent growth spurt. This period of rapid growth begins with the onset of puberty. All parts of the body are involved in this spurt, but not at the same rate and to the same degree. This uneven growth is often witnessed in students' clumsiness and misjudging distances.

A common myth of puberty is that "raging hormones" are responsible for all the changes experienced by adolescents. Although it is true that hormones affect many biological changes associated with adolescence, according to Dacey and Kenny (1994), they do not act alone. Psychological and social changes accompany an adolescent's physical development. Reactions to the physical changes associated with puberty vary by gender and in response to the differences in pubertal development from individual to individual. Being shorter or taller, heavier or slimmer than one's peers affects the psychological and social well-being of adolescents. Some adolescents respond more strongly to these physical changes than others (Lerner, Petersen, & Brooks-Gunn, 1991). But all adolescents express concern about how others see them.

Physical development that is judged to be early or late can greatly impact an adolescent's psychological and social development. Early-maturing boys have an advantage over late-maturing boys during the adolescent years. They have greater self-confidence and are viewed as more attractive than their peers (Tobin-Richards, Boxer, & Petersen, 1983). However, in later life, the advantage goes to late-maturing boys who develop a stronger sense of identity, often associated with personal achievement and career development (Simmons & Blyth, 1987). In contrast to the findings for boys, early-maturing girls develop independence and are pleased with their bodies during the middle school years, but by the senior high school years become dissatisfied. This dissatisfaction is often due to comparisons made with late-maturing girls whose taller and thinner bodies more closely match the current cultural ideal for feminine beauty (Santrock, 1995). Early-maturing girls, more so than their late-

maturing counterparts, are likely to experience depression and problems such as eating disorders and attain less educational and occupational success (Stattin & Magnusson, 1990). On-time boys and girls generally feel comfortable about themselves and are less susceptible to the psychological and social pressures often encountered by their early- and late-maturing peers (Balk, 1995). To be "normal," or on time, in their physical development is the desire of most young people.

Cognitive Development

Cognitive development is the general process that occurs as a result of natural maturation, social interactions, and the progressive differentiation of mental functions (Piaget, 1964). It provides the underlying foundation for learning. Key features of adolescent cognitive development are abstract, logical, and idealistic thinking. Cognitive development has been examined from several theoretical perspectives. In this section, three different theoretical perspectives are described.

Students should be given the opportunity to demonstrate their understanding of science principles with concrete objects.

Piaget's Stages of Cognitive Development.   In his theory of cognitive development, Jean Piaget describes four stages of thought: sensory motor, preoperational, concrete operational, and formal operational. They represent phases of intellectual growth from infancy to adulthood that individuals gradually pass through. The mental operations associated with these stages and their underlying structures become more complex as development progresses, permitting the individual greater range of thought and depth of understanding. Furthermore, these stages of development are invariant and qualitatively different. Only the concrete operational and formal operational stages will be discussed here, because most middle and secondary school students are operating at one of these two stages.

The concrete operational stage generally begins around the age of six and extends into the adult years for some individuals. This stage marks the onset of the ability to think logically and to perform mental operations that are tied to concrete objects and events. During this stage, individuals acquire the ability to order, classify, add, subtract, multiply, and divide. They acquire the ability to determine the cause of events and to represent spacial relationships. They also develop the ability to conserve, that is, to understand that one variable in a system can be altered while others remain constant and that the change can be reversed. One of Piaget's tests for conservation is presented in Figure 3.1. Concrete operational reasoning is necessary for learning a great deal of science course subject matter.

Students attain many concepts as they develop during the concrete operational stage. Early in this stage, they are able to classify plants, animals, and common objects based on perceptible attributes. As this ability improves, students can arrange concepts hierarchically, forming classes and subclasses. Forming classes and understanding their relationships facilitate learning the large body of organized knowledge that constitutes school science. These operations are only possible when students can manipulate objects and experience events directly. Students at this stage require concrete experiences before tackling hypothetical or abstract problems.

The formal operational stage begins about age twelve and is attained during early adolescence by some and by late adolescence and early adulthood by others. Individuals at this stage can think more abstractly and deal with many more variables than the concrete reasoner. They can make assumptions about hypothetical situations and reason logically about these assertions. Formal operational thinkers have a greater facility to deal with cause and effect in a multiple variable system, to formulate hypotheses, to use combinatorial thinking, and to use proportional reasoning than concrete operational thinkers. The formal operational reasoner has the capacity to use mental operations on abstract symbols

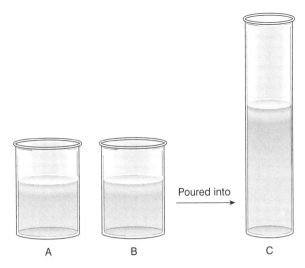

FIGURE 3.1   A setup used to assess for conservation of continuous quantity. After establishing that containers A and B have an equal amount of liquid, the liquid in container B is emptied into container C. The subject is asked to compare the amount of liquid in C with that in A.

with speed and accuracy. Individuals at this level of cognition have the potential to understand abstract and complex ideas through oral and written discourse.

Consider hypothetical-deductive reasoning as an example to illustrate the cognitive ability of the individual who has attained the formal level. Concrete operational individuals can deal with the real; they focus on what is—data and events that are observable (Flavell, 1963). Formal operational individuals, on the other hand, are inclined to deal with the possible; they focus on what could be. Formal thinkers recognize many possibilities, what could be and what is. Hypothetical-deductive reasoning is a strategy that involves deductive reasoning about hypothetical situations. Hypothetical refers to proposing what might be and deductive refers to determining what is. For example, if given the general hypothetical assumption is that all humans are vegetarians, then the student might generate specific implications such as no more beef cattle industry, healthier people, and new fast-food choices.

Although Piaget is credited with making an enormous impact upon the field of cognitive psychology, aspects of his developmental theory have been questioned by researchers in this field. One point of disagreement is that Piaget overestimated the effect of maturation on cognitive development. In other words, Piaget's theory gives less attention to the effects of culture and social interactions on learning, even though he recognized their importance (Inhelder & Piaget, 1958). It is thought by some that the achievement of concrete and formal operations in Western cultures is due in large measure to cultural expectations and the demands of Western schooling (Woolfolk, 1995). Other peoples may not develop these mental operations until later in life, if at all, because they are not needed to function in their culture.

A second point of disagreement is that the contribution of domain-general structures is not as great as Piaget believed (Carey, 1990). Carey posits that domain-specific structures make a greater contribution to children's thinking than domain-general structures. In fact, she states, "It seems that cognitive development is mainly the result of acquired knowledge in particular content domains" (p. 162). Carey points out that adolescents have many of the representational and computational capacities that Piaget believed they lacked. When researchers have controlled or provided for knowledge of certain concepts, some children demonstrate performance similar to adults. Additionally, theorists who have built onto the work of Piaget propose a fifth stage of postformal thinking. It is postformal thought that allows people to deal with everyday ambiguities and inconsistencies (Sternberg, 1995).

Vygotsky's Theory of Cognitive Development.   The work of Russian psychologist Lev Vygotsky has shed light on the influence of culture on cognitive development. Whereas Piaget acknowledged both biological maturation of the learner and the influence of the learner's environment, Vygotsky's work placed greater emphasis on the learner's environment. For Vygotsky, cognitive development is reliant on the learner's interactions with other people, and language is the critical feature of these interactions. An adolescent's interactions with parents, peers, and teachers provide the information and guidance needed for cognitive development to occur. Two ideas that are important to Vygotsky's theory are private speech and the zone of proximal development.

While trying to solve a perplexing molarity problem in chemistry you likely engaged in private speech. That is, you talked to yourself about the givens and the unknown and how to go about solving the problem. You probably even assessed your success at various steps along the way to the final solution. "Okay I know that I need to make 3 liters of a 0.2 molar solution. How many grams are there in 1 mole of $CuSO_4$?" This private speech, whether it was audible or silent, assisted you to regulate your thinking about the problem. If you found that you had reached a dead end when trying to solve the problem, your private speech may have enabled you to identify an alternative method to try. According to Vygotsky, private speech is important to cognitive development because it provides students with tools for the solution of difficult tasks and enables them to plan a problem solution prior to execution (cited in Muth & Alvermann, 1990, p. 32).

Sometimes learning can be accomplished independently; at other times it is beyond the learner's capability. Between these two points exists a level at which learning can occur when proper guidance is provided. This level is the zone of proximal development (Vygotsky, 1978). It is the level where instruction is most beneficial. A learner's zone of proximal development is in constant flux; it is dependent on the learner's cognitive ability and the nature of the problem or task. For example, a biology student's zone of proximal development will likely be different for understanding the production of ATP in the electron transport chain of oxidative respiration than for identifying animals as vertebrates or invertebrates. The link between Vygotsky's private speech and the zone of proximal development is most evident when a teacher or peer assists an adolescent to solve a problem. The learner is provided with structure, clues, information about steps to follow, and encouragement from the teacher or peer. The verbal exchange between the learner and helper will later be replaced by private speech when assistance is gradually withdrawn. Whether real or private, speech serves a helpful directive function in instances when additional cognitive effort is required to solve a problem or complete a task.

Information Processing.   Information processing is concerned with the ways in which the human mind takes in, puts together, stores, and makes use of information (Woolfolk, 1995). Information processing uses the operations of the computer as a model to describe the functioning of the human mind. An important question asked by the psychologists who study information processing is How do people of different ages process information? It probably comes as no surprise to you that one's capacity for information processing improves with age. Adolescents are better able to process information than young children. But maturation and the environment are not the only factors that affects one's capacity for information processing, according to information-processing theorists. To a great extent, a person's receptiveness to new information and memory capacity affect information processing (Sternberg, 1995).

Perception and attention are two factors that affect receptivity. In general, people are more receptive to information that is familiar to them or that is in agreement with what they already think (Dacey & Kenny, 1994). Adolescents often base their perceptions on the patterns they expect to find in a familiar context. For example, if a biology student sees a green oval inside an elodea leaf cell, she will likely identify it as a chloroplast, based on what she already knows about plant cells. Perception operates hand-in-hand with attention. According to Woolfolk (1995), attention is a limited human resource. But with age, people are better able to attend to multiple tasks simultaneously. This is possible because some tasks become automatic, that is, we carry out the tasks with little thought. The way in which chemistry students' familiarity with multiplication and division allows them to attend to the specifics of calculating the molality of a solution is but one example. The ways in which adolescents perceive phenomena of the natural world based on what they know and their ability to attend to multiple tasks simultaneously affect their receptivity and, in turn, their ability to process information.

Memory capacity also affects information processing. Adolescents have a greater ability to make use of memory strategies than do younger children. Summarizing information and creating mental images and analogies are memory-enhancing strategies used by early adolescents. These strategies assist adolescents to organize information that is more easily retrieved. Memory capacity is also affected by what is known about a topic. The more one knows, the easier it is to join smaller pieces of information into larger pieces, which makes retrieval easier. Additionally, memory capacity is influenced by an individual's metamemory, that is, the ability to know about and regulate one's own memory. Like memory capacity, verbal comprehension and fluency, quantitative skills, and the ability to mentally manipulate objects all improve with age and enhance information processing (Sternberg, 1995).

Maturation, social transmission, and experience are the three factors identified by Lawson (1995) as necessary parts of learning. It is these very factors that represent the variables of cognitive development. Each of these factors is considered by the three theoretical perspectives. Maturation was the most critical factor for Piaget, however, and for Vygotsky social transmission using language was most important. Information-processing theorists consider maturation, environment, and experience as important factors in cognitive development.

Personal and Social Development

Development during the adolescent years in not restricted to the physical and cognitive areas. Adolescents also develop in others ways as well—personally and socially. Adolescents' personal development is evident in their search for identity. Their social development is seen in their ability to consider what other people think and feel. Development in each of these areas is not based solely on maturation. Transition requires appropriate interactions with other people.

Personal Development.   Adolescence is often thought of as a time of conflict, rebellion, and turbulence. This popularized view grew out of the work of G. Stanley Hall, who in the early 1900s described adolescence as a period of "storm and stress." Erik Erikson's (1968) refinement of this view presents adolescence as a time of searching for personal identity. According to Erikson (1968), an individual passes through eight stages of psychosocial development over a lifetime. Associated with each stage is a unique psychosocial crisis, or "critical period of increased vulnerability and heightened potential" (Erikson, 1968, p. 286). The time of adolescence marks Erikson's fifth stage of development. At this stage, individuals struggle with the psychosocial crisis of identity versus role confusion as they try to answer the questions Who am I? (self-concept) and Do I like the person I am? (self-esteem). For adolescents, answers to these question are linked to school and occupational decisions, peer relationships, sex-role identity, and emancipation from adult authority (Vander Zanden, 1993).

Erikson (1968) suggests that all adolescents as they try to find themselves experience role confusion, a psychological state marked by mixed feelings about the social order of things and what the future holds. This personal "identity crisis" is a difficult one for adolescents in our society because of the conflicting expectations conveyed by parents, teachers, and other adults. Adolescents are not really treated like adults, but are told not to act like children. The favored outcome of this crisis is the development of a coherent sense of self, with its accompanying feelings of personal and social well-being.

Other psychologists do not consider adolescence as a time of storm and stress (Rosenberg, 1986; Waterman, 1982). They see changes in adolescent self-concept and self-esteem occurring as part of a gradual and continuous process extending throughout one's life. Substantiating this view is research by Offer and his colleagues (Offer & Offer, 1975; Offer, Ostrov, & Howard, 1981) and O'Malley and Bachman (1983). Their findings indicate that adolescence is no more stressful than other periods of life and that self-concept is well established during early adolescence and remains relatively stable throughout the high school years and beyond. Bandura's (1964) belief that the description of adolescence as a time of crisis best applies to only the "deviant 10 percent of the adolescent population" may serve to reconcile the two positions presented here. The individual who experiences adolescence as a time of crisis likely experienced childhood and will experience adulthood in the same way.

Social Development.   Adolescence is also a time of significant social cognitive development. Three characteristics of adolescents' social thinking were identified by Sprinthall and Collins (1988). The first is that adolescents' conceptions about themselves and other people are complex and abstract. For example, a child would describe a classmate as "a boy with brown eyes and brown hair in my science class," whereas an adolescent's description of a classmate would be "He's really smart in science, but he's not a nerd." The second characteristic of adolescents' social cognitive development is their ability to note discrepancies between what is real and what could be. "Science class is all reading and note taking, but wouldn't it be fun to do labs and go on field trips." The third characteristic is the ability to take account of others' perspectives on social situations. The teenager who offers an explanation for a friend's absence from a science club meeting based on what she or he knows about the friend's likes and dislikes is exhibiting this characteristic.

In line with Selman's (1976) five-stage model of perspective taking, early adolescents are capable of considering social situations from a third-party or neutral perspective, whereas older adolescents additionally are capable of societal perspective taking. That is, they recognize that third-party perspective taking is affected by societal influences that may range from superficial interests to abstract ethical concerns. These different capabilities of early and later adolescents correspond to the fourth and fifth stages of Selman's model, respectively. Progression from one of Selman's stages to the next is based both on maturation and environmental interaction.

Adolescents often respond in an immature manner to the realization that the perspectives of others are different from their own. Their thinking is egocentric (Elkind, 1984). Prominent during the middle school years and less so in high school, adolescent egocentric thinking is expressed in the following ways (Elkind, 1984; Papallia & Olds, 1992):

- attention-getting behaviors and dress
- risk-taking behaviors
- feelings that no one understands
- finding fault with authority figures
- argumentativeness
- self-consciousness
- self-centeredness
- indecisiveness

Elkind likened adolescent egocentrism to the Ptolemaic view of the earth as the center of the universe (in Sprinthall & Collins, 1988). As the Ptolemaic view was found lacking and discarded by Copernicus and other Renaissance thinkers of the sixteenth century, so too is egocentrism discarded by adolescents when they find it no longer useful for functioning in social arrangements. Nevertheless, recognizing that the behaviors associated with adolescent egocentrism seem to function as vehicles that facilitate social cognitive development makes

adolescents who exhibit these behaviors no easier to deal with.

Implications of Developmental Perspectives

Teachers who understand the developmental levels of the students are better able to address their needs and help them grow. In the area of physical development, there is much that science teachers can do. First, recognize that the rapid growth that students are experiencing, particularly middle school students, may cause them to be uncomfortable and fidgety if asked to sit for very long. This suggests that activity-oriented lessons that involve students in physical movement are very desirable. Hands-on lessons, laboratory work, and outdoor excursions all provide for the students' need for physical movement. Engaging students in several activities during a class period also tends to meet their needs for movement and stimulation. Second, the great variation in student height and weight makes standard desks and chairs unsuitable for some students. Students uncomfortable in standard desks could be assigned seats at lab tables or smaller desks could be secured for their use. Lab stations can also get very crowded when large students are asked to share a small work space. Third, teachers should consider students' physical capabilities when designing lessons. For example, early-maturing boys would enjoy participating in a lesson that focuses on muscle strength, whereas late-maturing boys might find it embarrassing to do so. Finally, teachers should not confuse physical maturity with social, personal, and intellectual maturity. Just because a student looks like an adult, doesn't mean that he or she thinks and acts like one.

The contributions of cognitive psychologists also have important implications for science teaching at the middle school and secondary levels. First of all, Piaget's theory suggests that most middle school students are concrete learners and most secondary students are concrete learners or transitioning to formal operations. The likelihood of having a wide variety of cognitive abilities represented in a single class is great and teachers should be prepared for this. It is possible that as many as 75% of the middle school students and that at least 50% of the high school students are concrete thinkers (Chiappetta, 1976). Therefore, both of these groups of students will benefit from concrete learning experiences, particularly when new concepts are introduced.

If science teachers wish to identify learning outcomes that students can attain, they must be aware of the cognitive operations and reasoning patterns required to learn a given amount of material. They must ask if the reasoning patterns possessed by their students are compatible with the complexity of the subject matter. Responses to questions asked in class can be used to gauge students' cognitive abilities and their readiness for instruction (Muth & Alvermann, 1990). Shayer and Adey (1981) advise that chemistry is perhaps the most difficult of the basic sciences for students to assimilate because it involves so many abstract ideas that are imperceptible. Also this discipline requires the use of abstract models in order to convey basic ideas to the learner. Biology and physics seem to make less of a conceptual demand on the learner than chemistry. However, the great integrating ideas of biology and physics are no less demanding than those of chemistry.

The implications drawn from Vygotsky's work complement those suggested by the work of Piaget. Cooperative learning groups should be used often, and they should include both concrete and formal learners, if possible. Interactions between group members and careful teacher monitoring will help students function in their zone of proximal development. Students' cognitive capabilities should also be considered when assigning independent work. The key to student success, according to Muth and Alvermann (1990), is to identify tasks that will challenge but not frustrate students. Additionally, teachers should verbally share their thoughts with students while working problems and engaging in tasks during science class.

Additional implications that center on content presentation and adolescents' understanding can be drawn from information-processing theory. Things to consider when planning science lessons include the adolescents' prior knowledge, the complexity of a task and how it can be broken down into smaller pieces, and ways to help adolescents become aware of how they can regulate their own memory processes (Muth & Alvermann, 1990). Additionally, Muth and Alvermann (1990) recommend that teachers focus not only on the products of adolescents' thinking, but also on the strategies they used to arrive at the product. This focus is helpful in illuminating students' errors, particularly in chemistry, physics, and genetics problem solving. For example, listening to a student think aloud as she works through a heterozygous $\times$ heterozygous dihybrid cross (BbSs $\times$ BbSs) might reveal that her misunderstanding of independent assorting led to her answer of a ratio different from the expected 9:3:3:1.

Science teachers also need to consider the personal and social development of their students. First, teachers should realize that adolescents are searching for their own personal identity and that an aspect of the search involves an answer to the question, Who am I with regard to science? For most students, their science self-concept is inextricably tied to school science experiences and contributes to their overall self-concept. Students' science self-concept can be positively or negatively affected by what happens in middle school and secondary science classes. For example, a student's poor science performance or uncomfortable science experience can lead to a negative science self-concept, which, in turn, can lead to poor science achievement and an unwillingness to continue in science. Second, science teachers should provide students with opportunities to view science experiences and science-related problems from the perspectives of others. Issues related to human health, evolution, and ecology are all good for this purpose. Such opportunities will help students advance to the highest stage of Selman's model. Finally, teachers must understand that most middle school and secondary students do not experience adolescence as a period of storm and stress. The egocentric thinking of adolescents, however, will manifest itself in a number of unwanted behaviors. Teachers must be willing to deal with these behaviors as a natural part of adolescence.

■ **STOP AND REFLECT!** ■

Before going further, answer the following questions:

- How should the realization that the majority of students in an upper-level high school science class are functioning at Piaget's concrete operational level affect a teacher's instructional practices?

- What does Ms. Kendall's journal entry (Box 3.1) reveal about the personal and social developmental levels of her students?

MIDDLE AND SECONDARY SCHOOLS

Secondary schools grew out of the tradition of the nineteenth-century academy, with its dual purposes of educating students for life and preparing students for college. Guided by the thinking of Benjamin Franklin, it was the academy that first included science as a curriculum area (in the forms of natural philosophy, astronomy, and navigation) and provided instruction for both girls and boys. Traditionally, a school that includes grades 7 through 12 in any combination has been called a secondary school. Today, however, a distinction is made between the high school and schools intended for young adolescents—middle schools and junior high schools.

High Schools

High schools generally house students in grades 10 through 12, with some also including grade 9 students. Most high schools are described as comprehensive in that they are intended to provide a general education for all, special vocational and college preparation programs, and enrichment experiences (e.g., band, sports, etc.). The size of a high school student body may vary from less than two hundred to more than two thousand. The typical high school science teacher teaches five or six classes a day for 180 days. If each of five classes has thirty students, the teacher works with 150 students each day. Generally, the school day runs from 8:00 A.M. to 3:00 or 3:30 P.M. and is broken into class periods of 45 or 50 minutes. Some high schools schedule optional classes before the start of the regular school day during what is called the **0 period**. Normally, teachers are required to arrive 30 minutes before school starts and leave no sooner than 30 minutes after school ends. High school science class offerings include biology, chemistry, physics, and numerous applied, special interest, and Advanced Placement (AP) courses. The diversity of the class offerings is largely dependent on teacher expertise, the size of the high school, and the distance learning capabilities available at the school. The science teacher at a large high school may have only one preparation, whereas a teacher at a small high school may have three or more. In most high schools, science teachers are organized as a content area department, with one teacher serving as the department head.

Junior High Schools

Junior high schools developed in the first half of the twentieth century in response to recognition of the different educational needs of the young adolescent. Students in grades 7, 8, and 9 are typically taught in these schools. Junior high schools were intended to provide young adolescents with a general education by making use of curriculum particularly suited to their interests, needs, and abilities. As Tanner and Tanner (1975) make clear, however, this focus was lost during the 1950s and 1960s as academic preparation for high school and beyond took precedence. The result was that the junior high school became a high school for young adolescents.

Middle Schools

The initial intention of the junior high school was resurrected in the middle school movement of the 1960s and 1970s. Most middle schools include grades 6, 7, and 8,

and some also incorporate grade 5. The differences between today's junior high school and middle school are quite profound. Jones, DeLucia, and Davis (1993) describe some of the differences with respect to science instruction. First, middle school science teachers participate as interdisciplinary team members rather than as members of a science department. The instruction provided by these teachers is student centered, not science centered, and often makes use of flexible block scheduling. Rather than separate content courses, the curriculum is organized into theme-based interdisciplinary units that emphasize science in addition to reading, writing, mathematics, social studies, and fine arts. Middle school science teachers represent a mix of certification levels, including secondary science, middle grades, and elementary. By comparison, most junior high and high school teachers hold secondary science (grades 7–12) certification.

In general, middle schools are viewed as providers of educational experiences better suited to the needs of young adolescents. But as Jones and her colleagues (1993) point out, interdisciplinary teams are no substitute for a strong science department when it comes to leadership for science instruction at the school level. Middle school science teachers need to compensate for the missing departmental structure by meeting regularly to discuss such issues as science clubs and fairs, equipment purchase and inventory, and science inservice opportunities.

School Restructuring

No one word better characterizes what is happening in schools today than restructuring. Restructuring efforts involve making organizational changes to both what is taught, that is, the curriculum, and how the curriculum is delivered to students. Whether school-based or systemwide, the ultimate goal of all restructuring is to improve student learning. Often seen as critical to improving student learning is the transformation of schools needed for the industrial age of the past to schools needed for the information age of the future. Based on a national study of school restructuring by Cawelti (1995), elements that seem to be key to the restructuring efforts ongoing in today's secondary and middle schools include

- interdisciplinary curriculum
- school-based shared decision-making teams
- block scheduling
- community outreach
- performance standards

■ authentic assessment

■ instructional technology

In the section that follows, the element of interdisciplinary curriculum will be discussed from the perspective of the organizational structure that makes it possible—the interdisciplinary, decision-making team. Next, the element of block scheduling is taken up. The focus of this discussion will be expanded to address alternative approaches to organizing the school day and school year, thus including the topic of year-round schooling. Finally, the element of community outreach will be discussed. The three elements of performance standards, authentic assessment, and instructional technology will not be covered here because they are discussed at length in other chapters of this book.

Interdisciplinary Teaming.   Interdisciplinary teaming involves "teachers from different subject areas working together to plan the curriculum for a common group of students" (Callahan, Clark, & Kellough, 1995, p. 6). An interdisciplinary team typically consists of teachers from the core areas of mathematics, English or language arts, social studies, and science. Fine arts and physical education teachers may also be represented. The practice of interdisciplinary teaming is prevalent in middle schools and many junior high schools. It is also used with ninth and tenth grades in some high schools. For the younger high school students, an interdisciplinary approach is seen as a way to help them transition into the discipline-centered classes of the junior and senior years (Cawelti, 1995).

A common planning time, having team members' classrooms in close proximity, and having a knowledgeable lead teacher are critical to the work of the interdisciplinary team. A common planning time allows teachers to meet regularly to plan interdisciplinary units, synchronize daily activities, and discuss the work of individual students. A common planning time is greatly facilitated by block scheduling. Having the classrooms of team members in close proximity allows for flexible scheduling and facilitates the movement of equipment, materials, and students to produce the most favorable learning environment. The lead teacher functions much like the head of a content area department would, planning team meetings, leading discussions during team meetings, ordering supplies and materials, and representing the team at school- and district-level meetings. An outgrowth of the interdisciplinary team approach is the concept of a school within a school, where teacher teams and their students function as independent learning communities located within a single school building. In some schools, like Elbert County Middle School in Elberton, Georgia, interdisciplinary teams stay intact for two or three years, as teachers and students move together from one grade to the next.

A major benefit of interdisciplinary planning and teaching is that through the integrated learning experiences, students are better able to see the relationships between science and other subjects. A second is that students are more likely to master the skills and understandings delineated in the science curriculum followed by the district because the skills and understandings will be stressed by all members of the team rather than just one teacher.

Block Scheduling.   Block scheduling offers an alternative to the traditional 50-minute class period. It means that some part of the daily schedule is organized into blocks of time of more than 60 minutes to permit instructional flexibility (Cawelti, 1995). Science teachers who have gone to block scheduling report numerous advantages, including more time for focused instruction and laboratory work and increased student-teacher interactions (Day, 1995). Other benefits associated with block scheduling are fewer class changes and less time lost checking attendance and cleaning up, fewer daily preparations for the teacher, opportunities for interdisciplinary work, and teachers and students who experience less stress and fragmentation (Canady & Rettig, 1995). Science teachers have also found the need to change their instructional strategies when using block scheduling. The increased class time provided by block scheduling is not conducive to lecture. The nature of instruction shifts from presenting information to guiding students in critical thinking and problem solving (Day, 1995; Gerking, 1995).

Block scheduling options for high school are almost limitless. Students on an intensive block schedule complete two courses in 60 days, then move on to two other classes. They can complete six courses in one school year. A 4 × 4 block schedule permits students to take four classes in a semester. In many schools following this schedule, each class meets for 90 minutes each day. Both the intensive block and 4 × 4 block make transfers from schools on traditional schedules difficult. Students on a block 8 or alternating day schedule meet for four classes one day and a different four the next day throughout the school year. In some schools, the basic block 8 plan is adjusted on Fridays to ensure a consistent weekly schedule. A modified block can be just about any arrangement. It could be a 4 × 4 block Monday through Thursday and a traditional six- or seven-period schedule on Friday. Or, it could involve a combination of blocked classes and those following a traditional schedule of meeting for 50 minutes every day. This latter schedule, shown in Figure 3.2, accommodates the preferences of many foreign language and band teachers who feel it is important to meet with students daily.

At the middle school level, the four-block schedule is seeing increasing use across the country (Canady & Rettig, 1995). According to Canady and Rettig (1995), students spend one 90-minute block in language arts, a second block in mathematics, a third in science or social studies, and a fourth block in physical education, fine arts, or exploratory classes. The science/social studies block is rotated in accordance with the preferences of the teaching team, for example, every other day or by semester. Following this schedule, the science teacher meets three groups of students daily and six groups for the year.

Year-Round Schooling.   Year-round schooling is an alternative to the traditional, agrarian-based school calendar. It has been proposed as a means of addressing the problems of summer learning loss and of overcrowded schools. A typical year-round calendar has four 45-day instructional sessions, with each session followed by a 15-day intersession or vacation. This calendar provides the 180 school days required by most state legislatures. During the summer months, many year-round schools start and end earlier than usual. In overcrowded schools, students and teachers may be assigned to two different tracks with daily schedules that vary. For example, one track starts at 7:00 A.M and ends at 2:00 P.M., and the other starts at 2:30 P.M. and ends at 9:30 P.M. During the 1994–95 school year, 2,252 schools in thirty-seven states followed a year-round calendar (Ballinger, 1995).

Other benefits in addition to reducing summer learning loss are associated with year-round schooling.

One is that students in need of remediation or desiring enrichment can take classes during the intersessions. Ballinger (1995) claims that the arrangement is particularly beneficial for students who need help learning English or who wish to prepare for the SAT. Student athletes benefit from year-round schooling in that a portion of the sport's season is free of homework and exams (Ballinger, 1995). Additionally, year-round schooling provides teachers with time for rest, reflection, and year-long staff development. Opposition to year-round schooling often centers on the need for breaking with tradition and the concern about the cost of keeping school buildings open during the summer months. Proponents claim that the benefits of year-round schooling far outweigh the disadvantages.

Community Outreach.   To better serve the needs of their students, many schools have broken with past patterns of isolationism and reached out to the local community for support. Community support for science education is based on the notion of that which benefits the school today, benefits the community tomorrow.

Community support for science education can take many forms. Organized groups may provide volunteers to work with students during classes and in after-school science programs. School-university partnerships can provide faculty to assist with science curriculum development and teacher inservice and help in using new technologies. Business and industry alliances can provide real-life science work experiences for students and teachers. They can also provide for needed science resources in the form of monetary contributions or equipment donations. Some industries may even loan

FIGURE 3.2   Modified Block Schedule

From BLOCK SCHEDULING, 1995, Canady and Rettig, published by Eye on Education, 6 Depot Way West, Larchmont, NY 10538, (914)833-0551. Reprinted by permission.

Holston High School Washington County, VA Combination Single-Period and Semester Block Schedule (2 Semester Blocks; 3 Single Year-Long Periods; 7 Courses Annually)		
Blocks	Fall Semester	Spring Semester
HR & Period 1 8:30–9:25 AM	Course 1 (Year-long)	
Block 1 9:30–11:10 AM	Course 2	Course 3
Period 4 & Lunch 11:15 AM.–12:45 PM	Course 4 and Lunch (Year-long)	
Block II 12:50–2:30 PM	Course 5	Course 6
Period 7 2:35–3:25 PM.	Course 7 (Year-long)	

employees to work with science teachers and students, as does the Pratt and Whitney Division of United Technologies in Hartford, Connecticut (Cawelti, 1995). More important than all other kinds of support, according to Cawelti's national study of school restructuring, is direct parental involvement. Parents can be the deciding factor for whether or not their children achieve success in science.

Magnet Schools

Maximum effort at school restructuring is often observed in magnet schools. Magnet schools are schools that specialize in an aspect of the traditional curriculum or offer a special kind of schooling that would be perceived as attractive to a wide cross section of students and their parents. Many magnet schools were created in response to the failure of district desegregation plans as a "more socially and educationally productive way to desegregate our schools" (Clinchy, 1995, p. 47). Others were envisioned as a way to hasten the process of change needed to create schools for the information age. For a high school science magnet, it is the availability of a wider range of science courses, an emphasis in higher mathematics, and other science-related experiences that constitutes its attractive, or magnetic, quality.

Magnet schools are typically the product of large school districts or states. The teaching staff of magnet schools comprises experienced teachers with advanced degrees and expertise in areas that coincide with a school's mission. The unique offerings of magnet schools are sometimes the result of collaborative partnerships with business, industry, universities, or the military, or funding from the U.S. Department of Education's Magnet Assistance Program. Through the use of electronic networks, it is also possible to organize virtual magnet schools for science and mathematics. The Regional Electronic Magnet School in Massachusetts is but one example of this new wave of opportunity (Goodrich, 1994).

In recent years, the success of magnet schools has spawned national movements to develop schools of choice and charter schools. Schools of choice are schools that have identified a curricular specialty that serves to attract students. Areas emphasized by these newly conceptualized schools include dance, accounting, economics, aerospace engineering, and marine biology, to name just a few. A way to think about the schools-of-choice movement is that all schools are magnet schools by virtue of their unique attractive qualities. Charter schools, through agreement with state or local governing bodies, are given considerable autonomy to organize and operate as they wish. The variety of curricular and organizational options offered by charter schools is almost limitless. Ongoing programs of research and development are integral to the operation of both schools of choice and charter schools. According to Clinchy (1995), within a decade or two magnet schools will disappear as the schools-of-choice and charter schools movements expand and become more influential.

ASSESSING AND REVIEWING

1. In 2061 Halley's comet will again be visible from the earth and science education will be radically different than it is today, so say the framers of the Project 2061 *Benchmarks*. Given what you know about today's school age population, what do you think will be the nature of this population in 2061? Will the factors that affect student success in science in 2061 likely be the same as they are today? Explain.

2. A common medical practice today is for a physician to prescribe a calcium supplement for a new mother to replenish the calcium lost during childbirth. In China, new mothers have traditionally been fed a thick broth, high in calcium ions, prepared by boiling pig's feet in vinegar. Even today, dishes of sweet and sour pork are eaten by many Asian American mothers in the weeks following childbirth (based on a description by Barba, 1995, pp. 61–62).

   a. From the multiculturalist perspective, would the Chinese practice be considered science and/or a product of science? What about from the universalist perspective? Explain your responses.

   b. How could a science teacher utilize the information about the Chinese practice to formulate a multicultural science learning experience for students?

3. What is feminist science education? How does it compare with girl-friendly science education and feminine science education?

4. Most of today's science classes will include students ranging from the learning disabled to the gifted and talented. How would you go about addressing the special science learning needs of these students? Identify two approaches for making science content

more accessible to learning disabled students. Additionally, describe two or three strategies for challenging the bright and highly motivated students.

5. As a new teacher at Bearhollow Middle School, you feel it is important to learn what you can about your students before the first day of classes. Mr. Sloan, whose classroom is right down the hall, taught many of your students last year. When asked, Sloan offered the following recollections of Jeffrey Martin:

> Jeffrey is shorter and weighs less than most of his classmates. He seemed to enjoy my class, but had difficulty with abstract science ideas, such as the Coriolis effect and seafloor spreading. His interest in rock collecting helped him when we studied the characteristics of common rocks and minerals. He got along reasonably well with other students in the class except when they called him "squirt" and teased him about being a "weakling." Jeffrey enjoyed working in groups, but was unable to see things from the perspectives of other students. He once destroyed the

glacial model constructed by his group because they wouldn't agree to build it the way he wanted.

a. Given this information about Jeffrey and assuming it to be accurate, what are three things you could do to help Jeffrey succeed in your science class? Justify your ideas to help Jeffrey in terms of what you have learned about adolescent development in this chapter.

b. How would you expect Jeffrey's eleventh-grade chemistry teacher's recollections of him to differ from those shared by Mr. Sloan?

6. The impetus for much of the current focus on school restructuring is to change the nature of schooling from that needed for the industrial age to that needed for the information age. Pick either interdisciplinary teaming, block scheduling, year-round schooling, or community outreach, and then describe how this one element of school restructuring may lead to the science learning experiences needed for the information age.

■

RESOURCES TO EXAMINE

Science Education For A Pluralist Society. 1993. Distributed in the United States by Open University Press, 1900 Frost Road, Suite 101, Bristol, PA 19007.

> In this 125 page-book, Michael J. Reiss paints a vivid picture of multicultural science education and describes the nature of science curricula for a pluralist society. An extremely valuable section of the book comprises three chapters that present many examples of how teachers can make science learning experiences truly multicultural experiences for students.

Block Scheduling: A Catalyst for Change in High Schools. Part of the Library of Innovations series from Eye On Education, P.O. Box 3113, Princeton, NJ 08543. Published in 1995.

> Robert Lynn Canady and Michael D. Rettig discuss how changes in school scheduling function as the catalyst for school reform. Their 266-page treatise includes numerous examples of 9-month and year-round school schedules actually used by hundreds of high schools across the country. Although they focus on high school schedules, the information presented is also applicable to today's middle and junior high schools.

A Practical Guide for Teaching Science to Students with Special Needs in Inclusive Settings. 1993. Distributed by PRO•ED, 8700 Shoal Creek Boulevard, Austin, TX 78757.

> This manual is an excellent resource for teachers with special needs students in their regular science classes. Margo A. Mastropieri and Thomas E. Scruggs describe general instructional and laboratory practices that have proven effective for working with learning disabled and physically challenged students. Also included are suggestions for adapting often-used life, physical, and earth science activities and information about suppliers of science equipment and materials for students with special needs.

Meeting the Challenges. 1995. Produced and published by the American Association for the Advancement of Science, 1333 H Street, N.W., Washington, DC 20005.

> This is a special supplement to *Science Magazine* that profiles scientists and engineers working in the areas of pharmaceuticals and biotechnology. It may be accessed through the SCIENCE World Wide Web Home Page: http://www.aaas.org. From the main AAAS menu, choose SCIENCE Magazine.

Barrier-Free in Brief. 1991. Produced and published by the American Association for the Advancement of Science, 1333 H Street, N.W., Washington, DC 20005.

This four-booklet series is distributed free of charge by the American Association for the Advancement of Science. The individual titles and their brief descriptions follow.

Access in Word and Deed provides information about appropriate language, courtesies, and stereotyping. It also includes a list of consultants on issues of science and disability.

Access to Scientific Literacy offers suggestions for making out-of-school science programs and experiences accessible to all students.

Laboratories and Classrooms in Science and Engineering includes recommendations for making laboratories and classrooms barrier-free for disabled students.

Workshops and Conferences for Scientists and Engineers provides information necessary for organizing a barrier-free meeting.

REFERENCES

Anderson, J. L. (1982). Chemical instrumentation for the visually handicapped. *Journal of Chemical Education, 59,* 871–872.

Atwater, M. M., Crockett, D., & Kilpatrick, W. J. (1996). Constructing multicultural science classrooms: Quality science for all students. In J. Rhoton & P. Bowers (Eds.), *Issues in science education* (pp. 167–176). Washington, DC: National Science Teachers Association.

Atwater, M. M., & Riley, J. P. (1993). Multicultural science education: Perspectives, definitions, and research agenda. *Science Education, 77,* 661–668.

Balk, D. E. (1995). *Adolescent development.* Pacific Grove, CA: Brooks/Cole.

Ballinger, C. (1995). Prisoners no more. *Educational Leadership, 53*(3), 28–31.

Bandura, A. (1964). The story decade: Fact or fiction? *Psychology in the Schools, 1,* 224–231.

Banks, J. A. (1994). *Multiethnic education: Theory and practice.* Boston: Allyn and Bacon.

Baptiste, H. P., Jr., & Key, S. G. (1996). Cultural inclusion: Where does your program stand? *The Science Teacher, 63*(2), 32–35.

Barba, R. (1995). *Science in the multicultural classroom.* Boston: Allyn and Bacon.

Belenky, M. F., Clinchy, B. M., Goldberger, N. R., Tarule, J. M. (1986). *Women's ways of knowing.* New York: Basic Books.

Bentley, D., & Watts, D. M. (1986). Courting the positive virtues: A case for feminist science. *European Journal of Science Education, 8,* 121–134.

Bireley, M., & Genshaft, J. (Eds.). (1991). *Understanding the gifted adolescent: Educational, developmental, and multicultural issues.* New York: Teachers College Press.

Callahan, J. F., Clark, L. H., Kellough, R. D. (1995). *Teaching in the middle and secondary schools.* Upper Saddle River, NJ: Merrill/Prentice Hall.

Canady, R. L., & Rettig, M. D. (1995). The power of innovative scheduling. *Educational Leadership, 53*(3), 4–10.

Carey, S. (1990). Cognitive development. In D. N. Osherson & E. S. Smith (Eds.), *Thinking: An invitation to cognitive science.* Cambridge, MA: MIT Press.

Cawelti, G. (1995). High school restructuring: What are the critical elements? *NASSP Bulletin, 79*(569), 1–15.

Chambers, D. W. (1983). Stereotypic images of the scientist: The draw-a-scientist test. *Science Education, 76,* 255-265.

Chiappetta, E. L. (1976). A review of Piagetian studies relevant to science instruction at the secondary and college level. *Science Education, 60,* 253–262.

Clinchy, E. (1995). The changing nature of our magnet schools. *New Schools, New Communities, 11*(2), 47–50.

Dacey, J., & Kenny, M. (1994). *Adolescent development.* Madison, WI: Brown & Benchmark.

Day, T. (1995). New class on the block. *The Science Teacher, 62*(4), 28–30.

Elkind, D. (1884). *All grown up and no place to go.* Reading, MA: Addison-Wesley.

Erikson, E. (1968). *Identity: Youth and crisis.* New York: Norton.

Flair, M. N., & Setzer, W. N. (1990). An olfactory indicator for acid-base titrations. *Journal of Chemical Education, 67,* 795–796.

Flavell, J. H. (1963). *The developmental psychology of Jean Piaget.* Princeton, NJ: Van Nostrand Reinhold.

Gerking, J. L. (1995). Building block schedules. *The Science Teacher, 62*(4), 23–27.

Goodrich, B. E. (1994). Creating a "virtual" magnet school. *T.H.E. Journal, 21,* 73–75.

Harding, J., & Parker, L. H. (1995). Agents for change: Policy and practice toward a more gender-inclusive science education. *International Journal of Science Education, 17,* 537–553.

Harvey, T. J., & Edwards, P. (1980). Children's expectations and realisations of science. *British Journal of Educational Psychology, 48*, 18–23.

Hodson, D. (1993). In search of a rationale for multicultural science education. *Science Education, 77*, 685–711.

Hofman, H. M. (1994). Learning disabilities. In J. Egelston-Dodd (Ed.), *Proceedings of a working conference on science for persons with disabilities* (pp. 71–87). Ames: University of Northern Iowa.

Inhelder, B., & Piaget, J. (1958). *The growth of logical thinking from childhood to adolescence.* New York: Basic Books.

Jegede, O. (1994). African cultural perspectives and teaching science. In J. Solomon, & G. Aikenhead (Eds.), *STS education: International perspectives on reform.* New York: Teachers College Press.

Jones, E. D., & Southern, W. T. (1991). Conclusions about acceleration: Echoes of a debate. In W. Southern & E. Jones (Eds.), *The academic acceleration of gifted children* (pp. 223–228). New York: Teachers College Press.

Jones, G., DeLucia, S., & Davis, J. (1993). From junior high to middle school: How science instruction is affected. *NASSP Bulletin, 77*(556), 89–96.

Kahle, J. B. (1996). Equitable science education: A discrepancy model. In L. H. Parker, L. J. Rennie, & B. J. Fraser (Eds.), *Gender, science and mathematics: Shortening the shadow* (pp. 129–139). Dordrecht, Holland: Kluwer Academic Publishers.

Keller, E. C., Jr. (1994). Science education for the motor/orthopedically-impaired students. In J. Egelston-Dodd (Ed.), *Proceedings of a working conference on science for persons with disabilities* (pp. 1–39). Ames: University of Northern Iowa.

Keller, E. C., Jr., Pauley, T. K., Starcher, E., Ellsworth, M., & Proctor, B. (1983). *Resource book: Teaching the physically disabled in the mainstream science class at the secondary and college levels.* Morgantown, WV: Printech Printing.

Kelly, A. (1985). The construction of masculine science. *British Journal of Sociology of Education, 6*, 133–153.

Kelly, A. (1987). Why girls don't do science. In A. Kelly (Ed.), *Science for girls.* Milton Keynes, UK: Open University Press.

Kirschenbaum, R. (1988). Methods for identifying the gifted and talented American Indian student. *Journal for the Education of the Gifted, 11*, 53–63.

Kozol, J. (1991). *Savage inequities.* New York: Crown Publishers.

Kucera, T. J. (Ed.) (1993). *Teaching chemistry to students with disabilities* (3rd ed.). Washington, DC: American Chemical Society. (ERIC Document Reproduction Service No. ED 383 131)

Lang, H. G. (1994). Science for deaf students: Looking into the next millennium. In J. Egelston-Dodd (Ed.), *Proceedings of a working conference on science for persons with disabilities* (pp. 97–109). Ames: University of Northern Iowa.

Lawson, A. E. (1995). *Science teaching and the development of thinking.* Belmont, CA: Wadsworth.

Lee, O., Fradd, S. H., & Sutman, F. X. (1995). Science knowledge and cognitive strategy use among culturally and linguistically diverse students. *Journal of Research in Science Teaching, 32*, 797–816.

Lerner, R. M., Petersen, A. C., & Brooks-Gunn, J. (Eds.). (1991). *Encyclopedia of adolescence.* New York: Garland.

Linn, M. C., & Hyde, J. S. (1989). Gender mathematics and science. *Educational Researcher, 18*(8), 17–27.

Loving, C. C. (1995). Comments on "Multiculturalism, universalism, and science education." *Science Education, 79*, 341–348.

Lynch, S., Atwater, M., Cawley, J., Eccles, J., Lee, O., Marrett, C., Rojas-Medlin, D., Secada, W., Stefanich, G., & Willetto, A. (1997). *An equity blueprint for Project 2061,* 2nd draft. Washington, DC: American Association for the Advancement of Science.

Mastropieri, M. A., & Scruggs, T. E. (1992). Science for students with disabilities. *Review of Educational Research, 62*, 377-411.

Mastropieri, M. A., & Scruggs, T. E. (1993). *A practical guide for teaching science to students with special needs in inclusive settings.* Austin, TX: Pro-Ed.

Mastropieri, M. A., & Scruggs, T. E. (1995, Summer). Teaching science to students with disabilities. *Teaching Exceptional Children,* 10-13.

Mathur, C. F. (1991). Factors influencing the underrepresentation of women in science. In S. K. Majumdar, L. M. Rosenfeld, P. A. Rubba, E. W. Miller, & R. F. Schmalz (Eds.), *Science education in the United States: Issues, crises and priorities* (pp. 503–513). Harrisburg: Pennsylvania Academy of Science.

Matthews, M. R. (1994). *Science teaching: The role of history and philosophy of science.* New York: Routledge.

Mertens, D. M. (1991). Instructional factors related to hearing impaired adolescents' interest in science. *Science Education, 75*, 429–441.

Muth, K. D., & Alvermann, D. E. (1990). *Teaching and learning in the middle grades.* Boston: Allyn and Bacon.

National Center for Educational Statistics. (1996). *The digest of education statistics 1996* (NCES 96-133). Washington, DC: U.S. Government Printing Office.

Offer, D., & Offer, J. B. (1975). *From teenage to young manhood.* New York: Basic Books.

Offer, D., Ostrov, E., & Howard, K. (1981). *The adolescent: A psychological self-portrait.* New York: Basic Books.

Ogawa, M. (1995). Science education in a multiscience perspective. *Science Education, 79*, 583-593.

O'Malley, P., & Bachman, J. (1983). Self-esteem: Changes and stability between ages 13 and 23. *Developmental Psychology, 19*, 257–268.

Papallia, D. E., & Olds, S. W. (1992). *Human development.* New York: McGraw-Hill.

Parkinson, J. (1994). *The effective teaching of secondary science.* London: Longman.

Patton, J. R. (1995, Summer). Teaching science to students with special needs. *Teaching Exceptional Children*, pp. 4–6.

Piaget, J. (1964). Cognitive development in children: Development and learning. *Journal of Research in Science Teaching, 2*, 176–186.

Rakow, S. J., & Bermudez, A. B. (1993). Science is "Ciencia" Meeting the needs of Hispanic American students. *Science Education, 77*, 669-683.

Reiss, M. J. (1993). *Science education for a pluralist society*. Buckingham, England: Open University Press.

Rennie, L. J., Parker, L. H., & Kahle, J. B. (1996). Informing teaching and research in science education through gender equity initiatives. In L. H. Parker, L. J. Rennie, & B. J. Fraser (Eds.), *Gender, science and mathematics: Shortening the shadow* (pp. 203–221). Dordrecht, Holland: Kluwer Academic Publishers.

Renzulli, J. S., & Reis, S. M. (1991). The schoolwide enrichment model: A comprehensive plan for the development of creative productivity. In N. Colangelo & G. Davis (Eds.), *Handbook of gifted education* (pp. 111–141). Boston: Allyn and Bacon.

Reynolds, M. C., & Birch, J. W. (1977). *Teaching exceptional children in all America's schools*. Reston, VA: The Council of Exceptional Children.

Rosenberg, M. (1986). Self-concept from middle childhood through adolescence. In J. Suls & A. Greenwald (Eds.), *Psychological perspectives on the self* (Vol. 3). Hillsdale, NJ: Erlbaum.

Rothman, R. (1990, August 1). Study of 8th graders finds 20% at high risk of failure. *Education Week*, p. 11.

Rowe, D., & Rodgers, J. (1989). Behavioral genetics, adolescent deviance and 'd': Contributions and issues. In G. Adams, R. Montemayor, & T. Gullotta, (Eds.), *Biology of adolescent behavior and development* (pp. 38–67). Newbury Park, CA: Sage.

Santrock, J. W. (1995). *Life-span development*. Madison, WI: Brown & Benchmark.

Selman, R. L. (1976). Social-cognitive understanding: A guide to educational and clinical practice. In T. Lickona (Ed.), *Moral development and behavior: Theory, research, and social issues* (pp. 299–316). New York: Holt, Rinehart, & Winston.

Shayer, M., & Adey, P. (1981). *Toward a science of science teaching*. London: Heinemann Educational Books.

Simmons, R. G., & Blyth, D. A. (1987). *Moving into adolescence*. Hawthorne, NY: Aldine.

Snyder, T. D., & Hoffman, C. M. (1995). *Digest of educational statistics 1995*. Washington, DC: U.S. Department of Education.

Sprinthall, N. A., & Collins, W. A. (1988). *Adolescent psychology*. New York: Random House.

Stanley, W. B., & Brickhouse, N. W. (1994). Multiculturalism, universalism, and science education. *Science Education, 78*, 387–398.

Stattin, H., & Magnusson, D. (1990). *Pubertal maturation in female development. Paths through life* (Vol. 2). Hillsdale, NJ: Erlbaum.

Sternberg, R. J. (1995). *In search of the human mind*. Fort Worth: Harcourt Brace College Publishers.

Suter, L. E. (Ed.). (1996). *Indicators of science and mathematics education-1995*. Arlington, VA: National Science Foundation.

Tanner, D., & Tanner, L. (1975). *Curriculum development*. Upper Saddle River, NJ: Merrill/Prentice Hall.

Tobin, K. (1996). Gender equity and the enacted science curriculum. In L. H. Parker, L. J. Rennie, & B. J. Fraser (Eds.), *Gender, science and mathematics: Shortening the shadow* (pp. 119–128). Dordrecht, Holland: Kluwer Academic Publishers.

Tobin-Richards, M. H., Boxer, A. M., & Petersen, A. C. (1983). The psychological significance of pubertal change: Sex differences in perceptions of self during early adolescence. In J. Brooks-Gunn & A. C. Petersen (Eds.), *Girls at puberty: Biological and psychological perspectives* (pp. 127–154). New York: Plenum.

Travis, J. W. (1990). Geology and the visually impaired student. *Journal of Geological Education, 38*(1), 41-49.

Troyna, B. (1987). Beyond multiculturalism: Toward the enactment of antiracist education in policy provision and pedagogy. *Oxford Review of Education, 13*, 307–320.

Troyna, B., & Hatcher, R. (1992). *Racism in children's lives: A study of mainly-white primary schools*. London: Routledge.

United States Commission on Civil Rights. (1992). *Civil rights issues facing Asian Americans in the 1990s*. Washington, DC: U.S. Government Printing Office.

Vander Zanden, J. W. (1993). *Human development*. New York: McGraw-Hill.

Vygotsky, L. S. (1978). *Mind in society: The development of higher psychological processes* (M. Cole, V. John-Steiner, S. Scribner, & E. Souberman, Eds.). Cambridge: Harvard University Press.

Waterman, A. S. (1982). Identity development from adolescence to adulthood: An extension of theory and a review of research. *Developmental Psychology, 18*, 341–358.

Weigerber, R. A. (1993). *Science success for students with disabilities*. Menlo Park, CA: Addison-Wesley.

Woolfolk, A. E. (1995). *Educational psychology* (6th ed.). Boston: Allyn and Bacon.

■

CHAPTER 4

LEARNING IN MIDDLE GRADES AND SECONDARY SCHOOLS

Students construct meaningful knowledge through their interactions with the physical environment and each other.

In our quest to produce an informed society, scientific literacy is a necessary goal. We want all students to graduate from high school with a good feeling about science, an interest in some of its fields, and an understanding of many major concepts. This aim necessitates changing the perceptions of many middle and senior high school students regarding science and helping them to form more correct notions about fundamental ideas. In order to achieve these ends, science teachers must draw upon and use the latest findings that are available on learning science. The contributions from researchers in the areas of cognitive psychology and constructivism have caused many educators to view teaching and learning from an entirely different perspective than from the tradition view of instruction.

OBJECTIVES

This chapter is designed to help the reader meet the following objectives:

- Better understand cognitive psychology and constructivist approaches to teaching and learning.
- Become more sensitive to the roles that attitudes, motivation, and alternative conceptions play in learning science. How to assess?
- Use students' prior knowledge, contradictions of beliefs, analogical reasoning, and concept mapping to stimulate learning and to make science more meaningful.

INTRODUCTION

Science teachers must know more than the subject matter they are assigned to teach. They must understand how students learn, what they think about, and what they know when they enter the classroom. In addition, science teachers must be sensitive to students' feelings toward science and how their interests can aid or interfere with learning this subject. They must be skilled at helping students to represent ideas, make connections, solve problems, and modify ideas. Fortunately, science teachers can turn to the fields of cognition and learning for guidance in these matters.

Today, cognitive psychologists and learning theorists place a great deal of importance on **meaningful learning.** They remind us that students must find their studies meaningful in order for them to invest the mental energy required to think deeply about the subject matter. Further, students must find relevance in the curriculum so that they can see how it connects with their lives. Students' attitudes and interests toward the subject matter, the teacher, other students, and instructional activities should become critical areas of concern for science teachers.

Cognitive psychologists and learning theorists also stress the importance of encouraging students to **think** deeply about the ideas under study. They advise educators to help students develop a disposition for critical thinking within a variety of contexts (Resnick, 1987) so that students will form patterns of thought and acquire substantive knowledge within specific domains of science and technology. Along with thinking, the **construction of knowledge** is a central theme of much of the work taking place in cognitive psychology research. This theme is based upon the notion that ideas, images, and skills are developed over time in the mind through mental activity directed toward the physical and social world. This is a two-way process whereby ideas can be assimilated into existing structures and existing structures can be altered to fit those which exist outside of the mind.

The construction of knowledge begins with what students know when they come to science class. This is where instruction begins. Whereas many science teachers say that students in the middle and even high schools possess little knowledge about science when they begin their courses, researchers say that students come to school with a great deal of personal knowledge about the natural world, and this **prior knowledge** is a critical element in their learning science. Prior knowledge is rooted deeply in students' minds and beliefs. These alternative conceptions, whether they are considered naive ideas or misconceptions or different from science, interfere greatly with intended learning outcomes.

A useful approach for determining what students know and how they think is to encourage them to represent their ideas. The **representation of ideas** is an ongoing process that starts at the beginning of instruction, takes place throughout, and is reflected upon at the end. Discussions, journal writing, analogies, and concept mapping are among many techniques that can be used to help students externalize their thinking and organize their ideas. In addition, teachers can introduce **contradictions** into the learning environment to get students to modify their ideas and cognitive structures.

■ STOP AND REFLECT! ■

Given this brief introduction to cognitive psychology and learning, read Box 4.1 titled "Do Rocks Have Ancestors?" Examine the teaching and learning that appears to have taken place in the science class and respond to the following questions.

- Did the teacher begin the unit with what the students know or with what is known in science about the age of the earth?

- What type of general thinking pattern was the teacher attempting to get students to practice?

- How effective was the teacher's attempt to approach the study of the rock cycle with an exercise pertaining to the ancestry of the students in the class?

CONSTRUCTIVISM AND TEACHING SCIENCE

> Pupils come to science lessons with ideas about the natural world. Effective science teaching takes account of these ideas and provides activities which enable pupils to make the journey from their current understanding to a more scientific view. (Driver, Squires, Rushworth, & Wood-Robinson, 1994, p. xii)

At present, constructivism is a popular idea associated with teaching and learning science. This notion is used to explain learning, guide instructional practices, and conduct research. The central thesis is that humans construct knowledge as opposed to knowledge being transmitted into their minds. Constructivism stresses the importance of considering what is already in the learner's mind as a place to initiate instruction. Learning is regarded as an active process whereby students construct personal meaning of the subject matter through

BOX 4.1

■

DO ROCKS HAVE ANCESTORS?

Mrs. Reyes is an experienced science teacher who has taught a variety of science courses at the middle and senior high school levels in the southwestern part of the United States. She has been reassigned to a large inner-city high school in an attempt by the district to restaff the school with teachers who are interested in changing a science program to better meet the needs of the students. Mrs. Reyes's task is to plan and teach a new science course, which is a combination of earth and environmental sciences. The teacher realizes the big challenge that faces her because of the student population and the course content.

The students at MacArthur High School show little interest in academic work. For a large percentage of the students, English is a second language. Even those who speak English are reading at the sixth-grade level or below. Many of the students have never traveled to other parts of the United States. A large percentage works after school and on weekends, causing them to neglect homework.

Mrs. Reyes thought hard about how she was going to get the students interested in geological changes in the earth over time, given that most of them had little acquaintance with different geological regions. She was concerned about connecting abstract science concepts with what students know. How can students relate to different land formations as a result of their prior experiences? Further, how do you make the subject matter meaningful?

An idea came to mind. Why not precede the study of changes in the earth and the rock cycle with an activity on ancestry. Since these students will readily discuss people, Mrs. Reyes reasoned that it might be wise to begin with the familiar. The following dialogue illustrates how she initiated the lesson:

MRS. REYES: I have written on the board the question:

Do rocks have ancestors?

With that the students immediately began to giggle and express a variety of opinions.

JUSTIN: Are you crazy! Rocks don't come from people.

MARISHA: We have ancestors—not rocks.

SIN: Rocks don't change much, but they do crumble.

MRS. REYES: All of your answers make some sense. Let's define ancestor.

After several students gave their definitions, the teacher used their ideas to define ancestor as a person whom we come from.

MRS. REYES: Can you trace your ancestry? Tell me where you come from, where your parents come from, your grandparents, and so on. For each person, including yourself, give the year and place of birth. In addition, give the year of death for your ancestors who have died. This information will also tell us the cultural background of the people who settled this land.

During the discussion that followed, some of the students identified the Spanish as the first settlers of the land. One student, Benny Martinez, asserted that his people have lived in the southern part of the state since the early 1800s. Another student indicated that she was one-eighth American Indian and her people, the Apaches, were here before any of the other settlers. The students' responses led to a heated argument as to which people settled the territory. After getting control of the class, Mrs. Reyes decided to group the students so that they could trace the people who came to live in the state.

MRS. REYES: Let's get into our small groups and produce a timeline, giving the names of the people who settled in the state and approximately when they arrived. Begin with yourself and go back in time. Identify one person in your group to use as an example. It should be the person who knows the most about his or her ancestral history. Write your timeline on notebook paper first, then transfer it to the butcher paper. Select someone in your group to write clearly on the large paper. Today is Friday, which will give you the weekend to obtain more information about your family history.

When the students returned on Monday, two of the groups had a timeline that could be presented. Below are the examples.

Claire White	My mother	My mother's father	My mother's father's father (Apache Indian)	
1980	1963	1942 to 1994	1915 to 1973	
New Mexico	New Mexico	Arizona	Arizona	

Tom Esquivel	Father	Grandfather	Great grandfather	Great, great grandfather
1981	1959	1928	1887 to 1950	1863 to 1909
New Mexico	New Mexico	New Mexico	New Mexico	Mexico

Over the next two days all of the groups had an opportunity to trace back their origins. Some of the students traced their ancestors to the northeastern part of the United States, then to western Europe. Some students and their families came from Asia, Vietnam, and China. At the end of the presentations, Mrs. Reyes brought up the question about who were the first people to settle Arizona/New Mexico and where did they come from. One student indicated that she remembered in her American history class that the teacher said the Native Americans came from people who traveled from Asia across the Pacific Ocean into Alaska and then down to the Southwest.

Through discussion the class came to an agreement that one accepted idea for the origin of the earliest people in the United States is that they originated in Africa, some moved into Asia, then into Alaska, and eventually down into the southern states.

Mrs. Reyes approached Mr. Butler, the American history teacher, who showed interest in the topic and said he would be happy to discuss it with her class. He pointed out that there is more than one theory about the origins of the first humans in North America. Mr. Butler had a time conflict, but he agreed to be videotaped. In the presentation, he reviewed the Clovis theory, which traces our origins to Asia. In addition, he brought up a new theory that traces Native Americans to South America. Mr. Butler discussed the evidence that is gathered by archeologists in order to make inferences about dates and life-style, pointing out that hand tools and weapons are artifacts that give us clues about early civilizations. The students were attentive to Mr. Butler's presentation and seemed to absorb the information.

After several class periods in which students were put into the position of having to "think back" in time, Mrs. Reyes was ready to get to the science topic in the curriculum. She set out three rocks and asked the students to gather around her for a close-up view.

MRS. REYES: Rocks have origins, just like people. Some are formed first and then others follow as the result of processes that occur over very long periods of time. Before we study the characteristics of these rocks in the laboratory, I want you to tell me which is the youngest, then move back to the oldest. In front of you are three types of rocks. Order them by placing the youngest rock here, then the rock that formed it here, and finally the oldest rock here.

The students immediately began to respond and to provide reasons for their ideas. Mrs. Reyes noted their interest. Now she was curious as to how attentive and interested they would be during the rest of the laboratory exercises on the rock cycle and the subsequent study of changes in the earth. Then she could evaluate how worthwhile it was to spend several class periods easing students into studying important scientific principles by beginning with a strange question: Do Rocks Have Ancestors?

their interactions with the physical and social world. It is the student who must make sense out of the experiences. Knowledge is not just out there in textbooks and in teachers' heads ready to be transferred into the minds of students. Instead, "out there" is where one finds information and experiences, which are formed by the mind into durable knowledge. This learning process is facilitated by the skilled teacher who engages students in thinking, questioning, testing ideas, explaining, and representing ideas. As stated in the quote above, effective science teaching must take into account what students know, then modify this knowledge so that it reflects scientific views.

Constructivism has been addressed by philosophers for centuries in **epistemology**—the study of the origins and nature of knowledge. Epistemologists asks questions such as

1. Where does knowledge come from?
2. How is knowledge expressed and communicated?
3. How truthful is the knowledge we claim?
4. How necessary is experience in the acquisition of knowledge?
5. What part does reason play in forming knowledge? (Angeles, 1981, p. 78)

During the last ten to fifteen years, constructivism has become popular among science and mathematics educators as they search for ways to better understand, explain, and guide teaching and learning. Some educators view constructivism as a theory (Fosnot, 1996), some as a model (von Glasersfeld, 1993), and others view it as a referent (Tobin & Tippens, 1993). Constructivism has taken on many meanings and will continue to evolve while it is popular.

Von Glasersfeld (1993) indicates that constructivism is a way of knowing that recognizes the real world as a source of knowledge. There is an external world made up of objects and events, which we want students to learn about. However, students as well as scientists can never fully know reality. They can form approximations of reality, but never a true picture of it. Absolute truth is not possible. What we can aim for is to build useful ideas about the world that are viable and can be used to understand and explain nature. Viable knowledge can be applied to further our purposes and the quality of life. This notion implies that reality is dependent upon the mind for its existence, hence knowledge is constructed by the mind rather than being a facsimile of reality (von Glasersfeld, 1995).

The theory that the mind constructs useful ideas of reality has implications for instruction. If people have to conceptualize reality, they need to process, organize, and reflect upon it. Thus learning becomes an active process that builds upon prior knowledge. What the learners know becomes as important as what we want them to know. Teaching and learning must be an interactive process that engages the learners in constructing knowledge. Negotiation takes place between the teacher and students, whereby the teacher moves students toward greater understanding of reality. Often these interactions take time, requiring many small steps toward reforming and building new ideas (Driver, Asoko, Leach, Mortimer, & Scott, 1994). Through this approach, students' ideas become more differentiated and more closely resemble scientific concepts.

There are at least two sources for constructing knowledge—personal experience with the physical world and interaction with others in our sociocultural world. Jean Piaget, Lev Vygotsky, and David Ausubel made significant contributions to these areas. During the last half of the twentieth century, Piaget's work on intellectual development has provided educators with a foundation for constructivism. His theory of cognitive structures and logical mathematical operations has given educators greater insight into development and learning. Importantly, the work underscores the significance of experience in developing internal structures. The interaction with objects and events stimulates the construction of knowledge, as opposed to passive listening. For Piaget, it is the learner who brings to bear mental operations in reaction to the environment, engaging learning and furthering cognitive development. In translating this theory into practice, science teaching has promoted more experiences with concrete materials, emphasizing manipulation of objects, testing ideas, and organizing data. More emphasis has been placed on the use of contradictions and discrepant events to cause cognitive dissonance, motivating students to wonder why and find out. Piaget's theory of equilibration has given teachers a

model to reflect upon in order to help students to assimilate information and to modify thinking.

Another dimension of learning and development is the role of peers and adults in facilitating the construction of knowledge. Whereas Piaget focused his attention on physical interaction, Vygotsky focused his attention on social interaction. He believed that peers and adults greatly influence learning and the acquisition of science concepts. The organization of ideas by others has enormous influence on what people learn. Although Vygotsky believed as Piaget that knowledge is constructed and developed over time, he stressed that the major contribution to cognition is social interaction. He used the idea of a zone of proximal development to focus attention on the potential (Sternberg, 1995) for learning and development via adult interaction. The zone of proximal (or potential) development is a range of possible development between what learners can do by themselves and what they can do with assistance from others at a more advanced level (Vygotsky, 1978).

For Vygotsky, direct instruction had a more influential role on the assimilation of ideas than for Piaget. Further, he stressed the importance of language in the mediation of ideas, which advances learning and development. Vygotsky emphasized that students learn about science from others. Similarly, scientists learn about their enterprise by interacting with other scientists and examining the ideas that they have contributed to the discipline. Thus, knowledge is a product of culture that has been constructed over time, growing and changing as the result of human interaction.

David Ausubel also promoted a cognitive approach to learning, except he focused on the conceptual rather than the operative forms of knowledge that were stressed by Piaget. He advocated that reception learning is directed toward discipline-based concepts that can be learned by students, and, in fact most of what is learned, both in and out of school, is acquired through the transmission of ideas rather than through discovering them. Ausubel, however, advised that reception learning must be meaningful in order for it to be effective. He cautioned educators that discovery as well as reception learning can be rote, and that they must avoid this situation and take every measure to make learning meaningful. However, he pointed out that students must relate the material under study to their existing cognitive structures of organized information (Ausubel, 1963). When students learn in a meaningful manner, they form mental connections between new ideas and the relevant elements within their existing cognitive structures.

Today, constructivism has taken on a different meaning for many educators from the one which was used widely over the past several decades. In the past, the Piagetian stage theory and his generalizable thinking skills dominated a great deal of teaching and learning in science education. The theory that developmental reasoning sets limits on what students can learn was central to the stage theory. As a result, considerable emphasis was been placed on general reasoning ability with much less emphasis on learning specific concepts. This movement is evidenced by the importance placed on learning science process skills, which has been observed in science education over the past thirty years. For some science educators, this stance tended to separate content and process, de-emphasizing the importance of subject matter content and elevating the importance of science process skills. As the result of the stress placed upon general reasoning skills and problem solving associated with the Piagetian psychology, neo-Piagetian researchers suggest that we modify our views regarding learning science and that we place more emphasis on the acquisition of subject matter content and science concepts.

For many who are participating in the constructivism movement, the focus is on the construction of content specific knowledge. "Children do not apply preexisting general cognitive structures to the tasks and materials encountered in schools, but they construct specific cognitive structures or organize their activities in each type of task or learning situation in which they participate" (Bidell & Fisher, 1992, p. 19). This statement implies that if a science teacher wants to teach students to measure, the question becomes Measure what? The "what" becomes an important focus of learning. You often hear science teachers say, "Every year we teach our students to measure, but when they go to math class or to science in the following year, the teachers indicate that they cannot measure." Change the context and the skill seems to disappear. For these reasons, the content or the context have taken a prominent role in the present constructivist movement.

Constructivism is a popular idea that is being used to guide teaching, learning, and research in science education. This idea places great emphasis upon what the learner already knows. Those teaching from a constructivist referent might view the learning process as a journey that begins where the student resides. The voyage is a collaborative effort between the learner and the teacher. The students designate the starting points of their excursion based upon what they believe and know. The direction for the trip is charted by the ideas students wish to test or territories teachers wish to explore. In some instances, opportunities are provided for students to stop along the way to interact with objects and observe events. In other instances, there are teachers, adults, and peers who share their ideas of the world and keep students moving. Since students **cannot** discover all important ideas on their own, social interaction is a vital part of their educational excursion. Students benefit from discussions with teachers and interactions with peers who can help them to acquire new concepts. Further, students can receive information that has been organized by others, so long as it is meaningful to their way of thinking and knowing.

Science teachers and educators need to remember that there are many useful ways to view teaching and learning science that have not been addressed here because of space. For example, behavior, practice, and reinforcement are aspects of learning that merit attention in the science classroom. These ideas are associated with behavioral approaches to learning that are different from cognitive approaches. Constructivism is only one way to view learning science. There are many ways of viewing reality and how people acquire scientific knowledge, beyond constructivism (Osborne, 1996). Further, constructivism may offer claims regarding teaching and learning science that cannot be substantiated by research (Matthews, 1994). In any event, as we carry out the science education reform, the ideas associated with constructivism can provide teachers with many important insights into how students can learn about and appreciate science.

AFFECTIVE LEARNING

If teachers want to help students construct their own science understandings, they must be cognizant of the attitudes and values that students bring with them to science class. Students' attitudes and values should not be discounted as unimportant nor should attempts be made to override them in the context of science instruction. The attitudes and values that students bring with them to science class are aspects of the affective domain, and as such they are critical indicators of the worth students place on science and how they view the scientific enterprise.

Not only should students' attitudes and values be considered as factors that affect science knowledge construction, but they should also be regarded as outcomes of science instruction. There is much that teachers can do to help students develop favorable feelings toward science, scientists, and science learning and strengthen commitment to certain science-related ideas and actions. Students should be engaged in instructional activities specifically designed to achieve affective outcomes. It should not be assumed that favorable feelings and strong commitments will develop as students learn more science content.

Affective Concepts

Attitude has long been one of the most important affective concepts in science education. Attitude represents a favorable or unfavorable feeling toward something (Koballa & Warden, 1992); therefore, **attitude** is primarily an affective concept that centers upon the evaluation of an idea. The word attitude is often confused with belief, value, interest, and opinion, which although related are somewhat different. **Beliefs** are the cognitive bases for attitudes and are the more informational and factual. In recent years, as the disciplines of social psychology and educational psychology have become more cognitively oriented, belief has replaced attitude as the most studied affective concept in science education. **Values** relate to moral and ethical issues of right and wrong, and are much broader than either attitudes or beliefs. Although the term **interest** is thought of as synonymous with attitude, it has a slightly different meaning and has been addressed in a different line of research. Interest addresses someone's willingness to respond to something and explains some aspects of motivation. **Opinion** is often used interchangeably with attitude and interest, but is seldom used as the focus of inquiry in affective studies in science education.

Affect and Action

Affective variables are important because of their links to behavior. By knowing about a student's science-related attitudes, beliefs, or values, a teacher is provided with some insight into the student's science-related actions. Whereas the correspondence between, say, a student's attitude toward science and his or her decision to engage in a science activity when other options are available is not absolute, the links between affective variables and behavior are considered strong enough to warrant instructional efforts that target affective variables. By systematically targeting affective variables in science instruction, students are likely to develop dispositions to think and act in responsible ways toward science learning and the scientific enterprise.

One model that illuminates various links between affective variables and behavior is Ajzen's (1989) model of planned behavior, shown in Figure 4.1. According to the model, the best predictor of behavior is one's intention to engage in the behavior. This means that if a person intends to attend a science club meeting, barring unforeseen circumstances, he or she will be there. Affective variables that are considered antecedents of intention include attitude toward the behavior, subjective norm, and perceived behavioral control. Attitude is concerned with personal feelings about engaging in the behavior, and subjective norm is concerned with impressions about the support coming from significant referents. Perceived behavioral control addresses the perceived barriers and facilitating factors that may make

engaging in the behavior difficult or easy. For any given behavior, the three variables may contribute equally to an individual's motivation to engage in the behavior, or one variable may contribute more than the other two. The following questions capture the essence of these three antecedents:

1. Attitude: What is in it for me?
2. Subjective norm: Who wants me to do it?
3. Perceived behavioral control: What factors may make it easy or difficult for me to do it?

Attitude, subjective norm, and perceived behavioral control also have antecedents, according to the model. The antecedents are based on the expectancy-value formulation of attitude proposed by Fishbein (1963) to show the link between attitude and belief. Consistent with the expectancy-value theorem, a student's attitude toward engaging in a behavior is the product of two forces, the beliefs that the student holds about engaging in the behavior and the value that he gives to the outcome associated with each belief. Likewise, subjective norm is the product of the student's beliefs about what people think he should do and his motivation to comply with their desires, and perceived behavioral control is the product of beliefs about factors that will facilitate or inhibit his action and the likely occurrence of these factors. These expectancy-value linkages reflect the cognitive processing that takes place prior to decision making and action, according to Crawley and Koballa (1994), and provide a means to target affective variables in science instruction and promote reflection and affective change.

Persuasion

Persuasion can be used to promote reflection and affective change in the science classroom. According to Reardon (1991), persuasion is the act of "encouraging someone to *choose* to make a change in beliefs, attitudes, and/or behaviors" (p. 12). Persuasion can also be used to influence value judgments (Goldthwait, 1996). The activities of persuasion are easily understood in the context of the question, Who says what to whom with what effect?. **Who** is the advocate and **what** is the advocate's message. **Who** is the audience, or message recipient, and **what** effect is the acceptance of the position presented in the advocate's message.

When considering the use of persuasion, it is critical to understand that all persuasion is self-persuasion (Larson, 1986). That is to say that people are persuaded by the messages that they themselves construct by relating what they know about the topic to the arguments and

FIGURE 4.1   Ajzen's Planned Behavior Model

Adapted from *Understanding Attitudes and Predicting Social Behavior* (p. 71), by I. Ajzen, and M. Fishbein, 1980, Englewood Cliffs, NJ: Prentice-Hall.

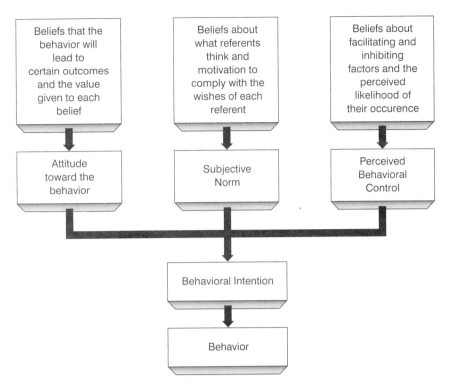

evidence presented by the advocate. The personal messages constructed by individuals may lead them to accept or reject the choice favored by the advocate. Persuasion is useful not only for modifying attitudes, but for forming attitudes where none exist and strengthening attitudes already held, according to Miller (1980). Persuasion ceases and coercion begins when choices are imposed rather than freely accepted or rejected. Of course, the focus of persuasion in the science classroom must be noncoercive, and students must be allowed to weigh the evidence presented and decide for themselves whether to accept the position favored by the advocate.

Ajzen's (1989) planned behavior model provides a framework for using persuasion in the science classroom. Persuasion is operationalized by means of the expectancy-value formulations of attitude, subjective norm, and perceived behavioral control. Key to persuasive appeals are the specific beliefs that students hold about outcomes associated with the behavior targeted in the appeal, about the wishes of significant referents, and about the likely occurrence of facilitating and inhibiting factors, and the value given to each belief.

active recipients of arguments and evidence. Petty and Cacioppo's (1986) elaboration likelihood model provides an explanation for why instruction to achieve affective objectives may or may not be successful. According to the model, students use two types of information-processing strategies: central route and peripheral route. **Central route** processing involves careful scrutiny of arguments and evidence, topic-relevant thinking, and, perhaps, a decision to act based on a combination of information from instruction and long-term memory. Use of this strategy requires ability and motivation to process the incoming arguments and evidence. **Peripheral route** processing relies on the use of heuristics and cues associated with the instruction and requires less cognitive effort than central route processing. Peripheral route processing is more likely when ability and/or motivation to engage in instruction are low, and it tends to result in affective change that is short-lived and very susceptible to contradictory arguments and evidence (Petty & Cacioppo, 1986). Therefore, to encourage central route process and thus achieve the most from instruction to achieve affective objectives, lessons must be both understandable and motivational.

Cognition in Affect

Even when using the strategies of persuasion, instruction to achieve affective objectives is not always successful. This is true because students function as cognitively

Motivation

Motivation is a central element of instruction to achieve both affective and cognitive objectives. According to Brophy (1988, p. 205), a student's tendency to find school work meaningful and worthwhile and to try to benefit from it is the essence of motivation to learn. In science, students are motivated to engage in activities for the personal satisfaction gained from them and for the rewards or punishment that may be linked to them. Motivation that comes from personal satisfaction, interest, or curiosity is called intrinsic motivation. Motivation that has little to do with the activity itself but rather with the associated rewards or punishment is called extrinsic motivation. One of the important jobs of teachers is to encourage students to engage in activities for the intrinsic benefits derived from them.

By observing a student's behavior it is impossible to determine if the motivation for engaging in an activity is intrinsic or extrinsic. Only by understanding the student's reasons for his or her action can it be determined whether the action is prompted by personal satisfaction, interest or curiosity, or by rewards or punishment. In some cases, teachers can develop intrinsic motivation in students by stimulating their interest in a topic or by gradually increasing the difficulty level of lessons to ensure continued success. For example, biology teachers are often successful in creating intrinsic motivation among their students to learn genetics by having them develop family pedigrees. It is also true that at times teachers must rely on rewards and external inducements to achieve their instructional objectives, such as when a reminder about slipping grades is used to encourage a student to work harder. But, teachers should always be looking for ways to help students shift the emphasis from extrinsic incentive to intrinsic satisfaction.

According to Woolfolk (1995, p. 349), intrinsic motivation is only one attribute that contributes to student motivation to learn. Four others are challenging learning goals, involvement in the learning task, achievement based on mastery learning, and feelings of control over effort and ability. All five attributes of motivation should be considered when planning instruction to achieve both affective and cognitive objectives.

In summary, the affective domain is an important dimension of science learning. Students need to leave science classes not only with science understandings, but with favorable feelings toward science learning and the scientific enterprise and with commitment to some science-related ideas and actions. Persuasion can be used by teachers to achieve affective objectives in science. Motivation to learn is an important affective concept because of its role in mediating the achievement of both affective and cognitive objectives. It is well for science teachers to be familiar with aspects of the affective domain in order to better address this dimension of learning in the science classroom.

EQUILIBRATION AND CONTRADICTIONS

Knowledge is not a copy of reality. To know an object, to know an event, is not simply to look at it and make a mental copy or image of it. To know an object is to act on it. To know is to modify, to transform the object, and to understand the process of this transformation, and as a consequence to understand the way the object is constructed. An operation is the essence of knowledge; it is an interiorized action which modifies the object of the knowledge. (Piaget, 1964)

This quote by Piaget underscores a central theme in cognitive psychology: Learning is an active process. It is not a transmission process whereby knowledge is photocopied by the nervous system, but an interactive process whereby mental actions lead toward the understanding of objects and events that make up our world. The growth of knowledge is tied to internal mechanisms and cognitive organization. What implications does this view have for teaching science? What can science teachers do to encourage students to think deeply in order to construct a body of knowledge that they can understand and can use?

Piaget used the concept of **equilibration** as a mechanism to explain learning and cognitive development (Piaget, 1971). He asserted that intelligence and learning have a biological mechanism, just as animal behavior—down to the most primitive instincts—can be traced to an organ and a set of functions. Thus, if physical behavior can be tied to biological structures, then knowledge can be tied to psychological structures. Further, we should explain how these structures form and elaborate over a human lifetime, especially during childhood and adolescence, thereby extending our understanding of how learning takes place. Piaget used the concept of equilibration, which was taken from the biological sciences, to theorize about learning and cognitive development.

The Piagetian notion of equilibration is that of a dynamic, continuous process that controls intelligence and learning (Furth, 1969). This process coordinates what infants, children, adolescents, and adults do when interacting with the world around them. It regulates their thinking and intellectual responses, and does so by affecting what individuals can react to and how they respond. Piaget used the terms assimilation and accommodation to explain equilibration, to suggest how learning and development progress.

When an individual takes in information from objects and events, he or she **assimilates** it into existing cognitive structures. The cognitive organism perceives (assimilates) only what it can "fit into" the structures it already has (von Glasersfeld, 1995). Note that this notion is central to constructivist psychology, which stresses the belief that new knowledge builds upon prior knowledge. Constructivistic thinking would question the value of a learning situation where the ideas to learn have no connection with existing ideas in the mind of the learner. For example, if a person were in a cafeteria line and saw a vegetable that she enjoyed eating, she would recognize it and perhaps take it. This individual would assimilate the idea right into her organization of foods. If she did not recognize a particular food, however, the chances are high that she would not place it on her tray. We would question a science teacher's effectiveness in trying to explain Einstein's theory of gravitation to a group of middle school students who have no sense or knowledge of space-time curvature. Where is the foundation for the geometry of curved space in the cognitive structures of these students? The presence of already existing knowledge increases the possibility for the learner to fit external ideas into their thinking, assimilate them into their schemata, and therefore find these ideas meaningful.

Along with assimilation, **accommodation** occurs (Piaget, 1971). When one assimilates information and events, he or she must also accommodate to it. Accommodation is the modification of existing cognitive structures to fit the ideas that one is internalizing. The degree to which individuals have to modify their existing beliefs and ideas depends upon the situation. Again, consider the cafeteria line. When people select a food that they eat regularly and place it on their tray, they accommodate the selection process with relative ease. However, if a friend suggests that you try an unknown vegetable, because it is a delicious food, similar in taste to a sweet potato, you may try it. As you reach for the dish, you will be convincing yourself that this vegetable is going to suit your taste. Regardless of how the vegetable tastes, you will have learned something new about this food as well as the trust you place in the friend. Now you have accommodated, modifying your knowledge about eating this food.

The continuous equilibration process of assimilation and accommodation is one way to envision the growth and differentiation of knowledge and is a mechanism for learning science. Now, how does this theory assist us to teach science in a manner that will help students to better understand important abstract ideas? Piaget and others (Lawson, 1994; Fosnot, 1996) recommend the use of **contradictions** to stimulate assimilation and especially accommodation. Situations that contradict what students think or believe may cause them to alter their thinking and to find out about the situation at hand. External events that challenge what people know or believe and create puzzlement or surprise motivate them

to think more deeply and to alter their world view (Kasschau, 1986). Even discussing ideas can cause cognitive perturbations, creating cognitive disequilibrium.

Discrepant events are used by science teachers to challenge students to think and encourage them to focus on a concept, law, or principle under study. For example, Bernoulli's principle is used to explain a phenomenon that many find difficult to comprehend. Demonstrations centering around this principle present contradictions to what people believe, thus putting them into a state of mental disequilibrium (Lawson, 1994). Note the demonstration setup in Figure 4.2 in which a sheet of paper is supported by two thick textbooks. Pose the question: What will happen to the paper when I blow hard between the table top and the paper? Many students will respond that the paper will fly off the books or move upward. Place the responses of the students on the board and take a count of those who hold certain ideas regarding what will occur.

Demonstrate what happens when you blow vigorously beneath the paper. Ask a few students to come forward and blow under the paper. Note the surprise and discrepancy between what most of the class believed would occur and what actually did occur. Now, how do you explain these results? Through a series of questions, develop a description of this event and an explanation of the principle involved. Many in the class will still be hooked to their beliefs with regard to the effects of rapidly moving air pushing directly on the paper. Write a scientific explanation on the chalkboard of what happened, then call on a few more participants to test the principle. Ask some individuals to blow under the paper and some to blow over the paper. Perhaps some participants will begin to incorporate a different view of a stream of air moving across an object.

Do not believe that this one demonstration will produce enough conceptual change for students to reach a level of equilibrium that solidifies scientific understanding of Bernoulli's principle. The task of the effective science teacher is to present many discrepant situations that produce disequilibrium, causing students to make many cognitive connections to accommodate to the events and information. For example, another demon-

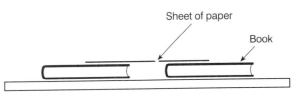

FIGURE 4.2   A discrepant event can be demonstrated by blowing under a sheet of paper supported by two books.

stration that can be conducted in order to study Bernoulli's principle is to drop playing cards into a box. You can demonstrate this card drop one or two times and then call on some members of the class to try it. There is a certain way to hold the cards so that they fall into the box. Most students will not know this technique, so the cards they drop will fall away from the box when released. This activity generates cognitive dissonance, and the participants will need to examine what they know about air pressure to figure this out. Examine and try the several discrepant event demonstrations on Bernoulli's principle in Appendix A that are written up for use with inservice and preservice science teachers.

Many of the most spectacular easy-to-present discrepant events are related to the physical sciences. However, with some thought, you can provide situations in the life sciences that will cause students to stop and wonder about the situation at hand. Most middle and high school students are not concerned about the presence of microorganisms in their everyday environment. Because these adolescents do not see microscopic cells, they are not perceived to be present. Many youth are not careful about washing their hands before eating and after using the lavatory or avoiding close contact with someone who has a cold or respiratory infection. A young person in middle or high school is likely to think, If I can't see it, it can't hurt me. Telling students about the potential harm that microorganisms can cause often does not make an impression. This form of direct instruction is not provocative enough to cause them to become alarmed (disequilibrated) and to alter their behavior. Consider showing students a culture of bacteria that appears particularly yucky. This will get students to think about the unseen world and to reappraise their ideas of microscopic creatures existing even though they are not visible in everyday life.

A teacher can prepare ahead of time a culture of microorganisms grown in Petri dishes. A swab from one's mouth, a dishrag, and pond water can be used to culture bacteria and other microorganisms. Cultures of microorganisms also can be obtained from a medical clinic or the biology department of a local college. (Exercise extreme caution when bringing pathogenic organisms into the classroom and ensure that the cultures are disposed of properly after viewing them). Show the microbial growth to students and note their reactions, especially when describing how the Petri dishes were prepared and the origin of the organisms. Many students will find it hard to believe that the air they are breathing contains organisms that will grow and end up looking like slimy creatures.

Let's return to the quote by Piaget at the beginning of this section. Note his emphasis on active learning and the skepticism toward direct instruction. Piaget did not believe that conveying information was adequate to

teach for understanding because this approach does not produce cognitive disequilibrium. A teacher must get the learner to think and reason differently. Piaget's theory of equilibration (which includes assimilation, accommodation, disequilibrium, and self-regulation) has motivated science educators to focus on instruction that provokes thinking through contradiction. Although equilibration is still a useful model for selecting methods and techniques for modifying students' beliefs and conceptions, Lawson (1994) indicates that Piaget's equilibration theory is built upon biological evolutionary concepts, not neurological concepts. Therefore, this researcher has put forth a neurological model for conceptual change and believes that in the future the profession will have a more valid theory of learning that will better explain how cognitive dissonance takes place in the brain.

ALTERNATIVE CONCEPTIONS AND CONCEPTUAL CHANGE

A critical aspect of scientific literacy is to develop students' understanding of science concepts in order for them to comprehend the biological and physical world in which they live. Even though most students will not become experts in a particular scientific field, we do expect them to learn a core of concepts from the major fields of science, which represents the most basic ideas of science (AAAS, 1993). By the time students complete their high school education, they should be able to provide correct explanations for these core concepts. All of this sounds so simple, but in reality it is difficult to achieve. The journey from where most students are to where we want them to be is far more intricate than most educators realize. A major hurdle is changing what students believe and think to what we would like them to believe and think.

Central to the problem of learning science appears to be what students **know** when they come to science class. All students have preformed conceptions about phenomena. Their minds are not empty, ready to be filled with a body of scientific knowledge. They already possess knowledge. Unfortunately, what students know frequently does not agree with scientific knowledge. Some researchers view students' ideas as primitive or naive or as misconceptions (errors in what has been learned). Others refer to students' knowledge as alternative conceptions, different from accepted beliefs, but nevertheless very important. Wandersee, Mintzes, and Novak (1994) provide science educators with an extensive review of alternative conceptions research in which they present a useful synthesis of eight knowledge claims

(Figure 4.3). A brief discussion of these claims highlights important findings regarding students' scientific conceptions.

There is a strong consensus that students possess alternative conceptions about the natural world before, during, and after school science instruction (claim 1). For this reason, students' conceptions must become a focus of instruction and their ideas the starting point for instruction. The task of science teachers is to **change** students' ideas that are not in line with science, ideas that will be prevalent among many students of different ages, abilities, genders, and cultures (claim 2). Even the most capable students hold ideas about basic science that are not correct. We simply cannot cover up these alternative conceptions by piling on new information, nor can we erase them by logical presentation. For some of the most important concepts, alternative conceptions persist beyond formal instruction. Yes, these alternative conceptions "hang on" even after science course participation (claim 3). With certain natural phenomena, alternative conceptions parallel the growth of that knowledge as evidenced by explanations put forth by scientists and philosophers in earlier times (claim 4).

Where do these alternative conceptions originate? In our diverse multicultural society, students from many different backgrounds arrive at the classroom. Their perceptions and beliefs vary widely (claim 5). Consider, for example, students' views of modern medicine. Those from families of means may hold the belief that going to the doctor for treatment of an illness is beneficial and, thus, is a common practice. Some students from poor immigrant families may hold the belief that doctors are to be avoided, and only in a life-and-death situation do they go to a doctor or hospital. Students from these different backgrounds and belief systems will interact with instruction on disease and medicine in different ways. Not only is family background a source for alternative conceptions, but textbooks, personal experiences, and teachers also contribute. Yes, science teachers often possess the same alternative conceptions as their students (claim 6).

The distressing fact is that students' alternative conceptions interact with the conceptions presented in school science, resulting in varied learning outcomes, some of which are not desired (claim 7). Today researchers are coming to accept the idea that learning science is not a matter of simply adding information or simply replacing existing information. After many days and even weeks of instruction, students fail to walk away with certain facts and beliefs, because they are still grounded in what they knew prior to instruction. Further, that which takes place during science instruction sometimes merely serves to reinforce what some students believe. Attempting to teach evolution of animal

FIGURE 4.3 This set of knowledge claims derived from the research literature on alternative conceptions can be used to guide teaching and learning science.

From "Research on Alternative Conceptions in Science," by J. H. Wandersee, J. J. Mintzes, & J. D. Novak, 1994, in D. L. Gabel (Ed.), *Handbook of Research on Science Teaching and Learning* (p. 195), Upper Saddle River, NJ: Merrill/Prentice Hall.

Knowledge Claims about Alternative Conceptions

Claim 1: Learners come to formal science instruction with a diverse set of alternative conceptions about natural objects and events.

Claim 2: The alternative conceptions that learners bring to formal science instruction cut across age, ability, gender, and cultural boundaries.

Claim 3: Alternative conceptions are tenacious and resistant to extinction by conventional teaching strategies.

Claim 4: Alternative conceptions often parallel explanations of natural phenomena offered by previous generations of scientists and philosophers.

Claim 5: Alternative conceptions have their origins in diverse sets of personal experiences including direct observations and perceptions, peer culture and language, and in teachers' explanations and instructional materials.

Claim 6: Teachers often subscribe to the same alternative conceptions as their students.

Claim 7: Learners' prior knowledge interacts with knowledge presented in formal instruction, resulting in a diverse set of unintended learning outcomes.

Claim 8: Instructional approaches that facilitate conceptual change can be effective classroom tools.

species from simple life forms to humans is a good example of how personal belief in special creation is very resistant to change. However, for many science topics, there are change strategies that seem promising in moving students toward more scientifically accepted ideas (claim 8).

How do science teachers help students to understand and explain major science concepts? A teaching strategy recommended by Driver (1988) to facilitate conceptual change, from a constructivist point of view, is shown in Figure 4.4. In the teaching sequence presented in the figure, the teacher begins with a brief **orientation,** which introduces students to what they will be studying. This is followed by the **elicitation** phase in which students are asked to present their ideas. This activity is effective when conducted in small groups because all students can participate and put forth their conceptions. Each group presents its descriptions and explanations and places them on large sheets of paper for the entire class to view and discuss. Similarities and differences among the ideas are noted. Here is where students' prior knowledge is made explicit and clear. This information is important because it is the knowledge base that must be restructured during the unit of study.

The **restructuring** phase is where students engage in a variety of learning activities. These tasks provide students with many opportunities to test out ideas and to compare and contrast the results with what they believe. Equally important, this phase of the teaching sequence permits the learner to determine what others believe, and what is accepted as valid knowledge. Deductive laboratory activities can be used to place students in the position to state what they believe will result when they examine situations or manipulate certain variables. Students can design experiments and engage in problem solving. They can be given writing tasks to encourage them to describe and explain their ideas. Discrepant events can be used to bring about cognitive conflict, which can serve to cause students to reexamine their ideas and to find out what is taking place.

During the restructuring phase, the teacher must provide students with a variety of experiences so they can test their ideas to determine how well the ideas fit reality. These activities should include individual as well as small-group work. As the result of a long series of instructional activities over time, the learner constructs new ideas. This is a creative process that requires time and experience. In addition, the teacher must do everything possible to avoid evaluating students' ideas and presenting the "correct" explanations, because this would end the restructuring process. At the end of each lesson, the teacher asks students to examine their findings and to compare them with what they stated at the

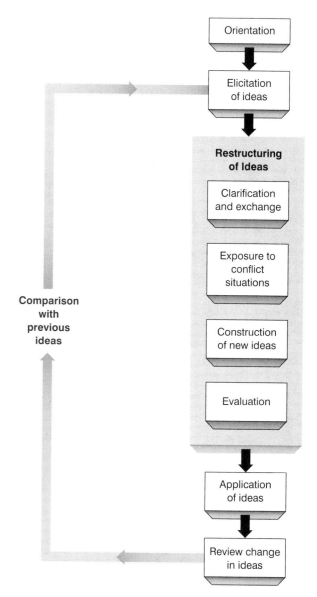

FIGURE 4.4   The General Structure of a Teaching Sequence Aimed at Bringing about Conceptual Change

From "Theory into Practice II: A Constructivist Approach to Curriculum Development" (p. 141), by R. Driver, in P. Fensham (Ed.), *Development and Dilemmas in Science Education,* 1988, Philadelphia: Falmer Press. Reprinted by permission. All rights reserved.

beginning of the unit on the large sheets of paper. Finally, there is a point in the instructional process at which the teacher examines the ideas that students possess, presents what is believed to be scientifically accepted knowledge, and compares the accepted knowledge with the students' conceptions.

With new conceptions and reformed ideas, the students are ready to **apply** them to new situations. This step can lend greater meaning to the concepts, principles, and theories under study and help to form richer cognitive connections in the minds of the learners. The unit ends with a **review** of ideas, permitting students to compare what they first thought regarding the topic under study with what they learned from the many experiences engaged in during the unit.

The teaching sequence just described may appear to be similar to that which effective science teachers use who instruct in conventional science programs. The instructional activities implemented in both of these situations are many and varied, and both include the application of new knowledge. However, the readers must **not** be deceived. The fundamental difference between the conceptual change strategy and traditional teaching is not so much the activities, but the underlying approach to learning (Needham, 1987, p. 1). The constructivist/conceptual change approach aims toward teaching a smaller number of science concepts and places greater emphasis upon understanding. The teacher begins with students' prior knowledge, urging them to reflect on the ideas and beliefs they possess regarding a given science concept or principle. Then many opportunities are provided for students to find personal meaning from interacting with objects, events, and people. In addition, there is a deliberate attempt to utilize relevant contexts with which students can identify. Finally, there is a realization by the teacher that students' misconceptions and naive ideas may continue after the completion of the unit of study.

Students come to science class with a "commonsense view of phenomena, which they have constructed through personal experiences and social interactions with others (Driver, Squires, et al., 1994). These commonsense views differ from scientific views and do not provide a coherent, accurate picture of the world. Nevertheless, these ideas serve the learner in everyday life and are difficult to replace. Science teachers can help students to acquire scientific conceptions with instruction that promotes both personal and social construction of knowledge through concrete experiences and teacher intervention. It is the teacher's role to introduce students into the culture of the scientific community, which cannot be discovered by students. The skillful teacher "introduces new ideas or cultural tools where necessary and provides the support and guidance for students to make sense of these for themselves" (Driver, Squires, et al., 1994, p. 11).

Science education is faced with an enormous challenge if it is determined to realize the goal of scientific literacy in the nation's schools. Literacy implies understanding ideas. From the substantial amount of research on conceptual change, the profession now realizes there are many difficulties associated with teaching some of the most fundamental ideas associated with science.

Strike and Posner (1992) indicate that many factors are related to changing students' conceptions so that they more accurately reflect science. For example, students' motivation to learn, their ability to represent what they know, and the complexity of the concepts under study are among many factors that affect learning science. Osborne and Wittrock (1983) point out other factors that we should note in our attempts to implement a new way of teaching when using conceptual change strategies. They remind us that many students do not have the desire to alter what they believe. Most students are satisfied with interpreting science terms to fit what they know, rather than modifying what they think. Students make only some of the connections that science teachers want them to make. Often students form isolated branches of knowledge that they use only in science class. Further, many students are either incapable of or unwilling to restructure their knowledge to coincide with that of science. This takes a great deal of mental effort. Nevertheless, science teachers should consider the following four conditions in order to improve the possibilities for students to acquire scientific concepts (Posner, Strike, Hewson, & Gertkzog, 1982):

1. Students must be **dissatisfied** with their ideas in order to consider changing them.

2. Students must believe that they can **comprehend** the conceptions.

3. Students must perceive that the concepts are **plausible.**

4. Students must feel that they can **find out** about the idea.

A great deal of the teaching and learning that takes place in secondary schools and at the college level centers around the presentation of information. This situation makes it difficult to implement or even to suggest another approach to teaching science. However, after studying this section on conceptual change and the other sections in this chapter, you should realize that there is a psychologically based body of knowledge to refer to when planning to teach science. Now perhaps you will think differently about the acquisition of scientific knowledge, realizing that this knowledge has taken centuries to construct and a great deal of thought on the part of those who have contributed to this body of knowledge. Consequently, should we expect adolescents, whose energies and interests are not on science course matters, to learn about the great ideas of science in a matter of several days or even months? The construction of knowledge is an interactive process, rather than a transmission process, requiring considerable time and effort to build.

The section on alternative conceptions and conceptual change should impress upon you the significance of this psychologically based body of knowledge as it relates to science teaching. Before rushing on to the next section in this chapter, do the following:

■   Make a list of important assumptions regarding the alternative conceptions that you should consider when teaching science.

■   Form a list of strategies and techniques that you will use to help students alter their conceptions of science ideas.

■   Identify a science principle, law, or theory, and design a sequence of instruction that will help a given age group of students to change their ideas and to guide them toward more correct scientific understanding. A beneficial approach to this activity might be to work with a partner or group of peers.

MEANINGFUL LEARNING AND CONCEPT MAPPING

Joseph Novak has translated and extended Ausubel's cognitive learning theories for teaching and learning science. He stresses the importance of meaningful learning and believes that effective learning occurs when the learner "constructs new and more powerful meaning" from educational experiences (Novak & Gowin, 1984, p. xi). Novak and many other researchers have focused on meaningful learning. Their psychological view of science teaching is that of the social constructivist who stresses the importance of learning scientific concepts from others who understand the field. They believe that there is a body of scientific knowledge that can be learned by the layperson. More importantly, this knowledge is most efficiently learned under the guidance of an experienced mentor. Therefore, one of the tasks of science teachers is to help students acquire a body of scientific knowledge in a meaningful way and to form correct explanations for these ideas.

One technique that is being used to get students to construct relationships between ideas is called **concept mapping.** This approach to learning science began in the 1980s. The technique helps students to visually represent meaningful relationships between science concepts (Novak & Gowin, 1984). In Figure 4.5, a concept map for water is presented. The key concepts are shown in ovals and words linking these ideas are placed along the lines connecting them. The picture presents the superordinate-subordinate relationships of the topic under study. It graphically places the knowledge structure of water into a hierarchy, with broad general concepts at the top and the more specific concepts at the lower levels.

A variety of spatial organizations can be formed for the same topic, depending on the nature of the learning outcomes and students. The concept map shown for water is probably appropriate for a middle school science course. A concept map for water in a high school chemistry class during the study of solutions would be much different, because of the emphasis on solubility, ionization, and polarity.

Novak (1995) recommends the following suggestions to science teachers who desire to incorporate concept mapping in their instruction:

■   Begin with a content or subject area that students are familiar with.

■   Identify the key ideas or propositions that form the conception under study.

■   Rank order the ideas from the most general to the most specific.

■   Construct a preliminary concept map using ovals or boxes.

■   Identify and label the linking lines between concepts, which serve to form propositions that relate ideas.

■   Make cross-link connections between different domains of knowledge.

■   Do not construct sentences in the boxed or closed-in areas of the map.

■   Continually revise maps and consider them never final.

Novak and Gowin indicate that concept mapping promotes meaning through active learning, because each student must make connections between the ideas in the picture and those in his or her mind. They emphasize that students must participate in the creation of the concept map. Consequently, the new knowledge the students gain is constructed, not discovered. These researchers state that "knowledge is not discovered like gold or oil, but rather it is constructed like cars or pyramids" (Novak & Gowin, 1984, p. 4).

Novak and Gowin (1984) indicate that concept maps can be used to:

1. Determine pathways for organizing meanings.

2. Negotiate meaning with students.

FIGURE 4.5   A Concept Map for Learning about Water

From *Learning How to Learn* (p. 16) by J. D. Novak and D. B. Gowin, 1984, New York: Cambridge University Press. Copyright © 1984 by Cambridge University Press. Reprinted with the permission of Cambridge University Press.

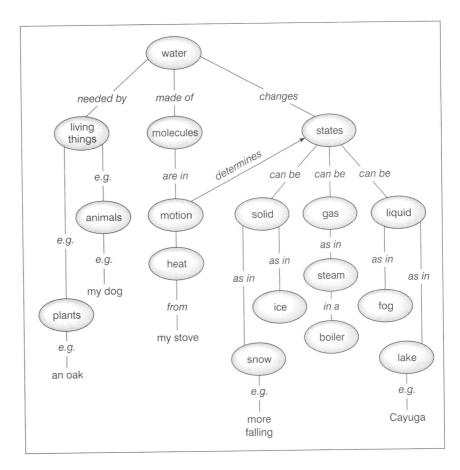

3. Point out misconceptions.

4. Promote higher level thinking. (p. 23)

Concept mapping is used in other fields besides science instruction. For example, it is used under the name of semantic mapping for language arts instruction.

Concept mapping is an effective way to engage students in finding meaning in the ideas that are under study in science courses. This tool encourages social thinking among students, and between teacher and students (Roth, 1994). Concept mapping can be used in a variety of ways and at many points during the study of a unit. Students can be asked to construct concept maps on their own and place them into their science notebooks. They can be asked to construct them with other students in collaborative learning groups. Students can be asked to construct a map at the beginning of an instructional sequence in order to determine their entry level of knowledge. Further, this map will identify alternative conceptions that they hold. During the instructional sequence, the students can be asked to revise their concept maps, which will permit them to externalize their thinking and illustrate the conceptual change that is taking place. At the end of the instruction for a given unit, concept mapping can be used as a review. Generally, as the mapping process progresses, students will make connections between concepts. In Box 4.2 is an illustration of how this tool was used by a life science student studying the animal kingdom. Note how the knowledge of the student increases through instruction and how the categories become more inclusive and differentiated.

IMAGES AND ANALOGIES

The study of imagery has been part of the history of psychology from the time of the early philosophers who attempted to describe the mind to the present (Kosslyn, 1980). Images can be thought of as thinking aids that help to transfer information. They are one way of representing objects that constitute the perceptible world. The ability to produce images in the mind offers the possibility for humans to construct meaningful connections with ideas. The representation of phenomena and concepts are important to comprehending science.

Many scientific conceptions are very abstract and, therefore, difficult to imagine and represent pictorially. Nevertheless, these ideas are central to learning science and necessary for students to understand and explain. Science textbooks and teachers often present ideas with which students are familiar in order to make the unfamiliar comprehensible. You probably have heard the phrase "now picture this in your mind" used to encourage students to imagine what they are about to learn. This prompt requests students to represent in their minds relationships that will transfer knowledge from one domain to another. Analogical reasoning encourages students to construct cognitive connections between the familiar and the unfamiliar. It facilitates meaningful learning of abstract subject matter by helping students to integrate new information with existing knowledge, thus forming new conceptions.

Pictures and diagrams are used frequently during science instruction to represent concepts and principles. Science textbooks are filled with these teaching aids. Teachers use them in their lectures. Visualization provides students with cognitive aids that make abstract ideas more comprehensible. Since we cannot observe directly the movement of electrons or ions, for example, we must find a way to illustrate these concepts. Abstract ideas must be made accessible by visual representation through diagrams or other means. You can find experienced chemistry teachers who weave diagrams into their presentations to help students conceptualize concepts like pH. Some teachers use a diagram similar to the one shown in Figure 4.6 to illustrate how the acidity and basicity of a solution changes as the relative concentrations of hydrogen ions (H^+) and hydroxide ions (OH^-) changes.

The use of diagrams for instruction can further be enhanced by interactive techniques such as analogical reasoning. Analogies are one tool for getting students to

BOX 4.2

CONCEPT MAPPING BY A MIDDLE SCHOOL STUDENT STUDYING THE ANIMAL KINGDOM

Mr. Jefferson is a new teacher who has taught life science for several years. His students seem to enjoy the study of plants and animals. He finds many students do not understand some of the most basic ideas associated with life science, however, even after he has spent considerable time teaching about the various life forms. For example, after spending several weeks on the animal kingdom, many students do not categorize humans with other animals. In searching for a solution to this problem, Mr. Jefferson discussed the situation with a high school biology teacher in the district who offered many suggestions regarding laboratory activities to perform, videos to watch, and field trips to take. In addition, the biology teacher discussed an instructional technique called **concept mapping** that she thought might help the students to better organize biology and to help them remember important relationships. The following two illustrations are concept maps done by one of Mr. Jefferson's students, one at the beginning of the study of animals and one toward the end of the unit. Note how the student's knowledge increased through instruction and how the categories became more inclusive and differentiated.

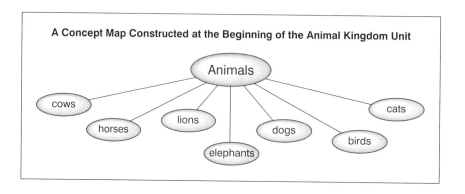

A Concept Map Constructed at the Beginning of the Animal Kingdom Unit

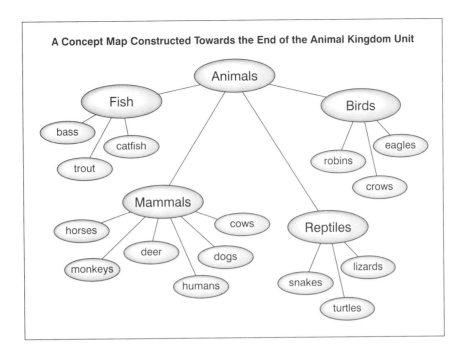

A Concept Map Constructed Towards the End of the Animal Kingdom Unit

make connections between what they know and what we want them to know. In some research studies, they have been reported to further students' comprehension of scientific concepts and to help them to construct meaning (Duit, 1991; Dagher, 1995; Glynn, Duit, & Thiele, 1995). An analogy forms a relationship between what the learners are familiar with and what they are expected to learn (the unfamiliar).

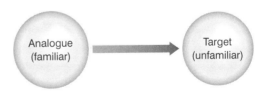

The familiar is referred to as the analogue and the unfamiliar the target. For example, science teachers have used the analogy of water flowing through a pipe (analogue) to help students comprehend electrical current (target).

David Ausubel (1963), an important educational psychologist, recommended the use of advanced organizers to facilitate the acquisition of knowledge. His idea of the comparative organizer serves to illustrate how we can show similarities and differences between what the students know and what they are expected to learn. This approach uses analogies to facilitate assimila-

Effective science teachers use common everyday materials and equipment to help students visualize ideas and construct science meaning.

FIGURE 4.6 A Visual Representation of the pH Scale Showing the Relative Concentrations of Hydrogen and Hydroxide Ions

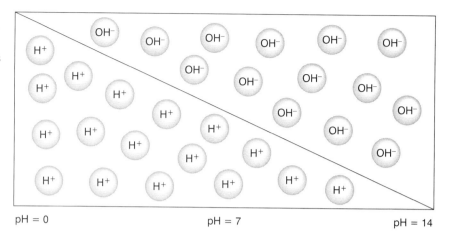

pH = 0   pH = 7   pH = 14

tion of new material into existing cognitive structures. Examine the analogy in Table 4.1 that a life science teacher might use to help students learn about the structure of the cell from their knowledge of a jail cell. We will examine six operations for teaching analogies, developed by Glynn (1995, p. 27) for his teaching-with-analogies model, to guide our discussion regarding this instructional strategy.

1. Introduce the target concept.
2. Review the analogue concept.
3. Identify the features of the target and analogue.
4. Map the similarities.
5. Indicate where the analogy breaks down.
6. Draw conclusions.

For the comparison given in Table 4.1 and the six operations just stated, let's examine a jail-cell analogy instructionally. A science teacher might begin by introducing the purpose of the exercise. This statement can

be accompanied by listing the structures of the cell (target) on the chalkboard (operation 1). Information can be given regarding the structure and function of cellular parts, similar to those shown in the left-hand column of the table. The teacher can pose a question to prompt students to search for an analogy in everyday life that is similar to the workings of a biological cell. Students may or may not come up with the jail cell as an analogy. They may provide an example that is more relevant to them than the jail cell, which would certainly be an important path to pursue. In any event, if the students do not offer the jail cell as a comparison, the teacher can present it (operation 2). Given the amount of television and western movies students are exposed to, the jail cell is likely to be familiar to them and a relevant analogue concept. Features of the jail and the biological cell can be discussed (operation 3). A diagram of these cells can be constructed and a discussion of how their structures are related can take place. In this manner a comparison of key features of the analogue and target are mapped by bridging similar features (operation 4). Other analogies

TABLE 4.1 An Analogy between a Jail Cell and a Biological Cell

Structure or function of the concept to be learned	Structure of the jail cell (familiar analogue)	Structure of the biological cell (unfamiliar target)
Outer structure	Walls and bars	Wall and membrane
Inner part	Air	Cytoplasm
Control center	Prisoner	Nucleus
Communication	Prisoner talking	Endoplasmic reticulum
Energy	Light bulb	Mitochondria
Waste removal	Toilet	Vacuole
Enzyme production	Prisoner's body	Golgi apparatus

can be discussed to help students widen their understanding of a living cell, which will help them to generalize and to form conclusions. For example, some life science teachers have used a house or a factory to provide an analogy for a living cell. After students have had a variety of instructional experiences with cells, aspects of the jail-cell analogy that are weak or erroneous should be discussed (operation 5). Finally, the teacher should draw conclusions about the cell that highlight the important functions carried out by this fundamental biological entity (operation 6).

The use of analogies is widespread in science lectures and textbooks. In some instances these examples are beneficial to students; in others they are less than effective. Glynn et al. (1995) have analyzed many textbooks for examples of analogies as well as analogies used by science teachers in their classrooms. These

researchers report that textbooks and teachers who were judged to be effective with analogies used the six operations of the teaching-with-analogies model. Further, these authors and teachers carefully relate the familiar with the unfamiliar so that erroneous ideas do not come into their comparisons. Glynn et al. (1995) point out that Paul Hewitt's *Conceptual Physics* textbook contains many excellent analogies.

The idea of teaching abstract concepts and principles using analogies has great instructional appeal. Nevertheless, this approach is not always effective. Students can and often do miss the connection between the analogue and the target concept (Glynn et al., 1995). Pedagogical skill is needed to map the important features of analogical comparisons in order for conceptual bridges to be established by the learner. Remember, the key connections must be made by the student. Further, teachers

---

Major Ideas in Science for Constructing Analogies

Target Concepts in Biology
- Lock-and-key mechanism of enzymes
- Active transport of molecules through the cell membrane
- Production of food during photosynthesis
- Replication of DNA double helix
- Coloration, camouflages, and selection
- Body structure, adaptation, and survival
- Gradual change in organisms over time
- Virus attacking a cell
- Breathing—filling and expelling air in the lungs
- Movement of electrical impulses along a nerve cell
- Digestion of food
- Blood pressure in the arterial systems

Target Concepts in Chemistry
- Bohr model of the atom
- Charged cloud model of the atom
- Dalton's law of multiple proportions
- Isotopes of chemical elements
- The periodic table of chemical elements
- The mole
- Kinetic molecular theory of gases
- The quantum concept
- Covalent chemical bonding
- Equilibrium in chemical reactions
- The pH scale of acidity and basicity

Target Concepts in Physics
- A vector quantity
- Newton's idea of gravity
- Einstein's idea of gravity
- Conservation of momentum
- Three states of matter
- Electromagnetic waves
- Sound waves
- Virtual and real images
- A charged particle
- Direct electrical current
- Alternating electrical current
- A magnetic field
- Radioactive decay of an element

Target Concepts in Geology and Space Science
- Geologic time scale
- Water cycle
- Rock cycle
- Erosion
- Sedimentation
- Layers of the earth
- Volcanic activity
- Movement of the earth's continents
- Air pressure
- Tornadoes
- Ocean currents
- The solar system
- Galaxies
- Black holes

FIGURE 4.7   These important concepts from the major fields of science can be used as targets to help students learn these ideas by reasoning analogically.

must be on guard so that students do not form misconceptions (Thagard, 1992). For example, when using the flow of water through a pipe to illustrate electrical current, students as well as many elementary and middle school science teachers have formed the idea that electrons "zip" through a wire, similar to water shooting through a pipe. With direct electrical current, electrons move very fast in the spaces between atoms, but their net movement in the direction of the positive terminal is relatively slow. Many misconceptions have been found in textbooks and in teachers attempting to use analogical reasoning to explain concepts and phenomena whose features cannot be perceived directly.

■ STOP AND REFLECT! ■

Consider the fields of science that you are teaching or preparing to teach. Identify a concept or principle to explain by analogy. Examine the list of important concepts presented in Figure 4.7 for possible choices. Use the six operations associated with the teaching-with-analogies model to assist in developing your analogy. Present the analogy to a group of public school students or peers and then critique the effectiveness of the instruction.

■

ASSESSING AND REVIEWING

1. What have you learned from this chapter about cognitive psychology as it pertains to teaching and learning science?

    a. Without referring to the chapter, write a paragraph presenting the major ideas associated with constructivism.

    b. Compare and contrast a constructivist and a traditional approach to teaching science using a table like the one below.

Constructivist approach	Traditional approach
Where is knowledge found?	
How is knowledge formed?	
What is the role of the teacher?	
Which teaching strategies are most effective?	
And so on…	

2. How would you use the Piagetian ideas of equilibration and contradiction to engage learning? In brief form, outline an activity to teach a science concept, principle, or law using

    a. a discrepant event situation with concrete materials, and

    b. a verbal or written statement that contradicts the beliefs of many people.

Share these examples with others so that everyone expands their knowledge of how to stimulate learning in the science classroom.

3. Find a teacher-developed instructional unit for a middle or high school science course. Examine the activities to determine the potential the unit holds for promoting conceptual change among the students who will participate in it. For this exercise, consider the conceptual change model discussed in this chapter. Focus on

    a. eliciting ideas

    b. clarifying knowledge

    c. examining conflicting views

    d. constructing new ideas

    e. applying new knowledge

    f. reviewing the knowledge restructuring that might take place

4. Construct a concept map to represent the major ideas presented in this chapter on learning.

5. Develop an analogy that you might use to teach a concept to either a middle or senior high school group of students. Refer to the teaching-with-analogies model discussed in the chapter. Present the analogy to a group of peers and get their feedback regarding the effectiveness of the instruction. Pay special attention to the potential for introducing misconceptions or incorrect notions about the target concept.

■

RESOURCES TO EXAMINE

"Conceptual Bridges." 1995, December. *The Science Teacher*, pp. 25–27.

Shawn Glynn provides a good explanation of how to use analogies to help students understand scientific concepts. He presents his teaching-with-analogies model and illustrates how the elements of this model have been used by scientists and effective teachers to further scientific understanding.

Science Teaching and the Development of Thinking. 1995. Belmont, CA: Wadsworth.

Anton Lawson gives a psychological basis for learning science. He emphasizes the importance for students to test their ideas in authentic learning situations. Lawson gives many examples of how to involve students in science activities to promote active learning and to develop thinking.

Making Sense of Secondary Science. 1994. New York: Routledge.

Rosalind Driver, Ann Squires, Peter Rushworth, and Valerie Wood-Robinson have assembled a com-

pendium of research on students' ideas of science. They discuss the construction of knowledge through conceptual change. The book gives many illuminating examples of the growth of concepts related to the major areas of science. Among the concepts described are nutrition, microbes, solids, air, particles, electricity, light, and sound.

"Doing Is Believing: Do Laboratory Experiences Promote Conceptual Change?" 1996, May. *School Science and Mathematics*, pp. 263–271.

Susan Westbrook and Laura Rogers describe a study that they conducted with ninth-grade students enrolled in physical science. They investigated the conceptual change among students who generated and tested hypotheses concerning flotation in the laboratory. Conceptual change was assessed by concept maps and work-sorting activities. Students who selected the hypothesis that weight determines an object's ability to float generally changed their notion of the relationship between weight and flotation.

■

REFERENCES

Ajzen, I. (1989). Attitude structure and behavior. In A. R. Pratkanis, S. J. Breckler, & A. G. Beckman (Eds.), *Attitude structure and function* (pp. 241–274). Hillsdale, NJ: Erlbaum.

American Association for the Advancement of Science. (1993). *Benchmarks for scientific literacy*. New York: Oxford University Press.

Angeles, P. A (1981). *Dictionary of philosophy*. New York: Barnes and Noble.

Ausubel, D. P. (1963). *The psychology of meaningful verbal learning*. New York: Grune & Stratton.

Bidell, R., & Fisher, K. W. (1992). Cognitive development in educational contexts: Implications of skill theory. In M. Shayer & A. Efklides (Eds.), *Neo-Piagetian theories of cognitive development*. New York: Routledge.

Brophy, J. (1988). *On motivating students*. In D. Berliner & B. Rosenshine (Eds.), *Talks to teachers* (pp. 201–245). New York: Random House.

Crawley, F. E., & Koballa, T. R. (1994). Attitude research in science education: Contemporary models and methods. *Science Education*, 78, 35–55.

Dagher, Z. R. (1995). Analysis of analogies used by science teachers. *Journal of Research in Science Teaching*, 32, 259–270.

Driver, R. (1988). Theory into practice II: A constructivist approach to curriculum development. In P. Fensham (Ed.), *Development and dilemmas in science education* (pp. 133–149). Philadelphia: Falmer Press.

Driver, R., Asoko, H., Leach, J., Mortimer, E., & Scott, P. (1994). Constructing scientific knowledge in the classroom. *Educational Researcher*, 23(7), 5–12.

Driver, R., Squires, A., Rushworth, P., & Wood-Robinson, V. (1994). *Making sense of secondary science*. New York: Routledge.

Duit, R. (1991). On the role of analogies and metaphors in learning science. *Science Education*, 75, 649–672.

Fishbein, M. (1963). An investigation of the relationship between beliefs about an object and attitude toward the object. *Human Relations, 16,* 233–240.

Fosnot, C. T. (1996). *Constructivism: Theory, perspectives, and practice.* New York: Teachers College, Columbia University.

Furth, H. G. (1969). *Piaget and knowledge.* Englewood Cliffs, NJ: Prentice-Hall.

Glynn, S. (1995). Conceptual bridges. *The Science Teacher, 62*(9), 25–27.

Glynn, S. M., Duit, R., & Thiele, R. B. (1995). Teaching science with analogies: A strategy for constructing knowledge. In S. M. Glynn & R. Duit (Eds.), *Learning science in the schools: Research reforming practices.* Mahwah, NJ: Erlbaum.

Goldthwait, J. T. (1996). *Values: What they are and how we know them.* Amherst, NY: Prometheus Books.

Kasschau, R. (1986). A model for teaching critical thinking in psychology. In J. Halonen (Ed.), *Teaching critical thinking in psychology.* Milwaukee, WI: Alverno College Institute.

Koballa, T. R., & Warden, M. A. (1992). Changing and measuring attitudes in the science classroom. In F. Lawrenz, K. Cochran, & J. Krajcik (Eds.), *Research matters . . . to the science teacher* (pp. 75–83). Manhattan, KS: National Association for Research in Science Teaching.

Kosslyn, S. M. (1980). *Image and mind.* Cambridge: Harvard University Press.

Larson, C. U. (1986). *Persuasion: Reception and responsibility.* Belmont, CA: Wadsworth Publishing.

Lawson, A. E. (1994). Research on the acquisition of science knowledge: Epistemological foundations of cognition. In D. L. Gabel (Ed.), *Handbook of research on science teaching and learning.* Upper Saddle River, NJ: Merrill/Prentice Hall.

Matthews, M. R. (1994). *Science teaching.* New York: Routledge.

Miller, G. R. (1980). On being persuaded: Some basic distinctions. In M. F. Roloff & G. R. Miller (Eds.), *New directions in theory and research.* Beverly Hills, CA: Sage.

Needham, R. (1987). *Teaching strategies for developing understanding in science.* Children's Learning in Science Project, Centre for Studies in Science and Mathematics Education, Leeds, England: The University of Leeds.

Novak, J. D. (1995). Concept mapping: A strategy for organizing knowledge. In S. M. Glynn & R. Duit (Eds.), *Learning science in the schools.* Mahwah, NJ: Erlbaum.

Novak, J. D., & Gowin, D. B. (1984). *Learning how to learn.* New York: Cambridge University Press.

Osborne, J. F. (1996). Beyond constructivism. *Science Education, 80,* 53–82.

Osborne, R., & Wittrock, M. (1983). Learning science: A generative process. *Science Education, 67,* 489–508.

Petty, R. E., & Cacioppo, J. T. (1986). *Attitudes and persuasion: Classic and contemporary approaches.* New York: Springer-Verlag.

Piaget, J. (1964). Cognitive development in children: Development and learning. *Journal of Research in Science Teaching, 2,* 176–186.

Piaget, J. (1971). *Biology and knowledge.* Chicago: University of Chicago Press.

Posner, G. J., Strike, K. A., Hewson, P. W., & Gertkzog, W. A. (1982). Accommodation of a scientific conception: Toward a theory of conceptual change. *Science Education, 66,* 211–228.

Reardon, K. K. (1991). *Persuasion in practice.* Newbury Park, CA: Sage.

Resnick, L. B. (1987). *Education and learning to think.* Washington, DC: National Academy Press.

Roth, W. M. (1994). Student views of collaborative concept mapping: An emancipatory research project. *Science Education, 78,* 1–34.

Sternberg, R. (1995). *In search of the human mind.* New York: Harcourt Brace College Publishers.

Strike, K. A., & Posner, G. J. (1992). A revisionist theory of conceptual change. In R. A. Duschl & R. J. Hamilton (Eds.). *Philosophy of science, cognitive psychology, and educational theory and practice* (pp. 147–176). Albany: State University of New York Press.

Thagard, P. (1992). Analogy, explanation, and education. *Journal of Research in Science Teaching, 29,* 537–544.

Tobin, K., & Tippens, D. (1993). Constructivism as a referent for teaching and learning. In K. Tobin (Ed.), *The practice of constructivism in science education.* Hillsdale, NJ: Erlbaum.

von Glasersfeld, E. (1993). Questions and answers about radical constructivism. In K. Tobin (Ed.), *The practice of constructivism in science education.* Hillsdale, NJ: Erlbaum.

von Glasersfeld, E. (1995). *Radical constructivism: A way of knowing and learning.* London: Falmer Press.

Vygotsky, L. S. (1978). *Mind in society: The development of higher psychological processes* (M. Cole, V. John-Steiner, S. Scribner, & E. Souberman, Eds.). Cambridge: Harvard University Press.

Wandersee, J. H., Mintzes, J. J., & Novak, J. D. (1994). Research on alternative conceptions in science. In D. L. Gabel (Ed.), *Handbook of research on science teaching.* Upper Saddle River, NJ: Merrill/Prentice Hall.

Woolfolk, A. E. (1995). *Educational psychology,* 6th edition. Needham Heights, MA: Allyn and Bacon.

■

PART TWO

Teaching Strategies and Classroom Management

CHAPTER 5

INQUIRY AND TEACHING SCIENCE

Wondering why and finding out are powerful motivators for learning.

All students should be given the opportunity to explore their world to learn about the wonders of nature. Most middle and senior high school science students become excited when they are placed in situations where they can examine physical and biological phenomena. For these experiences to be authentic and productive, they must reflect the nature of science and how new knowledge is acquired through investigation. Textbooks and other instructional materials must also present the thinking and investigative activities in which scientists and engineers engage as well as the knowledge and products they produce. Logically, therefore, science courses should include teaching practices that reflect scientific investigation. The word that captures the nature of finding out, which can serve as a guide for teaching and learning science, is **inquiry.**

OBJECTIVES

This chapter is designed to help the reader meet the following objectives:

- ■ Explain the general concept of inquiry, scientific inquiry, teaching science **by** inquiry, and teaching science **as** inquiry.
- ■ Describe many strategies and techniques for teaching inquiry-based science.
- ■ Demonstrate many instructional strategies and techniques that engage students in finding out.
- ■ Become familiar with concerns that are often associated with teaching science via inquiry.

WHAT IS INQUIRY?

> If a single word had to be chosen to describe the goals of science education during the 30-year period that began in the late 1950s, it would have to be inquiry. (DeBoer 1991, p. 206)

Teaching science must be consistent with the nature of science in order for course content and methods to reflect how scientific knowledge is constructed and established. Science is generally characterized as an active process whereby men and women, curious about nature, contribute to humankind's understanding of objects and events that surround them. **Inquiry** is a word that has been used over and over in the science education literature to characterize the active processes involved in scientific thinking, investigation, and the construction of knowledge. Consequently, inquiry has been used as a guide for establishing goals and objectives, selecting instructional strategies and teaching techniques, and assessment procedures. The term inquiry is ubiquitous among the ideas associated with many national, state, and local curriculum guidelines as well as course materials for the past thirty years, and it is still being used for these purposes.

The recommendations of national committees concerning the school science reform that is taking place across the nation stresses the inclusion of inquiry in the curriculum. Project 2061 of the American Association for the Advancement of Science (AAAS, 1990) reminds us that teaching science should be consistent with the nature of scientific inquiry. Their publication *Science for All Americans* urges science teachers to begin with questions about nature, actively engage students, concentrate on the collection and use of evidence, provide a historical perspective, insist on clear expression, use a team approach, do not separate knowledge from finding out, and de-emphasize the memorization of technical vocabulary. Further, this document points out the difficulty in describing scientific inquiry apart from the content of a particular investigation and that there is no set of procedures followed by scientists.

In the *National Science Education Standards* from the National Research Council (NRC, 1996), the term **science as inquiry** appears frequently throughout the publication. "The Standards call for more 'science as process' in which students learn such skills as observing, inferring, and experimenting. Inquiry is central to science learning" (p. 2). Science teachers must engage students in inquiry so that they ask questions, describe objects and events, test their ideas with what is known, and communicate what they are learning.

In the most **general sense**, inquiry is the act of finding out. It centers around the desire to answer a question or to know more about a situation. Humans have always been inquirers, searching for food and places to live. People from all walks of life inquire on a routine basis. Parents search for the best bargains when purchasing food and clothing for their families; business people look for customers who need their products and services. Journalists seek out people who can provide them with information to produce a good story, and detectives look for clues to the causes of accidents and homicides. Teenagers try to find friends with whom they like to associate. Inquiry, in general, is being used by people around us all the time.

Scientific inquiry also takes place in our society, but it has a specialized focus and is conducted by a group of people called scientists. As stated often in this textbook, scientific inquiry centers upon natural phenomena and is an attempt to understand nature by explaining it and applying that knowledge. However, the knowledge has to be more than personally satisfying; it has to pass the scrutiny of other scientists through verification. Scientists take many paths in their quest to answer questions. Thus, scientific inquiry is a creative process that is fueled by curiosity and hard work, often resulting in frustration and sometimes leading to useful knowledge.

By now you probably have gotten the idea that, in general, inquiry involves **finding out** about something, which includes seeking information and answering questions. With scientific inquiry, the process is often lengthy, whereby knowledge is pieced together by gathering information and reasoning about it. Part of the process involves knowing what ideas others have contributed, such as the knowledge and understandings of individuals during various historical periods up to the present. How did philosophers and scientists reason about ideas and how did this reasoning reflect the societies in which they lived?

A great deal of the science teaching that takes place in middle and senior high schools, as well as at the collegiate level, can be characterized as teaching science via the presentation of information. A major goal of this approach is to convey the products of scientific inquiry to students. This mode of teaching is designed to present an organized body of information that has been constructed by others. Unfortunately, this approach often omits the thinking that was used and the paths that were taken to form the knowledge under study. It also minimizes the firsthand experiences that students should be provided. Teaching science as a body of knowledge results in conveying the abstraction or the distillates of the learning process that others have gone through to construct a body of knowledge. The approach can convey ideas that have little meaning to students and result in rote memorization, especially when a great deal of subject matter is covered. Thus, one can realize why teaching science via inquiry offers such an appealing alternative to teaching science via the presentation of information.

Given the importance of inquiry, all science teachers must understand this idea in order to advance scientific literacy. Unfortunately, inquiry is often misunderstood and thus leads to unintended outcomes. Before we provide many examples of how to use this idea for teaching science, it is necessary to describe two ideas that must become clearer in the minds of educators. The first is teaching science **by** inquiry; the second is teaching science **as** inquiry.

Teaching Science **by** Inquiry

As one thinks about science and the excitement that can be associated with finding out, does it make good sense to give students many opportunities to learn science by inquiry? Will students gain a better feeling for science if they examine objects and events, and form their own impressions of what is taking place in the natural world around them? Many educators strongly believe that there are scientific attitudes and skills that can be developed by engaging students in inquiry. They also believe that direct involvement in the process of inquiry will help students to attain concepts. What do you believe?

■ Can science courses give students a feeling for inquiry by engaging them in the process of finding out?

■ Are there scientific attitudes or attributes of scientists that students should acquire as the result of practicing inquiry and that will benefit them in pursuing knowledge?

■ Is it critical for students to develop certain reasoning skills, patterns of thinking, and habits of mind that they can use throughout their lives?

If the answers to these questions is yes, then you will certainly want to be informed about one view of inquiry that pertains to school science, that of teaching science **by** inquiry.

Teaching science **by** inquiry is an idea that grew along with the inquiry movement during the post-Sputnik era of curriculum reform. This idea has also been called teaching science **through** inquiry or learning **by** discovery. Let's examine some of the thinking that promoted these ideas.

Jerome Bruner helped to galvanize the inquiry movement by extolling the virtues of finding out by doing, which was often referred to as learning by discovery. He claimed that students who practiced discovery learning would obtain efficient strategies for acquiring,

transforming, organizing, storing, and using information that is most useful in problem solving (Bruner, 1961). The reasoning behind this hypothesis began with the recognition that much information comes to the learner before the problem is solved. Success and efficiency in problem solving, therefore, depend upon the learner's ability to manipulate the information according to how it might have to be used. Bruner assumed that practice in discovery learning would develop efficient and powerful ways of information manipulation, which can be used not only in discovery learning but in other forms of learning as well. Bruner admitted that it is very difficult to describe the heuristics of inquiry. Nevertheless, he believed that the modes of discovery can be acquired only through the practice of discovery. There is no question that Bruner's work did a great deal to promote active learning.

Many educators who participated in the elementary school science reform during the post-Sputnik era were caught up in the inquiry/discovery learning movement. They believed in the efficacy of the processes of science and active learning. This can be observed in the words of Kessen (1964, p. 4):

> There is a joy in the search for knowledge; there is excitement in seeing however partially, into the workings of the physical and biological world; there is intellectual power to be gained in learning the scientist's approach to the solutions of human problems. The first task and central purpose of science education is to awaken in the child, whether or not he will become a professional scientist, a sense of the joy, the excitement, and the intellectual power of science.

He goes on to say that science is a way of testing one's ideas by observation and experimentation.

Richard Suchman (1966) also did a great deal to promote inquiry, especially in the middle grades. He provided a strong rationale for the merits of teaching science by placing the student in the position of finding out, rather than the teacher giving the answers. Suchman produced many instructional materials and teacher resources in a program that he developed to assist educators in implementing the inquiry approach in science classrooms.

> The Inquiry Development Program is designed to help students learn to formulate and test their own theories and to become aware of their own learning processes. Its goal is to help the naturally inquisitive child retain and develop this characteristic so that he will become an inquiring adult—self confident, reasonable person who can and will investigate the world for his own satisfaction. And it will permit the student to develop a sound foundation in the subject matter of science along the way. (Suchman, 1966, p. 3)

Suchman advocated that students learn by inquiry because of its motivational effects. His rationale was that learning, which consists of storing information, may not be stimulated by intrinsic motivation. Students who learn and store information usually do this for extrinsic rewards such as grades or praise. In contrast, student-initiated inquiry leads to meaningful learning, which is intrinsically satisfying. Teachers can stimulate this by providing situations that are puzzling, permitting students to devise creative ways to figure them out. Suchman emphasized that it is the student who should take the initiative to put forth ideas and to test them. If students generate theories, they will be meaningful, because these ideas will grow out of their own thinking.

Rakow (1986) discusses the growth of "teaching science as a process of inquiry" whereby the student is the active agent in the discovery of knowledge. He cites the work of John Dewey whose

> notion of discovery as a method of acquiring knowledge closely parallels the inquiry approach advocated by the curriculum reforms of the 1950s and 1960s. . . . This discovery approach espoused by Dewey places less emphasis on what information is learned and greater emphasis on the logical thinking processes by which new knowledge is acquired. (Rakow, 1986, p. 14)

Rakow goes on to stress the importance of student curiosity and hands-on investigation in learning science. Further, this student-centered approach can develop students' abilities to use science process skills, such as classifying, using numbers, communicating, measuring, predicting, forming hypotheses, controlling variables, and experimenting. In addition, the Learning Cycle can be

---

■ STOP AND REFLECT! ■

Before going further, do the following:

- Explain what is meant by teaching science **by** inquiry.

- Which teaching strategies and techniques can a science teacher use to teach science by inquiry?

- Recall the four themes of scientific literacy that were discussed in Chapter 1 on the nature of science: (1) science as a way of thinking, (2) science as a way of investigating, (3) science as a body of knowledge, and (4) science and its interaction with technology and society. Of these ideas, which are particularly relevant to the notion of teaching science **by** inquiry?

---

used to guide inquiry by initiating instruction with student exploration before teacher intervention.

Teaching Science **as** Inquiry

> When it comes to the teaching of science it is perfectly clear where we, as science teachers, science educators, or scientists, stand: we are unalterably opposed to the rote memorization of the mere facts and minutiae of science. By contrast, we stand foursquare for the teaching of the scientific method, critical thinking, the scientific attitude, the problem-solving approach, the discovery method, and of special interest here, the inquiry method. (Rutherford, 1964, p. 80.)

At the time of the science reform, during the Sputnik curriculum reform era, James Rutherford (1964) directed attention to the apparent misunderstanding that existed (and still exists) regarding the role of inquiry in science teaching. In the statement just quoted, Rutherford calls attention to the consensus on teaching science that is held among the members of the profession—science should be taught as a process rather than as content. He goes on to say that science is often taught as a body of content or as a set of techniques thought to resemble scientific inquiry. Neither approach is appropriate. Rutherford pointed out "that the conclusions of science are closely linked with the inquiry which produced them" and that is why we must "take into account the close organic connections between process and content in science" (p. 80). He stressed that we must illuminate how major conceptions were arrived at. For example, when the study of gravitation is undertaken, it is important to study the contributions of Galileo and Kepler as well as Newton. The work of many scientists who investigated motion is essential to understanding gravitation. Therefore, according to Rutherford, teaching science **as** inquiry rests heavily on the teacher's understanding of the topic under study. The teacher must have an in-depth knowledge of the scientific conception he or she is teaching—what is known, how it came to be known, and its historical background. Consequently, teaching science **as** inquiry can be distinguished from teaching science **by** inquiry.

Joseph Schwab, who was a curriculum theorist at the University of Chicago, exerted enormous influence on teaching science **as** inquiry. As a member of the Biological Sciences Curriculum Study Committee in the late 1950s and early 1960s, he discussed the "enquiry approach" (the term he used for inquiry) and how to use it in the classroom. At the time, Schwab urged science educators to take a different approach to science teaching and to adopt one that better reflects the way scientists go about their work. He stressed the belief that "scientific research has its origin, not in objective facts alone, but in a conception, a construction of the mind" (Schwab, 1962, p. 12), and he proposed that we should help students to realize how scientists interpret information and form ideas. Textbooks as well as science teachers should go beyond merely presenting the facts and the outcomes of scientific investigation; they must show how these products were derived by scientists. In doing so, both the "stable" and "fluid" aspects of enquiry would be characterized. Stable enquiry illustrates how a body of knowledge grows, whereas fluid enquiry illustrates how new conceptions come about. Schwab illustrated one way of teaching science as enquiry through discussion in the *Biology Teachers' Handbook* (Biological Sciences Curriculum Study [BSCS], 1978), including a set of sixteen oral activities called "Invitations to Enquiry", which biology teachers could use to engage students in thinking through problems and their solutions. Schwab felt that to teach science as enquiry would show students

1. how knowledge arises from interpretation of data;
2. that the interpretation of data—indeed, even the search for data—proceeds on the basis of concepts and assumptions that change as our knowledge grows;
3. that because these principles and concepts change, knowledge too, changes; and
4. to show students that, though knowledge changes, it changes for good reason—because we know better and know more than we knew before. (BSCS, 1978, p. 306)

An understanding of the nature of scientific inquiry is difficult to secure, let alone teach. Herron (1971) asserted that scientists and philosophers of science have not given educators enough help in this matter, because individuals within these groups who expound upon the topic of inquiry generally address only a segment of the idea rather than presenting a unified picture. He goes on to say that even the curriculum materials that were developed after Sputnik, which were supposed to be inquiry based, did not live up to their inquiry orientation, especially the laboratory exercises. No wonder science teachers are unclear about teaching science as inquiry.

Herron (1971) undertook the task to construct a more complete characterization of inquiry for educators. He drew on the work of Schwab, Dewey, Einstein, Peirce, and others for his synthesis, pointing out that there are commonalties as well as sharp differences between their beliefs. Nevertheless, Herron found five categories that seemed to be recurrent in the ideas associated with scientific inquiry. He cautioned that these

areas should not be condensed into the "five-step scientific method" or be held to any particular sequence. The categories that Herron identified are agent, subject matter, method, phenomenon, and scientific knowledge. A significant aspect of Herron's categories, which is often absent in treatments of this topic, is the agent. The **agent** is whoever carries out the inquiry. The implication is that there is an individual who wants to know and learns what others in the scientific community have claimed about the ideas under study. This body of knowledge defines the **subject matter** that is known up to that period of time. This knowledge permits the agent to pose problems and then to proceed on to devise **methods** for testing his or her ideas. The **phenomenon** is also central to the process, because the nature of this entity will bear on the inquiry. Finally, the **scientific knowledge** that is produced is revisionary (subject to change and modification), and, thus, not an end point in scientific enquiry.

Martin (1985) asserts that science teachers can benefit from the philosophy of science in their quest to better understand the notion of teaching science as inquiry. He also indicates that it is important to study the scientific enterprise for direction. Martin offers the position stated in Chapter 1 in this textbook, which states that the principle goal of science is to understand the physical and biological world. In order to achieve this goal, students and teachers must realize that scientific conceptions are tentative, open to question, and subject to revision. Thus, instruction must show the **way** ideas are arrived at because this will illuminate how fundamental scientific conceptions were invented, verified, confirmed, rejected, and modified. Martin stresses the significance of generating hypotheses and testing them. However, he cautions educators not to confuse discovery learning with teaching science as inquiry. Science teaching can provide students with a good idea of **how** scientific knowledge is constructed without having them discover or rediscover this knowledge.

DeBoer (1991) concurs with this opinion and points out some of the problems associated with inquiry teaching. He cautions us not to confuse the understanding of scientific inquiry with **methods** of teaching science. We should teach students about the nature of science and how scientific understandings are achieved; however, the problem arises in giving students the idea that a given instructional approach is "the" way to inquiry. In particular we should not offer discovery learning and inductive teaching as the way to teach science as inquiry. Perhaps there is no one way or best way to teach science as inquiry.

Matthews (1994) urges science teachers to become familiar with the history and philosophy of science so that they will be better versed about inquiry. He argues that only by having a good understanding of how major ideas have been developed over time, can science teachers help students to learn about these conceptions. This background can help teachers "to avoid much of the naiveté associated with the claims of discovery learning—naive and false views such as: that scientific method is inductive, that observation does not depend upon conceptual understanding, and that messing about with real objects can reveal the structure of the scientific theories that apply to those objects" (Matthews, 1994,

p. 28). Matthews points out that hands-on/discovery learning teaches students about the "structure of objects," but it does not teach them about the "structure of disciplines." He clarifies this with an example: "The structure of the leaf is one thing, the structure of photosynthesis theory is quite another. And two very different modes of contemplation and manipulation are required for the different objects; one is turned around in the hand, the other is turned over in the mind" (Matthews, 1994, p. 26).

■ STOP AND REFLECT! ■

Before going further, do the following:

▨ Explain what is meant by teaching science **as** inquiry. How does this idea differ from teaching science **by** inquiry?

▨ Does teaching science **as** inquiry specify the use of certain methods of instruction, such as lecture, discussion, reading, and laboratory?

▨ Go back and review Chapter 1 on the nature of science, especially the section on the many facets of science. Which of these facets would a science teacher need to be knowledgeable about in their content area in order to teach science **as** inquiry.

▨ Recall the four themes of scientific literacy that were discussed in Chapter 1: (1) science as a way of thinking, (2) science as a way of investigating, (3) science as a body of knowledge, and (4) science and its interaction with technology and society. Of these ideas, which are particularly relevant to the notion of teaching science **as** inquiry?

▨ In Chapter 4 on learning, constructivism was discussed at great length, indicating that there are at least two sources whereby individuals construct their knowledge. One source is experiences with the physical world (personal construction of knowledge), the other is experiences with the sociocultural world (social construction of knowledge). In order for science teachers to become adept at teaching science **as** inquiry, in which of the two modes of knowledge construction must they become proficient?

▨ Consider elementary, middle, and senior high school students with respect to teaching science **as** inquiry and teaching science **by** inquiry. Indi-

cate to what extent these approaches should be used at the various grade levels by shading in the areas shown in the matrix. Compare your shaded matrix with others in the class.

Grade level	Teaching science	
	by inquiry	*as* inquiry
K–2		
3–5		
6–8		
9–12		

▨ Examine the vignette in Box 5.1 that illustrates a science teacher using batteries and bulbs to promote inquiry in the classroom.

   a. Which approach is the teacher using, science **by** inquiry or science **as** inquiry?

   b. Do you believe this teacher understands these two approaches, and is he capable of using both of these approaches to help students learn about electricity?

   c. Evaluate the teacher's understanding of electrical current by considering the definition of this concept that he placed on the board and the manner in which he requested one of the students to demonstrate electric current by running between rows of seats in the classroom.

BOX 5.1

BATTERIES AND BULBS?

Mr. Sharp teaches physical science at Brook Middle School. He employs a variety of hands-on experiences to maintain student interest in science. One of the activities he uses to introduce electricity is "batteries and bulbs." For this experience, Mr. Sharp gives each student a battery, a bulb, and a large paper clip. First, he instructs them to use the materials to "get the bulb to light." When all of the students can accomplish this task, the teacher challenges them to determine different arrangements by which the bulb will light.

Invariably, the middle school students become actively engaged in this hands-on activity. They must concentrate on the task in order to position the bulb against the battery, using the paper clip to make electrical connections. Mr. Sharp gives the students plenty of time to establish various combinations that light the bulb. In addition, he spends time discussing the activity. One of the question that he poses is:

Can you trace the current that makes the bulb light?

The answer that the teacher establishes is that current flows from the base of the battery, through the wire, and into the top of the battery. A follow-up question is:

What is electric current?

This question usually results in a variety of student responses, all of which Mr. Sharp accepts. Then he proceeds as follows:

1. On the chalkboard he writes:

    Electric current is the flow of electrons through a wire; it zips from one end of the wire to the other at high speeds.

2. He calls a student to the front of the class and asks her to run between two rows of seats from the front of the class to the back to illustrate the rapid movement of electrons through a wire, thus producing electric current.

(*Note:* Mr. Sharp's definition of an electric current is very limited and incorrect in some respects. In the battery and bulb and wire system, there is no steady stream of electrons speeding straight through the wire. What occurs is the "banging around" of billions of electrons attempting to move away from the negative terminal of the battery through the wire toward the positive terminal. The net speed of electron flow is a slow drift toward the positive terminal, with individual electrons moving in many directions in three-dimensional space. With this alternative conception held by the teacher, he uses an incorrect physical illustration when he requests a student to run between the rows of seats to demonstrate the rapid movement of the electrons straight through the wire.)

STRATEGIES AND TECHNIQUES FOR CONDUCTING INQUIRY-BASED INSTRUCTION

Few classroom scenes are as exciting as those in which you find students actively engaged in inquiry. In these classrooms you are apt to observe students trying to make sense out of what they are finding, exchanging ideas, questioning each other, giving their opinions, disagreeing with each other, and manipulating equipment. Students' ideas often drive the instruction.

In an inquiry-based learning environment, the teacher takes on a different role than in the traditional science classroom. The teacher must plan for exploration and set up situations that will encourage students to wonder and want to find out. Provocative questions, discrepant events, and problems that beg for an answer are considered in advance in preparation for student encounters with science. These stimulating situations are often planned around topics set down in the curriculum, but there is always room for investigations that students formulate. When instruction is planned with the consideration of the students as the active agent of their learning, the probability increases that students will take more interest in science and find their learning more meaningful.

When science is taught as inquiry, there exists the probability for students to engage in "minds on science" whereby they construct knowledge by aligning what they think with objects and events they experience. An observer of this type of learning may get the feeling that students are developing favorable **attitudes towards science,** because they find it exciting to learn by doing. The students may even enjoy this approach to the extent that they would like to pursue a scientific or a technological career or a science-related hobby. These students may view science as a worthwhile enterprise. Many may **acquire scientific attitudes,** giving them the desire to acquire information on their own. Students may demonstrate curiosity and interest in scientific investigation when they are learning to question ideas and events. Learning science by the process of inquiry can help students to **develop reasoning skills,** which will help them to seek answers and gather information. Students can become proficient in graphing data, making inferences, stating hypotheses, and devising laboratory investigations. The inquiry approach can also help students to **construct scientific knowledge** as the result of studying objects and events in concrete learning experiences. This knowledge can be directly related to subject matter content that is central to many middle and senior high science programs.

There are many ways to bring inquiry into the science classroom. Science teachers have been doing this for many years, using a variety of strategies and techniques. These instructional approaches have been used to illustrate how important ideas have come about and how scientists go about their work, as well as how to get students involved in the process of finding out. These methods are instructive regardless of whether one's desire is to teach science **as** inquiry or to teach science **by** inquiry, or to combine both of these goals.

Asking Questions

Questions are fundamental to scientific inquiry as well as to science instruction. Asking the right question is critical in investigative work. Questions can engage thinking and orient mental activity toward meaningful ends. For instructional purposes, questions can be classified many ways. For example, there are the what, where, which, when, and why types of questions. The questions can be phrased to match Bloom's taxonomy—knowledge, comprehension, application, analysis, synthesis, and evaluation. Questions can also be asked to direct student thinking along the lines of the science process skills such as observing, inferring, hypothesizing, experimenting, and so on. These questioning techniques are discussed in this textbook.

One questioning technique that some science teachers use is to write questions on the chalkboard for the students to answer. These questions are few in number and guide the instruction for the period. Generally, they can be answered by all students by the end of the class period.

Ms. Sanchez placed a small transparent container filled with water before the class. She held up a paper clip and directed students attention to a question on the chalkboard:

What will happen when I place this paper clip on the water?

The class was silent for a short period of time, then one hand went up. When the student was given permission to answer, she indicated that the paper clip would drop to the bottom of the pan. The rest of the class seemed to support this prediction. With that the teacher asked all of the students to write their predictions in their notebooks. Then she requested every student to go back to the laboratory tables to test their prediction. She provided each student with a small container of water and three different size paper clips. At first, all of the paper clips were sinking to the bottom of the container when the students placed their clips on the water. With some guidance, the teacher was getting some of the students to float a paper clip on the water. The surface tension of water is great enough to suspend a medium size paper clip.

When most of the students were successful in floating the paper clip, Ms. Sanchez directed student attention to another question that she had written on the board:

What variables are related to your success in floating a paper clip on the water?

Needless to say, this activity kept students busy attempting to answer a few questions posed by the teacher. With the first question, the students were invited to make a prediction and test it out through a firsthand experience. With the second question, the students were asked to explain their observations and results, which will be used by the teacher to discuss the principle of flotation.

Science teachers who encourage students to state what they think, to find out what actually happens, and to explain outcomes are using pedagogy that reflects scientific inquiry and strategies recommended by cognitive psychologists who study conceptual development and the construction of knowledge. Let's continue by examining other inquiry strategies that can be used to promote learning through the use of questioning.

Yes/No Questioning Technique. Richard Suchman (1966), who created the Inquiry Development Program in the 1960s for the middle school, offers many suggestions to teachers who want to implement inquiry in their classrooms. His six rules for inquiry sessions reflect the openness and freedom that he believed students should possess in order to develop their inquiry skills.

Rule One: Encourage students to ask questions that the teacher can answer yes or no.

Rule Two: Permit students to ask as many questions as they wish when they initiate their question asking.

Rule Three: Avoid evaluating the worth or accuracy of students' explanations.

Rule Four: Allow students to test out their own ideas at any time.

Rule Five: Encourage interaction and discussion among students.

Rule Six: Permit students to "mess around" with lots of materials connected with a given inquiry session.

Suchman's suggestions provide us with a way to promote inquiry and discovery learning in the science classroom. His approach, which places the learner in the position of having to find out and explain how, shifts the responsibility for learning away from the teacher to the student. We want students to follow their hunches and to compose their own explanations for situations rather than memorizing what the teacher or the textbook says.

The following is a question-and-answer session centering around a demonstration on heat loss. The students have just observed the temperature reading from one thermometer in a silver metal container and one in a black metal container, both containers had hot water (85°C) poured into them. The students are asked to predict which container will give up its heat the fastest over a twenty-minute period. Temperature readings are taken every five minutes.

STUDENT: Why did the silver container lose less heat?

TEACHER: Beverly, please turn your question into a yes/no question and I will respond to it.

STUDENT: Do things that are painted white absorb less heat than those that are painted black?

TEACHER: Yes!

STUDENT: Is the black container black on the inside?

TEACHER: No.

STUDENT: What happens if you spray the inside of the black container black?

TEACHER: Remember the rule for asking questions.

STUDENT: Can I paint the inside of the black container black?

TEACHER: Yes.

During this type of dialogue, students must think before they speak. They must organize their thoughts and express them in a coherent manner. These sessions usually lead students to try out ideas through self-initiated investigations. Thus, this technique has great potential for moving students away from the reception learning end of the continuum and toward the inquiry-oriented end where they ask questions, suggest procedures, and find solutions.

Science Process Skills

One way to give students an appreciation for science is to get them involved with investigating, using certain reasoning skills, and presenting information. Useful approaches to this type of inquiry have come from elementary school science programs developed in the 1960s. One program in particular was called Science—A Process Approach (SAPA). The developers believed that science was best taught as a procedure of enquiry (sic). Science teaching, just as scientific inquiry, should be taught as a process of finding out, which would involve the development of certain attitudes and skills. The process approach places considerable importance upon the development of specific thinking skills believed to be used by scientists in their work.

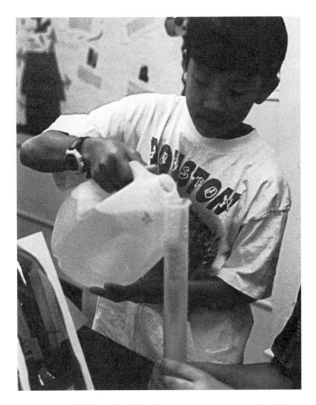

Effective middle school science programs emphasize science process skill development.

The process approach focuses on many skills that humans use to construct knowledge, to represent ideas, and to communicate information. For example, it promotes posing questions, stating problems, making accurate observations, classifying data, providing inferences, forming hypotheses, communicating findings, and conducting experiments. Many educators hold the belief that the acquisition of these skills will better enable students to solve problems, to learn on their own, and to appreciate science. Table 5.1 presents a list of many commonly used science process skills in science programs.

The process approach can be used to develop science concepts and to organize content knowledge. Although the major intention of the process skills approach was to develop the spirit of scientific investigation, it has been used in the middle school to guide students' thinking so that they process information and construct meaningful knowledge. In many instances, this approach has been successful in many science classrooms in transforming a reception learning environment into an inquiry, experiential-based learning environment.

Many middle school science programs place heavy emphasis upon science process skills development. These curricula use process skills as the content and learning outcomes of the instruction as well as the teaching methodology. They specify certain skills to teach and to test for, such as observing, inferring, classifying, measuring, graphing, controlling variables, hypothesizing, and experimenting. Some school districts devote four to six weeks to science skills, particularly at the beginning of the school year. These programs use a variety of science content and contexts within which students engage in practicing scientific reasoning skills. In the school districts where students have poor backgrounds in science or where they lack proficiency in the English language, the time spent on process skills seems to be worthwhile. Certainly a curriculum that includes a large body of scientific information for students to memorize in a lecture-based course will be ineffective.

Scientifically literate science students must be competent in using the science process skills. For example, graphing is an essential skill for all students to develop. Graphs organize information in an efficient manner. Graphing is a communication skill that is used throughout school science, from elementary school through college. Middle school science programs must ensure that all students are proficient in graphing before they enter high school. Some of the graphing subskills are:

- Identifying the appropriate type of graph—bar or line—to represent data
- Providing a useful title for a graph and correctly labeling the *x* and *y* axes

TABLE 5.1   Basic and Integrated Science Process Skills

Process skill	Definition
Basic skills	
Observing	Noting the properties of objects and situations using the five senses
Classifying	Relating objects and events according to their properties or attributes (This involves classifying places, objects, ideas, or events into categories based on their similarities.)
Space/time relations	Visualizing and manipulating objects and events, dealing with shapes, time, distance, and speed
Using numbers	Using quantitative relationships, e.g., scientific notation, error, significant numbers, precision, ratios, and proportions
Measuring	Expressing the amount of an object or substance in quantitative terms, such as meters, liters, grams, and newtons
Inferring	Giving an explanation for a particular object or event
Predicting	Forecasting a future occurrence based on past observation or the extension of data
Integrated skills	
Defining operationally	Developing statements that present a concrete description of an object or event by telling one what to do or observe
Formulating models	Constructing images, objects, or mathematical formulas to explain ideas
Controlling variables	Manipulating and controlling properties that relate to situations or events for the purpose of determining causation
Interpreting data	Arriving at explanations, inferences, or hypotheses from data that have been graphed or placed in a table (This frequently involves concepts such as mean, mode, median, range, frequency distribution, t-test, and chi-square test.)
Hypothesizing	Stating a tentative generalization of observations or inferences that may be used to explain a relatively larger number of events but that is subject to immediate or eventual testing by one or more experiments
Experimenting	Testing a hypothesis through the manipulation and control of independent variables and noting the effects on a dependent variable; interpreting and presenting results in the form of a report that others can follow to replicate the experiment

- Constructing a bar or line graph when given a data table

- Interpreting a graph by communicating its significance

- Interpolating and extrapolating information from a line graph

At first thought, graphing seems so simple to the college science major who is preparing to become a science teacher. This is deceiving because graphing is tied closely to the context in which it is learned and used. Change the context or content, and many students seem lost and unable to demonstrate this skill. Examine the table and axes for a graph provided in Figure 5.1. Fill in the missing data on the table and construct a graph to represent the information, complete with a title and labels for the axes.

In addition to the basic science process skills, inquiry is carried out by using the integrated process skills or more advanced reasoning skills. Let's read about

the process approach taken by two science teachers to gain an understanding of how this inquiry strategy might be used in the middle and the senior high schools when a more advanced level of thinking is intended, such as manipulating and controlling variables.

■

TEACHER 1.   Mr. Roosevelt engages his middle school students in the study of sound because it produces excitement and interest toward science. One reason for these positive outcomes is that he involves students in an extensive laboratory investigation, centering upon the "string telephone." Mr. Roosevelt initiates this activity by demonstrating how two metal soup cans connected with a wire transmit voice sounds between two people. He challenges the students to construct many different phones to determine which pair will transmit the

Volume of iron (milliliters)	Mass of iron (grams)
x	y
1	2
2	4
3	8
4	16
5	—
6	64

Title of graph:

FIGURE 5.1   This data table for the relationship between the volume of a piece of iron and its mass can be used to construct a graph to represent the information.

clearest voice messages. He also asks them to predict which phones will work best and to explain why. Working in groups, the students bring to class many cans and containers of various sizes and compositions—from small metal cans to large coffee cans, from small paper cups to giant soft drink containers, and from Styrofoam cups to plastic dairy containers. The students also bring to class a variety of lines to connect the phones such as thread, string, monofilament fishing line, and wire.

After the students have tested many combinations of phones and lines, they select a set of phones that produces very clear voice sounds. For example, a pair of paper cups connected by carpet thread produces amazing results. Mr. Roosevelt asks his students to identify the variables that seem to produce good sounds through these simple devices. He guides students' thinking so that they realize that they were conducting an experiment and controlling variables. The students not only come to realize that the size and composition of the phones are important, but that these variables affect the vibration of the transmitting material. Even though the students lack the scientific terminology to explain the effects of elasticity on vibration, they feel

good about conducting an investigation that seems scientific.

■

TEACHER 2.   Ms. Suki is a high school physics teacher who engages her students in the careful examination of variables that affect the transmission of sound in different media, but for the purpose of gaining conceptual knowledge. She begins the study of sound with a laboratory exercise in which she demonstrates the difference in clarity of voice in two "string telephone" systems. One pair of phones is made from paper drinking cups, the other pair from heavy plastic containers in which metal parts are packed for shipping. From the demonstration it is obvious that the paper cups are superior to the plastic containers in transmitting a conversation between two classmates. After this fact has been established, the students are given the charge to determine why the paper does so well in voice transmission. Ms. Suki asks: "What are the variables that affect the transmission of sound?" Before the students proceed, however, she requires them to explain in writing what factors in a medium promote sound transmission and why this is true.

In a large box, Ms. Suki has many pairs of phones, all made from materials different in composition, thickness, and flexibility. It does not take long for students to realize that the transmission of sound is directly related to the elasticity of the medium and inversely to its density or inertia. This discovery is reinforced when students find a chart in their physics textbook showing that sound travels much faster in steel (5,200 m/sec) than in lead (1,200 m/sec).

■

In the string phone examples, the two teachers differ in their purpose for using the process approach for science instruction. The middle school teacher uses experimentation and controlling variables to promote the spirit of inquiry centered on the topic of sound. This teacher desires that students gain only some familiarity with basic concepts of sound transmission. The high school physics teacher uses this approach to help students clarify any misconceptions they may have about the transmission of sound and to help them develop correct ideas about this phenomenon. For the physics teacher, the primary outcome is conceptual development, and she uses the identification and examination of variables to assist in achieving this end.

Discrepant Events

An attention-getting approach for initiating inquiry is through the use of discrepant events. A discrepant event is one that puzzles the observer, causing him or her to wonder why the event occurred as it did. These situations leave the observer at a loss to explain what has taken place. An inquiry session initiated with a discrepant event can begin with a demonstration or film, preceded by some directions to focus students' attention on what they are about to observe.

Discrepant events can be used to stimulate inquiry into numerous concepts and principles. Discrepant-event demonstrations of the laws of motion, center of gravity, Pascal's principle, density, and vacuum, to mention some, can be used to initiate inquiry sessions. The discrepant-event approach receives support from the cognitive psychologists, because of its potential impact on learning. Discrepant events influence equilibration and the self-regulatory process, according to the Piagetian theory of intellectual development. Situations that are contrary to what a person expects cause the individual to wonder what is taking place, resulting in cognitive disequilibrium. With proper guidance, the individual will attempt to figure out the discrepancy and search for a suitable explanation for the situation. When a person arrives at a plausible explanation for a discrepant event, he or she will establish cognitive equilibrium at a new cognitive level. The individual is now better equipped mentally to approach new situations that cause curiosity and puzzlement (Piaget, 1971).

For an idea regarding how to conduct a discrepant event activity, consider Newton's first law of motion. Examine the series of demonstrations in Figure 5.2a–d; they illustrate the phenomenon associated with the first law of motion. All science teachers should become familiar with these demonstrations and be able to explain the science behind them.

How would you conduct the demonstration shown in Figure 5.2a? Begin the discrepant event without a support under the board where the nail is positioned.

- Ask the participants:

  Can we hammer the nail into the board with one end secured to the table and no support under the nail?

- Request that all students write the answer to this question in their notebooks and that they explain the reason for their answer.

- Attempt to hammer the nail into the board with one end secured to the table.

- After illustrating that one cannot hammer the nail into the board, determine by a show of hands those who believed the nail could be hammered into the board and those who believed that the nail could not be hammered into the board.

- Bring forth the explanations regarding this event from both those who predicted the nail would go into the board and those who predicted it would not. Write them on the chalkboard.

- Attempt to verify what individuals believe by testing the beliefs. Compare what is observed with what is believed. How do they compare?

- Produce a statement of Newton's first law and write it on the chalkboard. Determine the alternate conceptions that were held by some of the individuals and discuss them using the eight knowledge claims regarding alternative conceptions in Chapter 4.

- Continue to present the other three demonstrations that pertain to Newton's first law of motion (Figure 5.2b–d), using a format similar to the one just outlined or one that you believe will be beneficial for helping science teachers present discrepant events with the intention of improving understanding of a science law or principle.

Science teachers must exercise discretion in selecting events and problems that bring about disequilibrium by devising situations that present a challenge to students but that can be understood by them given proper guidance and ample time. Some researchers have argued that the discrepant event approach can be used with homework problems, providing the following two factors are present:

> Problems must be chosen so that the student can partially but not completely understand them in terms of old ideas . . . and sufficient time must be allowed for the student to grapple with the situation, possibly with appropriate hints to direct his thinking, but allowing him to put the ideas together himself. (Lawson & Wollman, 1975, pp. 470–471)

These same two factors or guidelines should be considered for discrepant events, whether it be in the form of live demonstrations, filmed demonstrations, or word problems. Refer back to Chapter 4 on learning and the section on equilibration and contradictions for an in-depth discussion about this aspect of cognitive psychology.

Inductive Approach

The inductive approach provides students with learning situations in which they can **discover a concept or principle.** With this approach, the attributes and instances of an idea are encountered first by the learner,

FIGURE 5.2a–d This series of discrepant event demonstrations can be used to help stimulate thinking, inquiry, and learning about inertia.

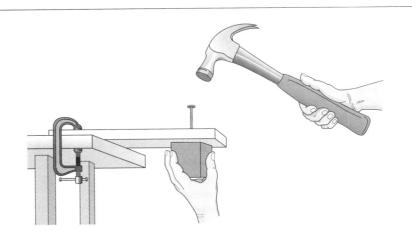

a. *Hammering the Nail through the Board.* Find a short board about 15 inches long and 1 inch thick. Extend the board past the edge of a table with about 3 inches resting on the table. Brace the end of the board that is on the table with a heavy clamp or ask a student to stand on the board so that it is secured to the table. Near the opposite end of the board, try to hammer a nail through the board without any support under it. Then try hammering the nail with the support of a large weight under the board at the point of the nail.

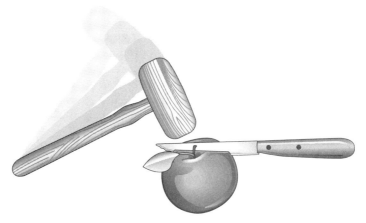

b. *Cutting an Apple in Mid-Air.* Take a large heavy kitchen knife and push the blade far enough into an apple so that the apple stays on the blade of the knife when the knife is held out away from the body. With a hammer or mallet, strike the blunt edge of the knife with a hard blow and notice what happens to the apple.

followed by naming and discussing the idea. This empirical-inductive approach gives students a concrete experience whereby they obtain sensory impressions and data from real objects and events. Now the learner can mentally record certain stimuli and is in a better position to make sense of a phenomenon than if he or she had received abstract information about the phenomenon solely from a lecture, for example. Empirically obtained information can be acted upon cognitively and organized in the mind where patterns may be discovered that are meaningful to the learner. This is how a concept is induced or discovered and how ideas are put forth to describe and explain a phenomenon under study. The

teacher serves as a guide who helps to bring into the discussion the appropriate terminology for naming the concept or principle and defining it.

The inductive approach can be thought of as an experience-before-vocabulary approach to learning. The inductive strategy is the opposite of the deductive approach, in which the name and explanation of a concept or principle are given first, followed by experiences that illustrate attributes and instances of the idea. Figure 5.3 contrasts inductive and deductive approaches to instruction.

An example of an inductive approach that can be used in biology is one in which students are introduced

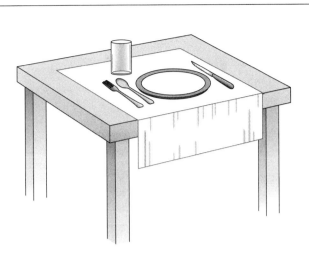

c. *The Table Setting.* Cut a piece from an old bed sheet approximately 18 inches by 24 inches. Make sure that there is no hem left on any side. Lay the sheet on a smooth table so that approximately 6 to 8 inches hangs over the edge. Place a table setting—fork, spoon, knife, plate, and glass—on the cloth. Grab both sides of the cloth that is hanging over the edge and with a quick downward jerk, snap the cloth from under the table setting. (You may wish to use a plastic dish and cup for this demonstration.)

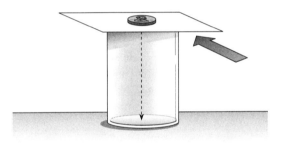

d. *Flicking the Card from under the Coin.* Place a glass or a beaker on the table. Place a 3-by-5-inch index card over the mouth of the glass and put a penny at the center of the card. Flick the card out from under the penny so that it drops into the glass.

to the theory of natural selection before it is mentioned or discussed in the classroom. They can form the notion that evolution can occur over time through the selection process. This is illustrated through the following outdoor activity.

■

Students are told that they will play the role of predators and will have an opportunity to go outside and feed on insects. For this exercise, the teacher scatters 400 small objects, 200 red and 200 green, over a grassy lawn on the school grounds.

(Soup macaroni, popcorn dyed with food coloring, or colored beads are often used in this exercise.) The students are given signals when to start and stop "feeding." Each feeding time might last one or two minutes. The students are instructed to walk upright, bending to pick up only one object at a time, and they must take two steps before picking up another object. It requires only a few time intervals of approximately one or two minutes in order to illustrate the intended outcome.

After the students return to the classroom, the data are entered on a table on the chalkboard. The total number of red and green "insects eaten" is

Inductive Approach to Instruction

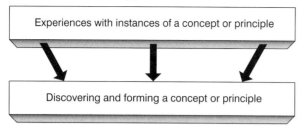

Deductive Approach to Instruction

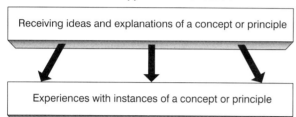

FIGURE 5.3 The inductive approach in the top diagram is contrasted with the deductive approach in the bottom diagram, indicating the different manner in which they initiate and carry through instruction.

entered in the table. Inspection of the data will show the number of "insects eaten" during each interval, the total number of "insects eaten," and the percentage of "insects" remaining (Table 5.2).

The question that can be asked is

What happened to the "insect" population?

After inspecting the data, the students may respond that the red "insects" were consumed at a higher rate (toward extinction) than the green "insects." They will realize that this situation is due to the colors of the "insects" and the grass. Because the red "insects" were easier to see, they were consumed faster than the green "insects."

As a result of this inductive activity, some students now have an idea of one aspect of natural selection—how color can serve to camouflage some species while exposing others to predators. For other students this activity merely broadened their knowledge of natural selection.

■

The inquiry-oriented teacher will extend this activity so that students can expand their knowledge of natural selection by discovering additional examples that seem to illustrate this theory with other traits and organisms. The teacher might present the following questions for further inquiry:

■ What traits have helped certain species of birds to survive?

■ What are some traits or behavior patterns that cause some species of birds to become scarce?

■ What traits have assisted sharks to survive over thousands of years with very little change?

■ Name some animals that have become extinct and explain what might have happened to these creatures.

■ Identify some animals or plants in your community that may soon become extinct and tell why this might occur.

■ Identify some animals or plants in your community that might thrive in the near future and tell why this might occur.

Students could be encouraged to select one of these questions and to find information to answer their question from books, magazines, television programs, newspapers, people, and personal observations. At a designated time the students can give a short report to the class concerning their findings.

The Learning Cycle.   The inductive approach is illustrated in an instructional strategy called the Learning Cycle. The Learning Cycle was developed as the primary teaching method for the elementary science program,

TABLE 5.2 Consumption of Insects	Number "eaten" in each interval		Total number "eaten"	Percentage remaining
Species	1	2		
Red	63	88	151	24
Green	21	34	55	72

Note: Initially there were 200 red and 200 green insects.

Science Curriculum Improvement Study (SCIS), produced in the 1960s under the direction of Robert Karplus (SCIS, 1974). In addition to the elementary level, the strategy has been used at the junior high, senior high, and college levels to promote inquiry and intellectual development (Fuller, 1980; Renner, Cate, et al., 1985). The Learning Cycle has three phases: exploration, invention, and application.

Exploration.   The exploration phase allows students to experience objects and events in order to stimulate their thinking about a concept or principle; students are placed in a context that will permit them to discover patterns and relationships. During this phase, students are given some guidance to keep them focused on the learning task. Questions are posed and cues are given to channel thinking. However, students are not given answers or labels. This phase is illustrated in the natural selection example wherein the students are directed to pretend they are birds and should "eat" the "insects" that have been scattered over the lawn.

Invention.   The invention phase allows students to determine relationships between objects and events that they have experienced. Initially, the teacher serves as a guide to channel thinking, encouraging students to construct appropriate labels for the relationships they have just discovered. At some point, however, it is appropriate for the teacher to provide labels and terms that are given in the curriculum guide and the textbook. This phase is illustrated in the natural selection example during the inspection of the data in Table 5.2. The students are asked to explain the consumption pattern of the insects. Why were more red insects eaten than green insects? Here the teacher discusses the terms natural selection and evolution.

Application.   The application phase allows the students to apply their knowledge of a given concept to other situations. The teacher encourages the students to find (discover or inquire into) examples to illustrate the concept they have just experienced. This phase permits students to generalize their learning, thus reinforcing newly acquired knowledge and attaining concepts. This is illustrated in the natural selection example whereby the students are encouraged to find additional examples of the theory in textbooks, magazines, television programs, first-hand observations, and so on, and to share this material with other class members.

The labels for the three phases of the Learning Cycle have been modified by different educators. Renner, Abraham, and Birne (1985) used the terms exploration, conceptual invention, and expansion of the idea. Rakow (1986) used exploration phase, concept introduction, and concept application. The terms used for these phases are not so important as giving students the opportunity to experience the sequence of instruction, which probably causes them to enjoy it and to believe they are learning more in science class (Renner, Abraham, & Birne, 1985).

Lawson, Abraham, and Renner (1989) have researched and written extensively about the Learning Cycle. They discuss three types of Learning Cycles in their work, which they term descriptive, empirical-abductive, and hypothetical-deductive. These strategies differ according to what the learner is expected to do with the data during the invention phase.

In the descriptive learning cycle, students discover empirical patterns during the exploration phase. The students are basically describing perceptible phenomena and telling "what" they have found out. With the empirical-abductive learning cycle, students also attempt to discover and describe empirical patterns. However, they go one step further by attempting to determine the cause of these patterns. The term abductive is used here to specify an activity where the learner studies data and patterns and attempts to explain "why." In the hypothetical-deductive learning cycle, students are asked to generate alternative explanations for phenomena and to design experiments to test them out. This approach certainly engages the students in more reflective and deductive thinking than the other two approaches.

Lawson et al. (1989) point out that the three phases and their instructional sequences are important. They recommend beginning with exploration and moving to the introduction of terms (invention), which is the inductive aspect of this approach. This sequence may be more effective with average students, whereas a more deductive approach may be better suited to the more able students. Furthermore, the inductive approach may be more effective when studying complex concepts that make a high intellectual demand on the learner.

Koran, Koran, and Baker (1980) warn that inductive approaches must be carefully planned so that students, especially those of low ability, recognize the relevant stimuli that constitute the concepts and principles being taught. The low-ability students need cues to direct their attention and to assist them in processing the information. These researchers reported success with an inductive cueing approach to teach the biological topic of monocots to ninth- and tenth-grade students. They used a slide-tape program and preceded each group of slides with one of the following cues:

a. "Pay attention to the appearance of the leaf views,"

b. "Pay attention to the petal number," or

c. "Pay attention to the fibrovascular bundle organization." (Koran et al., 1980, p. 167)

The inductive or discovery approach can increase student interest and motivation in science, but the right conditions must prevail. First, students must be able to discover the concept or principle under investigation. Then, they must be able to achieve this end with a modest amount of searching for relevant information. If the concept is too difficult, or if there is a great deal of irrelevant information, the discovery approach should give way to other approaches.

5 E Instructional Model.   The 5 E instructional model was developed for the elementary school science program *Science for Life and Living* by the Biological Sciences Curriculum Study organization (BSCS, 1990). This approach to teaching science through inquiry is an elaboration of the Learning Cycle and has application at the middle and senior high school, as is recommended by BSCS in their curriculum framework for teaching about the history and nature of science and technology (BSCS & Social Science Education Consortium [SSEC], 1992). As the name implies, the 5 E model has five phases: engagement, exploration, explanation, elaboration, and evaluation.

Engagement.   The first phase of the model serves to capture students' attention and to engage them in the study of a concept, principle, issue, or problem. These activities can be in the form of a question, discrepant event, problem, puzzle, or any other strategy used to focus thinking. The engagement phase introduces students to the investigation that they will undertake and the manner in which they will go about their inquiry. During this phase the teacher guides students to make connections between what they know and what they are about to study.

Exploration.   During the second phase of the model, students carry out investigations. Students gather information, test out ideas, record observations, experiment, and so on. This phase provides concrete, hands-on experiences that bring students into contact with the phenomena or situations they are studying. As a result, students should realize patterns and relationships and raise questions. The teacher serves as a facilitator of learning, helping students to find out and discover ideas.

Explanation.   The third phase permits students to make sense from their explorations. They are encouraged to find patterns, relationships, and answers to questions. Students are urged to explain their findings and to demonstrate their understanding. The teacher uses questions to guide thinking and reasoning. In this phase, it is important for students to use their own words to explain ideas, which may be followed by more precise terminology put forth by the teacher.

Elaboration.   This phase in the instructional sequence gives students opportunities to apply the concepts and skills that they have acquired to different situations. The applications of newly acquired information and skills are reinforced in new contexts, making learning more meaningful. Misconceptions are addressed. Cooperative group work and individual study are appropriate strategies to use at this point in the teaching sequence. The elaboration phase can take place over many periods of instruction and serve to enhance student cognition.

Evaluation.   The last phase of the 5 E instructional model calls upon students to demonstrate their knowledge and understanding of the ideas under study. These activities also serve to reinforce important learning outcomes. This assessment can be based upon the measurement of many types of cognitive and psychomotor behaviors such as producing written works, demonstrating laboratory skills and procedures, and completing projects.

The 5 E instructional model is similar to the conceptual change teaching sequence discussed in Chapter 4 where it was stressed repeatedly that science teachers must consider what the students know and believe at the start of an instructional sequence. This will increase the probability that the knowledge construction process begins with students' prior knowledge and their alternative conceptions. The inductive models of instruction offer science teachers a psychologically based approach to teaching and learning. Further, they support inquiry as well as the attainment of science concepts.

Deductive Approach

In contrast to the inductive approach to science teaching, there is the deductive approach that is frequently used in science courses. With the deductive strategy, a concept or principle is defined and discussed using appropriate labels and terms, followed by experiences to illustrate the idea. It can involve hypothetical-deductive thinking, whereby the learner generates ideas to be tested or discovered. However, the learner must first know about the phenomenon under study in order to propose hypothetical relations that may exist in the real world. The deductive approach is a vocabulary-before-experience model of teaching where lecture and discussion precede laboratory or field work.

The deductive approach can be used to promote inquiry sessions and to construct knowledge. The first phase presents the generalizations and rules about the concept or principle under study, and the second phase requires students to find examples of the concepts or principles. The following example illustrates an inquiry session in teaching acid-base chemistry by beginning deductively.

Phase one. Students are presented with definitions and properties of acids and bases. This presentation might begin with the definitions of acids and bases that are based on three theories. The first is the Arrhenius theory, which explains acids and bases in terms of ionization and should be given considerable discussion time. The second is the Bronsted-Lowry theory, which defines these disjunctive concepts in terms of proton acceptors and proton donors. The third definition is based on the Lewis theory, which defines acids and bases in terms of electron-pair acceptors and donors.

The discussion might also include the attributes or properties of acids and bases that distinguish them from other chemical compounds in aqueous solution. For example, acids turn the litmus indicator red, taste sour, and neutralize bases; bases turn litmus blue, taste bitter, and neutralize acids. The concept of pH is introduced to develop a quantitative idea of the acidity or basicity of a solution. Here, the pH scale would be discussed, stating that a pH of 7 indicates a neutral solution, a Ph of 1 indicates a strong acid, and a pH of 14 indicates a strong base.

Phase two. After a lecture/discussion regarding the definitions and properties of acids and bases, students are ready to gather information about these concepts through laboratory activities.

■

One of Mr. Beard's favorite laboratory experiments is on acids and bases. He introduces the laboratory experience like this: Today you are going to become experts on identifying acids and bases. On the laboratory bench to your right are many solutions, some of which are commonly found in a chemistry lab, some of which are commonly found in your home, and some of which are commonly found in industrial plants and factories. I want you to classify these solutions as either acids or bases and then order them by their pH. Further, I want you to predict what the pH of each solution is, that is, its approximate pH, by indicating its relative strength as an acid or a base. Think about the uses of the acid and base solutions provided, and then deduce what pH they might have for that particular function.

You can use these acid-base indicators—methyl orange, litmus, indigo carmine—to determine which is an acid and which is a base and to determine their relative strengths. Analyze data and order your chemicals from the strongest acid to the strongest base. Then check the pH of these solutions with the pH meter that is on the front demonstration table and reorder the solutions if necessary.

■

This method of teaching science as inquiry—a lecture/discussion phase followed by a firsthand experience phase—is a popular and common practice among science teachers. Nevertheless, the approach should be carried out with the spirit of "let's find out." It is an effective way to teach difficult content (Herman & Hincksman, 1978). With difficult subject matter, all students may not induce the rule or principle through an inductive approach; thus, a deductive approach may be more effective with the majority of students.

The traditional, lecture/lab, deductive approach is often overused in secondary school science teaching. Consequently, this method can become too routine and is often used when an inductive approach might be more effective. Furthermore, this approach loses some of its effectiveness when too much information is presented during the lecture phase. Perhaps elements of both the deductive and inductive strategies should be combined and used with the conceptual change strategy that was discussed in Chapter 4. Remember, the conceptual change strategy emphasizes that teachers initiate instruction with an **orientation** to introduce students to what they will be learning. During this segment of instruction, the teacher should **elicit** from students what they know about the topic under study, which will bring out alternative conceptions that will interfere with what students are about to learn. It is not advisable to spend too much time correcting students' ideas, but plenty of time should be given to getting students to the point of reasoning about what they are to be looking for in the laboratory. Here is where you want students to put forth their ideas to be tested in the laboratory.

Gathering Information

Scientific inquiry includes more than constructing knowledge through hands-on activities. Laboratory work and experimentation are only some of the ways in which we find out about reality. A great deal of the inquiry that scientists and engineers carry out involves reading and conversing with others. Many of these professionals probably spend more time gathering ideas and information from literature sources and other people than they spend in their laboratory.

Science teachers must encourage students at many points during the inquiry process to obtain information from a variety of sources. Information gathering can occur during the application phase of the learning cycle, for example, when students are assigned to read about a topic. Reading articles and reading the textbook may be appropriate at this point, because the students have had firsthand experiences from which to relate. In other

Science teachers should provide students with opportunities to gather information from printed matter.

instances, the teacher may ask students to bring in newspaper clippings on a topic just as the class begins to study it. Today, we also have the resources of the Internet system of electronic information that is available with the aid of computers. People can search the World Wide Web for information that can be accessed in seconds from any part of the world.

Reading Printed Material.   Newspapers and magazines are rich sources of information for students to improve their scientific knowledge. One science course requirement can request students to cut out or photocopy articles and organize them into a notebook. Another technique to improve knowledge and understanding of a given topic is to require a short written report. These reports can be compiled from a single source or a few sources. When long reports are desired, students should be required to use a variety of sources for their write-up such as newspapers, textbooks, magazines, encyclopedias, and journals. Students can research information in their homes, the school library, and the public library. They should be taught how to cite information sources in their reports. Effective science teachers require information gathering throughout the school

year, but are careful not to burden students with this type of work.

Assignments of this nature are not always successful, because student motivation and competence are involved. Therefore, some science teachers identify topics that students can investigate before giving these assignments. They arrange topics on three-by-five-inch index cards, and along with a topic title they list appropriate literature sources that are readily available to the students. Also, there may be many index cards with the same topic title, because there may exist a limited number of topics that can be researched on a given subject for a class of thirty students. Using this guided approach, students are led by the hand during their information-gathering experiences. However, as students gain more experience and competence with this procedure, they require less direction and guidance.

Seeking Information from Individuals.   Seeking information from individuals is an important aspect of knowledge acquisition and the scientific enterprise. People are a rich source of information and ideas. They can explain concepts to teenagers and improve their understanding of these ideas, often better than a textbook or science classroom explanation can. Older siblings, parents, aunts, uncles, pharmacists, lawyers, nurses, doctors, firemen, engineers, construction workers, electricians, bakers, mechanics, coaches, musicians, and florists are among those with whom science students can interact to learn more about a topic. These people are often willing to spend time with young people to explain how something works or to clarify ideas and concepts.

Inquiry techniques that engage students in gathering the opinions of others is an excellent way for students to find out what others believe about issues and problems. This approach can also teach students how to develop questionnaires and survey instruments. Furthermore, this is an excellent way to make science relevant and to illustrate its relationship to society.

■

Ms. Gelespie encourages her life science students to find out what others think about various issues that relate to living organisms. She has found that when students gather information, they feel as though they are conducting scientific inquiry. During the course, therefore, Ms. Gelespie requires her students to survey the opinions of others on at least four topics: nutrition, population, drugs, and chemical waste. She organizes students into groups to investigate these topics. Each group is assigned a particular segment of the population to investigate and they are encouraged to collect data from a wide variety of individuals such as peers, parents, and professionals in a given field. Students conduct interviews face to face, use the telephone, or send a survey form. For these data collection approaches, the teacher has the students develop a questionnaire to guide the interview process. Ms. Gelespie reports that her students enjoy this type of inquiry, especially using the telephone, which is one way to tap into what they do well—talk on the phone.

■

Accessing Information from the Internet.   The Internet is one of the great human inventions of the twentieth century. This electronic network is an enormously huge source of information at the fingertips of anyone using a computer. The Internet consists of massive quantities of information available electronically from locations throughout the globe. It also includes people and software programs. The Internet makes people available as well as information. This gigantic electronic network is giving information a new meaning.

Students, teachers, scientists, and others can facilitate their inquiries into most topics through the Internet. Most university scientists and science departments are on the Internet, as are exploratoriums, museums, planetariums, zoos, and government research facilities. Many people and sites will respond to inquiries pertaining to science. In addition, these facilities offer instructional materials that can be downloaded to personal computers.

Problem Solving

The problem-solving approach to science instruction has the potential to engage students in authentic investigations and to develop their inquiry skills. This strategy can give students a feeling for science and engineering and how professionals in these fields go about their work. Problem solving can also make science course learning more meaningful and relevant for teenagers.

Problem solving is often used synonymously with inquiry and science process skill reasoning (Helgeson, 1989, 1994). As such, this concept is associated with the nature of scientific inquiry as well as instructional methodology. The problem solving that will be addressed in this section involves situations that are relevant to students' lives and raise their doubt or uncertainty (Dewey, 1938). This type of problem solving often engages students in investigations where they raise questions, plan procedures, collect information, and form conclusions. These learning experiences can be short in duration or long, taking up to several months to complete. This approach is not the sort of activity that directs students to answer questions at the end of the textbook chapter or to substitute numbers into a formula and compute the answer.

After studying problem solving, Watts (1991, p. 3) pointed out:

> Problems come in all shapes and sizes, and from all areas of life. . . . They may be problems, or puzzles that need an explanation or simple "itches" that may be the first steps in an investigation to be followed by a few well-thought-out tests to reach an answer.

Watts also stresses that students who engage in problem solving take ownership for their learning and are motivated to find out.

In some science programs, problem solving can be used as a primary learning outcome as well as a major instructional strategy. In these programs of study, fundamental science subject matter is learned as the investigation ensues. Problem-solving-based science courses can sometimes be found in the middle school where the curriculum is more flexible and open-ended than in the high school.

■

Ms. Janis teaches seventh-grade life science in a neighborhood where many blue-collar families live. Part of the curriculum includes topics on nutrition and exercise. Ms. Janis begins the study of nutrition and exercise by referring to the bulletin board at the back of the room where the pictures of many teenage models, movie stars, and athletes are displayed. The students are attracted to these pictures and like to identify with the people in them. Ms. Janis poses the following question:

How do these people get to be where they are in life?

This question brings responses from everyone in the class. Students have many opinions regarding fame and success and are willing to express these ideas freely. During the discussion, invariably someone will mention a good diet and the advantages of exercise. The teacher then probes to find out what the students believe regarding a good diet and the diet of these famous people. Ms. Janis asks:

Do you have the same diet as some of these famous people?

This question leads to a great deal of uncertainty and many different opinions regarding what fashion models and bodybuilders eat. Consequently, one of the first investigations that the students undertake is to keep a record of what they eat. They arrange this information so that the number of calories consumed and the percentages of fat, proteins, and carbohydrates in their diet are clearly displayed. A food diary is kept for at least three weeks by every student.

While the students are keeping their own nutritional diary, they are asked to inquire about the dietary needs and recommendations for young people and adults. The students use the school and city library to gather this information. They also ask people in the community for information regarding the topic. Some of the students interview nurses, dietitians, physical therapists, coaches, bodybuilders, and doctors. The students are required to present the information and its source. Tables and bar graphs are used in the reports.

The results are always startling to the students when they compare the nutritional balance in their diet with what professionals recommend. The students eat a great deal more fat than is recommended; some students' diets consist of approximately 60% fat. These young people find it a bit

unsettling to learn that their diets are so high in fat, especially when the recommended intake is around 35%. Many of the boys in the class are shocked to learn about the diets of bodybuilders who consume many calories. A large percentage of calories are from protein, however, and only a relatively small percentage from fat and very little sugar. These activities lead many of the students to reconsider what they are eating and change their eating habits. As a result of these discussions, many of the food diaries of the students from this point on show a different pattern of eating than at the beginning of the unit.

■

In order to contrast the nutrition example where a middle school teacher implements a problem-solving-based curriculum, let us examine a senior high school teacher's instruction where problem solving is used only occasionally. Consider the following example taken from Mr. Morton's high school chemistry class.

■

After a short period of time into the study of water and aqueous solutions, one student brought up the question of the quality of the drinking water in the community. The student made statements to the effect that their tap water was contaminated and that it was unsafe to drink. Students reacted to this assertion, some seeming to agree with it, others thinking it was crazy and simply not true. This situation resulted in a heated debate and challenges that led the class to investigate the quality of the city's drinking water.

Mr. Morton helped the students turn their concerns about the quality of the drinking water into a research question: Is the city's water supply safe to drink? With this, students formed research groups to work on the question. Mr. Morton asked each group to design an investigation that they could carry out to answer the question. He wanted students to identify as many sources as possible from which to gather data regarding water quality. The students proved quite ingenious in this aspect of their inquiry. Some thought of going to the Water Department to find out how they analyze water to determine its purity. Some suggested that they take samples of their water and test it in the schools' chemistry laboratory. One group thought of obtaining information from local environmental activists who have made claims that industry is contaminating the drinking water. Someone brought up the idea of looking into the city's health records for any problems that might be related to contamination of the drinking water. During the water quality investigation, which was conducted mainly after school, the students continued to study the textbook unit on water and aqueous solutions presented in the textbook.

When the students completed their investigations about the city water, they were given class time to present their findings and conclusions. As a result of the investigation, the students seemed convinced that the water was safe to drink. Although they found that the water was not pure and contained many contaminants, the percentage was small and did not seem to affect the health of the public. One group did find a contamination problem that occurred several years ago in a rural area where families were drinking from well water that had been contaminated by fecal matter. In all, the students became excited about their findings and admitted that they learned a great deal more about the chemistry of water as a result of this problem-solving activity.

■

In the two vignettes just presented, examples of real-world problem solving are illustrated. This type of school science problem solving has been shown to enhance student learning, especially among younger students in the elementary and middle grades (Barr, 1994; Helgeson, 1994). In high school chemistry and physics, however, word problem exercises at the end of textbook chapters occupy a great deal of instructional time. These learning activities are also referred to as problem solving. They require mathematics for their solution and many students experience difficulty in working and understanding these exercises. In order to be successful with mathematical word problems, students must possess (a) conceptual knowledge, (b) procedural knowledge, and (c) representational ability (Gabel & Bunce, 1994). This is a complex area of cognition, problem solving, and inquiry that goes beyond the scope of this chapter.

Science Projects

Science projects are learning activities that require many hours of student involvement. They take place over many weeks and even months. Some science projects reflect "true" inquiry whereby students identify a topic to study, propose questions to be answered, designate procedures for carrying out a project, gather information and data, present the results, and form the conclusions. These projects entail a great deal of effort on the part of students, as well as guidance from teachers and parents. A science project can be undertaken individually, by a pair of students, by a group of students, or by an entire class. Science projects should be a common component of all science courses, whether or not they are tied to a science fair competition.

In many schools students are encouraged to complete a project for a science fair. These are big events for science teachers, students, parents, and members of the community. Science fairs stimulate enormous interest in science. They provide students with incentives to study problems in depth and to communicate their findings. In addition, they give students an opportunity to pursue investigations that they would not ordinarily be able to carry out during regular science class periods, because of limitations on equipment, space, and time. In addition to identifying the gifted science students, these events encourage all students to get involved in inquiry and to design products. Science fairs not only display the talents and interests of students, but they also reveal the orientation of a school's science program, the type of science teaching that is occurring, and the type of students in the school.

Science fair projects can take on many forms. The following are descriptions of activities that make good science projects:

1. **Hobby or pet show-and-tell:** A display of items of special interest to the student, such as arrowheads; seashells; photographs of cats, dogs, or horses; bee hives, and so on

2. **Display of a natural phenomenon:** Pictures and descriptions of lightning, a volcano, an earthquake, a hurricane, a tornado, and so on

3. **Model:** A three-dimensional model of a volcano, a brain, a heart, an internal combustion engine, a rocket, a space station, a 35 mm camera, the solar system, and so on

4. **Report and poster:** Photographs and pictures of objects with explanations and information taken from literature sources on such topics as nuclear power, HIV infection, movement of the earth's continental plates, how a computer works, living in space, a rain forest habitat, a biome, and so on

5. **Laboratory exercise:** The presentation of a laboratory exercise that illustrates a concept, principle, or law such as the frequencies of a pendulum, osmosis, crushing metal cans with air pressure, chemical and physical properties of acids and bases, behavior of light rays, determination of electrical current and resistance, and so on

6. **Observational study:** Extensive observations of a situation or phenomenon and reporting the findings, such as bird counting, whale reporting, weather conditions and patterns, driving behavior and accidents at a busy intersection, changes in ozone levels and pollution counts in an urban area, and so on

7. **Experimental study:** Manipulating a situation and determining the results of the intervention, such as the effects of x-rays on plant growth, temperature on food spoiling, moisture on the amount of corrosion, and so on

There are many types of science projects that students can complete, but not all students are capable of carrying out all of these projects. Some projects require much less imagination, intellectual ability, and adult guidance. When grading these projects for a course grade or judging them in a fair competition, it is best to form separate project categories, because they cannot be evaluated together. One cannot judge a model with the same criteria used to judge an experimental study. This should be evident from the following categories and points that are often used to judge experimental science projects:

- Creativity (20)
- Investigative procedure (30)
- Understanding of the topic (20)
- Quality of the display (15)
- Oral presentation (15)

Although experimental projects are a good way to promote inquiry, discretion must be used in determining what each student can accomplish, considering the resources that are available and the assistance from adults. Many at-risk students come from one-parent families with very low incomes. Generally, these students do not have the resources available to compete with students whose parents are professionals.

GROUPING AND COOPERATIVE LEARNING

Placing students in groups to work on a problem or to conduct an investigation is a recommended practice that is supported by research findings and by observing effective science teachers. The dynamics of group work can stimulate and sustain inquiry in many situations better than individual work. Not only can group work enhance student problem-solving ability, but it can improve con-

cept development (Lumpe, 1995). These results can be explained, in part, by the effects of cognitive conflict that student-to-student discussion brings about. According to Piaget, interactions that cause disequilibrium stimulate modification of knowledge in order for the learner to reestablish equilibrium. This increased learning can also be explained, in part, by the assistance that peers give to each other when working on a common task. Information and insights that are shared among students are essential for learning, according to Vygotsky's view of cognition.

Effective science teachers often group students and assign them tasks in order to facilitate inquiry in the science classroom. They organize academic work, because this approach seems to increase student involvement in the learning environment. When students have a specific task to carry out, they seem to have more direction and interest in their own learning. Grouping and role techniques have also been found to be a useful management strategy, because the teacher's role changes from a dispenser of information to a manager of student-directed learning where students tend to be more productive with fewer behavioral problems.

Grouping and assigning roles facilitate cooperative learning and hold the potential to result in important learning outcomes. For example, permitting students to work in groups to solve problems can promote scientific inquiry and develop in students a feeling for "doing" science. Cooperative learning can improve achievement and mastery of content (Slavin, 1989/1990). This approach can also develop team-building and a positive classroom environment (Kagan, 1989/1990). Cooperative learning, as its name implies, gets students to work together, eliminating some of the competitiveness and isolation that can exist in most academic environments.

Some of the critical elements of cooperative learning have been summarized by Watson (1992). He points out that cooperative groups have from two to seven students working together. The students can either be assigned different tasks or each student can study the same body of information. Groups are generally heterogeneous with respect to academic ability, sex, and racial background. Watson advises that incentives are necessary so that individuals and groups of students are rewarded for success. This reinforces learning and cooperation. However, students must be accountable for their personal achievements and contribute to the group.

Experienced teachers know well that it is easy for some students to defeat the cooperative work process, and teachers who are just beginning to use this strategy should be on guard against this occurrence. Solomon and Globerson (1989) tell us that free riders allow others to do the work. Some high-ability students do not want to contribute because they feel others are not doing their share. In other instances, students with high social status take control of the group. Then other students decide to do the least amount of work necessary to complete the task.

Cooperative instruction can take many forms with no set number of steps to follow. Nevertheless, the following steps are discussed to highlight important aspects of this strategy.

STEP 1   Organize students into groups, using criteria to make decisions regarding this process. Determine the desired cognitive and affective outcomes for the investigation to be undertaken, then place students into groups accordingly. For example, if you wish to assign tasks to individual students, identify students in each group who can carry out the task and who also work well together with others in the group.

STEP 2   Identify ideas or topics that will motivate student inquiry. Some science teachers provide a preliminary list of ideas for their students that relates to the course or unit under study, focusing their thinking process. However, this approach should encourage brainstorming in order to identify additional ideas for student investigation. Problem solving can focus upon many ideas such as science concepts or principles, science topics, STS issues and problems, products and services, and technological devices. Figure 5.4 lists some specific topics for consideration.

STEP 3   Ask each group to provide a preliminary outline of their project or study. This step immediately places students on a productive path. When you examine the outline, provide suggestions and guidance. Be sure each student in the group knows exactly what to do.

STEP 4   Monitor the investigations. You should have a good idea where each group is while the investigations are carried out. Some inquiries and projects will be conducted during class time, making them easy to monitor. Other investigations will take place after school and on weekends. For this type of work, take some time during class to ask for information to determine how groups as well as individuals are progressing.

STEP 5   Help students to prepare their final reports so that they do well and feel good about their work. Help students form an outline for these reports and designate who will do each part of the write-up. The report is an opportunity for students to demonstrate their science process skill reasoning through the questions they attempt to answer, the inferences and hypotheses they form, and tables and graphs they construct to communicate their findings. This phase of the work is ideal for helping students represent knowledge, visualize models, give explanations, and demonstrate understanding.

FIGURE 5.4   Examples of titles for science fair projects or long-term science investigations

The Effects of Electricity on Seed Germination
Electromagnetic Radiation and Bacterial Growth
The Study of Oral Bacteria
Does Music Affect Memory?
Fluoride in Your Water
How Does Food Spoil?
Antioxidants and Your Health
Pheromones and Ant Behavior
How Much Bacteria is on Your Kitchen Dishrag?
The Association between Alzheimer's Disease and Aluminum
Do We Need Food Additives?
Bugs That Eat Oil
Aerodynamics and Automobile Design
Which Flashlight Batteries Last the Longest?
Light and Photography
What Variables Contribute to the Strength of an Electromagnet?
What Does UV Radiation Do to Organic and Inorganic Materials?
Determining the Viscosity of Lubricants
How Does Acid Rain Affect the Growth of Plants?
Effects of Waves on Beaches

STEP 6 Assist each group to identify several, if not all, students to take part in presenting their report. This aspect of cooperative group work develops presentation skills and confidence in speaking before others. Try to avoid the same students making all of the presentations.

STEP 7 Evaluate the investigations and projects. This often takes the form of assigning points to groups and individual students and entering them into the grade book. Generally, students put a great deal of effort into the activities so they should be rewarded accordingly.

To illustrate the cooperative group role assignment approach, consider the investigation Mrs. Cox proposed to her sixth-grade students to involve them in an investigation about a consumer product.

■

Mrs. Cox posed this question to the class:

Here are five brands of paper towels I purchased in a supermarket. Which of the brands is the best?

She then divided the class into five groups of four students each. Mrs. Cox asked each group to brainstorm the question and come up with a list of characteristics that they would use to determine the quality of paper towels. She then asked each group to identify two characteristics they wanted to test to determine quality. The characteristics identified included softness, tensile strength, water absorption, and absorption of grease and oil. Mrs. Cox gave the following directions to one of the groups and similar directions but different assignments to the others:

Roger, organize the research project and be sure that everyone does his or her job.

Cindy, write up the report of the investigation and assign each person in your group a part in making the presentation to the class.

Barbara, gather the brands of paper towels to be tested and help Brian investigate the criteria established to determine the quality of paper towels.

Brian, work with Barbara to test the criteria used to determine paper towel quality. Gather materials necessary to the investigation. Clean up after the task has been completed.

The students obtained samples of the five brands of paper towels to test. They measured the absorp-

tion potential of the paper towels by rolling up a sample of each type and placing it into a beaker containing 100 milliliters of water. Each sample was treated in the same way. Students allowed their paper samples to absorb water for a 4-second interval. The amount of water absorbed by each sample was determined by finding the difference between the amount of water in the beaker before the towel was immersed and after it was removed (Table 5.3).

Mrs. Cox used this problem and others that center around the claims made in advertisements and commercials to improve her students' critical-thinking and problem-solving skills. She found that this approach prompted many students to feel and think like scientists. When she used commercials and advertisements as the focus of the investigations, the students seemed motivated and interested in their work. Of course, after the students felt comfortable with the group investigative approach, there was much more stress on specific course content in subsequent inquiry sessions.

■

Many years ago Seymour and Padberg (1975) emphasized the positive effects of group work in the science classroom in their research on the role approach. Their findings support those of other researchers who conclude that this approach improves communications, increases insight into scientific phenomena, develops cooperation and responsibility, and improves problem solving and task completion.

The Inquiry Role Approach (IRA) is a technique developed for secondary school biology courses at the Mid-Continental Regional Educational Laboratory in the early 1970s. It stresses inquiry in the laboratory by assigning students to specific roles. Biology content, scientific attitude, and inquiry skills are developed through group problem solving (Seymour, Padberg, Bingman, & Koutnik, 1974).

The IRA technique organizes students into teams of four. Each student is given one of the following roles:

TABLE 5.3 Paper Towel Absorption Test

Brand	Amount of water absorbed in mL			
	Trial 1	Trial 2	Trial 3	Mean
A	10.0	14.5	13.3	12.6
B	42.5	44.6	50.2	45.8
C	65.9	60.8	58.0	61.6
D	20.2	31.5	26.8	26.2
E	44.5	48.7	45.4	46.2

coordinator, technical advisor, data recorder, and process evaluator. Students change roles as they work on different investigations. In this manner they practice and acquire a variety of group problem-solving skills. The IRA approach begins with a great deal of structure and teacher direction and moves toward more student-directed activities during the course, with the teacher playing more of an advisory role (General Learning Corporation, 1974).

The Research Team Approach to Learning (ReTAL) is another group-role approach that has been used successfully with elementary, junior high, senior high, and college students. According to its developer, Bette Del-Giorno (DelGiorno & Tissair, 1970), ReTAL places emphasis on team learning and stresses an open-ended approach to science instruction. This technique is structured to fit into existing courses, extending science content and processes beyond a given textbook and traditional classroom experiences.

ReTAL consists of a four-phase process. The technique provides another method of facilitating inquiry through group procedures (DelGiorno, 1969). In addition, this is a deductive approach to inquiry that many science teachers may feel comfortable using. The phases of this technique are as follows:

1. **Lecture phase or the deductive process.** This is the telling phase where the teacher introduces a given science topic to the whole class. Key terms, concepts, and relationships are presented to the students.

2. **Independent study phase or the confrontation process.** The students are urged to find resource people, books, and films to extend their knowledge of the topic under investigation. Use of the library, field trips, brainstorming sessions, and consultation with experts in the field are stressed.

3. **Experimental phase or the inductive process.** Students design and conduct investigations or create models and products. In general, they try out their ideas.

4. **Discussion phase or the evaluation process.** At this point, individual teams meet to discuss their work and to determine if further research is needed for their topic. When the team determines that their investigation is complete, they write a research report. The reports can be given to the entire class in a final discussion of the topic(s) in a large group setting.

Science teachers can organize students in many ways to engage them in learning science. This should become a common practice in both the middle and senior high schools, because group and inquiry role activities can develop many valuable skills and attitudes associated with the scientific enterprise. Further, these strategies can complement other methods used to improve the acquisition of content knowledge.

CONCERNS ASSOCIATED WITH INQUIRY-BASED SCIENCE INSTRUCTION

In order for science teachers to make the transition from a traditional mode of instruction to an inquiry-based mode, they must better understand inquiry and its relationship to science teaching. This understanding will permit them to construct a personal rationale to justify the inquiry approach to themselves, to other science teachers in their school building, and to the parents of their students. An understanding of inquiry—its conception and strategies—is also necessary so that inquiry-based science can be adapted to the enormous differences among students and schools. The challenge that faces science teachers is to understand the meaning of inquiry, scientific inquiry, teaching science **by** inquiry, and teaching science **as** inquiry.

Science education researchers have provided us with valuable insights regarding the place of inquiry in science teaching. Welch, Klopfer, Aikenhead, and Robinson (1981, p. 46) point out:

> Our stance is that all students should not be expected to attain competence in all inquiry-related outcomes, which science educators (including ourselves) have advocated in the past. For some students and in some school environments it may not be appropriate to expect any inquiry-related outcomes at all.

Scientific thinking is not subscribed to by everyone in our society. Many people want answers and information given to them; they do not want to put forth the effort it takes to question, reason, find out, or reflect. Many in our society are concrete thinkers who reason in black-and-white and want certainty in their world view (Dutch, 1996). For these and many other reasons, implementing an inquiry-based science program offers an enormous challenge.

Some science teachers claim that they experience problems implementing the inquiry approach. Although they believe inquiry is important, they cite many obstacles in their attempts to use this form of instruction in the classroom. Some claim that this method is **too time-consuming** and that it does not permit them to cover the required amount of subject matter. Furthermore, these teachers believe that they **must teach many terms**

and definitions so that students will be successful on tests prepared by their science department, school district, or state education agency. Assessment is an important aspect of schooling, and it places a great deal of pressure on science teachers to teach toward the test, thus de-emphasizing inquiry.

Some **parents complain** when science teachers attempt to use inquiry strategies and science programs that stress investigation, thinking, and discovery, especially where hands-on instructional materials are used in place of textbook-based courses. These parents want textbooks to be used and for their children to be drilled on the vocabulary words that relate to the topic under study. They also want an assigned **textbook** that their children can refer to and take home to study. Many parents want their children to go to college and recognize only direct instruction of subject matter content as the most appropriate form of instruction for this preparation.

Materials and equipment are another aspect of teaching science through inquiry that can be problematic (Stake & Easley, 1978). Teachers who engage students in firsthand investigation must acquire and maintain materials. Funds are needed to buy equipment, which is often relatively expensive when purchased from science supply companies. Expendable materials are also needed throughout the school year. Middle school science programs often suffer from the lack of equipment and expendable materials for conducting a variety of science activities. Furthermore, the **facilities** in many middle and junior high schools are not designed for laboratory activities to be carried out in all rooms where science is scheduled.

Some science teachers have found that their attempts to use inquiry methods have not been successful because of **student confusion.** They report that many students seem to expect intended outcomes when they are investigating an idea. Their hands may be on materials, but their minds are not focusing on what it is they are to be discovering. The opportunity to explore and find out in the traditional classroom environment can also lead to **discipline problems,** because only the brightest students seem capable of handling investigative activities. Exploration and openness tend to remove control of the classroom from the teacher, allowing active and unruly students to become disruptive (Helgeson, Blosser, & Howe, 1977).

Throughout the years it has become obvious that many school systems are not organized to conduct programs that foster curiosity, discovery, and critical thinking. These systems often pay lip service to promoting creativity and learning how to learn, but they do not support their claims with an instructional program that fulfills these ideals. Their curricula are impoverished, and teaching for understanding is practically nonexistent. Many of the science teachers in these schools have little understanding of inquiry methods and how to use them. They are **inadequately trained** to teach science that promotes discovery and critical thinking. Some science teachers have not participated in scientific research, and the science courses they took in college did not model scientific inquiry.

Learning psychologists have identified at least two inherent problems with the discovery process that must be considered by those who desire to promote inquiry teaching. These problems center around **errors in learning** and **time spent on instruction** (Shulman & Keislar, 1968). Students who are left to discover ideas for themselves often make mistakes in their thinking (Glaser, 1968). They go up blind alleys in their search for answers to questions. Glaser cautioned educators about situations that involve too much exploration and error in learning. He emphasized that the teacher should maintain control over the learning environment to reduce errors and minimize student frustration, both of which can interfere with learning. Constructivistic and conceptual change approaches that are recommended by cognitive psychologists and science educators support this view (see Chapter 4). These professionals emphasize that instruction must begin with what students know by providing them with opportunities to discuss what they believe to be true about a given situation, before students attempt to test out their ideas. Carefully prepared questions can guide student thinking. The introduction of terms at appropriate places in the instructional process can facilitate concept development. Therefore, teaching inquiry-based science should be a guided approach to discovery rather than an unstructured search for answers (Wittrock, 1968). Furthermore, students should not be expected to discover all learning outcomes in the science courses they take, because certain facts and concepts can be given to them at the proper time in the instructional process (Gagné, 1968). Also, many of the major ideas of science (laws and theories) cannot be discovered by students; they are constructions of the mind, requiring considerable assistance from others who possess their understanding.

Today, science education continues to place a high value on inquiry-based science programs. Inquiry is no less important as a major theme in teaching science than it is as a way of knowing about the world in the scientific community. Further, there is evidence to support the efficacy of the new science programs of the 1960s and 1970s, which were inquiry-based. These programs were more effective in enhancing student performance than traditional textbook-based programs, namely in the areas of achievement, process skills, problem solving, and attitudes (Shymansky, Hedges, & Woodworth, 1990). For these reasons, science teachers must become knowledgeable about inquiry, scientific inquiry, teaching science by inquiry, and teaching science as inquiry.

FIGURE 5.5 This concept map suggests one set of relationships for inquiry in science teaching.

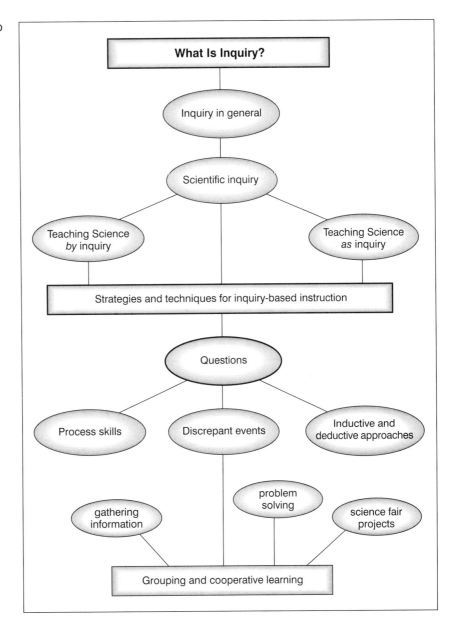

■

ASSESSING AND REVIEWING

1. Demonstrate your understanding of inquiry and science teaching by **explaining** the following concepts:

   a. inquiry in general
   b. scientific inquiry
   c. teaching science by inquiry
   d. teaching science as inquiry
   e. science process skills
   f. discrepant events
   g. inductive instruction

   h. deductive instruction
   i. gathering information
   j. problem solving
   k. science fair projects

2. Examine the concept map in Figure 5.5 that presents one way of illustrating relationships between many concepts associated with inquiry and science teaching. Reconstruct this visual to present your conception of how inquiry is related to school science.

3. Reflect upon the science and nonscience courses that you have taken, the science and education courses in which you are presently enrolled, and the science courses that you may be observing in the public schools. Indicate which of these courses were or are inquiry-based and which are not. Further, explain the type of instructional strategies that were used and whether the courses taught or teach science by inquiry and science as inquiry.

4. Conduct an analysis of laboratory exercises and other science instructional materials in order to determine the type of inquiry strategies emphasized and the extent to which they engage students in this method.

5. Organize a file of instructional activities that can be used to teach science by and as inquiry in your teaching area (i. e., life science, earth science, physics). These activities can be found in science textbooks, paperback books, and laboratory manuals. Some of the best inquiry-oriented activities will come to mind, however, when you reflect upon what takes place in your everyday surroundings.

6. Obtain for your own professional library textbooks, paperback books, magazines, journals, manuals, and so on that can provide ideas for inquiry sessions. These materials are good sources for discrepant events, problem solving, and inductive activities.

7. Plan and teach an inquiry lesson to your peers or to middle school or senior high school students that emphasizes one or more ways to initiate and carry out inquiry instruction: process skills, discrepant events, inductive activities, deductive activities, and problem solving. Participate in the critique and feedback of this teaching session with others.

8. Develop an inquiry activity that uses grouping, role assignments, and cooperative learning. Try out your activity with peers or middle or high school students to determine the effectiveness of this technique.

RESOURCES TO EXAMINE

Teaching Science through Inquiry. March 1993. David Haury. ERIC Clearinghouse for Science, Mathematics, and Environmental Education, EDO-SE-93-4. 1929 Kenny Road, Columbus, OH 43210-1080.

This compact, two-page publication contains a great deal of useful information about inquiry—what it is and its educational outcomes over the past several decades. It includes an excellent reference list of relevant literature on the topic. Haury has given science teachers and science educators a valuable summary of inquiry-based science teaching with which they should be conversant.

Introductory Science Skills. 1993. By Dorothy Gabel. Prospect Heights, IL: Waveland Press.

This is a 423-page book that addresses many of the science process skills, such as observing, classifying, measuring, inferring, predicting, controlling variables, testing hypotheses, graphing, using numbers, problem solving, and using models and theories. The workbook format can help teachers as well as their students to better understand inquiry and how to use skills to promote inquiry-based science teaching.

The Current NSTA Catalog for Membership and Publications. National Science Teachers Association. 1840 Wilson Boulevard, Arlington, VA 22201-3000. Phone (800)722-NSTA. http//www.nsta.org.

This catalog contains hundreds of booklets, teaching guides, and rescues for science teaching in grades K–12. These materials address the major science disciplines, providing background information as well as inquiry-oriented activities. All science teachers should possess this publication and be a member of the National Science Teachers Association.

The Complete Handbook of Science Fair Projects. 1991. By Julianne B. Bochinski. New York: Wiley Science Editions/John Wiley & Sons.

This paperback book contains fifty award-winning projects from actual fairs. It describes in detail the projects, plus it has hundreds of other suggested topics for students to investigate. The explanations and illustrations make this a valuable and easy-to-follow resource for science teachers or their students to use.

■
REFERENCES

American Association for the Advancement of Science. (1990). *Science for all Americans*. New York: Oxford University Press.

Barr, B. B. (1994). Research on problem solving: Elementary school. In D. L. Gabel (Ed.), *Handbook of research on science teaching and learning* (pp. 237–247). Upper Saddle River, NJ: Merrill/Prentice Hall.

Biological Sciences Curriculum Study. (1978). *Biology teacher's handbook*. New York: John Wiley & Sons.

Biological Sciences Curriculum Study. (1990). *Science for life and living: Integrating science, technology, and health, Grades K–6*. Dubuque, IA: Kendall/Hunt.

Biological Sciences Curriculum Study & Social Science Education Consortium. (1992). *Teaching about the history and nature of science and technology: A curriculum framework*. Colorado Springs: The Colorado College.

Bruner, J. (1961). The act of discovery. *Harvard Educational Review, 31*(1), 21.

DeBoer, G. E. (1991). *A history of ideas in science education*. New York: Teachers College, Columbia University.

DelGiorno, B. J. (1969). *The research team approach (ReTAL): A structure for openness*. Fairfield, CT: Fairfield Public Schools.

DelGiorno, B. J., & Tissair, M. E. (1970, December). The research team approach to learning (ReTAL), part II. *School Science and Mathematics, 70*, 833.

Dewey, J. (1938). *Experience and education*. New York: Macmillan.

Dutch, S. I. (1996). The standard model for reform in science education does not work. *Journal of Geoscience Education, 44*, 245–250.

Fuller, R. G. (1980). *Piagetian problems in higher education*. Lincoln: ADAPT, University of Nebraska.

Gabel, D. L., & Bunce, D. M. (1994). Research on problem solving chemistry. In D. L. Gabel (Ed.), *Handbook of research on science teaching and learning* (pp. 301–326). Upper Saddle River, NJ: Merrill/Prentice Hall.

Gagné, R. (1968). Varieties of learning and the concept of discovery. In L. S. Shulman & E. S. Keislar (Eds.), *Learning by discovery: A critical approach* (pp. 135–150). Chicago: Rand McNally.

General Learning Corporation. (1974). *Teachers' guide: Inquiry role approach*. Morristown, NJ: Silver Burdett.

Glaser, R. (1968). Variables in discovery learning. In L. S. Shulman & E. S. Keislar (Eds.), *Learning by discovery: A critical appraisal* (pp. 13–26). Chicago: Rand McNally.

Helgeson, S. L. (1989). Problem solving in middle school science. In D. Gabel (Ed.), *What research says to the science teacher: Vol. 5. Problem solving* (pp. 13–34). Washington, DC: National Science Teachers Association.

Helgeson, S. L. (1994). Research on problem solving in middle school. In D. L. Gabel (Ed.), *Handbook of research on science teaching and learning* (pp. 248–268). Upper Saddle River, NJ: Merrill/Prentice Hall.

Helgeson, S. L., Blosser, P. E., & Howe, R. W. (1977). *The status of pre-college science, mathematics, and social science education, 1955–1975: Vol. 1. Science education*. Columbus: Ohio State University, Center for Science and Mathematics Education.

Herman, G. D., & Hincksman, N. G. (1978). Inductive versus deductive approaches in teaching a lesson in chemistry. *Journal of Research in Science Teaching, 15*, 37.

Herron, M. D. (1971). The nature of scientific enquiry. *School Review, 79*, 171–212.

Kagan, S. (1989/1990). The structural approach to cooperative learning. *Educational Leadership, 47*(4), 12–16.

Kessen, W. (1964). Statement of purposes and objectives of science education in the elementary school. *Journal of Research in Science Teaching, 2*, 4–6.

Koran, J. J., Koran, M. L., & Baker, S. (1980). Differential response cueing and feedback in the acquisition of an inductively presented biological concept. *Journal of Research in Science Teaching, 17*, 167.

Lawson, A. E., Abraham, M. R., & Renner, J. W. (1989). *A theory of instruction: Using the learning cycle to teach science concepts and thinking skills*. NARST Monograph, Number One. National Association for Research in Science Teaching.

Lawson, A. E., & Wollman, W. W. (1975). Physics problems and the process of self-regulation. *The Physics Teacher, 13*, 470.

Lumpe, A. T. (1995). Peer interaction in science concept development and problem solving. *School Science and Mathematics, 96*, 302–309.

Martin, M. (1985). *Concepts of science education*. New York: University Press of America.

Matthews, M. R. (1994). *Science teaching: The role of history and philosophy of science*. New York: Routledge.

National Research Council. (1996). *National science education standards*. Washington, DC: National Academy Press.

Piaget, J. (1971). *Biology and knowledge*. Chicago: University of Chicago Press.

Rakow, S. J. (1986). *Teaching science as inquiry*. Bloomington, IN: Phi Delta Kappa, Fastback 246.

Renner, J. W., Abraham, M. R., & Birne, H. H. (1985). The importance of the form of student acquisition of data in physics learning cycles. *Journal of Research in Science Teaching, 22*, 303-325.

Renner, J. W., Cate, J. M., Grzybowski, E. B., Atkinson, L. J., Surber, C., & Marek, E. A. (1985). *Investigation in natural science: Biology teacher's guide.* Norman: Science Education Center, College of Education, University of Oklahoma.

Rutherford, F. J. (1964). The role of inquiry in science teaching. *Journal of Research in Science Teaching, 2,* 80–84.

Schwab, J. (1962). The teaching of science as enquiry. In J. Schwab & P. Brandwein (Eds.), *The teaching of science.* Cambridge: Harvard University Press.

Science Curriculum Improvement Study. (1974). *Science Curriculum Improvement Study (SCIS): Teacher's handbook.* Berkeley: University of California at Berkeley, Lawrence Hall of Science.

Seymour, L. A., & Padberg, L. (1975). The relative effectiveness of small group and individual settings in a simulated problem solving game. *Science Education, 59,* 297.

Seymour, L. A., Padberg, L. F., Bingman, R. M., & Koutnik, P. G. (1974). A successful inquiry methodology. *The American Biology Teacher, 36,* 349.

Shulman, L. S., & Keislar, E. S. (Eds.). (1968). *Learning by discovery: A critical appraisal.* Chicago: Rand McNally.

Shymansky, J. A., Hedges, L. V., & Woodworth, G. (1990). A reassessment of the effects of inquiry-based science curricula of the 60s on student performance. *Journal of Research in Science Teaching, 27,* 127–144.

Slavin, R. E. (1989/1990). Research on cooperative learning: Consensus and controversy. *Educational Leadership, 47*(4), 52-54.

Solomon, G., & Globerson, T. (1989). When teams do not function the way they ought to. *International Journal of Educational Research, 13,* 89–99.

Stake, R. E., & Easley, J. A. 1978. *Case studies in science education,* Urbana: University of Illinois Center for Instructional Research and Curriculum Evaluation.

Suchman, R. (1966). *Developing inquiry.* Chicago: Science Research Associates.

Watson, S. B. (1992). The essential elements of cooperative learning. *The American Biology Teacher, 54,* 84–86.

Watts, M. (1991). *The science of problem solving.* Portsmouth, NH: Heinemann Educational Books.

Welch, W. W., Klopfer, L. E., Aikenhead, G. S., & Robinson, J. T. (1981). The role of inquiry in science education: Analysis and recommendations. *Science Education, 65,* 33–50.

Wittrock, M. C. (1968). The learning by discovery hypothesis. In L. S. Shulman & E. S. Keislar (Eds.), *Learning by discovery: A critical appraisal* (pp. 33–76). Chicago: Rand McNally.

CHAPTER 6

LECTURE, DISCUSSION, AND DEMONSTRATION

Small group discussions led by students offer opportunities to exchange ideas, ask questions, and clarify misunderstandings.

Lecture, discussion, and demonstration are methods of instruction that play an important role in middle and secondary science classrooms. They tend to be teacher centered and make use of numerous instructional techniques, the most important of which is questioning. Constructivist theory suggests that the meaning that students construct from science lectures, discussions, and demonstrations is affected by their prior knowledge and experiences and their interactions with other students and instructional materials in addition to the teacher. It also suggests that unanticipated learning is likely if the students' perceptions of the purpose of the lesson do not coincide with those of the teacher. It is clear that the effectiveness of each method depends on the teacher's ability to use it appropriately and to relate it to the overall science instructional program and the needs of students.

OBJECTIVES

This chapter is designed to help the reader meet the following objectives:

- Determine when the lecture method should be used in science instruction and how to prepare for and present an effective lecture.
- Distinguish three types of discussion sessions and identify procedures that can be used to conduct meaningful discussions in science classes.
- Reflect upon the difficulties in asking oral questions and identify ways to overcome them.
- Describe the functions of science demonstrations and factors to consider when planning and presenting effective demonstrations.

The Lecture Method

The lecture method of teaching is commonly used in middle school and secondary school science classes. It is a traditional teacher-centered method that involves the didactic presentation of ideas and information (McLeish, 1976; Kindsvatter, Wilen, & Ishler, 1996). When using this method, a teacher must cope with its limitations and use its strengths to best advantage.

The lecture method has certain strengths that make it useful for science instruction. A large amount of material can be covered in a short period of time using the lecture method. It is an effective means for introducing a unit, clarifying understandings, and defining science terms (Flowerdew, 1992; Kyle, 1972; Thompson, 1974). The lecture is an efficient way to convey information to students who have difficulty reading textbooks and do not read assigned text materials. It is also an inexpensive method of instruction, since many students can be taught by a lecturer using few materials and resources (McLeish, 1976). In general, the lecture method is as effective as other instructional methods, particularly when the purpose is immediate cognitive gains (Gage & Berliner, 1992).

According to Gage and Berliner (1992, p. 390), it is appropriate to use the lecture method when:

- The basic purpose is to disseminate information.
- The material is not available elsewhere.
- The material must be organized and presented in a particular way for a specific group.
- It is necessary to arouse interest in the subject.
- Students need to remember the information for only a short time.
- It is necessary to provide an introduction to an area or directions for a learning task that is going to be taught through some other teaching method.

The effectiveness of the lecture method is based on using students' existing knowledge and presenting information in a logical manner to help them construct new understandings (Eggen & Kauchak, 1996). The lecture may also utilize questions to further facilitate the construction of new understandings by students. Students have a better chance of constructing new understandings from a lecture when there is a good match between their developmental level and the cognitive complexity of the science content under study.

Despite its usefulness, the lecture has been compared with other more "innovative" forms of science instruction and found to be lacking. It is associated with rote learning, bored and inattentive students, and authoritative and overly structured teaching. But Ausubel (1961, p. 16) believed that the weaknesses attributed to the lecture method are not due to the method itself but to the abuse of the method by teachers who use it. All too often the lecture is used inappropriately as a substitute for other forms of instruction. Teachers who substitute the lecture for laboratory work, for example, are denying students the opportunity to learn the methods of science and preventing them from understanding the ways scientists go about their work. Additionally, adolescents and preadolescents are restless by nature, preoccupied with immediate problems, and often handicapped by limited vocabulary and background of experience. They also have short attention spans. The teacher must consider that lectures to such an audience will be dull and meaningless unless these factors are taken into consideration during planning.

Lecture Forms

Kindsvatter and colleagues (1996) identify two types of lecture: the formal lecture and interactive lecture. The one-way presentation of information by the teacher is the centerpiece of both forms. The difference between the two is the amount of student involvement in the presentation.

Formal lecture.   The formal lecture is essentially a teacher monologue. It has much in common with a Sunday sermon. The focus of the formal science lecture like the Sunday sermon is on the speaker, be it the teacher or preacher, and his or her message. There is little audience involvement. Nothing interrupts the preacher's sermon, except perhaps the occasional chuckle or "Amen." Likewise, few, if any, questions are asked by students during a formal lecture. Jay Leno, host of *The Tonight Show*, delivers a formal lecture of sorts at the beginning of each evening's show. You may wish to think about yourself as the Jay Leno of your classroom when presenting a formal lecture. In saying this, we don't mean that science teachers should tell jokes and poke fun at people during their formal lectures. There is much to be learned, however, about how to present a formal lecture by watching Leno and other performers who are successful at delivering monologues to a large audience. The lecturer's physical movement, nonverbal behaviors, voice, pacing, and ability to present material in a well-organized and persuasive manner influence the effectiveness of the presentation (Kindsvatter et al., 1996).

The length of time spent lecturing is largely determined by the audience's attention span. In the case of *The Tonight Show*, the optimal length of Leno's monologue has been determined based on careful audience and marketing research. You will need to determine the optimal length for your lectures by researching your students. As a rule of thumb, a lecture of fifteen to twenty minutes is appropriate for most high school students, whereas ten minutes of lecture is about all that middle school students can handle. Formal lectures of up to thirty minutes may work for advanced-placement students. Fidgeting, talking, and other similar behaviors are indeed signals that you have reached the limits of your students' attention span and should bring your formal lecture to a close.

The best use of the formal lecture is in combination with other instructional approaches. In schools that follow a block schedule, a formal lecture is one of three or four instructional approaches that could be used during a ninety-minute block period. A biology teacher might start class with a ten-minute lecture about the laboratory activity on interpreting DNA fingerprints that will be completed that day. Or three biology classes that meet during the same block period could be brought together to listen to a genetic engineer present a twenty-minute lecture about goals of the Human Genome Project and the ethical issues the project raises. The remainder of the class time might be devoted to reading an article about the Human Genome Project and discussing the ethical issues mentioned by the speaker and in the article.

Interactive Lecture.   When science teachers speak of lecture they are more often than not talking about the interactive lecture. The interactive lecture differs from the formal lecture in that it is punctuated by teacher and student questions. As with the formal lecture, student attention span and instructional context must be considered when using the interactive lecture method. The increasingly common TV infomercials are examples of the interactive lecture. The infomercial host presents information about a product to be sold. Questions about the product raised by audience members are central to the infomercial presentation. These questions and their answers provide consumers with information about the product needed to make an informed purchase. Similarly, the interjection of questions encourages students to attend to the topic or issue that is the focus of the interactive lecture. It is hoped that the questions and their accompanying responses provide the arguments and evidence required by students to further develop their science understandings or change their science conceptions. Additionally, student questions and responses to teacher questions provide a check of student understanding.

According to Kindsvatter et al. (1996), the questions asked by the teacher during an interactive lecture are related to the objectives she or he has for the lecture. For example, a physical science teacher in an interactive lecture on the periodic table might ask students to name the three members of the alkali metal group and give their symbols. During an interactive lecture a week later, the teacher might give students information about the properties of lithium (Li) and potassium (K) and ask them to predict the properties of sodium (Na) based on their understanding of Mendeleev's work.

Preparing the Lecture

Lecture preparation involves checking your understanding of the content to be presented, preparing lecture notes to guide your presentation, and organizing the lecture in a logical manner for your audience.

Checking Your Understanding.   It goes without saying that teachers should be comfortable with their content knowledge in order to present a good lecture. However, knowing the content is not enough. Knowing how to teach the science content knowledge is equally important (Gage & Berliner, 1992). This "how to" knowledge, which Shulman (1987) calls pedagogical content knowledge, is reflected in the teacher's ability to explain ideas in more than one way, provide persuasive examples, use helpful metaphors and analogies, and recognize where students will likely have difficulty when studying a science topic for the first time. Pedagogical content knowledge is constructed by teachers as a result of a variety of experiences, including talks with other teachers, reading, science methods courses, and teaching the same content multiple times. Your own science learning experiences provide the foundation for the pedagogical content knowledge that you will use as a novice teacher to help students construct their science understandings.

Preparing Lecture Notes.   Lecture notes can be planned in prose form or they can consist of an outline of the key points that serve as a reminder of what should be covered. Some teachers feel comfortable about delivering a lecture only when they have written the complete lecture in prose form. The prose form provides teachers the security of knowing that all the information is at their fingertips should difficulty arise during the presentation. Other teachers, usually with more experience, prefer a skeleton outline that consists of a title and main headings with key terms and ideas organized under the headings. Still others feel most comfortable with an outline that provides more detail. It may consist of complete sentences of ideas and terms and be organized under specific headings.

A teacher may present a visual representation of the lecture notes to guide students through the lecture and to stimulate notetaking. The visual representation may take the form of information presented on the chalkboard or overhead projector or provided in a handout distributed to students. Research indicates that visual representations do help students follow lectures and can improve student achievement (Hartley, 1976). Research

An effective lecture is organized around a few major ideas and makes use of visual representations.

findings related to notetaking are not so clear-cut. A lecturer's use of visual representations does stimulate more notetaking, but student achievement may or may not be affected. Gage and Berliner (1992) report that notetaking helps students remember the material when the notes are studied in preparation for a test, but notetaking does not aid student comprehension of the material. This suggests that it is important for students to listen carefully to a lecture and that teachers may wish to distribute handouts that highlight important information. If handouts are not provided, then teachers may wish to cue students to the important points of the lecture.

Organizing the Lecture.   A lecture that is organized around a few major ideas or concepts that are presented in a logical sequence has been found to be effective for adolescents and preadolescent students. The effective lecture has an introduction, a main body, summaries within the presentation, and a conclusion. The **introduction** can serve to motivate students to attend to the lecture, and it cues them to what will be presented and emphasized. Announcing to students that this information will be on the test or explaining how the lecture topic is related to their personal lives are ways to heighten motivation. Instructional objectives and questions are often used by teachers to cue students about what to expect in a lecture. The introduction also serves

to help students ready themselves for the information presented during the lecture. Good and Brophy (1994) recommend the use of advance organizers for this purpose. Advance organizers help explain and interrelate the material they precede (Ausubel, 1963, p. 61).

Two types of advance organizers can be used in the lecture introduction. The **expository advance organizer** places the information to be learned into perspective with other information that is conceptually related. For example, for a lecture on the circulation of blood, an expository organizer might include a brief description of other systems in the body such as the lymphatic system and the renal/urinary system. A **comparative organizer** for the same lecture might compare the circulatory system with a hot-water system in a house. The simplicity of a hot-water system provides a concrete analogy for students to begin the study of a similar concept involving the human body.

The **body** of the lecture is characterized by the presentation of content in an orderly fashion, the use of visual aids to enhance the presentation, and the inclusion of questions and nonverbal cues to stimulate student attention (Kindsvatter et al., 1996). Remembering that the processing capabilities of middle/junior high school and high school students are not those of adults, it is best to have a simple plan of organization for a lecture. A complicated sequence can only cause confusion.

The organization for a science lecture may show how a main idea is composed of several subordinate ones, show how ideas or events are related chronologically or through cause and effect, or show the relationship of ideas through a central unifying theory (Gage & Berliner, 1992). Overhead transparencies, slides, graphs, pictures, and models are examples of visual aids that can enhance any lecture. Henson (1988, p. 92) reports that the most effective use of visual aids occurs when the "lesson is not predeveloped but built up in front of the students, who help develop the concepts . . . as the lesson develops." Nonverbal cues such as body posture, facial expressions, eye contact, gestures, and physical distance can help hold student interest and attention and stimulate their mental involvement in the lecture (Kindsvatter et al., 1996). Humor and teacher questioning can achieve these same ends.

Summaries within a formal lecture presentation are brief statements of important ideas. In the interactive lecture, summaries are typically question based. Whether statement- or question-based, lecture summaries are intended to motivate students and establish the relevancy of the material just presented. Questions asked by the teacher and students during an interactive lecture will preclude the possibility of a monologue continuing for long periods of time without a break.

The **conclusion** of the lecture is the place for the teacher to summarize major points and, in the case of the interactive lectures, to ask additional questions. The success of the lecture may be gauged from students' responses to these concluding questions. The emphasis on the important points during the conclusion will help students identify relationships needed to undertake future assignments and to be involved in other activities used during the future. Unfortunately, too many lectures lack conclusions because teachers run out of time while presenting the body of their lectures.

Presenting Successful Lectures

The success of a lecture depends largely upon the collaboration between the lecturer and the audience. The most successful lecture is an interaction in which the lecturer offers information and receives attention, and the audience offers attention and receives information (Clarke, 1987). Lectures that are presented at a slow pace will bore students, whereas those presented at a fast pace will prevent students from understanding the lesson. A moderate pace is recommended to ensure optimal learning.

To ensure a successful lecture, the teacher should use various techniques to make certain that there is a continuous interaction between the teacher and the student audience. The following nine suggestions adapted from Clarke (1987) should be helpful in maintaining student attention.

1. Emphasize important ideas by changing the rate, volume, and pitch of your voice.
2. Emphasize important statements by using pauses that allow time for the audience to respond to questions.
3. Enunciate words clearly.
4. Avoid repetition of words.
5. Avoid using such words or phrases as *um, er, like well, ah, you know, uh-huh,* and *okay.*
6. Maintain eye contact with the audience.
7. Scan the audience to observe reactions.
8. Interject humor and signs of curiosity and interest and other indications of your personality.
9. Keep the flow of visual aids smooth and free from distraction.

■ STOP AND REFLECT! ■

Before going on to the next topic, do the following:

■ Describe how you would prepare for an interactive lecture. How would your preparations be different if you were to deliver a formal lecture?

■ Examine the vignette in Box 6.1, "Decisions, Decisions—Teaching about Sexually Transmitted Diseases," and explain what you believe prompted Ms. Block to choose the interactive lecture method for a lesson to address the first three objectives.

THE DISCUSSION METHOD

The classroom discussion is one of the most powerful strategies that a teacher can use to facilitate cognitive and affective gains in students. It is the ideal instructional method for addressing science topics for which there are many options. The discussion can be used to initiate inquiry sessions, review material previously covered, explain or predict the results of laboratory experiments, solve problems, and allow students to plan for future class activities. A true discussion involves the free expression of viewpoints by the teacher and students about a topic that all are interested in and possess the

BOX 6.1

DECISIONS, DECISIONS—TEACHING ABOUT SEXUALLY TRANSMITTED DISEASES

Ms. Block teaches life science at a large middle school in a rural area. It's Sunday evening and she's looking over the section in her textbook on sexually transmitted diseases. The section will serve as the basis for a week long unit on the topic. After school on Monday, Ms. Block will participate in a cooperative planning meeting with three other life science teachers. These teachers are counting on Ms. Block to bring her ideas regarding the most appropriate teaching methods to address several of the objectives for the unit, which had been agreed upon at an earlier planning meeting. Ms. Block is responsible for the following objectives:

- Identify the ways by which HIV is transmitted.
- Describe ways to reduce the risk of HIV infection.
- Relate the symptoms of AIDS to HIV infection.
- Evaluate the benefits of the care provided AIDS sufferers versus their cost to society.

After looking over the chapter and other instructional materials, Ms. Block developed a plan to share with the other teachers. Before school on the day of the meeting, Ms. Block runs into Mr. Castle, a member of the cooperative planning team, in the hall and they have the following discussion:

CASTLE: Have you given much thought to how we can address those HIV objectives?

BLOCK: I have. If you have a few minutes, I'd like to tell you what I've come up with and get your reaction.

CASTLE: Sure. Go ahead.

BLOCK: Well, there are certainly no suitable demonstrations or lab activities to address the objectives. But I do know of a video that the district owns that would work well to address the first three. If we can get the video, working it into an interactive lecture may be our best bet. I've written some questions that I think will engage the students and help them achieve the objectives. I'll bring them to the meeting this afternoon.

CASTLE: The students will have questions about AIDS and HIV. How can we be sure that they are addressed?

BLOCK: If we go with the video, it could be stopped periodically to give them a chance to ask questions. I have a pretty good idea what questions they will ask based on last year's experience and the video addresses many of them.

CASTLE: Their questions would also allow us to detect their misconceptions about HIV and about the relationship between AIDS and HIV.

BLOCK: Good point.

CASTLE: I'm a little concerned about that last objective since we didn't address it last year. How do you think we should handle having students evaluate the benefits and cost related to AIDS?

BLOCK: That's a tough one. I thought about suggesting that we try either guided discussion or reflective discussion to handle that one. How do you think Ms. Alverez and Mr. Oliver will react to this suggestion?

CASTLE: I think they'll agree with you but will say that the students need more information than is presented in our textbook to really participate in a discussion on the topic.

BLOCK: Oh, there goes the bell. See you this afternoon in Ms. Alverez's room. Thanks for listening.

background knowledge to make contributions. Unfortunately, science teachers use the term discussion when they are engaged in almost any type of verbal interaction with their students. For example, when a teacher says, "We will now discuss the topic of population growth," what she or he may really mean is, "I am going to ask you questions about what you read in your textbook about the topic of population growth."

Discussion Types

Kindsvatter and colleagues (1996) identify two discussion types and one "quasi discussion" type that can be used by science teachers: guided discussion, reflective discussion, and recitation. They apply the characteristics of purpose, structure, interaction pattern, and level of student thinking to distinguish between these different types. Recitation is labeled as quasi discussion because it lacks the element of group conversation that characterizes true discussion.

Recitation.   A recitation has much in common with a TV quiz show (Roby, 1988). During a recitation, the teacher asks a series of questions and the students provide the answers. The questions are based on what students have read in their textbook or what has been presented by the teacher during class. The interaction pattern of a recitation is teacher question—student answer—teacher reaction (Wilen, 1990). The purpose of a recitation is for the teacher to determine whether students have learned what was presented in the textbook, lecture, or other assigned material.

The success of recitation sessions depends to a large degree on the quality of the questions asked by the teacher. Unfortunately, the questions asked during most recitations tend to be low level. How many chambers are there in the human heart? and What are three symptoms of tuberculosis? are typical of these low-level questions. Questions asked during recitations could but normally do not invite students to demonstrate their understanding or ability to apply what has been learned (Kindsvatter

et al., 1996, p. 239). Too often recitation periods become sessions of review and drill in which few students participate and many sit quietly without making any contributions. For this reason, both volunteers and nonvolunteers should be questioned. Only by questioning as many students as possible can the teacher assess what the class has learned. Feedback gained through a recitation can give the teacher insight into what ideas need further elaboration and explanation.

Recitations are generally fast paced and require less time than most other instructional methods. To maintain the flow of a recitation, teachers should limit the active participation to one or two students at a time and should not permit questioning to drag or student answers to become too involved and lengthy. Questions should be prepared in advance and sequenced in the order in which they will be asked.

Guided Discussion.   Science teachers can use guided discussion to help students construct for themselves the science knowledge that scientists have already constructed and agree upon. Important for the success of a guided discussion is that students have basic knowledge of the idea or topic to be discussed. Student preparedness to engage in a guided discussion can often be determined through a recitation.

Guided discussion differs from recitation in terms of the teacher-student interaction pattern and the types of questions asked. The teacher is the interaction leader and primary questioner, but the interaction pattern is more varied and flexible than that of a recitation (Wilen, 1990). Two or more students may respond to a single question during a guided discussion, and the teacher need not react to each student's answer. In some instances, students may ask questions of the teacher or classmates to extend an explanation or clarify something that was said. The pace of a guided discussion is slower than that of a recitation, fewer questions are asked, and students are typically given time to think about questions asked and to formulate answers before responding.

The questions asked during a guided discussion aim at a higher cognitive level and are broader than those asked during a recitation. They require students to interpret, explain, apply, illustrate, generalize, and conclude (Wilen, 1990). How does Gram stain help a physician prescribe treatment for a bacterial infection? and What evidence suggests that plants evolved from green algae? are examples of the types of questions asked during a guided discussion. Responses to questions may vary because the students come to the discussion with their own personal theories about the idea or topic under consideration.

Reflective Discussion.   The centerpiece of reflective discussion, or true discussion, is the open expression of ideas. The discussions that are featured on the nightly news program *Nightline,* hosted by Ted Koppel, have much in common with the reflective discussions that go on in science classes. If you have ever watched *Nightline,* you know that after acquainting the TV audience with the evening's topic or issue and introducing the guests, Koppel asks a question to get the discussion rolling. From that point on, he moderates the discussion and asks questions only when further explanation or clarification is required.

Controversial issues on which persons take a stand make excellent subjects for *Nightline* and for reflective discussions in science classes. In science classes, the issues may deal with matters of current interest such as abortion, the creation-evolution controversy, AIDS, genetic engineering, nuclear testing, human cloning, and others. Reflective science discussions may also center around questions that require problem-solving skills to answer. Questions such as the following two may serve this purpose well: (1) Some people feel that all complex behaviors are learned, whereas others believe that many behaviors are inherited. Which position do you support and why? (2) Sedimentary rocks can be distinguished from other classes of rocks on the basis of bedding, color, fossils, ease of breakage, and porosity. Which do you feel are the poorest criteria to use as distinguishing characteristics and why? Excellent reflective discussions may also center around conflicting laboratory data. Topics that are concerned with indisputable facts, although stock-in-trade for recitations, are not suitable either for *Nightline* or for reflective discussions in science classes.

In the science class, the purpose of reflective discussion is to challenge students to think critically and creatively at the highest cognitive levels and to consider their personal beliefs, attitudes, and values (Kindsvatter et al., 1996; Wilen, 1990). During a reflective discussion, a science student may help resolve a problem of local water pollution or may state and defend his or her position regarding euthanasia. The use of complex thinking processes, students holding leadership responsibility, and belief and attitude change are characteristics of reflective discussion (Gall & Gall, 1976).

No recognizable interaction pattern is associated with the reflective discussion. The discussion is initiated by a question posed by the teacher who, much like Ted Koppel on *Nightline,* functions thereafter to facilitate the discussion. The question must be carefully worded to trigger original and evaluative thinking on the part of students (Kindsvatter et al., 1996). Reflective discussion is slow paced, and student responses tend to be quite lengthy. The momentum of the discussion is not maintained by a series of teacher questions, but by students asking questions of each other and statements contributed both by the teacher and students and student questions (Dillon, 1990). Unlike recitation and guided discussion, participation by all students is not critical to the success of a reflective discussion. Students whose thoughts on the topic or issue under consideration are not well formulated may choose just to listen. As is true for guided discussion, however, the success of the reflective discussion rests on student interest and background knowledge. If background knowledge is lacking, the discussion becomes what Roby (1988, p. 170) called a bull session, where "participants ventilate their implicitly agreed upon right opinions with a certain passion but with little purpose and no reflection."

Preparing for the Discussion

In preparing for a discussion, the teacher should consider the nature of the topic, the physical setting, the optimal group size, and how the students should ready themselves for the discussion.

Nature of the Topic.   Students cannot discuss a topic unless they are interested in it and have the sophistication to understand it. The maturity level of students should be considered when the topic is selected. Topics that are of interest to eighth graders may not be of interest to twelfth graders and vice versa. The teacher should select topics with care before attempting to organize discussion sessions based on them.

The topic selected for discussion may be noncontroversial or controversial. Noncontroversial topics are typically the subjects of recitation and guided discussion sessions. In some instances, the social context in which noncontroversial science topics are embedded may become part of a guided discussion. Besides the knowledge and understandings acquired during discussions of noncontroversial topics, students benefit from the opportunity to practice expressing themselves and to hear, critique, and evaluate other students' successive approximations of an important idea (Gage & Berliner, 1992). As previously mentioned, controversial topics are excellent subjects for reflective discussion, where the purpose is not to establish scientific truth. The value of discussing controversial topics, according to Gage and Berliner (1992, p. 425), lies in their motivational effect, the need they create to withstand the force of another person's arguments, and the resultant process of students developing a better understanding of their own logic, information and position. Teachers should welcome the opportunity to address controversial topics in science classes, but should consider local community values, school policies and local laws, and the maturity level of the students when choosing topics for discussion.

Physical Setting. In order for students to engage in a discussion, it is advisable to seat them in a circle or other arrangement so that they are close enough to interact. The physical arrangement of desks or chairs should permit students to speak so that others can hear without raising their voices and to sit face-to-face so that they can observe each other's facial expressions. If the teacher plans a discussion based on a demonstration or class activities, it is recommended that the seating arrangement be around the demonstration table or other area where activities involving the entire class will take place. These considerations are most important for guided and reflective discussions, but the latter one may also prove helpful for facilitating recitation sessions. Recitation typically requires no special seating arrangements.

Also, the physical environment in which a discussion takes place has a great deal to do with its success. A dingy, hot room with uncomfortable seats will produce poor results. On the other hand, a light, airy, attractive room provides an atmosphere that will encourage students to engage in discussion activities. Further, discussion sessions should be held in areas where students and teachers have access to reference materials that may be needed. The availability of library and laboratory references will facilitate the collection of information at appropriate times as the discussion warrants.

Group Size. Because both guided and reflective discussions require considerable interaction and interchange among students, it is often necessary to limit the number in the group. A skilled teacher can probably conduct a good discussion session with up to twenty students. Too large a group prohibits maximum participation, so that the session become a recitation or lecture. The optimum number for a discussion group is between ten and twenty students. Below ten, the teacher will discover that the discussion can be stifled because of the limited amount of information that the small group of students can contribute. The optimal group size for a recitation is dependent on the time available to question students. Only when most, if not all, of the students have been questioned can the teacher assess the class's understanding of the assigned material.

At times a teacher may wish to divide the whole class into small discussion groups. This might be done to have each small group investigate one aspect of an issue or problem. For example, a middle school science class could investigate the advantages and disadvantages of using the metric system in the United States. Each small group could be assigned a different aspect of measurement: linear, volume, mass, and temperature. A spokesperson from each group could later present the highlights of the group's data-gathering efforts, discussion, and conclusions to the entire class. Small-group sessions may be especially useful if there are specialists at hand to help conduct discussions. These specialists may be other teachers or interested people from the community who have expertise in the area under consideration. One teacher may find it difficult to answer all the possible questions that might arise during small-group sessions, and the help of specialists would certainly be in order to guide students and answer their questions. In this way students will be able to contribute more and with greater authority during large-group sessions.

Small-group discussions led by students are sometimes more successful than class discussions. There are more opportunities for students to interact; however, care must be taken to ensure that the discussion will run smoothly. Teachers must assign leadership to students who will take its responsibilities seriously. Teachers must also be willing to have individual conferences with student leaders so that they know what to do and what outcomes are expected.

Student Preparation. The success of a discussion is also affected by the readiness of students to contribute to the discussion. According to Gage and Berliner (1992, p. 426), students and their teacher must have "common ground," that is, a shared experience that "provides information, perspective, or understanding" on the topic that will be discussed. Assigning Rachel Carson's book *Silent Spring* is one way to give students some common ground from which to discuss the environmental impact of pesticides. Computer games and simulations, teacher demonstrations, laboratory activities, videos, field trips, class projects, student reports, and guest speakers can all be used to establish common ground for science class discussions.

Additionally, students' attention should be directed to specific aspects of assigned readings or other activities that will be discussed (Gage & Berliner, 1992). Doing this will ensure that students are prepared to contribute to the discussion. For example, if the reading assignment for a ChemCom class is *Silent Spring*, the teacher would tell the class that the focus of the discussion will be on Carson's warning of the danger DDT poses to human food sources and the impact of her warning on the government's decision to ban the use of DDT. Or if a teacher is using the film *Race for the Double Helix* in a middle school life science class, she or he might ask students to pay particular attention to how information about Rosalind Franklin's X-ray diffraction image was obtained by Watson and Crick and how it was used to develop their model of DNA.

Conducting a Successful Discussion

A discussion is often viewed as a freewheeling exchange of ideas with no starting or ending points. However, as a teacher intent on using the discussion method effectively with science classes, it is wise to think of a discussion as consisting of four phases: entry, clarification, investigation, and closure (Kindsvatter et al., 1996). In the **entry phase,** the teacher identifies the discussion topic and tells the students what will be done and why. For example, a chemistry teacher might begin a recitation session on the properties of crystalline solids like this: "For the remainder of the period, I'm going to ask you some questions to find out what you have learned about the properties of crystalline solids. Your answers to my questions will let me know if you're ready for Thursday's quiz." When initiating guided or reflective discussions, many teachers also use attention grabbers to cognitively engage students and to arouse their interest. Attention grabbers that could be used to begin a discussion on the necessity for controlled use of antibiotics may range from statistics that show the prescription rates of certain antibiotics by physicians to a TV newsclip that reports on the death of a person from a new strain of a bacterium that before was easily treated with antibiotics. Questions, pictures, slides, personal testimonials, and role-plays can also be used as attention grabbers.

During the **clarification phase,** rules for the discussion are communicated and terms or concepts important to the discussion are defined and clarified. Students need to know how they will be recognized to speak and that showing respect for the views of others is expected. They also need to know what role the teacher will play during the discussion. Depending on the purpose to be served by the discussion, the teacher may choose to function as the chairperson, directing student conversation, or simply listen. Experience suggests that the more the teacher talks, the less students will contribute to the discussion. Furthermore, when engaging in guided and reflective discussions, students also need to realize that it is acceptable and appropriate to question the teacher and other students and to ask for clarification of and evidence for statements made

during the discussion. Defining difficult terms and clarifying students' understandings of complex concepts also facilitates discussion in science classes. For example, clarification may be necessary at the start of a reflective discussion on AIDS because of confusion regarding the difference between being HIV-positive and having AIDS.

The **investigation phase** is the heart of any discussion. The central elements of this phase are teacher questions and nonquestioning techniques, all intended to encourage student engagement and learning. The kinds of questions asked by the teacher during recitation, guided discussion, and reflective discussion will differ. Generally, the questions asked during a recitation are less complex than those asked during either a guided or reflective discussion. Probing questions that ask for elaboration or further explanation serve to enhance reflective discussions, but too many teacher questions can quickly change a reflective discussion into a recitation. Whereas it is impossible to anticipate all questions that should be asked during a discussion, it is helpful for the teacher to have written out questions considered critical to the discussion. Pausing after asking a question, expressing a personal point of view, adding on to a student's contribution, and using verbal encouragement are all nonquestioning techniques that can be used by a teacher to keep a discussion rolling and focused. Finally, student ability level, language skills, and home culture can affect a teacher's use of questions and nonquestioning techniques. White (1990) concluded that culturally specific discussion strategies should be used when the participant structures found in the students' home community differ from those found in schools. For example, when working with native Hawaiian students, choral responses to questions and overlapping speech should be accepted because they are features of indigenous Hawaiian verbal interaction (White, 1990).

Closure, the final phase of a discussion, is critical to the success of guided and reflective discussions, but is too often bypassed due to time constraints or just poor planning. It is during this phase that ideas are summarized, synthesized, and applied to situations not directly discussed and where meaningful learning occurs (Kindsvatter et al., 1996, p. 247). Closure is also when the outcomes of the discussion are related to previous lessons and lessons to come. In a reflective discussion, closure may include the evaluation of decisions arrived at during the discussion. Closure in a recitation has minimal importance compared to its stature in guided or reflective discussions. In a recitation, closure involves reviewing the topic under consideration and highlighting those areas were student responses revealed knowledge gaps or misconceptions. Closure in a small-group discussion is the time when the spokespersons present the results of the groups' work to the entire class (Kindsvatter et al., 1996).

When leading a discussion session, it is also important to consider how long discussion should continue. The length of any discussion is dependent on student interest and the quality of their contributions. A recitation should be terminated after about ten to fifteen minutes. Guided and reflective discussions may go on much longer. Small-group discussions may begin during one class meeting and conclude with group reports to the entire class during the next meeting. Middle school and high school students will show signs of restlessness and inattention and the number of students anxious to participate will start to dwindle if a discussion continues too long.

According to Gall and Gall (1990), the discussion method is very effective for advancing student learning outcomes in the areas of content mastery, problem solving, moral reasoning, attitude change and development, and communication skills. Teachers who are successful at using the discussion method tend to be tolerant of low classroom structure, intellectually agile, and willing to relinquish classroom authority (Gage & Berliner, 1992). The teacher's role during a discussion varies depending on the discussion type. The teacher's role is very directive during a recitation, less directive during a guided discussion, and usually that of a moderator during a reflective discussion. It is also very appropriate to turn the responsibility for leading a discussion over to students. In summary, to lead a good discussion session the teacher should be able to do the following:

- Seat students in a circle or horseshoe arrangement so that they interact easily and can observe each other's facial expressions. Facial expressions also indicate a type of communication among participants.

- Keep the discussion moving at a reasonable pace.

- Keep the discussion pertinent to the topic under consideration.

- Encourage all students to participate. Do not allow two or three students to monopolize the conversation.

- Acknowledge all contributions that the students make.

- Reject irrelevant comments with tact.

- Summarize always at the end of the discussion, and do so frequently or permit students to do so as often as is feasible.

- Terminate the discussion when the students begin to lose interest.

■ STOP AND REFLECT! ■

Revisit Box 6.1, "Decisions, Decisions—Teaching Sexually Transmitted Diseases" and answer the following questions:

- Suppose that at the afternoon meeting Ms. Block recommends to her colleagues that they should use the guided discussion method rather than the reflective discussion method to address the objective about the benefits and cost related to AIDS. What factors likely affected Ms. Block's decision?

- Ms. Block and her colleagues decided to use the recitation method to help students review for a test. Which of the four objectives assigned to Ms. Block would likely be targeted during the recitation? Why?

CONSTRUCTION AND USE OF ORAL QUESTIONS

The success of a lecture or discussion often depends on the questions teachers ask students. Teachers must be able to formulate good oral questions. This means that questions have to be well conceived, concise, and clearly stated. Students can answer only the questions they understand. They have to understand the intent of the question in order to respond correctly.

Oral questions can be used in a variety of ways during a lecture or discussion. They can be used to stimulate students' thinking and check for understanding during an interactive lecture. They can be used for review or drill during a recitation or to lead a guided discussion. They can be used to determine students' knowledge of a phenomenon before a demonstration or to clarify their understanding of the purpose of a demonstration. Additionally, questions can be used to focus students' attention during a lecture or discussion and to help students construct meaningful understandings. Higher-level questions—those that require students to give broad responses—can facilitate cognitive and affective development in students. This type of questioning during a reflective discussion helps students to clarify their values and make decisions about societal issues and problems.

Constructing Clear Oral Questions

An oral question should be simple and direct so that students can grasp the meaning and intent immediately.

Long, complex questions are often awkwardly worded and, consequently, confusing to students. Such questions are also difficult for students to keep in mind during a lecture, demonstration, or discussion, and their intent can be forgotten unless they are repeated or written on the chalkboard or overhead projector.

Oral questions must be constructed using words that are familiar to students. A word that they have not encountered before can make the question meaningless. Science teachers often overestimate their students' vocabularies and use scientific terms and other words that students do not understand. This is particularly true for teachers who are working with middle and junior high school students for the first time.

There are many instances when a teacher can improve a question by simply replacing an unfamiliar word in a sentence with one familiar to the students.

> **Original: What is the etiology of the disease?**
>
> **Improved: What is the cause of the disease?**

In this example the word *etiology* can be replaced with the more common word *cause,* which has the same meaning. It is not necessary for biology or life science teachers to use the language of physicians who might use the word *etiology* to describe diseases.

> **Original: Why does the mixture of the two chemical substances effervesce when the test tube is agitated?**
>
> **Improved: Why does the mixture of the two chemical substances bubble when the test tube is shaken?**

In this example, the word *bubble* is substituted for *effervesce,* and the word *shaken* is substituted for *agitated.* The question has the same meaning but is more simply stated.

A teacher must exercise great discretion in attempting to use simple and common words when asking questions, however, because making things too simple may minimize the vocabulary and concept development of students. The technical vocabulary of science that is part of the curriculum should be taught. Just because some terms are multisyllabic or new does not mean they should be replaced by simpler terms or avoided. The vocabulary of science should be used in the context of clear and simple language.

> **Original: What is your idea of an astronomical unit?**
>
> **Improved: What is the definition of an astronomical unit?**

In the example given, the original question is cluttered. "What is your idea of" can be easily replaced by "What is the definition of, " but the term astronomical unit should remain however complicated it might appear. Astronomical unit is a basic term used in the study of astronomy, and it should be freely used.

Finally, teachers should use questions that are well structured and complete.

> **Original: Proteins are made where? The equilibrium constant tells you what?**
>
> **Improved: Where in the cell are proteins made? What information does the equilibrium constant provide concerning the rate of a chemical reaction?**

In each instance the original questions are vaguely stated, and the students can provide many plausible answers. Rewording the questions gives the students a clear understanding of exactly what is expected.

Lower- and Higher-Order Questions

Many systems are used to classify different types of questions. One of the most widely used classification systems is Bloom's Taxonomy of Cognitive Objectives (Bloom, 1956). The six levels of Bloom's taxonomy are given in Table 6.1. Along with each level are the cognitive activities, key words, and sample questions. The knowledge and comprehension levels represent the lower levels in the taxonomy in which questions can be developed. The application, analysis, synthesis, and evaluation levels represent the higher levels of the taxonomy at which questions can be developed. The lower-order questions obviously require less thinking on the part of the learner than the higher-order questions.

Science teachers can improve their questioning skills by learning to classify their questions and by using a mixture of lower-order and higher-order questions (Rowe, 1978). Each type of question has its place in teaching science and one type should not be used exclusively in preference to other types. Teachers too often ask recall and factually oriented questions and avoid asking questions that are thought-provoking and probing. Students should be asked oral questions that encourage them to analyze problems, synthesize ideas and make assessments, criticize, and make value judgments. Teacher should not be overly concerned about matching their questions with levels of Bloom's taxonomy, but recognize that there are different cognitive levels of questions and that a relationship between questions and student thinking exists (Kindsvatter et al., 1996, p. 197). By asking concise and clearly worded higher-order questions, teachers are able to increase the thought level of students' responses.

TABLE 6.1   A Taxonomy of Classroom Questions

Level	Cognitive activity	Key words	Sample questions
1 Knowledge	Remember, recall, or recognize facts, ideas, information, or principles as they were taught	Define, identify, list, recall, quote	1. Define photosynthesis. 2. Who discovered a cure for rabies? 3. What is the autumnal equinox?
2 Comprehension	Comprehend, interpret, or translate information or ideas	Describe, explain, compare, summarize	1. How would you measure the distance between the earth and a planet in the center of a neighboring galaxy? 2. How can you explain the movement of the dye in the water?
3 Application	Solve problems, find solutions, and determine answers through the application of rules, principles, or laws	Apply, provide an example, use, determine	1. Determine the resistance in the circuits from the data given. 2. Find the molarity of the solutions, given their normality.
4 Analysis	Distinguish the parts from the whole, identify causes, find support and evidence. Construct hypotheses and draw conclusions	Identify causes or effects, draw conclusions, provide evidence	1. What are the effects of the two drugs on the mobility of the goldfish? 2. Present evidence that demonstrates the harm that has been caused by nuclear power plants.
5 Synthesis	Produce, design, make, and construct products. Synthesize ideas, produce ways, and determine how to…	Make, produce, create, write, build, design	1. Produce a scenario about life in your city if heart disease were eliminated. 2. Design an experiment to determine how much energy can be saved by using storm doors in a home in the winter.
6 Evaluation	Judge, appraise, assess, or criticize. Substantiate on the basis of a set of criteria or standards	Evaluate, judge, critique, substantiate	1. Evaluate the government's research on tobacco from a moral and ethical point of view. 2. Judge the merits of the research based on your criteria for conducting research.

Based on data from *Taxonomy of educational objectives. Handbook I. Cognitive domain*, by B. S. Bloom, 1956, New York: David McKay Co., Inc., and *Dynamics of effective teaching* (3rd ed.), by R. Kindsvatter, W. Wilen, & M. Ishler, 1996, White Plains, NY: Longman Publishing.

Science teachers can also help students respond to their questions at the desired level by teaching them to recognize key words often imbedded in questions (Costa & Lowery, 1989; Kindsvatter et al., 1996). For example, once taught to recognize the key words **judge** and **critique**, students would understand that when asked a question that includes one of these action verbs, they are being asked to engage in higher-order thinking, not simply to recall a fact. Key words in questions that students can be taught to recognize are shown in Table 6.1.

It is important that science teachers not be confused by the different methods by which questions are classified. Some educators classify oral questions based on the type of responses the questions evoke. Using this method, questions are classified as convergent or divergent. **Convergent** questions elicit short responses that are low in cognitive complexity; they focus on a limited number of correct answers. Convergent questions fall into either the knowledge or comprehension level of Bloom's taxonomy. What is one of the biomes found in North America? or What are the three ingredients needed in the atmosphere for a cloud to form? are examples of convergent questions. In contrast, **divergent** questions provide opportunities for students to give several correct answers to a question. Because there is more than one correct answer, students are more willing and able to respond to divergent questions (Montague, 1987). Divergent questions match with the middle levels of Bloom's taxonomy. For example, the question, What evidence exists that no-till farming is an improvement over conventional farming practices? can be classified as both divergent and at the analysis level of Bloom's taxonomy.

Questions are also classified as closed and open. **Closed** questions are similar to convergent questions, but allow for only one correct response. What formula do you use to determine the capacitance in a series circuit? is an example of a closed question. **Open** questions stimulate creative and personal responses, de-emphasizing the notion of correct and incorrect. Open questions match with the synthesis and evaluation levels of Bloom's taxonomy. For example, the question, Should the school institute a program to inform students about AIDS? can be classified as both open and at the evaluation level of Bloom's taxonomy.

Probing and Redirecting Questions

Much can be gained by asking students to provide detailed responses to questions. This can be accomplished by using probing questions. Probing questions can be used to encourage students to extend, clarify, or justify their response to a question (Montague, 1987). Students should be asked to extend incomplete answers. What comes next? and Please add more to what you've just said, are examples of ways to ask students to extend their answers. Seemingly memorized answers need clarification. Encourage students to clarify their responses by asking such questions as Would you tell us what you mean in words that we all can understand? and What does that mean to you? and Clarify what you just said. Justification is often needed for responses to open questions when none is provided. Examples of ways to ask for justification include What evidence can you offer for that? and Why do you believe that is true?

A second way to encourage detailed responses to questions and to foster student cognitive engagement throughout a lesson is by redirecting. In redirecting, the teacher asks other students to extend, clarify, or justify the response of the student to whom the initial question was directed (Montague, 1987). What evidence supports Juan's statement that some reactions of photosynthesis don't require light? and Hayden, would you please expand on Kendal's answer about the relationship between adhesive forces and meniscus formation? are examples of redirecting questions.

Probing and redirecting questions permit students to provide clear and expanded responses and to provide justification for what they say. They encourage analysis, synthesis, and evaluation of a problem. Both forms of questions can also stimulate inquiry and the clarification of personal attitudes and values.

Wait Time and Teacher Statements

One reason why question-and-answer sessions are ineffective is that teachers tend to ask too many lower-order rapid-fire questions. Studies by Mary Budd Rowe (1974a, 1974b) have shown that these sessions can be made more effective by using wait time. **Wait time** is defined as the duration of time between speakers. The pause that follows a question by the teacher is referred to as **wait time 1**. The pause that follows a student response to the teacher's question is referred to as **wait time 2**. Data gathered from many classroom situations indicate that the average wait time between a teacher's question and a student's response and the pause that follows students' responses is approximately one second (Rowe, 1974a).

Science teachers must learn to increase the wait time in their question-and-answer sessions when using higher-order questions. A series of lower-order questions in general does not necessarily require wait time between question and response. But for higher-order questions, wait time from three to five seconds should be employed to give students a chance to think and reflect. Increased wait time between teacher- and student-talk, student- and student-talk, and student- and teacher-talk will probably cause some uneasiness when first tried, but the payoffs of this change are worth the effort. Rowe (1974a, pp. 89–91) reported the following benefits when wait times were extended beyond three seconds:

1. The length of student solicited and unsolicited responses increased.
2. The failure of students to respond to questions decreased.

3. Student confidence and incidence of speculative responses increased.

4. The incidence of students comparing their responses and of evidence-inference statements increased.

5. The number of questions asked by students increased.

6. Slow learners responded with greater frequency.

7. The variety and type of verbal behavior of students increased.

8. The teacher's expectations for the performance of students rated as relatively slow learners changed.

9. The number and type of questions asked by the teacher changed.

Tobin's (1984) study of wait time in middle school grades indicates several advantages of extending teacher wait time in whole-class situations beyond those identified by Rowe. His findings showed that when a teacher extended wait time for an average of between three and five seconds, the quality of teacher and student discourse was improved, student achievement was increased, and teachers had a tendency to use strategies to push students into further discussions rather than "mimicking or evaluating student responses." According to Tobin (1984) the results of the study indicate that teachers should use an average wait time of three to five seconds when question-and-answer sessions are intended to stimulate higher cognitive processes. Based on the study he recommends that teachers use extended wait time in whole-class situations "to improve the quality of the learning environment and to increase achievement in subjects such as mathematics and science where higher cognitive level outcomes are often a concern" (p. 790).

Another technique that can be used by science teachers to enhance student discourse and thinking during science lessons is using statements in place of questions. Although not as well researched as wait time, Dillon (1990) recommended that statements be used rather than questions because students respond better to teacher statements than to their questions. Kindsvatter et al. (1996, p. 205) identify four types of teacher statements that can be used to foster classroom interactions:

1. Declarative statement—reflects on an idea related to what a students said

I know what you mean, I've also seen what a tornado can do to a mobile home.

2. Reflective statement—recasts or rephrases what a student has said

So you think that the winds of a tornado move in a counterclockwise direction.

3. Statement of interest—indicates that you would like to know more about what a student has said

Tell me what else happened when you tried to outrun the tornado in your car.

4. Speaker referral—links a student's statement with one previously made by another student

Your encounter with the tornado is very similar to Sharon's, even though your's was in Kansas and her's was in North Carolina.

Using statements to the exclusion of questions would be difficult for most teachers and might make students uncomfortable since they expect teachers to ask questions during most, if not all, lessons. Many teachers intuitively mix questions and statements during discussions, interactive lectures, and demonstrations. Making this a conscious practice is likely to increase the student participation during these types of lessons.

Target Students

Lectures and discussions typically involve a whole class of students interacting with the teacher. However, not all students interact equally with the teacher during these types of lessons. A study by Tobin and Gallagher (1987) revealed that teachers generally asked low-level questions at random and usually directed higher-level questions to more able students—target students. Two kinds of target students were identified: those selected because the teacher felt that students would give responses that would "facilitate learning and content coverage," and those who raised their hands to respond to questions or called out responses. These students, who were few in number (three to seven) in each class and typically male, dominated class interactions. According to Tobin, Tippins, and Gallard (1994, p. 50), target students engage in the higher cognitive-level work of the class and in so doing reduce the cognitive demand of the work for their classmates. Nontarget students listen to the interchange between the teacher and target students and then memorize correct answers.

The research on target students indicates that science teachers do not direct their instruction to the "middle of the class in order to cater to the majority of students and to cater to the needs of both more- and less-able students" (Tobin & Gallagher, 1987, p. 74). For this reason alone, science teachers should be very conscious of what occurs during whole-class interactions, particularly of the level of learning that takes place during instruction. They must make sure that all students are involved during instruction and that no particular type of student is disregarded or favored for any reason. When high achievers dominate classroom discourse, maintain the pace of a lesson, or monopolize the teacher's attention and time, the low achievers are short-changed. All students should be given the opportunity to interact and be involved at all times and at their cognitive level. Science teachers can facilitate the involvement of all students during lectures, demonstrations, and discussions through the questions they ask and the nonquestioning techniques they employ.

■ STOP AND REFLECT! ■

Before going on to the next topic, do the following:

■ Choose a discussion topic and write two higher-order questions that might be used during the discussion.

■ Write three statements that could be used to convince a novice science teacher to use wait time during either lecture or discussion sessions.

THE DEMONSTRATION

A science demonstration is a powerful instructional strategy. A demonstration is a concrete experience that can be considered an advance organizer for structuring subsequent information and activities into a meaningful, instructional framework for students. An effective demonstration can focus students' attention, motivate and interest them in a lesson or unit, illustrate key concepts and principles, and initiate inquiry and problem solving. Oral questioning, as addressed in the previous section of this chapter, is an important aspect of most demonstrations. Carefully planned and executed demonstrations can greatly enhance the learning environment and make special contributions to the teaching of science.

Functions of Demonstrations

Demonstrations may be used in several ways in science instruction. Each approach makes its own contribution to the learning environment.

Initiating Thinking.   Many science demonstrations, when presented for the first time to a group of students,

will leave them searching for an explanation. This type of demonstration, often called the discrepant event, can stimulate student interest and curiosity. To achieve the atmosphere of inquiry, the teacher must present the event as a problem to be investigated. "The intuition-offending event must be presented to the learner in such a way that the science principle underlying the event is not immediately revealed" (Liem, 1987). Physical science students experience a discrepant event when they expect a thin stream of water to be unaffected by a plastic comb held close by, but instead witness that the stream of water bends toward the comb, which has been rubbed on a wool sweater. (See Figure 6.1.) As a result of experiencing this counterintuitive phenomenon, the students are primed for learning about static electricity. Psychologists believe that discrepant events promote higher-level thinking and meaningful learning, and, when properly presented, the students will have better recall and retention of information. Even a simple presentation can initiate student inquiry.

Illustrating a Concept, Principle, or Point.   To illustrate a concept some teachers first state the concept and then parallel the statement with a demonstration that illustrates the idea. This is a direct and explicit way to clarify and explain ideas. This approach should be used only to illustrate the concept, law, or principle but not to develop the idea.

Consider a demonstration to illustrate what conditions are necessary for cloud formation. The teacher first tells the students that moisture, condensation nuclei, and a change in air pressure are needed for a cloud to form. She takes a clear two-liter plastic bottle and seals it with the bottle cap, holds it in front of a light so the

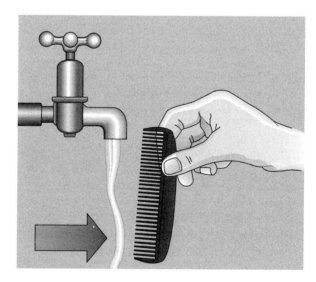

FIGURE 6.1   Bending Water Demonstration

inside of the bottle can be seen, then repeatedly squeezes and releases the bottle to change the pressure inside. The air pressure inside is increased when force is applied by pressing on the outside of the bottle, and decreased when the bottle is released. No cloud is formed. Next, she adds a couple milliliters of water to the bottle, seals it again, and then repeatedly squeezes and releases the bottle. Again, no cloud is formed. Then, she puts a lighted match inside the bottle. The match goes out once it hits the water already at the bottom of the bottle. The smoke from the match provides the condensation nuclei. Again, she repeatedly squeezes and releases the bottle to change the air pressure inside. The students observe that a cloud forms when the bottle is released after force has been applied. The teacher engages the students in a discussion about the conditions necessary for a cloud to form and the conditions in nature that mirror those observed in the plastic bottle.

Probably the most common use of a demonstration is to illustrate a point. For example, the students had observed the eclipse of the moon the previous night and asked the teacher to explain the event. The teacher proceeded to set up a readily available model to demonstrate the relative positions of the earth, moon, and sun during an eclipse. In cases such as this, the demonstration is not part of the lesson plan. Often the apparatus has to be set up on the spot and in a matter of minutes. If materials and/or apparatus cannot be gathered quickly, it is wise to postpone the demonstration until the next day, so that the continuity of the lesson is maintained and students' attention is not lost.

Teacher demonstrations can be useful to initiate thinking, illustrate a concept, answer questions, and review ideas.

Answering a Question.   Students sometimes ask questions that can be answered easily with a demonstration. These situations usually occur spontaneously and require teachers to have a large repertoire of demonstrations to draw from. For example, during a unit on oceanography, the topic of skin diving arose, and a student asked a question about the bends. To answer the question, the teacher demonstrated how a beaker of water in a vacuum chamber appears to boil. He explained that the bubbles released were analogous to the nitrogen bubbles that are formed in a diver's body as the diver moves up from an area of greater depth and higher pressure to the surface, a region of lower pressure. Such demonstrations should not be conducted spontaneously unless the teacher is positive that the demonstration will be presented successfully and that the materials are readily available.

Reviewing Ideas.   Demonstrations can be the center of excellent review sessions when combined with oral recitations. They can be performed to reinforce important ideas that were previously addressed during a lesson

or laboratory exercise. For example, during a recitation, a teacher might present as a demonstration the same lab on copper plating by electrolysis that students had difficulty with the week before. The teacher's recitation questions would focus on the students' lab work, how their lab results compared to those of the demonstration, and the reactions involved in electrolysis.

Introducing and Concluding Units.   Demonstrations can be used to introduce new topics and provide stimulating introductory discussions. They can promote creative thinking on the part of students by presenting them with a related or an apparently unrelated event for explanation. Interesting and exciting demonstrations are also excellent ways to conclude units of study. They can serve as a climax as well as a summary of the high points of a unit. They can also motivate and interest students in further study. For example, a teacher might demonstrate how chemical substances such as sulfur and magnesium burn in an atmosphere of pure oxygen to conclude a unit on air and to point out to students that high school chemistry involves the study of many exciting phenomena.

Addressing Students' Naive Conceptions. Demonstrations can be used to help students construct more scientifically accurate explanations of phenomena. In this type of instruction, teachers can elicit predictions from their students regarding a phenomenon and request explanations for their predictions. After students' conceptions have been put forth and recorded on the chalkboard or elsewhere, a demonstration can be performed that will contradict the students' predictions. The contradiction not only motivates students to resolve the discrepancy but also allows them to formulate their own logical explanations for the phenomenon. In using this approach, a teacher who finds that her students naively believe that all materials lose weight when burned, could suspend a piece of steel wool from each arm of an equal arm balance so that the arms balance, then direct the flame of a gas burner at one piece of the steel wool and allow students to observe that the balance arm tips downs on the side that was burned. She could then use the students' observations to guide them to the conclusion that burning does not always involve a decrease in mass (see BouJaoude, 1991).

Advantages and Limitations of Demonstrations

Demonstrations have several advantages that make them very useful in teaching science. Demonstrations can provide an exciting event that will capture most students' attention, and if conducted properly, a demonstration can involve all students in attempting to answer questions or in observing an event. Demonstrations are also useful to guide and channel students' thinking. They allow teachers to guide thinking by arranging the external and internal conditions of learning in a classroom through the use of concrete materials and carefully planned questions. Student thinking can be focused directly on the intended learning outcomes or guided to discover a relationship or answer a question through inquiry. Additionally, demonstrations enable the teacher to conduct activities that may be too dangerous for students to carry out themselves. For example, a chemistry teacher can demonstrate reactions that produce strong and toxic fumes under a well-ventilated hood rather than permit students to conduct the exercise themselves.

A demonstration can also save class time and teacher time and effort and stretch limited resources. Some laboratory activities can be conducted as demonstrations without any loss of student understanding. This eliminates time spent setting up and taking down apparatus, collecting materials, and giving directions. It

is certainly easier for the teacher to prepare materials for one laboratory activity than for twenty duplicate ones. It is also easier to perform one activity than to supervise twenty activities and more convenient to store materials for one activity than for twenty. Some items are too expensive or delicate for general use. Because of cost, many high school science departments, for example, have few electronic balances, one human skeleton, and only one oscilloscope, which is used to analyze electrical impulses in large-group presentations. When supplies and equipment are limited, teachers must often use a demonstration instead of a laboratory activity.

Demonstrations also have limitations that make them useful for only certain types of learning situations. Visibility is always a problem when demonstrations are presented. All students may not be able to see the details of the apparatus and of the procedures when the demonstration is conducted at a fixed location in the classroom and they are seated some distance from the demonstration table. Problems of visibility may be diminished by assembling students around the demonstration site or by passing materials around to the students before conducting the demonstration. Another limitation is that students can miss the point of the demonstration. Students often miss the point due to the swiftness of the pace and the smooth way in which demonstrations are presented. Students also miss the point because they are distracted by extraneous materials or events that are part of the demonstration. When observing the classic egg-in-the-bottle demonstration, for example, students may fail to see it as an illustration of the effect of changing air pressure but as a demonstration of fire or heat. This misinterpretation occurs because they are distracted by the flaming piece of paper dropped into the bottle to heat the inside air (Shepardson, Moje, Kennard-McClelland, 1994).

It also is difficult to maintain student interest during a demonstration because there are few opportunities for active student involvement. Students have a tendency to mentally disengage from a lesson when they are inactive in their seats. To maintain students' interest and ensure their understanding during a demonstration, the teacher must make provisions to involve all students through questioning procedures and other techniques.

A final limitation associated with the use of demonstration in science class is related to the equipment used and the manner in which demonstrations tend to be presented. The use of elaborate or professionally made apparatus adds a note of authority and often makes the results of a demonstration difficult to question. Elaborate demonstrations that require complex equipment and complex procedures are often very convincing to students. This situation may cause students to become uninvolved in the demonstration and misunderstand its purpose.

BOX 6.2

■

EGG-IN-THE-BOTTLE DEMONSTRATION

MATERIALS

one 1000-milliliter Erlenmeyer flask or bottle of comparable size

one peeled hard-boiled egg

one sheet of notebook paper

matches

water

SAFETY

This demonstration requires the use of fire. Perform the demonstration on a tabletop free of objects that may catch fire. Have a fire extinguisher near the demonstration table in case it is needed. Wear safety goggles.

PROCEDURE

1. Read the procedures before performing the demonstration.
2. Tear off half a sheet of notebook paper and roll it up tightly.
3. Light the rolled up notebook paper with a match and push the burning paper into the flask.
4. Quickly set the egg on top of the flask as shown in the figure below.

QUESTIONS & ANSWERS

1. What happened when the egg was placed on top of the flask?

    ANSWER: The bottle filled with smoke and the egg bounced on the lip of the bottle as the paper continued to burn. Once the fire went out, the egg slowly began to move into the flask. After only a few seconds, the egg passed through the mouth of the flask and landed on the smoldering paper.

2. What explanation do you have for what you observed?

ANSWER: The fire heated the air inside the flask, causing it expand and rise. The expanding and rising air caused the air pressure inside the flask to increase, which caused the egg to bounce on the lip of the flask. The bouncing egg, acting like a release valve, allowed some of the hot air to escape from the flask. When the fire went out, the air inside the flask began to cool and contract. As the air contracted, the air pressure inside the bottle decreased to become less than the air pressure outside the flask. The egg is pushed into the flask by the air trying to get into the flask, achieving equal pressure inside and outside the flask. *Note:* Some oxygen inside the flask is consumed as the paper burns, but the amount of oxygen consumed is not sufficient to explain the movement of the egg into the flask.

3. How can you get the egg out of the flask?

ANSWER: The key to getting the egg out is to increase the air pressure inside the flask. One way is to position the egg in the mouth of the flask with the mouth pointed down. Carefully insert a bendable drinking straw between the egg and the inside mouth of the flask. With the egg seated in the mouth of the downward pointed flask, blow into the flask through the straw. As the air pressure inside the flask increases, the egg will pass out of the mouth of the flask.

Planning a Demonstration

A demonstration is, in effect, a performance, and many factors must be considered before the event takes place. The first thing that a teacher should consider is whether the strategy is the best way to address a certain topic. It certainly would be inadvisable, for instance, to use a demonstration to show students the test for the presence of starch in carbohydrates when a laboratory exercise would ensure visibility by all and be both inexpensive and very safe. A second point to consider is whether the topic lends itself to the demonstration strategy. Are there elements of surprise or suspense? Will the demonstration take place at a reasonable pace? Is there enough variety to maintain interest? Are there long periods of inactivity? A third consideration is the size of the equipment and materials. Can the apparatus be seen by all the students? Once these considerations have been satisfactorily addressed and the decision has been made to use a demonstration, then other aspects of planning must be undertaken.

Materials and Equipment. Materials and equipment for a demonstration should be planned and collected well in advance of the actual presentation. Last-minute preparation may prove frustrating and cause either a delay in the presentation or no presentation at all. For example, the teacher may find that the apparatus has been lost or damaged or that chemicals are too old, exist in the wrong concentrations, or are in short supply. Potential problems should be recognized well in advance so that the demonstration can take place as planned.

Teachers or their students can construct the equipment needed for many demonstrations. When teachers construct devices for demonstrations, they are designed to illustrate and emphasize specific points and tend to be used with more frequency and with greater ease and finesse. When students construct demonstration apparatus, they benefit from the experiences of planning and building the devices and the presentation they make. Additionally, it is important to keep in mind that students are more likely to understand the demonstration if the apparatus used is closely related to things with which they are familiar. For instance, the effect of tension on vibrating strings can be illustrated using an actual guitar or banjo instead of an elaborate piece of equipment purchased from a scientific supply house.

Ensuring Visibility. Simple but large-scale apparatus are best for demonstrations. But even when large equipment is used, the teacher must take care to ensure that small and important details are made visible to students. The apparatus and/or materials on the demonstration table must be arranged to avoid blind spots. Before presenting the demonstration, it is a good idea for the teacher to view the setup from various points around the classroom to determine whether there are problems in viewing. Further, the background behind the apparatus and proper lighting should be considered to ensure good visibility. A partially erased chalkboard makes a very unsuitable background; however, white or colored cardboard or cloth backgrounds with suitable supports provide adequate contrasts for viewing. Good overhead lighting that eliminates shadows will make any demonstration easier to see.

Focusing Student Attention.   There are several ways to focus student attention on a demonstration. Some teachers begin a demonstration with a bare demonstration table and then proceed to remove the needed items from a box or other source. Items taken from a box, the contents of which are not visible, can introduce an element of surprise, for students will continue to wonder what will be removed next and how it will be used in the demonstration. A second way is to assemble the apparatus first, cover it with a cloth or a box before the students arrive in the room, and then unveil the setup to begin the demonstration. This technique works well when a large-scale apparatus is required for the demonstration. Another approach is to set in operation, before class begins, a scientific novelty or device that is used for the demonstration.

Student attention can also be focused by modifying the demonstration procedures. A student or several students can carry out a demonstration under the teacher's direction. A student or teacher from another classroom or an outside expert may be used to present a demonstration. The teacher can use special equipment such as an opaque projector, videocamera, or a projection microscope to add novelty and surprise during the demonstration procedure. The teacher can present demonstrations outdoors or in another room or in the hallway. Demonstrations that include unusual noises, lights, or motions are also useful in attracting student attention and maintaining their interest.

Trying Out the Demonstration Beforehand.   Unexpected complexities can arise even during a simple demonstration. A damaged pulley or dead battery can sabotage a demonstration. The only way to be certain that a demonstration will proceed smoothly is to set it up beforehand, try it out, and then use the same materi-

als during the actual presentation. The availability of backup materials such as additional batteries, pulleys and glassware will often allow the demonstration to proceed as planned without problems. The importance of trying out the demonstration well in advance to be certain that it will proceed smoothly when it is actually delivered cannot be overemphasized.

Presenting a Demonstration

A demonstration by its very nature allows for limited student participation. Depending on the level of student involvement encouraged, a demonstration may resemble a formal or informal lecture. As with the lecture, a demonstration has three phases: an introduction, a presentation, and a conclusion (Kindsvatter et al., 1996).

Introduction.   During the introduction, the purpose for the demonstration is established and students are acquainted with the materials and procedures. The recognition by the students of the purpose of the demonstration is essential to ensure cognitive engagement and to obtain the desired outcomes. The purposes of a demonstration should be kept simple and written on the chalkboard or overhead transparency in short, direct statements. For example, a physical science teacher's purpose for performing a demonstration using the Van de Graaff generator is to show students the effects of static electricity. Moreover, interesting problems often arise from the actions of the demonstration materials themselves. The students will discover the purpose of the demonstration from these problems.

Whether or not to tell the students of the outcome is a question pondered by the teacher with regard to many science demonstrations. Some teachers tell their students in advance of the demonstration what the outcome will be. This practice is not usually recommended but it is sometimes necessary to make the outcome more meaningful. Teachers who wish to use demonstrations to initiate student inquiry say very little during this phase. They prefer to allow their students to draw conclusions based on their own observations at a later point during the demonstration.

For most demonstrations, students require help in recognizing the materials that will be used as well as learning the function each item plays in the procedure. It is wise not to assume that students know the materials that will be used during a demonstration and their functions. To ensure success, each item should be identified and its purpose made clear, preferably during the introduction of the demonstration.

Presentation.   This is the main body of the demonstration, when the concrete event is shown and questions are asked. The presentation must proceed in a logical and organized manner and move along at a somewhat rapid pace. Procedures that may cause long pauses or delays should be avoided. If the demonstration requires boiling water, for example, prepare it beforehand so that it is available at the appropriate time. A very useful tactic to hold students' attention during this phase is to create suspense. Events leading to a dramatic climax such as an explosion will maintain student interest, give them a feeling of involvement, and motivate them to meet the objectives of the demonstration. Additionally, humor can be used to achieve a successful presentation. Students enjoy learning from demonstrations that end with unusual, unexpected, or humorous outcomes.

A momentary lapse of attention, blocked vision, or inaudible words due to laughter may cause a student to miss the point of the procedure or the significance of the demonstration. To ensure that students learn from the demonstration, there is much that the teacher can do during the presentation. One technique is to ask questions such as, What observations have you made up to this point? or What did I do during the last step? When asking such questions do not signify approval or disapproval but proceed to ask another student the same questions. If a disagreement occurs, then it may be necessary to repeat the demonstration or step. A second technique is to conduct brief, periodic reviews. A review can be done in several parts with one student reiterating the purpose, another describing the materials, and another describing the procedures. A third technique is to summarize what has taken place. If a demonstration consists of a number of distinct parts, then interim summaries, led either by the teacher or students, are helpful. Data and charts placed on the chalkboard or overhead projector can help summarize observations or results.

Depending on the demonstration, it may be possible to have students participate physically during this phase. Students can assist the teacher in some way during most demonstrations. If a number of manipulations or parts are involved, allow one student to carry out one part and then allow other students to conduct the subsequent manipulations or parts.

Conclusion.   During this phase of the demonstration, the teacher helps students construct new understandings about the concept or principle illustrated in the previous phase. One way to do this is by engaging students in a guided discussion of the application of the concept or principle to everyday life. This will make the instruction relevant to the students and make the purpose of the demonstration better understood. Be prepared to

describe several common situations that illustrate the idea, just in case the students do not suggest any. Questions should be asked to facilitate student conversation and meaningful learning during this phase of the demonstration. Discussion that challenges students' ideas and stimulates dialog is "necessary to promote a scientific understanding of a science demonstration" (Shepardson et al., 1994, p. 244). Too much teacher talk tends to stifle student conversation. If the demonstration is used to initiate inquiry, the questions should be carefully planned and asked that encourage intellectual speculation. Inquiry demands that teachers evaluate students' responses without being influenced by what they believe students should say or think.

Research indicates that the quality of science demonstrations improves as teachers grow in their science content knowledge and their understanding of science instructional practices and student characteristics (Clermont, Borko, & Krajcik, 1994). Nevertheless, there is much that beginning teachers can do to ensure the effectiveness of science demonstrations. In summary, to present an effective demonstration, the teacher needs to do the following:

- Select a demonstration that clearly fits the context of the lesson or unit.
- If a series of demonstrations is to be used, make sure that the demonstrations revolve around a single concept (Shepardson et al., 1994, p. 254).
- Make sure that all materials and apparatus are available and in good working order and that proper safety precautions are planned for.
- Clear the demonstration table of extraneous and irrelevant materials and make sure that the demonstration can be easily seen by all students.
- Speaks at a moderate pace, loud enough to be heard by all students, and enunciate clearly.
- State the purpose of the demonstration at the beginning or end or at the appropriate time.
- Describe and simultaneously show the steps of the demonstration.
- Ask questions to stimulate student thinking, to help them draw their own conclusions, and to initiate further investigation.
- Allow sufficient time for the demonstration to achieve the expected outcomes and to maintain student attention and interest.
- Conclude the demonstration with a discussion and, if appropriate, link the demonstration to applications in everyday life.

■

ASSESSING AND REVIEWING

1. Construct a table to help you organize the information about the different teaching methods presented in this chapter. Label the columns of the table: Teaching Method, Purpose, Teacher's Role, Students' Role, Strengths, and Limitations. Include the following teaching methods in your table: Formal Lecture, Interactive Lecture, Recita-tion, Guided Discussion, Reflective Discussion, and Demonstration.

2. When students have difficulty learning from lectures it is often because they are unable to organize the information presented in a meaningful way. How could the topic outline shown here be used by a teacher to facilitate student learning during a lecture on vascular plants?

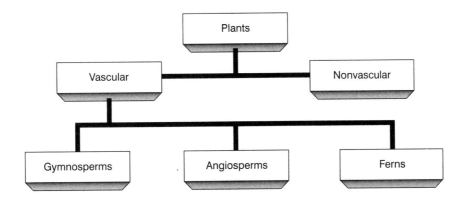

3. Why do you suppose that the recitation method is used more often by science teachers than either guided or reflective discussion even though research supports the superiority of discussion in facilitating meaningful learning?

4. It is important to recognize that a science lesson may be taught using only one instructional method or a combination of methods. Select a science concept that you are familiar with and explain how you could use two or more of the methods presented in this chapter to teach the concept.

5. Locate a description of a science demonstration that is of interest to you. Describe how you would pre-sent the demonstration to a class of students and the purpose it would serve. Include in your descrip-tion of the presentation how you would introduce and bring closure to the demonstration.

6. List five science and societal issues that lend them-selves to reflective discussion. Plan one of the dis-cussions to include (1) the lead question or ques-tions to be used to initiate the discussion, (2) questions and nonquestioning techniques to be used during the discussion, (3) activities to be con-ducted by students in small groups or as a whole class, and (4) the strategy to be used to bring clo-sure to the discussion.

■

RESOURCES TO EXAMINE

Questioning Skills, for Teacher. 1991. A part of the What Research Says to the Teacher series published by the National Education Association, Washington, DC.

This easy-to-read booklet of forty pages summa-rizes much of what is known about teachers' use of questioning and nonquestioning techniques. William Wilen discusses many important topics related to questioning, including purpose of questions, congruency of questions and thinking, and the use of teacher statements instead of questions.

Teaching and Learning through Discussion. 1990. Published and distributed throughout the world by Charles C. Thomas, 2600 South First Street, Springfield, IL 62794-9265.

Read the eighth chapter, "Involving Different Social and Cultural Groups in Discussion." Jane White reviews anthropological research on classroom interaction involving Native American, Hispanic, and other cultural groups and suggests a variety of strategies teachers can use to engage students from diverse cultural backgrounds in productive discussions.

"The Lecture Method." 1976. *The Psychology of Teaching Methods: 75th Yearbook of NSSE* (pp. 397–401). Chicago: University of Chicago Press.

This classic piece by J. McLeish provides an overview of the lecture method. He discusses the proper uses of lecture, what strategies teachers can use to motivate students and to help them organize content during a lecture, and the benefits of lecture compared to other instructional methods.

"Wait-time and Rewards as Instructional Variables: Their Influence on Language, Logic, and Fate control. Part I. Wait-time." 1974. *Journal of Research in Science Teaching, 11,* 81–94.

Mary Budd Rowe's original account of her early work on wait time is presented in this article. Her findings led to the strategy of wait time being used by hundreds of thousands of teachers around the world to enhance classroom discourse.

REFERENCES

Ausubel, D. P. (1961). In defense of verbal learning. *Educational Theory, 11,* 15.

Ausubel, D. P. (1963). Some psychological and educational limitations of learning by discovery. *New York State Mathematics Teachers Journal, 13*(3), 90.

Bloom, B. S. (Ed.) (1956). *Taxonomy of educational objectives. Handbook 1. Cognitive domain.* New York: David McKay.

BouJaoude, S. B. (1991). A study of the nature of students' misunderstandings about the concept of burning. *Journal of Research in Science Teaching, 28,* 689–704.

Clarke, J. H. (1987). Building a lecture that works. *College Teaching, 35*(2), 56.

Clermont, C. P., Borko, H., Krajcik, J. S. (1994). Comparative study of the pedagogical content knowledge of experienced and novice chemical demonstrators. *Journal of Research in Science Teaching, 31,* 419–441.

Costa, A., & Lowery, L. (1989). *Techniques for teaching thinking.* Pacific Grove, CA: Midwest Publications.

Dillon, J. T. (1990). Conducting discussions by alternatives to questioning. In W. W. Wilen (Ed.), *Teaching and learning through discussion* (pp. 79–96). Springfield, IL: Charles C. Thomas.

Eggen, P. D., & Kauchak, D. P. (1996). *Strategies for teachers* (3rd ed.). Boston: Allyn and Bacon.

Flowerdew, J. (1992). Definitions in science lectures. *Applied Linguistics, 13,* 202–221.

Gage, N. L., & Berliner, D. C. (1992). *Educational psychology* (5th ed.). Boston: Houghton Mifflin.

Gall, J. P., & Gall, M. D. (1990). Outcomes of the discussion method. In W. W. Wilen (Ed.), *Teaching and learning through discussion* (pp. 25–44). Springfield, IL: Charles C. Thomas.

Gall, M. D., & Gall, J. P. (1976). The discussion method. In N. L. Gage (Ed.), *The psychology of teaching methods: Seventy-fifth yearbook of the National Society of the Study of Education* (pp. 166–216). Chicago: University of Chicago Press.

Good, T., & Brophy, J. (1994). *Looking into classrooms* (6th ed.). New York: HarperCollins.

Hartley, J. (1976). Lecture handouts and student note-taking. *Programmed Learning and Educational Technology, 13,* 58–64.

Henson, K. T. (1988). *Methods and strategies for teaching in secondary and middle schools.* New York: Longman.

Kindsvatter, R., Wilen, W., & Ishler, M. (1996). *Dynamics of effective teaching* (3rd ed.). White Plains, NY: Longman.

Kyle, B. (1972). In defense of the lecture. *Improving College and University Teaching, 20,* 325.

Liem, T. (1987). *Invitations to inquiry.* Lexington, MA: Ginn Press.

McLeish, J. (1976). The lecture method. In N. L. Gage (Ed.), *The psychology of teaching methods: Seventy-fifth yearbook of the National Society of the Study of Education* (pp. 397–401). Chicago: University of Chicago Press.

Montague, E. J. (1987). *Fundamentals of secondary classroom instruction.* Upper Saddle River, NJ: Merrill/Prentice Hall.

Roby, T. W. (1988). Models of discussion. In J. T. Dillon (Ed.), *Questioning and discussion: A multidisciplinary study* (pp. 163–191). Norwood, NJ: Ablex.

Rowe, M. B. (1974a). Wait-time and rewards as instructional variables: Their influence on language, logic, and fate control. Part I. Wait-time. *Journal of Research in Science Teaching, 11,* 81–94.

Rowe, M. B. (1974b). Relation of wait-time and rewards to the development of language, logic, and fate control. Part II. Rewards. *Journal of Research in Science Teaching, 11,* 291–308.

Rowe, M. B. (Ed.) (1978). *What research says to the science teacher* (Vol. 1). Washington, DC: National Science Teachers Association.

Shepardson, D. P., Moje, E. B., & Kennard-McClelland, A. M. (1994). The impact of science demonstrations on children's understanding of air pressure. *Journal of Research in Science Teaching, 31,* 243–258.

Shulman, L. S. (1987). Knowledge and teaching: Foundations for the new reform. *Harvard Educational Review, 57,* 1–22.

Thompson, R. (1974). Legitimate lecturing. *Improving College and University Teaching, 22,* 163–164.

Tobin, K. (1984). Effects of extended wait-time on discourse characteristics and achievement in middle school grades. *Journal of Research in Science Teaching, 21,* 779–791.

Tobin, K., & Gallagher, J. J. (1987). The role of target students in the science classroom. *Journal of Research in Science Teaching, 24,* 61–75.

Tobin, K., Tippins, D. J., & Gallard, A. J. (1994). Research on instructional strategies for teaching science. In D. L. Gabel (Ed.), *Handbook on research in science teaching and learning* (pp. 45–93). Upper Saddle River, NJ: Merrill/Prentice Hall.

White, J. J. (1990). Involving different social and cultural groups in discussion. In W. W. Wilen (Ed.), *Teaching and learning through discussion* (pp. 147–174). Springfield, IL: Charles C. Thomas.

Wilen, W. W. (1990). Forms and phases of discussion. In W. W. Wilen (Ed.), *Teaching and learning through discussion* (pp. 3–24). Springfield, IL: Charles C. Thomas.

CHAPTER 7

SCIENCE, TECHNOLOGY, AND SOCIETY

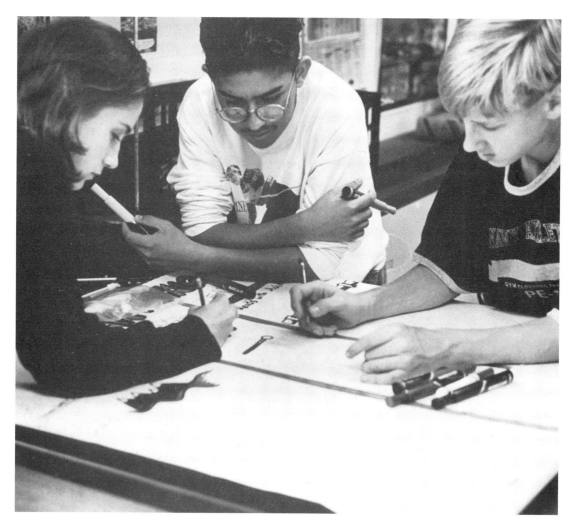

Students are motivated by projects that allow them to relate science learning to their lives outside the classroom.

The development of technology literacy can result only from learning experiences that go beyond those that center upon traditional science course subject matter. This goal calls for new instructional approaches that link science and technology together, stressing the application of knowledge. These approaches must focus on the work of engineers and technologists as well as scientists. Consequently, they must engage students in a variety of learning activities, including those that involve the design of products and systems. The new instructional approaches must also provide opportunities for students to analyze the impact of science and technology on society and to determine their costs and benefits.

OBJECTIVES

This chapter is designed to help the reader meet the following objectives:

- Develop a rationale for including technology in school science programs.
- Explain how technology is related to science and society.
- Describe several ways that designing products and systems can become an integral part of science course instruction.
- Describe examples of strategies and techniques that can help students become aware of science-technology-society issues—how to investigate them and make decisions regarding their findings.
- Reflect on important considerations for dealing with controversial issues and personal values in the classroom, especially evolution and creationism.

RATIONALE

Science and technology exert a profound influence on society. Scientific knowledge influences our thinking about human, political, and social affairs. It also affects how we think about ourselves. In general, scientific knowledge has had and continues to have both positive and negative impacts on individuals as well as society as a whole. Technology also influences individuals and society. It plays an important part in providing products that affect the quality of life. Social, political, and economic changes in society are often affected by new technologies.

Some people fear technology. They believe that the problems resulting from modernization through technology are growing faster than the solutions to these problems. In effect, the attitudes, needs, and values of these people, individually and collectively, can influence the use of existing technologies and the development of new technologies. New technologies often arise because there is a need or demand for them in society or because present technologies need to be improved upon. Society, therefore, exerts its control over technology by assessing its worth and calling for its products or rejecting them.

Science and technology must be understood better by everyone in our society. The development of accurate understandings of this relationship can be accomplished by first dealing with the unique attributes of each enterprise, then addressing their implications for society. It is therefore important to realize that to be functionally literate in science and technology one must understand and appreciate the interrelationships of science and technology as well as their relationships with society. The task of developing a scientifically and technologically literate society has become a major goal of science education.

A continued outcry from all sectors of society demands relevance in the classroom. This societal pressure mandates that science curricula introduce students to careers in the scientific, medical, and engineering fields and provide instruction to assess their cultural influence. Therefore, science teachers must go beyond the content and methods of science and demonstrate how the application of scientific knowledge can affect the welfare of society. This opinion was voiced by Hurd (1961) and other science educators more than thirty years ago when they proposed support for a society-centered biology curriculum.

> Our efforts as biologists ought to be toward the unity of biology with life as a whole; teaching what is required to illuminate biosocial problems and sustain a humane world under conditions of favorable culture and a supporting natural environment. Students want a biology course that says something about their own growth and development and shows their own well-being. Students seek experiences that will bring them into contact with the realities of man's existence and provide insight for future planning. (Hurd, 1961, p. 399)

Students are constantly exposed to environmental and social problems either through direct involvement or indirectly through the communications media. These social issues and problems relate to such areas as drug and alcohol abuse, cancer, AIDS, obesity, overpopulation, abortion, water quality, national defense, and hazardous waste. In order for science education to be relevant, students must be able to examine these issues and to apply the scientific principles and processes to them. They must be given many opportunities to discuss their beliefs and value judgments and to propose solutions to "real world" problems. It's only through this type of exposure and instruction that students will be able to engage in meaningful discourse about science- and technology-related societal issues and problems and go on to make informed decisions about them.

According to Yager and Lutz (1995), the content presented in middle school and secondary science classes is not seen as personally relevant. The traditional lecture/laboratory, science instructional format is antithetical to the educational goal of developing students who are independent thinkers (Gottlieb, 1976). Even widely used science texts have been criticized for containing too much information with little attempt to help students establish relevancy and, on average, devoting less than 7 percent coverage to interactions of science with social, economic, and political problems of contemporary society (Andrews, 1970; Chiang-Soong & Yager, 1993). The factual knowledge of science is of no value if it is stored and forgotten.

Science teachers must develop the content background of students so they can use this knowledge in their daily lives. The big question is: What type of content and how much do we teach our students? Many science educators believe that we are attempting to teach our students too much science information in our efforts to prepare them for courses they will never take and careers they will never pursue. Yager (1985, p. 21) says that preparing students for courses or careers in science, medicine, and related professions is misguided because "for at least 98 percent of all high school graduates such justification is not only inappropriate, it borders on being a hoax." He and many others suggest that we focus on social issues and what takes place in society. They urge science teachers to begin science lessons and units with real issues facing society and let the students define the problems, gather the information, and derive the solutions.

Many science education leaders (Bybee, 1986; Rubba, 1987; Yager, 1993) agree that the science-technology-society (STS) movement, now into its second decade, does a better job than traditional science instruction in educating young people for the world in which they live. An STS approach to teaching and learning involves beginning with student questions and addressing students' interests and concerns in ways that they understand. STS means dealing with science applications and making connections between the world in which students live and the traditional disciplines of science. It means that students are active learners who make use of a variety of resources, not just the textbook. An STS approach offers a broad set of educational goals that cluster around the following themes:

■ Science for meeting personal needs

■ Science for resolving current societal issues

■ Science for assisting with career choices

Learning experiences based on these themes, according to Yager (1993), are appropriate for most middle and secondary students and help them acquire the science content needed for further study in science. Bybee (1986) believes that attention to goals clustered around these themes will help to restore the public's confidence in science education.

Rubba (1987) also believes that STS has the potential to provide students with a variety of essential skills that they can apply to their everyday life. However, this will occur only if science teachers go beyond the awareness and the discussion of issues. He urges that science teachers help their students investigate issues and involve them in inquiry, problem solving, and action learning. Rubba states that "the issue is secondary; it is the vehicle to the development of investigations and action skills which students can incorporate into a decision-making strategy applicable to the STS issues they will face throughout life" (p. 183).

Central to the whole issue of incorporating STS into the science classroom is the attempt to provide students with the knowledge and skills to make decisions that will affect their lives. Ultimately, we as science teachers want people to make good decisions, which will impact them directly. We want young people, for example, to consider the consequences of taking drugs when they are urged to do so by others and then to act in favor of their own welfare. We want young adults to consider the importance of having a plentiful supply of good drinking water in their community, to study water-supply issues, and to vote responsibly when and if these issues are brought up in the community. We want teenagers to consider the consequences of not using seat belts when they drive so they will buckle up when they get into a motor vehicle.

How do we as science teachers provide students in our science classes with information and skills to act responsibly? Ajzen and Fishbein (1980) indicate that human beings are rational and systematic about their behaviors and use the information that they have internalized to make decisions. They stress that the antecedents of behavior are intentions, attitudes, and beliefs—in that order. If we subscribe to their model of reasoned action, we can begin by helping students to acquire information that provides them with a belief system that permits them to learn about the consequences of many behaviors that they may choose in their lives. We can organize learning environments that help students learn about the psychological and physiological effects of certain drugs such as crack cocaine and marijuana, for example. We can help them to clarify their attitudes and those of their peers toward taking these drugs. We can even permit them to resolve their own intentions to take drugs. Although it is naive to believe that we can prevent everyone who enrolls in a science class from using drugs, we can certainly help students acquire some knowledge and skills that can be used to make important decisions now and in the future.

Some science teachers have always introduced technology and social issues into their teaching. They have made their courses relevant, going beyond the facts of science and the assigned science textbook. Unfortunately, however, many science teachers hesitate to incorporate STS into their courses of study for one or more of the following reasons:

■ They depend upon textbooks that stress pure science.

■ They lack an understanding of the nature of science.

■ They are fearful of dealing with student expressions of values and beliefs.

■ They resist change.

■ They view themselves as scientists and defenders of their own personal beliefs about what a science course should include.

■ They feel unprepared to teach topics that they know little about.

■ They feel compelled to teach questionable content known to be included on standardized tests mandated for students. (Jarcho, 1985, p. 17; Ost & Yager, 1993, p. 284)

These are reasons for concern. When science teachers feel unqualified to handle new topics and approaches, constrained by standardized tests, and are afraid to get involved in issues that focus on values and beliefs, then we are shortchanging our students. These concerns have to be taken seriously and become focal points for change so that initiatives can be taken to make science courses more meaningful and useful for students.

WHAT IS TECHNOLOGY?

Just as science is not easy to define, neither is technology. Furthermore, the differences between science and technology are not clear-cut; science and technology are inherently intertwined. As a consequence, they convey different meanings to the professional as well as to the layperson. In general, science can be regarded as the enterprise that seeks to understand natural phenomena and to arrange these ideas into ordered knowledge, whereas technology involves the design of products and systems that affect the quality of life, using the knowledge of science where necessary. Science is a basic enterprise that seeks knowledge and understanding. It is aligned with observation and theory. Technology, on the other hand, is an applied enterprise concerned with developing, constructing, and applying ideas that result

in apparatus, gadgets, tools, machines, and techniques. The products of science are called discoveries; the products of technology are referred to as inventions.

Technology began when humankind invented tools and processes to make work easier and life better. Early technology was simple compared with today's high-tech products. Simple tools were made by primitive people to aid in hunting, farming, and fighting. Many of today's devices are complex, such as computers that present and manipulate information in amazing ways, making it possible for humans to explore the far regions of our solar system or to create new genes that perform special functions in living organisms. After centuries of interplay between technology and science, there exist a myriad of designs, goods, and services that benefit humankind. Today, technology and science are often so intimately related that they rely on each other. This interplay of science and technology was clearly evident during the American Industrial Revolution. Increased use of internal combustion engines and electrical devices before 1890 put into place the foundation for considerable technological advancement. During the years that followed, the internal combustion engine was developed and Westinghouse marketed the first electric generator. Such technological advances underscore the usefulness of scientific knowledge in the fields of thermodynamics and electricity.

The interplay of science and technology is clearly evident in the U.S. space program.
NASA

Americans have only to look back to the beginning of our nation to realize the important role that technology had in its development. Most people are familiar with the names of individuals who participated in promoting one or more technologies in America, such as Benjamin Franklin, Thomas Jefferson, Eli Whitney, Alexander Graham Bell, Thomas Edison, George Eastman, Ellen Swallow Richards, and Henry Ford. Individuals like these and others made possible mass production, which enabled mass consumption that changed our society (Purcell, 1981).

The practical and utilitarian nature of science and technology and their implications for science education are evidenced in the advice given by Benjamin Franklin to Dr. Thomas Cooper, who in 1812 was planning a chemistry course at Carlisle College:

> The chemists have not been attentive enough to this. I wish to see their science applied to domestic objects, to smelting, for instance, brewing, making cider, to fermentation and distillation, generally to the making of bread, butter, cheese, soap, to the incubation of eggs, etc. And I am happy to see some of these titles in the syllabus of your lecture. (cited in Meier, 1981, p. 73)

Recent technological achievements that can be addressed in school science programs are computers, microchips, compact disc players, automatic cameras, digital watches, guided missile systems, superconducting materials, nuclear power, genetic screening, organ transplants, artificial organs, superhighways, and plastics. Engineers design products and services that benefit society, often drawing on scientific information to assist in their work. They also engage in inquiry, use their imagination, and figure out solutions to problems. Engineers experiment, control variables, and make keen observations. These men and women possess a body of knowledge about their enterprise along with knowing many scientific disciplines. Most important, these individuals create their products and processes.

In addition to the benefits of technology, the costs must also be considered. Large-scale production of goods and services consumes valuable resources such as fossil fuels, forests, minerals, recreational areas, plant and animal species, and drinking and irrigation water. These resources are being depleted and are becoming more costly and difficult to obtain. Nations throughout the world must make decisions regarding the use of all resources so that this generation does not use or misuse valuable raw materials, leaving future generations without them. The problems and issues that reside with the use of natural resources that are essential to society must be part of a curriculum improvement movement to increase scientific literacy. The moral and ethical implications of how to apply science must be decided upon by

society—a society, it is hoped, that is well informed about critical science and societal issues.

INCORPORATING STS INTO THE CURRICULUM

Science teachers have several options for incorporating STS into their curriculum. They can include the study of products and systems to improve students' understanding of technology. They can also involve students in the investigation of issues that are related to science and technology, permitting them to analyze situations and to make decisions. It is this latter option that has been the primary thrust of the current STS movement and has served as a guide for the development of some innovative curriculum programs.

Designing Technological Products and Systems

The development of useful products and services illustrates the imagination of engineers, scientists, and technicians who attempt to affect the quality of life. Individuals who develop goods and services think, reason, and imagine in ways similar to those who theorize about natural phenomena. Often, these individuals learn to better understand basic science concepts and principles when they develop products that build upon established knowledge. Fortunately, many types of products and systems can be designed by students to help develop their technological literacy.

Products.   Some science teachers have always engaged their students in building working models of various machines and gadgets to further their involvement in science courses. For example, middle school students can build series and parallel electric circuits, wet cell batteries, electric motors, water clocks, and water pumps. Secondary students can build radios, remote-control gates, electrical generators, rockets, and simple robotic arms. Directions for constructing these kinds of machines are found in many books and on the World Wide Web. Students also enjoy the challenge of constructing gadgets or devices to achieve a particular objective. Building a thermometer that gives the same reading as a commercial thermometer or constructing a container that will hold an egg and keep it from breaking when the container is dropped from the roof of a three-story building are but two example of challenges enthusiastically pursued by students. Additionally, students marvel at the inventions of Rube Goldberg, like the one shown in Figure 7.1.

Constructing such a gadget will generate a wealth of excitement and result in students learning a lot about science and technology.

Library work is another form of inquiry that many science teachers use to study technology. Students can find a great deal of reading material to improve their understanding and stimulate their interest in this topic. The following list of prompts can help students organize their thinking and reporting during the study of technology and its relationship to science and society:

- Tell how the technology was discovered.
- Explain how the technology works and include the scientific principles upon which it is based. Include diagrams.
- Give some of its beneficial uses, such as entertainment, medical, defense, education, and so on.
- Cite any potential dangers of the technology.

Table 7.1 lists some of the many technological devices that students can gather information about from books, magazines, journals, and encyclopedias.

Systems.   A teacher can focus an activity upon systems made up of products and devices that already exist—systems that can be modified and improved to meet the needs of a given community. For example, a critique of a mass transit rail system can be incorporated in a physical science course that addresses energy, mechanics, and motion. Consider a mass transit system for an urban area that is congested with internal combustion engine vehicles that consume large quantities of fossil fuel and pollute the atmosphere. The location of the rail system, the type of power used to move the vehicles, and the economics of the system are but some aspects of the problem.

Rube Goldberg ™ and © property of Rube Goldberg, Inc. Distributed by United Media.

Self-Operating Napkin   RUBE GOLDBERG (tm) RGI 070

Professor Butts walks in his sleep, strolls through a cactus field in his bare feet, and screams out an idea for self-operating napkin: As you raise spoon of soup (A) to your mouth it pulls string (B), thereby jerking ladle (C) which throws cracker (D) past parrot (E). Parrot jumps after cracker and perch (F) tilts, upsetting seeds (G) into pail (H). Extra weight in pail pulls cord (I), which opens and lights automatic cigar lighter (J), setting off sky-rocket (K) which causes sickle (L) to cut string (M) and allow pendulum with attached napkin to swing back and forth thereby wiping off your chin. After the meal, substitute a harmonica for the napkin and you'll be able to entertain the guests with a little music.

FIGURE 7.1   Rube Goldberg Machine

TABLE 7.1 Technological Products That Students Can Study and Explain to Further Their Understanding of Science and Technology

Antenna	Artificial intelligence
Automatic focusing lens	Cardiac pacemaker
Chip	Compact disc player
Computer wafer	Digital watch
Fluorescent light	Fuel cell
Geiger counter	Hologram
Integrated circuit	Laser gun
Magnetic tape	Microwave oven
Nuclear reactor	Quartz clock
Radar detector	Solar panel
Solid-state wafer	Superconductor
Touch-tone telephone	Transistor

■ STOP AND REFLECT! ■

Before going on to the next topic, do the following:

- Formulate a definition of technology. Indicate in your definition how technology is related to science yet different from it.

- Use your definition of technology to examine Box 7.1, "Building Mousetrap Cars." Indicate the extent to which Mrs. Fellabaum's class activities help students develop an understanding of technology.

BOX 7.1

■

BUILDING MOUSETRAP CARS

Mrs. Fellabaum describes the instructional approach she uses in her eighth-grade general science course:

■

More than half of my course centers on basic physics, which includes electricity, light, motion, and sound. I begin the study of each of these topics by asking students what they know about these topics and what they would like to learn about them. The discussions are followed with several laboratory exercises to develop fundamental concepts and principles. With some background, the students begin to participate in design projects. When we study motion, for example, I always involve students in the construction of mousetrap cars. These vehicles are powered by the basic mousetrap sold at hardware stores. They are made from scratch or modified from toy cars and trucks. Since I attempt to associate this experience with speed, acceleration, and friction, one of the primary objectives is to design a vehicle that will accelerate the fastest from a stopped position to a line 2 meters away from the starting point. Another objective is to design a vehicle that will roll the farthest. Students have the option as to which type of vehicle they want to design. These activities are of high interest and they seem to reinforce the topic we are studying. I do not stop at the design phase of this activity because I want to further the hands-on and minds-on aspects of science and engineering. Therefore, all students are asked to write a short paper that requires them to analyze a real vehicle and explain the features that contribute to its acceleration, speed, efficiency, and so on. Some students use their family car for the analysis, others go to automobile dealerships and get the brochures on new cars. One of my students videotaped drag races from a TV show and used these visuals to illustrate features that contribute to the cars' acceleration. This activity also provides the opportunity for us to invite local guest speakers to discuss how people design, maintain, and repair automobiles. We have on occasion taken a field trip to a local garage where dragsters are built. Surprisingly, the girls as well as the boys are motivated by this approach to science and technology education.

Addressing Issues and Problems

The issue/problem focus is prominent in the National Science Teachers Association's (NSTA, 1995–96) position statement for STS programs. These guidelines emphasize that students identify issues and problems of local concern, study them, and make appropriate decisions based on their inquiry. Although the terms *issue* and *problem* are used interchangeably within STS instruction, they have a different meaning. An **issue** is an idea about which people hold different beliefs and values. Whether or not to make recycling mandatory, to limit the construction of multifamily apartment buildings in a community, or to fine drivers for not wearing seat belts are examples of issues. A **problem** is a situation that is at risk for a given population, for example, the poisoning of fish in estuaries that are receiving toxic waste from industry. In any event, the study of issues and problems has taken place for many years, primarily in the area of social studies and environmental education.

Social studies educators have long addressed issues and values in their curricula. A useful model of approaches in values education was described by Superka, Ahrens, Hedstrom, Ford, and Johnson (1976, pp. 4–5) to include five strategies: "(a) inculcation, (b) clarification, (c) moral development, (d) analysis, and (e) action learning." More recently, science educators drawing on work in environmental education have put forth a model that parallels the work in social studies, but that relates more directly to STS instruction: (a) STS foundations, (b) STS issue awareness, (c) STS issue investigation, and (d) STS action skill development (Rubba & Wiesenmayer, 1988, p. 42). The five instructional strategies described here are taken primarily from these models.

Inculcation.   One approach to values education is to instill certain values in students directly, which means that the teacher identifies a given value judgment and attempts to impart it to students. According to Goldthwait (1996), a value is "a conception of how something ought to be" (p. 42) and values are recognizable through the value judgments we make and our acceptance or rejection of them. For example, teachers are expressing a value judgment when they tell their students that they ought to ride the school bus rather than driving cars to school or that they ought to oppose the teaching of creation in science classes. Convincing others to accept your value judgments is a matter of persuasion that can be understood in the context of the question, Who says what to whom with what effect? **Who** is the advocate and **what** is the advocate's message. **Whom** is the audience, or message recipient, and **what effect** is the acceptance of a value judgment resulting from the arguments

and evidence presented in the advocate's message. One way to convince others to accept your value judgment is to present them with the same arguments that you found convincing.

Inculcation is an approach that can be used for values education, but one that has some inherent dangers. It is important to recognize that students may or may not accept the value judgments you proffer. This is true because all persuasion is self-persuasion in that people are free to accept or reject the value judgments held by others. Persuasion stops and coercion begins when value judgments are imposed rather than freely accepted or rejected. Statements that begin with words such as "You must" or "I expect this" when addressing value judgments suggest that persuasion has become coercive. Teachers should guard against using coercion when persuasion is ineffective.

A second danger associated with inculcation is the temptation to present only one perspective regarding a complex, multifaceted issue. The following example illustrates this point.

■

Mr. Clemens teaches high school chemistry in a community where steel mills and petrochemical plants have existed for many years. He often criticizes these industries for polluting the land, rivers, and air in the community. On every possible occasion, Mr. Clemens cites how the waste materials of the steel and chemical industries are "poisoning the environment." He often invites local environmental activists to speak to his classes about the problems of the smokestack industries and their effects on urban America. Mr. Clemens requires all students to write a report on the problems of environmental pollution in their community.

■

This example shows how a science teacher attempts to inculcate students with one point of view—the evils of industry and how industry is damaging the environment. Although few would deny that industry has contributed to environmental pollution, industry has also made great progress to clean up and to protect the environment. Many industries carefully monitor the wastewater they discharge into rivers and lakes and control the concentration of toxic substances in their waste emissions. Mr. Clemens could do a better job of educating his students regarding pollution by providing an opportunity for industries in the community to explain what they do with their waste and how they attempt to protect their workers and the surrounding community from potential health hazards. He should provide students with data and opinions from a variety of sources—industry representatives as well as environmentalists—giving students the opportunity to modify their own beliefs and value judgments and ultimately to act on them. One primary purpose for addressing societal issues is to encourage students to find out about science and technological problems so that they can evaluate them and draw their own conclusions. If the dangers inherent in inculcation are guarded against, this approach to values education can initiate reflection and discussion that can help students improve their understanding of social problems.

Issue Awareness.   Another approach to help students become more aware of issues and problems is through the clarification of these ideas. The clarification of personal values related to science and societal issues is one method that many science teachers might feel comfortable using when they address controversial issues. Values clarification is an approach to "help students to confront the various areas of conflict and confusion that are of specific concern to them, in a constructive and systematic way" (Simon, Hartwell, & Hawkins, 1973, p. 4). This approach provides students an opportunity to become aware of their own beliefs and those of other students. It helps students choose what values are right for them.

Values clarification can be accomplished through discussion techniques, which might be considered safe and prudent, especially in communities where parents are very sensitive to what their children are being taught in school. A relatively easy way to implement values clarification is to find a newspaper article on a social issue related to a science topic currently under study. Place the title of the article on a sheet of paper or on the chalkboard and list questions for students to answer. A good example of a social issue directly related to a science topic is "Awarding monetary damages to long-term smokers diagnosed with lung cancer." This can be discussed in a life science class during the study of respira-

tion. The following questions can be listed for discussion on this topic:

1. Do you smoke?
2. Does anyone in your family smoke?
3. Is it easy for people to quit smoking if they want to?
4. Is smoking a cause of cancer?
5. How can tobacco companies inform consumers of the health risks associated with smoking?
6. Should tobacco companies be held liable for the medical expenses of cancer suffers who were long-term smokers?
7. Should the government collect money from tobacco companies to pay for the cost of treating smoking-related illnesses?

A second values clarification technique is to use societal issue vignettes. Brinkerhoff (1986) recommends that science teachers prepare vignettes about science- and technology-related problems and use these vignettes frequently throughout the school year. His ideas have been implemented by some science teachers as part of their daily science teaching. Whether used daily or less often, teachers can follow Brinkerhoff's recommendation by distributing copies of a vignette to students or showing a transparency of the vignette on an overhead projector at the beginning of a class period. (A sample vignette is shown in Figure 7.2.) Students can begin immediately to respond to the vignette so that by the time the bell rings to start class, they are already thinking about the societal issue. After the roll is taken, the teacher can engage the students in a discussion of the issue. The discussion may be limited to five minutes, but some may take longer or may even last the full period. Students should be encouraged to keep a journal on societal issues, which can be collected periodically and examined for expression of feeling, clarity of writing, factual accuracy, and logical thought.

FIGURE 7.2 A Vignette on Science and Societal Issues

Adapted from *One-Minute Reading Issues in Science, Technology, and Society* by R. F. Brinckerhoff, 1992, Menlo Park, CA: Addison-Wesley.

Today's Science and Societal Issue

Great advances have been made in recent years in cryogenics, the area of physics that deals with very low temperatures. Today, many animals, including goldfish, can be quick-frozen and kept alive at temperatures around −200°C and then returned to good health by slowly warming to normal temperatures. All indications are that the process will work for humans. Suppose you found out that you had cancer and would die within one year. Would you consider having yourself frozen until a cure for cancer could be developed? If you think that having yourself frozen is a good idea, how long would you wait before being frozen? Should the government pay for the procedure, as it now pays for the treatment of many cancer patients?

Teachers who use this approach to develop awareness about science and societal issues indicate that this is one of the most positive aspects of their science course. Students develop knowledge and awareness of topics that they would not have become familiar with, except through this type of instruction. These written exercises and oral discussions stimulate interest in science. The beginning-of-class technique described also promotes effective use of class time because students begin to work as soon as they enter the classroom. Ordinarily, students would not begin to work on academic tasks until after roll is taken and everyone settles down and stops talking. There is little doubt that values clarification activities can be used to initiate the discussion of science- and technology-related issues in science classrooms. They can be infused into existing curricula and implemented in a manner that takes little time away from other types of instruction. Science teachers must not stop at the awareness level, however, but must continue on so that students will inquire further into issues and extend their learning.

Moral Development.   The moral development approach is used to improve the moral reasoning ability of students through the examination of issues. This approach is similar to the analysis approach in that it emphasizes reasoning and thinking. However, the moral development approach focuses on personal moral values such as fairness, justice, equality, and human dignity; the analytical approach focuses on social moral value issues such as global warming, nuclear weapons, and world hunger (Superka et al., 1976). The instructional approach that is used to develop moral reasoning centers around a moral dilemma, which is a factual or a hypothetical story. The moral dilemma is discussed in small groups before it is discussed by the whole class. The dilemma can be introduced in the form of a reading or a film, and it involves characters who are confronted with a personal moral dilemma. A dilemma is a situation that requires an individual to choose between two rather equal choices, each of which is accompanied by a difficult consequence.

Acquired Immune Deficiency Syndrome (AIDS), for example, is a topic that lends itself to discussion in science courses because of its moral implications and biochemical nature. AIDS is fast on its way to becoming the most serious epidemic since the plague. Understanding this disease requires study to understand its biological, clinical, and social aspects. Some students have already been confronted with the AIDS dilemma. In certain communities, students diagnosed as being infected with human immunodeficiency virus (HIV), which causes AIDS, have been prohibited from attending school because some people believe that their presence will result in the virus being spread to other students. In other communities, although HIV-infected students have been permitted to attend school, they have been shunned by classmates. This situation has been difficult for youngsters infected with the virus because they are faced not only with a serious illness but also with rejection by their peers. Situations like this are very real and exist in many communities. Science teachers can address the moral reasoning of their students by involving them in moral dilemmas in which students are asked to reason through these situations that may have personal relevance. They can give students information regarding the transmission of HIV. Science teachers can dispel many misconceptions about other diseases as well. Many other topics, such as drug abuse, alcoholism, abortion, organ transplants, genetic diseases, and obesity can be used to develop moral dilemmas that will get students to focus on issues of personal concern.

The degree to which students can deal with moral dilemmas depends upon their intellectual and moral development. Much of the original work in this area, which will be discussed later in this chapter, has been done by Jean Piaget and Lawrence Kohlberg. In essence, however, they found that the moral reasoning level of the individual will greatly influence how he or she responds to moral issues and social problems.

Issue Investigation.   The investigation and analysis approach goes beyond clarification in that it helps students learn a great deal about issues and technologies so they can understand them better. This approach stresses organization of factual information as well as the presentation of attitudes, beliefs, and values. The analytical approach requires students to participate in inquiry and to find out about ideas by doing library and field work and by determining other people's beliefs. It also encourages students to separate fact from opinion and to become aware of the values of individuals who hold different views regarding an issue. This approach promotes scientific inquiry and higher-level thinking—very important outcomes for science programs. The investigative and analytical approach culminates in students making decisions about important issues.

The analytical decision-making model developed by Oliver and Newman (1967) can be used by science teachers to provide in-depth experiences to students on environmental and technological issues. The following six guidelines can be considered for these purposes.

1. Identify and clarify the basic question.
2. Gather facts about the issue under study.
3. Evaluate the "factual" data.
4. Evaluate the relevance of the "factual" data.
5. Propose a tentative decision.
6. Determine the acceptability of the solution.

The analytical decision-making model can be used to involve students in examining important issues that will directly affect their lives. Some states, for example, are considering whether or not to use some of their land for long-term storage of radioactive waste from nuclear power plants. This is an important decision because of the impact it can have on the local economy, and because radioactive waste triggers such strong reactions from people regarding the environment and public health. The community near any proposed storage site must weigh the risks and benefits of the land use.

Students who undertake assessing whether or not the storage facility should be built near a given hypothetical community must investigate many aspects of the problem. They must learn about radiation and half-life and study the safety record of similar facilities in other states and countries. They must compare the potential danger associated with nuclear power with that of other industries. This inquiry will lead students to study the hazards of using coal and petroleum to produce electricity and the problems of disposing of chemicals such as polychlorinated biphenyls, lead, arsenic, and other industrial waste products that have been going into landfills.

Students must also research the beneficial effects of a storage site to the community. How will this project benefit the community economically? Local business will increase tremendously, at least during the construction of the storage site, to provide food and lodging for the construction workers, technicians, and engineers. Perhaps roads and rails will have to be improved or built. Then there will be the maintenance of the facility once it has been completed and placed in use.

Students should investigate the attitudes of the people in the community regarding the nuclear waste storage problem. Although they cannot survey the citizens of the hypothetical community for which the proposed site is being considered, there are studies that have polled a variety of groups regarding their feelings about nuclear power and radiation. These results will surely be a significant factor in the decision to accept or reject a nuclear waste storage site in the community. Students who undertake the analysis of issues and problems often need to find out the attitudes and beliefs of others regarding these ideas. This necessitates the construction and administration of questionnaires or the development of interview protocols and interviewing people, either face-to-face or by telephone. They can ask a set of questions that assess how knowledgeable individuals are about a given situation, which would address factual knowledge. They can ask a set of questions that assess what individuals believe to be true. And the students can ask a set of questions that assess how the individuals feel about a situation, which would address their attitudes. Beliefs are tied more closely to factual information, whereas attitudes are tied more closely to feelings. Attitudes represent one's likes or dislikes of an idea or event. The beliefs and attitudes of individuals provide insights into their values regarding the environment and society.

Analyzing newspaper and magazine articles is an excellent way to enhance student inquiry (Hungerford, Litherland, Payton, Ramsey, & Volk, 1988). Figure 7.3 presents a format that students can use to guide their analyses and organize the information they derive from written material or oral presentations. First, it is useful to know who the individuals are who are communicating and presenting their views because this makes it is easier to determine the position these individuals have taken on an issue. Listing the main points of each person's argument further clarifies each person's position and elucidates what he or she knows. Finally, it is revealing to determine each person's beliefs and values.

FIGURE 7.3 Format for Examining an Issue from Newspapers, Magazines, or TV Shows

The issue under analysis: _____

_____

The individuals involved:

The positions taken:

Main points of their arguments:

Their beliefs, attitudes, and values:

_____

An important learning outcome of issues investigation and analysis is decision making. Given all of the information that students have gathered, what will they decide to do regarding the situation they have studied? For example, if students have been studying the feasibility of placing a solid waste dump in their community, what do they believe should be done? Do they believe that more waste disposal areas are needed for their community, but that these facilities should not be constructed in their backyard? Decision making can result from a paper prepared by students or from a debate conducted before the class. Students should be asked to make these and many other types of decisions, and then to take some type of responsible action if this is their desire.

Action Learning.   Action learning involves more than thinking, reasoning, clarifying, and decision making. It stresses taking social action in the community, which extends instruction beyond the classroom. Action learning requires student participation in activities that benefit society. This approach is emphasized in the goal structure for precollege STS education, which stresses the need for "opportunities to take actions toward the resolution of an STS issue and to evaluate the effectiveness of those actions" (Rubba & Wiesenmayer, 1988, p. 43).

Some science teachers have, for many years, engaged students in ecology projects in their community. They have taken interested students to streams and beaches to clean up these areas and to collect samples of organisms to take back to the classroom for study. One example of this type of action learning is the Adopt-A-Stream program. Supported and directed in the state of Georgia by the Environmental Protection Division of the Georgia Department of Natural Resources, Adopt-A-Stream involves many teachers and students in a variety of activities related to stream monitoring and cleanup. Program volunteers are encouraged to investigate the origin of water quality problems and to report their findings to community officials and the regional office of the Georgia Environmental Protection Division.

Action learning is definitely a way to get students involved in issues that are important to their lives and to the community in which they live. This approach helps students to become active participants in society and to perform useful services. However, considerable thought and planning must go into action learning activities. Some activities may need to be carried out after school or on weekends, and some activities may be potentially dangerous and science teachers must weigh their risks as well as their benefits. Action learning, along with issue awareness, moral development, issues investigation, and

inculcation, offers science teachers many ways to make science relevant. These approaches provide numerous options from which to select a method that best accommodates their teaching style, student maturity, and community needs.

STS Programs.   STS has been used recently to guide the development of large-scale science programs. Two of these programs are *Biology: A Community Context* (Leonard & Penick 1998) and *Chemistry in the Community (ChemCom)* (American Chemical Society, 1993). Both programs emphasize environmental content while addressing the basic concepts, principles, and skills of biology and chemistry, respectively. They are intended for use with classes of heterogeneously mixed high school students, are strongly activity based, and press students to make personal decisions related to living in a scientific and technological society. *Biology: A Community Context* and *ChemCom* were written by teams of high school and college teachers, and field-tested in classrooms across the county. Financial support for the development of both *Biology: A Community Context* and *ChemCom* came in large part from the National Science Foundation.

Biology: A Community Context is organized into eight units: (1) Matter and Energy for Life, (2) Ecosystems, (3) Populations, (4) Homeostasis: The Body in Balance, (5) Inheritance, (6) Behavior and the Nervous System, (7) Biodiversity, and (8) The Biosphere. Each unit follows a six step sequence that begins with whole-class, problem-centered inquiry (step 1) intended to capture student interest. This is followed by hands-on investigations (step 2) that teach biological concepts and skills, which are related to the initial inquiry through a whole-class science conference (step 3). Next, individual or small-group inquires (step 4) are conducted to investigate questions generated during the science conference or to continue investigations initiated during step 2. Information collected during step 4 is compiled and consensus is reached among small groups of students during the science congress (step 5). Each unit concludes with a whole-class town meeting (step 6) during which students reach some resolutions to the problem introduced at the start of the unit. Stressed throughout the *Biology: A Community Context* program is students keeping logbooks that contain their data, ideas, and questions.

ChemCom is also organized into eight units: (1) Supplying Our Water Needs; (2) Conserving Chemical Resources; (3) Petroleum: To Build? To Burn?; (4) Understanding Food; (5) Nuclear Chemistry in Our World; (6) Chemistry, Air, and Climate; (7) Health: Your Risks and Choices; and (8) The Chemical Industry: Promise and

Challenge. Steps of the *Biology: A Community Context* instructional sequence are found in many of the *Chem-Com* units, but not in an organized manner. However, at the conclusion of each *ChemCom* unit, students use their newly acquired knowledge to tackle a specific chemistry-related problem, to propose solutions to the problem, and to assess the consequences of their proposed solutions.

A concern regarding the implementation of STS programs like *Biology: A Community Context* and *ChemCom* has been that students who take these courses in high school will perform poorly in college science courses. But reports suggest that they are not disadvantaged, and may be better off. According to Ware (1992, p. 2), "if a former *ChemCom* student later decides to major in chemistry, there is no evidence whatsoever that he or she has been intellectually harmed by studying chemistry the *ChemCom* way." Ware goes on to point out that better laboratory skills and more favorable attitudes toward chemistry are found among college chemistry students who took *ChemCom* in high school.

■ STOP AND REFLECT! ■

Before going on to the next topic, do the following:

■ List the salient characteristics associated with each of the five instructional strategies that can be used to address STS issues and problems.

■ Use your list of the salient characteristics to examine Box 7.2, "Mr. Bloom's Adventure," and indicate which of the five strategies is exemplified in the vignette. Provide reasons for your choice.

CONSIDERATIONS FOR STS INSTRUCTION

The examination of technologies and the discussion of social issues in the science classroom require careful

---

BOX 7.2

■

MR. BLOOM'S ADVENTURE

Mr. Bloom observed a great deal of water standing in a drainage ditch located several blocks from the middle school in which he teaches life science. The ditch was an unsightly area because of the dirty water and an accumulation of trash. Mr. Bloom had a hunch that some sewage water might be seeping into the ditch because of the age of the city's sewer system and that if they tested the water, perhaps fecal material would be found in it. When he proposed to students in his classes the idea of cleaning up the drainage ditch and analyzing the water for contamination, many students volunteered to participate in the project.

On a Saturday in October, Mr. Bloom took a large group of students, along with several parents, to the ditch to collect the cans, cups, and paper products that had accumulated there. He also directed some students to collect water samples to be given to the city water department to analyze for contamination and to be examined in the school's science laboratory.

Mr. Bloom had made prior arrangements with the city public works department for the use of their rakes, shovels, and trash bags to aid in the cleanup operation. The public works department also picked up the trash that the students collected. The city water department tested their water samples for fecal material and concluded that sewage was seeping into the drainage ditch.

The students derived a great deal of satisfaction from this project, especially when they observed the public works department digging up the broken sewage pipes and replacing them. They also benefited from examining water samples for microorganisms using their microscopes.

planning and good judgment. Science teachers must select topics that are directly related to the curriculum so that investigation into their relationships with science and society is legitimate. They must select topics that are relevant to students and that will impact the students' lives. The STS approach provides many opportunities to show teenagers how scientific and technological knowledge can make them better informed about themselves and the world they live in. In order for this approach to be successful, however, science teachers must implement instruction that considers the maturity level of the students. For example, middle school students will not be able to participate in discussions at the same level as senior high school and college students. In addition, science teachers must also be knowledgeable about the technologies and social issues that they wish to address in the classroom.

General Guidelines

Relevancy.   Science teachers should identify and study technologies and issues they wish to include in their curriculum. These topics should be related to concepts and principles that are part of the syllabus. In this manner the science subject matter under study will be reinforced by discussions that focus on these topics. For example, nuclear energy will have a different focus in a biology course than in a chemistry course. A biology teacher might stress radiation effects on human body tissues and how to determine the amount of radiation people receive from background radiation, dental X rays, and so on, during a given year. A chemistry teacher might stress radioactive decay and the types of radiation that are given off during the decay of various radioactive isotopes. However, both teachers might address the pros and cons of the transportation of nuclear weapons by rail through their city.

Science teachers should make every attempt to organize science subject matter so that it is relevant to the lives of students as well as pertinent to the curriculum. Experienced and successful science teachers often tell how excited students get when instruction is directed toward content and topics that teach students about themselves. Students want to learn about their bodies and how they can maximize their potential to compete with peers. That is why drugs, sex, nutrition, sports, and cosmetics are topics of high interest to teenagers. Try to select topics of immediate concern to students and try to avoid the approach that transmits to students the message that this information might not seem important now, but as you learn more you will understand.

Teacher's Abilities and Skills.   Science teachers must employ good interpersonal and group facilitator skills

when conducting guided and reflective discussions on controversial issues. They must create a positive and open classroom climate that will encourage students to discuss their feelings and beliefs (Barman, Rusch, & Cooney, 1981). Science teachers must train themselves to be good listeners so that their students will engage in open and meaningful discussions. They must avoid judging the responses of students or putting them down in any way, which is similar to what is expected of science teachers when they conduct inquiry and recitation sessions. If students are embarrassed by what they believe their teacher or their peers will think of them when they share their thoughts and feelings on a given topic, little or no dialog will take place. Science teachers must use great care when they attempt to distinguish fact from opinion during discussions. Students often confuse opinions for what they believe to be factual information, which obviously can distort their beliefs and attitudes.

Science teachers, especially those new to teaching, should ask administrators and colleagues for their opinions about the inclusion of issues that might be problematic to address in science class. They should discuss their plans with the principal, department head, and instructional team leader to determine the possibility of parents' concerns about what is taking place in their children's science classes. Whereas the principal is the one who usually receives complaints from parents regarding the experiences their children have in school, department heads and team leaders also receive them. Principals, department heads, and team leaders tend to have a great deal of experience dealing with problems of this nature and can be a good sounding board for instructional plans. Veteran science teachers, especially those who have taught in a given school or community for many years, can also be very helpful in making recommendations on the inclusion of social issues in the science curriculum.

Students' Intellectual Development.   The age and ability level of students must be considered when a societal issue is chosen for classroom discussion. Many social issues that are scientifically relevant cannot be presented to low-ability students or to those who are simply not mature enough to discuss them. Adequate treatment, as used here, is meant to imply more than a superficial mention of the underlying complexities of the social issue. A disregard for student maturation very often creates more distortion and misunderstanding than educational benefit. Discussions of genetic screening, for example, may not be appropriate for a group of sixth-grade students because they do not have the sophistication to handle the issue. It is true that such students can discuss the issue at some level, but the intricacies of the concept of personal freedom that underlies this issue would most likely be ignored or glossed over when dealing with such a group. The teacher must be very careful that student age and ability do not preclude a relatively complete discussion of the issue at hand. It is important to remember that inclusion of a social issue in science instruction is for the two-fold purpose of (1) helping students learn and understand science content and (2) enabling students to make informed decisions with regard to the scientifically based issues that will confront them in life.

Jean Piaget's work on the development of intelligence provides a conceptual framework to help science teachers understand the potential and limitations of their students to discuss certain ideas. His work indicates that intellectual competence is tied to the development of general reasoning patterns. The degree to which these thinking skills have been developed will set limits on adolescents' thinking. Science teachers should be aware that intellectual development has both cognitive and social dimensions. Although cognitive and affective reasoning develop together, there is not a one-to-one correspondence between these areas of competence. People in general, and young people in particular, may be more advanced in certain aspects of their physical world than in certain aspects of their social world. And, of course, the opposite is also true.

Lawrence Kohlberg furthered Piaget's work in the area of moral reasoning. He illustrates how moral reasoning is linked to values in the moral dilemmas he has developed. Each dilemma involves a character who is involved in a difficult situation and must choose between two conflicting values. It is these values that constitute one's moral reasoning. The ten basic moral values that Kohlberg incorporates into his moral dilemmas are as follows:

The Ten Universal Moral Issues

1. Laws and rules
2. Conscience
3. Personal roles of affection
4. Authority
5. Civil rights
6. Contract, trust, and justice in exchange
7. Punishment
8. The value of life
9. Property rights and values
10. Truth (cited in Reimer, Paolitto, & Hersh, 1983, p. 84)

Kohlberg uses these ideas to develop situations in which to study how people reason in the social dimension. He also believes that educators can enhance moral development by exposing students to moral dilemmas and asking them to present their reasons for how they would deal with a particular dilemma. This approach would require students to express and clarify their values.

Perhaps Kohlberg's biggest contributions to this field of study are the six "stages of moral judgment" that he has formed from his investigations. His six stages as presented in figure 7.4 have been adapted from Barman et al. (1981, pp. 11–15), and Reimer et al. (1983, pp. 58–61). Kohlberg's stages of moral development provide a useful framework to use when selecting and incorporating into the curriculum the five recommended approaches to values education discussed earlier in this chapter. Analysis of these stages will permit the teacher to maximize the match between any one of the values education approaches—inculcation, awareness, moral development, investigation, and action learning—and the students in a given science class. Although you may find that a large proportion of the students demonstrate decisions based on the conventional level, often students will display behavior either above or below their principal level of moral development. Zeidler and Schafer (1984) suggest that moral reasoning is influenced by the context or setting of a moral dilemma. For example, a group of students may demonstrate a higher level of decision making on an environmental issue that they are familiar with and interested in than an issue that they have little knowledge of and interest in. Therefore, it is possible to get students to become more sophisticated in their beliefs and actions by involving them in values education instruction that centers on their interests and considers their maturity.

EVOLUTION VERSUS CREATIONISM—DEALING WITH NONSCIENCE TENETS

The evolution/creationism controversy illustrates the influence society can have on science education. For more than half a century biology textbooks have de-emphasized the teaching of evolution because a very small percentage of people believe that the study of evolution threatens their religious beliefs regarding the origin of humankind. In addition, many science teachers have been so intimidated by the problems surrounding this societal issue that they have either de-emphasized teaching evolution or have excluded it from their course. Consequently, this section has been written to give science teachers a strong rationale for including evolution in their instruction and for not addressing nonscience tenets in their curriculum.

The biological theory of evolution was discussed and written about before 1800, but the first formidably structured statement concerning variation among organ-

FIGURE 7.4 Kohlberg's Six
Stages of Moral Development

Preconventional Level: Self-Centered Needs

Stage 1: *Avoidance of punishment.* In this stage, people follow rules to avoid punishment. They are obedient and do what they are told to avoid getting into trouble.

Stage 2: *Self-benefit.* In this stage, people follow the rules to serve their own best interests. They are aware of the motives and needs of other people and treat others in accordance with how that treatment will benefit themselves.

Conventional Level: Conformity and Maintenance of Law and Order

Stage 3: *Concerns for acceptance.* In this stage, people behave to meet the expectations of others. They are greatly influenced by peers and peer pressure and behave in order to meet the expectations of those close to them. Being good is important, as is demonstrating loyalty, trust, and respect.

Stage 4: *Authority orientation.* In this stage, people act according to what appears to be "right or best" for society. They are influenced by authority and rules and have the best interests of society as a whole in mind, as opposed to their own personal interests.

Postconventional Level: Consideration for the Values of Others

Stage 5: *Greatest good for the greatest number.* In this stage, people believe that the rights of others are of uppermost importance. They will act to change laws if they feel that the laws are injurious to the rights and well-being of society. They believe that laws should be useful and serve everyone—the greatest good for the greatest number of people.

Stage 6: *Conscience is the guide.* In this stage, people believe that individuality is supreme and the rights and freedom of each individual should be preserved. The equality of human rights must be maintained. They will do everything in their power, including breaking the law, to promote these universal principles.

---

isms was made by Charles Darwin with the publication of *On the Origin of Species* in 1859. Darwin's theory was presented as a grand and unifying theme of the biological sciences. Darwin was immediately criticized for what were interpreted as atheistic views, although he clearly reflected his theistic beliefs in the document. Thus, the current debate pitting evolution and creationism against one another was born. The controversial issue concerned with evolution and creationism centers around whether creationism should be presented as a valid alternative to evolutionary theory within science instruction. The issue did not always take this form, however. In the 1920s the debate was whether to present evolutionary theory at all in the public school science classrooms. The textbooks of that period (1910 to early 1920s) covered evolution, but did so forthrightly.

The original legal battle over the teaching of evolution in public schools took place in Dayton, Tennessee, in 1925 where John Scopes was accused of teaching evolution, which constituted a violation of a Tennessee law prohibiting such instruction. Much notoriety was given

to the trial, as Clarence Darrow defended Scopes against the Tennessee prosecution led by William Jennings Bryan. Much has been written about this landmark trial through the years. What has surfaced is a rather humorous account of a circus-type atmosphere. Indeed, the trial became known as the Monkey Trial and was the subject of a play and a movie. In reality, the legal aspects of the trial were rather undistinguished. There was clearly a law against the teaching of evolution, and Scopes had clearly violated it. (Actually, he only assigned the pages for students to read.) Thus, he was found guilty. Furthermore, Scopes had agreed to participate in the "incident" to test the merits of such a law. However, the legend of events past very often supersedes reality. Because Scopes was fined only $100, the trial has been considered a victory for evolutionists. However, even though many antievolution laws were repealed subsequent to the trial, the controversial nature of the issue prevented comprehensive coverage of evolution in biology textbooks before the 1960s. Then, as now, teachers often consciously avoided the teaching of evolution in an effort to avoid community backlash. This has been the legacy of the Scopes trial.

One of the most significant court decisions of recent times was *Epperson v. Arkansas* (1968):

Government in our democracy, state, and nation must be neutral in matters of religious theory, doctrine, and practice. It may not be hostile to any religion or to the advocacy of no-religion; and it may not aid, foster, or promote one religion or religious theory against another or even against the militant opposite. The First Amendment mandates governmental neutrality between religion and non-religion.

One debate concerning the teaching of evolution is not about banning such instruction but rather about providing equal time for the creation story as a valid alternative. Thus, the approach has changed, but the controversy continues. Mandates forcing science teachers to provide instruction regarding creationism strikes at the heart of academic freedom. Science teachers are exercising this academic freedom and choosing not to teach creationism. Furthermore, as Skoog (1985) points out:

Equal time policies are not necessarily fair or educationally sound. . . . Science teachers cannot treat all knowledge equally. We must select content based on its power to explain the natural world scientifically and its ability to unify, illuminate, and integrate other facets. We should not include ideas that cannot serve these functions. . . . The courts have ruled that laws prohibiting the teaching of evolution are unconstitutional and that teachers have no obligation to shield students from ideas that may offend their religious beliefs. Furthermore, it is possible to excuse students from classes where topics, offensive to their religious beliefs, are being presented. (p. 8)

This issue brings us to the nature of scientific theory. Creationists refer to evolution as only a theory. They appear to use the term as it is used in the American vernacular to mean an imperfect fact. Such use of the term implies a hierarchy of confidence that runs downward from fact to theory to hypothesis to guess. Actually, scientific theory is not placed in such a hierarchy. In science, theories are structures of ideas that explain and interpret scientific facts (data). Thus, using the term theory to mean an imperfect fact is not the sense in which scientists use it when they call evolution a theory. Scientists do not believe that evolution is an imperfect fact.

What constitutes a scientific theory actually touches the core of the current evolution/creationism controversy. Creationists believe that creationism is just as much a theory as evolution and that it is as scientific. Therefore, they feel that the creation story should be presented in science instruction as a valid scientific alter-

native to evolutionary theory. On the other hand, evolutionists believe that creationism is not science at all, but rather religion, and should not be included in the science classroom. In 1982 Judge William Overton interpreted the constitution and, in doing so, sided with a variety of individuals in the *McLean v. Arkansas* case that tried the constitutionality of a law requiring equal treatment of creationism and evolution. The verdict was simple. It was decided that creationism is religiously based and inclusion of it within public education would violate the separation of church and state.

More recently, the U.S. Supreme Court ruled against the equal treatment of creationism and evolution in public schools. The ruling, prompted by the 1987 Louisiana case *Edwards v. Aguillard*, indicates that mandating equal time to the teaching of creationism and evolution in science classes is unconstitutional. Known as "the Edwards restriction," this Supreme Court decision has been applied in court cases in California and Illinois to prohibit the teaching of creationism in science classes. Teachers need to be acquainted with such court cases and local challenges to them.

Because this issue is extremely controversial, it would appear to serve as an efficient vehicle for classroom discussion. Nevertheless it is *not* a good issue to debate because the creation aspect of the issue is not part of the science curriculum and according to court decisions and science educational guidelines it should not be part of the curriculum. Perhaps the NSTA position statement concerning "Inclusion of Nonscience Tenets in Science Education" is a worthwhile guide for science teachers to follow when dealing with a topic such as creationism versus evolution. The following statement was adopted by the NSTA Board of Directors in July, 1985:

People have always been curious about the universe and their place in it. They have questioned, explored, probed, and conjectured. In an effort to organize their understanding, people have developed various systems that help them explain their origin, e.g., philosophy, religion, folklore, theaters, and science.

Science is the system of exploring the universe through data collected and controlled by experimentation. As data are collected, theories are advanced to explain and account for what has been observed. Before a theory can be included in the system of science, it must meet all of the following criteria: (1) its ability to explain what has been observed, (2) its ability to predict what has not yet been observed, and (3) its ability to be tested by further experimentation and to be modified as required by the acquisition of new data.

NSTA recognizes that only certain tenets are appropriate to science education. Specific guidelines must be followed to determine what does belong in science education: NSTA endorses the following tenets:

I.   Respect the right of any person to learn the history and content of all systems and to decide what can contribute to an individual's understanding of our universe and our place in it.

II. In explaining natural phenomena, science instruction should only include those theories that can properly be called science.

III. To ascertain whether a particular theory is properly in the realm of science education, apply the criteria stated above.

IV. Oppose any action that attempts lo legislate, mandate or coerce the inclusion in the body of science education, including textbooks, any tenets which cannot meet the above-stated criteria. (NSTA, 1995–96, p. 253.)

Since this problem never seems to go away, Clough (1994, pp. 411–413) offers the following suggestions in *The American Biology Teacher* to reduce resistance to the teaching of evolution and to avoid unnecessary controversy:

- Demarcate biological evolution from debates concerning life's origin.

- When using the word **theory**, define it as a structure of ideas that explains and interprets scientific data. Make clear that a scientific theory is not an imperfect fact.

- Acknowledge that all scientific theories, including evolution, are open to revision and should be judged by their explanatory powers.

- Stress a functional understanding of evolution, not one based on beliefs.

- Point out that knowledge is not democratic. Fairness and equality are not criteria for selecting science content.

- Show how science provides natural explanations for phenomena and how creationism employs explanations that are beyond nature and include supernatural events.

- Avoid defining **fitness** as simply "differential reproductive success."

- Recognize the contradiction between the claim that evolutionary theory is not falsifiable and hence not science, and the evidence presented to falsify evolution.

- Explain that comprehensive theories, like evolution, should not be discarded simply because of several pieces of anomalous data, such as the incomplete fossil record.

- Show mutual respect for all students' views, whether or not they support evolution.

- Don't start the first day of biology class with a lesson on evolution. Teach students about the nature of science and give them a chance to get to know you.

In closing this section, we must stress the importance of evolution in science and the understanding of the universe. Although the topic is controversial, science teachers should not fall into the trap of attempting either to deal with evolution and creationism as a science and societal issue, or to demonstrate the inadequacies of creationism to explain the origin of life. This approach may be offensive and inflammatory to some students and their religious views. Stick to the discipline of science and teach it well.

Assessing and Reviewing

1. Suppose you were asked by parents to explain your reasons for including technology in your tenth-grade biology course. From your principal, you learned that the parents believe that their children are not learning the biology content that they should from the course. Write a paragraph that includes at least two arguments with supporting evidence that you would use to convince the parents of the need to include technology in your course.

2. The following ten statements describe aspects of science instruction. Which of the ten better characterize aspects of STS instruction than typical science instruction? Give reasons for your choices.

- Instruction is guided by student questions and interests.
- Instruction is teacher centered.
- Students are active participants in the learning process.
- Instruction makes use of all available resources, both material and people, to resolve problems.
- Instruction is guided by a textbook.
- Students work cooperatively to investigate issues and problems.
- An emphasis is placed on content mastery that is demonstrated on tests.

- Instruction is primarily directed to the upper third of the class.

- Students are given little autonomy in deciding what and how to learn.

- Students apply science concepts to new situations.

3. Two approaches for incorporating STS into the science curriculum are (1) designing technological products and systems and (2) addressing issues and problems. Select one of the following topics and describe how you might incorporate STS using the designing products and systems approaches. Then, use the same topic or select a second one and describe how you might incorporate STS using the issues and problems approach. Was it easier for you to think of how to incorporate STS using one of the approaches? Why do you think so?

- Motions and forces
- Chemical reactions
- Geochemical cycles
- Origin and evolution of the universe
- Behavior of organisms
- The cell
- Structure and property of matter

4. Your local newspaper prints a story of cockroach infestation in apartment buildings located in your town. You decide to use this story to incorporate STS into your unit on insects. Assume that some of your middle school students live in these apartment buildings and this is your first year teaching in this town. Which of the five strategies for addressing issues and problems would you choose to employ? Why? What instructional factors would you consider before implementing your teaching plan?

RESOURCES TO EXAMINE

One-Minute Readings Issues in Science, Technology, and Society. Published 1992. Menlo Park, CA: Addison-Wesley Publishing Company.

Richard F. Brinckerhoff presents eighty issues that address the social and ethical aspects of numerous topics in biology, chemistry, and physics. Each issue is to be read by students and is written to capture their attention and stimulate critical thinking. The issues can be used to expose students to science applications and to involve them in science-related decision making.

"Goals and Competencies for Precollege STS Education: Recommendations Based upon Recent Literature in Environmental Education." 1988. *Journal of Environmental Education, 19,* 38–44.

Peter Rubba and Randall Wiesenmayer describe the origin of STS education in environmental education and their rationale for the goal categories of foundations, issue awareness, issue investigation, and issue action skill. Additionally, the authors identify fifty-three student competencies for STS instruction in grades 7–12.

Scientists Confront Creationism. Published 1983. New York: W. W. Norton & Company.

This easy-to-read 324-page book edited by Laurie R. Godfrey includes fifteen chapters, all contributed by

leading scientists, that set forth the science that supports evolution. Chapter authors address such issues as how geology and paleontology disprove the notion of a global flood, why molecular evidence supports the arguments for evolution, why the second law of thermodynamics does not contradict evolution, and how punctuated equilibrium supports evolution.

STS Course Pack Archive. World Wide Web Address: http://www2.ncsu.edu/ncsu

This World Wide Web site provides access to complete citations for STS-related readings from science magazines and journals. The citations are accessed by selecting one of fifteen topics listed. Topics include global issues, computer and information highway, decision making, values, military issues, energy issues, politics, technological risk issues, and rhetoric, among others. The site is maintained by Patrick Hamlett and updates periodically.

NSTA Pathways to the Science Standards: Guidelines for Moving the Vision into Practice. Published 1996. Distributed by the National Science Teachers Association, 1840 Wilson Boulevard, Arlington, VA 22201.

Edited by Juliana Texley and Ann Wild, this 191-page book provides practical suggestions for operationalizing the National Science Education Standards. Of particular interest with regard to STS are the sections "Personal and Social Perspectives" and "Science and Technology" that are presented for each key area of life science, physical science, and earth and space science content standards. Ideas are offered about how to make connections between technology and society and the science content specified in the standards.

■

REFERENCES

Ajzen, I., & Fishbein, M. (1980). *Understanding attitudes and predicting social behavior*. Englewood Cliffs, NJ: Prentice-Hall.

American Chemical Society. (1993). *Chemistry in the community*. Dubuque, IA: Kendall/Hunt.

Andrews, M. D. (1970). Issue-centered science. *The Science Teacher, 37*(2), 29–30.

Barman, C. R., Rusch, J. J., & Cooney, T. M. (1981). *Science and societal issues: A guide for science teachers*. Ames: Iowa State University Press.

Brinckerhoff, R. F. (1986). *Values in schools: Some practical materials and suggestions*. Exeter, NH: Exeter Academy.

Brinckerhoff, R. F. (1992). *One-minute readings issues in science, technology, and society*. Menlo Park, CA: Addison-Wesley.

Bybee, R. W. (1986). The Sisyphean question in science education: What should the scientifically and technologically literate person know, value, and do—as a citizen? In R. W. Bybee (Ed.), *1985 Yearbook of the National Science Teachers Association*. Washington, DC: NSTA.

Chiang-Soong, B., & Yager, R. E. (1993). The inclusion of STS materials in the most frequently used secondary science textbooks in the U.S. *Journal of Research in Science Teaching, 30*, 339–349.

Clough, M. P. (1994). Diminish students' resistance to biological evolution. *The American Biology Teacher, 56*, 409-415.

Edwards v. Aguillard, 482 U.S. 587 (1987).

Epperson v. Arkansas, 393 U.S. 97 (1968).

Goldthwait, J. T. (1996). *Values: What they are & how to know them*. Amherst, NY: Prometheus Books.

Gottlieb, S. (1976). Teaching ethical issues in biology. *The American Biology Teacher, 38*, 148.

Hungerford, H. R., Litherland, R. A., Payton, R. B., Ramsey, J. M., & Volk, T. L. (1988). *Investigating and evaluating environmental issues and actions skill development modules*. Champaign, IL: Stipes.

Hurd, P. H. (1961). *Biological education in American secondary schools, 1890–1960*. Washington, DC: AIBS.

Jarcho, I. S. (1985). S-T-S in practice: Five ways to make it work. *Curriculum Review, 24*(3), 17–20.

Leonard, W. H., & Penick, J. E. (1998). *Biology: A community context*. Cincinnati, OH: South-Western.

McLean v. Arkansas, 529 F. Supp. 1255 (1982).

Meier, H. A. (1981). Thomas Jefferson and a democratic technology. In C. W. Purcell, Jr. (Ed.), *Technology in America*. Cambridge: The MIT Press.

National Science Teachers Association (NSTA). (1995–96). *NSTA handbook*. Arlington, VA: Author.

Oliver, D. W., & Newman, F. M. (1967). *Taking a stand*. Middletown, CT: Xerox.

Ost, D. H., & Yager, R. E. (1993). Biology, STS and the next step in program design and curriculum development. *The American Biology Teacher, 55*, 282–287.

Purcell, C. W., Jr. (1981). *Technology in America*. Cambridge: The MIT Press.

Reimer, J., Paolitto, D. P., & Hersh, R. H. (1983). *Promoting moral growth*. New York: Longman.

Rubba, P. A. (1987). Perspectives on science-technology-society instruction. *School Science and Mathematics, 87*, 181–185.

Rubba, P. A., Wiesenmayer, R. L. (1988). Goals and competencies for precollege STS education: Recommendations based upon recent literature in environmental education. *Journal of Environmental Education, 19*(4), 38–44.

Simon, S. B., Hartwell, M. R., & Hawkins, L. A. (1973). *Values clarification: Friends & other people: Teachers' manual*. Arlington Heights, IL: Paxcom.

Skoog, G. (1985). Editor's corner. *The Science Teacher, 52*(1), 8.

Superka, D. P., Ahrens, C., Hedstrom, J., Ford, L. J., & Johnson, P. L. (1976). *Values education sourcebook*. Boulder, CO: Social Science Education Consortium.

Ware, S. A. (1992). What type of student should take Chem-Com? *Chemunity News, 2*(5), 2–3.

Yager, R. E. (1985). Preparing students for the technological world. *Curriculum Review, 24*(3), 21–22.

Yager, R. E. (1993). Science-Technology-Society as reform. *School Science and Mathematics, 93*, 145–151.

Yager, R. E., & Lutz, M. V. (1995). STS to enhance total curriculum. *School Science and Mathematics, 95,* 28–35.

Zeidler, L., & Schafer, L. E. (1984). Identifying mediating factors of moral reasoning in science education. *Journal of Research in Science Teaching, 21*, 1–15.

■

LABORATORY AND FIELD WORK

Science teachers must demonstrate certain techniques to help students become capable in the laboratory.

Laboratory and field work are unique types of instruction that must be integrated into science teaching. These activities involve students in firsthand experiences, which can permit them to participate in science as a way of thinking and as a way of investigating. Laboratory and field work can also help students construct an important body of scientific knowledge and to learn about technology. They also provide concrete, real experiences that will help students to comprehend phenomena. These modes of instruction require careful planning, however, in order for them to fulfill their functions. Further, it takes considerable expertise on the part of science teachers to produce desired outcomes, whether they be from laboratory exercises conducted inside of school or field work in the community.

OBJECTIVES

This chapter is designed to help the reader meet the following objectives:

- Define and state the purpose of both laboratory and field work.
- Explain five types of laboratory approaches that should be used in science courses and construct exercises that illustrate these methods.
- Discuss teaching tips that can result in successful laboratory experiences.
- Plan a field trip for a group of students that will be productive and safe.

WHAT IS LABORATORY WORK?

> Members of the scientific community . . . agree that science, at its roots, is an active process, not facts or products, but the process of problem identification, experimentation, data interpretation, hypothesizing and testing. (Renner, 1966)

Laboratory work engages students in finding out and learning how through firsthand experiences. It can involve students in scientific inquiry by placing them in the position of asking questions, proposing solutions, making predictions, taking observations, organizing data, explaining patterns, and so on. This type of work permits students to plan and to participate in investigations or to take part in activities that will help them improve their technical laboratory skills. Some laboratory work engages students in hands-on activities in which they use specialized equipment. It can also engage students in activities in which they use ordinary equipment found in their everyday environment. Some laboratory work may occur in field and natural settings where little or no equipment is necessary and where there is little intervention from the observer.

The science laboratory is central to science teaching because it serves many purposes. Laboratory work has the potential to engage students in authentic investigations in which they can identify their own problems to investigate, design procedures, and draw conclusions. These activities can give students a sense as to how scientists go about their work, which in turn may influence their attitudes about the scientific enterprise. Along with attitudes about science, laboratory work can help students acquire a better understanding of concepts and principles as the result of concrete experiences. In general, laboratory work can be used to promote the following learning outcomes:

- attitudes toward science
- scientific attitudes
- scientific inquiry
- conceptual development
- technical skills

Science laboratory work seems to leave a lasting impression on students. "Many of them [students] enjoy labwork and prefer it to other modes of learning. This is not, of course, the universal reaction of all students at all times" (Gardner & Gauld, 1990, p. 136). This statement is especially true of the middle school students who prefer active learning experiences over listening to lectures. Science teachers who are highly regarded by students frequently include laboratory exercises in their courses. These teachers believe that laboratory work enhances concept development and promotes scientific attitudes. They also realize that lab work breaks up the instructional period, which limits the amount of lecturing and adds variety to the course.

The laboratory has always been emphasized in science teaching, and during some periods in the history of science education, it has been given a dominant role. During the major science curriculum reform movement of the 1960s, for example, some science educators felt that a considerable amount of laboratory work should lead, rather than lag behind, the classroom phase of science teaching (Schwab, 1964). Curriculum planners of the 1960s placed heavy emphasis on inquiry and the processes of science by suggesting that working on problems in the laboratory is more important than drawing conclusions and that science teachers should expose their students to certain amounts of doubt in science courses even though they and the students may not tolerate ambiguity well (Schwab, 1964). Henry (1960) indicated that more emphasis should be placed on how to process data and make predictions from data, and less stress should be placed on finding exact answers. Further, Hurd (1964) recommended that the laboratory should focus on major ideas related to class work and should precede textbook assignments. Even more recently, some science educators have advised science teachers to conduct laboratory work that emphasizes hypothesizing, predicting, developing concepts, model building, and developing positive attitudes toward science. They advise that lab work should de-emphasize illustration, demonstration, and verification (Lunetta & Tamir, 1979).

The recommendation to implement inquiry-based laboratories, such as those intended by the national curriculum projects of the 1960s, may be appropriate for some students and for certain purposes. As pointed out earlier, the curriculum reform projects of the 1960s were very laboratory oriented, but they did not necessarily provide students with experiences they needed to live in a changing society. The curriculum reform projects of the 1990s, on the other hand, emphasize scientific literacy and stress the need for students to have experiences that permit them to adapt to a changing world.

Laboratory work is not a panacea for improving science education. Although most science educators promote lab work, this strategy does not necessarily produce all of the outcomes believed by many educators (Blosser, 1981; Hegarty-Hazel, 1990) for a number of reasons. For example, a great deal of the lab work that takes place in schools is "aimless, trivial, and badly planned" (Hodson, 1985, p. 44). Laboratory work that is counter to what students expect does not necessarily produce new conceptions (Rowell & Dawson, 1983). Laboratory periods are often too short, and students do not complete their lab work (Gardner & Gauld, 1990).

Of course materials and equipment are always a problem in some schools where limited resources are available for this type of instruction. Some researchers who have studied the construction of scientific knowledge advise that the role of the laboratory needs to be reexamined, because student learning from firsthand experiences may not produce the intended learning outcomes that we believe them to produce (Driver, Guesne, & Tiberghien, 1985).

The ultimate success of laboratory work lies with science teachers who determine the frequency, importance, and purpose of this enterprise in a science course. If a teacher believes that laboratory work is important and has the competence and facilities to carry out this type of instruction, the chances are good that the students will frequently engage in meaningful firsthand experiences. If the teacher believes that the function of a science program is to transmit information, laboratories will be deductive in nature, occurring after textbook reading and classroom discussion; thus, the laboratory will serve only to verify existing knowledge. If the teacher believes that a science program should be investigative in nature, then some laboratories will be inductive and occur before textbook readings and teacher lectures (Pella, 1961).

Beginning and practicing science teachers should carefully formulate their professional philosophy of science teaching, taking into consideration the curriculum, the students, their approach to instruction, the facilities, and the materials available. Teachers must understand the various approaches to laboratory work so they can make good decisions regarding the type of laboratory to use with a given group of students in order to achieve a given purpose. Further, science teachers must learn to be able to analyze laboratory manuals, related exercises, and the laboratory work that is taking place in science departments where they are teaching in order to evaluate their potential to promote scientific inquiry (Lazarowitz & Tamir, 1994).

APPROACHES TO LABORATORY WORK

Science course laboratory work can be used to achieve many different learning outcomes. Some laboratory exercises, for example, might be employed to verify a concept previously discussed in class. Other types of laboratory exercises might be used to develop particular manipulative skills that are needed for subsequent lab work. Some laboratory exercises facilitate the attainment of concepts. The desired outcomes will dictate the type

of laboratory needed. Each type of laboratory approach has characteristics differentiating it from other approaches. In general, most approaches can be classified into one of five categories:

1. science process skill
2. deductive or verification
3. inductive
4. technical skill
5. problem solving

Science Process Skill Laboratory

A major purpose for including laboratory work is to develop in students a sense for the nature of science. This aim requires that students use inquiry skills to engage in investigation. Some of the mental processes associated with science and, in particular, with laboratory work are often referred to as science process skills. These skills include observing, classifying, using space/time relations, using numbers, measuring, inferring, predicting, defining operationally, formulating models, controlling variables, interpreting data, and experimenting (see Chapter 5). When the primary intent of a laboratory exercise is to help students develop the ability to use one or more science process skills, the laboratory can be classified as a science process laboratory. Certainly science process skills are involved in all types of laboratory work, such as observing, for example. Nevertheless, some laboratory work can be used to specifically improve students' awareness and competence in using skills that are related to scientific reasoning.

There are many skills that people use to think critically and reason logically. In Chapter 5, many of the cognitive reasoning patterns were discussed and a long list of science process skills were presented and defined. Table 8.1 provides a sample of science process skills that deserve the attention of science teachers, because these are skills that middle and high school students should be capable of using.

Consider observing and inferring, which are related. Often science teachers begin the school year with exercises that address these cognitive abilities. The exercise shown in Box 8.1 is one that can stimulate students' interests in observing and inferring and give them practice with these skills. Some creativity has been put into this exercise to help students visualize these concepts. Note that definitions and background information are provided along with several examples on distinguishing observations from inferences. Just as important, students are given experiences at lab stations to help them acquire these process skills.

TABLE 8.1   A Sample of Science Process Skills to Develop in Middle and High School Laboratory Instruction

Process skill	Learning outcome
Observing and inferring	Distinguish between observations and inferences. Make accurate observations that describe objects and events. Make plausible inferences that help to explain situations.
Measuring	Make measurements for length, mass, and volume, using SI or metric units.
Hypothesizing	Distinguish between inferences and hypotheses and know when to use each. Construct hypotheses that can be tested and for which enough data can be gathered for generalizing.
Communicating	Construct and label tables, bar graphs, and line graphs that are accurate and fit the situation. Keep a laboratory notebook and journal of activities with reflections. Write laboratory reports that are coherent and present procedures, results, and conclusions.
Experimenting	Test hypotheses and answer questions through controlled experimentation where independent and dependent variables are accounted for and properly controlled.

BOX 8.1

■

OBSERVING AND INFERRING CAN BE A SAFE ACTIVITY

An **observation** is the act of noting something that can be sensed directly or with the aid of an instrument. One can observe the color of a car, the final score of a basketball game, or the first snowstorm of the season. These and many other observations can be made, confirmed by others, and established as a matter of record. Direct observations are possible through the five senses—smell, taste, sight, sound, and touch. Although observations can be disputed, most everyday observations are accepted as fact. Indirect observations are made with instruments, such as microscopes, spectrophotometers, and multimeters.

An **inference** differs from an observation in a significant way, because it requires individuals to explain what they observe. An inference is an attempt to explain a particular event or object. It requires thinking and reasoning to make the leap from what is observed at the surface to what the observer believes is there and hidden from view or perception. An inference requires the observer to go beyond the obvious. Inferences, however, are not exactly hypotheses. A **hypothesis** is a generalization that relates to a class of objects or events, whereas an inference is related to a specific object or event. Let's develop the skill of distinguishing between observations and inferences.

Look at the illustration of the safe. Visualize yourself in a friend's home where you notice a similar safe in the master bedroom. The safe is thick, made of steel, and appears to be locked shut. Would you not wonder what is in this strong container? At best you could observe the size of this structure; however, you could not open it to see what is inside. You could infer or guess its contents. Perhaps it contains cash, jewelry, personal letters, and prized photographs. All of these ideas would be inferences made in an attempt to surmise what is inside the safe. Unfortunately, you cannot even pick up the safe and shake it to determine what rattles around inside.

Let's consider another example to distinguish between observations and inferences. Mr. Lee died on January 4, 1992, at 2:37 A.M. in San Jose, California. He was 48 years of age at the time of death. The cause of death was given as "natural" and no autopsy was performed. Mr. Lee did not indicate that he was sick. It is known that he had smoked one to two packs of cigarettes per day from the time he was 17 years old. It is easy to point the finger at cigarettes, but perhaps something else led to Mr. Lee's death. In this case, the fact that death occurred, when it happened, and where it happened is hard to refute. Many inferences can be put forth to explain his death, however, such as cigarettes, fat in the diet, or a hereditary disease that was eating away at Mr. Lee, about which he said nothing to his family and friends.

Now let's practice our observations and inferences. At lab stations 1–8 there are 35 mm film canisters in which one or more objects have been placed. You are to make many observations about each container and then infer what is inside. At the ninth lab station is a paper bag with something inside. You will be given an opportunity to smell the contents of the bag, but not to look inside. Record your observations and infer the contents. At the tenth station is a bag with objects inside. You will be given one of these objects to eat, during which time you must close your eyes and plug your nose. Record your observations and indicate what you ate. For each lab station exercise, write your observations on the left side of your lab notebook page and the inferences on the right side as shown below.

Observations   *Inferences*

Station 1:

Station 2:

Etc.

Box 8.2 provides an example of an exercise that a science teacher might develop to give students practice with measurement. Note again that some creativity has been put into this instructional material, as noted by the title: "What is Your Measurement Quotient (MQ)?" For this laboratory exercise students are first given common objects to determine if they have any ideas of their mass, temperature, or length. Then they have the opportunity to check their estimates using the metric system. Both the teacher and the students can determine the degree to which the students are fluent in metric measurement, which is their measurement quotient. Of course measuring must continue to be used throughout the year and become part of all laboratory work.

Perhaps no science course is complete unless each student has been given the opportunity to conduct an experiment. Experimenting is the most complex of the integrated process skills and one that requires students to use many process skills to test out an idea. A true experiment tests a hypothesis that states a relationship between variables. Experiments can range from simple to very complex procedures. In science teaching, experiments can be valuable activities for which students are prepared and realize their purpose. Quite often, the term **experimenting** is used loosely to mean simply "trying something out" or "messing around." Although trying something out and messing around might be encouraged, these activities should be distinguished from a true experiment.

Some science educators prefer to restrict the term experiment to the type of investigation known as the **controlled experiment,** in which every effort is made to control the variables involved. All factors, except for the independent variable(s), are held constant, and the

BOX 8.2

WHAT IS YOUR MEASUREMENT QUOTIENT (MQ)?

Directions: For each question provide two answers. Give an estimate even if you are not sure. Then, determine a more accurate quantity than your estimate by weighing, measuring, or going to a printed source.

Equipment and materials: aspirins, dimes, balances, metric rulers, measuring cups, graduated cylinders, a metric scale, and metric balances

	Your estimate	*Actual measurement*
1. What is the mass of an aspirin tablet in grams?		
2. What is the mass of your body in kilograms?	_____	_____
3. At what temperature does water boil in degrees Celsius?	_____	_____
4. What should your approximate body temperature be in degrees Celsius?	_____	_____
5. How many milliliters are in a 2-liter soft drink bottle?	_____	_____
6. How many milliliters are in a cup?	_____	_____
7. How many millimeters thick is a dime?	_____	_____
8. How many centimeters across is a dime?	_____	_____
9. What is the mass of a dime in grams?	_____	_____
10. On a rattlesnake hunt, six snakes were collected. The length of the snakes caught were: 35 cm, 43 cm, 62 cm, 72 cm, 85 cm, and 1.10 m.	_____	_____

a. Estimate the average length of these snakes.

b. Compute the average length of the snakes.   _____

c. Graph the data to display the lengths of the snakes. Label the axes and give a title to the graph.   _____

effects of the independent variable(s) on the dependent variable are observed. For example:

> To determine the effect of ammonium sulfate on plant growth, two seed flats containing soil from the same lawn are seeded using a standard lawn grass mixture. One flat is watered with rainwater and the other with rainwater containing a little ammonium sulfate. The flats are kept in the same area to ensure identical conditions of temperature and light.

In this experiment, the seed flat watered with rainwater alone is called the **control.** The seed flat watered with the rain water containing ammonium sulfate (fertilizer) is called the **experimental situation,** and the ammonium sulfate is the **independent variable.** The **hypothesis** being tested in this experiment is ammonium sulfate improves plant growth. The **dependent variable** is the growth of the plant.

Science teachers can use science-process-oriented laboratories to great advantage if they are sensitive to the intellectual development of their students. They should realize that there is a high correlation between the integrated science process skills and the ability to use formal operational thinking (Yeany, Yap, & Padilla, 1986). It may take considerable time to identify variables and formulate hypotheses. Thus the apparently less cognitively demanding skills, such as defining operationally, interpreting data, and graphing may be the initial focus of science-process-oriented laboratory exercises for many youngsters. With some thought and planning, science process skill laboratories can be very effective in motivating students to be successful inquirers and helping them build important cognitive skills and subject matter knowledge. This type of laboratory may also promote the spirit of science, especially among middle school students.

Deductive or Verification Laboratory

The deductive or verification laboratory is perhaps the most common approach to laboratory work in science courses. The purpose for this type of laboratory work is to confirm concepts, principles, and laws that have been addressed during classroom discussion and reading, as well as for students to gain firsthand experiences with them. Most science teachers present major ideas first, through lecture, discussion, and reading, followed by laboratory work to illustrate them with concrete activities. A biology teacher, for example, might use the deductive approach to discuss different types of bacterial cells, such as rod-shaped, spherical, and spiral-shaped.

The oral presentation might then be followed by a laboratory exercise during which students observe the different shapes of bacteria under the microscope. Or a physics teacher might use a verification laboratory to demonstrate to students how the intensity of light diminishes as the distance between the light source and the light receptor increases. In connection with the laboratory, a formula might be presented to students and problems solved on the chalkboard using various numbers to represent the distance between two points. Students are often convinced of the mathematical model of light intensity through verification of the law in the laboratory.

Many concepts, principles, and laws can be best developed through a deductive approach, whereby they are first discussed by the teacher, then followed by a laboratory activity to verify the relationships. Many of the laws of physics and chemistry, which are represented by mathematical formulas, can be illustrated in laboratory work. When the formulas for these laws are first presented in class, students begin to realize their meaning. Greater meaning is acquired when students gather data and use the data with the formula to verify the law or principle under investigation.

Verification laboratories have a positive feature in that they tend to provide students with some advanced organization of an abstract idea. With this approach, students are given some notion of what they are expected to find out. Many students, especially middle school students, do not tolerate ambiguity well, and therefore they need to know what they are looking for in their laboratory work. The deductive laboratory is preceded by the discussion of a principle or law (lecture phase), for example, followed by concrete exemplars and firsthand experiences (laboratory phase).

Consider the deductive approach used by a high school physics teacher during the study of light and electromagnetism.

■

Mrs. Beck begins her instruction on light and electromagnetism by providing students with a brief historical background and overview of this topic. She initiates this study with a lecture/discussion on three theories of light—particle, wave, and field. This segment is followed by a presentation on the work of the scientists who contributed to our understanding of these theories. Then Mrs. Beck carefully discusses the behavior of light, which she organizes in three main parts: (a) reflection, (b) refraction, and (c) diffraction. She provides students with a concept map to illustrate the order in which the behavior of light will be studied as well as the

FIGURE 8.1   This concept map can help students conceptualize the behavior of light through discussion and a verification laboratory exercise.

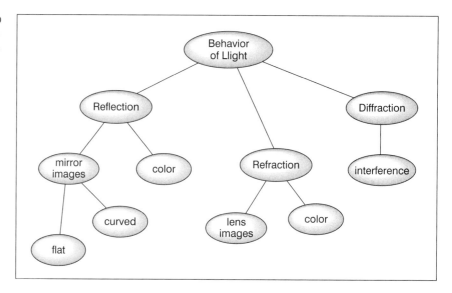

aspects of each that will be examined in the laboratory (see Figure 8.1).

After the background and overview, Mrs. Beck involves students in their first laboratory on the topic, which involves reflection. During the prelaboratory discussion, she calls on several students to explain reflection. Then Mrs. Beck specifies what the students are required to determine during the laboratory. A demonstration takes place on how to measure the angles of incidence and reflection. Again, she calls on several students to be sure that they know what to do during the laboratory experience so they will not need to constantly refer to the laboratory procedures.

The laboratory exercise requires students to work in groups and to determine the angle of reflection produced by imposing a beam of light on a reflecting surface. They are free to use many angles from which to strike the surface with a light beam. Although the students have a pretty good idea of what to expect as a result of their classroom discussions, they seem challenged by the activity because the teacher provides a variety of surfaces on which to study reflection. Some of the students display a lack of understanding about the principle, however, which is evident when they are asked to predict the reflection of a light beam that has a large angle of incidence.

■

You might agree from reading the description of this deductive instruction that the approach can help to reinforce subject matter content that is taken up in the classroom. In many instances science teachers have found this method to be beneficial, first to give students a conceptual organization of the topic and then to provide them with firsthand experiences. Also, note how Mrs. Beck attempted to avoid making this experience a cookbook laboratory by helping students to become familiar with the procedures so that they would not be preoccupied with following written directions during the laboratory and by giving them some freedom to "experiment" with the angle of the incident light beam.

Inductive Laboratory

The inductive laboratory is the opposite of the deductive laboratory. The inductive laboratory provides students with the opportunity to develop concepts, principles, and laws through firsthand experiences before these ideas are discussed in the classroom. The inductive approach places students in the position to search for patterns and to identify relationships among data, after which the ideas are discussed by the teacher and applications of the concepts are provided to reinforce the learning.

Although science teachers frequently use deductive laboratories, they should also use inductive laboratories to help students acquire fundamental science concepts and principles. Consider the following inductive approach taken by a high school science teacher and determine if you agree with this assertion.

■

The students who enroll in Mr. Fleming's chemistry course enter the tenth grade with very little understanding of basic science concepts and principles. He has had to be creative in order to provide concrete experiences that help students visualize abstract ideas and construct this form of knowledge. For example, Mr. Fleming had very little success in teaching the concept of pressure until he began to initiate the instruction in the laboratory.

Mr. Fleming begins the study of pressure with a series of stations set up around the laboratory. Students work in pairs and go to each of ten stations where they make observations and provide explanations for what they encounter (see Figure 8.2). At each station there are familiar objects to examine or manipulate and a set of directions with information (see Figure 8.3). The ten setups present students with a variety of situations to study, in which they receive firsthand, sensory experiences with pressure.

After the students have interacted with the instructional material at each station, Mr. Fleming conducts a discussion of the observations and explanations. Here is where he introduces the term **pressure,** and begins to use it to help students explain the phenomena they have observed. As the discussion proceeds, Mr. Fleming develops a definition for pressure. He also calls on all of the students in the class to participate. When students are not

clear about a particular occurrence or explanation, he asks them to go to a particular lab station to demonstrate what happens and to explain the events.

For the next day Mr. Fleming asks students to bring to class one example of pressure in their everyday life and how that pressure changes. These sessions address a large range of events from boiling water to diving into swimming pools. After the discussion of the pressure examples that students bring to class, he sends them to the laboratory sinks where two lengths of rubber tubing have been placed. One of the tubes is twice as large in diameter as the other. Mr. Fleming asks each student to predict the pressure in the two different sized hoses when they are attached to the faucet and the water handle is turned to the same position to let water flow into the tubes. After the students make their predictions and explain them, they test out their ideas. The findings are discussed with regard to pressure. At the end Mr. Fleming asks the students to write about this laboratory experience and to explain pressure in a variety of situations.

■

FIGURE 8.2 A laboratory worksheet is used for recording observations and making explanations at ten stations set up in the laboratory.

"The Pressure Is On"—Lab Worksheet

Instructions: A series of stations are located around the room. You and a partner should move from station to station and examine each situation carefully. Written instructions are at each station; follow them carefully. Record your answers and observations and explain them in the spaces provided below. If you are unsure about your explanation or if you have additional questions, be sure to record those as well.

Station	Observations	Explanations
1		
2		
3		
4		
5		
6		
7		
8		
9		
10		

FIGURE 8.3 These instructions are for a series of ten stations set up in the laboratory for students to examine situations that are related to pressure.

"THE PRESSURE IS ON"—LAB STATION INSTRUCTIONS

STATION 1:
Imagine that you are in a crowded store and two women are approaching. Both are the same height and weight. One woman is wearing tennis shoes and the other high heel dress shoes. All of you are converging on the same place in order to reach for the same item. You are certain that one of the women is going to step on your toe. Which woman would inflict more pain on your toe? Explain your answer.

STATION 2:
Each of the containers on the table is a tank filled with a different gas. All three tanks are of equal volume and all are at the same temperature. Each of the small wooden beads inside each tank represents a gas molecule in rapid motion. In which container would the pressure be greatest? How do you explain this?

STATION 3:
The container is filled with colored water. Look carefully inside and squeeze the container. Record your observations as you squeeze the container and as you release your grip on the container. Perform this squeezing and letting up many times and explain what you observe.

STATION 4:
Place your hand inside the plastic bag and try to pull the bag from the jar. What do you notice as you pull your hand out? Why does this happen?

STATION 5:
Gently pull down on the red balloon. What happens? How might this device simulate the actions associated with human breathing?

STATION 6:
Examine the marshmallow underneath the jar. Place both hands on the pump and start pumping. What is happening and how can you explain it?

STATION 7:
Fill the drinking glass with water. Place the index card over the mouth of the glass and press to form a seal. Quickly invert the glass over the sink. Yes, the sink! What happens? Explain the results.

STATION 8:
Select two clean straws from the box. Fill the drinking glass half-full with water. Hold the straws together, but place one straw inside and one straw outside the glass. Suck on both straws at once and attempt to draw up water out of the glass. Does any of the water go up the straws? Explain!

STATION 9:
Examine the tennis balls. One of these balls is new and one is old. Squeeze both of them. Do they feel different? Squeeze the can that contains new tennis balls, but do not open it. Why do you think tennis balls are stored in a pressurized can?

STATION 10:
Examine the tire. Using the tire pressure gauge, find the pressure of the tire. How does a tire pressure gauge measure the pressure of a tire?

Reflect on this teaching session and answer the following questions.

1. How effective is Mr. Fleming's attempt to introduce pressure through an inductive approach?

2. Contrast this inductive approach with the procedures that would be used to introduce pressure in a deductive manner.

3. Which aspects of this laboratory pertain to the *exploration*, *invention*, and *application* phases of the

Learning Cycle? (See Chapter 5 for a discussion on the Learning Cycle.)

Technical Skill Laboratory

Good laboratory techniques are essential for conducting successful laboratory activities and gathering accurate data. They require manipulative skills that involve the development of hand-eye coordination, such as focusing a microscope, sketching specimens, measuring angles, and cutting glass. Good laboratory work also includes experimental technique and orderliness. Although laboratory work often relies on students' abilities to manipulate equipment, some is highly dependent on the use of special equipment and techniques; therefore, the emphasis of some laboratories should involve the development and use of these skills and techniques.

Science educators have placed too little emphasis upon developing proficiency in laboratory skills and techniques (Hegarty-Hazel, 1990). All students and science teachers should master many basic laboratory techniques and manipulative skills associated with the science area in which they are involved, some of which are presented in Figure 8.4. Science teachers who plan and organize laboratory experiences ahead of time can identify techniques that require special attention. For instance, the microscope is used a great deal in biology laboratory work. Most adolescents have difficulty focusing the microscope and centering the specimen in the microscope field. Experienced biology teachers provide their students with laboratory exercises on the care and use of the microscope. This work permits students to view such objects as newsprint and human hair under the microscope in order to learn how to focus this instrument and how to move objects into view. Because of the lens system, everything viewed is reversed, which confuses students; therefore, they need practice focusing the microscope. Beginners, for example, have a tendency to crush the glass cover slips under the objective lens when attempting to bring a specimen into clear view.

Psychomotor and mental practice are beneficial in improving the accuracy and precision of a student's laboratory measurements (Beasley, 1985). Physical practice with laboratory equipment provides concrete experience with the apparatus and procedure. It gives the student a set of experiences upon which to build images that represent the skill under development. Because time is always critical to laboratory work, firsthand exposure to the equipment is essential. Then, during class time and discussion sessions, mental practice of the skill and procedures under study can ensue. Consider one high school science teacher's experience.

■

It is essential to precede the laboratory on measuring electricity with a laboratory on using the voltmeter and ammeter. If the students misread their meters when trying to determine voltage, current, or resistance, the lab is lost. This experience requires practice in reading meters first, then concentrating on collecting data and making calculations. It is too much to ask the teenagers that I have in my classes to determine the amps in a circuit before they are comfortable with the use of the meters. Remember, these youngsters do not use meters such as these in their daily lives. What makes matters worse is that the meters we use in our labs have three scales, which can be very confusing to students. Therefore, when laboratory work related to electricity is carried out in stages to develop specific competencies, my students are successful and enjoy their science experiences.

■

The same science teacher goes on to say that she uses the following steps when teaching Ohm's law: (1) use the ammeter to learn how to connect it in series in the circuit and how to read the scale accurately, (2) use the voltmeter to learn how to connect this device across the circuit and how to read the scale accurately, and (3) use the meters to find amperes and volts and then use the data for Ohm's law calculations.

Making a profile map can be a challenge for the concrete operational adolescents participating in a middle school earth science class. Translating topographic information from contour lines to a vertical/horizontal profile is a task that requires considerable mental as well as manipulative ability. Most students need practice before they gain competence in this task and are able to realize the three-dimensional nature of a contour map.

Making sketches and drawings is an essential part of laboratory work. This type of activity not only provides a record of observations, but it reinforces visual images that pertain to essential concepts and learning outcomes in a science course. Here are some guidelines that can be used when instructing students to draw what they see in a biology class (or any other science course):

■ Draw, using a pencil and unlined paper.

■ Make the drawing large enough so that important details are easily seen.

■ Place the drawing near the left side of the sheet so that the labels can be placed on the right side.

■ Print the labels one under the other.

■ Use a ruler to draw lines from the labels to the drawing, and do not cross lines.

General Science

Constructing and calibrating an equal-arm balance
Determining mass with an equal-arm balance
Constructing and measuring with a metric rule
Measuring temperature with a thermometer

Measuring volume with a graduated cylinder
Determining significant figures to indicate precision
  in measurement

Life Science

Dissecting a frog or a worm
Sketching an organism
Slicing a piece of tissue for microscopic
  examination
Preparing a wet mount slide
Focusing a microscope
Measuring dimensions under a microscope
Transferring a microscopic organism from one
  medium to another

Taking a pulse
Sterilizing instruments
Making a serial dilution
Germinating seeds
Using paper chromatography to separate chemicals
Counting the growth of microorganisms

Earth Science

Growing crystals
Orienting a map with a compass
Making and reading topographic maps
Making a profile map
Using a stereoscope
Using a Brunton compass
Testing the physical properties of minerals
Reading a classification chart for rocks

Estimating the percentage of minerals in rocks
Classifying fossils
Plotting data on a time chart
Analyzing soil
Reading an aneroid and mercury barometer
Reading an anemometer
Plotting the sun's path

Chemistry

Cutting, bending, and polishing glass
Boiling liquids in a beaker
Folding filter paper and filtering solutions
Heating liquids in a test tube
Pouring liquids from a reagent bottle and a beaker
Pouring hot liquids from a beaker
Dispensing caustic solutions

Transferring powders and crystals
Smelling a chemical
Preparing solutions of a given concentration
Titrating with a burette
Calibrating a test tube
Using an analytic balance

Physics

Soldering electrical connections
Connecting electrical devices in parallel and
  series circuits
Using electric meters
Measuring time intervals with electrical and
  water clocks
Measuring weight with a spring balance

Determining the focal length of mirrors and lenses
Locating images in mirrors
Constructing a simple telescope
Constructing a spectroscope
Setting up a siphon

FIGURE 8.4   Some Techniques and Manipulative Skills Necessary for Science Laboratory Programs

- Use light stippling or dotting to shade part of a drawing.
- Construct a title for the drawing at the top of the page.

The preceding discussion points out that many technical skills are necessary for improving students' ability to participate in and learn from laboratory work. Students need these skills to gain the unique learning outcomes associated with the science laboratory. If students have to struggle with basic manipulative procedures, they may lose sense of what they are trying to accomplish in the laboratory. Also, if students are so unfamiliar with basic lab procedures that they need to follow them in a rote manner, they will lose much of the cognitive and affective benefits of laboratory work because they are preoccupied with following directions.

Problem-Solving Laboratory

In some instances, science teachers should engage their students in problem-solving laboratory work where students are given opportunities to identify a problem, design procedures, collect information, organize data, and report the findings. This type of laboratory investigation can involve authentic inquiry experiences for students. This approach is also recommended on psychological grounds. Because students are involved in organizing their own learning, they may be inclined to better understand what they are doing. Students take more interest in their learning when they take part in organizing it.

Consider, for instance, a set of problem-solving laboratories at the middle school level in the life sciences. The teacher might recommend that students identify an insect to study over a 1- or 2-week period. The students select an insect they wish to study, then determine questions they wish to answer about the insect. Many students will be inclined to investigate what their insect eats. Most will attempt to determine their insect's reactions to various stimuli. For example, students who select mealworms to study might determine how these insects react to water, vinegar, salt, soap, bran flakes, cola, sandpaper, glass, electricity, sound, heat, and light. The students can be encouraged to bring from home additional materials needed to study their insect. Some students may return to the laboratory after school hours to continue their inquiry beyond the regular time set aside for in-class laboratory work.

Some science teachers use the problem-solving approach with students who wish to satisfy their curiosity about certain situations or with students whom the teacher wishes to motivate to study science. Science teachers can accomplish these ends outside of the regular laboratory time, usually after school when students can spend many hours engaging in hands-on experiences. For more information and examples on problem-solving instruction, study the section on problem solving in Chapter 5.

PREPARING STUDENTS FOR LABORATORY EXPERIENCES

Students must be prepared for laboratory experiences in order to benefit from them. They need to know why they are expected to participate in an activity and what they will derive from it. Science teachers who report difficulties with laboratory activities either do not prepare students for this work or do a superficial job of getting them ready. Inexperienced teachers often believe that the laboratory activity itself will carry the students through this experience and automatically produce the intended learning outcomes. Experienced science teachers have learned to plan laboratory work carefully, conduct prelaboratory discussions, give important directions, and end with a thorough postlaboratory discussion.

Prelaboratory Discussion

The prelaboratory discussion prepares students for the laboratory activity. This phase of instruction informs students as to why, how, and what they will be doing. The prelaboratory discussion is critical because it gives the students a mind-set for the laboratory. However, it does not always reveal what students should discover. This step in laboratory preparation should explain how the activity relates to the topic under study in the classroom. If, for example, a principle is being discussed in the classroom, it should be made clear to the students that the purpose of the laboratory is to examine the principle under consideration (provided it is a verification laboratory). If an inductive laboratory exercise is planned, then the prelab discussion should not present the principle, ideas, or patterns that students are expected to discover.

Consider the following discussion that might take place before a laboratory on qualitative chemical analysis to identify ions by the flame test.

> TEACHER: You are going to find out how chemists and laboratory technicians determine the presence of ions. We have been discussing ions in class, and now you have an opportunity to detect them in solutions. You might think of yourselves as chemists working in a crime lab. I will write the ions on the chalkboard that you will test for in today's lab: sodium, strontium, potassium, copper, and calcium.
>
> Thomas, can you tell me what color will appear in the flame test for each of these ions?
>
> THOMAS: I'm sorry, but I can't remember them.
>
> TEACHER: It is not so important that you memorize the flame tests for each of the ions, but that you know where to find these tests in your textbook or on a chart, because these resources will be available to you when you are given a test on this subject. Will all of you look up the flame test in your textbooks at this time? [Pause.] Thomas, please give me the flame tests for the ions listed on the chalkboard? I will write them down.
>
> THOMAS: Sodium is orange, strontium is violet, potassium is purple, copper is blue, and calcium is green.

Thorough prelaboratory discussions help students to understand what they are expected to accomplish in the laboratory.

TEACHER: Thank you. Now let me show you how to test for these ions with this platinum wire. Pour a small amount of dilute hydrochloric acid into a clean watch glass. Dip the platinum wire into the hydrochloric acid and heat it in the burner flame. Why do I heat the wire first until it glows?

STUDENT: To clean the wire so that it won't be contaminated.

TEACHER: Good! Now I dip the wire into the solution with an unknown ion and then put the tip of the wire into the flame.

Maria, what ion did I have in this solution?

MARIA: Calcium!

TEACHER: That's correct. Does anyone have a question about today's lab and how to proceed?

The prelaboratory discussion must give students the clearest possible picture and understanding of what they are to do in the lab. This will help the students concentrate to make the experience more meaningful. It will also prevent the experience from becoming a cookbook exercise in which the students must constantly refer to printed directions for guidance and thus become immersed in the mechanics of the laboratory instead of the excitement of finding out something for themselves. If special equipment and/or difficult procedures are involved, the teacher should show the students how to use the equipment and procedures and then call on

some students to see how they perform these tasks. Prelaboratory discussions should be as short as possible, yet long enough to thoroughly orient the students to the laboratory.

Giving Directions

The directions for laboratory exercises must be explicit. They can be given orally, distributed in written form, or discussed during the prelaboratory session. Any combination of these can also be used. Oral directions may be adequate when one-step activities are involved and when the directions are simple enough to be remembered.

■

Miss Stasson advised her earth science class that diluted hydrochloric acid reacts with substances containing carbonates. She gave each pair of students a dispensing bottle of dilute acid and a tray of assorted rocks, minerals, bones, and shells. She directed the students to test the items for the presence of carbonates.

■

Sometimes summarizing directions on the chalkboard that have already been given orally is helpful.

■

Mr. Bruhn set out test tubes, medicine droppers, a soap solution, and a liquid detergent. He showed the students how to test the effects of these solutions on hard water. He then summarized the directions on the chalkboard as follows:

1. Fill two test tubes nearly full of water.
2. Add four drops of soap solution to one test tube.
3. Add four drops of detergent to the other test tube.
4. Shake each test tube well.
5. Hold the test tubes up to the light and observe.

■

Written directions can be duplicated on paper and given to students or they may be found in the laboratory manuals used in the course. Regardless of the form, the activities should be broken down into several steps. Each step should consist of a brief set of directions followed by some questions, as shown in the following example:

■

Strike one of the tuning forks against the palm of your hand. Observe the fork carefully.

1. What observations can you make?
2. With which of your senses can you make observations of the vibrating fork?
3. Can you count the number of times the fork vibrates in one minute?

■

Postlaboratory Discussion

Students present and analyze their data during the postlaboratory discussion. Here the information can be analyzed and related to the objectives of the unit, the course, or both. The postlaboratory discussion is an excellent place to broaden students' understanding of the content and processes of science.

■

At the completion of an exploratory laboratory on the topic of work, Miss Blaskiewicz assembled her class into groups. She asked a representative from each group to go to the chalkboard and report their findings on work (see Figure 8.5). Miss Blaskiewicz also asked each group to identify the set of data that represented the greatest amount of work accomplished. The groups' activities were partially contrived by Miss Blaskiewicz to help the students understand work and to explore this principle by inspecting various data. A few students expressed some difficulty in believing that the girl who lifted the $4\frac{1}{2}$ pound dictionary ninety times from the floor to 6 feet above the floor actually did more work than the boy who similarly lifted the 90 pound barbell a distance of 6 feet four times. Some students were also surprised that no work was done when the class "strong man" tugged at the student desk bolted to the floor, but did not move it. By the end of the postlaboratory discussion, all of the students in the class realized that work is the result of a force moving an object over a distance and that if either the force or the distance is equal to zero, then no work is accomplished. Miss Blaskiewicz concluded the postlaboratory discussion by calling on several students to verify the work formula by using data illustrating positive and negative examples of work.

■

FIGURE 8.5 Example of Post-laboratory Data Examined by Miss Blaskiewicz's Class

	Work formula: Work = force x distance		
Group A	90 lb × 24 ft = 2160 foot-pounds		
	A boy lifting a 90 lb barbell a distance of 6 ft from the floor a total of four times		
Group B	4½ lb × 540 ft = 2430 foot-pounds		
	A girl lifting a 4½ lb dictionary ninety times from the floor to an overhead position 6 ft above the floor		
Group C	280 lb × 0 ft = 0 foot-pounds		
	A boy capable of lifting a 280 lb barbell, pulling up on a desk that is bolted to the floor		

The postlaboratory discussion presents an excellent opportunity to focus on important learning outcomes associated with laboratory work. For example, if the lab is designed to address conceptual knowledge, the teacher can check on misconceptions and the extent to which these alternative conceptions are being affected. Students can be called upon to state what they believed regarding a given idea before the lab and what they believe now as a result of their experiences and the data collected. Students can be requested to construct concept maps to help them show relationships between key concepts. The teacher can call upon students to identify the science process skills that they used to conduct their investigation and to speculate about how scientists and engineers might have conducted this laboratory exercise. A science teacher can make the decision to have students perform parts of the lab over again as the result of the postlaboratory discussion. Performing a given laboratory experience only once may do very little to enhance some students' knowledge and skills. These individuals may need a considerable amount of practice and exposure to basic procedures and ideas, especially students who speak very little English. Also, many students do not have time to complete their lab work. Their learning experiences are fragmented and they merely skim over the curriculum.

ENSURING SUCCESSFUL LABORATORY EXPERIENCES

Science teachers must carefully plan and organize their laboratory activities in order for students to attain important learning outcomes from this work. They must give serious attention to the relevance of laboratory work, the degree of structure involved in activities, the methods by which students record and report data, classroom management, and evaluation of student work. Failure to give proper attention to these critical factors can undermine the value of laboratory activity in a science course.

Relevance of Laboratory Work

The association between classroom and laboratory work may not be evident to students during the course of daily instruction. Laboratory work often becomes a fragmented entity that seems to have little or no relation to the real world. This aspect of science teaching can become merely another activity to complete. Laboratory activities that incorporate commonplace devices and have immediate applications in the real world, however,

are worthwhile to use. In laboratories where siphons, candles, electric bells, xylophones, household cleaners, mechanics' tools, over-the-counter medicines, and garden soils are studied, students rarely question the value of the work or its association with scientific principles.

Familiar objects provide a context that may be more interesting to students and serve to motivate their learning. The use of everyday materials demonstrates the applicability of science concepts and principles in daily life. These materials are usually inexpensive and easy to obtain. Often, students who are unmotivated in science classes are those who readily volunteer to bring in items for laboratory work. Also, when students study everyday phenomena in the laboratory, they are more inclined to acquire inquiry skills (Rubin & Tamir, 1988). If instruction begins with things familiar to students, the instruction is most likely to be related to the knowledge that students possess. Consequently, the instruction begins with what students know, which will facilitate their conceptual development.

Degree of Structure in Laboratory Activities

Structure refers to the amount of guidance and direction teachers give to students. It usually takes the form of written directions or questions that are prepared on duplicated sheets or in laboratory manuals. Experienced science teachers often employ highly structured laboratory exercises, especially during the first part of a science course. Highly structured exercises provide students with a great deal of guidance, which helps the teacher to manage the instructional environment. Science teachers emphasize that when they must instruct large numbers of students, short exercises that provide students with plenty of direction seem to work best.

The following comments are from science teachers regarding the structure of their laboratories:

- "Our labs are highly structured and the answers seem so obvious, but not to these sixth-graders."

- "In physical science we use highly structured labs that focus on specific objectives and reinforce specific concepts. This is important to our ninth-graders who need help adapting to the high school environment."

- "The labs for many regular students are highly structured with specific instructions and questions that are close-ended because most of my students are not very science oriented. They get easily frustrated if they do not understand exactly what they are to do."

A note of caution is in order regarding highly structured laboratory work. There is a problem with using too much structure over the entire course. If the teacher uses highly structured activities throughout a course, problem solving, conceptual change, modifying misconceptions, and motivation may be limited. Structure can stifle self-directed learning and decision-making behavior. Consequently, toward the middle and end of the course, science teachers should vary the structure of their laboratory work.

After students have acquired basic inquiry skills and techniques, the teacher should give them the opportunity to identify their own problems and devise their own procedures. Over time, students will learn to conduct complete laboratory experiments. Some science teachers have suggested that students can be given more autonomy during the eighth and ninth grades than during the sixth and seventh grades, and certainly many high school students are capable of conducting their own inquiries.

Leonard (1991) suggests that science teachers should attempt to "uncookbook laboratory investigations." He claims that too many procedures and written directions for students to follow can reduce advance organization by students, thus causing them to follow directions in a rote manner and to lose the meaning of the lab. Students can remember only so many directions and internalize only so much of someone else's procedures.

Student Recording and Reporting of Data

Students need assistance in recording and reporting their laboratory observations. When laboratory manuals are provided, the problem is somewhat reduced, because laboratory manuals usually provide space for student responses. When laboratory manuals are not provided, duplicated sheets or notebooks can be used to record data. Regardless of the form, recording must be kept simple. If students must devote too much time and effort to recording and reporting, they may develop an unfavorable attitude toward the laboratory.

Laboratory exercises vary in terms of their content and involvement. Consequently, recording and reporting these activities should vary. Some exercises focus on

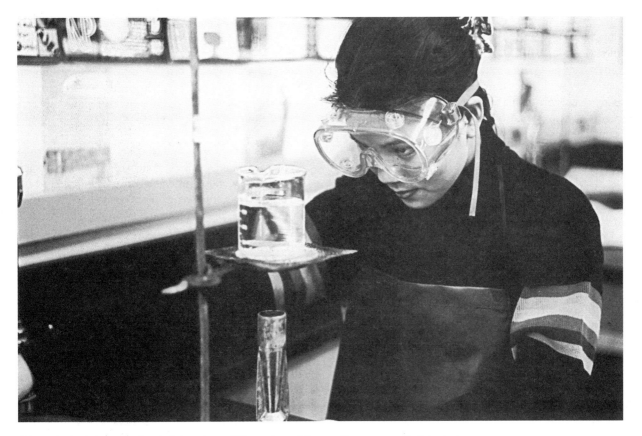

Once students acquire basic laboratory skills and confidence, they can undertake independent investigations.

techniques and motor skills and require very little written activity. For example, exercises developing competence in using the balance, microscope, graduated cylinders, burettes, voltmeters, ammeters, force measures, and dissecting instruments require careful manipulative skills, but little is required as far as reporting the outcomes in writing.

Exercises that involve students in a great deal of inquiry and open-ended investigations may require a more extensive type of report. In these situations, students may need to identify strategies that they will use to answer research questions. They should be expected to explain the procedures used to collect data when reporting their investigations. In addition, students must report data in a form that best communicates their value to the investigation. This usually requires the use of many communication devices used in science, such as graphs, tables, formulas, and figures.

Some science teachers require very little from students regarding the procedures used to carry out an investigation, because this information is usually written in the laboratory manual or on a handout. However, these teachers require their students to prepare a thorough explanation of (1) the results, (2) the significance of the results, (3) how the laboratory relates to the subject matter content that is under study in the classroom, (4) how the laboratory reflects the nature of science, and (5) how the concepts and principles apply to other situations. Teachers indicate that students benefit greatly from these exercises when they are required to determine the importance and derive something meaningful from their laboratory work. They also mention that this assignment is very time-consuming to grade.

A typical format for reporting science laboratory work includes the following six steps:

1. problem
2. materials
3. procedure
4. results
5. conclusions
6. applications

This format can become a highly stereotyped form for reporting laboratory work, however, and such an unvarying format may result in boredom and resentment from many students. Furthermore, students often mistake these steps as being synonymous with the scientific method. Science teachers are advised to vary their requirements for reporting laboratory work. Simple experiments require only simple records and reports.

Gardner and Gauld (1990) advise that teachers who emphasize correctness of data and conclusions might produce negative effects on students' laboratory performance and attitudes. They point out that students want to get the "right results" because their teachers use these results to grade them. Consequently, if students do not get good data or what is perceived to be the correct results, they may be penalized. This situation causes some students to copy data from other students so they will receive a good grade. Teachers should realize that getting the right answer can discourage curiosity and original thought. Science teachers must be acutely aware of the learning outcomes they are shaping from the type of laboratories they promote and the type of laboratory reports they require from students.

Management and Discipline During Laboratory Activities

Management is a critical factor for successful laboratory activities. This is especially true in the middle and junior high schools, where students are very active and perhaps cannot concentrate for extended periods. Laboratory room management may pose a special problem to the beginning science teacher, who may be a little lax in developing and maintaining rules for this type of activity. Some essential elements that need attention in the science laboratory include seating arrangements, grouping, discipline, and monitoring student activities. Desks and laboratory tables should be arranged so that they are not crowded, to allow for free flow of traffic. Keep students away from laboratory materials until they are ready to use them, especially during the time that the teacher is giving directions. Avoid placing work tables against walls.

Students can work individually, in pairs, or in small groups. The amount of equipment and materials usually dictates the working arrangement. Obviously, it would be best to have students work independently the majority of the time, but in most situations they must work in pairs or in small groups of approximately four students. Problems can arise when students within groups participate in very little laboratory work or when they interact between groups. Talking and fraternizing between groups usually results in a high noise level and disruptive behavior. It is best to require students to work and to talk only with those within their own group.

Noise level is a problem in open-space areas during laboratory activities. Noise creates distractions for classes in adjacent areas, causing fellow teachers to complain, and consequently resulting in negative reactions by administrators toward laboratory work. Science teachers instructing in open-space areas have had to work very hard to keep the noise level down. Those most successful at this task have instructed their students to speak quietly. These teachers help their students build a group esprit de corps, in which each group works quietly, guarding their findings, while remaining orderly.

Many laboratory activities can best be handled in groups. This is especially true for middle school students. Small-group laboratory activities will be most successful if every member is assigned a role. The following roles can be assigned to students within each group:

Coordinator: Keeps the group on task and working productively

Manager: Gathers and returns equipment and materials

Investigator: Helps conduct the investigation

Recorder: Records data and keeps notes on the investigation

Reporter: Organizes and reports the findings

The teacher should give students the opportunity to select roles that they wish to play in the investigation, giving them an opportunity to be actively involved in laboratory work. Students should rotate their roles, however, so that each is provided with a variety of experiences and responsibility for their learning. See chapter 5 for more information on grouping and cooperative learning.

Some science teachers are more successful than others at getting students to participate in orderly and productive laboratory experiences. Although successful teachers might begin laboratory activities with a great deal of control and structure, they soon begin to encourage their students to take more responsibility for their work and conduct in the laboratory. The most successful teachers are those who spend less time controlling their students and more time structuring them and giving them more opportunities to learn on their own (George & Lawrence, 1982). These teachers maintain a classroom atmosphere in which students develop a sense of ownership and control over their work.

The teacher plays a major role in developing and maintaining a well-disciplined laboratory environment. This is essential in promoting student productivity and safety as well as avoiding complaints from other teachers and administrators. Consequently, the science teacher must keep students on task and maintain a reasonable noise level. Continuous interaction between teacher and students can facilitate this process. Walking from student to student or from group to group is also helpful. Such contact urges students to work and gives the teacher the opportunity to help students with problems. It is important to move around the entire room so that all groups of students receive the necessary attention, rather than spending too much time with any single group of students. In addition, the well-managed lab

room has all of the necessary materials and equipment ready to be used. In some instances the items should be arranged on a table where they can be taken and returned, whereas in other instances they can be placed on a cart that can be moved to where students are working.

Rules and policies regarding safety and behavior are essential to the success of the laboratory. They must be stated verbally early in the course, preferably during the first laboratory period. Once stated, they should be posted in clearly visible locations in the laboratory areas. Students should be aware that they will be expected to follow the rules consistently and without exception and that the teacher will be firm but fair about this expectation. The rules should include statements regarding conduct, safety, laboratory reports, use of equipment and materials, and grading, and they should be stated as positively as possible. Student input may be desirable when teachers are establishing rules of conduct; this will increase the probability that students will know the rules and, consequently, adhere to them. It may also be a good policy to provide a set of rules to parents so they know what behaviors the students are expected to exhibit in the laboratory. See Figure 8.6 for rules that can be used for developing a set of guidelines for science laboratory conduct.

Evaluation

Evaluation of laboratory work as a part of the total science course grade is an essential part of science instruction. There are several techniques to employ in this situation. Paper-and-pencil tests, laboratory reports, notebooks, practical examinations, laboratory behavior, and effort can all be used to determine the laboratory component of the course grade. At least nine areas regarding laboratory work can be used to evaluate students:

1. Inclination to inquire and find out
2. Ability to ask questions that can be answered in the laboratory
3. Desire to design procedures to test ideas
4. Competence and mastery of technical skills
5. Competence and mastery of science process skills
6. Ability to collect accurate and precise data
7. Willingness to report data honestly
8. Ability to report patterns and relationships and to explain their significance
9. Thoroughness of laboratory reporting
10. Inclination to behave properly in the laboratory

FIGURE 8.6   This list of rules can be used to develop a set of guidelines for student conduct in the science laboratory.

Guidelines for Conduct in the Science Laboratory

1. Do your job well and assume your share of responsibility.
2. Keep the noise level to a minimum and speak softly.
3. Work primarily with members of your group; avoid interacting with other groups' members.
4. Raise your hand if you need help from the teacher. The teacher will come to you; do not go to the teacher.
5. Horseplay is not allowed in the laboratory at any time.
6. Eating or drinking in not permitted in the laboratory.
7. Follow all safety procedures that are posted.
8. Copy the rules concerning "Safety in the Laboratory" in your notebook for reference.
9. Carefully handle all equipment and return it to its proper place.
10. Report faulty or broken equipment immediately to the teacher.
11. Do not waste materials.
12. All dangerous organisms, chemicals, and materials must be handled as directed by the teacher. If you have any questions, ask the teacher.
13. Make certain that all glassware is washed and dried before being returned to storage areas.
14. Keep your work area clean and organized.
15. Clean your tabletop before leaving the laboratory.
16. Remove litter from the floor, particularly around the areas in which you work.
17. Strive for accuracy in making observations and measurements.
18. Be honest in reporting data; present what you actually find.

Short paper-and-pencil tests are often used to evaluate laboratory work. Five to ten items are often sufficient to assess information learned or reinforced in the laboratory. These assessments can also determine how well students have attained process skills and science concepts. Laboratory reports and laboratory notebooks are used to assess students' ability to record data and report findings.

Laboratory practicals are an excellent way to assess students' knowledge of laboratory work. Laboratory stations can be set up where information or techniques can be assessed. The teacher must allow time to prepare the laboratory stations and must take care to ensure that students do not receive answers from their classmates.

Science teachers use direct observation to assess student behavior in the laboratory. Some middle school science teachers give a grade for each lab period for conduct, for example, satisfactory or unsatisfactory conduct. The effort demonstrated by students in laboratory work should be rewarded by science teachers, particularly at the middle and junior high school levels. Giving credit for demonstrated effort can develop and maintain positive student behavior in the laboratory as well as reinforce laboratory work. The teacher, of course, determines what part of the total grade should reflect effort in the laboratory. In general, laboratory work accounts for 20 to 40 percent of the report card or course grade, and effort should be a part of this percentage.

FIELD WORK

Science teachers should incorporate field work into their curricula because it offers authentic learning experiences for students, giving them greater understanding of the natural and technological world in which they live. Field trips are perhaps the most enjoyable and memorable of academic experiences for students. Generally, field trip sites are somewhat familiar to students, which causes them to take a special interest in these events. Today there is renewed interest in field experiences because of their potential to contribute to the improvement of scientific literacy.

Planning Field Trip Experiences

Field trips permit firsthand study of many things, both natural and man-made, that cannot be brought into the classroom. Hospital operating rooms, electrical power generating plants, petroleum refineries, space centers, sewage treatment plants, observatories, and wildlife refuges are field sites that students can benefit from visiting. A trip to these and many other sites rival any video presentation or in-class lecture that students might receive about the activities that take place at these locations.

The Curriculum.   When science teachers entertain the idea for including field trips in their courses, they must examine the curriculum and decide which experiences relate directly to the course. Field trips require much time to arrange and conduct, so selection must be based on the goals and content of the curriculum. The question should be asked: Which topic(s) ought to be taught or reinforced by taking students into the field? If a science teacher can identify a topic in the curriculum that students should study outside of the classroom, the chances are good that she or he can make a case for organizing a field trip to that location.

Surveying Possible Sites.   Students should study indoors the things that are best studied indoors and study outdoors the things that are best studied outdoors. It should be obvious that far too much instruction takes place within the classroom walls. Fortunately, within and around most schools there are hundreds of things worthy of study—resources far more valuable than those available in the school science laboratories. Common objects and events are often the best to study in their natural environment. Science teachers can begin planning by making a list of field sites, beginning in the school, moving to the school grounds, streets, neighborhoods, community services, rural areas, small businesses, museums, hobbies, small manufacturing plants, and large industrial facilities. The places listed in Figure 8.7 present a large number of field sites, many of which are rather easy to access.

Administrative Policy.   Field trips within the confines of the school property are usually easy to arrange. Even for these experiences it is advisable to consult with the school administration so that you are informed about school policy. Further, incidents may have occurred in the past that the teacher should be aware of, because these events may have caused the administration to be concerned about field trips, even on school grounds.

Excursions off school property will certainly require administrative permission. Science teachers need to be fully informed of school and district policies regarding field trips to locations that require transportation. Liability is always a consideration. Policies governing trips away from school have usually been established. Some principals may possess negative attitudes about these events, however, because of problems that they have encountered. Science teachers should be aware of these matters. Most school policies require written notice, which includes purpose, location, times of departure and return, names of students, and so on. Written permission from parents is usually required as well.

Conducting a Field Experience

Since taking a field trip is viewed as a big event, considerable preparation is invested in this undertaking. Planning and instructional activities take place prior to the trip so that students are well informed of what they will be doing. The teacher and the students know precisely what to do once at the site. After they return to the classroom, there are follow-up activities to maximize the value of the experience.

Preparation.   Once a field trip has been decided upon, considerable planning should take place to ensure maximum benefit. Instruction is part of the preparation phase so that students have a clear idea of what they will be expected to observe and learn. Students need to develop the proper mind-set for this event so that they will be concentrating and learning important skills, procedures, and information. Read the following vignette to get an idea of how a high school biology teacher approached a field experience.

■

Ms. Walker spent three class periods getting her students ready for a field trip to a large pond located on the grounds of the school district's Science Center. During the first period, she described the purpose of the field trip and informed the students that parental permission is required for those who would be going to the center by bus. In the second class period, Ms. Walker introduced the study of ecology with a brief lecture on some major principles of the topic. Then students were given practice in identifying a small number of organisms that they might collect on the field trip day. They seem to require a great deal of practice focusing on specimens under

School building
Heating and cooling areas: heat, condensation, temperature
Electrical system: safety, wiring, voltage, current
Automobile shop: batteries, engines, brakes, safety
Cafeteria: food, nutrition, diet
Kitchen: hygiene, cooking, fire
Music department: sound, music
Auditorium: acoustics

School grounds
Lawn: plants, animals, habitats, ecology
Shrubs: effects of light and shade
Trees: seasonal changes, identification, classification
Flagpole: measurement, position of sun, seasons

Streets
Vehicles: types, stopping distances
Traffic: safety, patterns, intersections, lights
Pedestrians: patterns of walking and crossing
Streets: type of pavement, maintenance
Utility lines: service, safety

Residential dwellings
Gardens: topsoil and subsoil
Flower beds: identification, classification, conditions
Lawns: organisms, fertilizers, shade and light
Insulation: type, amount
Roofs: composition, pitch

Community services
Fire station: equipment, simple machines, ladders
Police car: computers, radar, engine, safety
Hospital: operating room, diet, sterilization
Nursery: plants, classification, seasons
Water works: purification, pipes, computer system

Small businesses
Supermarket: food, labeling, refrigeration
Building supply: materials, machines, tools
Dry cleaners: chemicals, cleaners, safety
Electronic repair: electronics, computers, recorders

Manufacturing and utility plants
Bakeries: baking, receipts, packaging
Dairies: refrigeration, pasteurization, production, packaging
Chemical plants: production, research
Electricity: furnaces, nuclear reactors, turbines, generators

Outside of the city
Beaches: wave action, marine life
Ponds: plant and animal specimens
Fields: flowers, birds, insects
Hillsides: erosion effects
Rivers: energy, sediments, movement
Woodlands: trees, classification, soil, succession

FIGURE 8.7   Examples of Field Study Locations and Related Situations

the microscope, especially those that are moving across the field of view. During the third period, the teacher organized the students into cooperative groups and gave all students a task to perform during the trip.

■

At the Field Site.   Everything must go as planned at the field trip site, because time is a critical factor. Students must get off the bus (or whatever mode of transportation they are using) and promptly assemble in the meeting area for an orientation. Business and industrial sites generally have public relations personnel to acquaint guests with their operations. Students must have a clear idea of what their role is on the trip and they must be apprised of any safety considerations. Let's continue with Ms. Walker's biology class to determine what occurred at the Science Center once they arrived.

■

As soon as they got off the bus, Ms. Walker and her students entered the main building of the Science Center for a brief orientation by one of the staff members. Safety and student conduct were addressed. Then Ms. Walker reviewed the purpose for the trip and performed a check to determine if each student knew his or her task. Then students were taken to the pond and the center's staff member recommended techniques to collect specimens. When the students completed all of their work at the pond and returned to the center, they entered a large room with fifteen microscope stations where they could view macroscopic as well as microscopic organisms. The staff member and Ms. Walker circulated among the students answering questions and guiding them in their work.

■

Back in the Classroom.   The last phase of the field experience involves follow-up activities to ensure that the objectives of the trip are achieved. Students should be given time to continue studying what they observed and brought back to the classroom. Examination of specimens, discussions, and written summaries are useful activities to ensure meaningful learning. Note the last phase of the field trip:

■

Ms. Walker devoted two instructional periods to the pond trip back in her classroom. She used the first period for laboratory work to give each student more time to examine the organisms that he or she gathered as well as those that others collected. Ms. Walker also set up four microscope stations with specimens for students to identify and for them to explain the role of biotic creatures in the pond's ecosystem. The second class period was devoted to group presentations to discuss the ecology of this aquatic biome. This session offered students another opportunity to construct more knowledge about important ecological concepts and principles.

■

Field experiences can last for more than several hours or one school day. The activities can extend for many days, even months. They can give students a great deal of experience in studying natural phenomena. Universities, museums, observatories, nature reserves, marine research stations, and the like usually carry on scientific investigations that are headed by scientists with a staff of assistants. Many of these facilities are willing to participate in the movement to improve the scientific literacy of our youth, and they may take on students to assist them in their research activities (Cunniff & McMillen, 1996). Science teachers should inquire about the possibilities of extended research experiences in their communities for their students as well as for themselves.

■

ASSESSING AND REVIEWING

1. Interview a few new and a few experienced teachers to obtain their views on the purpose and importance of laboratory work in the courses they teach. Also, determine the frequency of the laboratory work in their courses. Discuss this information with other members of your science methods class.

2. Analyze the laboratory activities for a science course and classify the laboratories into one of the following categories: process skill, deductive, inductive, technical skill, or problem solving. Evaluate the laboratory activities based on their variety and appropriateness for the students who are using them. Discuss your evaluation with other class members.

3. Develop an instrument to evaluate how a science teacher conducts a laboratory. Include ideas discussed in this chapter, such as the prelaboratory discussion, applicability, structure, recording/reporting, management, and evaluation. Establish a set of criteria from which you can make a judgment regarding the degree of inquiry that takes place during a laboratory exercise.

4. Survey how science teachers and science coordinators in a school district conduct inventories, order supplies and equipment, and maintain and store laboratory equipment, chemicals, and supplies.

5. Discuss with the other members of your science methods class the science teaching facilities that you believe are good or exemplify effective science teaching.

6. Develop a laboratory exercise illustrating one of the five types of laboratories described in this chapter. Conduct the laboratory with a group of peers or with middle or senior high school students enrolled in a science class.

7. Plan a field trip for several science classes of middle or high school students to a site in your community. Address the aspects of field work that were discussed in this chapter in order for the trip to be a productive and safe event.

RESOURCES TO EXAMINE

Science Education for Public Understanding Modules. Sargent-Welch *VWR Scientific*, 911 Commerce Court, Buffalo Grove, IL 60089. Phone: (800)676-2540.

This is one of the companies that distributes the Science Education for Public Understanding (SEPUP) modules that are described in chapter 2. The twelve modules were produced at Lawrence Hall of Science at the University of California at Berkeley to improve the public's understanding of chemicals and their relationship to everyday life. Each module contains many hands-on laboratory activities for middle school students (or high school students and adults). Some representative titles are *Risk Comparison, Investigating Ground Water, Toxic Waste: A Teaching Simulation, Plastics in Our Lives, and Household Chemicals.* These instructional materials are interesting and important to the lives of students.

National Association of Biology Teachers. 11250 Roger Bacon Drive #19, Reston, VA 22090.

This national biology teacher organization has produced many instructional materials for teaching biology. The following are among their publications that you should consider for your professional library:

Favorite Labs from Outstanding Teachers, Monograph VII (1991)

Favorite Labs from Outstanding Teachers, Volume II (1993)

Biology Labs That Work: The Best of How-To-Do-Its (1994)

Flinn Scientific Inc. P.O. Box 219, Batavia, IL 60510. Phone: (800)452-1261.

The *Flinn Chemical Catalog Reference Manual* contains a very large number of instructional materials that relate to teaching chemistry and basic science along with important information and listings of equipment, apparatus, and materials. This publication will be very useful to those who use chemicals in their instruction, especially chemistry teachers.

Kendall/Hunt Publishing Company. 4050 Westmark Drive, P.O. Box 1840, Dubuque, IA 52004. Phone: (800)258-5622.

Kendall/Hunt produces a large number of instructional resources for science teachers. This company, in particular, publishes innovative science curriculum projects that generally stress laboratory work and student activity. For example, they publish three innovative high school science courses that we described in the section on innovative programs in chapter 2. The textbooks and laboratory manuals for these course are resources that you should consider for your professional library.

BSCS Biology: A Human Approach

Insights into Biology

Chemistry in the Community

REFERENCES

Beasley, W. (1985). Improving student laboratory performance: How much practice makes perfect? *Science Education, 69,* 567–576.

Blosser, P. E. (1981). *A critical review of the role of the laboratory in science teaching.* Columbus, OH: ERIC/SMEAC Clearinghouse.

Cunniff, P. A., & McMillen, J. L. (1996). Field studies. *The Science Teacher, 63*(6), 48–51.

Driver, R., Guesne, E., & Tiberghien, A. (Eds.). (1985). *Children's ideas in science.* Philadelphia: Open University Press.

Gardner, P., & Gauld, C. (1990). Labwork and students' attitudes. In E. Hegarty-Hazel (Ed.), *The student laboratory and the science curriculum* (pp. 132–156). New York: Routledge.

George, P., & Lawrence, G. (1982). *Handbook for middle school teaching.* Dallas: Scott, Foresman.

Hegarty-Hazel, E. (1990). *The student laboratory and the science curriculum.* New York: Routledge.

Henry, N. B. (Ed.). (1960). *Rethinking science education: Fifty-ninth yearbook of the National Society for the Study of Education, Part 1.* Chicago: University of Chicago Press.

Hodson, D. (1985). Philosophy of science, science and science education. *Studies in Science Education, 12,* 25–57.

Hurd, P. D. (1964). *Theory into action.* Washington, DC: ERIC/SMEAC Clearinghouse.

Lazarowitz, R., & Tamir, P. (1994). Research on using laboratory instruction in science. In D. L. Gabel (Ed.), *Handbook of research on science teaching and learning* (pp. 94–130). Upper Saddle River, NJ: Merrill/Prentice Hall.

Leonard, W. H. (1991). A recipe for uncookbooking laboratory investigations. *Journal of College Science Teaching, 21*(2), 84–87.

Lunetta, V. N., & Tamir, P. (1979). Matching lab activities with teaching goals. *The Science Teacher, 46*(5), 22.

Pella, M. O. (1961). The laboratory and science teaching. *The Science Teacher, 28*(5), 29.

Renner, J. (1966). A case for inquiry. *Science and Children, 4,* 30–34.

Rowell, J. A., & Dawson, C. J. (1983). Laboratory counter-examples and the growth of understanding in science. *European Journal of Science Education, 5,* 203–215.

Rubin, A., & Tamir, P. (1988). Meaningful learning in the school laboratory. *American Biology Teacher, 50,* 477–482.

Schwab, J. J. (1964). *The teaching of science.* Cambridge: Harvard University Press.

Yeany, R. H., Yap, K. C., & Padilla, M. J. (1986). Analyzing hierarchical relations among integrated science process skills. *Journal of Research in Science Teaching, 3,* 277–291.

CHAPTER 9

SAFETY IN THE LABORATORY AND CLASSROOM

Using proper safety measures is critical for laboratory work.

Safety is one of the most important factors to consider in science teaching. The science laboratory and classroom are places where accidents can occur as a result of the mishandling and use of apparatus, equipment, chemicals, and certain live materials that are often maintained in these teaching environments. A program of safety should be in place that includes the training of teachers, students, and other personnel who may be involved in science instruction. Certain standard safety procedures should be implemented as a matter of course before, during, and after instruction, and these safety procedures must be given high priority to ensure a continuous and effective safety program.

OBJECTIVES

This chapter is designed to help the reader meet the following objectives:

- Understand the legal responsibilities with respect to safety in the science classroom.

- Point out the science teacher's responsibilities for maintaining safety in the classroom and laboratory.

- Know the preparations that should be made by the science teacher before the school year begins.

- Become familiar with a teacher's responsibilities for promoting safety awareness once the school year begins.

- Present specific safety guidelines for teaching biology, chemistry, earth science, and physical science courses.

- Discuss the necessity for teaching a unit on laboratory safety to develop students' awareness and responsibility toward safety. Also, discuss the importance of workshops and seminars on safety for teachers in order to keep them up-to-date.

INTRODUCTION

> Science teachers must have the opportunity to allow their students access to real understanding of science through hands-on activities and laboratory exercises. However, many science teachers are reluctant to allow this because of their fears of personal liability. (Reat, 1996, p. 4)

The preceding statement points out a reality that tends to cause science teachers to omit valuable science course experiences for students because of the liability involved. Lawsuits have become far too common and costly in our litigious society. This situation requires that science teachers devote considerable time and attention to safety in the science laboratory and classroom. Their concerns about safety must be related to liability as well as the students' well-being.

Science teachers have a moral obligation to promote safety awareness in the science classroom and laboratory. It is important that they recognize the legal implications when students are not properly supervised and when students are not trained to be responsible for their own safety and the safety of others. The teaching of safety and the use of appropriate laboratory procedures for safety should be an integral part of all science instruction. An accident or injury can spoil an enjoyable science learning environment.

SAFETY AND THE LAW

The science teacher must be aware of the legal responsibilities regarding safety in the classroom. The very nature of the science classroom and laboratory increases the probability of student accidents, and teachers must take every precaution to ensure the safety of the students and themselves. If an injury occurs in the classroom or in the laboratory, what do the courts commonly look for? First, the courts ask, Is there a duty (responsibility) owed? And the answer to that is yes. Next, the courts want to know the standard of care that was provided. Three areas determine the standard of care in education. A teacher owes his/her students (1) active instruction regarding their conduct and safety in the classroom, (2) adequate supervision, and (3) consideration of potential hazards. Merely posting rules in a classroom is not enough. "The common practice of laboratory science teachers instructing students on safety rules and requiring that they pass tests on this material makes good instruction and therefore legal sense is recommended for every grade and subject" (Vos & Pell, 1990, p. 34.).

The teacher must be well acquainted with state regulations regarding liability. Each state has specific statutes and requirements. If an accident occurs as a result of a teacher's noncompliance with such regulations, then the teacher is vulnerable to a legal suit, which injured students may choose to initiate. Such procedures can result in heavy fines or even the loss of a teacher's job. In addition to state regulations, the local board of education may have explicit policies and rules regarding the teacher's responsibilities. Very often, courts uphold such policies, even though they may not appear in the teacher's contract, and the science teacher is held liable for breaches pertaining to the health and safety of students.

Science teachers should also carefully read their contracts and take special note of any responsibilities concerning student health and safety. Thus, the first and most obvious step that the diligent teacher must take is to carefully investigate safety regulations that have been specified by state statutes, school board regulations, and the individual teacher's contract. Omitting this step is foolish, because any accidents that result from noncompliance may leave the teacher legally responsible.

Another source of teacher responsibility with regard to safety is common law, which refers to law that has been established by judges in actual courtroom cases. The law of negligence (which is the primary governing standard) derives mainly from common law. Because most states have waived common law immunity, the school board is usually named as the defendant in a suit, although it is not uncommon for a teacher to be sued based on common law (Vos & Pell, 1990, p.38).

One such case in California involved an explosion in a chemistry laboratory. A student had inadvertently substituted potassium chlorate for potassium nitrate, even though the textbook directions called for potassium nitrate. An explosion resulted, injuring the student, who sued the teacher for not providing specific instructions about the dangers of chemical substitutions. The court held the teacher liable and stated, "A teacher's duty goes beyond merely providing students with general instructions." A number of other interesting and informative legal cases are reported elsewhere (Joye, 1978).

If an injured student sues the teacher on the grounds of negligence, the teacher can raise a legal defense called **contributory negligence,** which holds that the injured student behaved in a manner that contributed to the injury. The teacher must, however, offer evidence to show that the injured student's behavior constituted gross disregard for his or her own safety. If such behavior can be established, traditional common law would prevent the student from recovering damages from the teacher. However, in some states this type of defense is being compromised by the doctrine of **comparative negligence,** which states that when contributory negligence is involved, both the plaintiff and the defendant will be held liable for damages consistent with their respective shares of the negligence. For example, if the plaintiff (student) committed 80 percent of the negligence, she or he could recover only 20 percent of the total damages from the defendant (teacher). Whatever the case, the teacher must be in a position to prove that he or she took every possible precaution to ensure the safety of the students.

Science teachers must always be prudent and demonstrate ordinary care in their teaching duties. During instructional activities in which certain safety hazards are known to exist, as in the use of corrosive or explosive chemicals in a laboratory exercise, for example, teachers must use **extraordinary care** to avoid any mishap that could injure a student. The teacher must prepare students for the activity, pointing out the dangers and stressing the importance of behaving properly in the laboratory. They must also supervise the students during the activity so that students carry out their procedures safely.

The best way for a teacher to avoid legal suits is, of course, prevention. Teachers must make a calculated effort to anticipate accidents and potentially risk-laden situations. In addition, the teacher should keep complete records of maintenance work, safety lectures, and specific safety instructions given during particular activities. This time and effort can reduce the teacher's liability. More important, the teacher can reduce the occurrence of classroom and laboratory accidents.

All science teachers must become knowledgeable about teacher liability and indemnification (protection against damages, loss, or injury). They can begin by requesting to see documents in the local school district(s) pertaining to this area. In addition, they should acquire information on these topics from such sources as the *Laboratory Safety Workshop* (James A. Kaufman and Associates) and Flinn Scientific, Inc., which are described at the end of this chapter in the section "Resources to Examine." *Safety in School Science Labs* (Wood, 1991) speaks directly to science teachers and is very informative with regard to liability.

GENERAL SAFETY RESPONSIBILITIES

Science teachers are responsible for safety in the science teaching environment; however, many take the charge lightly. It is not unusual to find many potentially hazardous violations. Inoperable fire extinguishers, safety showers, overhead sprinklers, or eyewash fountains; inadequate lighting; unlabeled chemicals; and faulty equipment are but a few common hazards found in the laboratory. Teachers must be aware of such problems in order to maintain a safe environment. They must be alert about what constitutes a safety hazard.

Accidents that occur in the laboratory are usually minor. The most common types are cuts and burns from glass and chemicals. Students will touch broken glass, handle hot vessels, and fail to wear safety glasses—all unsafe practices that can be avoided if teachers give students proper instruction and supervision. In addition, some students have a tendency to taste substances used for laboratory exercises. This is obviously dangerous. A general lab rule is no eating or tasting unless directed to do so by the teacher.

The teaching of safety must be done systematically and constructively. Many teachers introduce safety units at the very beginning of the school year. They instruct students on laboratory safety and how to conduct themselves during science classes. This approach is successful because it increases student safety knowledge and reduces the number of unsafe behaviors in the laboratory.

Teachers generally are not knowledgeable about safety, which makes teaching the topic problematic. Consequently, it is recommended that teachers take every opportunity to learn about proper safety procedures in the laboratory. They should attend special courses and seminars on safety, enroll in first aid and CPR courses, talk with other science teachers about safety problems, and read articles on safety in publications such as *The Science Teacher* and *Journal of Chemical Education*. Other important sources of safety information are the Manufacturing Chemists Association, the American Chemical Society, Flinn Scientific, the U.S. Department of Health and Human Services, and the *Laboratory Safety Program* produced by James Kaufman (see "Resources to Examine" at the end of this chapter).

Preparation before the School Year Begins

Before the school year begins, the teacher should inspect the classroom and laboratory to determine sites of potential danger. A checklist (inventory) such as the one shown in Figure 9.1 can serve as a guide for this purpose. A checklist ensures that the inspection will be organized and systematic and that critical safety aspects will not be forgotten. At the same time, the teacher has a record of direct responsibility and concern for safety in the event that litigation should arise in the future.

Conducting an inspection requires the cooperation of the school principal and must be coordinated to include the services of maintenance personnel, electricians, plumbers, and other skilled individuals. The teacher, in concert with the appropriate personnel, should inspect the laboratory and classroom areas for malfunctions involving gas lines, water valves, electrical lines and outlets, exhaust fans and hoods, and tempera-

	No attention needed	Attention needed	Comments
Gas valves and shutoffs			
Water valves and shutoffs			
Electrical lines and shutoffs			
Electrical outlets			
Exhaust fans			
Chemical storage			
1. Temperature of storage area			
2. Aisles cleared			
3. Chemicals properly stored			
4. Age of chemicals within expiration date			
Fire extinguishers			
1. Placed properly			
2. Label and seal show recent inspection			
3. Special type available for chemical fires			
4. Special type for electrical fires			
5. Type for ordinary fires not due to electrical or chemical causes			
Fire blankets			
1. Recent inspection			
2. Strategically placed			
Safety showers			
Eye wash fountains			
Sand buckets			
Student laboratory positions			
1. Gas outlets for leaks			
2. Water outlets for leaks			
3. Sinks have proper drainage			
4. Electrical outlets are functional and properly grounded			

FIGURE 9.1   Checklist for Safety Inspection of Science Facilities

ture controls in storage and classroom areas. Eyewashes, fire blankets, fire extinguishers, and safety showers also require inspection. It is best to engage qualified individuals to detect and rectify problems in laboratory facilities. It is not the teacher's responsibility to correct electrical or plumbing problems; such problems must be handled by qualified personnel.

Before the school year begins, have fire extinguishers inspected and placed in areas where they are visible and accessible. Examine labels and seals on fire extinguishers to determine when they have been inspected and if they are perceived to be operable. Special types of fire extinguishers should be available in the laboratory—those that extinguish ordinary fires not due to electrical or chemical causes and those that control electrical and chemical fires. Fire blankets are important in certain laboratory situations—particularly the chemistry laboratory. Place these blankets in strategic areas in the laboratory and check them often to see that they are in good condition.

Safety showers and eyewash fountains that have not been used for a period of time tend to malfunction because of corrosion. The teacher is responsible for seeing that they are clean, functional, and available in various areas in the laboratory in case of emergency.

Sand buckets can be useful in case of fire. Periodically check them during the school year to see that they are clean, full of sand, and readily available in areas where fires are likely to occur. In general, sand buckets are considered to be standard equipment in chemistry and physics laboratories but not in the biology facility. We strongly recommend that sand buckets should be standard equipment in **all** laboratories, regardless of the science discipline.

Inspect students' laboratory stations for gas leaks and electrical problems. All electrical outlets must be properly grounded and in good condition at all times. The teacher must correct electrical problems, preferably by engaging a qualified electrician. Gas leaks are detected by placing a soap solution around outlet joints and watching for the appearance of bubbles. Remember that merely "sniffing" the area is never adequate for detecting small gas leaks. Do not try to rectify gas problems without the help of qualified personnel.

Teachers must have easy access to master controls for gas and electrical sources in the laboratory in order to prevent serious mishaps when it is essential to cut off the power or gas supply quickly. The design of older facilities may make it difficult to satisfy this requirement, but if controls are accessible, their location should be known to the teacher.

Arrange movable laboratory tables so that there is sufficient area around them to avoid congestion and cramping. The placement of movable tables should allow students to work freely and without interference from other nearby students. Too much congestion may constitute a safety hazard.

Before the school year begins, make a plan for an orderly evacuation of a classroom or laboratory in case of emergency. Seek the assistance of a fire marshal and other competent individuals. There are a number of points to consider when developing the plan. For example, many science areas usually have only one exit into a corridor and only one door that leads into a storage area. It is important to ensure that exit doors and aisles in the classroom and laboratory are clear at all times to permit orderly exits. Discuss evacuation procedures and distribute a written plan early in the school year. Post diagrams and narratives describing the procedures throughout the science area. Successful evacuations can be accomplished only if students, teachers, teacher assistants, and other concerned individuals know the plans and practice their use in one or two mock situations during each school term.

The storage area deserves attention before school begins. It is often a catchall for anything that is not needed in the laboratory or classroom. Many are so cluttered that passage is virtually impossible. Aisles and exits should be clear and the storage area itself in good order before the school year begins. This sets a good example for the students. Rules on the use and maintenance of the storage areas are necessary to maintain a safe environment.

Safety Responsibilities during the School Year

The science teacher is responsible for promoting safety awareness once the school year begins. This responsibility has to be taken very seriously, particularity if students will be involved in activity-centered science. More accidents are likely to occur when students are exposed to hands-on activities during laboratory work. Consequently, more care and supervision is required when students are handling equipment, chemicals, apparatus, live animals, poisonous plants, and other hazardous items. Special preventive measures are required to operate a laboratory in which students are directly involved with the things of science.

Class size must be considered when planning laboratory activities. Classes that exceed the recommended number of students for the available space pose a safety hazard (Rakow, 1989). Unfortunately, few states have legislation that mandates class size in the science laboratory. Guidelines for lab space and class size are available from Flinn Scientific, Inc. (see "Resources to Examine" at the end of this chapter).

Because the trend is toward the implementation of activity-centered science courses, it is imperative for the teacher to establish a safety training program for students involved in such courses. Safety is the teacher's direct responsibility. The teacher must consider safety when planning and preparing courses of study and particularly when preparing and delivering science lessons. Audiovisual and reference materials regarding safety training and instruction in the secondary schools and middle schools are often available to teachers free of charge.

Pitrone (1989, S22) suggests the implementation of a safety learning center to teach safety issues to middle school students. The safety learning center consists of four stations where the students participating in the center (1) learn rules of laboratory safety and common hazard symbols, (2) learn to identify some basic laboratory equipment, (3) practice some simple laboratory procedures, and (4) take a quiz on safety and sign a safety contract. The safety contract is meant to be proof that safety procedures were stressed in case such evidence is needed.

The teacher must always exhibit a sincere concern for safety to set a good example for students. Everything the teacher does that models safety procedures should be visible and deliberate. The more safety is emphasized, the better students will understand the necessity of safety measures in the science teaching environment. The teacher's attitude and behavior toward safety will influence the students: If the teacher takes the laboratory experience seriously, so will the students. Do not expect students to follow rules that the teacher does not follow. The teacher must be a good role model in maintaining a safe environment.

There are certain inexpensive general precautions that a teacher can take to ensure a safer science teaching environment during the school year. The following are some suggestions regarding implementation of these procedures.

1. Develop a set of general safety rules to be in effect at all times in the laboratory. These rules should include a code for laboratory dress that requires safety goggles and gloves at appropriate times and should forbid careless activity, horseplay, and the wearing of contact lenses during certain activities. Post the rules in prominent areas in the laboratory and discuss the rules regularly, especially before laboratory activities (even the simplest activities can be hazardous). Encourage the students to add their own rules as they become more conscious of their own safety and the safety of others.

2. Safety posters are necessary in the science teaching environment. Posters that stress particular safety precautions are available commercially, but homemade posters may be more pertinent to the situation. The teacher can ask students to make safety posters as a project. Posters that include graphics are particularly effective when they illustrate the use of safety equipment such as a fire extinguisher, fire blanket, or safety shower. Post large signs that show the locations of safety equipment.

3. Schedule periodic safety inspections in the laboratory during the school year. Examine fire extinguishers, safety showers, fume hoods, and eyewash fountains. Check student laboratory stations to see that gas and water outlets and electrical sources are functioning properly. Report uncorrectable problems immediately to the

principal. Do not allow students to be subjected to any unsafe situations.

4. Inspect storage areas regularly to see that aisles are clean and chemicals are properly stored and labeled. Remember to store chemicals by class and then alphabetically.

5. Arrange laboratory furniture to allow enough working space for students to conduct activities. Inspect furniture to see that it is functional and not defective. Ask students to report any problems.

6. Inspect apparatus, equipment, and electrical devices before allowing students to use them. Electrical equipment and appliances must meet certain specifications and be approved by Underwriters Laboratories or another known organization. Homemade electrical devices can be hazardous; they must be inspected by a licensed electrician before using them.

7. Report problems in lighting immediately to appropriate personnel. Good lighting is necessary for a safe working environment.

8. Monitor ventilation in the laboratory regularly. Again, report malfunctions as soon as possible. Do not conduct laboratory procedures requiring good ventilation while the system is functioning improperly.

9. Post in several locations emergency procedures that are to be followed in case of fire, explosions, chemical spills, violent chemical reactions, and chemical toxicity. Review specific emergency procedures with students before conducting an activity and periodically rehearse evacuation procedures. Stress the precautions that must be taken to prevent problems, especially the fact that corridors, exit doors, and aisles should be clear at all times to allow for orderly efficient evacuation.

10. Instruct students in the use of safety equipment. Point out the location of such equipment and periodically demonstrate the use of fire extinguishers, safety showers, and eyewash fountains. Allow students to practice using the equipment.

11. Require students to behave in the laboratory. Ask them not to engage in horseplay or other careless activity and constantly supervise students to see that their behavior is consistent with your expectations. React quickly and bring unsafe practices to the attention of students. The teacher's reaction to an unsafe activity reinforces the seriousness and importance of the issue.

12.   Demonstrate and stress the correct procedures before permitting students to use certain types of equipment, materials, and supplies. Describe the procedures while students are seated at their desks, but do not place an array of laboratory instruments in front of each student and then attempt to explain the procedures. Students tend to devote more attention to the equipment than to the instructions for use. Prevent students from handling certain objects until they become familiar with their use.

13.   Prohibit students from performing unauthorized experiments or activities. Do not allow them to use materials, equipment, or supplies unless instructed to do so. Never allow students to open chemical storage cabinets, refrigerators, and so on. Only the teacher has this privilege.

14.   Perform potentially dangerous student activities as a teacher demonstration before allowing students to engage in the activity. Point out possible hazards and show students how to avoid certain pitfalls that may occur while they are conducting the exercise.

15.   Report and describe all accidents, even minor ones, to the administration. Keep details on file for reference in case of future inquiries or litigation. Request witnesses to supply their signed versions of the accident, including the circumstances that caused the accident, if known. Ask them to include the names of the individuals involved and a description of the supervision the teacher provided during the time the accident occurred. Inform the students of this procedure at the beginning of the course; do not wait until an accident occurs.

16.   Do not allow students to transport chemicals outside of the laboratory without permission. Chemicals, equipment, and apparatus should be used only in areas that are constantly supervised by the teacher.

17.   Control the use of chemicals by storing them in safe places and allowing only required amounts to be available in the laboratory as needed. Students are not to touch or use dangerous chemicals such as potassium, sodium, and mercury unless they have permission. Toxic chemicals such as benzene and carbon tetrachloride are no longer permitted for use in science instruction.

18.   Plan and discuss cleanup operations prior to laboratory performance and reinforce them at the conclusion of the exercise to avoid problems such as crowding and rushing. Accidents occur when jobs are done in haste. Prepare and discuss logistical procedures such as how many people will work together at the sink, where

to place glassware to dry, and how to safely dispose of chemicals. Monitor cleanup operations closely to elicit the appropriate student behavior during this potentially dangerous function.

19.   Include first-aid kits as standard equipment in all science classrooms. Kits should be large enough to hold the proper materials and arranged to permit quick access to items without unpacking the entire contents. Carefully wrap unused materials to avoid contamination. A first-aid kit should contain the following items:

antiseptics	tweezers
sterile gauze	scissors
tape	burn ointment
bandages	ampules of ammonia
cotton	boric acid
gauze roller bandage	bicarbonate of soda
alcohol	

20.   After reviewing first-aid procedures with students, post a list of the procedures near the storage rooms and other strategic areas. Do not allow students to use first-aid kits without permission. In the event of a serious injury, avoid the use of any medication or manipulation of the victim until the school nurse or a physician is consulted. The materials in first-aid kits should be used only for minor injuries, burns, cuts, or other conditions that are not serious. In all cases, carefully evaluate the situation before using any first-aid procedures or medication to avoid future litigation. Report all accidents immediately to the principal.

21.   Be careful when using demonstrations or hands-on activities in middle school science that require the use of chemicals or equipment that may pose a possible danger. Consult a secondary school science teacher if there is any question about danger in the use of such activities in the middle grades.

22.   Be cautious about using laboratory exercises and demonstrations described in old publications because they may be considered dangerous by today's safety standards.

SAFETY GOGGLES AND EYE PROTECTION

The eye is a precious organ and obviously is irreplaceable. It is formed of soft tissue and exposed to the environment outside of the body. We must do everything possible to avoid situations that might result in any type of an eye injury. Because of the serious nature of protecting students' eyes, eye protection is **mandatory.**

Safety goggles are the standard eyewear protective device. They are designed to prevent the following from coming in contact with the eyes:

- corrosive gases and fumes
- corrosive liquids
- hot liquids
- sharp objects
- small particles
- fire and heat

Science teachers **must require** students to wear safety goggles whenever the possibility exists that foreign material may come in contact with the eye. **This is the law.** Safety goggles must be available, in good condition, and fit students properly. When the elastic bands break or become stretched so that they no longer hold the goggles to the face, they should be replaced or new goggles purchased. After students use the goggles, they should be placed in a goggles sanitizer that uses UV radiation to destroy organisms that may be transferred among the students (see photo). If a UV sanitizer is not available, use an appropriate disinfecting agent to clean the areas of the goggles that come in contact with the skin.

Contact lenses are generally not allowed in science laboratories (Segal, 1995). The belief is that vapors, liquids, and tiny particles can lodge between the contact lens and the eye, causing irritation and even damage. Also, soft contact lenses present a risk because they can absorb and retain chemical vapors. It may also occur that when foreign materials are splashed into the eye, removing the contact lens may become a problem. Irrigating or washing the eye can be a problem if a person is unconscious and you are not aware that he or she is wearing contact lenses. Science teachers must have a list of students who wear contact lenses and make sure they remove the contact lenses and use eyeglasses during a laboratory activity that requires the use of safety goggles.

"Numerous industries, educational authorities, and organizations have arbitrarily restricted the use of contact lenses within their respective administrative domains (Cullen, 1995, p. 24)." Therefore, today the absolute requirement forbidding the wearing of contact lenses is being relaxed, because in some situations contact lenses may benefit the wearer in that he or she can see better with them than without them. Cullen (1995) urges us to weigh the situation to assess the risks:

Safety goggles must be worn and maintained properly.

It is improbable that the corneal response to volatile substances would be affected significantly by the wearing of a rigid contact lens, because these substances would be eliminated rapidly by tear flow; however, water-soluble gases, fumes, and substances capable of binding to or being absorbed into, hydrogel lens materials would be expected to produce prolonged exposure resulting in a more severe or chronic response.

Contact lens wearers who experience symptoms should not wear their lenses in such environments and they should ensure that their lenses are properly cleaned and rinsed before reuse. Severely soiled lenses must be replaced. (p. 23)

Some school districts prepare a form to advise parents about the potential risks involved if their child wears contact lenses in the lab. The parents must read and give their disposition on whether to permit the child (a) to wear contacts along with safety goggles or (b) not to wear contacts along with safety goggles. This form also helps to identify which students wear contact lenses. Remember, regardless of the decision about wearing contacts in the science laboratory, safety goggles **must** be worn in the laboratory when eyewear protection is necessary.

SPECIFIC SAFETY GUIDELINES FOR BIOLOGY

Precautions for Using Animals

Animals such as rats, mice, guinea pigs, hamsters, and rabbits must be handled gently and with thick rubber or leather gloves. There is always a danger that animals will become excited as they are being handled, particularly if they are injured or pregnant, or if foreign materials are being introduced into the cage. Animals should not be provoked or teased. If animals feel threatened, they will defend themselves, sometimes to the point of biting or scratching. Animals will exhibit violent behaviors if poked with fingers, pens, and other objects through the wire mesh of their cages. Discourage such actions because they can result in the injury of an individual or an animal.

Only those who know how to handle animals should be responsible for them. This means that before giving students the responsibility for handling animals, the teacher must instruct students in their proper care and maintenance.

It is illegal to use animals for instruction that are poisonous or known carriers of disease. Avoid using poi-

Science teachers should weigh the advantages and disadvantages of using animal specimens for laboratory instruction.

sonous snakes, scorpions, and Gila monsters. If snakes are used, be certain that they are not dangerous to individuals concerned. In some cases, poisonous snakes can be treated to prevent the production of venom, so that they can be used without danger. In general, do not use wild animals that are known carriers of rabies and parasites unless reasonable cause can be shown. In such cases the animals must be inoculated before they are permitted in the classroom or laboratory. Obtain mice, rabbits, rats, guinea pigs, and gerbils from reputable supply houses that will guarantee inoculation against rabies.

A teacher should have good reason for keeping animals and insects in the classroom or laboratory. Safety, feeding requirements, replication of natural environments, and unjustified confinement must be considered before using animals in classroom work, all of which make the proper maintenance of animals in cages a problem. Maintain all animals in clean cages and feed and water them on a daily basis or as required. Make provisions for feeding animals on weekends and vacation periods. Often, teachers or responsible students take animals home over extended periods of time to ensure their proper care.

All animals used in teaching must be acquired and maintained in accordance with federal, state, and local laws. Most states require permits to acquire and maintain wild animals in captivity. If permission is granted to maintain a wild animal in the laboratory, it is important that the animal be returned to its natural environment as soon as its use is not required.

Perhaps the best known set of guidelines for animal use in precollege education is from the Institute of Laboratory Animal Resources (ILAR). The ILAR has published the ten principles that are shown in Figure 9.2. These principles clearly delineate the responsibilities of those desiring to use animals for instructional purposes. You should note the restrictive use of vertebrates for animal study. The *Principles and Guidelines for the Use of Animals in Precollege Education* from ILAR are endorsed by the National Association of Biology Teachers (NABT). Although the ILAR guidelines are rather restrictive, NABT acknowledges the importance of animal studies and their use for science instruction. Figure 9.3 presents NABT's stance on the use of animals in biology education.

Science teachers must become more knowledgeable about the use of animals, particularly vertebrates, in the study of biology. Only then will they be able to guide instruction that achieves optimal educational value, but not at the expense of inhumane treatment of animal life. Orlans (1995) encourages science teachers to acquaint themselves with a large range of animal investigations that do not involve harming or destroying life. She points out that there are reasons for the concerns regarding the use of animals in school science. Twenty and

The humane study of animals in precollege education can provide important learning experiences in science and ethics and should be encouraged. Maintaining classroom pets in preschool and grade school can teach respect for other species as well as proper animal husbandry practices. Introduction of secondary school students to animal studies in closely supervised settings can reinforce those early lessons and teach the principles of human care and use of animals in scientific inquiry. The National Research Council recommends compliance with the following principles whenever animals are used in precollege education or in science fair projects.

Principle 1

Observational and natural history studies that are not intrusive (that is, do not interfere with an animal's health or well-being or cause it discomfort) are encouraged for all classes of organisms. When an intrusive study of a living organism is deemed appropriate, consideration should be given first to using plants (including lower plants such as yeast and fungi) and invertebrates with no nervous systems or with primitive ones (including protozoa, planaria, and insects). Intrusive studies of vertebrates with advanced nervous systems (such as octopi) and vertebrates should be used only when lower invertebrates are not suitable and only under the conditions stated under Principle 10.

Principle 2

Supervision shall be provided by individuals who are knowledgeable about and experienced with the health, husbandry, care, and handling of the animal species used and who understand applicable laws, regulations, and policies.

Principle 3

Appropriate care for animals must be provided daily, including weekends, holidays, and other times when school is not session. This care must include
   a. nutritious food and clean, fresh water;
   b. clean housing with space and enrichment suitable for normal species behaviors; and
   c. temperature and lighting appropriate for the species.

Principle 4

Animals should be healthy and free of diseases that can be transmitted to humans or to other animals. Veterinary care must be provided as needed.

Principle 5

Students and teachers should report immediately to the school health authority all scratches, bites and other injuries, allergies, or illnesses.

Principle 6

Prior to obtaining animals for educational purposes, it is imperative that the school develop a plan for their procurement and ultimate disposition. Animals must not be captured from or released into the wild without the approval of the responsible wildlife and public health officials. When euthanasia is necessary, it should be performed in accordance with the most recent recommendations of the American Veterinary Medical Association's Panel Report on Euthanasia (*Journal of the American Veterinary Medical Association*, *188*(3): 252–268, 1986, et seq.). It should be performed only by someone trained in the appropriate technique.

Principle 7

Students shall not conduct experimental procedures on animals that
   a. are likely to cause pain or discomfort or interfere with an animal's health or well-being;
   b. induce nutritional deficiencies or toxicities; or
   c. expose animals to microorganisms, ionizing radiation, cancer-producing agents, or any other harmful drugs or chemicals capable of causing disease, injury, or birth defects in humans or animals.

In general, procedures that cause pain in humans are considered to cause pain in other vertebrates.

FIGURE 9.2   Ten Principles for the Use of Animals for Instructional Purposes

Principle 8

Experiments on avian embryos that might result in abnormal chicks or in chicks that might experience pain or discomfort shall be terminated 72 hours prior to the expected date of hatching. The eggs shall be destroyed to prevent inadvertent hatching.

Principle 9

Behavioral conditioning studies shall not involve aversive stimuli. In studies using positive reinforcement, animals should not be deprived of water; food deprivation intervals should be appropriate for the species but should not continue longer than 24 hours.

Principle 10

A plan for conducting an experiment with living animals must be prepared in writing and approved prior to initiating the experiment or to obtaining the animals. Proper experimental design of projects and concern for animal welfare are important learning experiences and contribute to respect for and appropriate care of animals. The Plan shall be reviewed by a committee composed of individuals who have the knowledge to understand and evaluate it and who have the authority to approve or disapprove it. The written plan should include the following:

   a.   a statement of the specific hypotheses or principles to be tested, illustrated, or taught;

   b.   a summary of what is known about the subject under study, including references;

   c.   justification for the use of the species selected and consideration of why a lower vertebrate or invertebrate cannot be used; and

   d.   a detailed description of the methods and procedures to be used, including experimental design; data analysis; and all aspects of animal procurement, care, housing, use, and disposal.

Exceptions

Exceptions to Principles 7–10 may be granted under special circumstances by a panel appointed by the school principal or his or her designee. This panel should consist of at least three individuals, including a science teacher, a teacher of a nonscience subject, and a scientist or veterinarian who has expertise in the subject matter involved.* At least one panel member should not be affiliated with the school or science fair, and none should be a member of the student's family.

April 1989

* In situations where an appropriate scientist is not available to assist the student, the Institute of Laboratory Animal Resources (ILAR) might be able to provide referrals. For more information write to the ILAR, National Research Council, 2101 Constitution Avenue NW, Washington, DC 20418, or call (202)334-2590.

Principles and Guidelines for the Use of Animals in Precollege Education from the Institute of Laboratory Animal Resources, Commission on Life Sciences, National Research Council, National Academy of Sciences, and the National Academy of Engineering. Institute of Laboratory Animal Resources, National Research Council, 2101 Constitution Avenue NW, Washington, DC 20418.

thirty years ago, it was common for students to receive science fair awards for projects that subjected vertebrates to poisons, electrical shocks, gases, drugs, and to surgical procedures. These "scientific projects" resulted in pain and even death to the animals. This approach to science fair competition and science laboratory work must be carefully evaluated, and in many instances stopped. Orlans (1995) recommends the following policy for consideration:

Beginners should start projects that do not involve ethical costs. Studies of invertebrate species offer a vast array of possibilities and numerous vertebrate experiments do not involve harming the animals in any way. At the primary

and secondary school level, projects should not involve harm to vertebrate animals. Only as their educational level advances should students progress to vertebrate studies involving minimal animal pain. At a later point in the student's training, the goal of the experiment shifts from being solely educational to the search for new, significant knowledge. Most commonly this occurs at the graduate school level. Before educational institutions permit any students to conduct intrusive animal experiments, they should require training in humane techniques, the concepts and application of the three R alternatives, and ethical analysis of the justification for animal experiments. In any particular instance, the student's supervisor should determine what is appropriate. Procedures involving moderate or significant vertebrate animal pain should be

---

The Use of Animals in Biology Education

The National Association of Biology Teachers (NABT) believes that the study of organisms, including non-human animals, is essential to the understanding of life on Earth. NABT recommends the prudent and responsible use of animals in the life science classroom. NABT believes that biology teachers should foster a respect for life. Biology teachers also should teach the interrelationships and interdependency of all things.

Classroom experiences that involve nonhuman animals range from observation to dissection. NABT supports these experiences so long as they are conducted within the long established guidelines of proper care and use of animals, as developed by the scientific and educational community.

As with any instructional activity, the use of nonhuman animals in the biology classroom must have sound educational objectives. Any use of animals, whether for observation or dissection, must convey substantive knowledge of biology. NABT believes that biology teachers are in the best position to make this determination for their students.

NABT acknowledges that no alternative can substitute for the actual experience of dissection or other use of animals and urges teachers to be aware of the limitations of alternatives. When the teacher determines that the most effective means to meet the objective of the class do not require dissection, NABT accepts the use of alternatives to dissection including models and the various forms of multimedia. The Association encourages teachers to be sensitive to substantive student objections to dissection and to consider providing appropriate lessons for those students where necessary.

To implement this policy, NABT endorses and adopts the "Principles and Guidelines for the Use of Animals in Precollege Education" of the Institute of Laboratory Animal Resources (National Research Council). Copies of the "Principles and Guidelines" may be obtained from NABT or the ILAR (2101 Constitution Avenue, NW, Washington, DC 20418: 202-334-2590).

FIGURE 9.3   This policy supersedes and replaces all previous NABT statements regarding animal use in biology education.

National Association of Biology Teachers' Board of Directors, October 1995.

reserved for the acquisition of new knowledge: that is, for research. (p. 34)

The three R alternatives to using animals in research are **replacement, reduction,** and **refinement** of experimental procedures. This approach is being taken by more and more biological research institutions as well as companies that produce products requiring toxicity testing. Zurlo, Rudacille, and Goldberg (1994, p. vi) point out "that *in vitro* methods act together with whole-animal and clinical (human) studies to advance science, develop products and drugs, and treat, cure, and prevent disease." For more information (newsletters, booklets, technical reports, etc.) on this topic, contact the Center for Alternatives to Animal Testing, Johns Hopkins School of Public Health, 111 Market Place, Suite 840, Baltimore, MD 21202-6709.

Precautions for Specific Biology Procedures and Activities

Certain procedures and activities carried out in the biology laboratory require special mention. Activities involving the use of dissection instruments, sterilizing equipment and instruments, decayed and decaying plants and animal material, pathogenic organisms, and hypodermic syringes must be carefully monitored by the teacher. Activities involving blood-typing and field trips also have unique problems that can cause them to be potentially dangerous.

Care During Animal Dissections.   Certain cautions and procedures must be observed when conducting animal dissections. Use only rustfree instruments that have been thoroughly cleaned and sterilized. Dirty instruments are not safe and may cause infections. Instruct students thoroughly in the proper use of the instruments. Scalpels are generally used for dissection; if none are available, single-edged razor blades can be substituted. Some teachers recommend using scissors instead of scalpels. The teacher should demonstrate the proper techniques for using scalpels and dissecting probes before permitting students to use them. It should be stressed when students use a cutting instrument such as a scalpel that the direction of the incision must be away from the student's body.

Cuts can occur during the cleaning of scalpels and needles, so use care during the cleaning process. The use of rubber gloves while cleaning equipment will protect the student against cuts and infection.

Using Live Material.   The following list describes procedures and precautions to follow when using live material in the biology lab:

1. Do not use decayed or decaying plant or animal material unless every precaution is taken to ensure its proper handling. Improper handling may expose students to infection or accidental ingestion.

2. Warn students not to touch their mouths, eyes, or any exposed part of their body while using decayed or decaying material. Disposable gloves and forceps should be used to prevent physical contact.

3. Store decayed or decaying material in the refrigerator if it is to be used over a period of several days.

4. Use fungi with care to avoid the release of spores into the classroom environment. Spores may cause some students to have allergic reactions upon exposure. Excessive numbers of spores can bring on asthma, sneezing, and other respiratory problems.

5. Avoid weeds and plants that may induce hayfever and other pollen allergies. Large amounts of plant pollen can produce adverse effects.

6. Do not maintain cultures of pathogenic bacteria, viruses, or fungi in the laboratory. To do so may expose students to infection, particularly if they are not trained in proper laboratory techniques for handling microorganisms.

7. Avoid the use of blood agar, which can induce the growth of pathogenic bacteria.

8. Avoid the use of viruses in the laboratory because they may infect other living organisms in the school building.

9. Do not allow students to inoculate bacterial plates with human oral material. This simple exercise involves certain risks because it could lead to the production of pathogenic organisms.

10. Warn students to be extremely careful when using pipettes to transfer microorganisms. It is best to use safety bulbs instead of pipettes.

11. Use precautions when transferring by inoculating needles or loops. When a heated needle or inoculating loop is placed in a culture medium, the material tends to splatter and produce aerosols, causing the release of microorganisms into the air. Instruct students to remove as much of the culture material as possible before sterilizing the loop or needle.

Sterilizing.   A pressure cooker is excellent for sterilization purposes if an autoclave is not available. An improperly operated pressure cooker may pose certain dangers, however, so it is important to thoroughly understand the directions for operating a cooker before attempting to use it. Clean the safety valve on a pressure cooker and make sure it is operable before using it. Strictly follow the safety limits indicated in the directions or on the pressure gauge. Turn off the heat so that air pressure in the cooker will gradually be reduced to normal level before removing the cover. Do not remove the cover until the pressure is at a safe level. Do not allow students to operate a pressure cooker without proper supervision.

In the absence of an autoclave, sterilize glass petri dishes and test tubes that have been used for culture growth by placing them in a strong solution of Lysol, creosol, or other chemical disinfectant for a period of time before washing. Wear rubber gloves when washing glassware or instruments used for inoculation.

The disposal of cultures in glass petri plates can be a problem if an autoclave is not available. Use disposable petri plates instead of glass plates for laboratory exercises in which students carry out their own procedures.

Using Hypodermic Syringes.   The use of hypodermic syringes by students requires close monitoring. The syringe is a potentially dangerous instrument to use in science teaching and, because of its drug-related implications, the teacher must weigh the benefits of using it in instruction. If syringes are to be used by students, the teacher should warn them beforehand about harmful effects such as hepatitis or embolism that can result from an accidental skin puncture with an unsterilized syringe. The best advice is either to avoid their use altogether or use them in a controlled situation such as a teacher demonstration.

Securely lock syringes in storage areas when they are not being used. If students will be using them, the teacher must account for all syringes that have been distributed for a laboratory exercise. In general, the syringe is an instrument that must be selectively used and carefully controlled. All rules that apply to the use and handling of sharp instruments also apply to hypodermic syringes.

Blood-typing.   Blood-typing has often been performed in the biology laboratory using student subjects. The question often arises as to whether this type of activity should take place in secondary schools. Before performing blood-typing on students, the teacher should ask the principal or other administrator whether there are any restrictions on using students as a source of blood. Some schools have imposed such restrictions following legal suits brought because of science laboratory mishaps.

If students are used as subjects, the teacher must obtain a written statement from parents indicating their willingness to allow the procedure as well as affirming that their child is not subject to fainting, epileptic seizures, or other conditions. Only sterile lancets or needles should be used to prick the finger from which blood is to be drawn. Alcohol is applied to the entire finger using a saturated cotton wad or piece of cloth. Blood should be drawn from the fleshy portion of the fingertip. Alcohol is again applied, and the wound is covered with a bandage. Lancets or needles should not be resterilized by dipping them into alcohol. Each needle or lancet should be used only once and discarded.

It must be emphasized that conducting blood-typing on student subjects can be risky. This practice is not recommended, particularly with the current focus on AIDS and hepatitis. If this activity is carried out in the school laboratory, it is best for teachers to obtain blood samples from other sources, including themselves. It is best to take the safest route and avoid the use of student subjects.

Precautions during Field Trips.   Field trips have inherent problems that require special attention to safety. Biology field trips take place in different types of environments, each of which has a unique set of problems. Consequently, it is essential that the teacher know beforehand what precautions are needed to conduct a safe field trip. This requires that the teacher first visit the area to evaluate it for potential hazards.

Students need a list of specific rules of conduct to follow during the course of a field trip. Each trip will probably require the development of a specific set of rules. The following are some general safety guidelines for a biology field trip.

1. Brief students about the area they will visit. Instruct them about the areas that they are prohibited from visiting without supervision, such as ravines, cliffs, and bodies of water.
2. Tell students the type of clothing they are permitted to wear or take with them. Appropriate footwear is essential to avoid accidents.
3. Instruct students about the plants they should not touch, such as poison sumac, poison ivy, and certain mushrooms. Familiarize the students with poisonous plants that they may encounter on the trip. If possible, bring specimens of such plants into the classroom before the trip so that students can learn how to identify them. Warn students not to touch specimens in the classroom.
4. Warn students not to touch or pick up reptiles or other animals or touch dead carcasses of animals or birds.
5. Caution students about eating any plant material in the field unless it is identified by an expert as safe. Poisonous plants often appear very similar to edible ones, and even experts can make serious mistakes in identification. Alert students not to touch fungi and decaying material unless they are informed to do so.

Additional Considerations for Safety in Biology Teaching

Some additional safety considerations that apply to biology teaching are listed here.

1. Use indirect sunlight or a lamp when viewing with a microscope. Avoid direct sunlight on the mirror, which could cause damage to the eyes while viewing.
2. Avoid the use of alcohol burners in the laboratory; they are hazardous. Use Bunsen burners or hot plates instead.
3. Require that appropriate clothing be worn during the laboratory period and especially avoid long-sleeved or loose garments. Lab coats or aprons are advisable when students are working with caustic materials.
4. Require students to wash their hands after using chemicals and at the end of every laboratory session to avoid ingestion of chemicals.

Other suggestions for safety that are applicable to the teaching of biology can be found in various sections of this chapter. For example, the section on chemical safety describes a number of protective measures that can be implemented in the biology laboratory. The location and use of safety facilities such as showers, eyewashes, and fire extinguishers are discussed in detail in other sections. The discussion of earth science safety may be useful in planning aspects of biology field trips and laboratories.

SPECIFIC SAFETY GUIDELINES FOR CHEMISTRY

A number of activities commonly conducted by students in the chemistry laboratory are potentially hazardous. The teacher must weigh the risks involved before allowing the students to perform certain activities. If the risks are too high, there are alternatives. If alternatives are not possible, then abandon the activity or perform it as a teacher demonstration. In some cases, even as a teacher demonstration, the risks might still be too great.

Chemistry Safety Precautions

The majority of accidents in science instruction involve activities in the chemistry laboratory or the use of chemicals in other areas of science. Many accidents occur because teachers are careless about requiring students to wear goggles. In some instances students might be requested to remove contact lenses, yet required to wear safety goggles, during laboratory activities. Proper dress and use of laboratory aprons are often disregarded. The teacher should check students' attire to see that they are not wearing loose jackets, long neck-ties, or sandals.

The precautions listed below are further suggestions for a safe environment when using chemicals in the laboratory.

1. When inserting glass tubing into a rubber stopper, always lubricate the glass with glycerin beforehand. Otherwise, the glass tube is likely to break, possibly sending tiny glass fragments into the eyes or skin.

2. When bending glass tubing, keep the burner flame low and heat the material gently. Do not force the glass to bend; it may suddenly break or shatter, possibly causing injury to an individual.

3. When using a match to light a Bunsen burner, always light the match **first,** then turn the gas on **slowly.** Turning on the gas before lighting the match can result in accumulated gas, which might be explosive. Keep arms, hair, face, and other body parts as far away from the burner as possible while it is being ignited.

4. When heating any substance in a test tube, point the mouth of the tube away from the body. Boiling often occurs quickly and without warning, causing the boiling substance to spew the hot vapor on individuals in the vicinity.

5. Clean used test tubes meticulously. Residue left in test tubes could sabotage future experiments, either by altering results or, worse, by causing unexpected dangerous reactions.

6. Clean chemical spills immediately. There are potential dangers if laboratory tables are not cleaned. For instance, if spilled hydrochloric acid is not cleaned from the surface, an individual could lean on the table, causing burns to clothing or skin. A spilled substance also could accidentally be mixed with another spilled substance, which may result in a violent reaction.

7. Make absolutely certain that students do not attempt to remove a beaker, test tube, porcelain dish, or other glassware from a flame without using proper utensils. Tongs, test tube holders, and heat-resistant gloves are designed precisely for this purpose. No student should use bare hands during these tasks.

8. When diluting acids, always add the acid to the water, and not the reverse. The reaction of acid with water is exothermic, that is, large quantities of heat

It is important for science teachers to make sure that safety equipment is in proper working order.

are released. If water is added to the acid, the water will tend to remain on the surface of the acid because it is less dense and, consequently, will not mix. It may produce a violent reaction, which in turn may cause the acid to splatter into the eyes or onto the skin of individuals nearby. To add the acid to the water safely, place a stirring rod in the water and hold it at an angle. Pour the acid slowly down the length of the rod above the water. This procedure prevents splashing while pouring. Be sure to wear safety glasses.

9. When heating materials, always use open vessels during the heating process. Do not heat vessels that have been stoppered. When heating liquids, it is good practice to use boiling chips to prevent bumping.

10. When evaporating a toxic or dangerous solvent, use a well-ventilated fume hood.

11. Avoid subjecting flammable materials to any open flame. Open flames are dangerous in the presence of flammable substances.

All laboratory activities or demonstrations, whether performed by students or the teacher, must be considered potentially dangerous. Before using an activity, the teacher must first weigh whether the educational benefits are worth the risks that may be involved. The teacher must exercise extreme care no matter how many times he or she has performed the demonstration or conducted the laboratory; repeated performance of an exercise does not reduce the risks. Common laboratory exercises or demonstrations can be just as dangerous as those requiring unusual apparatus or infrequently used chemicals. It is essential that the teacher always be on the defensive and practice preventive measures when working with chemicals.

Storing and Using Chemicals Safely

Many accidents occur in the classroom or laboratory because of improper storage and use of chemicals. Those who use chemicals in their teaching must be knowledgeable about what substances are potentially dangerous. To avoid unforeseen problems, know what facilities are required for storage of chemicals, the safety procedures to employ when using them, and the safety procedures to use to properly dispose of them.

Today, many chemicals should not be used or even stored in a science laboratory because of the growing concern for people's health and better understanding of the potential risks involved with these chemicals. Science teachers who are not experienced with chemicals should discuss their use and storage with experienced chemistry teachers and they should become familiar with the literature recommended at the end of this chapter.

Combustible substances, poisonous materials, acids and bases, and other dangerous chemicals have special storage requirements and, in most cases, must be securely stored to avoid potential accidents. Always securely lock combustible substances, such as methanol and ethanol, in metal cabinets. Acids and bases should be stored on the proper type of shelving, such as metal, in cabinets or in a closet. Do not store in the same area chemicals that may react with each other; their caps may corrode so that they cannot be removed. In addition, acids and bases must be stored close to the floor to minimize the possibility that they might fall, crashing onto the floor, spattering their contents on someone. Glycerin and nitric acid, acids and cyanides, potassium chlorate and organic substances should not be stored in close proximity.

Science teachers must refer to accepted organizational schemes for organizing and storing chemicals, for example, the one developed by Flinn Scientific (see "Resources to Examine" at the end of this chapter). Teachers must not organize a chemical storage area by placing chemicals in alphabetical order because some chemicals can react with each other. The categorization

of organic and inorganic compounds, volatile liquids, and acids and bases have been worked out by experts and should be followed.

There is a list of poisonous substances that by law cannot be maintained or used in the lab, including substances such as benzedrine, benzene, arsenic, vinyl chloride, and asbestos. Other poisonous substances that are considered to be carcinogenic cannot legally be part of the chemical inventory, including formaldehyde, carbon tetrachloride, phenol, xylene, and lead compounds. Again, refer to the sources at the end of this chapter to determine what chemicals to use and store and how to inventory them.

Do not use chemicals that are suspected of causing physical or functional defects. Do not use any known carcinogens. Warn students of the possible harmful effects of such substances. See Table 9.1 for a partial list of such chemicals to avoid.

Teratogenic chemicals—those that cause physical or functional birth defects—should not be used. Again, teachers should warn students of possible harmful effects of these substances. These substances include aniline, phenol, carbon tetrachloride, and xylene (see Table 9.1).

Other Suggestions for Safety

All chemicals must be treated as if they are potentially dangerous. Do not downplay the problems that can result if chemicals are exposed to the skin or caustic fumes are inhaled. Neither should the teacher allow situations that may result in explosions or fires. The precautions needed to avoid potential hazards require knowledge about the nature of the chemicals stored in the laboratory as well as common sense in their use. The following suggestions can help prevent potential problems.

1. Keep the laboratory and other areas where chemicals are stored or used well ventilated and maintain a relatively cool temperature.

2. Use approved safety cans and metal cabinets to store flammable liquids.

3. Store cylinders of compressed gases by type and mark them as highly toxic, corrosive, or flammable. Store in cool and well-ventilated areas. Limit the amount of flammable liquids and gases maintained in the laboratory.

4. Store large bottles of acids and bases on shelves that are no more than two feet above the floor, and store them away from each other to prevent corrosion and other chemical reactions.

TABLE 9.1   Some Hazardous Chemicals

Toxic substances	Teratogens
Ammonium dichromate	Aniline
Ammonium thiocyanate	Benzene
Arsenic and arsenic compounds	Carbon tetrachloride
Barium salts	Lead compounds
Benzene and benzene compounds	Phenol
Beryllium	Toluene
Bromine	Xylene
Cadmium and cadmium salts	**Irritants**
Carbon disulfide	Ammonium dichromate
Carbon tetrachloride (also possible	Borane
carcinogen)	Ether
Chloroform	Hydrogen peroxide
Chromic acid	Methylene chloride
Chromium trioxide	Nitrogen dioxide
Cyanides (water soluble cyanides)	Toluene
Dimethyl sulfate	Xylene
Hydrogen chloride	Zinc chloride
Hydrogen fluoride	**Carcinogenic substances**
Hydrogen iodide	Asbestos
Hydrogen sulfide	Benzene
Lead and lead compounds	Carbon tetrachloride
Manganese compounds	Formaldehyde
Mercury and mercury compounds	Lead compounds
Molybdenum compounds	Nickel and nickel compounds
Naphthalene	Phenol
Nickel and nickel compounds	Xylene
Nitrogen dioxide	
Styrene	
Corrosive substances	
Bromine	
Hydro-halogens	
p-dichlorobenzene	
Sodium	

5. Inspect chemicals annually to see whether they are properly identified or outdated. Properly dispose of contaminated, unlabeled, and deteriorated chemicals.

6. Do not leave chemicals in areas where students are working, unless they are going to use the chemicals.

7. Keep chemicals in storage until they are ready to be used.

8. Store only small quantities of flammable substances in areas where they will be used. Large quantities are difficult to handle in case of a fire or accident.

9. Do not concentrate large quantities of flammable substances in any area in the laboratory.

10. Do not store chemicals in hallways and other heavy-traffic areas. Students are often curious about what is stored in boxes and cabinets. Mishandling can cause accidents.

11. Do not store chemicals on shelving above eye level unless there is easy access with ladders or stools. Individuals trying to remove chemicals from out-of-reach shelves run the risk of dropping chemicals and causing mishaps.

Using Reagents and Liquids.   Handle all corrosive substances with caution. Concentrated sulfuric acid, nitric acid, glacial acetic acid, and caustic alkalis are dangerous. When pouring liquid chemicals of this type, one must know the nature of the chemical in order to avoid potential problems. The following rules apply when using liquid corrosive chemicals.

1. Never place vessels anywhere near the face when pouring corrosive liquids into them. This will prevent splashing of the liquids into the eyes or onto the skin.

2. Use properly sized funnels during pouring operations—small funnels for small vessels, large funnels for large vessels.

3. Hold bottles containing the liquid very securely during the pouring operation.

4. Always pour into containers that are placed on protective surfaces. Never pour concentrated acid into a beaker that is held in the hand or placed on a surface that can be damaged, such as marble or wood.

5. Always pour small amounts of acids or bases when making dilute concentrations of these substances. Stir continuously while pouring. Always pour slowly and wipe up spills immediately.

6. Place reagents and liquids in small reagent bottles for student use. Large bottles are difficult to handle and may contribute to spillage and breakage.

7. After the liquid has been poured, return the chemical to the storage area to avoid improper handling by others.

Heating Substances in Test Tubes. The following rules should be used when heating substances in test tubes.

1. Always hold test tubes that are being heated with test tube holders.

2. Direct the mouth of the test tube away from others as well as oneself when heating substances in test tubes.

3. Agitate liquids gently during the heating process. Apply the heat just below the surface of the liquid in the test tube.

4. Heat toxic and noxious substances under a ventilated hood. Do not allow fumes to enter the classroom area.

5. Do not use open flames to heat flammable liquids.

Storing and Handling Sodium, Potassium, and Phosphorus. Chemicals such as sodium, potassium, and phosphorus require special attention because of their unique properties. The following suggestions can prevent potential dangers.

1. Store metallic sodium and potassium in kerosene or heavy mineral oil and avoid exposure to water solutions, containers of water, or sources of water. Even high humidity in the atmosphere can induce a reaction when the metals are exposed to the air.

2. Store white phosphorus under water and in a double container.

3. Cut white phosphorus under water because it may ignite in open air, causing serious consequences.

4. Use red phosphorus instead of white whenever substitution is permissible.

5. Burn residues of phosphorus under a ventilated hood before placing them in a waste container.

6. Do not expose sodium, potassium, or phosphorus to the skin; they are very corrosive.

Disposing of Chemical Wastes

To avoid unnecessary risks, remove waste materials from the laboratory that accumulate as a byproduct of scientific investigations and become useless because they are improperly labeled or have aged. Chemicals that are no longer used or needed also must be properly removed from the inventory.

Disposing of chemicals requires certain important procedures. Before disposing of chemicals, consider the federal, state, and local rules and regulations, the effect of the chemicals on the environment, their level of toxicity, and the degree to which they are hazardous. In addition, consult with an experienced chemistry teacher, a science supervisor, or use the reference information given at the end of this chapter. The following suggestions might be useful when disposing of chemicals.

1. Do not pour strong acids and flammable liquids down a drain without first diluting them. Do not dilute acids by pouring water into them; pour acids into the water for dilution. Neutralize or dilute all hazardous wastes before disposing of them.

2. Do not pour volatile substances and chemicals that produce obnoxious odors down the drain. They may lodge in interconnected drains located in other areas of the building, causing odors in these areas.

3. Always label solid wastes as such and place them in suitable containers, making certain that the containers will not react with the wastes.

4. When there is doubt about the proper handling of solid wastes, seek advice from scientists at universities or nearby industries or call commercial disposal firms. Chemical supply houses are also good sources of information.

5. Use care when disposing of carcinogens, radioactive materials, and other hazardous substances. If you do not know the procedures for handling these materials, seek help from the science coordinator, principal, or local fire department. They may provide the proper disposal method or suggest someone who knows.

6. Return unused chemicals to the supplier if possible.

7. Use an incinerator to safely dispose of certain substances after checking with an expert to see that the substance can be disposed of in this manner.

8. Dispose of some wastes by placing them in a landfill, but only after asking an expert whether the substance can be disposed of in this way.

It must be emphasized that the disposal of chemicals requires very careful planning. If there is any doubt about proper disposal, do not hesitate to ask experts for the safest way to remove wastes from school laboratories. In certain geographic areas, a number of schools have formed disposal pools that are administered by science teachers to properly dispose of hazardous and potentially dangerous chemical wastes. These arrangements have proven to be very effective, particularly in areas with a high concentration of schools. Teachers can exchange information through these pools and, in some cases, provide expert handling and disposal of materials. Contact science coordinators, university chemistry departments, or chemical industry representatives for assistance with the disposal of chemicals in addition to reading the literature recommended at the end of this chapter.

SAFETY IN THE EARTH SCIENCE LABORATORY

In addition to safety practices normally involved in all secondary science laboratories, possible hazards associated with the teaching of earth science require special attention. Teachers are under the misconception that nothing dangerous can possibly be associated with the activities that occur in the earth science laboratory, but rocks and minerals commonly used in the laboratory can and do present certain health hazards. The tasting of minerals and rocks, chemical procedures and analysis, crushing procedures, and the mere handling of rocks and minerals in the laboratory are potentially dangerous activities.

Warn students not to taste unidentified materials, rocks, or chemical substances. Before substances are tasted, they must be positively identified as not dangerous if ingested in small quantities. Students can make taste tests using minerals that contain halite (salt) or other common substances known not to be harmful. Students should be cautioned not to taste minerals that are known to contain antimony, lead, copper, mercury, zinc, nickel, or aluminum. Many minerals containing these elements resemble and can be mistaken for halite, and they are very dangerous when tasted (Puffer, 1979).

Minerals containing arsenic and several that contain calcium, copper, lead, or zinc arsenates are poisonous. Acute arsenic poisoning can produce gastrointestinal disturbances, muscle spasms, dizziness, delirium, and coma. Minerals containing lead also present health hazards because lead is poisonous in all forms. The ingestion of lead minerals in large quantities can produce cramps, muscle weakness, depression, coma, and even death. Lead poisoning can be cumulative, and effects can range from moderate to very severe.

Ingesting common substances such as calcite has been known to cause death in human beings. On the other hand, the amounts of halite taken orally during taste tests will not normally cause any disturbance unless individuals are sensitive to salt. However, always take great care even in instances that are normally regarded as nonhazardous (Puffer, 1979).

Inhalation of certain mineral and rock dusts can also cause certain health problems. Minerals containing manganese, asbestos, and quartz are hazardous in dust form, so avoid inhalation. Manganese dust can induce headaches, weakness in the legs, and general irritability when inhaled. Silica dust can cause silicosis (a lung disease), which has symptoms similar to those of tuberculosis. Asbestos dust fibers are known to cause cancer and asbestosis in human beings.

Appropriate signs that warn of the presence of asbestos or dangerous mineral dust should be posted in the laboratory. The following are examples of such warning signs.

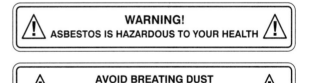

A charcoal block test that is often performed in the earth science laboratory requires extreme caution. Substances containing mercury, such as cinnabar, produce mercury vapors when subjected to charcoal block tests. The vapors can cause excitability, anxiety, irritability, delirium, and other symptoms. The mercury produced during such tests also creates handling problems; it is difficult to dispose of because it is insoluble in water, dilute acids, and common solvents. Do not allow students to handle substances containing mercury or subject them to any mineral containing the chemical. Minerals containing copper, lead, nickel, and uranium, when subjected to charcoal block tests, can produce hazardous substances. Use care when handling them.

The following safety guidelines pertain to earth science laboratory practices. The teacher should use them whenever appropriate.

1. The teacher and students should wear goggles when crushing rock with a hammer or other instruments.

2. Do not crush rocks or other minerals unless they are wrapped in a cloth. This precaution prevents rock fragments and dust from being dispersed in the laboratory area and may prevent injuries to the eyes and other parts of the body.

3. Require students to wear gloves when handling large rock samples, particularly when moving or crushing the samples. Jagged rocks can produce both surface and deep wounds.

4. Do not allow students to lift heavy rock samples alone. Instruct students to help each other when lifting large or cumbersome samples. Use dollies or other equipment to move large and awkward objects.

5. Warn students not to wear open-ended shoes or sandals during field trips. Require them to wear long pants for protection. Gloves are essential when collecting materials on field trips.

6. Before taking a field trip, provide a special set of rules regarding the conduct of students during the trip. Oral directions are not substitutes for written directions. Written rules are constant reminders to students and ensure proper behavior in the field.

SAFETY GUIDELINES FOR PHYSICS AND PHYSICAL SCIENCE LABORATORIES

Accidents from electrical sources in physics and physical science laboratories are not uncommon. The mishaps can range from minor burns to death. Burns caused by electrical sources are usually slow to heal and often require several months of treatment for recovery. Thermal burns caused by high temperatures near the body, such as those produced by an electric arc, are similar to sunburn and are usually not severe unless the body has been exposed for long periods of time.

Impulse and electric shocks are not only unpleasant; in some cases, shock intensities produced by higher currents passing through the chest or nerve centers may produce paralysis of the breathing muscles. Excessively high currents will cause death, but it is also possible for amounts of current as low as 0.1 amps to stop the heart

from beating. Currents that blow fuses or trip circuit breakers can destroy tissue and produce shock and damage to the nervous system. The following safety procedures are guidelines for working with electricity.

1. Know the total voltage and current of the electrical circuit before using a piece of electrical equipment.

2. Use extension cords that are as short as possible, properly insulated, and of a wire size suitable for the voltage and current involved.

3. Service electrical apparatus and devices only when the power is turned off. Make certain that power is not accidentally turned on during servicing.

4. Do not permit students to service electrical equipment or apparatus.

5. Do not permit students to be in the vicinity of electrical apparatus or equipment being serviced.

6. Do not turn power on after servicing until all students are moved to a safe area. Notify students when it is safe to return to their positions.

7. Use properly insulated, nonconducting tools that are in good condition when working with electrical equipment. Use only appropriate tools—those that have specifications indicating that they can be employed for servicing electrical devices.

8. Properly mark all electrical equipment, using letters two or three inches high to indicate the voltage.

9. Make sure electrical contacts and conductors are enclosed at all times to avoid accidental contact and check them periodically for compliance.

10. Periodically inspect electrical outlets to see that they are in good order. Constant use may cause wear and loosening of outlets.

11. Avoid using metallic prongs, pencils, and rulers when working on an electrical device.

12. Do not wear rings, metal watchbands, or metal necklaces in the vicinity of an activated electrical device.

13. Never handle activated electrical equipment with wet hands or while the body is wet or perspiring.

14. Do not use highly volatile or flammable liquids to clean electrical equipment. There are cleaning solvents that can be used safely, but investigate whether they are suitable for electrical devices.

15. Allow only qualified electricians to perform electrical wiring and maintenance of electrical outlets and devices. Do not allow students or unqualified teachers to perform these functions.

16. Do not store volatile and flammable liquids in the vicinity of activated electrical equipment. The heat generated by equipment may cause a fire or explosion.

17. Do not handle electrical equipment that has been in use for a long period of time. It may be very hot and could cause serious burns; or the hot equipment may be dropped, causing damage to some of its parts.

18. Use electrical appliances that are approved by Underwriters Laboratories or another known laboratory.

19. Have homemade equipment inspected by a licensed electrician before using it. Always regard homemade equipment as potentially dangerous until it is checked by the electrician.

20. Use indoor equipment inside, not outside. The same is true for indoor and outdoor outlets, and indoor and outdoor electrical wires. Do not use outdoor equipment or wire when the ground is wet or when it is raining.

21. Make sure power tools used in the laboratory are in excellent working order. Check the cord or plug periodically for fraying. Check tool switches only when standing on a dry, insulated floor away from grounded objects.

22. Service tools that have shocked anyone or that have emitted sparks. Do not use such tools until they are in good working order.

23. Before using an electric motor, check to see that it conforms to the specifications of the National Electric Code. Three-phase motors require proper wiring for actual voltage levels in a particular facility.

24. Employ licensed electricians periodically to inspect and service all motors to detect possible defects that could cause problems.

25. Make sure all permanently installed motors have an accessible, quick disconnect switch.

26. Have all electrical devices properly grounded. Grounding can be complicated and must be done by a licensed electrician.

27. If possible, have ground fault interrupters (GFI) installed to prevent possible electrocution. Many state electrical codes now require outlets to have a GFI.

Some important precautions and potential problems associated with electrical wall and floor outlets require special attention. Teachers often disregard the importance of keeping outlets clean and in good order. Teach-ers should also be aware of problems associated with electrical equipment such as high voltage step-up trans-formers, refrigerators, and vacuum pumps. Such equip-ment requires proper maintenance and use to avoid safety problems.

1. Have floor outlets inspected routinely to see that there is no accumulation of foreign material in the underfloor conduit. Place safety caps in unused out-lets and, if necessary, have new gaskets installed to prevent damage to floor boxes. Avoid flooding areas around floor outlet boxes when mopping and advise the janitor to use only a damp mop in these areas.

2. Periodically check wall and table outlets and appro-priately mark them as 110V, 220V, 440V, and other appropriate voltages. There should be a sufficient number of outlets in the laboratory to minimize the use of extension cords.

3. Teach most electrical concepts in the laboratory using low voltage in the 0–6 volt range rather than the 110–120 volt range from regular outlets. This range is recommended to reduce risks of shock.

4. Avoid conduction of 120-volt current through solutions. Use lower ranges.

5. Do not expose students to situations that require high voltage. High voltage from step-up transform-ers, induction coils, and static charges is potentially dangerous, and only the teacher should perform the activities requiring their use.

6. Recognize the potential danger of glass tubes such as cathode-ray tubes that are to be evacuated. When conducting evacuation procedures, make certain that students wear safety goggles and are properly garbed.

7. Provide belt guards for motor-driven devices such as vacuum pumps and rotors.

8. Warn students of the potential hazards in working with materials under low pressure, such as experi-ments and demonstrations using bell jars and ther-mos bottles. Require students to wear safety goggles when performing such activities. Also warn them to follow directions carefully and not to exceed the specifications indicated for the activities.

9. Use refrigerators to store flammable liquids but make sure the appliances have been approved for this use. Do not use any home refrigerator for this purpose.

10. Make sure ovens have proper, functional thermosta-tic controls. Do not dry out materials saturated with volatile substances in ovens that have open flames or exposed electrical hearing coils. Dry such materi-als only in ovens suitable for this purpose.

RADIATION SAFETY

Secondary school biology, physics, and chemistry courses include topics that involve radiation. Physics and chemistry courses involve experiments that deal with radiation emission of radioactive isotopes, X-ray diffraction apparatus, Crookes tubes, Laser beams, ultraviolet rays, infrared rays, and microwaves. Biology courses sometimes involve experiments exposing biological materials to radiation sources. Apparatus and materials that generate radiation can be hazardous unless precautions are taken to avoid radiation exposure.

To avoid excessive radiation exposure during activities involving radiation sources, limit the time of exposure to short periods. Lead sheets or bricks provide appropriate shielding between the students and the radiation source. To avoid great intensities of primary radiation, the distance between the radiation source and students should be as great as possible but still allow the activity to be carried out effectively. To avoid risks, the teacher should not attempt any activity without the advice of an expert.

The inclusion of laboratory activities that involve radioactive materials in secondary school science is controversial; some feel that such activities are inappropriate at this level. This is not the place to discuss the pros and cons of such activities. However, the teacher should carefully weigh the benefits of these types of activities against the potential dangers of subjecting students to radioactive sources. In any event, it is imperative that teachers know how to handle apparatus and materials so that the laboratory is a safe place for teachers and students to work. Teachers should be properly trained in the use of materials and apparatus before attempting to use them in the laboratory. Self-taught teachers must be certain that their teaching techniques are safe and appropriate. Radiation experts and scientists, university professors, and other qualified individuals can provide invaluable assistance for formally trained and self-taught teachers. Furthermore, permission from the school administration to use radiation sources in teaching may be required. Some school districts have regulations that prohibit the use of such materials.

Using Live Animals in Radiation Work

Vertebrate animals should not be used in radiation work in secondary school science. Subjecting animals to small doses of radiation can induce cancer, tumors, and other conditions that cause discomfort or pain. Animals should be treated humanely, as specified in the guide-lines of the National Association of Biology Teachers and the Institute of Laboratory Animal Resources.

Storing and Using Radioactive Materials

Because of the potential dangers radioactive materials pose, the teacher must take special care when using, storing, or disposing of them. The following is a list of precautions that apply to radioactive materials.

1. Store radioactive materials in cupboards or refrigerators that are labeled **radioactive.** To ensure safety, have the cabinets properly shielded and locked at all times.
2. Refer to the United States Energy and Development Administration's list of radioisotopes approved for secondary school science activities before engaging in any activity.
3. Label radioactive material with the date received and type and quantity of material.
4. Handle radioactive materials and equipment only while using proper shielding devices. Use thin plastic gloves when radiation to the hands is not a significant factor. The level of radiation used in secondary school work usually does not necessitate the use of remote handling procedures (i.e., specially shielded radiation chambers).
5. Thoroughly wash glassware subjected to radioactive substances in detergent solutions especially developed for this purpose.
6. Dispose of used materials promptly and appropriately.
7. Do not store radioactive material for any length of time beyond what is required. Place such materials in labeled containers and store in a locked room reserved for this purpose.
8. Consult an expert at a university or industrial scientific facility who is familiar with such materials or a radiation expert associated with a state or federal agency if there are any questions regarding the disposal of radioactive wastes.

Personal Work Habits during Radiation Exercises

The use of radioactive materials requires special work habits, which are contained in the following list.

1. **Never** allow eating or drinking in a laboratory where radioactive substances are being used.

2. Do not lick labels or pipette solutions.

3. Require protective clothing.

4. Do not expose cuts or abrasions to radiation sources.

5. Thoroughly wash hands after using radioactive materials and equipment. Keep fingernails trimmed closely; radioactive materials can accumulate between the nails and supporting skin.

Suggestions for Use of Nonionizing Radiation

Using nonionizing radiation requires special precautionary measures (Mercier, 1996). A list of these measures follows, including some special recommendations for using laser beams.

1. Laser beams are very dangerous. If the intensity is high enough, severe burns can result. Preventive measures are extremely important because laser beams can cause blindness in less than one second. The teacher must become skillful in handling the equipment and know the safety measures required. The following are safety recommendations for the use of laser beams in the classroom.

   ▪ Keep students away from all sides of the path of laser beams.

   ▪ Warn students and other individuals not to look into the laser beam.

   ▪ Do not aim laser beams directly into the eyes.

   ▪ Do not allow laser beams to hit the exposed skin of an individual.

2. Ultraviolet radiation is harmful below 310 nm. Mercury arcs and other sources can produce radiation below 310 nm, and the teacher should take care to use proper shielding and adequate filtering materials.

3. Radiation from microwave ovens can cause severe damage. Although high frequencies cause heat sensation on the skin, low frequencies do not, and thus an individual is not aware that tissue damage is taking place. Microwave ovens should be equipped with adequate interlock mechanisms.

4. Ultrasonic beams of high intensity can also be extremely harmful; use them with caution.

SAFETY UNITS FOR STUDENTS

The work of Dombrowski and Hagelberg (1985) suggests that a unit on laboratory safety increases students' safety knowledge and reduces the number of unsafe behaviors. Safety units that can develop student awareness and responsibility toward safety are best presented during the early stages of a laboratory course. Throughout this period, students can learn how to use safety equipment such as safety showers, fire extinguishers, eyewash fountains, and fire blankets. They can be indoctrinated to use laboratory coats, eye goggles, and gloves at appropriate times. They can be shown how to handle broken glass, chemicals, and electrical equipment and how to light a Bunsen burner. Stress the importance of housekeeping as well as the necessity of maintaining a clutter-free work environment. During the course of the unit, the students can develop a set of safety rules, which the teacher can supplement.

The unit can vary in length, but three or four class periods would probably suffice. The unit should be general, dealing with aspects of safety that apply to the laboratory course that will be offered. The use of visual aids, demonstrations, and hands-on activities will meet the unit objectives. Active student involvement is necessary to make this unit an effective experience. Other safety considerations specific to a laboratory exercise can be dealt with as the course progresses.

The teacher can administer pretests and posttests using questions similar to those in Figure 9.4 before and after the unit to determine whether the unit improves students' safety awareness, knowledge, and sensitivity. The same questions can be used for both tests, or questions can vary, depending on what has been stressed.

After teaching the unit, require students to sign a safety contract such as the one in Figure 9.5. The students should not take the signing of the contract lightly. It is an agreement that the students will behave as required to maintain a safe environment. To make the document more meaningful, it is suggested that the parents read and sign the contract as well, so they, too, understand the implications of its contents. The safety contract is a valuable record for the teacher to have in case of future litigation. It will show that the teacher has been responsible in attempting to instruct, promote, and maintain a safe working environment for all concerned.

The teacher can effectively teach safety only with the proper background. Units cannot be presented in a haphazard fashion; they must be well organized and taught by knowledgeable individuals. A teacher's background knowledge should be extensive before embarking on a safety unit. Safety knowledge can be strengthened by attending courses, workshops, and lectures as they are offered by safety experts. Background can also be acquired by talking with science teachers, scientists, fire marshalls, and others who have the expertise on particular aspects of safety.

Laboratory Safety Quiz

Directions: The following questions are either true or false. In the blank to the left of each statement, write the letter *T* if the statement is true, or *F* if the statement is false.

_____ 1. It is required by law to wear safety goggles in the area where chemicals are stored.

_____ 2. When diluting acids, water is always poured into the acid.

_____ 3. A chemical is considered dangerous only if it is toxic or flammable.

_____ 4. The teacher is the only individual responsible for safety in the laboratory.

_____ 5. A fire that involves a solvent should be extinguished with a carbon dioxide fire extinguisher.

_____ 6. The disposal of chemical wastes produced from an exercise should be done by flushing the material down the drain.

_____ 7. Prescription glasses can be used instead of safety glasses when working in the laboratory.

_____ 8. It is permissible for students to use beakers for drinking purposes after they have been sterilized.

_____ 9. It is permissible for responsible students to remove chemicals from the storage areas.

_____10. The student should be able to operate various types of fire extinguishers.

_____11. In general, it would be permissible for students to substitute one chemical for another in the case of a shortage of a particular substance.

_____12. It is permissible to store reagents and chemicals in student lockers.

FIGURE 9.4 Sample Laboratory Safety Quiz

Student Safety Contract

I agree to follow all my teacher's instructions regarding safety procedures during laboratory work. I will conduct myself in responsible ways at all times while working in the laboratory and not engage in any horseplay.

While in the lab I will do the following:

1. Carry out the required housekeeping practices.
2. Know the location of fire extinguishers, safety showers, eyewash stations, and safety blankets and learn how to operate and use them.
3. Wear appropriate safety goggles when performing potentially hazardous activities.
4. Wear appropriate dress, as required by the teacher, during laboratory activities.
5. Know where to get appropriate help in case of emergency.
6. Agree to follow all printed and verbal safety instructions as given by the teacher and/or principal.
7. Agree to take and pass the safety test administered by the teacher.

I have carefully read this contract and agree to its conditions. My parents have read and signed this contract, and fully understand the implications of its contents.

______________________________ ______________________________

Signature of student Signature of parent

________________ ________________

Date Date

FIGURE 9.5 Sample Student Safety Contract

ASSESSING AND REVIEWING

1. Prepare an inventory of the possible storage hazards associated with any one or more of the following courses: physics, chemistry, biology, earth science, physical science. After preparing the inventory, visit a local school and seek permission to examine the storage areas associated with the course you chose.

2. Outline a safety program that you would institute if you were the chairperson of a science department in a middle or secondary school. Ask a science chairperson in a local school to critique the program. Discuss the results with your methods class.

3. Prepare the safety rules you would post in a prominent place in one or more of the following areas: (a) a chemistry laboratory, (b) a physics laboratory, (c) an earth science laboratory, (d) a biology laboratory. Prepare an example of the poster you would use for one of the areas. Ask a member of the class to make suggestions for improving the poster.

4. Observe a chemistry, physics, biology, or science laboratory while students are performing hands-on activities. What safety practices are obviously in effect? What safety hazards are evident while students are working? What precautions do students take to avoid accidents? Discuss the observations with members of your methods class.

5. Ask permission to inventory the electrical equipment that is used for a physics course offered in a secondary school. Determine if the equipment meets specifications determined by law. If there is homemade equipment, has the teacher asked an electrician to determine its safety? Discuss the results with members of your methods class.

6. Design a safety contract that would be suitable for students taking middle school science. Compare the contract you have designed with the one found in this chapter. What are the differences? Discuss the differences between the two contracts with the students in your methods class. What did you stress in the contract you prepared that was not stressed in the one found in this chapter?

RESOURCES TO EXAMINE

American Chemical Society 1155 16th Street NW, Washington, DC 20036. Phone: (800)227-5558.

The American Chemical Society provides a wealth of information regarding chemical safety. Their pamphlets and books are useful resources for science teachers who desire to learn more about the proper use and storage of chemicals.

FLINN Chemical Reference Manual Obtain the most current edition. Flinn Scientific, Inc., P.O. Box 219, Batavia IL 60510-0219. Phone: (800)452-1261. Fax: (708)879-6962.

Flinn is a recognized company that provides schools with equipment, information, and assistance to make their science program safe and successful. Some of the information and supplies that a science teacher can obtain from Flinn's catalog or by contacting the company are:

- safety equipment, such as goggles, cabinets, sanitizers, eyewashers, showers

- student safety contracts, labels for chemicals, safety posters

- material safety data sheets (MSDS) that provide important information about chemicals

- Federal Right-to-Know Law or Hazardous Communication Standards

- standards and designs for school science laboratory facilities

- a scheme for organizing, labeling, and storing chemicals

- procedures for identifying unlabeled laboratory chemicals

- suggested laboratory chemical disposal procedures

Laboratory Safety Workshop James A. Kaufman & Associates, 101 Oak St., Wellesley, MA 02181. Phone: (617)237-1335. Fax: (617)239-1457.

Professor Kaufman has produced many useful materials to help science teachers and industrial workers better understand hazardous materials and situations that place people at risk. He and his associates conduct safety workshops across the country to educate workers and professionals about safety in the workplace. Kaufman also publishes a safety newsletter.

National Safety Council 1121 Spring Lake Dr., Itasca, IL 60143. Phone: (708)285-1121.

This organization provides a large assortment of printed matter regarding many aspects of safety that pertains to schools, the workplace, and homes. They produce magazines and pocket handbooks that are appropriate for the lay audience.

National Association of Biology Teachers 11250 Roger Bacon Drive #19, Reston, VA 22090-5202. Phone: (800)406-0775 or (703)471-1134.

This is an important organization for providing information regarding the use of animals and all organisms. Periodically the NABT Board issues position statements on teaching biology, such as the use of human body fluids and tissues products in biology teaching, the use of animals in the classroom, and dissection of animals. Their periodicals, *The American Biology Teacher* and *News & Views* (a newsletter), are very informative.

Occupational Safety & Health Administration
200 Constitution Ave., Washington, DC 20210. Phone: (202)523-7075.

This governmental organization has produced many regulations and guidelines for safety in the workplace. OSHA has many documents that pertain to all aspects of safety hazards. In some states OSHA's regulations hold for public schools, whereas in other states OSHA's regulations are superseded by the state's Hazardous Communication laws and standards. There are many regional offices across the United States that a science teacher can contact for assistance.

■

REFERENCES

Cullen, A. (1995, January–February) Contact lens emergencies. *Chemical Health & Safety*, pp. 22-24.

Dombrowski, J. M., & Hagelberg, R. R. (1985). The effects of a safety unit on student safety, knowledge, and behavior. *Science Education, 69,* 527–534.

Joye, E. M. (1978). Law and the laboratory. *The Science Teacher,* 45(6), 23–25.

Mercier, P. (1996). *Laboratory safety pocket guide.* Natick, MA: James A. Kaufman & Associates.

Orlans, F. B. (1995, October). Investigator competency and animal experiments: Guidelines for elementary and secondary education. *Lab Animal,* pp. 29–34.

Pitrone, K. (1989). Safety: A Learning Center. *Science Scope, 13*(3), S22.

Puffer, J. H. (1979). Classroom dangers of toxic minerals. *Journal of Geological Education, 27,* 150.

Rakow, S. (1989). No safety in numbers. *Science Scope, 13* (3), S5.

Reat, K. (1996). Liability issues regarding science teachers. *The Texas Science Teacher,* 25(2), 4–8.

Segal, E. (1995, January–February). Contact lenses and chemicals: An update. *Chemical Health & Safety,* pp. 16–21.

Vos, R., & Pell, S. W. (1990). Limiting lab liability. *The Science Teacher,* 57(9), 34–38.

Wood, C. G. (1991). *Safety in school science labs.* Natick, MA: James A. Kaufman & Associates.

Zurlo, J., Rudacille D., & Goldberg, A. M. (1994). *Animals and alternatives in testing.* New York: Mary Ann Liebert.

CHAPTER 10

■

COMPUTERS AND
ELECTRONIC TECHNOLOGY

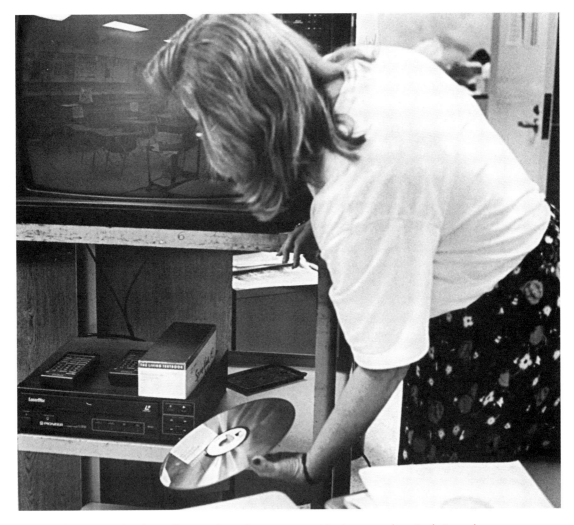

Electronic technology offers a variety of resources to aid science teachers in their work.

With a reformation under way in science education, new methods, materials, and instructional delivery systems must be considered. The computer has become a key instrument in this reformation to improve science teaching and learning. Computers play a multitude of curricular roles from personal tutor to learning and management tool. In recent years, the power and versatility of the computer has been significantly enhanced with the coming of age of multimedia systems and telecommunications capabilities. The amount of software available for use by science students is growing almost exponentially, and what can be accessed via the Internet is virtually limitless. It is important that science teachers learn about the capabilities of computers and other electronic technologies and consider how best to use them to lessen some of the burdensome tasks associated with teaching and to enhance the science learning experiences of their students.

OBJECTIVES

This chapter is designed to help the reader meet the following objectives:

- Investigate several computer and technological systems that can be used to teach science, such as computer-based instruction, multimedia systems, computer-based laboratories, and telecommunications systems.

- Analyze examples of computer software and multimedia that can be used to enhance science learning, including drill-and-practice, tutorial, simulation, and problem-solving software.

- Consider how computers can be used for record keeping, preparing instruction, and assessing.

- Reflect on aspects of software and multimedia that should be examined when considering it for use in science instruction.

USEFULNESS OF MODERN TECHNOLOGY FOR TEACHERS AND STUDENTS

Computers and electronic technology have great potential for enhancing the science education received by middle and secondary students. This technology can help science teachers perform their jobs more efficiently and instruct students in a variety of ways. Computers and electronic technology can engage students in many forms of learning that will help them process information and construct understandings in ways more meaningful than with conventional instruction. Microcomputers, videodisc players, and CD-ROM players can bring sights and sounds to the classroom that ordinarily would not be experienced in daily life by most students. These devices present spectacular images of natural phenomena from the far regions of the universe to the depths of the atom. They can simulate or show actual events that would be too expensive or impossible to present firsthand in the classroom. Additionally, telecommunications access through a microcomputer can be used to communicate with people around the world and to access databases with useful information that can aid in inquiry and problem solving. Computers can accomplish many useful tasks with lightning speed and accuracy, and our access to the Information Superhighway provides endless opportunities and resources for science teaching and learning.

For the student, computers and related technology can be used along with other forms of instruction to enhance learning. These devices help individuals visualize concepts and principles. Interactive microcomputer programs, for example, can be used to help students restructure and modify their conceptions by presenting a more accurate illustration of scientific ideas than what they hold in their minds. Videodisc and CD-ROM presentations can provide advance organizers for subsequent instruction through lecture/discussion and laboratory work or they can be used to illustrate natural phenomena previously discussed in class. Microcomputer-based laboratories provide a means for students to collect accurate measurements, manipulate data, and construct graphs in real time. Using computers and software packages such as *Inspiration*, students can build concept maps of their interrelated ideas and then convert their concept maps into outlines to facilitate the writing process.

Computers and related technologies offer many benefits to science students and teachers. Computers can provide immediate feedback to students who are trying to master a given concept. These electronic devices are "patient" and can provide an endless amount of instruction or drill-and-practice. Individuals or small groups of students can also confront an approximation of a real-life situation in a computer simulation, some accessed via CD-ROM. The simulation provides a realistic experience without the risk, discomfort, or cost associated with the real thing. Additionally, students and teachers can use computers to access information via telecommunication networks and use multimedia systems that combine text, pictures, and sound to present what they have learned to others. Students who are ill and confined at home can be provided with software to use on their own computers that addresses material they normally would receive in the science classroom. Not all students will have access to a home computer, however. With the quality and quantity of software that is available for science teaching, microcomputers can assist in daily instructional tasks as well as eliminate some of the drudgery involved in basic teaching functions such as designing instruction, record keeping, and grading.

The potential of technology for substantially improving science teaching and learning is recognized as an important element of today's science education reform movement. Infusion of technology into the science classroom is being called for at the national, state, and district levels. This desired technology goes well beyond basic drill-and-practice exercises and tutorials. According to Adams, Krockover, and Lehman (1996, p. 66), it involves "(a) access to information via the Internet or a commercial service such as Prodigy or CompuServe, (b) the use of technology for simulations and laboratory based experiences, and (c) the retrieval of media sources via CD-ROM or laser disc." This level of infusion cannot possibly be achieved with only a single microcomputer with a floppy disk drive. Much more is required. At the very least, the computer must have 8MB RAM and a 500MB hard drive. The science classroom also should be equipped with a CD-ROM drive and laser disc player, a high-speed modem and telephone access, a computer-based laboratory system with multiple sensor options, and a large color monitor or liquid crystal display (LCD) panel (Adams et al., 1996).

The infusion of technology into the science classroom is best accomplished when a need for the technology is demonstrated. It is wise to establish a technology infusion strategy before purchasing hardware and software. Ball (1996) advises science teachers to (1) begin with a vision, not machines; (2) use technology to do something different; and (3) start locally and then go global. A vision for what you want to accomplish leads to fiscally responsible purchases. Using the technology for something that cannot be done without it generates excitement and enhances its educational benefit. Beginning small allows students and teachers to learn how to use the technology effectively. And, it is a strong start that helps build the confidence needed to tackle more demanding and far-reaching activities. Ball's advice is well worth following to avoid the pitfalls of apathy and obsolescence too often associated with technology infusion efforts.

There is little doubt that computer usage in science teaching is on the rise. Consequently, this chapter describes many uses for computers and related technology that can help science teachers cope with the task of educating students to live and work in a technologically oriented world in the twenty-first century.

COMPUTERS AND ELECTRONIC TECHNOLOGY IN SCIENCE INSTRUCTION

There is virtually no limit to the ways in which computers and electronic technology can be used in the science classroom. They can be used by individuals, small groups, or an entire class. Their uses can also be described as tutor, tool, and tutee (Taylor, 1980). As a tutor or instructional device, the computer helps students learn skills and acquire understandings. In its role as a tool, the computer may function as a calculator, word processor, and information retriever and manager, and when connected to sensors, it can gather, organize, and analyze laboratory data. As a tutee, the computer is programmed to carry out particular operations and to direct the operations of other electronic devices. Figure 10.1 shows examples of the many applications of computers and other electronic technology in science classes. These multiple and overlapping applications will be examined in greater detail under the categories of microcomputer-based instruction, microcomputer-based laboratories, interactive multimedia systems, telecommunications, and virtual reality.

Microcomputer-Based Instruction

Microcomputers loaded with quality software can help students develop abstract concepts and principles. The power of these instructional resources lies in their interactive capabilities whereby students can manipulate what takes place on a video screen. Students seem to gain greater understanding of a science law, for example, when they can alter variables or parameters and then observe the effects. Microcomputer-based instruction permits students to predict what they believe is going to take place as a result of their intervention and then observe what actually happens. Using a computer in this way can help students develop scientifically acceptable

notions of concepts and principles through the use of critical thinking skills.

Consider a biology course in which genetics is a topic in the curriculum. Genetics is one of the most abstract and complex areas of biology. Concepts such as the gene and the chromosome cannot be easily taught. Phenotypes and genotypes are often confused by students. The molecular composition of DNA is complex even when simplified. Most high school students enrolled in biology courses require a great deal of instructional time to master these fundamental concepts and principles of genetics, especially when very little laboratory work and firsthand experiences are provided.

Using computer-based instruction, for example, students can be schooled on the effects of radiation on a drosophila (fruit fly). On the monitor, students are given opportunities to select the trait to be altered, the sex of the fly, and the amount of radiation to be given. After each trial, the results appear on the monitor. The learner can conduct repeated trials to select the appropriate level of radiation so that the organism is not rendered infertile or killed outright. From the computer-based lesson, students get a sense of what research biologists think about when they perform their work. As students work through the lesson, they can produce a variety of phenotypes, for example, wingless, short body, and curly wing, all of which can be observed on the computer monitor. The students who experience this type of lesson, along with classroom discussion and textbook reading, will likely gain greater understanding of sex chromosomes, sex linkage, somatic mutation, and other concepts than they would without computer-based instruction.

The results of research on computer-based instruction in science tend to support the outcomes depicted in the genetics example. When computers are used to supplement the instructional efforts of teachers, student science achievement is improved and students view computers more favorably (Berger, Lu, Belzer, & Voss, 1994). Additionally, the use of computers complements school and science education reform in that it encourages and facilitates eight instructional shifts noted by Collins (1991):

- A shift from whole-class to small-group instruction
- A shift from lecture and recitation to coaching
- A shift from working with better students to working with weaker students
- A shift toward more engaged students
- A shift from assessment based on test performance to assessment based on products, progress, and effort
- A shift from a competitive to a cooperative social structure
- A shift from all students learning the same thing to different students learning different things

Large Group		
Tutor • Demonstrations • Graphing software/calculators • Presentation hardware/software • Videodiscs	**Tool** • Demonstrations • Graphing software/calculators • Presentation hardware/software • Videodiscs	**Tutee** • Hypermedia project development • Spreadsheets or computer programs for problem-solving
Small Group		
Tutor • Groupware (e.g. Tom Snyder software) • Multimedia (CD-ROM and videodiscs) • Simulations	**Tool** • Databases • MBLs • Multimedia (CD-ROM and videodiscs) • Spreadsheets • Telecommunication	**Tutee** • Hypermedia project development • Spreadsheets or computer programs for problem-solving
Individual		
Tutor • Drill and practice • Multimedia (CD-ROM and videodiscs) • Simulations • Tutorials	**Tool** • Databases • Graphing software/calculators • Multimedia (CD-ROM and videodiscs) • Spreadsheets • Telecommunication • Word processors	**Tutee** • Hypermedia project development • Spreadsheets or computer programs for problem-solving

FIGURE 10.1 Uses of Computers in the Science Classroom

Reprinted with permission of NSTA Publications from *Issues in Science Education* edited by Jack Rhoton and Patricia Bowers. Copyright © 1996 by the National Science Teachers Association, 1840 Wilson Boulevard, Arlington, VA 22201-3000.

■ A shift from the primacy of verbal thinking to the integration of visual and verbal thinking (cited in Berger et al., 1994, p. 473)

Microcomputer-Based Laboratories

Microcomputer-based laboratories (MBLs) involve laboratory and firsthand experiences using the microcomputer, software, and peripherals to gather, display, and analyze data. These laboratories may be used to quantify a variety of biological, physical, and chemical phenomena such as temperature, force, relative humidity, heart rate, light intensity, radiation level, and brain waves. MBLs offer science teachers a powerful technology to enhance laboratory work, often making it more exciting and meaningful to students. Students can explore science phenomena in more accurate and precise ways

than are possible by traditional laboratory methods—at least for certain experiences. As a laboratory tool, this technology permits students to be engaged actively in their laboratory work and to focus on the data almost immediately. Their true benefit, according to Adams and colleagues (Adams et al., 1996, p. 68), is that "MBLs reduce the time needed for tedious data acquisition and organization, thereby allowing more time to be devoted to experimental design and interpretation."

Unlike simulated labs in which the computer is not employed to make actual measurements, MBLs require students to manipulate equipment and to collect data using probes or sensors. The data can be displayed in real time as a graph or table on the computer monitor. Consider, for example, a laboratory exercise to measure temperature. With a simulation, a student might see several objects on the monitor, each having a different temperature. The temperatures are displayed along with questions about the causes of these differences. However, with MBLs students are required to take temperature measurements from real objects. They gather these data with a temperature-sensitive device called a thermocouple. Thermocouples that are properly interfaced to a computer are accurate instruments that can measure temperatures to within less than one-tenth of a degree Celsius. The student immediately observes the temperature readings and graphical or tabular changes on the monitor.

Many standard and innovative laboratory activities can be carried out with the microcomputer. Hundreds of these labs are already prepackaged and sold by software companies to run on IBM-compatible, Apple II series, and Macintosh computers. Although some science teachers prefer to write their own data acquisition and analysis software and build their own sensors for a fraction of the cost of most commercially available MBL packages, the commercial programs have many advantages. They are pretested, preassembled, come with detailed user instructions and student laboratory sheets, and are covered by warranty (Stringfield, 1994). Any science teacher can learn to use this technology.

In addition to the necessary software, commercially available MBL packages come with an interface system and a device called a sensor to pick up the data from the environment. The sensor converts physical or chemical changes into electrical signals. Sensors are available to detect changes in pressure, sound, light, temperature, pH, and so on. Analog signals entering the interface box or the microcomputer communication or game port from sensors are converted into digital signals before they are processed by the computer. Once the signal from the sensor is digitized, the data can be analyzed and displayed on the monitor and calculations can be performed. The graphical display function that accompanies most MBL programs transforms the data into graphs that help students see trends and anomalies.

The potential uses of MBLs in science instruction cannot be overemphasized. MBLs facilitate students' understanding of graphing; further their development of science concepts such as acid, base, pH, heat, and temperature; and enhance their understanding of scientific experimentation by providing them more time to think about what their data actually mean (Huetinck, 1992; Nakhleh, 1994). Not only do MBLs make a difference in students' learning, but students are fascinated by the labs. MBLs get students' attention, improve their attitudes toward computers, and motivate them to participate in science laboratory work (Adams & Shrum, 1990; Bross, 1986).

A science teacher might wonder how to conduct MBLs if many microcomputers are not available. If only one computer is available, pairs or small groups of students can use it on a rotating basis to conduct laboratory

measurements while the other members of the class are engaging in other types of work. Three microcomputers can accommodate twenty-four students. For example, consider an MBL that uses the thermocouple to study heating and cooling. The students can be organized into six groups of four students each. Two groups of students can connect their thermocouples to an interface box that, in turn, is connected to one computer. Each of these two groups can independently input the thermocouple data into the one computer and observe it separately. If two groups of students can use one computer, six groups of students can use three computers. Nevertheless, it would be easier to have six computers, one for each lab group. Many science teachers borrow five or six microcomputers from other classrooms or from the school's microcomputer lab so that they will have enough for a special MBL they wish to conduct. Planning ahead can facilitate all of these arrangements.

Hardly a month goes by when a new MBL package is not introduced for sale by a commercial software vender. Many are designed to provide students with specialized learning opportunities. For example, the Dyna-Pulse 200M Education Edition, based on a system used widely by medical professionals, is designed to engage students in laboratory experiences related to cardiovascular monitoring (Pankiewicz, 1995). Others are more universal in nature and provide for flexible instructional uses from a single computer platform.

The IBM Personal Science Laboratory (PSL) is a microcomputer-based laboratory designed for science instruction from middle school through college (IBM Educational Systems). This program provides its users with two options when electronic technology is employed to conduct laboratory work. Individuals can select experiments that are already designed, or they can create an experiment. The former is ready to go and comes with preset parameters. The latter allows the user to set the parameters for an experiment. Probes are available for collecting data on distance, temperature, light, pH, and time.

The Science Tool Kit is available from Broderbund Software for the Apple II series of computers. Using this MBL program, students can collect temperature and light data for numerous predesigned experiments or design their own. Ones that test the effects of light and temperature on seed germination and plant growth allow data collection to continue when students are not available to monitor the equipment, including overnight (Stringfield, 1994).

For the Apple Macintosh, Vernier Software has developed the Universal Interface. This is a flexible MBL program that is user friendly (Sneider & Barber, 1990). The computer display consists of simple pull-down menus. The data can be displayed in one, two, or four graphs. The probes that are available for investigating phenomena are as follows: photogates, voltage sensors, thermocouples, temperature probes, and radiation monitors. Users can also build a magnetic field sensor and pressure strain gauge to extend the capabilities of the program.

New developments in computer-based laboratories are occurring with regularity. One development involves the use of a digital multimeter (DMM) for portable data-acquisition. It is possible to connect sensors from some existing MBLs to a digital multimeter, available from Fry's Electronics or Radio Shack, to make a portable, computer-based data-acquisition system (Albergotti, 1994). Data collected in the field using the system can then be transferred to a laptop computer, where they can be recorded and displayed as a function of time when appropriate software is used. Albergotti (1994) describes how he collected, analyzed, and displayed direct measurements of automobile acceleration, bicycle speed, and brake pad temperature using this system.

Similarly, Texas Instruments' CBL (calculator-based laboratories) System also permits data collection outside of the laboratory. The CBL System consists of the small CBL unit to which probes can be attached to three different channels. The CBL unit is connected to a TI-82 or TI-85 graphing calculator that is used for data display and analysis. Adams et al. (1996) report that data collected using the CBL System can also be exported to a Macintosh or IBM-compatible computer, but that the CBL System is not as versatile as existing MBL systems at this time. With refinements on the horizon and a cost of less than half of the standard MBL system, it is suspected that the CBL System and others like it will soon be used in more and more science classrooms.

■ STOP AND REFLECT! ■

Before going on to the next topic, do the following:

■ List as many possible uses of modern technology in science teaching as you can.

■ Examine Box 10.1, "Technology in Motion," and indicate which item from your list most closely matches Ms. Roper's use of technology in her physical science classes.

Computer-Based Multimedia

The computer and other electronic technology can be combined to provide some of the most powerful curriculum resources that science teachers can have at their fin-

gertips. In a computer multimedia system, the computer serves to link other media forms so that the utility of the system is greater than that of any one element operating by itself. As the central element of the system, the computer functions as display device, management tool, or source of text, picture, and sound (Heinich, Molenda, Russell, & Smaldino, 1996). Multimedia systems useful to the science teacher include interactive video, CD-ROM, and hypermedia. It is clear from research that these multimedia systems not only influence the manner in which instruction is delivered but also influence student learning in desirable ways (Berger et al., 1994).

Interactive Video.   In this form of multimedia, the computer controls the delivery of pictures, short films, and sound provided through a 12-inch laser videodisc, although input may come from videocassette or compact disc. Individual systems differ in complexity, but the trend is toward providing fully interactive instruction that is controlled by the learner. Branching to different instructional sequences based on the learner's responses to questions is a feature common to this type of instruction and made possible by the computer. Interactive video programs are ideal for individualized or small-group instruction and many are available with both an English and Spanish audio track for use with students with limited English proficiency.

Interactive video may also be used for whole-class instruction. Images can be viewed in full color on a large TV monitor. The system can be used to introduce new material that requires a visual explanation and can be stopped at any point for questions or discussion. Science teachers or students can select still pictures and view them as they would colored slides or view the short films over and over again. Some of these multimedia systems, like The Living Textbook series from Optical Data Corporation, have been referenced to many commercial textbook series so that teachers can access the system with a bar code device.

There is a movement at the middle school level to promote interdisciplinary teaching. Instructional programs that combine science with other curricular areas are often organized around themes that facilitate contextualized student learning. Middle school science teachers need a variety of resources to instruct students in these programs. Consider, for example, a unit of study concerning ecosystems and the environment. Most likely the assigned textbook provides only definitions and explanations of common ideas related to this area such as niches, adaptation, competition, food webs, and biomes. Laboratory exercises would probably accompany the textbook, with additional hands-on activities from the teacher's resource files. However, an interactive multimedia system could be used to enhance this unit of study.

BOX 10.1

TECHNOLOGY IN MOTION

Computer technology is no novelty at Stonewall Jackson High School. Its use has been strongly encouraged by administrators and well supported with local monies and several privately funded projects. The high school media center and science department are well equipped when it comes to technology. Many software and multimedia programs have been purchased in recent years for use in science classes, along with a videodisc player and two CD-ROM players. All science classrooms have at least three microcomputers, a 25-inch monitor, and telephone lines for Internet access via a modem. Parents and visitors alike marvel at the amount of up-to-date technology available at the school for science instruction.

Despite the plethora of computer technology, most Stonewall High science students see the use of computers and other electronic technology as just a different way for teachers to teach the same boring stuff. Given this prevailing student attitude, most of the school's eight science teachers have become disillusioned with the technology's educational promise and are using it less than they were even one year ago. Many of the science faculty cannot see the point of incorporating technology into science classes if it does nothing to motivate students to learn science.

Ms. Roper is one teacher who does not share this view. She thought hard about how she could get students interested in using technology to study motion and forces, the next topic in her curriculum. She was concerned about connecting abstract science concepts with what her students knew and had an interest in. She knew that the technology available at her school could help her, but she did not want to use it in a way that would turn students off.

An idea came to mind. Why not begin the unit on motion and forces by allowing students to use the Internet to learn more about the concepts that will be addressed, such as speed, velocity, and acceleration? She knew that her students were interested in many activities to which these concepts could easily be related.

MS. ROPER: I have written on the board several activities: car racing, gymnastics, dancing, baseball, sailing, volleyball, space travel. What do they all have in common?

DAVA: They all would be fun to watch or do.

KENDAL: Some use special equipment or machines, but all involve quick movement.

PETE: I think that car racing is the most exciting of them all.

After several more students expressed their opinions, the class consensus was that they all involved people moving, sometimes with the help of machines. Other activities were added to the list until about thirty were identified.

MS. ROPER: To start this unit, I would like you to form three-member teams and use the Internet to find out what you can about one of these activities. To access the Internet, you can use the computers in the media center or the one here in the room. As you browse the Internet for information on your topic, save what you find about motion, speed, velocity, and acceleration. And, don't forget to check for bulletin boards related to your topic. Let me know when your team has decided on a topic, so that we don't have two teams working on the same one.

Two days later, the student groups presented what they found. The teams were encouraged to use the LCD panel connected to one of the classroom computers to show some of the Internet sites and bulletin board messages that were considered particularly interesting and informative. The wealth of information that the students collected in just two days surprised even Ms. Roper. The student presentations led to a number of questions related to motion and forces that the students now had a reason to find answers for.

That afternoon Ms. Roper told two of her fellow science teachers about the success she had had with her physical science classes. Her enthusiasm caused the other teachers to wonder if they could do what Ms. Roper had done. It also led Ms. Roper to wonder about how she might use motion detectors, force probes, and toy cars such as Hot Wheels to help students answer some of the questions that were raised during their presentations.

A videodisc program on ecology and the environment can take students to different parts of the world to illustrate simple and complex relationships between organisms. A video of the logging industry in British Columbia and the northwestern United States can show that cutting down large trees affects certain bird populations. Furthermore, students can view the extent of this deforestation and then discuss how it appears to be affecting other animal life. The scene can be changed to South America, where students can view the relationships between plants and vertebrates as well as the economic conditions of people who live in these areas. Since environmental factors and economic development are interrelated, this multimedia technology shows these interactions in a very powerful instructional format. The science teacher can team with a social studies teacher to reinforce student learning in both disciplines.

CD-ROM.   CD-ROM systems offer a very useful delivery format because they can store large amounts of pictorial and textual material on a 12-cm disc. As for videodiscs, a special player is required and the read-only format of CD-ROM makes it impossible to change the information on the disc. Many newer computers come with built-in CD-ROM players, and CD-ROM discs tend to be less expensive than videodiscs. The amount of information that can be housed on a CD-ROM disc is literally encyclopedic—over two hundred thousand pages of typewritten text. Early versions of CD-ROM programs merely produced printed material on the screen. Today's programs can provide action and pictures in vivid color along with textual material.

An example of a spectacular CD-ROM package that has been developed jointly by the National Geographic Society and IBM is called *Mammals: A Multimedia Encyclopedia* (Salpeter, 1990). The program is available for both IBM-compatible and Macintosh platforms and contains sound, photographic images, text, and film clips. The user can select and view hundreds of different species of mammals from around the world. For each animal, the program provides information about its habitat, diet, survival status, life span, and reproductive patterns. This teaching resource supplies the user with the quality of animal study that has characterized the National Geographic Society's long tradition of excellence.

Hypermedia.   Hypermedia is a computer-based format for linking information. It is unique in that the user simply clicks on a button with a mouse to follow an idea from one piece of information to another. The information may be in the form of graphics, text, audio, or video and can be viewed in any order by the user. For example, a computer user interested in hurricanes may decide to view a film clip that shows what it is like to fly through the eye wall of a hurricane, then read an account of a person's near-death experience with a hurricane, and later study a graphic that shows the Saffer-Simpson scale.

Hypermedia applications have been developed for many science areas. One developed for secondary biology illustrates the principles of osmosis. The Osmosis Program is highly interactive and intended to help students uncover and correct their misconceptions about osmosis by examining critical underlying concepts, including concentration gradients, equilibrium, and differential membrane permeability (Jensen, Hatch, Somdahl & Wilcox, 1993). HyperCard based, the program setup uses a Macintosh computer, a laser disc player, Optical Data Corporation's *The Living Textbook* laser disc, and a large monitor. A second hypermedia application is the Jasper series developed by the Cognition and Technology Development Group at Vanderbilt University (Van Haneghan et al., 1993). Designed for middle school students, the six-episode series involves students in solving problems that stem from the adventures of the character, Jasper Woodbury. In one adventure, introduced by a high-quality movie presented via videodisc, students are challenged to help Jasper construct a swing set frame of a specified height. To solve the problem, students construct models of the swing set frame using drinking straws and with guidance provided by information embedded in the adventure. This feature of embedded information allows teachers to use the videodisc over and over again to help students figure out what they need to know to solve the problem (Cognition and Technology Group, 1990).

Hypermedia shows great promise for improving science teaching and learning. An attractive feature of hypermedia is that its design matches cognitive scientists' models of how people learn and store knowledge in the brain. It allows for the organization of information into small chunks that can be linked in ways that are meaningful to the learner. There is no sequential presentation of information as in a textbook. According to Marsh and Kumar (1992, p. 5), "It is this ability to organize and manipulate irregular structures of information that seems to make hypermedia applications ideally suited for a variety of scientific applications ranging from classroom science to engineering." Software packages, such as Apple's HyperCard and IBM's Linkway, provide the omnidirectional structure for users to navigate through the information without changing it, form new linkages within the information, and create their own assemblage of information from existing or newly created text, diagrams, and film or audio clips.

Multimedia is well suited for whole-class instruction. Multimedia presentations using a hypermedia system, video disc, or CD-ROM can benefit a large number of students at a given time, if they can see what is taking place. Several devices are available for classroom presentations that permit large groups to view multimedia presentations. Large-screen monitors ranging in size from 26 to 35 inches provide excellent color images for student audiences. Video projectors can be used in large meeting rooms or auditoriums because they can project images directly onto large screens. A flat liquid crystal display (LCD) can provide images produced from computers and laser discs, which can be projected on a screen by a device similar to an overhead transparency machine. This device can be transported easily from classroom to classroom and used for large-group instruction.

Telecommunications

Electronic technology has made it possible for communications to take place between classrooms across the globe. Every day more science classrooms are being con-

nected to the Internet. This electronic system permits students and teachers to retrieve information in the form of text, images, and data and to communicate with others living in different locations. Now it is possible for schools, planetariums, museums, educational centers, and other facilities to share programs and exchange ideas through this network.

The Internet is a worldwide collection of access points for information acquisition and exchange (Krockover & Adams, 1995). A computer, a modem, a telephone line, the computer's systems software, and telecommunications software are all that is needed to access the Internet. Internet access may be gained through a local area service provider or through a commercial online service like America Online, CompuServe, or Prodigy. Both local and commercial services provide the necessary software and charge a user fee. The Internet also can be accessed directly through computers at colleges and universities and in some school districts. The Internet can be thought of as a large shopping mall where each store provides a different product or service. And as in all shopping malls, some stores attract more business than others. Parts of the Internet that have attracted the most business include electronic mail, telnet, FTP, WAIS, gopher, and the World Wide Web.

Many science classrooms have computers available to students who use them routinely to gather information off the Internet.

Internet Features.   Electronic mail, or e-mail, facilitates the personal exchange of messages between computer users and can be accessed on the Internet using programs such as Eudora and Pine. For example, middle school students can use e-mail to share on-the-spot weather data with other students around the country and to contact scientists to ask questions about the patterns observed in the data. E-mail can also be exchanged among groups of people who share a common interest using listservs and bulletin boards. A listserv is simply a computer-based mailing list to which many people subscribe. A bulletin board is a lot like the editorial page of a major city newspaper (Engst, 1995). Many science education-related listservs and bulletin boards exist where comments, questions, rebuttals, and opinions are posted on a daily basis. USENET is a very useful bulletin board for science teachers because it includes discussions of many science topics, such as oceanography, biology, and geology (Shepardson, 1995). A limitation of USENET is that for several discussion groups messages are deleted after only a couple of days due to the high volume of daily postings.

Telnet is an Internet access program that enables the user to connect to another computer and run a program located at that site. It can be used to gain entry to library catalogs, online journals, and sources of weather information among other things. The University of Michigan's Weather Underground is one source of weather information that can be accessed using telnet (Krockover & Adams, 1995). In contrast to telnet, file transfer protocol (FTP) allows the user to copy files back and forth from a computer at another site. The catch with both telnet and FTP is that you must know the full file name and address in order to run a program or retrieve a file. Getting the full name and address of a file through FTP is possible with the help of Archie. Archie provides a listing of file names and addresses located on other computers by searching for a specified key word in their names. Archie has indexes for more than one thousand servers with about 2.5 million files (Krockover & Adams, 1995, p. 37).

Gopher is another Internet search program that can be used to get files from other computers much like FTP. But because it allows a user to access files directly from a menu, it is much easier to use than FTP. Other advantages of gopher are that it allows the user access to Internet resources of many types, including pictures and audio, and provides indirect access to FTP and telnet. Accessing information through gopher is done using Veronica and Jughead (also names of characters in the Archie comics). Of the two search engines, Veronica provides the most comprehensive list of resources because its searches extend to all gopher sites (Engst, 1995). WAIS, the acronym for wide area information service, is a lot like gopher in what it can do. The advantage of

WAIS is that it employs an automated search system that allows the user to find documents on a topic in one of over five hundred libraries and, once found, to display the documents (Krockover & Adams, 1995).

The World Wide Web (WWW, or the Web) is the newest of many Internet services and is responsible for much of the Internet's notoriety. It is different from the other Internet services in two important ways. It provides hypertext links between documents and provides access to movies, audio, onscreen pictures, and full font and styles for text (Engst, 1995). Web browsers, such as Netscape, Mosaic, and Lynx, are used to navigate the Web, with Lynx providing text-only access. With the emergence of the Web and its increasing versatility, Internet users are finding fewer reasons to use programs such as telnet, FTP, and WAIS. These programs are still being employed as behind the scenes search engines through Web page interfaces, however, and they will continue to be used by those without access to the Web.

Internet Resources and Applications.   The Internet can be used to address many of the challenges associated with improving middle school and secondary science education. It enables information reception, information selection, and collaboration between students, teachers, and science content experts (Reynolds & Barba, 1996). The Internet is particularly helpful as a resource for up-to-date science information. Through the Internet, teachers can get information about most science topics included in the middle school and secondary science curriculum from government agencies, universities, museums and science centers, scientific societies, and other teachers. Many Internet sites are connected to other sites that can be accessed with a simple mouse click when using the World Wide Web. "NASA Spacelink" (http://spacelink.msfc.nasa.gov/), "Frog Dissection" (http://curry.edschool.Virginia.EDU.go/frog/), and "Hands-On Universe" (http://hou.lbl.gov/) are but three examples of Internet sites where up-to-date science information is available. New sites useful to science teachers are being added almost daily as others are being deleted. Most can be easily located through a keyword search. Given instruction on using the Internet, students also can access these resources.

Through the Internet teachers can also access information about science teaching ideas and materials. For example, The Eisenhower National Clearinghouse for Mathematics and Science Education's World Wide Web site is one of the many access points to an almost limitless cache of science teaching resources. Through the Clearinghouse's Web site (http://www.enc.org./), teachers can search an online catalog of thousands of science teaching resources and access a dozen high-quality science and mathematics Internet sites that are updated monthly (Roempler, 1996).

A true advantage of the Internet is its ability to make science classes come alive by facilitating student investigation of real world problems. For example, Internet access enables science students to participate in national and international scientific monitoring projects (Bartlett & Bartlett, 1996). Classes can collect data on the weather, acid rain, water quality, road kills, butterfly migration, and other phenomena and share their data with other science classes and scientists using a computer bulletin board. The data collected can be analyzed to show trends and relationships among variables. Monitoring projects provide a meaningful context for science learning and serve to get students online with a purpose (Cleaver, Barnes, Mitchell, & Winn, 1996).

The Internet is also a source of easily accessible data for use in science classes. Real-time and archival data can be accessed from a number of Internet sites. Students can easily become proficient at accessing the data themselves and at making decisions about what form of data—numerical values, or graphic display—is most appropriate for answering specific questions. Numeric data pulled from some Internet sites can also be downloaded as a spreadsheet that enables students to construct graphs of the data and run statistical analysis. Live Access to Climate Data from NOAA's Pacific Marine Environmental Laboratory (http://ferret.wrc. noaa.gov/) and the University of Rhode Island's Sea Surface Temperature Satellite Images Archive (http://rs.gso.uri.edu/avhrr-archive.html) are just two of the many sites of accessible data on the Internet (Clemmitt, 1996).

There is little doubt that the Internet is changing the character of science teaching and learning. Teachers and students no longer need to rely exclusively on a textbook to study science. They can use the Internet to bring exciting, real-time science to the classroom on any day. Active student learning is the norm in the Internet environment. Where else can one read from a text description of dinosaur fossils and, with a single mouse click, jump to a video clip of a *Tyrannosaurus rex* stalking its prey or to the home page of a dinosaur paleontologist. Activities that involve students using the Internet help them learn to think the way scientists do. The Internet also provides students with an outlet for telling others about their accomplishments. Multimedia reports can be constructed and published on the Internet. Graphics and photographs obtained from sites on the Internet can be included in reports, and the reports can be updated as new information and photographs become available. More importantly, access to the Internet can bring the resources of the world to all science classrooms at a relatively low cost. This will do much to ensure that students in poor and rural schools have the same science learning opportunities provided to students in affluent communities.

A concern of many teachers when using the Internet in their science classes is student access to pornography and other information unsuitable for adolescents. The availability of offline browsing and content delivery applications, such as ForeFront's WebWhacker, should lessen this concern. Using WebWhacker, a teacher can download entire Web sites and store them on a computer's hard drive for later access without an Internet connection. This capability allows the teacher to control what students are able to access, eliminates the hassle of trying to access the Internet during class, and provides an Internet experience, complete with information navigating and viewing.

Because of the newness of the technology, little research has been conducted regarding the influence of the two-way communication facilitated by the Internet on science learning, but early findings are indeed encouraging. Reynolds and Barba's (1996, p. 14) summary of research findings indicates that technology-mediated communication:

- increases student satisfaction with instruction
- provides students with additional avenues for communicating with instructors, peers, and content-area experts
- improves students' writing ability and reading comprehension
- increases students' interest in educational activities
- improves students' dialectical thinking processes
- provides disabled students with additional means for communication

These findings lend support for increasing the opportunities for student use of telecommunications in middle and secondary school science classes.

Virtual Reality

Perhaps the most powerful instructional resource for science education is what is termed "virtual reality" or "virtual environments" or "virtual worlds." A virtual reality environment is created to simulate a real environment but is not the real thing. Virtual reality technology goes beyond the common visual and auditory experiences from computer and multimedia technologies; it includes perceptual and tactile interactions as well. By wearing a special helmet (or headgear) and gloves, the learner can experience a new world, a virtual world, different from anything experienced before. During the past decade, military and space programs have used this technology to train individuals in flying and space travel. Also, it has been used to provide critical training for medical professional and police officers. The hardware for this technology exists at certain federal government-supported science and technology centers such as the Johnson Space Center in Houston, Texas, and private corporations that develop and support high-tech industries, medical schools, and state and city governments.

Today, software is in the design and testing stages for science education purposes. It features pseudovirtual environments that use CD-ROM technology that is not fully interactive (Heinich et al., 1996). In the not too distant future, virtual reality may play a major role in science teacher education and provide science students with the opportunity to explore places and events not accessible from the classroom. What would it be like for students, through virtual reality, to visit a live volcano or walk in space?

■ STOP AND REFLECT! ■

Before going on to the next topic, do the following:

▨ Describe two ways in which computer-based multimedia can be used to enhance science instruction.

▨ Revisit Box 10.1, "Technology in Motion." How could Ms. Roper's instructions to her students be revised to ensure that they accessed the Internet through more than one access point?

SCIENCE SOFTWARE AND ITS INSTRUCTIONAL USES

Students can interact directly with science lessons delivered by a computer alone or in combination with other electronic technology. The software can be accessed using a floppy disk, CD-ROM, or videodisc. This application of computers has traditionally been called computer-assisted instruction (CAI) and can be discussed in terms of the instructional method used.

Drill-and-Practice

The microcomputer can help students improve their performance in the science classroom. Many students who do not study or complete their homework and other assignments often do poorly on tests. These students fail to learn new vocabulary words and concepts that are

found in their science textbooks or that are presented during a unit of study. They need to practice identifying, defining, writing key words, and solving word problems. Many students need repetition to achieve retention of the subject matter. Drill-and-practice software provides valuable practice for these students.

Drill-and-practice programs provide the learner with exercises that review subject matter. The list of commercial and teacher-prepared programs for this purpose is long. For example, practice programs are available in biology for taxonomy, human anatomy, cell structure and function, protein synthesis, respiration, mitosis, digestion, parts of a flower, food chains, bacterial diseases, and more. Chemistry programs are available on various topics, such as significant figures, properties of matter, symbols of elements, naming compounds, balancing equations, and determining molecular formulas. A variety of programs is also available in other areas of science. Built into most drill-and-practice programs are several levels of difficulty and provisions for providing correction, remediation, or encouragement (Heinich et al., 1996).

Tutorial

Tutorial programs go beyond drill and practice. They are used to teach concepts, skills, and new information. These programs tend to be highly interactive and require active participation from the learner. They may involve reading, solving problems, analyzing graphics, simulating laboratory experiments, and completing word problems. Every science course has certain concepts and principles that give students problems. Many students have trouble understanding density, genetic crosses, Ohm's law, balancing chemical equations, solving mole problems, and determining acceleration, for example. Tutorials are excellent for helping students learn difficult concepts and principles.

Tutorial programs carefully guide the learner through the steps necessary to develop the subconcepts that underlie the major learning outcomes. For example, a good tutorial program on balancing chemical equations might begin with writing chemical formulas, proceed to discussing chemical equations, continue with writing chemical equations, and end with balancing chemical equations. Authors of good tutorial programs analyze the learning tasks involved in performing a given learning outcome. They break the learning into steps to increase the probability of the student performing the terminal task. These authors also include much practice after each step to promote understanding and retention. Branching is an important aspect of good tutorial programs because it provides appropriate remediation based on the student's incorrect answers.

Tutorial programs can be used by individual students or small groups during the school day or after school. They can also be used in large-group instruction. An LCD panel used with an overhead projector permits a class of students to view the computer output on an AV screen. An entire class also can use tutorial programs in the microcomputer lab when many computers are available.

Simulations

Computer simulations permit science teachers to bring rich learning experiences into the classroom. Simulations illustrate real-life or hypothetical situations that help the learner to visualize concepts and principles in action that would not be possible or as meaningful if presented through other modes of instruction. They often permit learners to manipulate variables or parameters and then to observe the consequences of their choices. Additionally, simulations can bring into the classroom aspects of the world or universe that are too expensive, too dangerous, too difficult, or too slow or too fast in occurrence to be experienced firsthand (Tamir,1985/1986). Objects in space, molecular motion, radioactive material, electrical current, predator/prey relationships, and breeding are just some of the topics around which science simulations have been developed.

Science simulations vary greatly and serve different purposes. The learning experiences provided by some simulations are easily achievable by other means during regular class periods. For example, Operation: Frog allows students to dissect and reconstruct a frog by following the same sequence of operations as in an actual lab. The advantage of this simulation is that it eliminates the need for purchasing large quantities of preserved frogs and may appeal to individuals who object to the killing of animals for educational purposes. Other simulations depict the operations of systems that are not normally visible. For example, a simulation of the heart can show the path of blood flow, highlighting the function of the chambers and values. With the use of color graphics, oxygenated and deoxygenated blood is traced as it flows through the chambers and vessels of the heart. Still other simulations are more sophisticated in that they allow learners to manipulate otherwise uncontrollable aspects of the environment or universe and to observe the effects. These manipulations often involve speeding up or slowing down time and increasing or decreasing distance. For example, simulations of weather fronts show in the span of minutes the movement of cold and warm fronts across regions and continents that in nature take days or weeks.

Recent advances in science computer simulations include the use of simulation software engines and the development of role-playing software, called groupware, that can be used to initiate whole-class or small-group simulations. A simulation software engine is the prominent feature of the software of the Explorer series by LOGAL Software. The engine allows the learner to design simulations, run them, examine the results, and use the results to design new simulation parameters. The Explorer series includes biology, chemistry, and physics programs, and each program contains learning modules that explore abstract concepts typically addressed in secondary science classes. An example of groupware is The Environment, a program of the Decisions, Decisions series offered by Tom Snyder Productions. When using this program, students are presented with a simulated local crisis—a polluted pond used by the community for recreation—through critical reading. The students attempt to clarify their values and evaluate the consequences of possible actions by interacting with the software, engaging in discussions, and reading relevant historical pieces provided as part of the package. By the time students reach the final decision-making step in the simulation, they have learned quite a bit about such issues as waste disposal, recycling, and endangered species. A unique feature of the Decisions, Decisions series is that only one computer is required to engage an entire class.

Some science computer simulations involve users in playing a game of some sort. Called computer-based simulation games, these programs combine the role-playing or mock reality of a simulation with the rules and challenges of a game. An example is Where in Space Is Carmen Sandiego? by Broderbund Software. In this computer-based simulation game, students make use of an array of resource materials while playing the role of detective to track down and catch members of Carmen Sandiego's gang. The game takes the detective on a journey through the universe and explores understandings from the areas of astronomy, space exploration, and the history of science.

Problem Solving

Problem solving requires the learner to use previously acquired skills and knowledge to resolve a challenging problem (Heinich et al., 1996). Science problem solving requires considerable involvement and interaction by the students before solutions are proposed and results are determined with the aid of the computer. This involvement and interaction often includes making sense of the problem, collecting relevant data, generating hypotheses, and testing the hypotheses in some fashion. The role of the computer and other electronic technology in science problem solving may include posing the problem, providing a mechanism for data storage and retrieval, and offering clues to help the learner resolve the problem.

One commercially available science problem-solving program is Science Sleuths from Videodiscovery. It provides middle school students with four mysteries to solve, with each mystery containing six solutions that vary in degree of difficulty. Students can work individually, in pairs, or in small groups. The mysteries are tied to real-life situations and require students to use their knowledge of life, earth, and physical science concepts and science process skills to arrive at a solution. The program does not promote a fixed problem-solving model; students utilize different resources, including video interviews, still pictures, documents, and maps to arrive at the six different solutions provided for each mystery. Students are introduced to the program through a humorous character and a tutorial. Science Sleuths is packaged in two volumes, each containing two mysteries. Volume 1 includes the mysteries of the "Blob" and the "Exploding Lawnmower." Mysteries of the "Biogene Picnic" and the "Traffic Accident" are in volume 2. The multimedia kit for each volume includes a CD-ROM, student case sheets and worksheets, assessment materials, and a teacher's manual.

Another problem-solving technology-based program is The Voyage of the Mimi developed by the Bank Street College Project in Science and Mathematics. Used by science teachers for more than ten years, it combines television video, microcomputer software, and printed materials to engage students in the study of whales during a sea voyage. The instructional package consists of thirteen video episodes, each lasting fifteen minutes and paired with a fifteen-minute documentary. The students use printed guides and interactive software to explore selected concepts in depth. They also engage in LOGO activities (a special type of graphics program) and microcomputer-based laboratory simulations. Printed materials and software that accompany the TV series stimulate problem solving by encouraging students to experiment with the elements of the natural world as observed through this instructional package.

Few problem-solving programs are as extensive as Science Sleuths or The Voyage of the Mimi, which has been shown on PBS. Nevertheless, there are many

---

■ STOP AND REFLECT! ■

Before going on to the next topic, do the following:

■ Describe the teacher's role when using drill-and-practice software in science class.

■ Describe the nature of simulation software. How does it differ from software that facilitates student problem solving?

---

worthwhile problem-solving programs for science teachers to preview for use in their teaching. One excellent technology-based problem-solving program can generate a great deal of student excitement in a science class.

USING COMPUTERS TO SUPPORT SCIENCE INSTRUCTION

There are many tasks performed routinely by science teachers that do not involve actual teaching but rather support the instruction provided to students or are required by the school. Tasks such as record keeping, planning, and assessment are ones that can be made easier or accomplished in a more efficient manner with the aid of computer technology.

Record Keeping

Entering and averaging grades, maintaining daily attendance records, and recording information about students can consume a great deal of teacher time and be very tedious. Fortunately, many computer programs can be used to simplify these tasks and to save considerable time. Most computer grading programs permit the teacher to list alphabetically the students in a given class along a left-hand column of the page, and allow the entry of grades across the top of the page, as in a traditional grade book. These programs also permit the teacher to weight the grades and to find numerical averages. For example, some science teachers count laboratory work one-third, daily work one-third, and tests and quizzes one-third. Others may count a portfolio twice as much as a major test grade. Whichever way teachers desire to weight the grades, the program will compute the averages. Figure 10.2 shows an example of the kind of display that can be obtained from a computer grading program, in this case Grade Machine.

Teachers do not necessarily need to use a predeveloped software grading package. Spreadsheet programs can also be useful. Spreadsheets are commonly used in business for record keeping. They produce rows and columns, neatly displaying many data. Not only do spreadsheets permit freedom and flexibility, but they also save time. Fortunately, many individuals in local communities and schools can help a teacher get started in using the microcomputer for record keeping.

In addition to grading, the computer can be used to generate charts to keep attendance. The seating chart shown in Figure 10.3 is a matrix with squares that represent desks in the classroom. When teachers place stu-

#	Assignment	Date Due	Category
1	HW-Ch. 14		Daily Grades
2	Prac. Set 1	1/20/93	Daily Grades
3	Ch. 14 Test, P1	1/22/93	Tests
4	Prac. Set 2	1/24/93	Daily Grades
5	Ch. 14 Test, P2		Tests

Name	Scores 1	2	3	4	5	First six weeks Daily Grades	First six weeks Tests	First six weeks Exam
Ammons, David	100	100	98	100	100	100.0%	95.1%	100.0%
Basawa, Philip	80	100	100	100	88	95.5%	92.0%	100.0%
Blount, Kendal	80	80	93	100	82	92.1%	82.3%	100.0%
Bryant, Joseph	90	80	96	80	61	75.3%	79.2%	100.0%
Ervin, Marybeth			76	90	34	62.0%	66.6%	90.9%
Floret, Andrew	90	80	87	90	84	91.6%	88.5%	
Hough, Yue	90	90	88	90	92	71.7%	75.4%	70.0%
Nickson, Jerry	80	90	91	90	72	93.9%	87.3%	
Pyle, Matthew	ex	ex	ex	ex	ex	95.0%	88.4%	100.0%
Staton, David	80	70	77	80	67	76.1%	62.1%	70.0%
Smith, Jacquelyn	80	80	98	80	82	67.8%	76.5%	100.0%
Summers, Ray	90	100	100	10	95	98.8%	96.7%	92.2%
Waverly, Erin	90	90	92	100	92	84.8%	81.9%	
CLASS AVERAGE	73	74	84	85	73	85.0%	82.5%	
POSSIBLE POINTS	100	100	100	100	100			

Key to special scores: ab=Absent ch=Cheating √=Completed dr=Dropped ex=Excused (blank)=Incomplete
+=Outstanding tr=Truant –=Unacceptable

FIGURE 10.2 Display Generated by Grade Machine, a Microcomputer Grading Program

dents' names in the appropriate spaces, they can take attendance easily while learning students' names.

Preparation of Instruction

One of the most satisfying uses of the personal computer is for the preparation of instruction. Science teachers can use the computer's word-processing and graphics capabilities to construct lesson plans, unit plans, paper-and-pencil exercises, lecture notes, laboratory exercises, assignments, word puzzles, and so forth. Using the computer requires much less time than it would take to prepare these instructional materials with pencil or using a conventional typewriter because modifications can be made in minutes. Corrections can be made without retyping the entire text or reconstructing the complete graphic. Since textual materials are stored in files, they can be saved and recalled for use at a future time. This capability saves a great deal of time retyping and modifying an exercise or a lesson plan.

Many school districts require teachers to prepare daily lesson plans and to submit plans to the principal or department head. This requirement provides both the administration and teachers with a record of what is expected of the students and the activities that will be used to help students achieve the objectives. These lesson plans always call for a list of instructional objectives, which can be prepared quickly with the computer because it permits the teachers to make changes and minor modifications on the screen. Some school districts also require that unit objectives, teacher expectations, and safety precautions be given to students so that they and their parents can review them. Using the computer, teachers can easily prepare these documents, modify them to meet the needs of different classes, and save copies of them for their personal records.

Assessment

The emerging applications of computers and hypermedia to science assessment are many. Using computer technology, science teachers can structure assessment tasks to provide immediate feedback to students, monitor student homework and laboratory activities, and design both formative and summative assessment opportunities that are realistic and engage students in problem solving (Helgeson & Kumar, 1993). Nevertheless, test construction remains the predominant use of computers by science teachers for assessment applications.

Tests can be constructed using a microcomputer's word-processing capability. Since the test is stored as a file, teachers can easily modify a test before administering it if they so desire. They can easily make two versions of a single multiple-choice item by taking the first version, modifying either the stem or the choices, and then saving it as a second item. This procedure can be repeated several times to produce several versions of a given item or two versions of the same test. Software and textbook companies have developed test generators for many science courses. These test packages are versatile

FIGURE 10.3 Computer-Generated Seating Chart

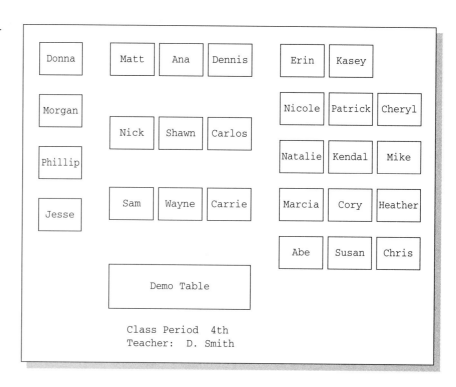

and easy to use. They can produce many types of test items, such as multiple choice, matching, true/false, and short answer. The programs also randomize test items, construct several test versions, and produce an answer key for each version of the test. Test generators that are designed for specific textbooks are keyed to the objectives for each chapter, and the user can select the objectives for the test items desired.

SELECTING QUALITY SOFTWARE AND MULTIMEDIA

Instructional software and multimedia are provided on floppy disk, CD-ROM, and videodisc, and can be accessed via the Internet. The quality of instructional software and multimedia is a major factor in determining the benefits derived from them. The quality must be high—that is, the product must be easy to use and instructive—otherwise the computer and other electronic technology will make little contribution to science education. Many education software and multimedia programs are available, but not all of them are effective for instruction. A number of programs appear to be useful when first examined, but a closer look will lead science teachers to conclude that they have little educational value. It is easy for commercial software and multimedia developers to make colorful, flashy programs that appear useful; however, in the final analysis some of these teaching aids have little instructional significance. Careful analysis of software and multimedia programs is essential before this technology is used in science instruction.

Perhaps the first thing that science teachers should do before selecting a program is to reflect on the course they are teaching or will be teaching. They must identify key concepts, principles, laws, and science process skills that they wish students to master or what aspects of the nature of science and technology that they want students to explore. This process will give purpose to their search for quality software and multimedia and will help them incorporate computer technology into the curriculum as opposed to using it because it seems to be the thing to do.

To examine a piece of software or multimedia, science teachers should read the author's description of the product's purpose. What is the program trying to teach? Some programs, for example, try to teach scientific laws. Chemistry programs instruct students on rates of reaction, stoichiometry, and chemical equilibrium. Life science programs instruct students on plant growth and human anatomy. Other programs emphasize problem solving and critical thinking. Next, science teachers must

decide on the type of instructional program they want to use, such as drill-and-practice, tutorial, or simulation. Then from the program description, teachers must determine for whom the software or multimedia is intended. Usually the grade level is given for the program but often this information is too general. In addition to determining the merits of various important aspects of the software or multimedia, teachers may wish to consider its cost.

Teachers reviewing software or multimedia should ask the following questions (Heinich et al., 1996, p. 277):

- Is the software or multimedia accurate and current?
- Is the language used clear and concise?
- Does the program enhance motivation and maintain interest?
- Does the program engage the learner as an active participant?
- Is the software or multimedia of high technical quality?
- Can the developer provide evidence of its effectiveness?
- Is the program free from objectionable bias?
- Are the program's teacher's guide and documentation of high quality?
- Are clear directions provided for loading the software and using it for the first time?
- Does the program stimulate creativity?

Make sure a program is easy to use before purchasing it. Are the instructions easy to follow, or does the user need to spend a great deal of time figuring out what to do? Good programs must be user-friendly or students will become frustrated and avoid using them.

Science teachers need to be concerned about content accuracy of software and multimedia. They should become mindful of programs that contain factual errors and outdated information. They should also seek programs that use appropriate statistics and accurate graphs. Graphs are an important consideration because graphing is one of the process skills stressed in science education. Often computer programs use graphs that are attractive, yet difficult to read. Remember that not all software and multimedia intended for science instruction have been developed or carefully reviewed by classroom teachers before they have been placed on the market. Individuals with programming background, who often play the major role in software and multimedia development, may not know the type of graphing skills, for example, taught at a particular grade level. Also, these people are often not subject matter specialists.

Sethna (1985) suggests that an easy way to evaluate software is to develop a form and rate its important aspects. He recommends that users rate software in at least the following five areas: (a) ease of use, (b) documentation, (c) graphics, (d) content, and (e) instruction. Each area can be rated on a one-to-ten scale from low to high.

Sethna points out that perhaps the best people to assess the merits of science instructional software are the students. He suggests that students be given the program to work through. The same recommendations should be heeded when considering multimedia. The following are some items that Sethna (1985, Appendix A) has given to students to evaluate science simulations.

▨ The program was easy to use without help from the teacher.

▨ The program helped me learn what I was supposed to learn.

▨ The program was related to other work on the same topic.

▨ The meaning of special symbols used in the program could be displayed on the screen when needed.

▨ The program told me when I had control over waiting time or not.

▨ Helpful shortcuts were given when I was expected to run the program many times.

Computer technology and the right software or multimedia package can assist teachers in enhancing their instructional programs. Nevertheless, science teachers must be keenly aware of the technical and the instructional quality of the software or multimedia they wish to adopt. Technically, it must be easy to use, and the screen display and graphics must be easy to view. Instructionally, the content of the program must be accurate and appropriate for the students. Good software and multimedia can be selected only through systematic inquiry into what is available and careful evaluation of it for a given group of students.

ASSESSING AND REVIEWING

1. Indicate your agreement or disagreement with each of the following statements. For those you disagree with, write a brief paragraph to convince others of the need to agree with your position.

   a. All science teachers will need to develop some basic level of understanding in using MBLs.

   b. In selecting software and multimedia for use in science classes, teachers should begin by asking the question: What concepts and skills are addressed by the program that match those that I address in my course?

   c. Sooner or later, all science teachers will need to be able to program new software.

   d. Microcomputers should be incorporated into science lessons whenever possible.

   e. The Internet is a fad that will become less useful to science teachers and students in the coming years.

2. Construct a table that will allow you to compare the different forms of science software and their instructional uses in science teaching and learning. Label the columns of the table: Software Type, Purpose,

   Teacher's Role, Student's Role, Computer's Role. Include drill-and-practice, tutorial, simulation, and problem-solving software among the types addressed.

3. Analyze a teaching situation to determine which use of computers and electronic technology discussed in this chapter is emphasized. Make an outline of the major ideas associated with (i) microcomputer-based instruction, (ii) microcomputer-based laboratories, (iii) computer-based multimedia, (iv) telecommunications, and (v) virtual reality. Then, use your outline as an aid to analyze the following paragraphs.

   a. Middle school students studying earth science can communicate with other students around their state to gather real-time data concerning the weather. They can construct regional weather maps by contacting students in other schools that are fifty to two hundred or more miles away to determine weather conditions in these locations. Students can provide information about the temperature, cloud formations, wind direction, and wind speed that exist in these locations. The students can attempt to forecast the weather. They can provide students in the rest of the school with daily weather reports over the announcement system. Furthermore, the students can attempt to predict the next day's weather from the information they gather and can determine which factors seem to provide the most useful information for this purpose.

b. Consider an introductory chemistry course in which Boyle's law is a topic in the curriculum. An interactive lesson on Boyle's law can be used to assist students to better understand the relationship between pressure and volume of a gas at a constant temperature. On the computer monitor, the students observe the motion of particles in a container with changeable volume. By altering the initial condition of pressure, students see the resulting changes in the gas volume. As

motion of the particles in the container (representing pressure change) and container volume are observed on the screen, a graph of the relationship between volume and pressure is shown in the upper right corner of the monitor. Points of the volume × pressure graph are plotted for each measure of pressure (kPa) entered into the program. An added benefit of this lesson is derived when the students must predict the volume at a given pressure, and then can verify the relationship by running the program to observe the graphic simulation and resulting point on the graph.

4. Identify five shortcomings or limitations resulting from using computers and electronic technology in middle school and secondary science teaching and learning. How might the shortcomings or limitations be changed into benefits?

■

RESOURCES TO EXAMINE

"Thinking Like a Scientist on the World Wide Web." 1996. *Science Scope*, 19(6), 38–41.

Cynthia Peterson and her colleagues discuss how the World Wide Web can be used to engage students in science investigations that help them develop important scientific thinking skills. During the investigations, students conduct searches, determine the usefulness and relevance of what they find, and draw conclusions. A model investigation developed by the authors and used with their students is presented as part of the article.

The IT in Secondary Science Book. A Compendium of Ideas for Using Computers and Teaching Science. 1994. Distributed in the USA and Canada by Data Harvet Educational, Inc., 267 Romark Mews, Mississauga, Ontario, Canada L5L 224.

This 132-page sourcebook includes a wealth of information about the many uses of information technology (IT) for teaching biology, chemistry, and physics. Roger Frost provides examples and activities to help the reader become proficient with the many applications of computers in science teaching, including databases, spreadsheets, sensors, modeling, and graphics.

"Data Collecting Calculators." 1996. *The Science Teacher*, 63(3), 18–20.

Carole Forkey describes her earth science students' experiences with Texas Instruments' CBL System as they investigated exothermic and endothermic reactions. Included in the article are her directions for the lab and the sequence of calculator commands used by her students.

Internet Starter Kit for Macintosh. 1996. Published by Hayden Books, 201 West 103rd Street, Indianapolis, IN 46290.

If you have questions about the Internet and no one you ask has the answers, this is the book for you. This 713-page volume by Adam Engst provides detailed information about connecting to the Internet via modem, the limitations of commercial services, troubleshooting your Internet connections, and full Internet access, including e-mail, gopher, and World Wide Web. A sister volume is available for IBM-compatible systems.

References

Adams, D. D., & Shrum, J. W. (1990). The effects of micro-computer-based laboratory exercises on the acquisition of line graph construction and interpretation skills by high school biology students. *Journal of Research in Science Teaching, 27,* 777–787.

Adams, P. E., Krockover, G. H., & Lehman, J. D. (1996). Strategies for implementing computer technologies in the science classroom. In J. Rhoton & P. Bowers (Eds.), *Issues in science education.* Arlington, VA: National Science Teachers Association.

Albergotti, C. (1994). Real-world physics: A portable MBL for field measurement. *The Physics Teacher, 32,* 206–209.

Ball, J. (1996). Technology infusion strategy. *The Science Teacher, 63*(3), 51–53.

Bartlett, B. M., & Bartlett, M. L. (1996). Scientific monitoring via telecommunications. *Science Scope, 19*(6), 36–37.

Berger, C. F., Lu, C. R., Belzer, S. J., & Voss, B. E. (1994). Research on the uses of technology in science education. In D. L. Gabel (Ed.), *Handbook of research in science teaching and learning.* Upper Saddle River, NJ: Merrill/Prentice Hall.

Bross, T. (1986). The microcomputer-based science laboratory. *Journal of Computers in Mathematics and Science Teaching, 5*(3), 16–18.

Cleaver, T. G., Barnes, B. E., Mitchell, C., Winn, D. E. (1996). Online water science. *The Science Teacher, 63*(3), 44–47.

Clemmitt, S. (1996). Accessible internet data. *The Science Teacher, 63*(3), 48–50.

Cognition and Technology Group at Vanderbilt. (1990). Anchoring instruction and its relationship to situated cognition. *Educational Researcher, 19*(6), 2–10.

Collins, A. (1991). The role of computer technology in restructuring schools. *Phi Delta Kappan, 73,* 28–36.

Engst, A. C. (1995). *Internet starter kit for Macintosh* (3rd. ed.) Indianapolis: Hayden Books.

Heinich, R., Molenda, M., Russell, J. D., & Smaldino, S. E. (1996). *Instructional media and technologies for learning.* Englewood Cliffs, NJ: Prentice Hall.

Helgeson, S. L., & Kumar, D. D. (1993). *A review of educational technology in science assessment* (Monograph Series No. 7). Columbus, OH: National Center for Science Teaching and Learning. (ERIC Reproduction Services No. ED 366 507).

Huetinck, L. (1992). Laboratory connections: Understanding graphing through microcomputer-based laboratories. *Journal of Computers in Mathematics and Science Teaching, 11*(1), 95–100.

Jensen, M. S., Hatch, J. T., Somdahl, C., & Wilcox, K. J. (1993). A multimedia lesson for osmosis in introductory biology. In G. Marks (Ed.), *Mathematics/Science Education and Technology, 1994. Proceedings of the International Symposium on Mathematics/Science Education and Technology, San Diego.* (ERIC Document Reproduction Service No. ED 375 801)

Krockover, G. H., & Adams, P. (1995). Navigating the Internet. *Journal of Computers in Mathematics and Science Teaching, 14*(1–2), 35–49.

Marsh, E. J., & Kumar, D. D. (1992). *Hypermedia: A conceptual framework for science education and review of recent findings* (Monograph Series No. 3). Columbus, OH: National Center for Science Teaching and Learning. (ERIC Document Reproduction Service No. ED 370 799)

Nakhleh, M. B. (1994). A review of microcomputer-based labs: How have they affected science learning. *Journal of Computers in Mathematics and Science Teaching, 13*(4), 368–381.

Pankiewicz, P. R. (1995). Software review: The DynaPulse 200M. *The American Biology Teacher, 57,* 121–123.

Reynolds, K., & Barba, R. (1996). Science, interactivity, and mediated communication. *Science Scope, 19*(6), 12–15.

Roempler, K. S. (1996). Connecting to science resources. *Science Scope, 19*(6), 26–27.

Salpeter, J. (1990, October). Multimedia spreads its wings: New applications for the Amiga and PS/2. *Technology & Learning,* 40–44.

Sethna, G. H. (1985). *Development of an instrument for evaluation of microcomputer-based simulation courseware for the high school physics classroom: Appendix A.* Unpublished doctoral dissertation, University of Houston.

Shepardson, D. P. (1995). Mathematics and science teaching and learning on the Information Superhighway. *Journal of Computers in Mathematics and Science Teaching, 14*(1–2), 9–26.

Sneider, C., & Barber, J. (1990). The new probeware: Science labs in a box. *Technology & Learning, 11*(2), 32–39.

Stringfield, J. K. (1994). Using commercially available, microcomputer-based labs in the biology classroom. *The American Biology Teacher, 56,* 106–108.

Tamir, P. (1985/86). Current and potential uses of microcomputers in science education. *Journal of Computers in Mathematics and Science Teaching, 5*(2), 18-28.

Taylor, R. P. (Ed.). (1980). *The computer in the school: Tutor, tool, tutee.* New York: Teachers College Press.

Van Haneghan, J., Brannon, L., Young, M., Williams, S., Vye, N., & Bransford, J. (1993). The Jasper series: An experiment with new ways to enhance mathematical thinking. In D. Halpern (Ed.), *Enhancing thinking skills in the sciences and mathematics.* Hillsdale, NJ: Erlbaum.

◼

CHAPTER 11

CLASSROOM MANAGEMENT

Keeping students engaged in academic tasks is an important aspect of good classroom management.

A classroom environment that promotes learning centers around the teacher's ability to monitor and guide the behavior of a classroom full of students. Too many variables exist in a classroom situation to provide a set of rules that will take care of all problems that arise. Teachers must understand adolescent and preadolescent behavior to be effective managers. Preadolescent and adolescent students are a product of our diverse society and at times can be difficult to handle, so middle and secondary teachers must be dedicated, warm and affectionate, have a good sense of humor, and recognize that their students need to be treated as individuals. Additionally, teachers must consider the causes of misbehavior and use this information to determine the procedures they will use to help students manage their own behavior. All in all, teachers must have an in-depth understanding of the dynamics of classroom management in order to provide a proper learning environment for their students.

OBJECTIVES

This chapter is designed to help the reader meet the following objectives:

- Identify teacher practices that contribute to well-managed classrooms.
- Reflect on the causes of misbehavior among early adolescent and adolescent students.
- Compare and contrast three categories of approaches to classroom management that may be useful when dealing with early adolescent and adolescent students.
- Analyze some suggestions and techniques on classroom management that have been found successful in many teaching situations.

PLANNING FOR WELL-MANAGED CLASSROOMS

Well-planned and well-implemented lessons are the bedrock of effective classroom management. Well-planned and well-implemented lessons will prevent management problems and may solve those that have already arisen. Kounin (1970) found that a teacher's ability to prepare and conduct lessons that prevent boredom, misbehavior, and inattention is crucial to classroom management. Successful teachers present well-prepared lessons that proceed smoothly from one activity to the next with little waste of time or loss of focus. In addition, such teachers are quite adept at providing activities appropriate to their students' interests and abilities.

Julie Sanford (1984) reported certain patterns of behavior that are exhibited among effective teachers, regardless of the subject, type of students, or grade level they teach. She pointed out that good classroom managers establish and carry out workable rules of behavior. These teachers give clear directions and deal quickly with inappropriate student behavior. Effective managers are well organized and pace their instruction so that activities and events flow smoothly from one activity to the next with minimal loss of time on task.

Sanford (1984) emphasized that the best science teachers observed in her field studies required students to complete many tasks during each class period. In these teachers' laboratory classes, students could be observed busily working at hands-on activities. The teachers were frequently observed monitoring students' work. The best science teachers were those who were "task oriented, businesslike, and congenial" (p. 196), and ran orderly and productive classrooms.

A synthesis of research into teacher practices that contribute to well-managed classrooms, by Emmer, Evertson, Clements, and Worsham (1994) in their book *Classroom Management for Secondary Teachers*, provides guidance for developing the classroom conditions and student behaviors that both Kounin and Sanford speak about. Their guidance centers on the classroom setting, rules and procedures, and instructional practices. Additionally, teachers should consider how the curriculum can contribute to the well-managed classroom.

Classroom Setting

There is much that the teacher can do to ensure a well-managed classroom before meeting with students. The classroom arrangement can be considered in light of the learning activities in which the students will engage. For whole-class instruction, desks should be positioned so that all students can see the teacher and chalkboard or overhead projector screen without twisting and turning. During large-group discussions, desk or chairs should be positioned so that students can see one another's faces. Alternate seating arrangements should be considered for small-group work or special projects. Regardless of the nature of the class interaction desired, the seating arrangement must permit the teacher to see all the students. Aisles must be wide enough to allow for easy passage so that the teacher can monitor student seat work and respond to a student's question without disturbing others. Ample space should be provided in areas around the door, bookshelves, computers, and teacher's desk to allow for heavy student traffic.

Laboratory work requires additional considerations. Laboratory work may be done in the same classroom space used for other purposes, in a special area within the classroom, or in a separate laboratory room. Conducting lab in the same classroom space used for general instruction requires attention to special details. Furniture needs to be moved to accommodate the demands of space and student movement that accompany most laboratory activities. Since desks or chairs must often be moved within a single class period, students must be instructed how to arrange the room for laboratory work. One strategy used by many middle school teachers is to display a chart of the laboratory furniture arrangement on a bulletin board. Laboratory groups are identified by numbers on the chart and the same numbers are suspended from the classroom ceiling. When students are instructed to form laboratory groups, they move their desks together under the number that corresponds to the arrangement shown on the class chart. After becoming familiar with the system, students are able to arrange the classroom furniture for laboratory instruction in just a couple of minutes.

Whether laboratory activities are conducted in a traditional classroom or special laboratory setting, the management of materials and equipment must be considered. Frequently used materials such as thermometers, rulers, small beakers, test tubes, and graph paper should be readily accessible. Some high school teachers choose to have students keep their materials in laboratory drawers or lockers. Often used equipment such as electronic balances and microscopes should be kept in a location easy for students to reach. Other equipment used for particular labs, such as a Van de Graaff generator or MBL probes, should be stored in a cabinet or storage closet and checked to make sure it is in proper working order well in advance of when it will be used. Instructional and safety considerations require that the teacher and students be able to move easily between lab stations, material distribution points, and equipment storage areas. Every science classroom should be equipped to ensure student safety during laboratory work. The first aid kit should be well stocked and the eyewash, safety shower, and fire blanket should be in proper working order.

Rules and Procedures

Just as highway safety is based on drivers understanding and obeying traffic laws, good classroom management relies on students understanding and following a planned system of classroom rules and procedures. Both rules and procedures communicate a teacher's expectations for students. Establishing rules for the sake of rules is poor practice, but those that help create a good atmosphere for teaching and learning are desirable. For example, rules may be established that state specifically when students are permitted to talk, how students should conduct themselves with respect to others, and what students should do to maintain safety in the science laboratory. Rules should be kept as simple as possible, be direct, realistic, and understandable, and be enforced once established. They should be few in number and stated in a positive fashion rather than as what not to do. Emmer and colleagues (1994, pp. 22–23) listed a set of classroom rules that may serve as a starting point for beginning teachers:

- Bring all needed materials to class.
- Be in your seat and ready to work when the bell rings.
- Respect and be polite to all people.
- Listen and stay seated when someone else is talking.
- Respect other people's property.
- Obey all school rules.

Many teachers involve their students in helping to set classroom rules. This practice is encouraged because it allows students to take ownership of the rules and know the reasons for having them (Kohn, 1996). Students will want to know the teacher's understanding of each rule and often wish to have a hand in deciding the consequences associated with breaking a rule. It may take several days or weeks before students become accustomed to the rules and make them a part of their normal behavioral pattern. If a rule does not work for one reason or another, it is the teacher's business to discuss changes with students that will make the rule more realistic and enforceable. If it is not realistic, it should be abandoned. Arbitrary rules set up to create a stifling and unappealing environment will only induce undesirable behaviors in students. By linking class rules with school rules, the teacher communicates to students that the classroom is part of the larger school community and that all students must abide by the rules of the community.

Most teachers post a copy of their class rules on a wall or bulletin board in the classroom to remind students what is expected of them. This practice is strongly recommended for classes of middle school students and ninth-graders who may not be aware of the behavioral expectations of the new school setting (Emmer et al., 1994). Many teachers also send a copy of their class rules home for parents to examine and ask that they be returned with a parent's signature. Acquainting parents with class rules at the beginning of the school year makes it easier to discuss rule violations with them later on if the need arises.

Some classroom activities can create confusion if they are not handled properly and efficiently. Activities such as passing out papers, organizing students into groups, and assigning student tasks can be considered routine but can also create problems unless they are handled efficiently. Teachers who spend unnecessary amounts of time passing out papers and collecting them create situations in which students keep themselves occupied by talking loudly and engaging in play. Many routine situations can cause a great deal of confusion unless simple procedures are established beforehand. Simple procedures that communicate the teacher's expectations for starting and ending class, whole-group instruction, grading, and laboratory work can prevent unnecessary misbehavior.

Most teachers feel that how they start a class sets the tone for the entire class period. For this reason, many teachers insist that students be in their seats and prepared to begin work when the bell rings. Starting the lesson at the sound of the bell is not usually possible due to the administrative duties that must be performed by the teacher, such as checking attendance. Good classroom managers plan activities that engage students as soon as the bell rings, allowing the teachers time to deal with the necessary administrative tasks. Some teachers start class with questions related to yesterday's lesson written on the chalkboard or presented on the overhead projector screen. Students are expected to answer these questions during the first three to five minutes of class. Once this practice is routinized, the teacher is able to take care of administrative tasks without wasting class time. Good classroom managers also favor the practice of dismissing students themselves rather than allowing students to leave the room when the bell rings. When students are dismissed by the teacher, final instructions regarding homework, classroom cleanup, or tomorrow's test can be given with the assurance that all students have received the information.

With science class sizes exceeding twenty-five students in most public schools, teachers need to establish procedures for ensuring that large-group instruction proceeds smoothly. First of all, it is important to communicate to students how they should behave during lecture,

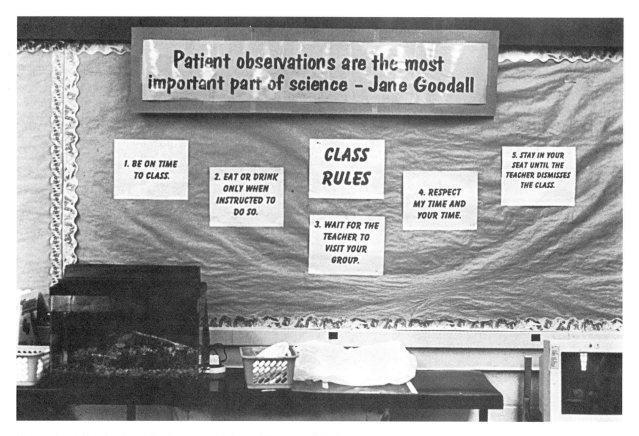

Rules should be kept as simple as possible and be posted in the classroom.

discussion, and independent work sessions. For example, students will want to know when and how they will be recognized by the teacher. They will want to know when talking among themselves is permitted. Students will also want to know under what conditions they can leave their seats to sharpen pencils, collect papers, and go to the restroom. In many classrooms students must raise their hand and be recognized before asking a question or making a comment during a lecture or discussion. A no-talking policy is enforced in some science classrooms, whereas in other classrooms students are allowed to talk quietly to others seated around them. Some teachers insist that students sharpen pencils and collect papers before the bell rings and allow students to go to the restroom during class only in an emergency.

Consideration should also be given to procedures related to grading. Students will want to know how their work will be graded, and the teacher will want to be prepared to discuss personal grading practices with students. A gradebook will need to be established and a system developed for recording daily grades, scores for major tests and projects, and student absences and tardies. A decision will also need to be made regarding how different assignments and tests will be weighted. Some teachers allow test grades to count for 30 percent

of the student's overall grade and allow daily work to count for 50 percent. Many school districts put limits on category weights, for example, tests 40–60 percent, final exam 10 percent, and so on. Finally, it is important to explain major class assignments and grading practices to parents. This information will enable parents to better monitor their children's progress and to assist with learning problems that may arise.

Routines are also essential in the science laboratory. Routines should be organized to carry out classroom work efficiently. When students are asked to obtain materials and supplies from storage areas, they should not be allowed to go to these areas in large groups. They should be directed to secure supplies in an efficient way—that is, individually or in small groups. If students are allowed to go to secure supplies en masse, not only will discipline problems be created, but safety problems will also develop.

In the laboratory students will encounter many practices that are new to them. It is for this reason that science teachers need to attend to procedures related to such concerns as appropriate dress, disposal of chemicals and specimens, keeping a notebook, and laboratory cleanup. Standards established by the Occupational Safety and Health Administration (OSHA) provide guidance for many aspects of laboratory work. Teachers should use OSHA standards in formulating their laboratory policy regarding the wearing of laboratory aprons, eye goggles, shoes, and hair bands for students with long hair. OSHA standards also provide guidelines that should be shared with students for the disposal of chemicals and used laboratory specimens. For many students keeping a science notebook will be a new experience and they will need to be told how to do so. Good managers provide guidance regarding notebook form and neatness. For example, some teachers require students to record procedures and results on the left page of the notebook and inferences and conclusions on the right page. They also stipulate that notebook entries be made in pen and that errors be crossed through with a straight line and not erased. Good managers also have procedures for guiding other aspects of laboratory work, including how students should make up missed labs, what to do when equipment is broken or chemicals are spilled, and when to begin to clean up the lab area in preparation for the end of class.

Instructional Practices

Beginning teachers must enter a classroom with the confidence of knowing what is to be done during each minute of the teaching day. Plans must be laid out in detail. Overplanning lessons can provide the comfort and ease needed to enter the classroom with confidence. It is good practice always to plan more work than can possibly be covered during the period. It is not uncommon for beginning teachers to underplan at first and find that they have nothing to do for more than fifteen or twenty minutes at the end of the period. They stand before the class embarrassed and frustrated, not knowing what to do next. Good planning involves overestimating what can be accomplished over a period of time. It also means that teachers should provide stimulating, interesting, and relevant experiences so that students are eager to learn. It also is good practice to have an alternative plan available in case of emergency. Students will become uninterested and uninvolved when poor planning is evident. Problems such as inattention, increased talking, and class disruption may result. Teachers who communicate organization and confidence, however, will avoid many potential discipline problems.

When planning for instruction, teachers must decide what content to teach and how the content should be presented to students. Content will need to be matched with the most appropriate presentation format. For example, a discussion may be the best way to address the pros and cons of using animals for medical research, whereas laboratory work is more suitable for testing the effects of soil moisture on seed germination. Careful consideration of the desired learning outcomes and discussions with experienced teachers about their own practices will provide guidance in making these decisions.

Teachers also must consider how to begin and end learning activities, how to transition from one learning activity to another, and how to begin and end a class period. One way to think about organizing instructional activities is to break the class period into smaller segments and plan for each. The class period might begin with students doing a warm-up activity that may consist of copying the day's objectives and agenda while the teacher takes attendance and deals with other administrative tasks. Next, the student's initial work could be quickly checked before beginning the lesson. The lesson may consist of one or more activities. For example, a lesson may be initiated by a teacher or student question, which leads to a hands-on investigation and ends with a discussion during which the teacher helps the students construct meaning from the investigation. Finally, the period is closed with the teacher giving students homework instructions, reviewing the day's lesson, and presenting an overview of the lessons for the next several days.

Two critical times of group instruction are when transitioning from one activity to the next and when communicating directions and information (Emmer et al., 1994). To prevent misbehavior and wasted time, transitions need to be smooth and brief. Good managers establish expectations for students' behavior during transitions. For example, when moving from desks to lab stations, students know to go directly to their lab stations without sharpening pencils or visiting with friends. Smooth transitions are also more likely to occur when materials and equipment needed for the next activity are at hand. The possibility of student misbehavior is further reduced when lesson objectives are clearly communicated, activity directions are presented in an orderly sequence, and the teacher checks to ensure that students understand the purpose of an activity by asking questions or having students summarize the main points (Emmer et al., 1994).

Keeping contact with students during the lesson is also an important aspect of managing group instruction. Teachers should be aware of what is taking place in the classroom at all times. This means there must be constant contact between the teacher and students while a lesson is being presented or during any other activity. Many teachers find that eye contact is a very effective way to deter misbehavior. By using eye contact, the sensitive and alert teacher is able to spot behaviors in students that indicate a discipline problem is about to occur or has already developed. If the teacher recognizes the problem early, he or she can handle it effectively and with discretion. Sometimes a simple long pause, combined with a stare in the direction of the situation, will curb the activity. These techniques can often prevent a problem from developing into something serious.

Maintaining contact with students during a lesson or activity can be accomplished only if teachers have complete confidence in what they teach and how they teach. Teachers who prepare their lessons well, know the content, know what to do next, and display interest in their lessons will have no difficulty in keeping contact with their students. Teachers who are so insecure about their teaching that they fumble through a lesson or other activity become oblivious to the behavior of their students. They do not sense how students are reacting to the lesson because they are so unsure of themselves. When students recognize a teacher's insecurity, they soon lose respect for the teacher and become inattentive and uninterested, causing behavioral problems.

Few educators would argue with the idea that middle and secondary students need a variety of experiences and activities in order to have a productive learning environment. The teacher should be flexible enough so that students can pursue some of their own interests as well as the learning outcomes of the existing curriculum. The teacher should give students opportunities to help them extend the cognitive skills they already possess, rather than spend all their time developing new skills. Because these students are constantly seeking independence, it is imperative that teachers recognize the necessity to provide activities that challenge their students in order to help them express themselves and grow intellectually.

Middle and secondary school students behave best in an environment that promotes self-control (Kohn, 1996). Teachers who are very rigid and control behavior through fear establish an atmosphere that will not permit students to practice self-discipline. Students must be given liberty in the classroom in order for them to develop as responsible and reliable individuals who practice self-discipline. At the same time, by giving students latitude, the teacher cannot allow behavior that will disrupt the learning environment. The students must recognize their responsibility to work with the teacher to maintain a healthy and productive learning environment.

A teacher who provides a supportive environment that is friendly and promotes cooperation among students will foster proper classroom behavior. A variety of learning experiences that are intellectually demanding and will allow students to use their mental skills will also help them to develop into self-disciplined, secure, and well-adjusted individuals. Figure 11.1 presents a set of characteristics of middle and secondary school students as well as the curriculum and administrative considerations that should be used to plan an orderly and productive classroom environment.

Curriculum

The curriculum, or what students are asked to learn, may be the source of discipline problems. Good classroom managers recognize this fact and use their knowledge of students to make sure the curriculum matches their abilities and interests. When the curriculum is too difficult, too easy, or perceived as boring by students, they give up on learning and find something else to do in class. Often the something else is viewed as misbehavior by the teacher. But when students see the curriculum as worthy of their time and effort, behavior problems are almost nonexistent. Stories are told in teachers' workrooms about the troublemaker in science class whose behavior improved dramatically when the lesson topic was of particular interest to him or her.

Making changes to the curriculum is often no simple matter. State legislatures, school boards, and administrators have as much to say about what is taught in science classes today as do teachers. Nevertheless, teachers must consider the relationship between the curriculum and student behavior. Minor adjustments to the curriculum could mean the difference between constantly reprimanding students for being off-task and inattentive and having a lively discussion among a class of enthusiastic adolescents. The importance of the curriculum to a well-managed classroom cannot be overstated. According to Kohn (1996, p. 21), "How students act in class is so intertwined with curricular content that it may be folly even to talk about classroom management or discipline as a field unto itself."

Effective classroom managers are those teachers who have thought about the classroom setting, the rules and procedures they want students to follow, and their instructional practices and curriculum. They are prepared to communicate their ideas to students and to solicit student input regarding the condition and operation of the classroom. They recognize that the key to a

■ STOP AND REFLECT! ■

Before going on to the next topic, do the following:

- List at least five techniques or strategies that a teacher might plan for and implement to encourage student self-discipline.

- Use your list of techniques and strategies to examine Box 11.1, "Investigating Mitosis Using the Microscope." Indicate the extent to which Mr. Thomas's instruction reflects good classroom management.

Intellectual Characteristics of Preadolescents and Adolescents

Design instruction appropriate to students' reasoning ability. Early adolescents and many adolescents are at the concrete operational level of development, which limits the amount of abstract information they can process and find meaningful. These students benefit from firsthand experiences that provide concrete exemplars of concepts and principles.

Expect a short attention span. Many middle and secondary students attend to a given learning task for a short period of time, then seem to be ready for a new experience.

Be aware that these students possess many interests. Students are motivated to engage in learning tasks when their interests are addressed. Their interest and knowledge schemas are tied together and form important mental structures to hook into during instruction.

Social-Emotional Characteristics

Don't be surprised when students display a variety of moods. Students may appear mature and orderly at one moment, followed by childish and disruptive behavior the next.

Take advantage of their tendency to seek peer acceptance. Students respond to and are attracted to their peers and friends. They spend considerable effort to gain peer approval.

Be prepared for students' tendencies to ignore and reject adult standards. Students want to gain their independence and show their maturity, which can manifest itself in a rebellious and inconsiderate manner.

Science Curriculum

Provide a balanced curriculum. There should be a variety of learning outcomes. The first outcome should be to produce positive attitudes toward science, technology, and school. In addition, the curriculum should develop mastery of basic skills and knowledge fundamental to science and technology.

Center upon relevant topics. The curriculum should address topics that are meaningful to the lives of students. Identify topics that have immediate interest and use science and technology to increase students' knowledge and understanding of these ideas.

Emphasize an inquiry-oriented mode of instruction. Use science process skills to help students process information and represent knowledge. Use problem solving and projects to provide relevant contexts for learning and to cause students to assume more ownership in their work.

Use a variety of measures to evaluate learning. Assess many learning outcomes to help these students. Some do well on paper-and-pencil tests whereas others may do well on performance tests, especially students with limited proficiency in the English language.

Organizational Structure

Plan and organize the curriculum. Middle and secondary school science teachers must be given time to form their own curriculum so that they can provide for the unique needs of this population.

Provide for the integration and coordination of subjects. Teachers in all of the subject areas should be cognizant of each others' curriculum and reinforce the learning outcomes designated in their own curriculum.

Use a variety of organizational patterns in the school. Multiage grouping, developmental grouping, homogeneous grouping, heterogeneous grouping, alternate scheduling, block scheduling, school-within-a-school, and so on must be considered to meet the needs of middle school and secondary students. The faculty should be free to experiment with different organizational arrangements.

FIGURE 11.1 Four Important Aspects to Consider when Teaching Science to Preadolescents and Adolescents

classroom environment that promotes learning is a management plan that encourages student self-discipline.

IDENTIFYING CAUSES OF STUDENT MISBEHAVIOR

Even under the best classroom conditions, student misbehavior will still occur. As teachers work and associate with boys and girls, they will gain an insight into the causes for misbehavior. If Jane reads a book instead of performing the specific activity assigned to the class; Ladonna throws spitballs; Mary cheats on a test; Andrew horses around in the chemistry laboratory, causing safety problems; or Jorge dozes off during the class period, there are reasons these students behave as they do. It is important for the teacher to determine the basic reasons for the misbehavior before applying measures to correct it.

BOX 11.1

■

Investigating Mitosis Using the Microscope

Mr. Thomas said, "The laboratory exercise will involve the use of prepared microscope slides and the microscope. You are to work in pairs and while I distribute the microscope slides, one member of each pair will go to the storage cabinet and get a microscope." Following this brief introduction, twelve students charged to the storage cabinet located in the back of the room to get microscopes. The first student flung the storage cabinet door open and almost broke the glass front. The students reached over each other to get their microscopes. One student bumped a microscope into one of the laboratory tables as he rushed back to his partner and then proceeded to knock off the reflecting mirror on the microscope. Mr. Thomas's reaction to this was, "Hey, kids, take it easy."

After Mr. Thomas distributed the microscope slides to each pair of students, the students set about the task of identifying and studying the stages of mitosis. Most of the students were performing the assigned task, except Mohammed and Jeff, who were laughing loudly and playing with their microscope. They were attempting to locate their fingerprints on a slide, but at the same time were abusing the microscope. Meanwhile, another pair of students asked Mr. Thomas for another box of slides because most of the slides in their box were damaged. Mr. Thomas spent about five minutes in the storage room searching for another box of good slides, and during this time the students became noisy. Some of the girls were discussing nonacademic matters. Matt tossed his gym bag halfway across the room to Wesley, and Ken demonstrated to his classmates how he could crush a microscope slide under one of the objective lenses of his microscope. When Mr Thomas returned from the storage room, the situation had degenerated into chaos.

Mr. Thomas was angry, and he lashed out at the students, "Look, you dummies, all of you will stay after school unless you shut up and get down to business. Can't I leave the room for a few minutes without you going wild? Now get back to your work." The students quieted down for a while, trying to appear interested in their work. Rose and Jennifer got Mr. Thomas's attention and kept him at their laboratory table until they were sure that they could identify all of the structures and phases that they were supposed to know as a result of the laboratory. During the period of time that Mr. Thomas spent with these two girls, the other students had another opportunity to get into mischief. The class became noisy again, and Jamal and Robert on the other side of the room slid a textbook across the laboratory bench with great velocity. Mr. Thomas snapped at the boys, "You two report here after school. I've had enough of both of you today."

Five minutes before the bell rang to dismiss the class, Mr. Thomas asked the students to stop their work, return the microscopes to the storage area, and clean up their work areas. The students again rushed to the storage cabinet to see who could get their microscopes put away first. A few students neglected to remove the microscope slides from the stage of the microscope. Others did not lower the body of the microscope completely so that the eyepiece struck the lower part of the shelf above, possibly doing damage to the microscope. As students were about to return the slides to the teacher, the bell rang. As a result, some students returned the slides in a disorderly fashion, and many simply left the slides at the work table. Mr. Thomas also attempted to announce the next day's assignment, but half the class had already left the room.

Misbehavior observed in students can usually be attributed to underlying conditions that are not necessarily obvious. A teacher should try to identify the deeper problems that are causing the misbehavior before attempting to deal with it. If only the symptoms are treated without knowing the conditions causing them, more undesirable behaviors may result, which may be more of a problem than the behavior first observed.

Students, as all human beings, interact with their environments, and the forces and pressures they encounter in and out of school can generate many of the misbehaviors exhibited in the classroom. The home environment, teachers, administrators, other students, and others not in the school setting can all influence student behavior. Additionally, factors such as academic aptitude and mental and physical health can have a great bearing on how a student behaves in a classroom.

Home Background

Desirable and undesirable classroom behavior may be partially attributed to the home environment. Relationships with parents, siblings, and other relatives all influence students' conduct. Parents establish rules of conduct that are generally accepted by their children and have a direct influence on how they act in a school setting. Many of the problems exhibited in the classroom stem from standards of conduct acceptable in the home. Swearing may be an acceptable form of speaking at home but is certainly not acceptable in the classroom. Fighting may be an acceptable behavior at home but is far from acceptable in school. Consequently, young people may be exhibiting behaviors they consider to be normal and

that reflect their parents' standards and rules of conduct when they act the way they do in the classroom.

The student who comes from a home environment with strict parents may react differently to the authority exhibited by a teacher. A student from such a home may resent authority at first and consequently resent the teacher. On the other hand, some students who come from a strict home atmosphere may be accustomed to authority figures and will readily accept them without question. Teachers, then, must learn how the behavior of students is managed at home before they can deal with the discipline problems that seem to stem from the home environment.

Students from homes where there is constant family friction and quarrels often develop into discipline problems. These students may be very emotionally involved in these situations and develop problem behaviors. The unsettled home environment is one variable that a teacher should consider when analyzing a student's behavior.

Often the attitudes of parents toward education have a bearing on how students behave in school. Parents who do not consider an education important may communicate such feelings to their children, who, in turn, will have little or no respect for teachers or school. On the other hand, students who come from homes where an education is considered very desirable may exhibit misbehaviors because their parents have established unreasonable expectations for their academic performance. Both situations may generate problems. In the first instance, the students may not be motivated to learn because they, too, regard the need for an education lightly. In the second instance, students who cannot meet their parents' high expectations may soon become

Desirable and undesirable behavior may be attributable to students' activities outside of school.

frustrated, which often leads to low self-esteem, poor motivation, and behavioral problems.

Students who are allowed to stay out late at night or surf the Internet until the early morning hours often become inattentive or fall asleep during the class period. They may have the aptitude to do the work but lack the energy they need to remain attentive. Other inattentive students may be involved in afterschool jobs, which require much energy and effort. For many high school students, it is the desire to own a car or wear the latest fashions that leads them to work at afterschool jobs. These students may find it difficult to keep up with the work in class and to do the homework assignments. Teachers should identify the causes of inattentiveness. They will often find that these students can do the work without difficulty and are even interested in learning but lack the energy needed to carry out the assignments. A conference with the student during which the teacher emphasizes the need for rest may correct the problem. If it does not, then the parents of the student should be contacted.

Academic Ability

Students in a class have differing degrees of academic abilities, and some of the discipline problems the teacher encounters are due to the type of classwork the teacher provides. The teacher who attempts to focus the classwork solely on the average students is not providing for the range of individual differences inherent in the typical classroom. The brighter students are usually not challenged and motivated in such classes and end up bored, irritable, and restless and exhibit contempt for the teacher, the school, and classmates. These students are potential discipline problems because they often become mischievous and interrupt classwork.

Students with low academic abilities may also exhibit behavioral problems if the teacher's lessons are presented at too high a level. These students become frustrated and their motivation suffers, possibly resulting in inappropriate behavior. It is the teacher's job to try to challenge all the students in a classroom. Each lesson must include portions that are at a level high enough to challenge those with high ability but at the same time offer the low-ability student a reasonable opportunity to master the material. This is not an easy task, but teachers must strive toward this end if they wish to avoid behavioral problems associated with academic ability.

The Teacher

Teachers often reprimand students who are engaged in noisy activities such as talking, chewing gum, scuffling feet, and shuffling paper. These are common behaviors among young people in a school setting, but many teachers consider these behaviors to be out of place and nonconforming. Such teachers often create discipline problems for themselves by insisting that their students be perfectly quiet and inactive in the classroom. Students in such a rigid environment end up irritable, restless, and threatened and eventually become behavioral problems. They must find an outlet for their energy. In general, it is best that teachers not insist on an unreasonable degree of physical inactivity in the classroom if they wish to avoid behavioral problems. Not all physical activity should be allowed, but common sense should be one's guide.

Teachers should also show respect for students and refrain from ridiculing them, both in front of their peers and privately. They should exercise self-control at all times and not derogate a student in public even when the situation appears to warrant it. Teachers who use humor at inappropriate times, sarcasm, or ridicule often cause discipline problems by backing students into a defensive posture in front of their peers.

Teachers who do not plan their lessons well, do not start their classes on time, deviate often from science lessons, and engage in useless talk and activity during a class period will soon lose the respect of their students and incite undesirable behaviors in them. In short, an atmosphere of disorder will promote disorderly behavior.

Many teachers find it difficult to understand students who come from socioeconomic backgrounds different from their own. Students, in turn, may have difficulty understanding the value system of the teacher. It is the teacher's responsibility to make the initial attempt at understanding the values of students. If students sense that the teacher does not respect or ignores their deeply ingrained values, resentment will be felt and discipline problems will arise. Alternatively, students will respect a teacher who respects their beliefs and values. This mutual regard, of course, will help diffuse many potential discipline problems.

Teachers can also cause discipline problems in the classroom as a result of their own personal problems. Teachers who have health, home, or work problems can allow them to affect their patience and relationships with students, which almost always leads to difficulties in the classroom. A teacher should always try to determine whether student misbehavior is due to the teacher's own problem. Once identified as such, the teacher should diligently work to eliminate his or her own behavior that causes undesirable behavior in the students.

School Administration

The school administration may be responsible for problems that a teacher experiences in a classroom. Administrators who are unrealistic about the standards of conduct in a school setting, such as noise levels in the classroom or corridors, dress codes, and other codes of behavior, will cause students to resist and defy authority. Many causes of misbehavior can be attributed to unrealistic rules of conduct. Students in general will adhere to the established rules if they are within reason, even though they may be strict. Students will rebel when the administration constantly bombards them with new and unrealistic regulations.

Frequent interruptions over the intercom system made by school administrators can also generate problems. Students become uneasy, inattentive, and noisy as a consequence. Administrators may need to be reminded to avoid frequent use of the intercom system during class time. Interruptions should be restricted to certain times of the day unless emergencies occur.

Health-Related Reasons

Some students exhibit serious health defects such as poor eyesight or heart, hearing, or respiratory ailments. They also exhibit health problems associated with their teeth and with allergies and malnutrition. Some illnesses are so severe that students are not able to exert the energy to work on assignments. Other conditions such as hyperactivity can cause restlessness and inattention. Hearing-impaired students who are supposed to wear hearing aids may be psychologically affected by the requirement and may avoid wearing the aid in school so as not to appear different from fellow classmates. As a result, these students may become inattentive and show a lack of interest.

A student who is inattentive in class may have a health problem; the inattention may be due to pain caused by a minor or severe illness or disability. It is important that teachers train themselves to be aware of such problems and refer these students to the school nurse, principal, and/or parents to avoid confrontations with these students.

Personality-Related Reasons

Many student discipline problems can be attributed to immaturity and poor judgment. They are also caused by insecurity, lack of recognition, lack of self-respect, lack of a sense of responsibility, and lack of self-control. The discipline problems caused by these situations may vary in magnitude, and are as common among high school students as among middle school students. Students who talk constantly and listen occasionally are inconsiderate of others, lack maturity, and have no sense of responsibility to their fellow students or teachers. If students do

not carry out assignments in and out of class, they lack maturity, motivation, and a sense of responsibility. These behaviors may seem minor, but when they are exhibited daily by the same students, they can create problems that eventually get out of control. These minor infractions should be dealt with as soon as possible to avoid more serious situations.

Some students exhibit misbehavior just to get attention and will go to any extreme to obtain attention from the teacher or classmates. Undoubtedly, these students are not getting the attention they require from their parents and others and will use the school setting to get it. More serious problems such as stealing chemicals and equipment, cheating on tests, and talking back to the teacher stem from deep underlying causes. A teacher must identify the causes of the problem behaviors before dealing with them.

■ STOP AND REFLECT! ■

Regarding the causes of student misbehavior that were just discussed, do the following:

■ Revisit Box 11.1, "Investigating Mitosis Using the Microscope." What factors could be eliminated as the underlying cause of Mohammed and Jeff's misbehavior in Mr. Thomas's biology class?

■ Organize the causes of students misbehavior discussed in the section along a continuum based on the control a teacher has to rectify them.

Teacher controls cause   Teacher has no control of cause

Which cause does the teacher have the most control over? least control over? Provide support for your choices.

MODELS FOR CLASSROOM MANAGEMENT

There are many approaches that a teacher can use to successfully manage the science classroom. Teacher Effectiveness Training, assertive discipline, discipline with dignity, behavior modification, and positive discipline are the names of just a few. All are based on psychology theory to a greater or lesser extent, present ideas about what motivates students and their unruliness, and identify strategies for dealing with misbehaving students. The approaches also differ in the amount of power used by the teacher to obtain student compliance (Wolfgang, 1995).

Ultimately, the approach to be used can be determined only after thoughtful consideration of the teacher's and students' characteristics. After all, one method of classroom management might be highly successful with one group of students and a dismal failure with another group. An approach stressing permissiveness and student freedom, for example, would not meet with much success if the students were too immature to handle such freedom in a responsible manner. Alternatively, some teachers might not feel comfortable with a particular approach, and any attempts to use it will eventually fail. A teacher whose personality is not confrontational by nature would find it quite difficult to succeed in managing a classroom following a management model based on a confrontational style. Because the proper approach to classroom management is so highly contingent on both teacher and student characteristics, it is difficult to make any general prescriptions with respect to which model is "best." However, it is quite useful for teachers at least to be familiar with different options.

With this knowledge, the teachers are in a better position to make an informed decision as to which approach is appropriate for their classroom.

The number of classroom management approaches is too great to discuss each one here, but a sense of the variety of approaches can be developed by examining three widely accepted interpretations of child development. McQueen (1992, p. 7) has pointed out that psychologists' ideas about child development serve as the cognitive basis for the vast majority of approaches to classroom management and described the three different interpretations of child development as follows:

- children are intrinsically motivated to develop their potential;
- children are shaped and molded by external forces of the environment and other powers; and
- children develop and are shaped through interactions between their intrinsic motivation and external forces.

Wolfgang (1995) has grouped and labeled classroom management approaches according to these interpretations of child development as relationship-listening, confronting-contracting, and rules and consequences. Table

TABLE 11.1   Classroom Management Approaches Grouped by Interpretations of Child Development

Relationship-Listening
1.   Thomas Gordon's Teacher Effectiveness Training
     Gordon, T. (1988). *Teaching children self-discipline: At home and at school.* New York: Times Books.

2.   Eric Berne's Communication Model
     Berne, E. (1964). *Games people play: The psychology of human relations.* New York: Grove Press.

3.   Thomas Harris's Transactional Analysis
     Harris, T. A. (1969). *I'm OK—You're OK: A practical guide to transactional analysis.* New York: Harper & Row.

Confronting-Contracting
1.   Rudolf Dreikurs's Social Discipline Model
     Dreikurs, R. (1972). *Discipline without tears: What to do with children who misbehave.* New York: Hawthorne Books.
     Dreikurs, R., & Loren, G. (1968). *Logical consequences.* New York: Meredith Press.

2.   William Glasser's Reality Therapy Model
     Glasser, W. (1975). *Reality therapy: A new approach to psychiatry.* New York: Harper & Row.

Rules and Consequences
1.   Alberto and Troutman's Behavioral Analysis Model
     Alberto, P. A., & Troutman, A. C. (1990). *Applied behavior analysis for teachers (3rd ed.)* Upper Saddle River, NJ: Merrill/Prentice Hall.

2.   Canter and Canter's Assertive Discipline
     Canter, L., & Canter, M. (1992). *Assertive discipline: Positive management for today's classroom.* Santa Monica, CA: Lee Canter & Associates.

3.   Dobson's Love and Punishment Model
     Dobson, J. (1970). *Dare to discipline.* Wheaton, IL: Tyndale House.

11.1 shows several of the different approaches that are grouped together under these three labels.

Relationship-Listening

Approaches in this category are based on the premise that children are intrinsically motivated to develop their potential. Teacher actions must be therapeutic and project minimal authority. Teachers who favor these approaches believe in supportive, exciting, and challenging classrooms where students are able to work and express themselves freely. They also share the belief that student misbehavior is due to obstacles that prevent students from thinking rationally and that by removing the obstacles, student misbehavior will desist (Wolfgang, 1995). In other words, when students view the classroom as a good place to be, they will work hard, enjoy themselves, and be well behaved. Nonverbal cues and nondirective statements are the primary means used by teachers to curb student misbehavior when employing relationship-listening approaches. The teacher's role is that of a nonjudgmental facilitator who helps students propose their own solutions to problems.

A closer look at Gordon's (1974) Teacher Effectiveness Training (TET) model will provide some insight into how relationship-listening approaches are operationalized. The first step in TET is to look at the misbehaving student to communicate to her that you see what is happening and that you are available to help with the problem if needed. When verbal communication is needed, the teacher encourages the student to talk about the problem while listening carefully and summarizing the student's thoughts and feelings. Nonverbal signals like head nodding and leaning toward the student and using "door opener" questions—Is there more that you want to tell me?—are strategies used to facilitate verbal communication.

A key issue that guides the use of nondirective statements in the TET model is problem ownership. When a student's problem endangers others or affects the personal rights of the teacher or classmates, the use of I-messages is recommended. For example, when lab groups are told to follow the procedures specified in the lab directions, two students begin to mix chemicals to see what will happen. The teacher's I-message might be: When students mix chemicals arbitrarily, I am fearful that a test tube might explode and a student would be injured, and my job as the teacher is to keep people safe. As a rule, I-messages specify the undesirable behavior and express the teacher's feelings and the likely effects of the undesirable behavior.

A limitation of the TET model and other relationship-listening approaches is that they are heavily dependent on language ability. If students are unable or unwilling to verbalize their thoughts, the approach will be minimally effective. An additional criticism of relationship-listening approaches in general is that they have limited applicability with large classes because it could take thirty minutes or more to listen to and solve one student's problem (Wolfgang, 1995).

Confronting-Contracting

Confronting-contracting approaches are based on the notion that children develop and are shaped through interactions between their intrinsic motivation and external forces. Teachers who feel comfortable using approaches that fall into this category believe that learning and behavioral management is the shared responsibility of teacher and student and that they must work cooperatively with students to resolve their problems. They also believe that an underlying cause exists for student misbehavior and that through interactions with the teacher and classmates misbehaving students will come to learn appropriate behaviors (Wolfgang, 1995). Some of the approaches within this category rely on the strength of group norms to curb student misbehavior. When using a confronting-contracting approach, the teacher often stipulates behavioral boundaries for students while allowing them to make choices within the range set by the boundaries. Solutions to problems must be acceptable to the teacher and to classmates as well as to the misbehaving student. Interactions between teacher and student occur through verbal communication, with teacher questions and, to a lesser extent, directive statements guiding the interactions.

Dreikurs's social discipline model will be used to illustrate aspects of the confronting-contracting approaches. According to Dreikurs (1968), four subconscious goals that arise from a student's inability to obtain social acceptance are at the root of misbehavior: attention getting, power, revenge, and helplessness. When using this approach, the teacher first attempts to figure out what goal is directing the student's misbehavior. Information gathering to determine the goal may involve observing the student, speaking with other teachers who have worked with him in the past, and questioning the student directly in a calm setting. Dreikurs, Grunwald, and Pepper (1982, p. 29) recommend that the teacher use questions like these to help identify the goal directing the student's misbehavior:

- Attention getting: Could it be that you want me to do more for you?
- Power: Could it be that you want to show me that you can do what you want?

- Revenge: Could it be that you want to hurt me and the pupils in the class?

- Inadequacy: Could it be that you want to be left alone?

Once the teacher is fairly comfortable that the student's reason for misbehaving has been correctly identified, a plan to help the student correct the misbehavior can be developed. The plan will differ depending on the goal underlying the student's misbehavior but will almost certainly involve modeling the practices of a democratic society and reinforcing desirable behaviors through natural and logical consequences. Class meetings where problems are discussed and resolved provide students with opportunities to model the practices of a democratic society and to address concerns about their own misbehavior and the misbehavior of classmates. The actions to be taken to help a student function as part of the class community are developed through consensus.

If a student's misbehavior seemingly resolved through a class meeting persists, natural and/or logical consequences serve to reinforce the desired behavior. "A natural consequence is an inevitable occurrence that happens by itself, whereas a logical consequence is arranged but directly related to the preceding behavior" (Wolfgang, 1995, p. 78). For example, if a student fails to bring her lab notebook to class, the natural consequence is that she has no notebook in which to record the procedures and results of the day's laboratory activity. Similarly, if a student's horseplay results in a broken piece of laboratory equipment, a logical consequence would be to have the misbehaving student pay for or replace the broken equipment. In Dreikurs's model, natural and logical consequences function as substitutes for punishment and serve to reinforce the point that the student is ultimately responsible for his or her behavior. Natural and logical consequences are often coupled with encouragement from the teacher or classmates that focuses on the student and his or her efforts to engage in socially acceptable behavior.

That the misbehaving student must truly wish to be a member of the class is seen as a major limitation of the social discipline model (Wolfgang, 1995). If the student's need for social belonging cannot be used as leverage, misbehavior is unlikely to be curbed. Also, as is true for the TET model, the heavy reliance on verbal interactions makes the social discipline model difficult to operationalize with nonverbal students. Finally, the distinction between logical consequences and punishment may not be apparent to students. When students are unable to see the relationship between their misbehavior and the teacher's actions, hostility and aggression toward the teacher may result.

Rules and Consequences

The major assumption involved in the approaches that fall into this category is that children are shaped and molded by external forces from the environment and other powers. Therefore, the teacher's role is to control the student's environment carefully through explicit standards of conduct, which will in turn shape the student's behavior. Teachers who feel comfortable using rules-and-consequences approaches believe that it is their responsibility to regulate student behavior and do not consider the student's inner motives when dealing with misbehavior. When using a rules-and-consequences approach, a teacher regulates student behavior by administering positive reinforcement, negative reinforcement, or punishment. Consistent with B. F. Skinner's behaviorist theory, advocates of rules-and-consequences approaches believe student behavior that the teacher wishes to influence must be followed by one of these three consequences, which will in turn affect the frequency of that behavior by increasing or decreasing it.

As the assertive discipline model is widely used in today's public schools, it will be presented here as an example to illustrate aspects of the rules-and-consequences approaches. Canter and Canter (1976a, 1976b) indicate that teachers have certain basic rights that legitimately allow them to control classroom behavior. They have the right to establish clear expectations, insist on correct or acceptable behavior from students, and, if needed, follow through with appropriate and reasonable consequences that have been established. These authors also emphasize that students must know their limits and that the teacher has the authority and right to set and enforce the limits.

Assertive discipline is often considered to be synonymous with forcefulness and intimidation. However, it need not degrade the student or involve harsh punishment. In its purest sense, assertive discipline simply involves the establishment of a clearly stated set of rules and the consequences to be expected if the rules are not followed. The rules should serve to guide and limit student behavior and may be jointly formulated by students and teacher (Charles, 1985). Rules tell the student what is and what is not acceptable. In short, they communicate to students what is expected of them. It is important that these rules be reasonable and enforceable and written in a clear, concise way so that all students understand what is and is not acceptable. In addition, the students should be well aware of the penalties that accompany breaking the rules.

Rather than severe punishment, mild alternatives are advocated. The terms **mild desist behavior** and **corrective** are often employed to describe the type of punishments used in the assertive discipline model. Such forms of mild punishment amount to the teacher informing students that they are misbehaving and that they should behave according to the rules that have been established. Such punishment is not intended to be a forceful or hostile way of handling an unacceptable behavior but rather a humane method to promote acceptable behavior. Such mild punishments, according to many researchers, are more effective than their harsh counterparts in promoting acceptable classroom behavior.

There is little question that assertive discipline and other rules-and-consequences approaches work to reduce the incidence of student misbehavior. But critics question whether the approaches achieve the goal of teaching students to manage their own behavior (Wolfgang, 1995). Observations that students revert to their undesirable behaviors when rewards and punishments are removed suggest that they are responding only to the external stimuli and not reflecting on the causes of misbehavior and reasons for changing it.

Using the Models Advantageously

It is possible for a teacher to select a model of classroom discipline that falls into one of the three categories, become well schooled in the model's techniques and strategies, and apply the techniques and strategies consistently with students. This practice is strongly recommended for new or inexperienced teachers. Before adopting a model, however, the teacher should make sure that the model fits her philosophy of discipline. For example, if she strongly believes that young people need to be controlled and that their classroom behavior should be governed by "her" rules, she should consider adopting a rules-and-consequences discipline model. If she chooses or is forced to use a model that does not fit her philosophy of discipline, she will likely do a poor job implementing the techniques and strategies advocated by the model and her students will recognize her discomfort and perhaps exploit it.

Once the teacher feels comfortable with one model of discipline, he may wish to learn more about the techniques and strategies associated with other models. Becoming acquainted with other models, particularly ones that fall under different categories, may help a teacher deal more effectively with difficult discipline problems. For example, Wolfgang (1995) notes that it is possible for a teacher to escalate from techniques and strategies suggested by relationship-listening approaches to methods suggested by confronting-contracting approaches and then to those suggested by rules-and-consequences approaches in a matter of minutes when dealing with a single classroom incident. As shown in

Figure 11.2, Shrigley's (1979, 1985) list of coping skills provides a sequence of teacher actions that operationalize Wolfgang's recommendation. Notice that coping skills 1–7 come from relationship-listening approaches, 8–11 follow roughly from confronting-contracting approaches, and 12–14 are linked to rules-and-consequences approaches. Research indicates that 40 percent of 523 classroom disruptions investigated were curbed by using the first four coping skills—ignoring behavior, signals, proximity, and touch control (Shrigley, 1985). Teachers considering the use of Shrigley's coping skills should also heed his warning: "The teacher majoring in coping skills and minoring in excellent teaching will wind up constantly reacting, constantly putting out brush fires. Coping skills serve to rescue the teaching act, and they usually focus on the symptoms. They may do little to answer the deep-seated problems of disruptive individuals" (Shrigley, 1979, p. 3).

USEFUL SUGGESTIONS FOR GOOD CLASSROOM MANAGEMENT

Shrigley (1979) stated that teachers must know their "vulnerability quotient." That is, they must recognize when their actions put them in a vulnerable situation with unwelcome consequences. He shares the example of the teacher whose vulnerability quotient is near the disaster level when she plans a class discussion on a complicated topic at 2:30 on Friday afternoon before the big football game.

Experienced teachers in general have the foresight to recognize that situations like this one lead to a host of classroom management problems. They can also analyze problems as they are developing or as they are encountered and make quick decisions to maintain classroom order and keep the learning act afloat. On the other hand, inexperienced teachers do not have this background and consequently cannot anticipate many of the problems that normally arise during the course of a day. Their lack of experience also prohibits them from planning adequately to prevent the occurrence of management problems. Until they gain experience, they must rely on suggestions and techniques that have been tested and found successful in many classroom situations.

Many of the following suggestions and strategies for classroom management have been gleaned from various approaches already discussed. Other procedures presented have been used by effective classroom managers in many different situations and subject areas. The strategies, procedures, and suggestions are not guaranteed to work in all cases and therefore should be modi-

1. *Ignore behavior*. An annoying behavior will often abate if ignored by the teacher.
2. *Signal interference*. Body language, such as a stare, can indicate that a behavior is unacceptable.
3. *Proximity control*. The teacher stands near a misbehaving student to provide the adult support needed to diffuse a disruption.
4. *Touch control*. By placing a hand on the shoulder of a student, the teacher can relieve tension and anger. Discretion must be used when applying this coping skill.
5. *Gordon's active listening*. The teacher listens carefully to the student describe the problem and acknowledges the student's concerns and frustrations.
6. *Gordon's I-messages*. An I-message reveals the problem and the teacher's feelings and is best used when rapport has been established between teacher and student. "When students play around Bunsen burners in the lab (behavior), I am afraid (feelings) that someone will get burned (effect)."
7. *Speak to the situation*. The teacher describes the problem but does not directly address the students. "Shoving tapes in the VCR can break the machine."
8. *Direct appeal*. Often in the form of a question, the statement attempts to appeal to the student's sense of logic and fairness. Two examples are, "John, you're disrupting others with your singing and drumming," and "Is it fair to disrupt others because you want to sing and drum on your books?"
9. *Interrogative*. A question can be used to indicate that the student has a choice regarding his or her behavior. "Will you please return to your seat?"
10. *Glasser's questions*. "What are you doing? What should you be doing?" When used in combination, these questions help students analyze their misbehavior and take corrective action.
11. *Logical consequences*. The teacher responds directly and logically to the student misbehavior. If two students make a mess of the classroom by throwing paper, then a logical consequence would be to have them clean up all paper from the floor for a week.
12. *Contrived consequences*. This teacher response to student misbehavior is punitive. If two students make a mess of the classroom by throwing paper, then a contrived consequence would be for the students to stay after school for a week.
13. *Canter's broken record*. The teacher repeats an assertive command two or three times rather than arguing or trying to reason with the student. "Michael, put down the thermometer and return to your seat...put down the thermometer and return to your seat."
14. *Compliance or penalty*. "Michael, put down the thermometer and return to your seat or go to the office... Michael, if you don't put down the thermometer and return to your seat I'll call for Mr. Big who will help me escort you to the office." The student is given the choice to comply with the teacher's request or pay the price.

FIGURE 11.2 Shrigley's Coping Skills Useful for Curbing Student Misbehavior

Based on "Strategies in Classroom Management," by R. L. Shrigley, 1979, *NASSP Bulletin, 63*(428), 1–9, and "Curbing Student Disruption in the Classroom—Teachers Need Intervention Skills," by R. L. Shrigley, 1985, *NASSP Bulletin, 69*(479), 26–32.

fied as needed to fit each teacher's style and circumstances.

Seek Student Cooperation

Most students are basically responsible human beings and will react positively to teachers who show that they, too, are good decent human beings. Teachers who have the respect of their students will find that their students will generally cooperate without hesitation. Teachers who seek student cooperation must show that they are firm and serious about their requests. They must display authority yet be proper and professional in the way they ask their students to cooperate.

Several leaders in classroom management recommend that teachers consciously make use of authority bases other than coercion, which is the basis for punishment, when seeking student cooperation. French and Raven's (1959) bases of social power are often presented as options for teachers to employ. Shrigley (1979, p. 7) described French and Raven's four alternatives to coercion in this way:

1. *Reward*. Positive verbal feedback and grades are examples of the authority to reward students.

2. *Legitimate*. The teacher's contract makes that teacher the adult in charge of classroom teaching.

3. *Referent*. Students who identify with the teacher as a person are extending to a teacher referent authority.

4. *Expert*. When we ask the beginning teacher to over prepare a teaching assignment, we are strengthening this authority base.

Consider the School Calendar

There are certain times during the school year when students are apt to have a higher energy level than usual. The day of an important basketball, soccer, or football game; the morning before an afternoon assembly involving an important entertainer; two days before the Thanksgiving recess; and the week before Christmas are periods when teachers should take steps to avoid potential problems. These are times when students must be kept involved and motivated. They should be given assignments that challenge and interest them and keep them active in order to compete with other interests associated with various events. It is essential that teachers identify periods during the school year when other interests and enthusiasms compete with classwork, and plan suitable lessons and activities that will produce desirable student behaviors.

The beginning of the school year is another time when teachers need to give extra attention to classroom management concerns. These days can be particularly trying for new teachers who are overwhelmed by the demands of the profession. Some students will use the first days of school to test a teacher's resolve. To help teachers ready themselves for the beginning of school, Emmer and his colleagues (1994) recommend attending to the twelve questions presented in Figure 11.3.

Become Familiar with the School Routine

Familiarization with normal school routines can help a teacher avoid a great deal of confusion and difficulty. Teachers should learn these routines as soon as possible so that they can handle them efficiently when they arise. If a routine is not known, mistakes can be made that can place both teachers and students in problematic positions. Many discipline problems can arise, for example, if the teacher does not know the procedures for issuing passes for students to leave the room or the building or when to send a student to the office.

In general, school procedures are usually established for the following: (1) how to take attendance and keep records of attendance; (2) how to handle passes that permit students to leave the classroom; (3) how to deal with students who are tardy; (4) how students must check out books from the science library or school library; (5) what to do when a student is injured in the science laboratory or if the student becomes ill during the class period; (6) how to take classes on an extended or short field trip; (7) when to send a student to see the school psychologist, principal, or guidance counselor; and (8) what to do in case of an emergency involving a laboratory accident.

Routines that must be followed by all teachers are generally pointed out early in the year and probably are described in some written format by the administration. If the procedure is not known, teachers should find out **before** acting. Routines that are not carried out as specified tend to jeopardize a teacher's position as well as create situations that can result in discipline problems.

Know the Students

It is good practice to learn students' names as quickly as possible. Teachers who demonstrate early that they know their students by name also show that they have a definite interest in them. It is not easy to learn 30 or 40 names in a hurry, and if science teachers have five classes, then they must learn 150 or more names. Seating charts are a help in learning names quickly and in associating names with individuals. It is advisable, at least at the beginning of the term, to ask students to use a particular seat. Once names have been learned, other seating arrangements can be made that may be more desirable.

In addition to knowing names, it is also advisable to know more details about students. Teachers should have information available regarding academic aptitude and achievement levels; health problems; family particulars such as number of siblings, occupation of father and mother, and status of the marriage; types of extracurricular activities in which the students are engaged or interested; handicaps such as hearing or visual impairments; and vocational plans.

Student files containing much of the information mentioned are usually available to teachers. Much information can be learned about students through individual conferences, observations made by the teacher in and out of class, and discussions with parents, guidance counselors, and other teachers. Misbehavior in students can be attributed to causes that are unapparent, and knowledge of student background can often permit teachers to detect the underlying causes of misbehavior so that they can be dealt with effectively and efficiently.

Check When Complete	Item	Notes
❏	1. Are your room and materials preparation complete?	_____
❏	2. Have you decided on your class procedures and rules and their associated consequences?	_____
❏	3. Are you familiar with the parts of the building to which you may send students (e.g., library, bathrooms, etc.) and do you know what procedures should be followed?	_____
❏	4. Have you decided what school policies and rules you will need to present to students?	_____
❏	5. Have you prepared a handout for students or a bulletin board display of rules, major class procedures, and course requirements?	_____
❏	6. Do you know what bell schedule will be followed during the first week?	_____
❏	7. Is your lesson plan for the first few days of school ready for each class?	_____
❏	8. Do you have complete class rosters?	_____
❏	9. Do you have adequate numbers of textbooks, desks, and other class materials?	_____
❏	10. Have you decided on the procedures you will use for checking out textbooks to students?	_____
❏	11. Have you prepared time fillers to use if the period is extended?	_____
❏	12. Do you know if any of your students have some handicapping condition that should be accommodated in your room arrangement or instruction?	_____

FIGURE 11.3   Preparation for the Beginning of School

From E. T. Emmer, C. M. Evertson, B. S. Clements, and M. E. Worsham, *Classroom Management for Secondary Teachers* (p. 85). Copyright © 1994 by Allyn and Bacon. Reprinted by permission.

Involve Students

The more involved students are during a lesson, the less likely teachers are to have serious discipline problems. The teacher should use a variety of strategies and activities to keep students actively involved during a class period. The involvement of students during a lesson, for example, "can take the form of asking questions, encouraging students to make comments about a lesson, allowing students to fulfill tutoring roles for those who need additional assistance in mastering a concept or skill and allowing students to work in large and small group settings" (Purvis & Leonard, 1985, p. 351). Getting students involved in various types of activities, such as demonstration work, leading discussions, delivering short lectures, presenting reports on projects, showing films and filmstrips, participating in games, and planning field trips, can take care of a variety of interests and abilities of students represented in a classroom. Many behavior problems occur when students are bored and have no involvement in what is taking place during the class period.

Practice Self-Control

Teachers should show self-control at all times. Teachers who have a tendency to explode over minor misbehaviors are not very good examples to students. Good and effective teachers are those who can control their emotions even when major problems arise. Teachers who are unable to control themselves and thus lose their tempers cannot deal with problems objectively, constructively, and professionally. These teachers in the long run become ineffective and lose student respect. Once students recognize that things are not under control, they are apt to create more problems that incite further misbehaviors.

It should be remembered that self-control is just as important for teachers as it is for students and that it is the teacher's responsibility to be civilized at all times. The best course to take when a discipline problem occurs is to underreact, avoid losing one's temper, and certainly not display any uncontrolled emotion. One should deal with the problem with concern, acting as an intelligent, rational, and mature adult.

Follow Good Testing Procedures

The administration of a test or quiz should involve a set routine. Students will learn the routine after several tests have been given. In general, this routine involves procedures to use to avoid cheating, to use while papers are being distributed, and to follow when students need clarification of a question. Students should also learn the type of behavior they should exhibit while the test is in session. There should be a procedure for alerting students when the test is over and a routine to follow to collect papers at the end of the test.

Usually, teachers establish methods to avoid cheating. Some use alternate seating arrangements, others use two different forms of the same test, and some use both procedures at the same time. Students should know that the routine requires them to be quiet while papers are being handed out and that all books and notes should be placed under or in their desks. They should also be warned to avoid any activity that may give the appearance of cheating. Teachers should also be alert to see that no cheating occurs while questions are being asked and answered for clarification.

When teachers respond to students who require clarification of test items, they should learn to handle them without disturbing the rest of the class and to keep the noise level at a minimum. The amount of information that a student receives as clarification of a question should be limited. Certainly, disclosure or hints of the correct answer to a question are unfair to other students and should be avoided.

Closing a test can be handled in a variety of ways. Once it is announced that the test is over, the students should immediately stop so that papers can be collected. Usually, to avoid confusion, it is desirable for the teacher to ask the students in each row to pass the papers forward to the first student in the row. Other routines can be used, but teachers should establish one and use it consistently so that students become used to the routine and know what to do once a test has been concluded.

Give Encouragement and Praise

Some teachers tend to devote a great deal of time to reprimanding and disciplining students for their misbehaviors and often neglect rewarding them through verbal praise or a smile or a gesture for tasks well done. Classroom management procedures should include techniques that acknowledge that:

- a class has performed well on a test
- a student has answered a difficult and probing question well
- a student has done outstanding work on a project or homework assignment
- a student has mastered a particular skill in the laboratory
- a class is doing well on a laboratory exercise
- a class is well behaved when the teacher is out of the classroom

A number of instances afford teachers the opportunity to praise their students for appropriate behaviors. The acknowledgments should be made as frequently as the opportunities arise, and they should be made verbally, if possible. Praise and reward should not be reserved for special occasions but should be used as a matter of course. The frequent use of encouragements creates excellent learning environments in which students strive to receive rewards in one form or another as they achieve certain desirable levels of performance.

Techniques that teachers sometimes use to reward students include the following six methods:

1. Giving students time to work on projects instead of devoting a full period to teacher-designated activities
2. Permitting students to go to the library to obtain more information about a topic that the students will present to the class
3. Rewarding students by taking them on a field trip to a nearby industrial site or other facility
4. Giving students an opportunity to work on interesting homework activities

5. Permitting students to engage in education-oriented games

6. Canceling homework assignments because the students have already attained the desired level of performance on a topic, making further work repetitious and unnecessary

Teachers should give serious consideration to the use of praise and rewards. They should use them with discretion and only when students rightfully deserve the attention for outstanding work and performance. Teachers should always make certain that students fully understand the reasons for a reward, flattery, a pat on the back, or other indication of praise, and that it is given with sincerity.

Project Personality and Enthusiasm

A truly effective teacher is one who is able to accept students as they are—on bad days when they display their faults and lack of interest and on good days when they display their enthusiasm and interest, eager to work and learn. We all have good days and bad days, and as teachers we must consistently show enthusiasm and interest in students as well as the subject. Teachers who display their enthusiasm for students and their subjects will learn that students, too, will show enthusiasm and interest in their classwork.

The type of learning environment in the classroom is based on how the teacher interacts with the students. An ill-tempered teacher will only create an environment that is threatening and not conducive to learning. On the other hand, warm, friendly, and energetic teachers who understand their students and know their subject matter will motivate students to behave in cooperative and meaningful ways.

Being a warm, understanding, and friendly teacher does not mean that one cannot display a firm, businesslike attitude. One can be interesting and humorous and still give the students a feeling that business is the order of the day. As a matter of fact, introducing occasional humor is a good tactic to use during a lesson or activity. Students learn that teachers are real live human beings when they display humor.

The most important thing to remember, however, is that teachers must be consistent in the way they handle their students, so that the students know what to expect. Teachers who display inconsistencies by unpredictably reacting to student behavior with anger, laxness, rigidity, or apathy will only create problems because students have difficulty in adapting to these changing behaviors. On the other hand, teachers who are consistently calm and yet firm are less likely to have discipline problems.

Control Noise Levels

There are many situations in the science classroom that by their nature may produce relatively high noise levels. Discussion sessions, for example, can degenerate into periods during which students yell, scream, or shout their answers, jump out of their seats, and move about, all indicating complete confusion and disorganization. The noise levels result in teachers shouting and yelling above student noise to maintain order. To avoid behaviors such as those mentioned, a discussion session should be as well planned as a demonstration or other science activity. Good planning for this type of activity should include the rules and procedures for maintaining a desirable learning environment. Students must be informed that chorus responses are not acceptable and that they will be ignored. Allowing chorus responses can cause discussion or recitation sessions to degenerate into chaos. Teachers may shout, yell, or slam books on the demonstration table to keep the noise level down. By this time the situation is out of control and almost impossible to handle.

Unusual noise levels also occur during laboratory sessions. Again, rules of conduct and procedures for laboratory should indicate the appropriate and acceptable noise level. Students should have a chance to talk and interact during these sessions. They should not be inhibited from discussing their work and results when they are broken up into pairs or groups. However, they should be told what is the acceptable noise level and the consequences associated with getting too loud.

Discuss Misbehaviors with Students

It is sometimes desirable to ask students who continuously misbehave to remain after class to discuss the reasons for their persistent disruptions. It is also appropriate to ask them to appear when more time can be devoted to the problem. A meeting after school or during a study period can be scheduled if an after-class meeting is not good. During these discussions, teachers can find out the specific causes underlying the student's misbehavior and act accordingly to correct the situation.

Individual conferences are often advisable to avoid student embarrassment and even teacher-student confrontations during class. Students will regard the situation seriously when the teacher asks for a private conference to discuss persistent misbehaviors. Conferences are particularly effective to handle problems that cannot be settled quickly and reasonably when they occur. During the conference, both the teacher and student can discuss the situation amicably and reasonably to correct the behavior.

Under certain circumstances, individual conferences are more effective if school administrators are involved. Many students require this type of conference to realize the seriousness of the situation. In order to resolve certain types of misbehavior, Sauer and Chamberlain (1985, p. 42) use the following three types of conferences involving school authorities:

1. Informal chat during which a school administrator talks to the offending student and tries to reach an agreement as to how the student is expected to behave

2. School conference that involves one or more school officials during which the student must agree to change his or her behavior

3. Parent conference that involves the parent or legal guardian of the student along with the student, teacher, and school administrator

Conferences that involve school administrators are generally very threatening to students and should be used as a last resort. Teachers can usually handle most behavioral problems effectively without the assistance of school administrators.

Change Seating and Isolate Students

Minor discipline problems can often be corrected by simply asking a student to take a seat away from a student or students with whom he or she interacted. Placing students who misbehave closer to the teacher where they can be monitored often does the job. Or placing them in areas where there are empty seats—away from other students—sometimes works as well.

Reseating students becomes a problem when all seats in the class are occupied and well-behaved students have to be displaced. The well-behaved student may react negatively toward the teacher, particularly if the student enjoyed the position in the classroom.

This technique works well on certain occasions when one or two students are involved. It is not a good procedure to use when many students are involved. Before locating a student in another area, make certain that the new seating arrangement does not create a more undesirable situation. The teacher should study the new seating arrangement carefully before acting and then determine if the misbehaving student can cause problems for students in the new location or whether the new location includes students who are also troublemakers.

Persistent misbehavior cannot often be corrected by new seating arrangements. Perhaps students may need to be isolated in a remote area of the classroom or even another room reserved by the administration for problem students. Persistent misbehavior that cannot be controlled in any reasonable way may have to be dealt with more severely. Students who are persistent problems and do not respond to other corrective measures may require complete isolation. Students react differently to this technique. Some are ready to change their behavior immediately; others will not admit their faults and are not willing to cooperate and make desirable changes. The teacher must be patient with this type of student who insists on innocence, because this situation may require counseling over a period of time to obtain the desired behaviors.

Know When and How to Use Punishment

The recommendations and suggestions made up to this point regarding classroom management can probably take care of the majority of classroom discipline problems. There are instances, however, when more drastic measures must be used to help students manage their misbehavior. When students continue to misbehave after the teacher has considered and tried all the previously discussed approaches, it is probably time to use punitive measures.

Punitive measures can often have negative side effects; thus it is essential to use them only as a last resort. The teacher should also be sure to check the school policy regarding the use of punishment before proceeding. Usually schools have rules that teachers must follow when severe measures must be taken.

Punishment is any stimulus that is perceived as adverse by an individual. What is punishment to one individual may not be punishment, and may possibly be rewarding, to another individual. Punishment is used to decrease the frequency of a particular behavior that may be considered disruptive, and possibly even dangerous, to the class or to the teacher. Under certain conditions, punishment may be the preferred method to permanently suppress behavior. If the type of misbehavior is dangerous to the point that the student will be harmed or is harmful to others, severe punishment may be warranted. For example, suppose a student throws concentrated sulfuric acid out of an eyedropper in the direction of another student. This type of behavior should not be tolerated at all and must be stopped immediately.

What should be done in such instances? Teachers should take the positive approach first but react to the misbehavior immediately. The student, as well as the class, should be shown what happens when sulfuric acid is placed on a piece of cloth. Once the student and classmates observe the reaction, they will probably think twice before repeating the incident. If this procedure does not work and the student insists on repeating the misbehavior or continues to perform dangerous acts in the laboratory, the teacher must take more severe measures. The student should be removed from the laboratory situation and isolated from other students during the period until the behavior is corrected. Repeated conferences with the student may also be in order. If again these avenues are not effective, the teacher should refer the student to the school psychologist (if there is one), principal, guidance counselor, or other administrator responsible for discipline. A parent conference is also desirable. Some might consider this approach to be harsh, but the unique nature of the laboratory compels the students to respect the rights of others. Squirting concentrated acid on a neighboring student is hardly analogous to shooting spitballs across the room.

Other types of behavior that may warrant punishment include continually horsing around and disrupting classroom routines and procedures; deliberately destroying or damaging laboratory equipment, school property, and the property of others; repeatedly preventing other students from conducting normal classroom activities; and cheating on tests. Punishments for the acts mentioned are certainly justified, but only after other avenues of discipline have been pursued. Of course some of the misbehaviors listed are more serious than others, but they must all be dealt with in one way or another. When considering the use of punishment as opposed to another approach, the teacher must weigh the overall effects of the behavior that is undesired. If it is decided that punishment must be used, Shrigley (1979, p. 6) recommends that it should be legal, infrequent, prompt, appropriate, impersonal, private, just, and mild.

Time-out is one kind of punishment that can be effective under certain circumstances, and it can take on many forms in a teaching situation. For example, the teacher can deprive students of working on a science project or participating in discussions, laboratory activities, field trips, science fairs, or school assemblies. Teachers regard these as mild forms of punishment because they do not involve undesirable and distasteful stimuli. The teacher is removing an activity that a student enjoys and replacing it with one that is unpleasant. The student may be asked to go to a time-out room designated by the administration that is devoid of all external stimuli. Instead of going on a field trip, attending an assembly, or working on a project, students will be asked to go to the time-out room while the activity is taking place.

Sometimes time-out results in a reward for some students, however. Students may deliberately cause a problem to avoid doing work, resulting in a reward instead of a punishment. Teachers must use care when employing this type of approach because it may be an effective discipline measure for certain students but not

for others. Time-out may also be used in a nonpunitive way. The student who cannot stop giggling or who is extremely frustrated by a task can be asked to take a note to the office or to get a drink of water. This type of time-out provides the student with an opportunity to gain his or her composure before returning to the classroom.

When considering punishment, the teacher should determine if other students are positively reinforcing the student who is misbehaving. Sometimes the punishment is not severe enough and the positive reinforcement on the part of other classmates outweighs the punitive measures. In this case, the student continues to misbehave to gain the attention of the classmates and teacher.

Teachers who have constant discipline problems and must frequently resort to punitive measures should examine their teaching situation. They should determine the causes of the misbehaviors. How often are the misbehaviors repeated? Are they teacher induced? That is to say, is the teacher doing a good job of teaching? Are the lessons stimulating, interesting, and relevant, or are they boring, uninteresting, and irrelevant? Do the lessons provide for individual differences in the class, or are they geared for only the bright student? Are a variety of activities used during the course of a science lesson, or does the teacher spend all the time asking students to read out of their textbooks or copy material written on the chalkboard into their notebooks?

A search for reasons for frequent discipline problems is certainly in order. Causes other than teacher-induced misbehaviors should be examined. The school situation may also be responsible for misbehaviors in the classroom. Students may know that they can get away with something if they know that the administration does not normally back up teachers' actions. The administrator who condones student misbehavior, serious or not, is only causing an atmosphere that can promote problems in the classroom. On the other hand, an administrator who is known to be firm, understanding, nonthreatening, and fair, and who will not condone misbehavior regardless of degree, will create only a good teaching atmosphere in which teachers can work effectively and without fear of lack of support.

Student Violence

Regrettably, there are some discipline problems that teachers encounter in middle and secondary schools that cannot be controlled by the approaches discussed in this chapter. Every teacher sooner or later will face the challenge of dealing with a violent student. The impetus for the violent behavior will probably not be known to the teacher.

Teachers are likely to encounter two kinds of violent students. A small number of students have little or no control over their violent outbursts. They experience drastic mood swings and may have psychological problems. While receiving special counseling services during part of the school day, these students are often infused into regular science classes. The special services provided for these students may consist of a class that helps them deal with their psychological problems through individual and group therapy and behavioral contracts. A violent eruption by these students, whether it be a fight or something else, is dealt with in a special way since it is viewed as a symptom of the disorder. Typically, the student is removed from the situation and sent to a school administrator who may refer the student to the school counseling center for therapy.

Many more students who exhibit violent behavior are able to control their actions. Violent acts committed by these students are usually prompted by some external situation or stimulus. After just a couple weeks of school, teachers usually know their students well enough to recognize who is prone to violence. Some violent behaviors call for the teacher to react with compassion, such as when a normally cooperative and friendly student begins throwing books and cursing the teacher who asks her to stop talking to her neighbor. In this case, the best immediate solution might be to send the student to the guidance counselor. It is also a good idea

to discuss the outburst with the student's parents as soon as possible.

Other violent behaviors, such as fighting, require a rapid and planned response. The teacher's first action should not be to try to stop a fight, but to call for help. Common sense suggests that one teacher is unlikely to stop a fight between two or more enraged students, who in high school may stand over six feet tall and weigh more than two hundred pounds. When several teachers and school administrators arrive on the scene, the combatants often come to their senses and stop fighting. If physical force is required to separate and restrain students, teachers and administrators in many schools seek assistance from resource officers. These off-duty police officers are employed by the school to deal with violent students. Fighting in most middle and secondary schools means automatic suspension. Students who engage in repeated acts of violence are often required to attend an alternative school, where staff psychologists and sociologists are available to help them with their problems. While student violence can be terribly upsetting, and in some instances frightening, teachers should try not to take it personally. The best that the teacher can do is to foster a classroom environment that encourages students to settle their differences in nonviolent ways, and to be prepared to act quickly and responsibly if violence erupts.

ASSESSING AND REVIEWING

1. An inexperienced teacher you know is taking over a science class that is known to be disruptive. What advice would you give him regarding how to manage student behavior when he first takes over the class? What types of procedures would you suggest he use to ensure a productive learning environment throughout the term?

2. Prepare a list of class rules for a science class of your choice using a relationship-listening approach to classroom management. Do the same for a science class using a rules-and-consequences approach. How do the lists differ? Explain the differences that you find.

3. Kensey is a ninth-grade student who came to class late three times in the last week. How would you help Kensey improve her attendance?

4. What course of action would you take when a student ignores your directions and uses profanity in front of the class?

5. Suppose you are assigned to teach science to a group of seventh-grade students and you have prepared a series of twenty laboratory exercises that will require the use of chemicals, a microscope, electrical equipment, plant material, insects, rocks, and glassware. How would you divide a group of twenty students in groups of three if half are boys and half are girls? What criteria would you use to group the students? What rules of conduct would you establish for such a laboratory program?

6. Draw the floor plan for a high school chemistry or physics classroom that would facilitate quality science instruction and reduce the probability of student misbehavior. On the floor plan, show the location of the students' and teacher's desks, student laboratory stations, safety equipment (e.g., first aid kit, fire blanket, etc.), material and equipment storage, chalkboard or overhead projector and screen, and doorways. Also, draw lines to represent student traffic patterns.

7. Describe the instructional activities you would plan and other steps you would take to ensure that your science classes are productive and orderly on the day before the Christmas holiday.

8. In *Beyond Discipline*, Alfie Kohn states, "A huge portion of unwelcome behaviors can be traced to a problem with what students are asked to learn." Do you agree or disagree with Kohn's statement? Provide support for your position.

■

RESOURCES TO EXAMINE

Solving Discipline Problems.   1995. Distributed in the USA and Canada by Allyn and Bacon, a Simon & Schuster Company, 160 Gould Street, Needham Heights, MA 02194.

Before deciding on a discipline approach to implement in your classroom, examine Charles Wolfgang's exacting descriptions of them. This 354-page volume presents over a dozen major and lesser known approaches in terms of their progression along a continuum of teacher's power. Additionally, the models' strengths and limitations are discussed and the decision to adopt a particular approach is examined from the perspective of personal fit.

Beyond Discipline.   1996. Published by the Association for Supervision and Curriculum Development, 1250 N. Pitt Street, Alexandria, VA 22314.

Alfie Kohn questions the premise that the teacher must control the classroom and argues that classroom management is little more than techniques and strategies devised by adults to ensure student compliance. He calls for classrooms governed by collaborative problem solving, with the goal of students' becoming self-disciplined, caring members of society.

Classroom Management for Secondary Teachers. 1994. Distributed in the USA and Canada by Allyn and Bacon, a Simon & Schuster Company, 160 Gould Street, Needham Heights, MA 02194.

Ed Emmer and his colleagues present practical suggestions for effective classroom management. The thesis of their work is that few discipline problems occur in a well-managed classroom. Classroom organization, rules and procedures, managing student work and special groups, and beginning the school year are among the topics addressed in chapters of this book.

■

REFERENCES

Canter, L., & Canter, M. (1976a). *Assertive discipline*. Santa Monica, CA: Canter and Associates.

Canter, L., & Canter, M. (1976b). *Assertive discipline: A take charge approach for today's educator*. Santa Monica, CA: Canter and Associates.

Charles, C. M. (1985). *Building classroom discipline*. New York: Longman.

Dreikurs, R. (1968). *Psychology in the classroom*. New York: Harper & Row.

Dreikurs, R., Grunwald, B. B., & Pepper, F. C. (1982). *Maintaining sanity in the classroom*. New York: Harper & Row.

Emmer, E. T., Evertson, C. M., Clements, B. S., & Worsham, M. E. (1994). *Classroom management for secondary teachers*. Boston: Allyn and Bacon.

French, J. R. P., & Raven, B. H. (1959). The bases of social power. In D. Cartwright (Ed.), *Studies in social power* (pp. 150–167). Ann Arbor: University of Michigan Press.

Gordon, T. (1974). *T.E.T.: Teacher effectiveness training*. New York: Peter H. Wyden.

Kohn, A. (1996). *Beyond discipline*. Alexandria, VA: Association for Supervision and Curriculum Development.

Kounin, J. S. (1970). *Discipline and group management in classrooms*. New York: Holt, Rinehart and Winston.

McQueen, T. (1992). *Essentials of classroom management and discipline*. New York: HarperCollins.

Purvis, J. S., & Leonard, R. (1985). Strategies for preventing behavioral incidents in the nation's secondary schools. *Clearinghouse, 58*(4), 349.

Sanford, J. (1984). Science classroom management and organization. In C. A. Anderson (Ed.), *1984 AETS Yearbook. Observing science classrooms: Observing science perspectives from research and practice.* Columbus: ERIC Clearinghouse for Science, Mathematics and Environmental Education, Ohio State University.

Sauer, R., & Chamberlain, D. (1985). Follow these six steps and learn to manage student discipline. *The American School Board Journal, 172*(1), 42, 45-46.

Shrigley, R. L. (1979). Strategies in classroom management. *NASSP Bulletin, 63*(428), 1–9.

Shrigley, R. L. (1985). Curbing student disruption in the classroom—Teachers need intervention skills. *NASSP Bulletin, 69*(479), 26–32.

Wolfgang, C. H. (1995). *Solving discipline problems.* Boston: Allyn and Bacon.

PLANNING FOR INSTRUCTION

■

CHAPTER 12

PLANNING AND TEACHING
SCIENCE LESSONS

The importance of carefully planned instruction cannot be overemphasized.

Planning and teaching are primary functions that all science teachers perform. The quality of planning and teaching is based on the skills, beliefs, and understandings of teachers and determines what students learn. Understandings critical to effective planning and teaching are a teacher's pedagogical content knowledge, which includes knowledge of the subject matter and materials, instructional methods, and the students. In many school districts, teachers are assessing their own effectiveness based on guidelines put forth in recent reform documents. These reform documents suggest that the focus of planning and teaching be on the learning experiences of students rather than on the teacher's organization and delivery of the lesson. Consistent with this focus, preservice science teacher preparation programs devote considerable time to planning, practice teaching, and opportunities for reflection. Planning links the current goals of science teaching and learning with clearly stated instructional objectives that are addressed through student-oriented activities. It is through the experiences of planning and practice teaching and reflecting on these experiences that teachers grow professionally.

OBJECTIVES

This chapter is designed to help the reader meet the following objectives:

- Critique examples of ineffective and effective science teaching practices.
- Define teacher knowledge and describe the relationship between teacher knowledge and effective science teaching and planning practices.
- Reflect on the content of science lessons, especially on their relevance, interest, and potential to engage student thinking.
- Reflect on the methodology of a science lesson and discuss the instructional strategies and teaching skills that are directly related to science teaching.
- Develop short- and long-form lesson plans and distinguish lesson plans from a daily plan book.
- Discuss the benefits for the professional development of a science teacher of planning and practice teaching and reflecting on these experiences.

HIGHLIGHTING EFFECTIVE AND INEFFECTIVE PRACTICES

Science teachers face a big challenge when they plan and teach science lessons because their instruction must reflect the dynamic nature of science, teaching, and learning. The task would be easy if they could transmit knowledge directly to students and if that knowledge would be learned, understood, and recalled with accuracy. The record is clear. The knowledge-presentation approach is not effective with most students in middle and secondary schools. Science teachers must go beyond telling and teaching terms and facts. They must create learning environments that help students to understand science principles and theories, to explain scientific and technological ideas, to find personal meaning from the content and processes, and to apply this knowledge in their daily lives (National Research Council [NRC], 1996). In addition, science teachers must engage all students in instruction, not only those who seem disposed to science and respond enthusiastically (McCormick & Noriega, 1986; Oakes, 1990).

Fortunately, a great deal of useful information is available to science teachers and educators that can highlight effective practices as well as those that interfere with students' learning (Tobin, Kahle, & Fraser, 1990; Tobin & McRobbie, 1996; Tobin, Tippins, & Gallard, 1994). Effective science teachers use a variety of instructional strategies to help students build upon their prior knowledge and construct knowledge from sensory experiences. They use demonstrations, laboratory exercises, hands-on activities, discussions, and lectures, and implement these strategies in a thoughtful and thorough manner. Effective science teachers use questioning and wait time to engage students and to maintain their interest throughout their lessons. They encourage all students to participate in learning activities and ask questions. In their role as mediator of student learning or provocateur, they also demonstrate the desire to help all students to learn a great deal about science and technology and to believe that science and technology are worthwhile enterprises in which they can participate. Additionally, effective science teachers show greater concern for their students than the discipline that they teach. They tend not to be bound by the cultural myths that impede student learning. For example, they believe that meaningful student learning is more important than content coverage and that students should have a say in the enacted science curriculum (Tobin & McRobbie, 1996).

New science teachers, as well as experienced teachers, can benefit from practice in planning and teaching lessons and receiving feedback regarding these teaching functions. Planning, teaching, and feedback sessions can identify understandings, skills, and beliefs about science teaching and learning that need to be developed, reinforced, or altered. This aspect of pre- and inservice teacher education can be very useful to a science teacher's success in the classroom and growth in the profession.

Later on in the chapter in Box 12.1, you will be presented with a science lesson and be asked to analyze the teacher's practices. The two vignettes and accompanying critiques that follow should help you prepare to do so by highlighting some ineffective and effective science teaching practices.

■

Mr. Stam teaches biology in an urban high school. He sits behind the desk as students file into the room and take their seats. After the bell, Mr. Stam takes roll and asks for yesterday's homework, which directed students to answer selected questions at the end of the textbook chapter just studied.

Today, Mr. Stam begins the chapter on the blood. He uses the overhead projector, writing on transparency material to present the lecture notes. Mr. Stam uses the assigned textbook as his lecture outline. He writes down key terms (e.g., plasma, red blood cells, white blood cells, and platelets) and provides a few phrases for each to highlight important information. The lecture moves at a rapid pace. Occasionally, Mr. Stam relates a personal note to embellish his lectures. For example, during today's session the students are told how he transported medical supplies and blood to the combat zones during the Vietnam War.

Once in a while Mr. Stam calls on a student to determine the student's knowledge of the content. He favors the males in the class, especially those whom he knows. For example, Mr. Stam frequently calls on Philip because Philip is on the cross-country track team that Mr. Stam coaches. Philip is also a good student who has expressed the desire to become a doctor. Mr. Stam scowls at the girls because many of them are inattentive during his lectures. He warns that if they do not pay attention, they will fail his test. Mr. Stam is known for long, difficult tests.

■

How would you evaluate Mr. Stam's teaching? From the vignette, one can conclude that Mr. Stam presents biology as a body of knowledge, using the lecture method as his primary instructional strategy. He believes that giving students large amounts of information is an appropriate way to teach. Therefore, Mr. Stam is an informer and a giver of information. He relies on the textbook and does not seem to be able to take advantage of the numerous resources and strategies available. In this situation, the teacher does all of the explaining and takes the primary responsibility for the conceptual organization of the subject matter. Given the teacher's philosophy and limited approach to instruction, the students are likely to find little meaning in the subject matter and to achieve little understanding of it.

Mr. Stam discourages the girls from taking part in class discussion. He even puts the girls down when they say something that is not entirely correct or when they are not paying attention to the lectures. On the occasions when Mr. Stam seems to include the girls in discussions, he does so with the more attractive females. Nevertheless, Mr. Stam favors his interactions with the boys, especially those he knows through athletics. He is a buddy to the boys with whom he is acquainted from the cross-country team that he coaches and the track team he assists. An observer of these teaching practices can easily recognize that the teacher turns off many students in the class by discouraging participation, especially from certain students such as females and males who do not take part in sports. Many science teachers are guilty of reinforcing sex roles and sexual stereotypes (Kahle, 1996).

Mr. Stam rarely organizes students into small groups, except for laboratory work. He conducts one laboratory exercise per week. Given the enormous potential that cooperative grouping holds for increasing the interaction between students and the learning environment, it is unfortunate that Mr. Stam does not use this strategy. Just as unfortunate is the fact that he does not use the computer or conduct demonstrations. However, there are many science classrooms like this across the nation, where the presentation of information predominates and where many other useful teaching strategies and techniques are not implemented (Tobin et al., 1994).

Let's look into the classroom of Mrs. Willis, another biology teacher just down the hall from Mr. Stam.

■

Mrs. Willis stands at the classroom door and greets students as they enter class, taking attendance as students pass by. The students head straight to the lab bench areas to begin work immediately in their small groups. The class is studying blood and students are assigned to a given group based upon special interests.

Mrs. Willis forms groups to build on academic strengths and individual interests. The task for each group is to create an advertisement to promote the sale of blood and its constituents, for example, plasma, red blood cells, white blood cells, and platelets. Each group is expected to study the composition of blood and to make a presentation that would urge others to buy their product, at the same time demonstrating knowledge of this important body tissue. Students are encouraged to make posters, videotapes, and audiotapes, or to present skits. The students cooperate in their group functions, each carrying out a particular task and working diligently to prepare for their presentation to the other class members.

Mrs. Willis provides many resources for students to examine in order to learn about the composition of blood. On a table at the front of the room, she provides textbooks, pamphlets, and journal articles for students to study. A videodisc program is available that students can use on their own to view a program about the composition of blood. The classroom is a beehive of student activity.

Mrs. Willis stops the class fifteen minutes before the end of the period and asks the students to take their seats. At this point, she determines each group's progress. She also checks for understanding of certain key concepts, calling on many students to demonstrate their knowledge and understanding. This is often accomplished by asking the students to construct a concept map or a concept circle. In addition, Mrs. Willis refers the students to the laboratory they conducted a few days before in order to reflect upon how well the information they gathered from the printed material and videodisc program confirms what they observed firsthand during the laboratory exercise.

■

How would you assess the teaching effectiveness of Mrs. Willis? From the vignette, it is obvious that Mrs. Willis serves as a facilitator of instruction, helping students to seek, construct, and organize their own knowledge. She employs a variety of strategies and techniques to help students derive personal meaning from the study of biology, especially techniques that enhance their conceptual organization of the subject matter (Novak & Gowin, 1994; Texley & Wild, 1996). Mrs. Willis initiates the study of blood with a laboratory exercise that permits students to examine different blood cells under the microscope so that they can use this sensory data to build the notion that blood is a tissue composed of cells and other constituents. Often students carry the naive conception that blood is really a liquid. A large percentage of class time is spent with students working in groups. This small-group work has improved the class-room climate as well as achievement. However, Mrs. Willis has fine-tuned the small-group work so that off-task behavior is at a minimum and students are productive during these sessions (Fraser, 1990).

Over the past five years the student body has changed dramatically. Now the school population comprises over 60% Asian, Black, and Hispanic Americans. As a result of this demographic change, the research she has read regarding equity in the classroom, and her awareness of the lack of participation by females and minorities in many technical careers, Mrs. Willis has modified her instruction so that girls and minorities are active participants in the class. She is aware that females, for example, may be reluctant to take an active role in classroom discussions or to assert themselves in small-group activities. Mrs. Willis strives to help all of the students realize that biology is a meaningful discipline and that they can participate in careers in this field as well as other scientific and technological fields. By the end of the school year, many of the students realize that they may be suited to become nurses, pharmacists, opticians, and ecologists.

Mrs. Willis provides a great many resources for students so that they can seek out information in the classroom. She has a storehouse of textbooks, magazines, paperbacks, and pamphlets that students can read in order to find out information and to answer their own questions. One magazine included an article about Charles Drew, the Black American whose work led to the establishment of the first blood banks in both England and the United States. She permits the students to use the computer, videodisc, and video equipment on their own. The confidence and trust that Mrs. Willis places in the students to use expensive equipment did not come easily, but she has found that students do not abuse equipment or the freedom that she has given them in the classroom because of the respect she has earned. In addition to the instructional resources already mentioned, a few laboratory stations are set up in the room where students can study and review important ideas through firsthand experiences.

Would you choose to be a student in Mr. Stam's or Mrs. Willis's class? Your choice is most likely an easy one. For the most part, Mr. Stam's practices are both ineffective and undesirable. His practices suggest that he believes that the teacher is the source of and transmitter of knowledge, the teacher must control students, and girls are not as capable in science as boys. In contrast, Mrs. Willis's practices are more consistent with those recommended by the *National Science Education Standards* (NRC, 1996). She believes that science lessons should be interesting and meaningful to students and that students should have the opportunity to learn in different ways and from one another. Her practices also

indicate that she feels comfortable sharing power with her students and that she is student centered in her thinking and planning.

■ STOP AND REFLECT! ■

Before going on to the next topic, do the following:

■ Describe three instructional practices used by Mrs. Willis that you believe would improve the quality of instruction received by Mr. Stam's students if he chose to implement them.

■ Examine Box 12.1, "Mr. Jake's Electrifying Lesson," and perform your own critique and compare it with those prepared by your peers.

SCIENCE TEACHER KNOWLEDGE

Conducting a lesson that resembles that taught by Mrs. Willis requires more than just content knowledge. In addition to content knowledge, it requires knowledge of the students, knowledge of teaching materials, knowledge of instructional methods, and pedagogical content knowledge (Shulman, 1987). Knowledge of students includes an understanding of their likes and dislikes, their background, and the conceptions they hold about science concepts to be taught. Knowledge of instructional methods involves an awareness of instructional strategies and basic teaching skills and how to match them with the needs of learners in order to facilitate the construction of meaning from the lesson. Knowledge of materials includes an understanding of what instructional materials are available and how they can be used in teaching. Pedagogical content knowledge refers to "that special amalgam of content and pedagogy that is uniquely the province of teachers" (Shulman, 1987, p. 8) and includes the teacher's understanding of how concepts and principles can best be represented to make them clear to students. All the types of knowledge work together to enable the teacher to plan well and conduct effective lessons. From this view, if teachers lack any of these types of knowledge, their planning and teaching abilities will be diminished. Fortunately, a teacher's knowledge base is constantly changing as a result of teaching experience and reflection. It is the teacher's reflection on aspects of the lesson that went well and those that need improvement that can lead to better planning and teaching and improved student learning.

BOX 12.1

■

MR. JAKE'S ELECTRIFYING LESSON

Mr. Jake teaches physical science in a new high school in a fast-growth suburban area. His class has just completed a series of laboratory activities involving series and parallel circuits. He wanted to relate their study of circuits to issues of safety at home and chose to address the topic of fuses in order to do so.

Mr. Jake held up a fuse in front of the class and asked, "Does anyone know what I am holding?" A boy seated near Mr. Jake in the front row raised his hand and yelled, "It's a fuse!" "That's right," said Mr. Jake. "How many of you have seen or heard of fuses before?" Only the same boy raised his hand. "How many of you have seen electric fuses in your homes?" Again, only the same boy raised his hand. The other students looked bewildered by Mr. Jake's question and one asked, "What's a fuse and what is it for?"

Upon hearing this question, Mr. Jake described where the electric fuse box was located in his boyhood home and how a fuse would blow when a circuit was overloaded. He even told how his father had almost set the house on fire by sticking a penny in a fuse receptacle so that the lights in their kitchen would work. After about ten minutes, Mr. Jake's story about his boyhood experiences was interrupted by a girl who asked, "Are fuses something like circuit breakers?" "Yes, they work a little differently, but serve the same purpose—to prevent a circuit from becoming overloaded," replied Mr. Jake. All of a sudden about half of the class said, "We have circuit breakers in our house!"

The proverbial light bulb went on in Mr. Jake's head as he realized why his students were not participating in the discussion. Fuses were replaced by circuit breakers in new home construction decades before most of his ninth-graders were born. Mr. Jake said, "Okay, then, let's talk about circuit breakers." Then the students were anxious to tell about the experiences they had in their homes. One boy told of the time he plugged the cord from an electric blow dryer into an outlet, which caused a spark that frightened him, and then he said that all the lights went out in the bathroom. His mother went to the circuit breaker box and examined each circuit breaker to see which one had tripped and then she reset it. Another student told of the occasion when the air conditioner at her home stopped working and that her father did not know what to do, so he called a repairman. The repairman showed them where the circuit breaker box for the air conditioner was located on the outside of the house and at the same time replaced the old circuit breaker with a new one. The period ended with students agreeing that circuit breakers are less hassle and safer than fuses in home circuits.

It is important for beginning teachers not to become discouraged as they try to prepare lessons that take into account all the many factors that make for an instructionally sound and effective lesson. Just compare your present state in learning to teach to when you were first learning to drive a car. As a beginning driver, you may have found it difficult to keep the car on the road while tuning the radio, talking to a passenger, or eating french fries. But as an experienced and reflective driver, who has learned from your mistakes, you are able to do all these things and keep the car on the road at the same time. Similarly, as you gain experience in lesson planning and teaching and reflect on these experiences, you will find that you will be able to design meaningful learning experiences that combine your growing understanding of science content, instructional methods, and students.

STUDENT-CENTERED PLANNING

Teacher planning functions as the critical juncture between teaching and learning. The science curriculum, national and state standards, best instructional practice, and current learning theory all need to be considered when planning for student learning. More importantly, according to Lubber (1994, p. 47), effective planning involves knowing how students will interpret the information presented in a lesson and what they will learn from it. He urges that the focus of lesson planning be on the successful learning experiences of students rather than on the teacher's delivery of the lesson.

As a beginning teacher, focusing on student learning rather than personal performance will be difficult to do. Studies of teacher concerns clearly reveal that personal concerns must be dealt with before addressing concerns about student learning (Hall, George, & Rutherford, 1979). It may take several years for a teacher to become comfortable enough with his or her own performance to give total attention to student learning. Nevertheless, the teacher's job is to facilitate student learning, and planning must be undertaken so as to ensure that due consideration is given to students' culture, science conceptions, needs, and feelings. Examples of questions suggested by Lubbers (1994, p. 49–50) that may help teachers maintain a student-oriented focus in their planning are:

- What concepts are most relevant to the students' needs and interests?
- What can I expect the students to know about this topic?
- How will students react to specific directions or tasks?
- What possible misconceptions might students have and what might be the best way of eliciting misconceptions?
- What can I do to ensure that students do not mindlessly memorize terms and definitions?
- What ideas or experience might students confuse with the new ideas being taught and how will those ideas and experiences be differentiated from the new ideas?
- What misconceptions might arise during the instruction and how will these misconceptions be addressed?
- What are the essential indicators that students have meaningfully understood the ideas, concepts, and processes?

These are just a few of the many questions that a teacher can ask about science content, students' prerequisite skills and understandings, and instruction strategies useful for maintaining a student-centered focus in their planning. Honest answers to these questions will lead to the preparation of lessons that address the true purpose of teaching—that is, student learning.

REFLECTING ON THE PEDAGOGICAL CONTENT OF A SCIENCE LESSON

What should science teachers think about, besides the students, to prepare a science lesson? Obviously, they must determine what it is they want to teach. If a course syllabus or district curriculum is to be followed, part of the decision regarding what to teach has already been made. If, however, science teachers are free to choose any topic, then they have a great deal of freedom to select ideas about which they are knowledgeable. Regardless of the situation, science teachers should carefully select the content, skills, and attitudes to be taught so that students will perceive them as meaningful and worthwhile. This approach to planning holds more potential to stimulate student interest and to motivate them to learn science than one that communicates the notion: Learn this now because you will need to know it later.

Let's examine the relevance of a lesson plan prepared by a prospective science teacher, Bill Cummings. Bill submitted to Ms. Schultz, the student teacher supervisor, a lesson plan on the endocrine system, which he was going to teach in about one week to a high school biology class as part of his field experience. The instructional objectives for the plan were as follows:

1. Define the terms endocrinology, hormone, and pituitary gland.
2. Name ten endocrine glands and identify their location in the body.
3. Describe the anatomy of the pituitary gland.
4. Explain and recognize the action of nine hormones produced by the pituitary gland.

Although these objectives are clearly stated, they actually have little meaning for the students. They do not emphasize the importance of the endocrine system and how necessary the hormones are to maintain a healthy body. A better set of instructional objectives would stress the function of the endocrine system, the way hormones regulate physiological processes, and how abnormal growth and disease result when the system malfunctions.

When a science lesson is relevant, it will most likely capture and hold students' attention. Students will participate and respond favorably if the information they receive and the activities they perform interest them. For these reasons, the student teacher supervisor met with Bill Cummings. Ms. Schultz identified several aspects of his lesson plan that required attention. One was the need to place greater emphasis on the function of the endocrine system and how its hormones affect the human body. She discussed the importance of male and female hormones and their contribution to athletic performance, relating how some athletes use drugs to increase the muscle mass and improve endurance. Ms. Schultz pointed out the availability of many magazine articles and pictures of athletes who have used and abused anabolic steroids and how these teaching aids can be used in the introduction of the lesson to stimulate interest. She suggested that Bill address physical abnormalities stemming from the endocrine system that students might recognize, such as giantism and dwarfism—problems of hyperpituitarism and hypopituitarism respectively. She further recommended that Bill mention myxedema as a condition observed in some older people whose thyroid gland has become inactive, causing puffiness around the eyes, drooping facial features, loss of hair, and a general lack of vigor. Ms. Schultz also mentioned that the lesson plan could include another abnormality known as testicular feminization. This syndrome results in a genetic male with female characteristics. After the discussion with Ms. Schultz, Bill was able to develop a new lesson focus that would make his instruction more meaningful and interesting to students. The payoff for the time and effort Bill put into developing the new lesson focus was the attentiveness and interest shown by students during the lesson.

Prospective and novice teachers are often inclined to focus their instruction on facts and definitions, minimizing or omitting application and significance. This orientation should be reversed, if one believes that science instruction should be meaningful and student centered. The science education profession recommends that science teachers help students to come to see science as useful in their daily lives. This is not always an easy task, but it is especially important to strive for in the introductory lessons in a unit. Every time a science teacher plans a science lesson, he or she should consider the importance and relevance of what is to be taught from the students' perspective. A question addressing this issue appears first on the list of those suggested by Lubber (see the preceding section).

Inspection of the instructional objectives for the prospective teacher's original lesson plan reveals that the learning outcomes reflect lower-order thinking. The objectives are primarily at the knowledge level, typical of much instruction in many science classrooms. It is unfortunate, but too much science teaching stresses facts and definitions when thinking and understanding should be the focus of science instruction (Tobin & Fraser, 1987; Tobin & McRobbie, 1996). Exemplary science teachers work diligently to encourage students to think and to comprehend science course material. With this in mind, Bill, the prospective teacher, was requested to rewrite his instructional objectives to stress higher-order thinking skills, specifically, learning outcomes at the application and analysis levels of Bloom's taxonomy.

Often novice as well as experienced science teachers believe that the first few lessons of a unit of study should teach students "the basics." These individuals believe that fundamental facts, definitions, and concepts should be taught first so this information can be used to learn and understand the rest of the topic. Although this rationale sounds logical, these teachers fail to consider that students already know something about the topic they are presenting. Students possess some knowledge related to most science topics, even though some of the knowledge may be limited or incorrect. Therefore, science teachers should design introductory lessons with this assumption in mind and gradually develop the definitions, facts, concepts, and vocabulary words as the unit progresses. Sound curriculum planning must begin with what the learner already knows (Ausubel, 1963) and build and reform the knowledge with relevant contexts. Again, we find a question related to this important understanding in our list of questions introduced in the previous section.

The amount of content covered during a science lesson is an important consideration for both middle school and secondary school instruction. Science teaching must stress thinking and understanding important scientific, technological, and mathematical concepts (American Association for the Advancement of Science, 1989). It must also emphasize student mastery over content coverage and the development of environments that foster science learning (NRC, 1996). Lesson plans must reflect these ideals through activities that engage students in reasoning and seeking answers to questions and that foster the creation of communities of science learners. Lessons that cover a great deal of subject matter, include many details and vocabulary, and encourage learner isolation must be reexamined for their potential effectiveness.

In addition, a science lesson should reflect inquiry (NRC, 1996). An effective science lesson must stimulate student involvement, as evidenced by examining the instructional activities as well as the instructional objectives. Unfortunately, little active learning could be inferred from Bill's original lesson plan on the endocrine system. Consequently, Ms. Schultz referred him to Chapters 4 and 6 in this textbook in order to reconstruct the instructional activities in a manner that would require students to observe, analyze, and explain. The prospective science teacher was asked to reflect on the *National Science Education Standards* discussed in Chapter 2 of this methods textbook, and he was requested to determine how science process skills can be brought into the lesson to help students gather information and organize it. For example, Ms. Schultz suggested using pictures from athletic magazines and geriatric journals so that students could examine them for conditions brought about by too little or too much of a given hormone in the body. Bill and his supervisor discussed an inductive inquiry session that would encourage students to find patterns from exploratory activities. Strategies and techniques were considered that would help students build upon what they know, represent concepts in their minds, and organize ideas so that they have personal meaning. All too often, science teachers conduct lessons in a way that suggests that knowledge is something that can be telepathically transmitted from the head of the teacher to the heads students (Tobin & McRobbie, 1996). These teachers seem to overemphasize science as a body of knowledge and de-emphasize science as a way of investigating and a way of thinking. They also demonstrate a lack of understanding as to how students learn best.

REFLECTING ON THE METHODOLOGY OF A SCIENCE LESSON

As teachers decide what to teach, they also focus attention on how to teach it. Effective science teachers at both the middle and secondary levels use a variety of instructional strategies, teaching skills, and materials within a given lesson (Rosenshine, 1990; Texley & Wild, 1996). As opposed to lecturing the whole period, these teachers may begin with a demonstration, move on to a brief lecture, conduct a short hands-on activity, and end with a review of major points. They ask questions that require students to think, and they encourage all students to participate in the lesson. This variety and transition from activity to activity within a single class period is critical to the success of science courses.

In addition, when using a variety of instructional strategies within a given lesson, effective science teachers properly implement each strategy they plan to use. Whether they conduct a discussion session or a demonstration or a laboratory exercise, these teachers carry out each strategy well and thoroughly. The quality of their instruction is evidenced by the amount of student engagement, as reflected in the amount of student learning that occurs. All students, regardless of their intellectual ability, benefit from the implementation of good teaching strategies (Roadrangka & Yeany, 1985).

Instructional Strategies

An instructional strategy designates the way that a major segment or the entire lesson is approached. It is the general plan that will be used to achieve a given set of learning outcomes. Some lessons are planned around the presentation of information, and thus the lecture is used. Some lessons are planned around activities that require students to find out about ideas, and thus selected inquiry and discovery strategies are used. Some lessons are planned around the illustration of science principles or laws through the use of a demonstration. And, of course, some lessons are designed to use several instructional strategies.

Effective science teachers are those who use models to plan a lesson, selecting instructional strategies based on their potential to accomplish certain goals and objectives (Eggen & Kauchak, 1996). Science teachers have a variety of teaching strategies from which to choose to match appropriate teaching plans with various learning outcomes. If the appropriate selections are made and the plan is executed well, students will actively engage in the lesson and benefit greatly.

The traditional science teaching approach whereby students are presented new information, verify what was presented, and then practice with the new information makes use of a combination of instructional strategies. The new information is often introduced through a lecture or demonstration; laboratory is the primary means by which students verify the accuracy of the new information; and practice may involve students in discussions or answering questions or working problems provided by the teacher or from a textbook. Following this sequence, recitation may be used to check student understanding and provide corrective feedback.

Two alternative science teaching approaches that make use of these same instructional strategies but are organized differently are the Learning Cycle and the Generative Learning Model. You will recall from Chapter 5 that the Learning Cycle is an inductive approach that includes three phases: exploration, invention, and application. Whereas the Learning Cycle is generally considered an inquiry strategy, it makes use of other instructional strategies to operationalize the desired inquiry effect. The exploration phase most often involves some type of a laboratory or demonstration; the invention phase, where students construct meaning from their exploration, involves discussion; and the application phase of the cycle may utilize the strategies of laboratory, discussion, or reading (Abraham, 1992).

The Generative Learning Model has proven useful for teaching for conceptual change and includes four phases: preliminary, focus, challenge, and application (Kyle, Abell, & Shymansky, 1992). The preliminary phase occurs prior to instruction and involves questioning students to determine their conceptions pertinent to the lesson. In the focus phase, students are presented with a problem, often through a demonstration or laboratory experience. The problem is presented so as to encourage students to explore their conceptions. The challenge phase is similar to the Learning Cycle's invention phase. It involves students discussing their ideas and may include the teacher demonstrating a discrepant event related to the concept under investigation for the purpose of encouraging students to consider alternatives to their own explanations. The application phase may involve laboratory work, demonstrations, or discussion for the purpose of helping students view the concept from different perspectives. Whether using the traditional approach or an alternative, science lessons typically use a combination of instructional strategies, although the arrangement of the strategies may be different.

Let's review the instructional methods discussed earlier in this textbook so that teachers can plan carefully for the inclusion of these approaches in science lessons.

1. **Inquiry.** Inquiry is a broad strategy. Actually it is more than a strategy because it is fundamental to the scientific enterprise. Nevertheless, teaching science as inquiry suggests many strategies that can be used to help students construct knowledge, such as the use of science process skills, discrepant events, inductive and deductive methods, and problem solving.

2. **Demonstration.** Demonstrations illustrate and help to explain ideas through concrete means. They focus attention on key ideas and are an efficient means for guiding thinking and engaging participation.

3. **Laboratory work.** The laboratory involves students in hands-on or firsthand activities. This strategy can be approached in a variety of ways, such as using process skills, inductive or deductive methods, problem solving, and technical skills.

4. **Lecture.** Lectures involve the presentation of ideas and information, especially to large numbers of people. Lecturing is an efficient way to instruct a large group of students.

5. **Discussion.** Discussion permits students to express their views and to clarify their ideas. It can increase student involvement with instruction.

6. **Recitation.** The recitation session requires students to demonstrate their knowledge through their responses to teacher questions. It usually takes place toward the end of a lesson.

Teaching Skills

Teaching skills are specific behaviors that teachers use to conduct lessons and implement instructional strategies. Specific skills are needed to introduce lessons, ask questions, give directions, provide feedback, and end lessons. Teaching skills must be developed to conduct effective science lessons. These are the behaviors that promote student engagement during instruction.

In addition to student engagement, good teaching skills can help make learning more concrete. Exemplary science teachers use these skills frequently to give students concrete examples, ensuring the opportunity to construct understandings (Treagust, 1987). For example, these teachers use expository and comparative advance organizers to help students construct meaning from explanations and to integrate what they are about to learn with what they already know. They constantly give students analogies so they can perceive abstract ideas that are common to the science curriculum (Glynn, Duit, & Thiele, 1995). One might add, these teachers incorporate teaching aids such as diagrams, charts, and slides to help students visualize key concepts during their presentations. The following list reviews the major teaching skills that a science teacher should consider when planning and teaching a science lesson.

1. **Set induction.** The set induction prepares the students for learning. It focuses attention on what will be taught and attempts to interest students in the lesson. Other labels given to set induction are anticipatory set and attention grabber.

2. **Questioning.** Questions involve students in their learning by causing them to think and respond. Students' responses to questions aid in the construction of understandings.

3. **Giving directions.** Giving directions communicates what is expected and directs students to proper and productive behavior.

4. **Interpersonal interaction and management.** Effective personal interaction between teacher and students is necessary to establish a positive, productive learning environment. Accepting learner feelings and thoughts, giving corrective feedback, reinforcing student participation, and eliminating disruptive behavior are critical skills to use during science instruction.

5. **Closure.** The closure brings a lesson or teaching segment to an end. This act helps students to review what has been presented, reinforcing main ideas and constructing additional meaning from the instruction.

Teaching Materials

An important consideration when planning and teaching science lessons is the gathering of teaching materials. Materials and equipment are required for student laboratory work as well as for teacher demonstrations. The materials needed for many science lessons may be inexpensive and very accessible. For example, cotton balls, batteries, isopropyl alcohol, seeds, and corn starch can be purchased from local grocery or hardware stores. Some science equipment, such as balances, barometers, and motors, may be constructed by the teacher or students, whereas other equipment must be ordered from a science supply company.

In addition to ensuring that materials are available when needed, science teachers need to be cognizant of the conflicting messages their choice of materials might send to students of different cultures (Dagher, 1995). Most science teachers are aware of the need to provide alternatives to animal dissections for students who find this practice objectionable. Fewer teachers are probably aware that certain materials used in science activities might conflict with students' home values or teach unintended lessons. For example, some students might view breaking perfectly good clay pots to use in an archeological simulation or using food to construct a cell model as

wasteful. Others might be fearful of the spiritual repercussions of handling either animal or human bones. An insect collection may suggest to students that killing is okay just as long as it serves an educational purpose. Dagher (1995) encourages science teachers to think about the values as well as the content communicated to students in activity-based science lessons. Her questions should help teachers in their selection of materials:

- Are they offensive to any cultural group?
- Are they offensive to any religion?
- What hidden lessons do they have the potential to impart?
- What social implications do they neglect to address?
- Are they necessary to make the point?
- If any of the above answers are yes, are these materials really necessary?
- If the materials are necessary, what other options could I make available for students who cannot participate?
- What thoughts do I need to discuss with my students to alter them to the ethical dimensions of dealing with a sensitive medium (even when alternatives are provided)? (Dagher, 1995, p. 50)

An aspect of good planning is to practice one's delivery and to become familiar with the teaching materials.

■ STOP AND REFLECT! ■

This section on teacher knowledge and the different parts that are integrated to form this knowledge base should help you see that an effective science teacher is one whose knowledge extends far beyond that of the science content he or she teaches. Before going on to the next section in this chapter, do the following:

- Make a list of the components of "teacher knowledge" that should be considered when planning a lesson.

- Reread the section that describes Bill Cummings's meeting with Ms. Schultz, his student teaching supervisor, about his lesson plan on the endocrine system. Identify aspects of their discussion about the lesson plan that illustrate the difference between Bill's "teacher knowledge" and that of his supervisor.

- Reexamine Box 12.1, "Mr. Jake's Electrifying Lesson," and your critique of the vignette. Then, rate Mr. Jake's "teacher knowledge" on a scale from 1 (low) to 10 (high). Provide a rationale for your rating.

CONSTRUCTING
INSTRUCTIONAL OBJECTIVES

Instructional objectives are an integral part of most lesson plans. They focus instruction and describe what the learner should know and do as a result of a lesson, unit, or course of study. Some educators refer to instructional objectives as performance objectives; others call them behavioral objectives. In any case, most educators agree that instructional objectives should be stated in terms so specific that they can be measured or assessed. This section emphasizes the development of clearly stated objectives that can guide instruction and assessment.

Instructional objectives can be placed into three categories or domains—cognitive, affective, or psychomotor. Objectives in the cognitive domain relate to intellectual abilities and skills such as recognition, recall, comprehension, and problem solving. Most of the objectives in science course work are written in the cognitive domain. Objectives in the affective domain relate to attitudes, interests, beliefs, and values. Objectives in this area are beginning to appear more frequently in science curricula because they relate to critical aspects of school learning. Objectives in the psychomotor domain reflect motor skills and hand-eye coordination. They occupy a special place in the teaching of science, especially in the laboratory.

A good instructional objective must describe a learning outcome that states what the student will be able to do, know, or believe as a result of the instruction. This must not be confused with an instructional activity, which indicates how the student will be taught. For example, watching a film on different types of sharks is an activity that should not be confused with the objective of naming different types of sharks or describing their behavior, which may be learned by viewing the film. One way science teachers can understand what is meant by a learning outcome is to determine what they want the students to be able to do, think, or know after they instruct them. The teacher should then write these outcomes in precise terms. The teacher should keep in mind several criteria when constructing objectives. A good instructional objective is one that is

1. student oriented
2. descriptive of a learning outcome
3. clear and understandable
4. observable (TenBrink, 1990, p. 75)

Some science teachers still write objectives that reflect what the teacher will do rather than what the students are expected to learn. Somehow, teachers who construct these objectives have misunderstood the purpose of instructional objectives. These teachers describe what they believe they will be doing in the classroom instead of describing what the students should be able to do as a result of the instruction. As mentioned earlier, the focus of instructional objectives, like all aspects of a lesson plan, should be the student. An example of an objective that might be considered teacher oriented instead of student oriented is as follows: Explain the steps in making a parabolic reflecting surface. If this statement refers to what the teacher does and the teacher has no intention of assessing it, the statement can then be considered a teacher direction. The statement refers to the instruction that a science teacher might use to prepare students for a science project that involves the use of solar energy for heating objects. The student-oriented instructional objective for this activity might read: Construct a solar cooker with a parabolic reflecting surface that will cook a hot dog.

Those who construct instructional objectives must be skilled in their work, similar to writers who wish to communicate well with their reader using verbs to specify action. Verbs give clarity and understanding to instructional objectives, just as they give action and color to written and spoken communication. The proper use of a verb can convert a vague statement intended for use as an instructional objective into a clearly understood learning outcome. Examine each pair of the following statements and observe how the second statement of each pair is made clearer by the replacement of one or more action verbs:

Original	**Improved**
<u>Learn</u> the parts of a cell.	<u>Name</u> the parts of a cell.
<u>Know</u> Ohm's law.	<u>Use</u> Ohm's law to <u>calculate</u> voltage, resistance, and amperage in a circuit.
<u>Understand</u> weather charts.	<u>Interpret</u> weather charts.

Finally, good instructional objectives are observable; that is, they state learning outcomes that can be recognized. The actions specified by objectives are those that are overt, such as talking, writing, moving, stating a rule, and drawing. Some action verbs that are useful in stating objectives in behavioral terms are as follows:

construct	devise	state
demonstrate	make	graph
identify	measure	calculate
locate	estimate	predict
diagram	interpret	express
classify	infer	gather
show	hypothesize	

When teachers get into the habit of using appropriate action verbs to construct instructional objectives, they will avoid using vague terms and actions that are difficult to observe and measure. Some of these vague outcome terms are know, understand, learn, appreciate, and familiarize. These terms are more appropriately used in goal statements associated with unit and course plans, not with instructional objectives.

Instructional objectives that are clearly written statements of observable student learning outcomes serve many important functions. They can define what the teacher should teach because instructional objectives must reflect the goals and purpose of the lesson. They also serve as a guide to instruction. Activities are developed to ensure that the students achieve the objectives. Some teachers use objectives to focus attention on what the students are expected to learn in the lesson. Others use objectives as study guides. The objectives are also used to guide the evaluation process. Assessment procedures are based on the objectives and not the actual instruction.

Robert Mager (1984) provides a useful technique to prepare and analyze instructional objectives. He indicates that clearly stated instructional objectives have three characteristics:

1. **Performance.** Specifies the observable behavior that the learner is to exhibit.

2. **Condition.** Specifies the conditions under which the learning outcomes will be assessed and what the learner will be given or denied.

3. **Criterion.** Specifies the minimal level of acceptable performance that the learner will be expected to exhibit.

Using these three characteristics will likely result in clearly stated objectives. Furthermore, their use will help teachers specify objectives in the three educational domains. Although most objectives written by science teachers for daily lesson plans include only the performance component, these objectives can be clarified in many instances by including the condition and criterion components.

Performance Component

The first and most important characteristic of an instructional objective is the performance component because it describes the behavior that the learner is expected to demonstrate as a result of the instruction. Action verbs are generally used to specify the performance component. Many of these verbs are listed in Table 12.1. They can be used to prepare objectives in the three domains: cognitive, affective, and psychomotor. The following list gives nine examples of instructional objectives with the verb of the performance component underlined:

1. <u>Label</u> the structures of the heart.
2. <u>Give</u> the name of the chemical elements.
3. <u>Analyze</u> a compound.
4. <u>Determine</u> how well different materials stop radiant energy.
5. <u>Identify</u> the factors that influence the period of a pendulum.
6. <u>Find</u> the voltage of batteries.
7. <u>Make</u> a tapered glass tip.
8. <u>Write</u> a report on cloning in humans.
9. <u>State</u> your opinion on abortion.

All these objectives contain a performance term that indicates what the learner is expected to do. Some verbs that specify the actions desired of the students are label, write, analyze, construct, and state. Although these objectives are concise, greater clarity can be gained by adding a conditional component to them.

Condition Component

The second characteristic that should be used to construct objectives is the condition component. This component gives the conditions under which the learner will be assessed or the circumstances under which the learner must perform. The condition component states what the learner will be given or denied or what the learner should have done to achieve a given objective. The following instructional objectives have been taken from the preceding list and given a condition component. Notice that the objectives attain greater clarity than they had when only a performance component was used. Parentheses are placed around the condition components, and the performance components are underlined.

1. (Given a diagram of the heart), <u>label the structures of the heart</u>.
2. (With the aid of a periodic table of chemical elements), <u>give the names of the elements</u>.
3. (When given the structural formula for an unknown compound), <u>analyze the compound</u>.
4. (With black construction paper, white construction paper, aluminum foil, and glass), <u>determine how well different materials stop radiant energy</u>.

TABLE 12.1   Performance Terms for Writing Instructional Objectives in the Three Domains of Educational Goals

Cognitive	Affective	Psychomotor
Knowledge Define, describe, identify, label, list, locate, match, measure, name, select, state	**Receiving** Ask, attend, choose, describe, follow, listen, give, name, locate, select, reply	Adjust, build, construct, calibrate, display, dismantle, dissect, focus, manipulate, measure, organize, prepare
Comprehension Alter, classify, convert, distinguish, estimate, explain, extrapolate, generalize, infer, predict, summarize, translate	**Responding** Answer, assist, discuss, do, help, perform, practice, read, recite, report, select, talk, watch, write	
Application Apply, calculate, compute, determine, predict, solve	**Valuing** Accept, argue, complete, commit, do, follow, explain, initiate, join, propose, report, study, work, write, differentiate	
Analysis Analyze, differentiate, compare and contrast, relate	**Organizing** Adhere, alter, argue, change, defend, modify, organize, relate, combine, explain, integrate	
Synthesis Arrange, compile, compose, construct, devise, design, reorganize, summarize, synthesize	**Characterizing** Act, confirm, display, propose, question, refute, solve, use, influence, perform, practice, verify, serve	
Evaluation Appraise, assess, conclude, evaluate, interpret, compare, criticize, explain, summarize, justify		

Based on information from *Taxonomy of Educational Objectives. Handbook I. Cognitive Domain,* edited by B. S. Bloom, 1956, New York: David McKay Co., Inc., and from *Taxonomy of Educational Objectives. Handbook II. Affective Domain,* by B. S. Bloom, D. Krathwohl, and B. B. Masia, 1964, New York: David McKay Co., Inc.

5. (Using two bobs of different masses and two strings of different lengths), <u>identify the factors that influence the period of a pendulum</u>.

6. (Using a voltmeter and a variety of good and bad batteries rated from 1.5 V to 9 V), <u>find the voltage of the batteries</u>.

7. (Using a piece of glass tubing, a Bunsen burner, and a triangular file), <u>make a tapered glass tip</u>.

8. (Using information from at least three articles on cloning and from a discussion on this topic with four laypersons), <u>write a report on cloning in humans</u>.

9. (After studying the unit "Human Reproduction"), <u>state your opinion on abortion</u>.

The condition component adds clarity to an objective in specifying what is expected of the learner. For example, in the case of objective 2, by adding the condition "with the aid of a periodic table of chemical elements," one finds that the student does not have to memorize the names of more than one hundred chemical elements but can instead refer to the periodic chart, which provides the symbols for all the elements. In the case of objective 6, by adding the condition "using a

voltmeter and a variety of good and bad batteries rated from 1.5 V to 9 V," the student can better realize the intent of the learning outcome that appears to relate to the practical knowledge of science. Here the student is given an opportunity to learn how to determine the voltage of batteries with a voltmeter. The batteries specified in this objective are those used for electrical devices commonly found in the home, such as flashlights, cameras, and radios. Voltmeters are commonly used by electricians, auto mechanics, and electronic technicians, and young people should become familiar with them. Nevertheless, without the condition component, the student could completely miss the intent of this objective. With only the performance component, "find the voltage of the batteries," the student could accomplish this objective simply by reading the voltage specifications printed on each battery.

Criterion Component

The third characteristic that should be used in the construction of an objective is the criterion. The criterion further defines the learning outcomes in behavioral terms. It gives the minimal acceptable level of performance that is expected. Speed, accuracy, quality, quantity, and reference to an established standard are used in the construction of the criterion component. A criterion component added to the conditional and performance components of an instructional objective gives greater clarity to that objective. In the examples that follow, the criterion component is bracketed, the condition component is enclosed in parentheses, and the performance component is underlined.

1. (Given a diagram of the heart), label the structures of the heart [to include the chambers, valves, and vessels].

2. (With the aid of a periodic table of chemical elements), give the names of the elements [with 100 percent accuracy].

3. (When given the structural formula for an unknown compound), analyze the compound, [giving the names of its functional groups].

4. (With black construction paper, white construction paper, aluminum foil, and glass), determine how well different materials stop radiant energy [by presenting the data collected on this problem on a bar graph].

5. (Using two bobs of different masses and two strings of different lengths), identify the factors that influence the period of a pendulum [by demonstrating how each factor influences the period of the pendulum].

6. (Using a voltmeter and a variety of good and bad batteries rated from 1.5 V to 9 V), find the voltage of the batteries [with an accuracy of ± .5 V].

7. (Using a piece of glass tubing, a Bunsen burner, and a triangular file), make a tapered glass tip [that can be used as an eyedropper].

8. (Using information from at least three articles on cloning and from a discussion on this topic with four laypersons), write a report on cloning in humans [that is at least three typed, double-spaced pages in length and either supports or condemns cloning].

9. (After studying the unit "Human Reproduction"), state your opinion on abortion [in one or two paragraphs].

The criterion components add greater understanding to the educational outcomes that are expected from the learner. For example, adding the phrase "with 100 percent accuracy" to objective 2 specifies that the chemistry students must learn all of the names of the chemical elements with complete accuracy. Adding the phrase "that can be used as an eyedropper" to objective 7 specifies that a certain quality must be achieved in making the tapered glass tip. If the taper is too narrow, liquids will not pass through, and if it is too wide, liquids will squirt

out of the tip. Adding the phrase "that is at least three typed, double-spaced pages in length and either supports or condemns cloning" to objective 8 specifies both size and purpose for the report. The report must be a three-page position paper.

It is extremely important to recognize that instructional objectives do not have to be written in the form presented here. The three components may be shuffled and presented in an order different from that just described. Or, the condition and/or criterion components may be omitted entirely. This latter practice is not recommended for beginning teachers who typically need experience in writing objectives that provide themselves and their students with explicit directions regarding desired learning outcomes. Some teachers actively encourage student participation in the construction of instructional objectives, and the acceptable level of performance that is expected for each student is individually negotiated. An instructional objective is like any other written statement—the intent is to communicate. Therefore, teachers should constantly change and revise their objectives, using as many components as needed and using the order necessary to communicate what it is that students should be able know or do at the conclusion of a lesson.

■ STOP AND REFLECT! ■

Before leaving this section on instructional objectives, do the following:

- Explain why objectives should be stated in terms of expected student behaviors and not teacher behaviors.

- Indicate whether you agree or disagree with each of the following statements and explain your decision.

  An objective that is vaguely written is less useful than one that is precisely and clearly written.

  A lesson plan should include objectives from the cognitive, affective, and psychomotor domains.

  An objective helps the teacher communicate to students what they are expected to know or do at the end of the lesson.

- Select a science topic that interests you and write three objectives that you would like to see students achieve as a result of participating in lessons on the topic. Write your objectives to include performance, condition, and criterion components and two different educational domains.

DAILY PLAN BOOK

Many school districts require teachers to keep a daily plan book. A daily plan book is often confused with a daily lesson plan, which it is not. The plan book merely sketches what will occur during each lesson. It provides the minimum detail and number of elements. Usually, school districts require their teachers to briefly outline the teaching plans for each week. This gives the teacher, administrators, or a substitute teacher some idea of what should be taught on each school day. Figure 12.1 is an example of a daily plan book for five class sessions of a unit on chemical names and formulas. These lessons are intended for high school chemistry students. Inspection of the example reveals that space is limited to describe the elements associated with the lesson. The elements contained in this particular plan book are as follows: instructional objectives, procedures, resource materials, and evaluation. Because so little information is given in the plan book, it is difficult to determine exactly what will take place and to critique it.

DESIGNING A SCIENCE LESSON PLAN

The planning process may begin with designing a course based on a state or district framework and continue

---

Monday
Instructional Objective: Explain the organization of the periodic table.
Procedure: Students read and discuss Section 5.1 "The Periodic Table". Students locate groups, periods, representative elements, and transition elements
Resource Materials: Addison-Wesley Chemistry: Chp. 5, pp. 107–108. Transparency of Period Table
Evaluation: Have students explain how properties of elements vary from the one side of the chart to the other and from top to bottom.

Tuesday
Instructional Objective: Define cation and anion and describe how they are different.
Procedure: Teacher demonstration, 5.2 "Ionization of Sodium Metal". Students discuss demonstration and the production of ions.
Resource Materials: Addison-Wesley Chemistry (TE): Chp. 5, pp. 106B. Na metal, 0.1% phenolphthalein, safety goggles for all
Evaluation: Have students explain how the magnesium ion differs from a magnesium atom and how a bromine ion differs from bromine atom.

Wednesday
Instructional Objective: Distinguish between chemical formula and molecular formula.
Procedure: Students view video. *Chemical Symbols: Formulas and Equations,* and practice writing chemical and molecular formulas.
Resource Materials: Videocassette player and monitor Video #4FS.
Evaluation: Provide chemical and molecular formulas and ask what information can be obtained from the formulas.

Thursday
Instructional Objective: Infer the charge on an ion from the periodic table.
Procedure: Students construct table of ionic charges of representative elements by group.
Resource Materials: Transparency of Period Table
Evaluation: Have students name the ionic charge of an element when given its group.

Friday
Instructional Objective: Learn the names and formulas of polyatomic ions
Procedure: Students read and discuss Section 5.7 "Polyatomic Ions". Students construct models of polyatomic ions and ion complexes.
Resource Materials: Addison-Wesley Chemistry (TE): Chp. 5, pp. 122–123. Polystyrene balls of various sizes, toothpicks
Evaluation: Have students match the names and formulas of 3 polyatomic cations and 3 polyatomic anions.

FIGURE 12.1   Daily Plan Book for One Week of Instruction

Based on information from *Chemistry* by A. C. Wilbraham, D. D. Staley, and M. S. Matta, 1995, Menlo Park, CA: Addison-Wesley.

through to the selection of unit themes or topics, but the central and fundamental element of the planning process is the daily lesson plan. Beginning teachers almost always question the merit of developing comprehensive written lesson plans, particularly after having seen the sketchy plans developed by many experienced science teachers. The reasons for emphasizing lesson planning for beginning teachers are straightforward. Beginning teachers do not have the pedagogical content knowledge that will allow them to go before a class and "wing it" or make good on-the-spot decisions. A lesson plan can provide the teacher with a guide to follow in teaching the lesson. The more detailed the plan, the more guidance it can provide and the less information the teacher will need to remember. A detailed lesson plan also enables experienced teachers and your field experience supervisor to critique your plans and provide feedback before the lesson is taught. Most beginning teachers also find it comforting to have a carefully prepared lesson plan to refer to when responding to student questions, transitioning from one activity to the next, and checking materials needed for a demonstration or laboratory. Glancing at a lesson plan during class is nothing to be ashamed of, as it indicates to students that you have prepared for the day's instruction. Also, a written lesson plan can be kept as a record of your work and used again.

There is no accepted format for designing a lesson plan. The sequence, number of elements, and amount of detail in a lesson plan vary considerably. The short-form lesson plan incorporates more detail than that found in the daily plan book. It is usually about one page long. In contrast, the long-form lesson plan describes all aspects of each lesson in detail, including the handouts, work sheets, and assessments. It contains many pages and gives great detail. The long form is much more useful than the short form to analyze and reflect upon the potential effectiveness of an instructional plan. The long-form plan is very helpful for teachers who wish to develop and teach exemplary science lessons. Whether using the short or long form, however, teachers should recognize that a lesson plan represents their best intention of what should occur during a lesson to achieve the desired learning outcomes. From this perspective, a lesson plan should be viewed as a guide for teaching, not as an inflexible set of rules and procedures that must be followed.

Short-Form Lesson Plan

The short-form lesson plan includes a moderate amount of detail about a lesson. Figure 12.2 shows an example of a short-form lesson plan concerning weather vanes

that is part of a junior high school earth science unit on wind and weather. It also shows the teacher's intended use of the learning cycle model to have students explore different weather vane designs and to construct an understanding of the important features of a weather vane by means of discussion.

Analysis of this example reveals the advantages and disadvantages of the short-form lesson plan. The time schedule gives the teacher an idea of what to do during each time segment of the class period. This will help the teacher gauge the length of each activity and realize how much can be accomplished during the period. There is plenty of room in this lesson plan to write the assignment, list the materials that are needed, and mention the references that will be used.

This type of plan has two major shortcomings. First, the objectives are usually abbreviated in that only the performance component is given, and the conditional and criterion components are left out because of space constraints. When the conditional component of an instructional objective is omitted, the conditions under which the students will be assessed are not revealed. Using this form, it would be difficult to describe the lesson's beginning, the major instructional activities, directions for weather vane construction, or the closure. It is possible to provide the necessary detail for these elements, however, by adding additional pages to describe these activities more fully.

Long-Form Lesson Plan

The long-form lesson plan is a complete and detailed plan of instruction that includes many elements (Figure 12.3). The plan may be many pages in length and provides a thorough description of the instructional plan: purpose, objectives, activities, and so forth. The long-form gives the teacher an opportunity to formulate a thorough and meaningful plan of instruction. This type of plan is often used in teacher education programs because it can be analyzed to determine the extent of the preparation, appropriateness of the activities, the relevance of the learning outcomes, and the continuity among lesson plan elements. The long-form format is ideal for designing a lesson to stimulate student interest and to achieve specific learning outcomes that can be analyzed to determine the extent to which these ends might be attained or have been attained at the conclusion of the lesson. There is no accepted format for the number of elements and the amount of detail in a long-form lesson plan. The following list suggests elements that the teacher might incorporate in a thoroughly prepared science lesson plan.

Class: Earth Science, section II

Unit: "Wind and Weather"

Topic: Weather Vanes

Instructional Objectives: Students should be able to:
1. Construct a weather vane using simple materials.
2. Determine wind direction using a standard weather vane and a compass.
3. Describe how the size and shape of the weather vane's point and tail affect its operation.

Time	Activity
9:15–9:25 A.M.	Use color slides of different weather vane designs to introduce the topic of weather vanes. Ask students: Does changing the size and shape of the point and tail of a weather vane affect how it operates? Record student predictions.
9:25–9:40	(*Exploration*) Give instructions regarding use of the compass and have student groups construct a standard weather vane and weather vanes having the following features: a) large point and small tail, b) small circle and large circle in place of point and tail, and c) squares of the same size in place of point and tail.
9:40–9:50	Students test the different wind vanes and record their results on activity sheet. Use blow dryers for wind source if winds are calm.
9:50–10:10	(*Intervention*) Class discussion of results. Guiding questions: How are the compass and weather vane used to determine wind direction? How does the shape and size of a weather vane's point and tail affect its performance? What rule can we state about the performance of weather vanes based on our work?

Assignment
1. (*Application*) Construct a weather vane different from the ones constructed in class. Does its performance provide support for our rule?
2. Ask for volunteers to interview a friend or family member about how a weather vane works and share the results of their interview in class.
3. Textbook pp. 205–206 "Weather Vanes and Weather Forecasting"

Activity materials needed

   45 note cards, 15 pairs of scissors, 15 pencils with erasers, 15 straight pins, 15 compasses, 3 blow dryers, 3 rolls of transparent tape

Resources
1. Weather vane slides
2. Teacher made activity sheet
3. Bulletin board (pictures of weather vanes)

FIGURE 12.2 A Short-Form Lesson Plan

Title

Purpose

Instructional objectives

Major concepts

Materials and equipment

Instructional activities

   set induction

   other instructional activities

   closure and review

Assessment of instructional objectives

Reflective Planning

Recent reforms in science education call for teachers to become more reflective. This call is based on the fact that experience **must** be coupled with systematic examination of teaching for professional growth to occur (Posner, 1985). Reflection involves the systematic process of exploration that leads to a rational decision. Teachers often engage in reflection-in-action as they teach. That is, they gather data about what is happening during a lesson and use the data to make on-the-spot decisions intended to improve their own teaching and, consequently, student learning. Many teacher educators con-

The Electrical Nature of Matter

An Introduction to Charging Objects and Static Electricity

Purpose:
Most individuals do not perceive matter in terms of charged particles. Instead, they perceive the objects in their everyday life as either hard or soft, large or small, serving this or that function, but not as electrically charged. One does not think of a table, wall, chair, shirt, or finger as electrical in nature. Matter, with the exception of certain subatomic particles, is composed of atoms, which in turn are composed of electrons, protons, and neutrons. This lesson introduces middle school students to the electrical nature of matter and static electricity, keeping in mind that students possess the naive notion or misconception that only certain materials and objects are electrically charged. This knowledge must be restructured and elaborated upon so that there is a better correspondence between what the learner believes and what exists in reality.

Instructional Objectives:
1. Put forth one's beliefs regarding the potential for objects to become charged, test these ideas, and compare the findings with what one believes.
2. With objects found in and around the home such as balloons, combs, or baseball bats, demonstrate how to produce a static electrical charge on an object and to determine the type of charge acquired—positive or negative.
3. Design and test at least ten objects to determine which objects in one's everyday environment can be charged at their surface and what charge is induced on the object.

Major Concepts: Atom, electron, proton, neutron, charged, attract, repel, induce, polarized, and static electricity.

Materials and Equipment: Balloons (one for each student), jar of Rice Krispies, rubber and glass rods, pieces of silk and wool cloth, scissors, PVC pipe, combs, fur, scrap paper.

Instructional Activities:
1. a. *Set induction demonstration.* Blow up a balloon and stroke it with a piece of wool cloth. Ask the students what will happen if the balloon is placed against the chalkboard. Many of the students will probably guess that the balloon will fall to the floor. Now place the balloon against the chalkboard. It will "stick" to the board and not fall to the ground (see figure A). The students will be amazed at this event. They believe that the balloon should fall to the ground. The discrepancy in their thinking will cause them to wonder why the balloon is sticking to the board; now the students will be engaged in the lesson.

FIGURE A: The negatively charged balloon polarizes the molecules on the surface of the chalkboard, creating positive charges that attract the negative charges on the balloon.

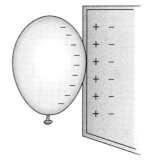

FIGURE 12.3 A Long-Form Lesson Plan

cur that deep reflection is not possible during the delivery of a lesson, however, and recommend lesson planning as a way to foster deep reflection and sustained professional growth (Ho, 1995; Chung, Mak, & Sze, 1995).

The process of reflective lesson planning described by Ho (1995) extends the procedures for lesson planning presented in the preceding section. First, a lesson plan is written. Either the short- or long-form lesson plan can be used. Below the lesson plan or on a separate sheet of paper, reflective notes are written after the lesson is taught. Numbers are used to match the reflective notes with corresponding lesson plan entries. Reflective notes may describe the teaching practices used during the lesson, beliefs that guide these practices, and concerns that extend beyond what occurs in the classroom.

As much space as needed should be allowed for reflective notes. Figure 12.4 shows how a lesson plan may be expanded to make it a reflective lesson plan.

The reflective lesson plan is very useful for the teacher who teaches two or more classes of the same science course. The lesson plan is prepared for the first class and written on the left side of the page. After the lesson is taught, reflective notes on parts of the lesson that need improvement are written on the right side of the page. Based on what is learned from the reflective notes, changes are made to the first lesson plan. This revised lesson plan can then be used to teach the second class. This process is repeated as many time as is possible throughout the day. A teacher's planning period is often the best time to write reflective notes and make

     b. Ask the question: *Why does the balloon stick to the board?* Require the students to write the answer to the question in their notebooks. Circulate among the students as they think about the question and write their responses in their notebooks. When all students have put forth their ideas, call on them to respond. Encourage responses but do not evaluate them. Some students will likely indicate that rubbing the balloon produces "static" and that is the reason for it clinging to the chalkboard. Check to determine how many students propose the static hypothesis. In addition, determine the other reasons students give for the balloon adhering to the board.

     c. At this point indicate the purpose of the lesson without telling the students that practically all matter is made up of charged particles, because they should arrive at this generalization as the lessons in the unit take place.

2. *Individual participation.* Pass out one balloon per student and give each person a small quantity (five to eight) of Rice Krispies. Demonstrate how to place the Rice Krispies into the balloon. Direct everyone to blow up the balloons so that they are firm. Stroke the balloons with a wool cloth or pass it through the hair several times. Observe what occurs with the cereal inside the balloon. You will note that the rice Krispies cling to the inside surface of the balloon.

3. *Discussion session:*

     a. Ask: *Why do the Rice Krispies cling to the inside surface of the balloon?* Solicit many answers from students and write them on the chalkboard. Try to build on the answer that comes closest to the ideas that the balloon has an excess of one type of charge and the molecules on the surface of the Rice Krispies have been polarized electrically with the opposite charge. Then present the following information:

       • The skin of the balloon has a negative charge from being stroked with the hair or wool.

       • The negatively charged balloon induces positive charges to occur on the surface of the Rice Krispies.

       • The positive end of the polarized charged surface of the Rice Krispies is attracted to the negatively charged balloon. Opposite electrical charges such as protons and electrons attract each other. Like charges such as negatively charged electrons repel each other.

       • Charges that build up on objects are stationary. They are called static charges and produce static electricity.

     b. Ask: *Why do the Rice Krispies "jump away" from the inside surface of the balloon when you bring your finger up to them?* Solicit answers to the question. Encourage the students to observe carefully how the cereal jumps away as their finger approaches it.

     c. Present information to the students that will cause them to reflect upon this topic and realize that charged particles exert enormous forces on each other. Consider the following:

> Your body contains more than 10^{28} protons and nearly an equal number of electrons. The protons have a positive electric charge; the electrons have a negative charge. The electrical force between these charges is one of the most important forces in nature.
>
>   Suppose for a moment that you could borrow all the electrons from a friend's body and put them into your pocket. The mass of the electrons would be about 20 grams. With no electrons, your friend would have a huge positive charge. You, on the other hand, would have a huge negative charge in your pocket. If you stood 10 m from your friend, the attractive force between the two of you would be about 10^{23} tons—more than 100,000 times greater than the gravitational force between the earth and sun. Obviously, your pocket would be ripped off long before you had gathered even a tiny fraction of your friend's electrons. (Heuvelen. 1986, p. 475)

4. *Small-group work.* Form the students into small groups.

     a. Request each group to design a set of activities to determine which objects in their everyday environment can be charged, using a charged balloon and other charged objects. The students in each group are to collaborate and

revisions to a lesson plan, but the five to ten minutes between back-to-back classes can also be used for this purpose.

    Use of the reflective lesson plan encourages teachers to operationalize the reflective spiral of "reflect→plan→act→observe" recommended for action research (Kemmis & McTaggart, 1982). The cycle can be carried out repeatedly during a single day as several classes are taught or extended into the next year when the same lesson is taught again. Reflective lesson planning takes little time when compared to reading teaching journals, listening to or viewing audio or video recordings, and other means of reflection. Reflective lesson planning also may be further streamlined by replacing reflective notes with key words and outlines (Ho, 1995). Another advantage

of reflective lesson planning is that it can be done without assistance from others.

TEACHING AND RECEIVING FEEDBACK

Teachers also benefit greatly from receiving feedback on their performance from peers and more experienced colleagues. There is little doubt that teaching a lesson and receiving feedback on its effectiveness is one of the most useful exercises in which a prospective or an experienced science teacher can participate. This type of activity pro-develop a data sheet for the activity. Some of the objects that students can charge and use to produce static charges on other objects are *balloons, combs, PVC pipes, plastic rulers, and baseball bats.* Some of the objects that students can attempt to charge are: *plastic bags, TV screens, refrigerator doors, automobile doors, automobile windows, wooden doors, rugs, string, and water rushing out of a faucet.* Encourage students to list as many objects to test as feasible.

    b. When each group has its data sheet designed, the group must show it to the instructor for approval. When the chart is approved, each student must produce one so that each individual can collect and record his or her own data. Ask the students to begin to test some of their ideas in class and record the results. Use the balloon to determine what charge is induced on a given object. Remember when you stroke the balloon through your hair that it produces an excess negative, static electrical charge.

5. *Closure and review.* Review the intended learning outcomes of the lesson. Ask students to respond to the following statements on a sheet of paper with their name at the upper right corner:

    • What did you believe regarding the potential for objects to become charged before today's lesson, and what do you believe now after you have had some experience with the phenomena of charging objects and static electricity?

    • List several objects that you charged which surprised you because before this lesson you did not think that a static electrical charge could be placed on the object.

    Request the students *to hand* in these responses before you go further with the review session.

    During the session, call on many students and solicit their responses to the above statements. When students tell about the objects that they charged, ask them to *explain* how this phenomenon occurs. Encourage students to tell the class what excess charge the charging object has, what charge it induces on another object, and where these charges exist that are attracting or repelling.

    The homework assignment is to carry out the exercise initiated in class at home and to bring back the completed data sheet for discussion and to hand in.

Assessment of the Instructional Objectives:

The instructional objectives to be assessed for this lesson are identical to the instructional objectives stated at the beginning of the lesson plan.

1. Put forth one's beliefs regarding the potential for objects to become charged, test these ideas, and compare the findings with what one believes.
2. With objects found in and around the home such as balloons, combs, or baseball bats, demonstrate how to produce a static electrical charge on an object and to determine the type of charge acquired—positive or negative.
3. Design and test ten objects to determine which objects in one's everyday environment can be charged at their surface and what charge is induced on the object.

The teacher will assess instructional objectives 1, 2, and 3 from the written responses requested at the beginning of the review session. The teacher will examine the responses that students wrote and handed in and will identify students who may be experiencing difficulty understanding the topic or what is expected of them. This assessment of students' progress will help the teacher prepare for the next lesson. Further assessment of students' achievement regarding the lesson's objectives will be ascertained from the homework assignment, requesting students to charge many objects in and around their home.

FIGURE 12.3, *continued*

vides an opportunity to "put it all together" and to demonstrate how to teach a good science lesson. Microteaching or miniteaching—a scaled-down version of teaching a complete lesson—is widely used in teacher education. This type of teaching exercise focuses on the development of one or a few skills at a time, often within the context of presenting a lesson to a small group of peers for a short time period (ten to twenty minutes). Microteaching permits one to implement a particular instructional strategy and to develop specific teaching skills and techniques. Some science microteaching sessions involve student focus on attention-getting set inductions, discrepant event demonstrations, discovery sessions, and discussion of societal issues. In these minilessons, asking questions, using wait time, calling on many students, using the chalkboard or overhead projec-

tor, providing materials, and so forth are observed, analyzed, and used in the feedback given to the person teaching. Some science teacher educators require prospective teachers to teach four or five minilessons before they ask them to teach a complete lesson.

    Reflective teaching, described by Cruickshank and colleagues (1984), is an extension of the microteaching approach and one that can be used to give prospective teachers many insights into the teaching process. Its purpose, like that of reflective lesson planning, is to bring about professional growth in teachers. This approach focuses on planning, teaching, evaluating, and receiving feedback with special emphasis on what the students (peers) have learned and how satisfied they are with the instruction. Reflective teaching has the following five characteristics (Cruickshank et al., 1984, pp. 3–4):

Class: Earth Science

Unit: "Wind and Weather"

Topic: Fog formation

Instructional Objectives: Students should be able to:

1. Describe the relationship between dew point and temperature.

2. Determine the dew point temperature using the sling psychrometer.

3. Measure and record the dew point temperature indirectly using a sling psychrometer and the dew point temperature chart in the text.

4. List and describe at least three types of fog.

Time		Activity
9:15–9:20 A M	1	Use demonstration to introduce the topic of fog formation. Demonstration of fog formation. (Teacher leads demonstration with help from two students.)
9:20–9:35	2.	Class discussion of demonstration. Student discussion of experiences with fog.
9:35–9:55	3.	Break students up into pairs to determine dew point using sling psychrometer. Ask them to repeat the procedure three times and compare results. (Laboratory exercise no. 23)
9:55–10:05	4.	Students practice using dew point data to determine relative humidity. Use temperature and dew point charts in textbook.
10:05–10:10	5.	Assignment
	5.1	Textbook pp. 308–313.
	5.2	Appoint two weather observers from the class to observe cloud formation in vicinity during the daylight periods of the next 24 hours.
	5.3	Ask for volunteers to perform the demonstration on cloud formation as described in the textbook for the next class period. Meet with students after school to go over the demonstration.

Laboratory materials needed

10 sling psychrometers
10 thermometers
Water
Bottles

Resources

1. Relative humidity tables from text
2. Bulletin board (photographs of various types of fog formation).

Reflective Notes

1. Need about 10 minutes to introduce demonstration. Pick at least one girl to help with demonstration.

2. Discussion was limited to only 8 students. Perhaps having student discuss in small groups before the whole class discussion will make more students feel that they have something to contribute.

3. About a third of the groups didn't soak the "wet bulb" of the sling psychrometer in water. As a result, their data were inaccurate. I should have repeated the lab directions and checked with each group as they worked. I think it would be helpful to write the instructions about the wet bulb on the board so that I don't forget to remind the students and to check their work.

4. Students were able to use the chart to determine relative humidity, but when I questioned them about relative humidity and its relationship to dew point most couldn't tell me. I guess I misjudged their understanding of these concepts. I should have addressed the relationship between dew point and relative humidity earlier in the lesson.

5.1 This assignment was clearly written on the board. I think they all got it.

5.2 Did this while students were working with dew point charts.

FIGURE 12.4 A Reflective Lesson Plan

1. It teaches a small group of peers.
2. Each prospective teacher teaches toward the same instructional objectives.
3. Each prospective teacher teaches a lesson that is approximately 10 to 15 minutes in length.
4. The teacher must strive to accomplish two outcomes, learner achievement and learner satisfaction with the lesson.
5. The peers are asked to play themselves and not to play the role of school-age children or adolescents.

The reflective teaching approach is very instructive because prospective teachers can compare their approaches and become aware that some approaches are more effective than others. This realization quickly comes to the forefront when learner achievement and interest in the lesson are analyzed. In these sessions, prospective science teachers discover that inquiry-oriented science lessons are often perceived to be more stimulating than lecture-oriented science lessons and that careful attention to learning outcomes is important to student achievement.

Title of lesson: _____

Name of individual teaching: _____ Date: _____

Rating scale:	Poor		Fair		Good			Excellent	
6.0	6.5	7	7.5	8	8.5	9	9.5	10

Elements to look for during the lesson

Provides a set induction   Provides practice
Asks many questions   Gives feedback
Uses wait time   Provides opportunities for reasoning
Calls on many students   Uses teaching aids
Maintains student interest   Organizes the learning environment
Uses time effectively   Relevant lesson for the audience
Gives clear explanations   Demonstrates knowledge of subject
Paces lesson well   Summarizes key point

Elements observed during the lesson

Summary of postlesson feedback

Effective aspects of the lesson   Suggestions for improvement

---

FIGURE 12.5   Feedback and Evaluation Form for a Science Lesson.

The presentation of a complete lesson is often the final step in the preservice preparation of a prospective teacher, before student teaching. Many teaching skills and several instructional strategies can be demonstrated in a complete lesson. This assignment should be completed when the prospective teachers have polished their teaching skills to the point where the chances are high that they will be perceived by peers and the instructor as effective teachers. If the presenters have not developed their teaching skills and give a poor lesson, the feedback may be too harsh and extensive. This situation should be avoided because it is not an effective approach to teacher education. Break lesson-teaching into small learning tasks, and require prospective teachers to master prerequisite skills that prepare them to be successful in the delivery of an exciting science lesson with activity that engages students in the acquisition of worthwhile knowledge and skills.

The feedback to presenters is a major element in the education process. It should be given as soon after the presentation as possible, and objectivity is essential. In order to promote objectivity, the feedback must be based upon a list of ideas that were discussed as being essential to a good lesson presentation, and of course these ideas should be the skills, strategies, techniques, teaching aids, and so on, that were stressed in the teacher education program. An example of a form that can be used for evaluating a lesson and providing feedback appears in Figure 12.5.

A technique that may work well is first to provide feedback on the effective aspects of the lesson. This approach sets the stage for a positive feedback session. Both the instructor and peers identify the skills and techniques that were executed well. These are listed on the chalkboard and on the feedback and evaluation form. The presenter is also encouraged to participate in the activity. Then suggestions for improvement can be given to the presenter focusing on specific elements of the lesson and on the skills that should be considered in future teaching.

ASSESSING AND REVIEWING

1. A school administrator asks your opinion about a hiring decision. Formulate a response based on your understanding of the relationship between pedagogical content knowledge and effective science teaching practices. The teacher applicant has a strong physics background but knows nothing about science teaching methods and materials and has never worked with adolescents.

2. Analyze Figure 12.3, the long-form lesson plan on static electricity designed for a middle school science course. Critique the lesson plan and compare your assessment with critiques constructed by your peers.

3. Design a lesson plan to be taught to a class of middle or high school students or to your peers.

   a. Organize the content so that it will be relevant to the audience and identify strategies and skills that will actively engage the learners in the lesson.

   b. Carefully review this chapter to be sure the lesson plan is thoroughly prepared and will be perceived by the students to be a good or an exemplary science lesson.

   c. Give the lesson plan to an instructor or colleague for evaluation and feedback. Respond to suggestions by modifying the plan.

4. Prepare to present a science lesson.

   a. Gather all the necessary equipment and materials, checking to ensure that no conflicting messages are being communicated by them to the intended audience.

   b. Practice the lesson in front of a peer, spouse, or friend, and determine perceptions regarding the potential effectiveness of the lesson.

   c. Present the lesson to the intended audience and record your reflective notes regarding the lesson on your lesson plan.

   d. Compare your lesson and reflective notes with the lessons and reflective notes of other students.

   e. Teach the same lesson again and compare your first and second performances.

5. Use Figure 12.5 or another feedback and evaluation form to critique a lesson taught by a peer. After the lesson, provide feedback to your peer regarding elements observed during the lesson, effective aspects of the lesson, and suggestions for improvement. Be particularly sensitive to your peer's receptivity to constructive feedback when offering suggestions for improving the lesson.

6. Construct a concept map to represent the major ideas presented in this chapter on lesson planning and teaching.

◼

RESOURCES TO EXAMINE

"A Constructivist Cloud Lab." 1996, October. *Science Scope*, pp. 18–19.

Dave Emery describes a student-centered laboratory activity he designed for his middle school students. The lab starts not with a prelab discussion, but with students generating hypotheses and later involves students deciding how to proceed through the investigation. A lesson plan for the lab is included in the article.

"Cultural Myths as Constraints to the Enacted Science Curriculum." 1996, February. *Science Education*, pp. 223–241.

Kenneth Tobin and Campbell McRobbie's study of cultural myths identifies beliefs held by teachers that tend to inhibit them from planning and teaching in ways that support the reform initiatives. The beliefs depict constraints that are both personal and social constructions; center on the transmission of content knowledge, teaching efficiency, course rigor, and exam preparation; and have broad support among educational stakeholders, including students, parents, and school administrators.

"The Process of Planning for Science Learning." 1994. Columbus, OH: ERIC Clearinghouse for Science, Mathematics, and Environmental Education. In Larry Schafer (Ed.), *Behind the Methods Class Door: Educating Elementary and Middle School Teachers in Science. Association for the Education of Teachers of Science (AETS) Yearbook*, pp. 47–53.

James Lubber presents a framework for developing lesson plans that focuses attention on student learning rather than teacher presentation. The framework is based on constructivism and assumptions put forth in today's reform documents. Questions presented to guide student-centered planning efforts are clustered under the headings of subject matter, student understandings, student-centered instructional methods, and assessment.

"Those Who Understand: Knowledge Growth In Teaching." 1986, 15(2). *Educational Research*, pp. 1–32.

Lee Shulman presents his thoughts about pedagogical content knowledge—the unique knowledge base that teachers develop as a result of experience and reflection.

◼

REFERENCES

Abraham, M. R. (1992). Instructional strategies designed to teach science concepts. In F. Lawrenz, K. Cochran, J. Krajcik, & P. Simpson (Eds.), *Research matters . . . to the science teacher* (pp. 41–50). Manhattan, KS: National Association for Research in Science Teaching.

American Association for the Advancement of Science. (1989). *Science for all Americans: Project 2061.* Washington, DC: Author.

Ausubel, D. P. (1963). *The psychology of meaningful verbal learning.* New York: Grune & Stratton.

Chung, C. M., Mak, S. Y., & Sze, P. (1995). Reflective lesson planning in refresher training programs for experienced physics teachers. *Journal of Science Education and Technology, 4*(2), 151–161.

Cruickshank, D. R., Holton, J., Fay, D., Williams, J., Kennedy, J., Meyers, B., & Hough, J. B. (1984). *Reflective teaching.* Bloomington, IN: Phi Delta Kappa.

Dagher, Z. R. (1995). Materials speak louder than words. *Science Scope, 19*(1), 48–50.

Eggen, P. D., & Kauchak, D. P. (1996). *Strategies for teachers* (3rd ed.). Englewood Cliffs, NJ: Prentice-Hall.

Fraser, B. J. (1990). Students perceptions of the classroom. In K. Tobin, J. B. Kahle, & B. J. Fraser. (1990). *Windows into science classrooms: Problems associated with higher-level cognitive learning.* New York: Falmer Press.

Glynn, S. M., Duit, R., Thiele, R. B. (1995). Teaching science with analogies: A strategy for constructing knowledge. In S. M. Glynn & R. Duit (Eds.), *Learning science in the schools: Research reforming practice* (pp. 247–274). Mahwah, NJ: Erlbaum.

Hall, G. E., George, A. A., Rutherford, W. L. (1979). *Measuring stages of concern about the innovation: A manual for the use of the SoC questionnaire* (2nd edition). Austin: University of Texas.

Heuvelen, A. V. (1986). *Physics: A general introduction.* Boston: Little, Brown.

Ho, B. (1995). Using lesson plans as a means of reflection. *ELT Journal, 49*(1), 66–71.

Kahle, J. B. (1996). Equitable science education: A discrepancy model. In L. H. Parker, L. J. Rennie, & B. J. Fraser (Eds.), *Gender, science and mathematics: Shortening the shadow* (pp. 129–142). Dordrecht, The Netherlands: Kluwer.

Kemmis, S., & McTaggart, R. (1982). *The action research planner.* Victoria, Australia: Deakin University Press.

Kyle, W. C., Jr., Abell, S. K., & Shymansky, J. A. (1992). Conceptual change teaching and science learning. In F. Lawrenz, K. Cochran, J. Krajcik, & P. Simpson (Eds.), *Research matters . . . to the science teacher* (pp. 29–40). Manhattan, KS: National Association for Research in Science Teaching.

Lubber, J. D. (1994). The process of planning for science learning. In L. E. Schafer (Ed.), *Behind the methods class door: Educating elementary and middle school science teachers.* Association for the Education of Teachers of Science (AETS) Yearbook. Columbus, OH: ERIC Clearinghouse for Science, Mathematics, and Environmental Education.

Mager, R. F. (1984). *Preparing instructional objectives.* Belmont, CA: Fearon Pitman.

McCormick, T. E., & Noriega, T. (1986). Low versus high expectations: A review of teacher expectation effects on minority students. *Journal of Educational Equity and Leadership, 6,* 224–234.

National Research Council. (1996). *National science education standards.* Washington, DC: National Academy Press.

Novak, J. D., & Gowin, D. B. (1984). *Learning how to learn.* New York: Cambridge University Press.

Oakes, J. (1990). *The underparticipation of women, minorities, and disabled persons in science.* Santa Monica, CA: The RAND Corporation.

Posner, G. J. (1985). *Field experience: A guide to reflective teaching.* New York: Longman.

Roadrangka, V., & Yeany, R. H. (1985). A study of the relationship among type and quality of implementation of science teaching strategy, student formal reasoning ability, and student engagement. *Journal of Research in Science Teaching, 22,* 743–760.

Rosenshine, B. (1990). On using many materials. In A. C. Ornstein (Ed.), *Strategies for effective teaching.* New York: Harper & Row.

Shulman, L. S. (1987). Knowledge and teaching: Foundations of the new reform. *Harvard Educational Review, 57*(1), 1–22.

TenBrink, T. D. (1990). Writing instructional objectives. In J. M. Cooper (Ed.), *Classroom teaching skills* (pp. 52–83). Lexington, MA: Heath.

Texley, J., & Wild, A. (Eds.). (1996). *NSTA pathways to the science education standards.* Arlington, VA: National Science Teachers Association.

Tobin, K., & Fraser, B. J. (1987). Introduction to the exemplary practices in science and mathematics education study. In K. Tobin & B. J. Fraser (Eds.), *Exemplary practices in science and mathematics education.* Perth, Western Australia: Curtin University of Technology, Science and Mathematics Education Centre.

Tobin, K., Kahle, J. B., & Fraser, B. J. (1990). *Windows into science classrooms: Problems associated with higher-level cognitive learning.* New York: Falmer Press.

Tobin, K., & McRobbie, C. J. (1996). Cultural myths as constraints to the enacted science curriculum. *Science Education, 80*(2), 223-241.

Tobin, K., Tippins, D. J., Gallard, A. J. (1994). Research on instructional strategies for teaching science. In D. Gabel (ed.), *Handbook of research on science teaching and learning* (pp. 45-93). Upper Saddle River, NJ: Merrill/Prentice Hall.

Treagust, D. F. (1987). Exemplary practices in high school biology classrooms. In K. Tobin & B. J. Fraser (Eds.), *Exemplary practices in science and mathematics education.* Perth, Western Australia: Curtin University of Technology, Science and Mathematics Education Centre.

CHAPTER 13

PLANNING A SCIENCE UNIT

Teaching units are carefully organized instructional plans that sequence content and experience for students.

Effective teachers plan well. They have a good idea of what they want to occur in the classroom before they begin instructing students. Consequently, teachers who organize their courses into units and plan them will be better able to provide meaningful learning experiences for their students than science teachers who follow a curriculum that others have organized and planned. The process of planning science units gives teachers opportunities to think deeply about what they are going to teach, how to actively engage students, and how to assess their performance. In addition, planning gives teachers ownership of the curriculum and empowers them to be creative in their teaching. Few activities are as useful for science teachers as organizing their own instruction through unit planning.

OBJECTIVES

This chapter is designed to help the reader meet the following objectives:

- Review some of the recommendations aimed at reforming science teaching in order to improve the scientific and technological literacy of students in the United States.

- Develop an awareness of many resources that a science teacher can go to for ideas in planning for instruction.

- Examine a science unit that was planned by a science teacher and assess its potential to promote scientific literacy among high school students.

- Become familiar with many elements that should be used to construct an effective science unit.

- Plan a science unit that actively engages students in learning about fundamental science principles and important topics that are relevant to their lives.

Introduction

A unit organizes the curriculum into a cohesive and meaningful instructional plan. Units of instruction break up a course of study into segments that are larger than a lesson plan. A unit may comprise one or more topics. Each topic consists of facts, concepts, principles, theories, and skills. Perhaps the most efficient units are those of short rather than long duration. Two types of unit plans can be used in science teaching—resource units and teaching units. Resource units are designed to identify a variety of resources that can be used to teach a particular topic. The resources can be drawn from many sources and organized in a variety of ways. Teaching units are specifically designed to contain only those resources that are used for teaching a particular topic. They are carefully organized teaching plans that sequence content and experiences for students. Teaching units that are designed around relevant topics will most likely stimulate student interest and motivate them to achieve the intended learning outcomes.

The Science Reform and Planning Science Instruction

As discussed at the beginning of this textbook, the science education reform is aimed at reshaping science programs in grades K–12. A major goal of the reform is to alter the content, instruction, and assessment associated with traditional science courses. A traditional science course is conceived to be one in which a great deal of subject matter is covered over the school year, and the content is dictated by a science textbook. Teachers spend a great deal of instructional time presenting information and getting students to learn terms. Laboratory work is interspersed among class periods and is generally used to verify ideas discussed in class. Assessment relies heavily on paper-and-pencil tests.

The national science education reform documents recommend that science courses cover fewer topics and give students more time to study a smaller number of ideas in greater depth (American Association for the Advancement of Science [AAAS], 1990). The curriculum should be approached in a multidisciplinary manner by using many fields of science to study topics, drawing from biology, chemistry, earth/space science, and physics (National Science Teachers Association, 1992). In addition, mathematics, technology, social sciences, history of science, and personal perspective should be integrated into courses in order for them to become rich learning experiences. An important aim is to help all students to understand science concepts within the context of everyday life.

Science teaching should take on a different form from the one where students sit in straight rows, receive information during most class periods, and take part in laboratory work once a week. Instruction must be centered around questions that are meaningful to students, stimulating them to search for answers over extended periods of time. Science should be taught **as** inquiry, which centers around learning ideas that can be tested against established scientific knowledge (National Research Council [NRC], 1996). Thus, students will be constructing their own knowledge and explanations, testing these ideas against reality, and comparing them with established conceptions.

The evaluation of student achievement and progress should be based on a more authentic assessment system than that which presently exists (Clark & Star, 1996). Many learning outcomes should be measured in situations in which the knowledge and skills will actually be used. If students are expected to become familiar with metric measurement in everyday situations, they should be assessed using 2-liter soft drink bottles, for example, which they encounter frequently in grocery stores and homes. Assessment must occur with real-life objects rather than substituting paper-and-pencil measures for the sake of convenience. Projects should be common products in science courses and judged using rubrics and criteria that are agreed upon by teachers and students. Portfolios should also be used to show students' work, evidencing their achievement and charting their academic growth.

Resources to Consider for Unit Plans

Ideas for what to teach are most important when planning lessons, units, or courses of study. For those individuals with many years of teaching and curriculum experiences, these ideas come to mind quickly. For those who are new to teaching, however, ideas do not just appear; they are produced only after a great deal of searching and thinking. The following list includes some people and places that may serve as useful resources for unit planning.

- Experienced science teachers
- University science and science education professors
- Scientists working in industry
- Public relations managers for science and technology related industries
- Innovative curriculum project materials
- High school and college science textbooks
- Laboratory manuals
- Science paperbacks

- Professional organizations
- Aquariums
- Museums
- Planetariums
- Nature centers
- Public libraries
- Internet
- Local utility companies and municipal treatment plants
- National Science Teachers Association publications
- Science magazines such as *ChemMatters*, *Scientific American*, *Science News*, *The New Scientist*, *Science Digest*, *Discover*, and *Technology Review*
- Science magazines for secondary school students, such as *Current Science*
- Newspapers and other periodicals (e.g., "Science Times" section of the *New York Times*)
- Television programs such as *Nova* and those on the Discovery Channel

AN EXAMPLE OF A TEACHER-PLANNED SCIENCE UNIT

■

Mr. Zimble had only two years of teaching experience when his principal asked him to plan a new science course, primarily for high school freshmen. For over twenty-five years, most of the freshmen have taken physical science, which consists of a half-year of basic physics and a half-year of basic chemistry. The principal feels that a change is needed in order to provide students with a more interesting interdisciplinary experience as an introduction to high school science. Another reason for this change is to encourage more students to take high school chemistry and perhaps even physics after their introductory course.

■

After the shock of being given the big assignment to develop a new course, Mr. Zimble began to reflect on this task. He recalled the science methods course that he was required to take for certification and the unit plan that he had to prepare for the course. One idea that stuck in his mind was the instructor saying repeatedly to the class: Teach students fundamental science within a

relevant context. In other words, teach basic ideas and make them meaningful to students. With fundamentals and relevance on his mind, Mr. Zimble decided to form a list of unit topics that he could draw from to form the new science course.

Mr. Zimble began to brainstorm ideas for the course. In the process he contacted many science teachers for their recommendations. He talked with biology, chemistry, and physics teachers in his school building as well as a few high school science teachers in other schools. Mr. Zimble also contacted a middle school science teacher who had given a dynamic district inservice workshop at the beginning of the school year. He borrowed as many innovative curriculum materials as he could find as well as the state's new science curriculum framework and the national science reform guidelines: *Benchmarks for Science Literacy* (AAAS, 1993) and *National Science Education Standards* (NRC, 1996). It did not take long before ideas for the course topics and units began to flow. The following is a list of science related topics that represents his initial thinking.

> electrical power generation
> building supplies and materials
> city parks and gardening
> water in the community
> dry cleaning and laundering
> medical diagnosis with X-rays and MRIs
> beauty supplies and cosmetics
> climate, weather, and atmosphere
> vehicles, transportation, and safety
> health and sanitation

With these topical ideas for starters, Mr. Zimble realized their potential to integrate biology, chemistry, earth science, and physics for teaching fundamental science concepts that relate to phenomena that are familiar to students.

Mr. Zimble could not wait to finalize the course listing of topics because he wanted to start planning immediately a unit on water. He felt that water would be the ideal topic to begin the new integrated science course. Mr. Zimble quickly gathered many resources for ideas with which to plan the first unit.

Instructional Activities

One of the recommendations that Mr. Zimble recalled from his methods course was the instructor emphasizing the importance of first identifying activities for students that would teach them important ideas. This prompted

Time Frame
"Water in Our Community"

Day 1
- Initiate the study of water with a puzzling situation for students to figure out, which will stimulate student interest in water and illustrate important properties of this chemical compound. All students are requested to place a drop of water on a piece of wax paper and to determine if the water rolls or slides across the waxed surface.
- Discuss structural, chemical, and physical properties of water.
- Conduct a brainstorming session to list all of the uses of water in the community, leading to the purpose and overview of the water unit.

Day 2
- Continue the study of water with a laboratory exercise to study adhesive and cohesive properties of water. Each student is requested to predict how far the water will rise in glass tubes of different diameters, then to test their predictions while working in small groups.
- Continue to discuss structural, chemical, and physical properties of water.
- Present the class with the assertion from an angry citizen who claims the local drinking water is not fit to drink. Use this situation to plan investigations to study water in many areas of the community.

Day 3
- Continue the study of surface tension of water with a laboratory activity. Each student is given the challenge: Determine if you can float a small, medium, and large paper clip on the surface of water.
- Continue to discuss structural, chemical, and physical properties of water.
- Continue planning activities to study water in the community and formalize the investigative groups.
- Plan for a laboratory exercise to filter dirty water. Ask students to bring some of the equipment and materials needed for the lab in order to increase their involvement.

Day 4
- Discuss the class field trip to the municipal water treatment plant.
- Ask students to list the steps in the water purification process, which represent those used at the municipal water treatment plant. Urge students to think logically, express themselves clearly, and then build on what students say.
- Conduct a laboratory exercise to purify dirty water.

Day 5
- Discuss the filtration and purification of water from the laboratory exercise of the day before and relate it to what is likely to be observed on the field trip to the municipal water treatment plant.
- Conduct a lecture/discussion of structure of water molecules and solution chemistry.

Day 6
- Continue to conduct the laboratory exercise to purify dirty water.

Day 7
- Review the chemical and physical properties of water to check on students' understanding of these ideas.
- Place students in their investigative groups and help them to plan their water studies.
- Prepare for the field trip to the water purification plant. Ensure that all students know what to do and have ready the questions they want to ask. Check for signed parental approval forms, permitting students to take the field trip.

Day 8
- Take field trip to the municipal water treatment plant. Bus leaves school at 8:30 A.M. and arrives back at school for the last lunch period at 12:20 P.M.

Day 9
- Discuss the field trip by reviewing the treatment plant's filtration process and the properties of water. Address student beliefs and issues associated with the sanitary conditions of the community's drinking water.
- Plan for students to collect water samples throughout the city and community to analyze in their science laboratory.

Day 10
- Present a short lecture on the importance of water on earth that leads into acid/base chemistry.
- Conduct a short laboratory exercise on determining the acidity and basicity of solutions.

Day 11
- Continue with a lecture/discussion of the importance of water on earth and acid/base chemistry.

FIGURE 13.1   This time frame shows the scope and sequence of instructional activities for the science unit centered around water in a community.

Day 12 • Conduct a laboratory activity to determine the pH of an assortment of items found in the home, e. g., soft drinks, fruit juices, liquid detergents, hand soaps, shampoos, floor cleaners, etc.
        • Lecture on ions in solution, focusing on metal ions, salts, cations, and anions.

Day 13 • Conduct a laboratory on the identification of metal ions in solution.
        • Review the properties of water, water purification, pH, and ions in solution.
        • Remind students to bring in water samples from various parts of the city and rural areas.

Day 14 • Administer the quiz on properties of water, water purification, pH, and ions in solution.
        • Begin the laboratory investigation to determine the impurities, pH, ions, etc., of the water samples taken from various parts of the city and adjoining areas.

Day 15 • Continue the laboratory to determine the impurities, pH, ions, etc. of the water samples taken from various parts of the city and adjoining areas.
        • Return the quiz and discuss basic chemistry and the chemistry of water.

Day 16 • Conduct a lecture discussion of elements, compounds, ions, and the periodic chart. Practice naming some common elements and compounds.
        • Set out examples of elements, compounds, and ions for students to examine and identify.
        • Give students a homework sheet for naming elements, compounds, and ions, and for writing symbols and formulas.

Day 17 • Continue lecture/discussion of elements, compounds, ions, and the periodic chart. Practice naming some common elements and compounds.

Day 18 • Continue building students' knowledge of elements, compounds, and ions.
        • Plan for a mock town hall meeting regarding the water purity of the drinking water in the community.

Day 19 • Conduct a laboratory investigation to examine and identify the microorganisms in the water samples collected from ponds, drainage ditches, rivers, and streams.

Day 20 • Permit the investigative groups to plan for the town hall meeting. Urge students to construct charts and tables to convey their data and to present logical arguments.

Day 21 • Conduct a recitation and review session on the properties of water, steps in the water purification process, ions in solution, microorganisms living in water, and naming and writing the formulas for basic elements and compounds.

Day 22 • Continue to review the important ideas studied during the unit. Help students to find personal meaning in what they have been learning.

Day 23 • Administer the unit test.
        • Plan for the town hall meeting to address the purity of the municipal water supply.

Day 24 • Conduct the town hall meeting to discuss the municipal water supply and the claim by one of the citizens that the water is unsafe to drink.

him to examine the resources that he had gathered and to begin to list instructional activities, sequencing them as shown in the time frame in Figure 13.1. He wanted to start the unit with an attention grabber that he remembered from his science methods class. For his introduction to the study of water, Mr. Zimble would conduct the "Drop of Water" activity, whereby all of the students are given a piece of wax paper and requested to place one large drop of water on it. Students are then instructed to tilt the wax paper in order for the water drop to move over the paper. Mr. Zimble would pose the following question:

Does the drop of water *roll* or *slide* across the wax paper?

He felt strongly that the students would be challenged by this puzzling situation and they would want to figure out the answer to the question. Further, he felt that the exercise would stimulate student interest and the desire to study water. (Refer to Appendix A for a detailed description of how to conduct this simple activity, which you should try out and include in your science teaching resource file.)

On Day 1, Mr. Zimble would follow the "Drop of Water" activity with a discussion of structural, chemical, and physical properties of water. He planned a question-and-answer session on adhesive and cohesive properties of water that would help students to understand the action of water on the surface of the wax paper and its ability to rise up narrow glass tubes, which will occur in the laboratory exercise scheduled for Day 2.

Along with introducing the properties of water, Mr. Zimble would address common uses of water in everyday life, which would open up the learning environment for considering science and societal issues that might be relevant to the study of water in their community. Note that this new science teacher has several science education strands running throughout the unit, such as knowledge of fundamental chemistry, investigation of ideas, and consideration of societal issues.

Mr. Zimble feels strongly about requiring students to participate in group investigative projects, because he believes this will make the study of water more meaningful and serve to integrate fundamental science into the instruction. After considerable thought, he came up with a plan for the group projects. He would bring up the assertion of an irate citizen who claims that the city's tap water is not fit to drink because it is contaminated. After students react to this issue, Mr. Zimble will ask the class to examine all of the water in the entire community. During this process, they will collect data to debate the drinking water purity question. For this investigative inquiry, he will organize the class into five groups on

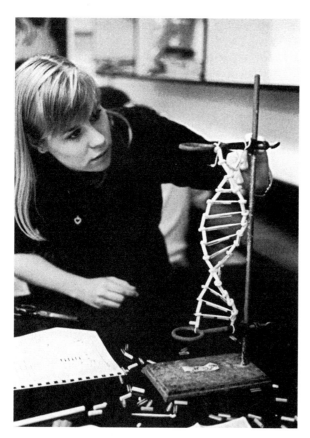

Effective planning often begins with identifying activities that can be used to help students construct meaningful understandings.

Day 3 and inform them that they will analyze samples of water from a particular part of the community. The results discovered by the entire class will provide an overall picture of the contents and quality of the water for the entire community. Further, each group will perform many basic water tests, which will give them practice with a variety of analytical procedures. The following are the group investigative projects that the teacher conceived.

1. **Tap water group.** This group will obtain samples of water from homes in various parts of the city. The students can ascertain the status of the drinking water and make a case for or against its suitability for drinking.

2. **River group.** There are several rivers and streams in and around the city from which samples can be taken. The data can be used to provide a measure of the contamination that might be found in these waters, thus determining if industry, farming, or other human activities might be contributing to this pollution.

3. **Lake group.** The municipal water treatment plant receives the water that it processes for the community from an 18-mile long lake on the northeast side of the city. This lake also serves as a recreational area for residents. The investigation of water from the lake will provide information regarding the suitability of the lake's water for swimming and fishing.

4. **Pond group.** Several large ponds can be found in the city's parks and on private lands on the edge of the city. Ponds generally have a large variety of macroscopic and microscopic organisms living in harmony that illustrate ecological relationships.

5. **Swimming pool group.** There are several municipal swimming pools and many private pools from which water samples can be taken for analysis. The students can determine whether or not these swimming environments are up to standards.

In order to personalize this activity, Mr. Zimble plans to give students some say about which group they would like to join.

On Day 3, Mr. Zimble planned to conduct another hands-on laboratory activity, also pertaining to adhesive properties of water and surface tension. For this exercise, students will be challenged to float paper clips of different sizes on the surface of water. This activity will require manual dexterity. It will also cause students to think more deeply about the bonding of water molecules, especially after they are instructed to add a drop of liquid detergent to the water and observe what happens to objects that are floating on its surface.

Gathering materials in sufficient quantities and organizing them for students to use is an important aspect of efficient planning.

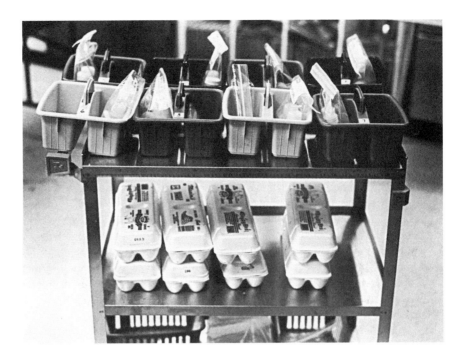

Following the lab, Mr. Zimble plans to carry out another laboratory exercise to filter dirty water. Before reading on or discussing the filtration process, he will ask students to list a series of processes that they believe are used to filter and purify muddy water. He will show the class a sample of disgusting looking water that he has placed in a large glass container on the demonstration table. Students will be urged to use their common sense to figure out ways to remove debris and contaminants from the muddy water. They will be requested to order the steps in the process of purifying the water, similar to the process used at the municipal water treatment plant. Mr. Zimble will permit students to change their proposed filtration process many times. After giving students time to modify their steps, he will present the following transparency:

STEP 1: SCREENING LARGE OBJECTS   Use a screening material to remove large objects from the water, such as soda cans, plastic bottles, sticks, and fish, so that they do not clog the filtration system.

STEP 2: PRECHLORINATION OF WATER   Add chlorine to the water to kill organisms that might cause disease.

STEP 3: FLOCCULATION OF SUSPENDED PARTICLES   Add chemicals to settle out suspended particles. This process begins to clear up the water.

STEP 4: SETTLING OF PARTICLES   Let particles settle out so that they fall to the bottom of the collection tanks.

STEP 5: SAND FILTRATION OF WATER   In this process water moves downward due to gravity through a bed of sand, which removes any particles that were not taken out of the water in the settling process.

STEP 6: POSTCHLORINATION OF WATER   Adjust the chlorine concentration to ensure that harmful microorganisms cannot live in the water.

STEP 7: ADDITIONAL TREATMENTS OF WATER   Other treatments can be used with water, such as fluoridation, pH adjustment, and aeration, in order to make it fit for drinking and other uses.

Mr. Zimble imagined that the laboratory exercise scheduled for Day 4 would run smoothly, given the advance preparation.

Let's skip over to Days 10, 11, and 12 when Mr. Zimble plans to address acids and bases because of their direct relationship with water and solution chemistry. He saw this as an opportunity to present a short lecture on the importance of water and its intimate relationship with fundamental chemistry. Mr. Zimble's **organized lecture** on water follows.

■

Water plays a key role in the support of life. If you consider where the great societies of the past have flourished over the past one thousand years, you will note that many of their major cities have existed near bodies of water where they are connected to other parts of civilization through travel by ship. For example, Athens, Venice, Barcelona, New York, San Francisco, Hong Kong, and Bombay are port cities that are served by sea travel that brings people and goods to these locations. In addition to seaports, many of the great cities of the world are located on major rivers, for example, Rome, London, Cairo, and Shanghai.

Water is the part of the biosphere that contains the majority of the life on our planet, where an enormous variety of plants and animals exist. Marine biomes cover most of the earth. Fish, whales, and algae support life as chief sources of food for humans and aquatic animals. People in many parts of the world eat fish as their major source of protein.

A large percentage of the human body is made up of water. Water carries nutrients to all parts of the body. It facilitates chemical reactions in cells and in the bloodstream. Furthermore, water assists in the elimination of waste from the body. Without water, neither plant nor animal life can be sustained.

Water serves as the medium through which acids and bases manifest their characteristics. When an acid or a base dissolves in water, it forms ions in solution that have many functions. For example, acids play a central role in our everyday lives. Many of the foods that we eat are characterized by their acidity. The sour taste that you experience when you eat citrus fruits such as lemons and oranges is an example. Vinegar contains acetic acid. Malic acid is found in apples. Lactic acid in found in buttermilk. Hydrochloric acid is one of the active ingredi-

ents in the gastric juices in the stomach that break down food during digestion. In industry, hydrochloric, sulfuric, and nitric acids are manufactured and used in enormous quantities. They are used as cleaning agents and for making plastics, metals, textiles, explosives, dyes, drugs, fertilizers, and many other chemicals.

In one sense, bases are the opposite of acids and they play an essential role in the body as well as in everyday life. In many situations, bases act to balance acids in our living systems. Bases are used in industry to make a variety of products, including household cleaners. They are used to produce soaps, paper, and synthetic products. For a list of common acids and bases, along with their formulas, common names, and uses, examine the table [Table 13.1] that I have constructed on the overhead transparency.

■

One of the activities that Mr. Zimble plans to conduct with students is to assess the concentration of acid and base solutions. Note in Table 13.2 that the students will be using at least seven indicators to produce color reactions. For this activity, Mr. Zimble will ask each group of students to prepare the color indicators that they will be using. In this manner, the students will gain experience in combining chemicals. He suspects the students will be interested in the vivid colors that are produced from acid/base indicators derived from common food products, such as grape juice, tea, and red cabbage juice. Further, students will be amazed at the color reac-

TABLE 13.1 Common Acids and Bases

Acid	Formula	Common name	Use
Acetic	$HC_2H_3O_2$	Vinegar	Cooking
Boric	H_3BO_3	Boric acid	Medicines
Carbonic	H_2CO_3	Carbonated water	Soft drinks
Citric	$H_3C_6H_5O_7$	Lemon juice	Foods
Hydrochloric	HCl	Muriatic acid	Cleaning agents and chemicals
Nitric	HNO_3	Aquafortis	Dyes and chemicals
Sulfuric	H_2SO_4	Oil of vitriol	Automotive batteries and chemicals

Base	Formula	Common name	Use
Ammonium hydroxide	NH_4OH	Ammonia water	Household cleaners
Calcium hydroxide	$Ca(OH)_2$	Slaked lime	Make mortar
Magnesium hydroxide	$Mg(OH)_2$	Milk of magnesia	Neutralize stomach acid
Potassium hydroxide	KOH	Caustic potash	Manufacture of soap and glass
Sodium bicarbonate	$NaCO_3$	Baking soda	Cooking, baking, and household use
Sodium hydroxide	NaOH	Lye or caustic soda	Manufacture of rayon and soap

TABLE 13.2   Color Reactions from Acid and Base Indicators

Indicator	Very acid	Slightly acid	Neutral	Slightly basic	Very basic
Flower petals from _____ _____					
Grape juice					
Litmus paper:					
red					
blue					
Phenolphthalein					
Red cabbage juice					
Other indicators					

tions produced from acid and base solutions by indicators made from the petals of flowers that can be found in a home garden, at the supermarket, or from the florist shop.

Mr. Zimble will gather several water quality and water testing manuals that the students can use for reference when they study their water samples. These manuals will help them in their analytical chemistry work on Days 11, 12, and 13. He will also borrow a few water analyses test kits from a science teacher who teaches an environmental science course in another high school in the district. Some of the tests that the students can carry out are as follows:

odor	iron
color	magnesium
turbidity	nitrate
acidity	nitrite
alkalinity	phosphate
ammonia-nitrogen	salinity
calcium	sulfate
carbon dioxide	sulfide
chlorides	zinc
chromium	dissolved oxygen
hardness	

Mr. Zimble will make available microscopes and reference material for students to use in identifying pond life and microorganisms that may be in their water samples. In addition, he will ask the municipal water treatment plant lab supervisor to perform the fecal coliform tests on the water samples collected by all of the groups.

Mr. Zimble expects that by the time Days 19 and 20 arrive, the students will be prepared to demonstrate their knowledge of fundamental water chemistry and also address the question regarding the purity of drinking water. Remember, he organized the group investigations so that the class would study water from many places in the community—water pipes, rivers, streams, ponds, lakes, and swimming pools. Further, students would examine many aspects of water, from its structural properties to the microorganisms that often inhabit it. Mr. Zimble felt that the mock town hall meeting would be an excellent activity to end the water unit.

Instructional Objectives

Many educators find it useful to state learning outcomes in instructional objective form. They believe these statements provide succinct descriptions of what students should be able to know and do by the end of the instruction. Instructional objectives are used to guide instruction as well as assessment. Few teachers are able to list all of the instructional objectives for a lesson or unit first, then produce the instructional activities that result in their achievement. Usually teachers find it easier to lay down some of the instruction, then begin to construct the objectives to reflect the desired learning outcomes. Writing and modifying instructional objectives is a continual process. The following list of objectives were constructed by Mr. Zimble for his water unit, after he had developed many of his instructional activities.

1. Predict the behavior of water moving across, up, or down various surfaces and explain the reasons for these occurrences based on the structural and molecular properties of water.

2. Demonstrate capillary action of water and its tendency to rise up in narrow tubes and explain this action based on structural and molecular properties of water.

3. Show the effects of surface tension of water and how it can permit objects to float.

4. Given a list of water filtering and purification processes, order them in a sequence that most likely would be used by municipal water treatment plants to make water safe for drinking.

5. Define an acid and a base and give uses for at least four common acids and four common bases.

6. Given a list of common household products, match the products with their corresponding pH values.

7. Explain what an ion is and give an example of a metal, a salt, an acid, and a base ion.

8. Given the symbol of a common element or the formula for a common compound, name the element or compound. Also, when given the name of a compound, write the formula.

9. Participate in a group investigation to analyze water taken from a particular place(s) in the community. Provide a written report of the investigation, giving the reason for conducting the inquiry, the procedures followed, the information gathered, the analyses of the data, and the conclusions.

10. When presented with an article from a newspaper or magazine, or one that would likely appear in these printed sources, interpret the information and evaluate it for factual accuracy and usefulness to the general public.

Grading Specification

Mr. Zimble planned to evaluate the success of the water unit by assessing student performance in a variety of ways. He believes that by using many assessment techniques, a realistic idea of student learning can be ascertained. Further, he believes that the measures he was going to use would reinforce authentic learning as well as help him to evaluate how much students gained from the study of water. The assessment scheme that Mr. Zimble was planning to use is as follows:

Quiz (properties of water, water purification, pH, and ions)	15%
Laboratory exercise (capillary action of water)	5%
Laboratory exercise (filtration and purification of water)	5%
Laboratory exercise (determination of pH in common solutions)	5%
Unit test (water, basic chemistry, and purification and analysis)	35%
Group investigation	35%
Total:	100%

Assessment and Testing

Mr. Zimble had to think deeply about the assessment process, because it must help him to achieve the goals of the new interdisciplinary course that he was assigned to develop. One of the main goals of the course is to help students gain more positive attitudes toward science during their first year in high school. In order to accomplish this aim, the first unit that the freshmen study must set the tone for their high school science course experiences. If the testing and grading are too easy, the students will take science too lightly and they will not be challenged intellectually. If the testing and grading are too difficult, many of the students will be turned off to science.

As Mr. Zimble reflected on the discussions that occurred during his teacher education courses, the words **authentic assessment** and **portfolio assessment** came to mind. He remembered that instruction and assessment should be closely associated and they should reflect real-life situations. He realized that the group investigation could serve as a vehicle to begin a portfolio for the students that would contain evidence of what they had learned during their high school science courses (Collins, 1991). Students would be assembling many items for their group investigations that would start a good portfolio, such as photographs, maps, and diagrams of where they obtained their water samples; charts and tables constructed to present water analysis data; sketches of microorganisms that live in the water samples collected; written arguments regarding the purity of the community's water used during the mock town meeting; and an overview of the inquiry. Mr. Zimble felt that the investigations and the town hall meeting would provide an ideal stimulus to motivate students to do their best work; thus, he would give students as many points for their participation in the group investigation as he would for the unit test. With the help of another teacher and after some discussion with students, he arrived at a point system for grading each student's work and contribution to the group investigation.

In order to make his paper-and-pencil tests promote scientific literacy, Mr. Zimble would provide some realistic situations to which students could apply their knowledge and evaluate information that they might encounter in real life. The thought came to mind to either find a newspaper article for students to examine or to create an article that might appear in a newspaper and require the students to analyze it. Figure 13.2 is a contrived newspaper article that Mr. Zimble wrote for his students to examine and evaluate based on their study of water in the community. In addition to the newspaper article analysis, he included a few test items that involved reading graphs, because he wanted to reinforce science thinking skills throughout the course.

A Concept Map

When all is said and done, what will the students learn from the water unit? Mr. Zimble pondered this question as he thought about the new science course he was responsible for planning and the first unit that he had just developed. He wondered if there were too many activities in the water unit, which might cause the students to focus on the excitement of doing and finding out but miss the science he was attempting to teach them. This introspection motivated him to construct a concept map (shown in Figure 13.3), giving a visual picture of the important content that he felt was embedded

in his unit plan. Do you believe the teacher included enough basic chemistry in this unit, which was designed to familiarize students with some fundamental terms and concepts of solutions chemistry and basic chemistry? In addition, will the students learn some valuable information about water in general?

■ STOP AND REFLECT! ■

As you think about the water unit that Mr. Zimble developed, what is your reaction to his instructional plan?

- Does the "Water in Our Community" unit illustrate the type of high school science education recommended in the reform documents (see Chapter 2), or does it represent a repackaging of traditional science instruction with few changes?
- To what extent does the unit introduce students to fundamental chemistry and teach these facts, concepts, and principles?
- How relevant is the water unit to a high school freshman?
- To what extent does the unit develop scientific literacy?

MEADVIL

Vol. 85 No. 6
Residents Cautioned No Swimming in Green Lake

By Max Pringle
Staff Reporter

Due to recent weather conditions and heavy rains, the bacterial count in Green Lake has risen. The Health Department warns residents against swimming in the lake. Their lab reports show that the coliform count is over 1,000 FC/100 mL, which is higher than normal. Some children and adults may get ear infections at this level of contamination from swimming in the lake. Officials feel this condition is temporary and the bacterial count should go back down in the near future. They advise that swimming in properly chlorinated swimming pools should be safe.

Read the article that appeared in our local newspaper last summer. Based on what you have learned about water purification and water analysis, respond to the following questions.
a. Does the article provide adequate information to average citizens to inform them whether they should or should not go swimming in Green Lake?
   Circle Yes or No. Then explain your response in a short paragraph.
b. Should the coliform count information—1,000 FC/100 ml—be given in parts per million or some other way to convey concentration?
   Circle Yes or No. Then explain your response in a short paragraph.

FIGURE 13.2   This contrived newspaper article was presented on a paper-and-pencil test to students, requiring them to apply what they learned during the study of water in their community.

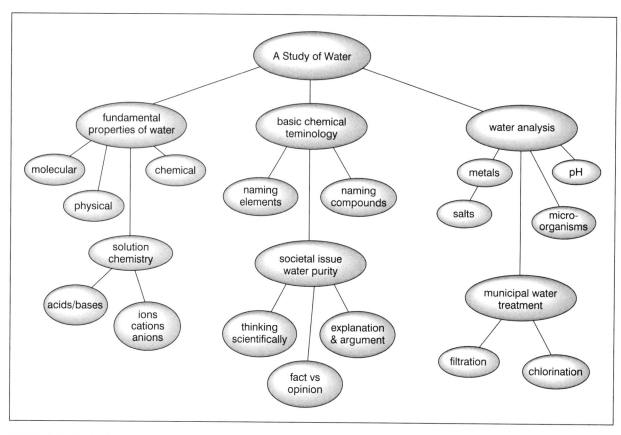

FIGURE 13.3   This concept map highlights the important content contained in the unit, "Water in Our Community."

IDEAS AND ELEMENTS TO CONSIDER FOR PLANNING A SCIENCE UNIT

As stated frequently in this textbook, planning instruction is a key factor in effective teaching. The typical science class contains from eighteen to twenty-five students; some even have over thirty students. These are adolescents, many of whom attend school for reasons other than the desire to learn science. They are concerned about their appearance and how they relate to their friends. These teenagers frequently watch television and are accustomed to entertainment with a great deal of action and sound. Because of their lifestyle, many of the students place little value in studying what they perceive to be science. Given this situation, what type of science course would you present to these students that would engage them in the learning process whereby they construct meaningful knowledge?

New and even experienced science teachers are faced with an enormous challenge to gain students' attention and keep them interested in learning topics that are useful to their lives. How do science teachers organize their courses so that they appeal to students,

yet follow school district and state curriculum guidelines and produce authentic science learning? This is not a trivial question, and it has occupied the thinking of science educators for decades.

The responsibility for planning one's course or even a unit is large, because it requires considerable time, effort, thought, and creativity. These factors often cause teachers to freeze up when engaging in planning. Consequently, they end up following the teaching plans of more experienced colleagues and hastily outline textbook chapters, which they "cover" rather rapidly in the classroom, teaching primarily by definition and explanation to convey a body of science content.

Should science teachers adopt the approach taken by Mr. Zimble? Recall that he began planning by listing many possible topics to include in the new science course. When he identified one of them that he thought would be of high interest to students, he spent a great deal of time selecting activities that would support interest, yet develop students' knowledge of fundamental chemistry. He believed that beginning a unit of study with engaging activities is a good way to get started.

After Mr. Zimble identified many student-centered activities, he then incorporated many other instructional elements into the unit plan. Figure 13.4 shows a list of elements that Mr. Zimble and other science teachers can use to form a complete teaching plan. Again, it must be emphasized that the ten elements listed in the figure are not developed in the order presented during the construction of a unit plan. However, these elements eventually end up as part of the plan after a considerable amount of adding, changing, or omitting material. Given this list of instructional elements, what would you add, change, and omit as you think about the next science unit that you will plan in order to improve the scientific literacy of students and contribute to the science education reform movement that is under way in the United States?

Elements of a Science Teaching Unit Plan

1. Place a **cover page** at the front that gives the title of the unit, the subject, and grade level for which it is intended. Also include your name, professional affiliation, and address.

2. On the next page, write one or more paragraphs giving the **purpose** and **scope** of the unit.

3. Construct a **concept map** or a **visual** representing the concepts and skills to be learned.

4. Present a list of **instructional objectives**, which state all of the learning outcomes for the unit.

5. Provide a list of special **materials/equipment** so that they will be on hand when teaching the unit.

6. Construct a **time frame** that lists the major activities for each day of instruction. Begin with Day 1, Day 2, Day 3, and so on.

7. Present the **grading specifications** for all assignments, labs, tests, effort, and so on with their respective points or percentages.

8. Describe the **instructional activities**.

   a. Partition the unit into sections, each of which includes all of the instruction for a given period or day.

   b. Produce a *detailed* instructional plan, ready to be used without further preparation.

   c. Include many of the following instructional activities plus others that you believe are useful.

   - lecture notes
   - pre- and postlab discussions that engage students in thinking, planning, and connecting what they know with the laboratory work
   - laboratory exercises that you develop or are developed by others
   - readings from textbooks, journals, magazines, and the like
   - videos and films
   - computer simulations, microcomputer-based labs, and so on
   - demonstrations
   - Internet and Web addresses
   - quizzes
   - role-playing and games
   - review and recitation sessions
   - remedial instruction (feedback and correctives)
   - assignments

   Note: You may photocopy items to be included in the unit, such as laboratory exercises, work sheets, games, and the like. However, do *not* photocopy more than 30–50 percent of the pages in the unit. Remember to describe in your own words how each day of instruction will begin, the instructional activities (even if accompanied with photocopied material), questions for review, and pre- and postlaboratory discussions, and so on.

9. Prepare a **unit test**, complete and ready to administer to students. Construct your own quizzes and tests, which must assess the instructional objectives of the unit. Do *not* use a commercially prepared test or quiz that comes with the textbook!

10. **Other assessment instruments** such as those that address attitudes, interests, and projects should be included if they pertain to the unit.

FIGURE 13.4 These elements should be considered when planning and constructing a science teaching unit plan.

ASSESSING AND REVIEWING

1. Scientific literacy is a central idea discussed in this middle and secondary school science methods textbook because scientific literacy has been used by educators for over fifty years to promote the ideals of science education. In Chapter 1, "The Nature of Science," a definition for science is presented along with four themes of scientific literacy. For the definition of science and each of the themes, identify key terms to help you recall their meaning. Then, evaluate the extent to which Mr. Zimble's water unit reflects these aspects of science teaching, which are:

   a. What is science?

   b. Science as a way of thinking

   c. Science as a way of investigating

   d. Science as a body of knowledge

   e. Science and its interactions with technology and society

2. Sharpen your analytical skills further by taking a unit from a science textbook or a teacher-made unit and examining it carefully. From the ideas in this chapter on unit planning, construct a matrix to use in the analysis. Then, analyze the unit based on the extent to which it promotes scientific literacy.

3. Either working alone, with another member of the class, or with a colleague, reorganize a traditional science course in a manner that better reflects a science experience that will significantly improve the scientific literacy of the students for whom it is intended.

   a. List the major topics to be studied and order them in the sequence they will be taught during the school year.

   b. Select one of the topics that you would like to develop into a teaching unit.

   c. Seek out ideas on the unit plan from as many people as possible.

   d. Assemble a large number of resources for ideas of activities and content to include in the unit.

   e. Plan the entire unit so that it is ready to use when the time arrives to implement it. Although you can photocopy some of the material for the unit, it is best to design as many of the activities yourself as possible in order to give the unit your own personal flavor.

RESOURCES TO EXAMINE

Carolina Science and Math Catalog. Carolina Biological Supply Company, 2700 York Road, Burlington, NC 27215-3398. Phone: (800)334-5551.

Carolina is an established science supply company that has a wealth of materials, equipment, and supplies for most every science teaching program. This company also provides a large range of living specimens, which are shipped by air to schools. The company has an extensive list of printed material for instructing students in science. Their catalog will offer many ideas to teach a variety of science topics and principles.

Chemistry in the Community (ChemCom). 1993. Produced by the American Chemical Association and published by Kendall/Hunt Publishing Company in Dubuque, Iowa 52004-1840. Phone: (800)258-5622.

This course is designed to help students realize the important role that chemistry will play in their personal lives and perhaps in their work. Knowledge of chemistry is used during instruction to assist students to make informed decisions about science and technology. The textbook topics are relevant to everyday living. The instructional activities and laboratory exercises can be used in other science courses in addition to chemistry. Because of the useful activities and information it contains, the *ChemCom* textbook is one that all middle and high school science teachers should have in their professional library.

Lawrence Hall of Science.   Registration Office, University of California at Berkeley, Berkeley, CA 94720. Phone: (510)642-5134.

The Lawrence Hall of Science has produced a large number of innovative instructional materials for the science classroom. The Lawrence Hall of Science has many other instructional materials to examine for use in improving the scientific and mathematics literacy of students.

National Science Education Standards.   1996. National Academy Press, 2101 Constitution Ave. NW, Box 285, Washington, DC 20055. Phone: (800)624-6242 or (202)334-3313 (in the Washington area).

This 243-page booklet gives an overview of what should take place to achieve a successful science education reform. It gives science standards for teaching, professional development, assessment, science content, and science programs. All science teachers should have a copy of this booklet for frequent reference.

Science For All Americans.   1990. Produced by the American Association for the Advancement of Science, New York: Oxford University Press.

Read the first chapter, "The Nature of Science." This important document offers a very clear presentation on what science is. All science teachers should have a copy of this book in their professional library and refer to it for guiding their understanding of science teaching.

REFERENCES

American Association for the Advancement of Science. (1993). *Benchmarks for science literacy.* New York: Oxford University Press.

American Association for the Advancement of Science. (1990). *Science for all Americans.* New York: Oxford University Press.

Clark, L. H., & Star, I. S. (1996). *Secondary and middle school teaching methods.* Upper Saddle River, NJ: Merrill/Prentice Hall.

Collins, A. (1991). Portfolios for assessing student learning in science: A new name for a familiar idea? In G. Kulm & S. M. Malcolm (Eds.), *Science assessment in the service of reform* (pp. 291–300). Washington, DC: American Association for the Advancement of Science.

National Research Council. (1996). *National science education standards.* Washington, DC: National Academy Press.

National Science Teachers Association. (1992). *Scope, sequence and coordination of secondary school science. Volume 1: The content core.* Arlington, VA: Author.

■

PART FOUR

ASSESSMENT IN SCIENCE TEACHING

CHAPTER 14

Assessing Learning Outcomes

ASSESSING LEARNING OUTCOMES

Good assessment programs should include investigative projects.

An important aspect of the current reform in science education involves reforming science classroom assessment. For decades, paper-and-pencil tests have served as the primary—and in some classrooms, the only—means of assessing students' science understandings. They are now viewed as woefully inadequate for the job of assessing all of what students know and can do in science. Alternative assessment methods, including portfolios, open-ended questions, and performance tasks, are now used by many teachers to provide a more comprehensive picture of students' science understandings and capabilities. Scoring rubrics are used in conjunction with alternative assessments to make judgments about students' work. An important consideration in the use of these assessments is their authenticity with regard to the world beyond the classroom and the work scientists do.

An expanded view of assessment also makes it an integral part of the teaching and learning process. Assessment is used not only to determine final achievement and grades, but is applied before and during instruction to diagnosis student learning problems, monitor student progress, and guide teacher planning. This expanded view of assessment and the use of alternative assessment methods have the potential to make learning and assessment a seamless process and to greatly improve the science education received by all students.

OBJECTIVES

This chapter is designed to help the reader meet the following objectives:

- Distinguish between alternative, authentic, and performance assessment and compare them to traditional assessment practices.

- Describe several concepts important to the implementation of an effective classroom assessment program.

- Devise procedures for assessing outcomes in the affective and psychomotor domains.

- Write test items of various types that can be used to assess student thinking at the six levels of Bloom's taxonomy.

- Describe alternatives to paper-and-pencil tests that can be used to assess learning outcomes in science.

- Explain useful procedures and techniques for scoring assessments and assigning final grades.

RECONCEPTUALIZING ASSESSMENT

Assessment is much more than testing and giving grades. It is the guiding force in what and how teachers teach and what students learn. Teachers organize their lessons to ensure that students do well on classroom and standardized tests. Students tend to be more focused during lessons when they know they will be tested on the material covered. It is this critical relationship between assessment and teaching and learning that has led to an expanded view of assessment, one brought to the forefront of the reformation that is now sweeping science education.

There are a number of reasons for rethinking assessment in science education at the present time. Hein and Price (1994, pp. 3–7) identify four of them. First of all, traditional paper-and-pencil tests are inadequate to assess all the outcomes associated with science learning. Tests tend to provide information about what students do not know rather than what they know and can do. Second, the content of the science curriculum is changing. The focus is no longer on learning isolated facts and concepts but on learning less content and only the content that will be important for students in the future. Third, everyone from the man on the street to the president of the United States is calling for increased accountability in schools. People want to know what they are getting for their tax dollars. Assessment is necessary to determine what science American students are learning and how they compare with students in other countries. Finally, according to Hein and Price, much has been learned in recent years about how students learn. Notions about how students construct knowledge by interacting with materials and each other have greatly influenced current thinking about learning and thus about assessment.

The *National Science Education Standards* (National Research Council [NRC], 1996) speak forcefully about classroom assessment. According to the *Standards*, the focus of assessment should not be limited to student understanding of scientific facts, concepts, principles, and theories. Assessment must provide information about students' ability to inquire and reason scientifically, to use science to make decisions that are both personal and society related, and to communicate effectively about science. Additionally, the *Standards* stress the use of multiple methods to systematically gather information and the need to involve students as active participants in the assessment process. It is this broadened view of assessment that has led to questions about what kinds of information teachers need to adequately assess student capacity and progress, how the information will be obtained, and how to help students engage in self-assessment.

Contemporary assessment involves the use of many data collection methods, including portfolios, journaling, concept mapping, observation, drawing, and open-ended problems. These various methods and many more are called **alternative** assessments because they offer alternatives to traditional paper-and-pencil tests. Alternative assessments are not meant to replace paper-and-pencil tests but to complement and supplement them. Alternative assessments are **authentic** if they "require students to apply scientific knowledge and reasoning to situations similar to those they will encounter in the world outside the classroom, as well as to situations that approximate how scientists do their work" (NRC, 1996, p. 78). A type of authentic assessment is **performance** assessment, where students are asked to make use of what they have learned (Ochs, 1996). Having students devise a method to purify a sample of river water following a unit on water purification and treatment or set up a saltwater aquarium after learning about ocean life are but two examples of performance assessment. Students come to understand the purpose for their learning when they work with the teacher to devise evaluation criteria for these tasks. Authentic assessment also implies compatibility between instructional objectives and assessment procedures (Rakow, 1992). For example, consider this objective: Students will construct a weather vane and an anemometer and use them along with a compass to determine wind speed and direction. An authentic assessment for this objective is to have students actually build the weather instruments and use them. Having students take a paper-and-pencil test to assess their ability to construct and use these weather instruments is not compatible with the instructional objective.

These contemporary methods have their advantages and disadvantages, and the teacher has to decide on the method or methods best suited to obtain the needed information. To carry out the assessment process, Ten-Brink (1990, p. 339) suggests the following steps:

1. *Preparing.* Determine the kind of information that is needed in addition to deciding how and when to obtain it.
2. *Gathering information.* Collect a variety of information as accurately as possible.
3. *Forming judgments.* Make judgments by comparing the collected information to select criteria.
4. *Making decisions and preparing reports.* Record important findings followed with appropriate forms of action.

These steps should be considered in both the formative and summative phases of the assessment process.

There is little doubt that assessment is one of the most sophisticated teaching functions, and, therefore, there is a definite need to understand the process and its concepts in the role of a teacher. Understanding the assessment process means that teachers should not regard testing and assessment as synonymous. Paper-and-pencil tests represent only one of the many methods of assessment. There is no one best way to assess the outcomes of learning in the cognitive, affective, and psychomotor domains. A multitude of alternative assessment methods exist for use in science classes. The important work for science teachers is to select appropriate assessments that match their learning objectives and to use them well to obtain information that tells what students know and can do.

OBJECTIVES AND ASSESSMENT

Effective science teachers know that well-constructed assessments can serve many purposes, particularly focusing attention on specific learning outcomes, reinforcing learning outcomes, and assessing learning outcomes. They are careful to construct assessments that correspond with the objectives they have stated for their units and course of study.

Instructional objectives specify what students should know and be able to do at the end of instruction, and assessments are used to determine if objectives have been met. Effective science teachers construct assessments that assess the outcomes specified by their instructional objectives. They do not, for example, use test items that require low levels of thinking to assess objectives that specify complex understandings. They do their best to match assessments with their objectives. They may, on occasion, develop an assessment that addresses the broad understandings of a topic (involving a set of objectives) even though an instructional objective had not been constructed originally for this purpose. It may have been omitted accidentally by the teacher during planning. The teacher will then revise the original objectives for a course or unit to include the missing objective. In general, some flexibility is sometimes necessary during assessment development, but congruence between instructional objectives and assessments should be the rule.

■ STOP AND REFLECT! ■

Before going on, do the following:

- Think back on how you were assessed in your middle school and high school science classes. What assessment methods were used? Were the assessments authentic?

- Examine Box 14.1, "Energy and Matter in Mr. Farmore's Class." How do the assessment practices used by Mr. Farmore compare to those that you remember from middle school and high school?

IMPORTANT CONCEPTS IN ASSESSMENT

There are several important concepts in assessment that teachers must understand in order to implement assessment as an integral part of the teaching process. Diagnostic assessment, formative assessment, and summative assessment are three of these concepts. Other important concepts are norm referenced measurements, criterion-referenced measurements, reliability, and validity.

Diagnostic Assessment

Diagnostic assessment can occur before the beginning of a unit of instruction or sometimes during the course of instruction, particularly when the teacher anticipates that students will have difficulty with the subject matter. Some teachers prepare and administer pretests or interview students to determine their level of knowledge and understanding of a particular science topic before beginning instruction on that topic. This information helps the teacher plan instruction to take into consideration the cognitive level at which students are functioning before starting a unit. Some teachers prefer to interview students or have them draw pictures in order to collect information about their understanding of and feelings about a science topic at the beginning of a course or in some cases at the beginning of a unit. Journals, concept maps, and solutions to open-ended problems can also be examined to provide insight into students' thoughts, skills, and feelings.

Diagnostic measurements can also be useful to collect information about a student's knowledge and understanding during the course of instruction. Teachers who find that students are functioning at a high level based on the information gathered can provide them with enrichment activities to take care of their needs. Students who are having difficulties and/or are functioning at a low level can be given remedial work to help them overcome their problems.

Formative Assessment

Formative assessment is usually carried out during instruction in order to assess student progress and learning. The teacher can use the feedback to reinforce students in areas in which they are performing well and indicate to them where they can make improvements. Formative assessments should be used throughout the entire instructional period to guide student learning and provide continuous feedback to help students shape

BOX 14.1

■

ENERGY AND MATTER IN MR. FARMORE'S CLASS

Students entering Mr. Farmore's classroom at the start of the school year knew what to expect, after all they were eleventh and twelfth graders. In chemistry, they knew they would listen to lectures, take notes, discuss chemistry topics, work problems, and engage in laboratory work. They also knew that their understanding of chemistry would be assessed by weekly quizzes, homework, laboratory reports, unit tests, and an occasional project.

Mr. Farmore's students were not at all ready for what they experienced. Before starting the unit on energy and matter, Mr. Farmore interviewed groups of students to find out what they knew and wanted to know about energy and matter. He also gave them some algebra problems to work to find out if he needed to review how to solve for the variable X. He used this information to modify his plans, tailoring his instruction to the needs of the students.

During laboratory, Mr. Farmore walked around with a checklist. The checklist enabled him to monitor the work of the entire class and to indicate the accomplishments of individual students. On occasion, he would also conduct brief interviews with groups of students or individuals as they worked in lab. Different types of checklists were used to document the dialog that occurred during these interviews. Laboratory reports not only asked students to describe their procedures and report their results, but to speculate about how the laboratory could be modified to produce different results.

Homework was not entirely what the students expected, either. In addition to answering the questions found at the end of the chapter, students were asked to draw pictures and construct concept maps to show their understanding of the relationships between energy and matter concepts. Homework often included open-ended problems that encourage higher-order thinking but have no right or wrong answers.

Some of Mr. Farmore's tests were performance based. On one test, students were presented with a problem having to do with recycling metals. The problem involved determining the density of the different metal pieces to identify the metals and into which recycling bin they should be placed. Another item on the same test asked students to use objects in the classroom to demonstrate their understanding of kinetic-potential energy transformations. One student used the spring from the inside of her ballpoint pen, and another used his ruler to demonstrate his understanding of kinetic-potential energy transformations. Another test was given during a laboratory session. Students were presented with a question and asked to design and conduct an experiment to address the question. Scoring rubrics were used to assess student work. Of course, Mr. Farmore approved all experiment designs before the students did the work. Students had difficulty determining where instruction ended and assessment began.

Mr. Farmore also required the students in his chemistry classes to maintain a portfolio. He explained that the portfolio was to be a collection of each student's chemistry work. He instructed the students to put into a working portfolio all of their completed homework assignments, completed work sheets, concept maps, weekly quizzes, laboratory reports, and the lecture notes they personally took during class. Near the end of the grading period, students selected ten items from their working portfolios to include in their permanent portfolios. The items were chosen to show individual progress during the grading period.

their own behavior and improve their learning. Formative assessment is not high-stakes assessment. Many teachers choose not to give grades for formative assessments. Those teachers who do tend not to weight the grades on formative assessments heavily when determining final grades.

Summative Assessment

Summative assessment is the final phase in an assessment program. It occurs at the end of instruction and assesses the overall situation or achievement. It often focuses on a comprehensive range of behaviors, skills, and knowledge. The most common examples in education are the unit test and final exam. The results of summative assessments are used to determine final achievement or performance and grades.

It should be virtually impossible for a classroom observer to know if an assessment is diagnostic, formative, or summative. The same questions or assessment task could serve all three functions. What distinguishes the three is how the information gathered from the assessment is used.

Norm-Referenced Assessments

Norm-referenced measurements are used to discriminate among individuals and often to categorize them. They rank and compare students in areas such as scholastic aptitude, language proficiency, and academic attainment. Norm-referenced data can be used to group students by ability and knowledge. The SAT (Scholastic Aptitude Test) and IQ test, for example, are norm-referenced instruments that provide scores that show students how they compare with others in a prescribed population. Standardized science achievement tests are also norm-referenced, and some can be used to predict how well a student will perform in a particular science area or a course.

Often, norm-referenced achievement tests are developed by drawing from a large and general body of subject matter, and the items are selected for their ability to discriminate among students. There are certain test items that high-scoring students will answer correctly, and low-scoring students will answer incorrectly. In common practice, many teachers do not adhere to this process for developing a test to be used for norm-referenced purposes, but they will use it for norm-referenced grading. Norm-referenced grading is discussed later in this chapter.

Criterion-Referenced Assessments

Criterion-referenced measurements asses how well a particular student is progressing or achieving the objectives in a course. These measurements are used to assess knowledge and skills developed in specific areas. The test items are developed from a limited body of subject matter, and success on these items is judged against predetermined criteria or standards. Students are judged to be successful or unsuccessful based on their performance relative to criteria that have been stated for success or mastery. For example, a science teacher may indicate that students who receive at least seventeen out of twenty possible points on a laboratory practical will receive an S (satisfactory), and those students who receive less than seventeen points will receive a U (unsatisfactory).

Criterion-referenced programs were popular in the 1960s when individualized instruction was being implemented in many schools throughout the country. These programs focused on student achievement of specific learning outcomes. One particular approach, mastery learning, allowed students to work at their own pace to master a body of science material. In these courses students were required to achieve a certain percentage of the objectives specified for a unit or block of work. The mastering of the material was determined after the students took a test in which they were required to receive a certain percentage, such as 70 percent, 80 percent, or another predetermined score, before going on to the next topic. If such competence was not demonstrated, students were required to continue studying the topic until mastery was achieved. Remedial instruction was also provided to help students achieve a level of proficiency. The teacher in these courses predetermined the standards for earning an A, B, C, D, or F before the students began the course. Therefore the teacher did not need to compare test results of students or grade them on a curve to arrive at a grade.

Reliability

Reliability is another word for consistency. When speaking about assessment, reliability refers to the stability of a measuring device over time (Borg & Gall, 1983). An example of unreliability would be a chemistry test on which a student scores 50 percent on one day and 85 percent four days later without receiving any instruction on the topic. Likewise, a genetics test consisting of one essay question would also be an unreliable test because equally strong biology students may or may not know the answer to the particular question. A more reliable test would be one that includes multiple questions on a variety of genetics topics.

Reliability must also be considered when two forms of the same assessment are used. Would a student's score be the same for Form-A of a test as for Form-B? Alternate forms of the same test should match one another in terms of question type, content, and thinking skills required. Comparisons between students may also be made when nonparallel assessment forms are used so long as the assessments address the same broad content or inquiry standard, according to the *National Science Education Standards* (NRC, 1996). This means, for example, that a student should be able to formulate a testable hypothesis in either a biology or chemistry context having had equal opportunity to study both subjects in high school.

Closely related to reliability is the issue of confidence. Confidence in the judgment made regarding a student's performance can also be increased by collecting data on more than one occasion and using multiple data collection methods (NRC, 1996). This means that a teacher ought to be more certain of his or her decision in assigning grades when the grades are based on information gathered from five different assessments over a three-week period than on information from only one test given on Friday of the third week.

Validity

Validity is the degree to which an assessment measures what it is supposed to measure. For example, a valid test on the earth's landmasses would include questions about continents and topography. However, a test reported to assess students' understanding of the earth's landmasses that included questions about wind currents, properties of ocean water, or layers of the atmosphere would be invalid. In the same vein, a valid assessment of students' ability to design and conduct an experiment to test the effect of moisture on seed germination would not be a paper-and-pencil test. A more appropriate form would be a performance task in which students actually design and conduct an experiment. These two examples illustrate **content** and **form validity**, respectively (NRC, 1996). Both types of validity are important to consider when writing or selecting science assessments.

A third type of validity important to teachers is **predictive validity**. Assessments of high predictive validity are often used in schools for placement of students into special programs or classes. An example of an assessment with high predictive validity would be one where students who performed well on the assessment administered before beginning a chemistry class did well in the

class, and students who performed poorly on the assessment performed poorly in the class.

As the brief overview of these concepts reveals, assessment is a broad teaching function involving more than averaging scores and assigning grades. Assessments can be used to diagnose student ability and readiness to learn, guide teacher planning, gather information about student learning, and determine the level of student accomplishment. Assessments can be used to compare and categorize students and to determine their attainment relative to a specified objective. Furthermore, assessments must be both reliable and valid for people to have confidence in assessment data and the judgments made from them.

■ STOP AND REFLECT! ■

Before going on to the next topic, do the following:

▪ Reexamine Box 14.1, "Energy and Matter in Mr. Farmore's Class." What assessment practices used by Mr. Farmore do you consider formative? summative? Detail the reasons for your choices.

▪ Compare and contrast norm-referenced assessment and criterion-referenced assessment. How are they the same? How are they different?

▪ Describe an assessment for the following objective that is valid in both content and form.

Objective: Using two bobs of different lengths, identify the factors that influence the period of a pendulum by demonstrating how each factor influences the period of a pendulum.

Assessing Affective Outcomes

Most school science programs emphasize cognitive goals and neglect goals in the affective domain, which are concerned with attitudes, interests, and values. Only recently have middle and secondary school science programs been interested in the identification of goals within the affective domain, because it is evident that student interests and attitudes play an important part in the learning environment and in the learning process. Science teachers and science educators believe that the affective domain should not be neglected even though outcomes are difficult to measure.

Taxonomy of Educational Objectives, Handbook II, by Krathwohl, Bloom, and Masia (1964) is concerned with the affective domain. The taxonomy is divided into five levels: receiving, responding, valuing, organizing, and characterization by a value or value complex. These terms and levels of taxonomy present problems when science teachers attempt to translate what they really mean. Also, clear-cut boundaries within the domain cannot be exactly defined because they do not exist. How does one separate attitudes and adjustments, or attitudes and feelings, self-reliance and confidence, thoroughness and precision? Klopfer (1976), Gronlund (1973), Nay and Crocker (1970), and Eiss and Harbeck (1969) have analyzed the affective domain and its levels. Their analyses are useful to science teachers who are interested in measuring affective outcomes and will aid them in understanding the five levels stated by Krathwohl and colleagues.

Measuring Affective Outcomes

Using scales is one way to assess affective outcomes. Scales are easy to administer and they provide quantitative scores that enable student and class comparisons. Semantic differential and Likert scales are the two most commonly used types.

Semantic Differential Scales.   One technique by Osgood, Succi, and Tannenbaum (1967) that has been extensively tried makes use of a set of bipolar adjectives that are relevant to and describe a situation (e.g., classroom environment), an idea, or a school subject, such as science or mathematics. The adjectives or terms relate to the situation, idea, or object to which the student reacts. The adjectives used in the measures are contrasting terms such as *bad/good*, *right/wrong*, *heavy/light*, and *fast/slow*. The terms are arranged in pairs (opposites), and the students check a space along a continuum between the contrasting extremes that describes their perceptions. Measures of this type can be constructed to determine students' likes and dislikes. The bipolar adjectives or descriptive phrases are listed in two columns, and the students are asked to respond to a collection of terms by checking or writing a number between the contrasting terms. Such a scale made up of bipolar terms is referred to as a **semantic differential instrument.**

Standard directions given to students when using a semantic differential instrument are as follows:

Please describe the feelings you have in biology class. There are no right or wrong answers. On the next page you will find the heading "BIOLOGY is. . . . " The rest of the page shows pairs of words you can use to describe your feelings about biology. Each pair of words is on a scale like this:

good   7   6   5   4   3   2   1   bad

Circle the number that best represents how you feel about biology. If you think biology is extremely good, you would circle 7. If you think biology is neither good nor bad, circle 4. If you feel that biology is bad, then circle 1.

Your first impressions are desired, so work rapidly and do not go back and change any marks. Be sure to circle only one number for each item.

BIOLOGY is...

good	7	6	5	4	3	2	1	bad
useful	7	6	5	4	3	2	1	useless
important	7	6	5	4	3	2	1	unimportant
interesting	7	6	5	4	3	2	1	boring
easy	7	6	5	4	3	2	1	hard

Another set of adjectives can be used to measure a student's self-perception in a science class. The extremes in an instrument of this type might consist of (In science class, I am . . . ") good/bad, interested/bored, involved/uninvolved, happy/sad, careful/careless, lazy/industrious.

Bipolar adjective scales are also used to operationalize Fishbein and Ajzen's (1975) reasoned action model. This model has been used in science education to assess students' intentions toward such science-related behaviors as enrolling in high school chemistry, participating in science fairs, and becoming the partner of a classmate who might have AIDS (Simpson, Koballa, Oliver, & Crawley, 1994). The basic instrument is constructed by first specifying the behavior of interest in terms of the (a) overt action, (b) the object of the action, (c) the situation in which the action is to take place, and (d) the time at which the action is to occur. An example that illustrates the inclusion of these four components in an action statement is: To enroll (action) in high school (context) AP physics (target) next school year (time). Items are then constructed to measure intention to engage in the behavior, attitude toward the behavior, and subjective norm, which reflects the influence of significant others. These three variables are measured because, according to the model, intention is the best predictor of behavior, and personal attitude and subjective norm are the two determinants of intention. The strength of the attitude and subjective norm scores indicates whether personal feelings or significant others are more influential in determining one's intentions. Items that would be used to assess the three components specified by the model are shown in Figure 14.1. The determinants of attitude and subjective norm can also be identified by questioning students about their beliefs regarding the behavior of interest. The following questions can be used for that purpose:

- What do you see as the advantages and disadvantages of your (insert target behavior)?
- Who are the groups or people who would approve or disapprove of your (insert target behavior)? (Crawley & Koballa, 1994, p. 43)

Likert Scales.   Science attitudes can be measured using a scaling method devised by Renis Likert (1932). Likert scales are easily constructed by using declarative statements in either positive or negative terms relevant to the area, subject, or topic being assessed. A five-point scale is used, and the student checks or circles a position on the continuum. The terms usually used are strongly agree (SA), agree (A), undecided (U), disagree (D), and strongly disagree (SD). Other symbols such as numbers can be used—5, 4, 3, 2, 1.

Standard Likert scale directions and an attitude-toward-science scale follow:

Each of the statements on this questionnaire expresses a feeling or attitude toward science. You are asked to indicate on a five-point scale the extent of your agreement between the attitude expressed in each statement and your personal feelings. The five points are: strongly agree (SA), agree (A), uncertain (U), disagree (D), and strongly disagree (SD). Draw a circle around the

letter or letters to indicate how closely you agree with the attitude expressed in each statement as it concerns you.

1. I am always under terrible strain in science class.   SA A U D SD
2. I enjoy science class.   SA A U D SD
3. Science is fun.   SA A U D SD
4. I have a good feeling toward science.   SA A U D SD
5. I really like science.   SA A U D SD
6. Science is the subject that I dislike the most.   SA A U D SD
7. I am happier in science class than in any other class.   SA A U D SD
8. I feel more relaxed in science class than in any other class.   SA A U D SD

There are a number of ways to interpret results of such scales. One could compute a weighted mean for each statement or make a frequency distribution of the number of individuals checking each position for each item.

In summary, a great deal of useful information can be derived from semantic differential and Likert-type scales. Assessment of student intentions and attitudes toward a particular science subject or science-related behavior and the influence of significant others, including family and friends, can be determined at the beginning of a unit or science course. The same or a similar

---

Intention

I intend to enroll in high school AP physics next school year.

likely _____:_____:_____:_____:_____:_____:_____unlikely
        extremely quite slightly neither slightly quite extremely

Attitude

My enrolling in high school AP physics next school year is…

good _____:_____:_____:_____:_____:_____:_____bad
valuable _____:_____:_____:_____:_____:_____:_____worthless
beneficial_____:_____:_____:_____:_____:_____:_____harmful
pleasant _____:_____:_____:_____:_____:_____:_____unpleasant

Subjective Norm

Most people who are important to me think I should enroll in AP physics next school year.

likely _____:_____:_____:_____:_____:_____:_____unlikely
        extremely quite slightly neither slightly quite extremely

FIGURE 14.1   Items Used with Fishbein and Ajzen's Reasoned Action Model

instrument can be given at the end of the unit or course to determine if intentions or attitudes have appreciably changed. Similar procedures can be used to determine what interests or values a student has in the beginning of a course and how they have changed by the end of the course. The fact that students often respond to these instruments in ways they think teachers want them to is a reality that must be considered when interpreting the results.

Direct Approaches to Determine Values and Attitudes

The personal interview is another method often used to determine student attitudes, interests, and values. Teachers must take care in the way they pose questions, however, because students have a tendency during interviews, as they do when responding to scales, to answer in such a way as to please the teacher. Questions such as Do you like biology? and Why do you think biology is useful? will produce responses that are intended to please a biology teacher. More honest replies can be obtained by asking questions such as What subjects do you feel secure about? What subjects do you study more than others? Do you like animals? Would you like to dissect a frog? Do you like plants? Does it make you nervous to perform an experiment in the science laboratory? Such indirect questions can give teachers much information about a student, usually more than is possibly obtained from responses to a scale. An excellent battery of questions can be constructed if teachers know their students well—particularly their hobbies, interests, and career choices. Questions can be constructed to help the teacher identify values without suggesting to students the types of responses the teacher might consider desirable.

Student values, appreciations, and attitudes can also be determined by reading students' science journals. Desired information can be obtained by guiding students' writing through prompts such as one of the following: (a) "Physics is a very interesting area of study. I like it more than any other subject I am taking." State why you agree or disagree with this statement. (b) "Chemistry is boring and useless to me." Do you agree or disagree? State and explain your reasons. (c) State why you like or dislike performing an experiment in the physics laboratory.

What students say during interviews and write in their journals can help teachers determine the type of teaching environment they are providing for their students. These responses can also give teachers information about the effectiveness of their teaching and the attitudes of their students toward a subject or unit of study. They can help teachers determine how interested stu-

dents are in the subject being taught. The feedback can help teachers improve their instruction and revise the science curriculum.

ASSESSING PSYCHOMOTOR OBJECTIVES

The laboratory is the place where students design and perform experiments, manipulate equipment, and use the processes of science—ask questions, formulate hypotheses, interpret data, and so on. It is the place where they use higher-order thinking skills such as analysis, synthesis, and logical reasoning. The skills that students apply in the laboratory cannot be adequately assessed when using paper-and-pencil tests alone (Tamir, 1990).

Laboratory outcomes are concerned not only with the cognitive and affective domains but also the psychomotor domain, the third major area of objectives categorized by Krathwohl et al. (1964). The psychomotor domain is very relevant to science, because laboratory activities require students to perform such tasks as manipulating equipment, mixing solutions, preparing slides for observation under a microscope, and using computers and calculators. The list is almost endless.

The teacher can assess students' abilities and skills in the laboratory by observing students engage in certain performance assessment tasks. These tasks may be embedded in the actual work done by students in the laboratory. The observations shown in Figure 14.2 can be made by the teacher to determine how well a student can manipulate, focus, and use a microscope. The teacher checks one of three categories as the observations are made.

Such checklists involving observations made by the teacher in a one-to-one situation are time-consuming. However, checklists or scales of this type can be developed for different situations involving the assessment of laboratory skills. The degree to which a student can perform a given task or skill on such checklists can be determined by checking Yes or No, or one of a set of alternatives, each of which represents a particular level of skill performance for a particular task or aspect of the task. For example, 1, 2, 3, 4, and 5 could represent (1) excellent, (2) good, (3) fair, (4) passable, and (5) inadequate.

Some teachers prefer to assess laboratory skills through different types of laboratory assessment tasks or practicals. When students perform these tasks, teachers may use a checklist similar to those involving direct observations but adapted to assess laboratory performance or use a scoring rubric. The use of a checklist or scoring rubric gives the teacher a more objective evalua-

E = excellent; A = adequate; I = inadequate

Gross body movements

1. Removes microscope from its case or space in the storage cabinet. Grasps the arm of the instrument with one hand and places the other hand under the base.   E   A   I
2. Sets the microscope down gently on the table with the arm toward student and stage away from student. The base should be a safe distance from the edge of the table.   E   A   I
3. Uses a piece of lens paper to wipe the lenses clean.   E   A   I
4. Clicks the lower power objective into viewing position.   E   A   I
5. Adjusts the diaphragm and mirror for the best light.   E   A   I
6. Places a prepared slide of human hair on the stage so that it is directly over the center of the stage opening.   E   A   I
7. Secures the slide in place with the stage clips.   E   A   I
8. Looks to the side of the microscope and slowly lovers the low-power objective by turning the coarse adjustment wheel until the objective almost touches the slide.   E   A   I
9. While looking through the eyepiece, with both eyes open, slowly turns the coarse adjustment so that the objective rises. The hair should become visible.   E   A   I
10. Brings the hair into sharp focus by turning the fine adjustment wheel.   E   A   I
11. Shows the properly focused slide to teacher.   E   A   I
12. Focuses the hair under high power and shows this properly focused slide to teacher.   E   A   I
13. Prepares to return microscope to storage area; turns the low-power objective into viewing position and adjusts it approximately 1 cm above stage.   E   A   I
14. Returns the microscope, handling by the arm and base, to storage place.   E   A   I

Finely coordinated movements

The following observations are made by the teacher, who judges how well a student can prepare and stain materials for observation under a microscope.

Preparation and staining of an onion cell wet mount slide

1. Rinses a microscope slide with water and wipes both sides with a clean, soft cloth.   E   A   I
2. Rinses and dries a cover glass.   E   A   I
3. Cuts an onion lengthwise and removes a thick slice.   E   A   I
4. Peels the delicate tissue from the inner surface.   E   A   I
5. Uses a medicine dropper to place a drop of water in the center of slide.   E   A   I
6. Places a small section of onion tissue in the drop of water.   E   A   I
7. Lowers the cover glass over the onion skin.   E   A   I

8. Staining the specimen: adds a drop of iodine stain along the edge of the cover glass.   E   A   I
9. Places a small section of a paper towel on the opposite side of the cover glass. This will draw the stain across the slide by capillary action.   E   A   I

FIGURE 14.2   Example of a Checklist to Assess Psychomotor Objectives

tion in assessing students' understandings related to laboratory work. The teacher can measure psychomotor responses and other outcomes when using checklists or scoring rubrics. The time factor when using such forms of assessment should be considered. It is not unusual to devote several hours to set up and administer performance assessments to groups of students. The other considerations for using performance assessments include availability of enough equipment for class members, availability of equipment that is in good condition, and a set of clear and concise directions that the students can follow.

Checklists and scoring rubrics can be structured to assess practical laboratory skills such as setting up apparatus to produce chlorine in the chemistry laboratory or conducting an acid-base titration. Several models of checklists and scoring rubrics are available in the literature and some are discussed later in this chapter. These models can be used not only to assess practical psychomotor skills but also for other outcomes such as the ability to design experiments, make quantitative and qualitative observations, handle certain calculations, analyze and interpret, predict, formulate hypotheses, and apply techniques to new problems.

■ STOP AND REFLECT! ■

Before going on to the next topic, do the following:

■ Describe one way to assess affective outcomes of science instruction.

■ Explain what a teacher might do to ensure that the affective information she or he gathers is reflective of students' actual feelings and not an attempt to please.

■ Identify several psychomotor skills associated with laboratory work that a teacher may wish to assess. How can checklists or scoring rubrics be used to make the evaluation of psychomotor skills more objective?

SCIENCE TESTS

Tests are an important part of science assessment. Science teachers need to be able to construct tests that do an effective job of assessing student progress. Test construction may involve teachers writing test items or selecting items from computer test banks. Most new science programs now come with test banks that provide a wide array of items. Science teachers must prepare or have access to a variety of test items that can be used to assess lower and higher levels of cognitive thinking and laboratory skills. In order to construct valid and reliable tests that assess student achievement and instructional effectiveness, teachers need to be familiar with the different types of test items and know how test items can be used to assess a variety of cognitive processes.

Classifying Test Questions

Many classifications for describing different types of test questions have been developed. These classification systems provide a framework for examining test questions. One system widely used by teachers is Bloom's (1956) taxonomy of cognitive objectives.

Bloom's taxonomy classifies educational objectives and questions into six cognitive levels, each of which requires the use of different types of thought processes. The six levels are:

1. Knowledge
2. Comprehension
3. Application
4. Analysis
5. Synthesis
6. Evaluation

Teachers who understand the taxonomy and learn what encompasses each of the six levels are able to write questions that require students to use a variety of cognitive processes, not only those that involve factual recall.

The knowledge level of Bloom's taxonomy requires students to remember facts they have already learned, whereas the comprehension level of the taxonomy requires students to select facts that have been learned and to organize, arrange, and interpret them. Words often used in constructing knowledge-level test items are *when*, *where*, *who*, *what*, and *define*. Even though knowledge-level questions stress the acquisition of information, they also encourage the memorization of facts that are later forgotten. In contrast, comprehension-level questions ask students to make comparisons, rephrase information using their own words, and interpret graphs, tables, and cartoons. Comprehension questions often make use of such words as *compare*, *contrast*, *describe*, *show*, and *explain*. Teachers should include both knowledge- and comprehension-level questions on their tests but not overuse them. Examples of knowledge- and comprehension-level test question follow.

Knowledge

1. Which of the following is a disaccharide?
   a. Glucose
   b. Glycerol
   c. Cellulose
   d. Sucrose

2. Define the following:
   a. Erg
   b. Work
   c. Mass
   d. Weight
   e. Power

Comprehension

1. $Li_2O + 2HF \rightarrow 2Lif + H_2O$

   The above reaction is best shown by
      a. $A + B \rightarrow AB$
      b. $AB \rightarrow A + B$
      c. $AB + CD \rightarrow AD + BC$
      d. $AB + CD \rightarrow BA + CD$

2. If a red blood cell is placed in a concentrated salt solution, it will most likely

    a. swell

    b. shrink

    c. remain the same

    d. divide by mitosis

The next four levels of Bloom's taxonomy (level 3, application; level 4, analysis; level 5, synthesis; and level 6, evaluation) are concerned with higher-level thinking. They involve such science skills as examining variables, problem solving, critical thinking, hypothesis generating, hypothesis testing, and drawing conclusions. These same reasoning skills tend to be the focus of open-ended questions and performance assessment tasks described later in this chapter. Tests that purport to assess science process skills are characterized predominately by application, analysis, synthesis, and evaluation questions. They require considerable thought and imagination to develop and construct. Some questions can be constructed to assess only one skill at a time; others can be more complex, involving the use of several process skills.

The application level requires that students solve problems by identifying relevant information and rules to arrive at a solution. The analysis level requires that students separate an idea into parts or elements and demonstrate an understanding of the relationship of the parts to the whole. Words frequently used in application questions include *solve*, *which*, *use*, *classify*, *choose*, *how much*, and *what is*, whereas words often found in analysis questions include *analyze*, *give reasons*, *why*, and *provide conclusions*. Application and analysis questions are frequently used in biology, chemistry, and physics, as the following examples illustrate.

Application

1. In very cold conditions up to 80 percent of the heat generated by the body can be lost through the surface of the head and neck. Which would be the best way to preserve the greatest amount of body heat if you were suddenly caught outside in below-zero weather and all you had to wear were boots, shorts, a T-shirt, and light jacket.

    a. Wrap the jacket around the uncovered portion of your legs.

    b. Leave the jacket on as you usually wear it.

    c. Wrap the jacket around your head and neck.

    d. Use the jacket to keep the nearby air moving.

2. Two disk magnets are arranged at rest on a frictionless horizontal surface as shown in the following diagram. When the string holding them together is cut, they move apart under the magnetic force of repulsion. When the 1.0 kg disk reaches a speed of 3.0 m/sec, what is the speed of the 0.5 kg disk?

    a. 1.0 m/sec

    b. 0.50 m/sec

    c. 3.0 m/sec

    d. 6.0 m/sec

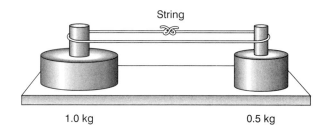

Analysis

1. The following table gives the electrical resistance of five coils of wire at two temperatures. The resistance of each coil changes uniformly between 10 °C and 300 °C. For each of the items written below the table, write in the letter for the coil that satisfies the specification given.

Coil	Resistance at 10 °C (ohms)	Resistance at 300 °C (ohms)
A	100.0	100.3
B	2.50	2.650
C	1.10	0.999
D	0.250	0.300
E	0.021	0.015

___ The coil whose resistance remains most nearly constant as the coil gets hot.

___ The coil whose resistance in the temperature range from 10 °C to 300 °C is to be not greater than 2.5 ohms or smaller than 0.25 ohms and to show as little variation in resistance as possible.

___ The coil whose resistance is most influenced by temperature.

___ The coil whose resistance is to be as low as possible and not decrease along with temperature.

2. Which of the following statements concerning mountain building is largely a hypothesis rather than the statement of fact based on extensive observational evidence?

    a. Deposition of large quantities of erosional material has accumulated in geosynclines.

b. Mountains have been produced by faulting on a gigantic scale.

c. Heavy minerals have tended to sink toward the center of the earth, forcing the lighter segments upward.

d. Mountains have been produced by the differential erosion of rocks.

Questions on the synthesis and evaluation levels promote creativity and require complex thinking. At the synthesis level, students are involved in analyzing patterns and formulating hypotheses to explain them. Evaluation questions require students to make judgments about the value or merits of an idea, purpose, solution to a problem, procedure, method, or product. Synthesis and evaluation questions do not necessarily have one correct answer, but a variety of answers, all of which may be plausible. Unfortunately, some teachers seldom address synthesis and evaluation level objectives in their courses. Consequently, synthesis and evaluation questions are seldom used in their testing programs. The directions used in synthesis questions often use words such as *write*, *predict*, *develop*, *design*, *synthesize*, *produce*, *solve*, *devise*, and *construct*. Words and phrases often found in questions involving evaluation include *assess*, *decide*, *judge*, *argue*, *what is your opinion*, *appraise*, *do you agree or disagree*, *give an evaluation*. Examples of synthesis and evaluation questions follow.

Synthesis

1. Substance X is known to move through cell membranes. You suspect its movement is accomplished by simple diffusion. Design an experiment to test your hypothesis.

2. Dry gases X and Y react readily when mixed in a glass flask. However, if the flask is heated and cooled just before the gases are introduced, no reaction takes place. Develop two hypotheses to explain these observations and state how you would test such hypotheses.

Evaluation

1. Two hypotheses that account for the diversity of species on earth are (a) gradual accumulation of mutations and (b) punctuated equilibrium. Which hypothesis do you favor and why?

2. Sedimentary rocks can be distinguished from other classes on the basis of bedding, color, fossils, ease of breakage, and porosity. Which of these do you feel is the poorest criterion to use as a distinguishing characteristic? Defend your position.

Types of Test Items

Science teachers use many types of test items when constructing tests for their students. Among the most frequently used test items are true-false, multiple-choice, matching, completion, and essay questions.

True-False. True-false items allow students to judge a statement for accuracy. True-false statements are scored either right or wrong and can be used to determine how well students understand a concept, principle, or theory. They can also be used to determine if students can make decisions, evaluate variables, and understand the nature of science and the scientific enterprise. True-false items are easy to write and to grade. A great number of items can be answered in a short period of time, permitting a broad sample of understandings. Unfortunately, much of the subject matter that lends itself to this type of item is relatively unimportant and often tests minutiae. Also remember that the probability of guessing the right answer is 50 percent, which gives unprepared students an excellent chance to provide the correct answer. As the following statements illustrate, true-false items are usually written with a blank to the left of the statement in which students write *T* if the statement is true and *F* if the statement is false.

 F The chemical digestion of starch begins in the stomach.

 T The liver secretes hormones that regulate the storage of glucose.

Multiple-choice. Multiple-choice items include a stem or statement with four or five options or distracters from which the student selects the best answer. Multiple-choice items may involve a lead statement or stem that is incomplete, and the student selects from the options or distracters listed below the statement to make it complete or correct. The lead statement may be in the form of a question, and the student must select the best answer to the question from the options listed. The lead or stem may also be a diagram, a graph, or a chart. Well-written distracters are simple, closely related to the same idea, randomly ordered, and about the same length. Distracters should not include the words *never*, *always*, and *all* because they tend to indicate that the option is not an acceptable response.

The multiple-choice form is very versatile because it can be used to measure both higher-order thinking and knowledge of factual information. These items are also easy to score. Multiple-choice tests usually have a higher validity than other types of tests because test items can be constructed that require the learner to demonstrate fine discrimination. A limitation of multiple-choice items is that they are difficult to construct. It is often difficult to write four or five plausible distracters for each item. When responding to multiple-choice items, students are instructed to write the letter of the correct answer in the blank provided to the left of the stem. Multiple-choice items are presented as examples of knowledge-, comprehension-, and application-level questions in the preceding section.

Matching Items.   Matching-type items are a special kind of multiple-choice question. Instead of having a single stem with its own list of options, as is the case with multiple-choice items, matching items list words, problems, or phrases in one column that must be matched with corresponding items from another column. When responding to a matching item, for example, students are to choose the word or phrase from the list in column B that is most closely related to the word or phrase in column A. Then they write the number of the correct word in the appropriate blank. In the following example, some blanks may contain more than one number.

A	B
__ White light	1. Lens
__ Refraction	2. Mirror
__ Reflection	3. Sun
__ Diffraction	4. Black cloth
__ Absorption	5. Spectrum
	6. Clear glass

To write good matching questions, items selected should include statements, words, or phrases that cover the same general topic or category and be arranged in long lists in some logical order. It is a good idea to make the number of choices greater than the number of statements to which they are to be matched. Matching-type questions are relatively easy to construct, particularly if they are to assess lower-level learning. The difficulty of constructing a matching-type exercise increases if one goes beyond lower-level learning. Also, matching questions take up less space than a series of multiple-choice questions and they keep guessing to a minimum. As is true for multiple-choice items, a well-constructed matching item makes guessing difficult, particularly if the teacher has eliminated most of the clues and has included a sufficient number of items to match.

Completion Items.   Completion or fill-in-the-blank items involve a statement with one or more blanks in which the student provides information to make the statement complete and correct. Completion items usually require recall of information, unlike matching, multiple-choice, and true-false items, all of which involve recogni-

tion. Items can also be written that require a student to perform certain calculations, the results of which go into the blank in the statement. Problems in physics, chemistry, and genetics that require calculations lend themselves to this type of item. Well-written completion items are statements that are not copied directly from a textbook or workbook and they provide an answer blank at the end of the statement that is long enough for the answer.

1. The chemical formula for potassium hydroxide is _____.

2. The number of different types of gametes that can be produced by a male guinea pig whose genotype is BbLlrrSs is _____.

3. The kinetic energy increase of an electron that has been accelerated to a potential difference of 20 million volts is _____.
   (Assume that $1 \text{ eV} = 1.6 \times 10^{-19}$ J.)

There are both advantages and limitations associated with using completion questions. Completion statements are easy to score and permit testing for a wide range of material in a short period of time. However, it is difficult to write unambiguous statements because in many instances several words may be correct responses even though they were not considered during the test construction. Completion statements can rarely be used to test for upper levels of Bloom's taxonomy.

Essay Questions.   Essay questions usually ask students to formulate responses in their own words. Two general types are the restricted type, which limits the scope of responses, and the nonrestricted type, which gives students free rein to respond to the question. In the restricted type, the student either is given an outline that directs the response or is asked to stress certain points in the essay. Examples of restricted essay questions follow:

1. Discuss, compare, and contrast mitosis and meiosis. Point out in your discussion the basic differences between meiosis I and mitosis and between meiosis II and mitosis. Also, discuss the significance of each process. Include diagrams to illustrate and support your discussion.

2. Explain in detail three methods for preparing a base and two methods for preparing an acid.

In contrast, the unrestricted type of essay question gives the student considerable latitude to discuss the topic with no directions. An example of an unrestricted essay question is:

Discuss the statement: The sun is the source of all energy on earth.

In general, essay questions are useful to assess the higher levels of Bloom's taxonomy—analysis, synthesis, evaluation—outcomes that cannot be measured easily through objective-type items. They are excellent to judge the organizational ability of students, as well as determine how well students are able to handle themselves at the higher levels of the cognitive domain. They are also useful for detecting misconceptions.

Essay questions take less time to write than multiple-choice, matching, and completion questions; however, great care must be taken in their construction. Essay questions are more difficult to score objectively because of the variety of responses given by students. It is wise to determine the criteria to be used for scoring while constructing the question. The restricted type questions channel student responses, making them easier to score. When using essay questions, it is important to allow sufficient time for students to respond.

Regardless of the type of question used, the best test questions are simple and direct. Each additional adjective and qualifying clause increases the complexity of the statement and the possibility for misinterpretation and ambiguity. The words used in the test item should be those used while teaching the topic. Generally, the use of short familiar words minimize reading problems associated with test items. It is also important to consider such factors as vocabulary, sentence complexity, the ability of students to understand the question, and the use of diagrams and illustrations to make the questions precise and clear. Factors that may be helpful in rating test questions, particularly multiple-choice types, are listed in Figure 14.3. This list can be used to rate a question to determine its suitability for a particular group of students. According to Rakow and Gee (1987), teachers who use the checklist to examine test items can reduce the reading difficulties that may be preventing students from demonstrating their science knowledge.

■ STOP AND REFLECT! ■

Before going on to the next topic, do the following:

▪ Write two multiple-choice, two true-false, and two completion items that assess comprehension or application of science information. Show your questions to classmates to see if they agree with your classification of the questions as assessing comprehension or application.

▪ Write one essay question that assesses students' ability to synthesize science information. Is it a restricted or nonrestricted type question?

Rate the questions using the following system:

5—Excellent
4—Good
3—Adequate
2—Poor
1—Unacceptable
NA—Not applicable

_____ 1. Students would likely have the experiences and prior knowledge necessary to understand what the question calls for.

_____ 2. The vocabulary is appropriate for the intended grade level.

_____ 3. Sentence complexity is appropriate for the intended grade level.

_____ 4. Definitions and examples are clear and understandable.

_____ 5. The required reasoning skills are appropriate for the students' cognitive level.

_____ 6. Relationships are made clear through precise, logical connections.

_____ 7. Content within items is clearly organized.

_____ 8. Graphs, illustrations, and other graphic aids facilitate comprehension.

_____ 9. The questions are clearly framed.

_____ 10. The content of items is of interest to the intended audience.

FIGURE 14.3 Test Item Readability Check

Reprinted with permission of NSTA Publications from "Test Science, Not Reading," by S. J. Rakow and T. C. Gee, from *The Science Teacher*, November 1987, p. 28, published by The National Science Teachers Association, Arlington, Virginia.

ALTERNATIVE ASSESSMENT

Alternative assessment refers to methods of assessment that are not paper-and-pencil tests. Alternative assessments now being used by science teachers include portfolios, journaling, concept mapping, oral interviews, and many more. Alternative assessments provide the teacher with information about students' backgrounds, cultural differences, and strengths and weaknesses in learning science (Tippins & Dana, 1992). They also provide teachers the opportunity to assess process in addition to product and to gain richer understandings of what students are thinking and how they construct meaning. Alternative assessment methods are **authentic** if they ask students to make use of skills and abilities that are applicable to real-life situations or problems. Reasons for the increasing interest in alternative assessments include their ability to reflect real student learning, create equity in assessing students, and bridge the apparent division between teaching, learning, and assessment (Oppewal, 1996, pp. 125–126). We recommend that alternative assessments be considered along with paper-and-pencil tests as arrows in a teacher's quiver. They can be "pulled out and shot" when their use matches the intended learning objectives and provides the desired information to chart student capability and progress. Let's now examine several of the alternative assessments available to science teachers.

Observation

Science teachers are continuously observing students at work, either at their desks or in the field or laboratory. Observation provides a wealth of information about what students know, need help with, and can do. For example, during a laboratory on chromatography of food dyes, the chemistry teacher might observe if the dye spot is uniformly circular and placed at the correct distance from the bottom of the filter paper strip, if students are wearing safety goggles, or if they are having difficulty measuring the distances traveled by the solute and the solvent. To make observation an effective assessment tool, decisions must be made regarding what informal observations to use to assess student progress or capability. In most cases, it is the teacher who decides what will be observed. Hein and Price (1994, pp. 24–25) offer the following suggestions for deciding what student actions to observe to assess progress in three areas:

- Knowledge Application—Observe how students solve problems, troubleshoot malfunctioning equipment, or try to figure out why an experiment is unsuccessful.

- Information Assimilation—Notice when and how students relate information from trade books [magazines, movies, television, sports events, fun activities, etc.] to what they are doing in class.

- Use of New Vocabulary—Listen to conversations and discussions.

Using observation as an assessment tool in science classes may be difficult. Many middle school and high school teachers meet with more than one hundred different students a day and their instructional objectives are many. To make this form of assessment manageable, a systematic procedure to keep track of observations must be adopted. Many teachers use checklists for this purpose. For example, the checklist shown in Figure 14.4 provides just enough space for check marks to indicate individual student accomplishments and can be used to monitor the work of an entire class of students. It can be used by the teacher while circulating around the room as students work. In contrast, the checklist shown in Figure 14.5 can be used to chart the progress of a single student and includes space for check marks and teacher comments.

Interviews

An effective way to find out what students are thinking and learning in science class is to interview them. An interview is a verbal exchange between the teacher and a student during which the teacher asks questions. It may be open-ended or partially structured (Martin, 1996) and used before, during, or after instruction (Bell, 1995). In an open-ended interview, the teacher asks few questions and listens carefully to what the student has to say. Questions such as What do you know about . . . ? Can you explain your ideas? and Could you tell me how that is used outside of school? are often used in open-ended interviews because they provide insight into how students construct understandings.

A partially structured interview is not as free flowing as the open-ended interview. It is organized around a set of questions written by the teacher ahead of time. Responses to the prepared questions tell the teacher what the student is thinking and understanding and suggests areas for further probing. Probing questions are generated based on the teacher's hypotheses about what the student understands. Often it is the verbal exchange that results from probing questions that reveals the most about what a student has learned from a lesson and where remediation is needed. Questions that a teacher might use for a semistructured interview to determine a student's understanding of continental drift follow:

Class Profile: *Finding the Density of Objects Lab*				
Student's name	Measures mass	Measures volume	Calculates density	Correct units for density (g/ml)

FIGURE 14.4   Checklist for Gathering Information from a Class of Students

- In your own words, what is the theory of continental drift?

- How do scientists explain the existence of the same animal and plant fossils on continents separated by thousands of miles of ocean?

- What rock evidence supports the theory of continental drift?

- How does ocean-floor spreading help explain how continents drift?

- Where are the youngest rocks on the ocean floor found?

- What did scientists learn from their study of the magnetic strips on both sides of the mid-ocean ridge?

The teacher should make the student feel comfortable and describe the purpose of the interview before questioning. When questioning, the teacher should be nonjudgmental and alert to obstacles such as unfamiliar vocabulary and wordy or leading questions that may affect student responses. Using pictures or diagrams as prompts, offering encouragement, and suggesting different ways to think about the question are ways to help students reveal more of what they have learned and understand. It is also helpful to take notes or tape-record the interview so that the student's responses are not forgotten. The interview is a very useful method for gathering information from students who have difficulty expressing themselves in writing.

Lengthy individual interviews are ideal, but hardly practical for use in typical science classes. Berenson and

Checklist of Student Progress for *Finding the Density of Objects Lab*		
Student: _____	Period: _____	

Learning Goals	Checklist	Observations
Using instruments • Uses a balance to measure mass of object • Uses a graduated cylinder to measure volume of object • Uses ruler to measure length of object		

Collecting and recording data
• Determines mass and volume of
  wood block
  metal block
  plastic block
  water
• Organizes data and uses them to calculate density
• Uses correct units of measure for mass, volume, and density		

Identifying relationships • Observes the density of water is 1 g/ml • Observes that objects having a density of <1 g/ml float in water and objects having a density > 1 g/ml sink in water		
Applying understandings • Predicts if the density of a paraffin block is > or < 1 g/ml • Calculates the density of a paraffin block to check prediction		

FIGURE 14.5   Checklist for Gathering Information on a Single Student and Recording Comments

Carter (1995, p. 184) offer suggestions for modifying the one-on-one interview to accommodate the constraints of schools:

1. Interview three or four students as they work together on a project or class assignment.
2. Conduct short, individual interviews while other students are engaged in tasks.
3. Interview students after school, before school, or during lunch, recess, and study periods.
4. Tape student-to-student interviews; provide the questions to student interviewers.

Concept Mapping

Concept mapping is a strategy that can be used for assessment as well as instruction. As presented in Chapter 4 of this textbook, a concept map graphically shows meaningful relationships between science concepts. A concept map can be used in assessment to show growth in understanding as a result of instruction and to infer misconceptions held by a learner either prior to or after instruction (Roth, 1992).

Vargas and Alvarez (1992) present a scoring scheme for concept maps based on a map's **hierarchy, relationships** between concepts, **branching** between one concept and two or more concepts, and **cross-links** that show parallelism between concepts. According to their scheme, one point is awarded for each correct level of the map, for each relationship drawn between two concepts and described by a proposition, and for each cross-link. Additionally, one point is awarded for the initial level of branching and three points are awarded for each incident of branching that occurs at Level 2 or below. For an example of their scoring scheme, examine the concept map shown in Figure 14.6. As can be seen in the figure, the map has three hierarchical levels (three points). It includes seven relationships connected by propositions, such as "Plants are vascular" (seven points). It also includes branches to two concepts at Level 1, yielding one point and, at Level 2, "Vascular" branches once, yielding three points (four points). There is one cross-link between "gametophyte" and "sporophyte" that yields one point. The total score of the map is sixteen points.

When students are asked to construct concept maps, the concepts may be provided for them or they may be asked to generate them without assistance. Students may also be provided with partially completed concept maps and asked to fill in the missing concepts. Additionally, teachers may use a student's concept map as a prompt during an interview. Here the student can be asked to explain the relationships shown on the map. Before using concept maps in assessment, it is important that students be taught how to construct concept maps and provided with opportunities to practice the technique.

Journals

In recent years, more and more science teachers have asked their students to keep science journals. Journal writing is an effective way for teachers to find out what students are thinking and feeling, to provide feedback to students, and to help them improve their writing skills. Many students have come to recognize the journal as a sure way to dialog with the teacher on a one-to-one basis.

A journal has no special format or content requirements. A journal may be kept in a notebook, consist of sheets of paper in loose-leaf binder, or contained on a computer disk. It may include responses to questions given by the teacher, questions written by students that they wish to have answered, reactions to class activities and homework, or spontaneous reflections. Diagrams and drawings may also be included in journals. To promote journaling among science students, particularly those with limited English proficiency and poor writing skills, spelling and grammatical errors should be overlooked (Tippins & Dana, 1992).

When first asked to keep a journal, many students have no idea what to write because they have not been asked to keep one before. Experienced teachers often help students begin journal writing by discussing their expectations for the journal, showing sample journal entries, and providing class time for students to write in their journals (Berenson & Carter, 1995). Questions—for example, What are your feelings about dissecting frogs?, What is the relationship between volume and mass when determining the specific gravity of a mineral? or How would you tell someone the process for determining the dissolved oxygen level in a water sample?—are also used by teachers to prompt student journal writing. As students become comfortable writing in their journals, they should be allowed to have a say in what is included.

Many teachers are reluctant to ask their students to keep science journals because they believe that they do not have time to read them. There are several strategies,

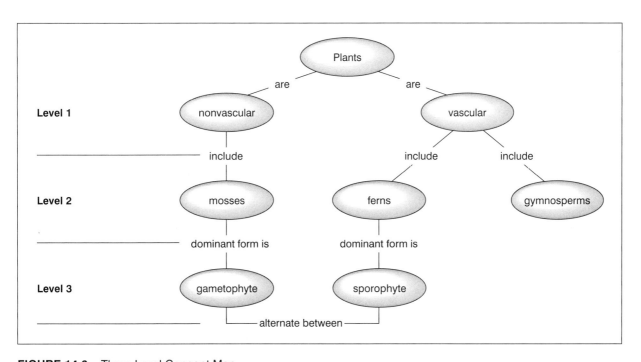

FIGURE 14.6 Three-Level Concept Map

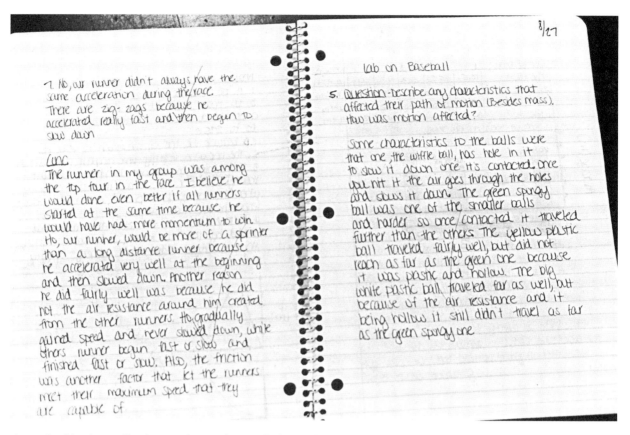

8/27

7. No, our runner didn't always have the same acceleration during the race. There are zig-zags because he accelerated really fast and then began to slow down.

Conc.
The runner in my group was among the top four in the race. I believe he would done even better if all runners started at the same time because he would have had more momentum to win. Ho, our runner, would be more of a sprinter than a long distance runner because he accelerated very well at the beginning and then slowed down. Another reason he did fairly well was because he did not the air resistance around him created from the other runners. He gradually gained speed and never slowed down, while others runner began fast or slow and finished fast or slow. Also, the friction was another factor that let the runners meet their maximum speed that they are capable of.

Lab on Baseball

5. Question -Describe any characteristics that affected their path of motion (besides mass). How was motion affected?

Some characteristics to the balls were that one, the wiffle ball, has hole in it to slow it down once it's contacted. once you hit it the air goes through the holes and slows it down. The green spongy ball was one of the smaller balls and harder so once contacted it traveled further than the others. The yellow plastic ball traveled fairly well, but did not reach as far as the green one because it was plastic and hollow. The big white plastic ball traveled far as well, but because of the air resistance and it being hollow it still didn't travel as far as the green spongy one.

Journal writing is an effective way for teachers to find out what students are thinking and feeling, to provide feedback to students, and to help them improve their writing skills.

however, that can be employed to help keep journals from becoming a burden. One is to read only a dozen or so randomly selected journals a week. Doing this allows the teacher to sample student reactions to lessons and their personal reflections. Over the course of a couple of months, every student's journal will be read. Other strategies to use with journals is to have students read each others' journals and provide feedback or have journals that are circulated through a class, with each student contributing to the dialog (Tippins & Dana, 1992). The teacher could periodically read these journals to gauge student thinking and lesson quality, correct misconceptions, and react to matters that are of concern to the students. It is the recommendation of all who encourage the use of science journals that they not be considered in summative assessment or graded, but rather used exclusively by teachers to become better acquainted with their students and to help these young people succeed as science learners.

Performance Assessment Tasks

Outcomes of science learning include the ability to inquire and problem-solve when using materials, equip-

ment, and models. These outcomes can only be adequately assessed with performance tasks. The laboratory practical exam stands as an early attempt to make use of performance assessment in science (Ochs, 1996). When engaging in a performance assessment task, a student works with "some material to produce a product that illustrates conceptual understanding" (Carter & Berenson, 1996, p. 101). A student's conceptual understanding may be assessed by observing her perform a task, such as determining the mass of an object using an electronic balance or focusing a microscope.

Given the nature of scientific activity, science performance assessment tasks vary considerably and may have multiple solutions or a single correct one. Designing a model insect that will go undetected in the wooded lot next to school is just one example of a performance task that has multiple solutions; there is only one solution to the problem of determining the amount of product produced in a chemical reaction based on beginning amounts of reactants. Science textbooks, laboratory manuals, and activity books are replete with examples and ideas for developing performance assessment tasks. Guidelines for the development of performance-based assessments offered by Shavelson, Baxter, and Pine (1991) include the following:

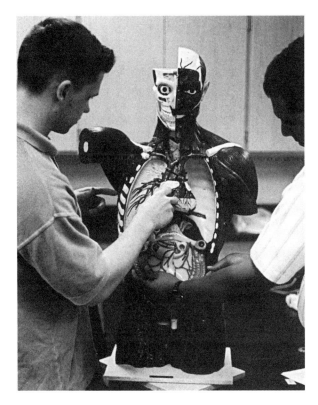

Laboratory practical exams are one type of performance assessment.

- Focus on complex cognitive behaviors.
- Assess students' knowledge structures that reveal science understandings and misunderstandings.
- Use manipulatives and scientific equipment.
- If possible, reduce the time demanded for assessment by making use of computers and other technologies.

The logistics and management problems associated with performance-based assessment are often cited as barriers to classroom implementation. But the teacher who recognizes that much of what is learned in science classes cannot be adequately assessed using paper-and-pencil tests works to overcome these barriers. Performance assessment tasks can be set up at stations around the room and students can alternate between visiting the stations and working on written test questions at their seats (Berenson & Carter, 1995, p. 185). Additionally, teachers can assess student performance of certain tasks, such as the construction of pulley systems in physics or the proper use of a Bunsen burner in chemistry, during regular class activities using a checklist. Computer simulations offer yet another alternative for performance assessment. Using computer simulations, students can demonstrate their understanding of complex systems such as a cell or the earth's atmosphere and how chang-

ing one aspect of the system affects others. Some of these computer simulations have the capacity to record the students' manipulations and the results on the simulated system and store them on separate files for later review by the teacher.

Open-Ended Problems

Many and varied solutions and ways of arriving at a solution are the hallmarks of open-ended problems (Berenson & Carter, 1995). In general, the solutions to open-ended problems are communicated in writing, although a solution may be presented as a product, such as an invention or blueprint. Open-ended problems are often associated with real-world issues or problems that confront scientists or communities, making them most appropriate for assessing student learning in areas of science-technology-society. They engage students in making connections between the world in which they live and the traditional disciplines of science. Open-ended problems also encourage active learning as students make use of a variety of resources, not just the textbook, when problem-solving. The following are some examples of open-ended problems.

- Describe how you would design a container that has a mass of 5 kg or less and that will keep an ice cube from completely melting for two hours.
- Several students who got sick after eating salad in the cafeteria blamed their illness on the process used to keep the salad ingredients cool. What kind of experiment could be conducted to find out if their assumption is correct?
- The cost of health care is becoming more expensive by the day. As a result, many insurance companies require persons applying for life insurance to submit to a medical examination. Coverage may be denied based on the results of the examination. Should this practice be stopped? Support your position.
- Given an ammeter, light bulb, batteries, and wire, describe how you could use these materials to demonstrate the relationship between bulb brightness and current reading on the ammeter.
- Environmentalists contend that the construction of a new housing development will overtax the existing wastewater treatment facility. What type of experiments could be conducted to test this contention?

As with other forms of alternative assessment, it is wise to guide students through some examples that will help them form a schema for the type of thinking required to solve open-ended problems. They will quickly learn that solutions to open-ended problems are not found in the pages of their textbook but require creative and imaginative thinking. Working with a partner or in small groups may provide the added encouragement needed by some students to engage in this type of thinking.

Drawings

Much can be learned about what students are thinking and feeling by studying their drawings. Drawing exercises tend to be nonthreatening to students and simple to administer. They are extremely useful for assessing the understandings of students for whom English is their second language and for students who have reading and writing difficulties. Students are often encouraged to annotate their drawings or to write a brief description of the drawing on the back of the paper.

Drawings have been used to determine students' perceptions of scientists and the work that they do. Stereotypic images of scientists as diabolical looking men wearing lab coats and thick eyeglasses and surrounded by books and bubbling beakers appear frequently in students' drawings (Chambers, 1983). When compared to written descriptions, student drawings of scientists minimize the possibility of socially desirable responses, provide compelling evidence of conceptual change, and sensitize teachers and students to the need to think differently about scientists and their work (Mason, Kahle, & Gardner, 1991; Schibeci & Sorensen, 1983).

When investigating biological concepts using WOWBug materials, students begin by drawing a picture of wasps and how they live. This activity is repeated at the end of the unit. Pre- and postunit drawings showed differences on the factors of

- combinations of proper and improper anatomy
- associations with social and aggressive bees and wasps
- expressions of human fear, flight or pain
- gender identification clues
- changes in wasp anatomy drawn
- wasps shown as insect parasites or predators, rather than as attackers of humans

- wasps shown as insects that undergo complete metamorphosis
- variability in wasps size
- evidence of changes in feelings toward wasps (Matthews, Koballa, Flage, & Pyle, 1996, p. 21)

The drawings in Figure 14.7 exemplify the richness and striking differences often seen between students' pre- and postunit drawings as the result of learning more about an idea. This growth in knowledge illustrates conceptual change, which signifies the construction of meaningful learning.

Portfolios

A portfolio is more than a collection of a student's classroom work. It may showcase classroom work and items directly tied to classroom learning activities, such as clipped newspaper articles and photographs. More importantly, a portfolio involves organization, synthesis, and summarization for the purpose of capturing the essence of student learning.

Portfolio development usually involves dialog between teacher and student, with both having input into the purpose of the portfolio and what is included. Portfolios may present evidence of student capability or progress and can be used in formative assessment, to stimulate student and teacher reflection, or as a summative evaluation of student work for a semester or an entire course. A portfolio may include many of the assessments already described, including drawings, concept maps, journals, and open-ended problem solutions in addition to other items ranging from laboratory reports to homework to videotaped interviews. These items and many more could be included in a portfolio, but only to the extent that the student can rationalize their inclusion. A science notebook that includes collections of notes copied from the chalkboard or transparency display is not a portfolio because it does not contain evidence of original student work. When well designed, portfolios can provide a sensitive portrait of authentic student work that requires complex thinking

FIGURE 14.7 Student Pre- and Postunit Wasp Drawings That Illustrate Conceptual Change

Preunit drawings

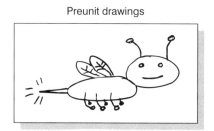

Postunit drawings

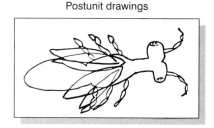

(Herman, Gearhart, & Baker, 1993). The most compelling reasons for using portfolios are that they involve the student in the assessment process and permit assessment of the total student rather than isolated test scores and assignments.

To make a portfolio a useful assessment tool, it must be accessible to students and attended to on a regular basis. Many teachers recommend that students keep both working and permanent portfolios (Willis, 1996). The working portfolio is a personal repository, which could be a folder or a box, into which students deposit work on a daily or weekly basis. Some of the items placed in the working portfolio are eventually put into the permanent portfolio, whereas other items that do not meet the criteria for appropriate evidence are discarded. The permanent portfolio should include a "table of contents, a paragraph describing the contents and what the items show, and a self-evaluation paragraph when it is time to assess the portfolio (Martin, 1996, p. 275).

The nature and number of the items included in the permanent portfolio should be congruent with the intended purpose of the portfolio. If the purpose is to assess student capability, a portfolio should include pieces of a student's best work. But if the purpose is to assess progress, then pre- and postunit assignments that focus on the same knowledge or skills should be included. Most permanent portfolios include fewer than a dozen items. For example, to demonstrate capability to design and conduct experiments, a class of middle school students decided in cooperation with their teacher to pick eight items that show their best work in this area. Items included in the students' portfolios were statements of research questions and hypotheses, drawings of experimental setups, tables of measurements made during experiments, graphs, and reflective paragraphs on what was learned by designing and conducting an experiment. Not all portfolios included the same items.

A portfolio may be assessed by the teacher, student, parent, outside evaluator, or a combination of these persons, and judgments applied to a portfolio may be holistic or analytic. A holistic judgment is rendered on an examination of the portfolio collection as a whole, whereas an analytic judgment is based on careful ratings of individual items contained in a portfolio (Herman et al., 1993). The teacher's contribution to students' work needs to be taken into consideration when portfolios are assessed. Having examples of well-done portfolios on hand to show students should relieve their anxiety about what is expected.

In summary, a number of new and innovative assessments are available for use by science teachers, several of which have been described here. Because they are so new, much is yet to be known about their effectiveness.

What is known, however, is that alternative assessments provide information on a wide range of outcomes not captured by paper-and-pencil tests. Use of alternative assessments also affects the ways that teachers teach and students learn, according to Khattri, Kane, and Reeves (1995). The results of their three-year national study indicate that when teachers use alternative assessments they shift from being information disseminators to learning facilitators, emphasize problem solving in their instruction, and collaborate more with other teachers on issues of instruction and curriculum. Students in these teachers' classes also engage in more project-based tasks and are highly motivated by this type of instruction. Research also indicates that quality performance assessment tasks take time to develop and to administer, and most seem to be context dependent (Baxter, Shavelson, Herman, Brown, & Valadez, 1993). That is, students will likely do much better on a performance assessment task related to something they have studied than something they have not studied. Perhaps the most important research finding related to the use of the many performance assessments is that successful implementation means changing traditional classroom routines (Gitomer & Duschl, 1995). For this reason, you will want to learn all that you can about how to use alternative assessments, seek advice and help from experienced teachers and administrators, and proceed slowly. It is also important that you communicate with parents about how students in your classes will be assessed. Based on their work with portfolios, Gitomer and Duschl (1995) recommend that a teacher start with one class and one unit rather than full-scale implementation in all classes and partner with other teachers to work through the difficulties related to science teaching and learning that arise.

SCORING RUBRICS

If you have ever watched a gymnastics competition, you have witnessed the use of a scoring rubric. The athlete's performance is judged by an expert using a set of well-defined criteria. The gymnast who scores a ten on the balance beam has performed at the highest possible level. Students' science work can be assessed in much the same way. Performance assessment tasks, portfolios, and open-ended questions are among the alternative assessments that result in student performance that must be judged using defined criteria.

A scoring rubric makes explicit the criteria by which student performance will be judged by an expert, usually the teacher. It presents the criteria as lists of descriptors for the performance along a numbered scale. The scale for most scoring rubrics has between three and five points. On a scale that runs from 1 to 5, a score of 5 would represent the highest level of performance and a score of 1, the lowest level of performance. Most rubric developers set a minimal acceptable level of performance, such as 3 on a 5-point scale.

Developing a scoring rubric takes considerable time and effort. But before a rubric can be developed, the task to which it will be applied must be known. Specified in the task description, whether the task is a performance task, portfolio, open-ended question, or laboratory activity, are the objectives (or standards) that students are expected to meet. Students are usually given the task and the scoring rubric at the same time. Figure 14.8 shows the description of a phase change task, the setup used in the task, and objectives in the areas of collaborative work, scientific literacy, and systems analysis. In the case of this example, the task is designed to assess student performance on three objectives, thus three sets of rubrics are presented.

The process of developing a task-specific scoring rubric can be greatly simplified by starting with a generic rubric and modifying it to match the task. In Figure 14.9, a general rubric for scoring student observation of a teacher's science demonstration is shown on the left and one developed from it for use in assessing students' written or oral descriptions of an acid/base demonstration is shown on the right. Generic rubrics from which task-specific rubrics can be developed for assessing complex thinking, communication, habits of mind, collaboration/cooperation, and science content and process skills are presented in *Assessing Student Outcomes* by Marzano, Pickering, and McTighe (1993).

The true value of scoring rubrics lies in their ability to communicate to teachers and parents what students know and can do and to provide students with understandable performance targets (Marzano et al., 1993, p. 29). Scoring rubrics must be clearly worded and match the objectives set forth in the task. Well-crafted scoring rubrics allow students to answer for themselves the questions, How will we be graded? and How am I doing?

GRADING AND REPORTING GRADES

The determination of grades is a serious responsibility. Grades, once entered in the records, have great impact on the lives of students. They represent degrees of success and failure. They are used to compare one student with another. They determine promotion and graduation and fitness for college or other advanced training. They are taken into account in awarding scholarships, and they are usually determined by one person—the classroom teacher.

A good assessment system should include assessments of many different types of learning outcomes.

Knowledge and understanding of facts, concepts, laws, and theories should be a part of this assessment. Problem solving should also be a part of the assessment process, as should communication, critical thinking, and attitudes. These outcomes can be measured using a variety of means, including paper-and-pencil tests, laboratory reports, portfolios, journals, observation, and drawings. An important concern of teachers when thinking about grading is whether grades should reflect what a student has actually learned or how the student's performance compares with the performance of classmates. This is the main difference between criterion-referenced and norm-referenced grading.

Criterion-Referenced Grading

In criterion-referenced grading, student achievement is judged relative to performance against an established set of criteria, rather than performance relative to others. Following this system, grades are recorded as is and not adjusted in any way. The teacher will allow as many As, Bs, Cs, Ds, and Fs as students earn. The same would be true for scores of 1, 2, 3, 4 and 5 obtained by using a 5-point scoring rubric. If the raw score for a test differs from 100 points, students should learn how to interpret their grades when they are given a raw score based on the total number of points. Accepting raw scores for performance tasks is easier for students because interpretation is not necessary as expectations are communicated in the scoring rubric.

Criterion-referenced grading is also used in mastery learning. In this case, students are expected to attain a certain level of performance. If this level of performance is not met, they are given the chance to receive remedial help to reach the objectives. For example, if a student received a 2 on a scoring rubric for which 3 is the minimal acceptable level of performance, the student is then given remedial work to reach the minimal level when the performance task is next administered.

Criterion-referenced grading presents challenges for teachers. The assumption that all students can earn As if they reach the set objectives is regularly questioned. Some administrators and parents expect to see a distribution of grades in a class and may insist that grading practices be altered to produce Bs, Cs, Ds, and Fs. Teachers who use this system of grading must be prepared to defend their practices.

Norm-Referenced Grading

Another procedure that some teachers use to grade students' work is to base grades on a normal curve. In this grading procedure a student's grade depends on how

Task: This is a three-day activity in which students observe and perform a distillation to demonstrate phase change, explain energy transformation, and identify key components in the system. On day one, a group of students writes a description of the distillation equipment that is placed in a location that the other class members cannot see. The rest of the class assembles the equipment laying on the lab tables according to this description. On day two, the lab groups use the setup to experiment with the phase change of water from liquid to gas and back to liquid. Each group writes their own statement of the problem, hypothesis, procedure, data table, and conclusion. On day three, each student describes individual components of the setup and explains how each part is used to cause water to change phase.

Rubric:

Topics	Scores			
	4	**3**	**2**	**1**
Collaborative Worker: Student can take charge of his/her own behavior in a group	Student stays on task; offers useful ideas and can defend them; can take on various roles; participates without prompting.	Student stays on task; offers useful ideas and can defend them; can take on various roles; rarely requires prompting to participate.	Student does not attend to the lab. Student accepts group view or considers only his/her own ideas worthwhile. Student needs regular prompting to stay on task.	Student does not respond to the group. Student is not involved or may try to undermine the efforts of the group.
Scientific Literacy: Student uses processes and skills of science to conduct investigations.	Student identifies the question, forms a possible solution, writes out steps to test the possible solution, designs a data chart, collects data, and concludes about the validity of the possible solution.	Student identifies the question and forms a possible solution. Procedure and data chart are complete but lack clarity and/or creativity. Student concludes about the validity of the possible solution.	Student identifies the question but does not form a complete solution. Procedure and data chart are incomplete and the conclusion does not speak to the possible solution.	Student does not identify the question. No possible solution is given. Procedure and data chart are incomplete or missing. The conclusion is incomplete or missing.
Systems Analysis: Student describes how a system operates internally and how it interacts with the outside world.	Student identifies how parts of the system interact and provides personal insight into the interacting of the parts. Student relates how the system interacts with the outside world.	Student identifies how parts of the system interact and relates how the system interacts with the outside world.	Student does not identify some parts of the system. Student does not understand how the parts interact and does not relate how the system interacts with the outside world.	Student incorrectly identifies the parts and cannot describe how they interact either within or outside the system.

Distillation setup:

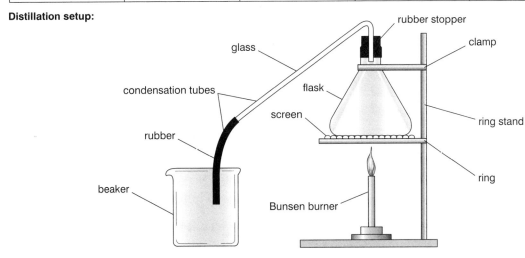

FIGURE 14.8   Scoring Rubric for Phase Change Task

Reprinted with permission of NSTA Publications from "Effective Rubric Design," by K. Jensen, from *The Science Teacher, 62*(5), 1995, p. 36, published by The National Science Teachers Association, Arlington, Virginia.

FIGURE 14.9 Generic Scoring Rubric and Task-Specific Scoring Rubric

Reprinted by permission of NSTA Publications from "Demonstration Assessment," by D. L. Radford, L. L. Ramsey, and W. C. Deese, from *The Science Teacher*, 62(7), 1995, p. 54, published by The National Science Teachers Association, Arlington, Virginia.

Score	Accomplishments
0 points	Makes no observations or inaccurate observations.
1 points	Makes accurate observations, but no accurate inferences.
2 points	Makes accurate observations, uses some appropriate vocabulary to draw some accurate inferences.
3 points	Makes accurate observations, accurate inferences, cites evidence, uses appropriate vocabulary.
Score	Accomplishments
0 points	Makes inaccurate observations or no observations.
1 points	A colorless liquid is poured into a second colorless liquid. The mixture turns pink. The pink solution is poured back into the first contained and the solution becomes colorless.
2 points	(The above description plus) One solution was probably an acid and the other was a base. The color change was due to an indicator.
3 points	(The above plus) The indicator was colorless at one pH and pink at the other. Because the color changed to pink and then back to colorless, there must have been an excess of the reagent in which the indicator was colorless.

A good assessment system should include assessments of many different types of learning outcomes.

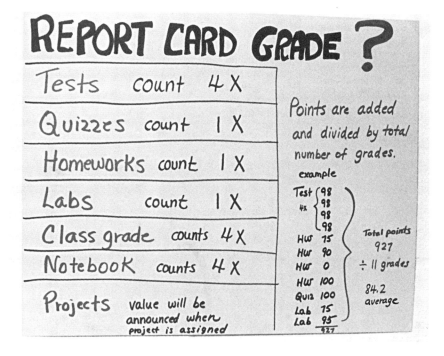

well she has performed with respect to other members of the class. When the teacher uses this system, he has in mind a predetermined percentage of students who will receive As, Bs, Cs, Ds, and Fs. This procedure, sometimes called grading on the curve, assumes that students in a typical class can be categorized in a normal distribution.

The normal distribution curve is a mathematically defined theoretical distribution. As shown in Figure 14.10, the curve is symmetrical with the mean in the center and with roughly 68 percent of the distribution clustering within one standard deviation of the mean. When using the normal curve for grading, the teacher would assign 68 percent Cs, 14 percent Bs, 14 percent

Ds, 2 percent As, and 2 percent Fs. Modifications to this standard procedure are common. One involves shifting the average grade for the class. For example, if the teacher believes that B was the average grade for the class on a particular assignment, then the resulting distribution might be 68 percent Bs, 14 percent As, 14 percent Cs, 4 percent Ds, and no Fs. A second modification involves giving one-third of the students Cs rather than two-thirds as roughly reflected by the 68 percent of the distribution clustering within one standard deviation of the mean. This change results in more students receiving both higher and lower scores. A possible distribution of scores resulting from this modification would be 34 percent Cs, 21 percent Bs, 21 percent Ds, 12 percent As, and 12 percent Fs.

Norm-referenced grading has been severely criticized, particularly when teachers use it to assign grades to small groups of students. The size of classes in which the procedure is used is often too small to expect a normal distribution. Another criticism is that teachers seldom produce tests or other assessments that yield normally distributed scores. Where students are homogeneous, with similar aptitudes, as is often the case in Advanced Placement classes, a normal curve does not apply. This system of grading is also inappropriate when a teacher bases grades on student mastery of specified objectives. Norm-referenced grading should not be used to cover up poor achievement resulting from inadequate instruction. The cause of poor achievement should be identified, and proper steps taken to rectify the situation.

Keeping Records of Performance

Constant records are essential for arriving at grade reports. Record forms or grade books should permit a variety of entries and notations as to the different types of achievement that students demonstrate. A portion of a grade book adapted for science records is shown in Figure 14.11. The grades are recorded on a daily basis and reflect items from these four general categories:

1. *Tests*. Chapter tests and unit tests may include paper-and-pencil items and performance tasks. Unit tests are given more weight than chapter tests.

2. *Projects*. The grades given for work that students undertake largely on their own time are recorded. Portfolios, long-term problems, science-fair projects, and inventions are examples of the types of work included in this category.

3. *Laboratory work*. Grades are entered for laboratory-based performance tasks, open-ended problems, laboratory reports, drawings, and other laboratory work that demonstrates cognitive and psychomotor learning.

4. *Daily work*. Student performance on such assignments as homework, in-class assignments, journals, and quizzes can show trends in student understanding and attitudes. For example, daily grades may reveal that a student's performance has dramatically improved over the last three weeks of the term.

Some teachers choose to treat daily work as a checklist, with the exception that number or letter grades are given for work that surpasses the minimum. Extra-credit work that students undertake spontaneously and do with little teacher assistance may also be treated as a checklist or acknowledged by adding points to a daily grade or final grade.

A grade book is convenient to carry around and store. The records are compact and easily examined. However, there is usually not enough space in grade books to specify the nature of student performance. Consequently, a busy teacher has difficulty in calling to mind precisely what each student has done; she is hand-

FIGURE 14.10 The Character-istics of the Normal Curve

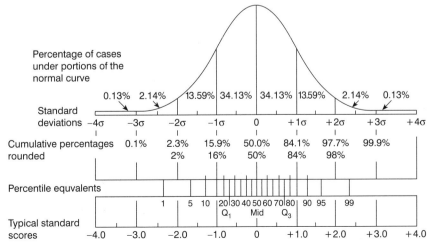

Name	11/5 Homework 1 pt.	11/6 Quiz 10 pts. max.	11/7 Lab Drawing 5 pts. max.	11/10 Homework 1 pt.	11/11 Lab Report 50 pts. max.	11/12 Chap. 6 Test 100 pts. max.	11/15 Quiz 10 pts. max.	11/18 Portfolio 100 pts. max.	Term Grade
Armstrong, Mike	√	10	4	√	38	96	7	100	
Coleman, Carolyn	√	9	5	√	48	92	7	80	
Joseph, Patrick	√	6	3	√	42	67	9	80	
Kendall, Caroline	√	9	4		35	89	10	60	
Lindsey, Chuck		8	5	√	25	58	9	80	
Olssner, Donald	√	7	3	√	37	75	7	100	
Ruiz, Jane	√	8	2		38	69	9	80	
Slocum, Gordon	√	10	2	√	28	90	8	100	
Williams, Louise	√	6	4		47	94	7	60	

FIGURE 14.11 A Teacher's Grade Book

358

icapped in arriving at final grades without having detailed records. Thus, some teachers prefer to keep their records on computer. A computer grade book program that tracks numeric scores can be used in conjunction with a word-processing program for recording and keeping up with notes regarding student performance on particular tasks.

Assigning Final Grades

The traditional practice for reporting science grades is to combine all the results of a student's work. For example, test grades are averaged, with unit tests being given more weight than weekly tests or quizzes. Grades for lab reports, portfolios, and other required work and for extra credit work are then averaged, with proper weight being given according to the nature of the assignment. Ultimately, these results are combined with the test average to give a final grade. This time-honored practice of producing a numerical average as a final grade has served science teachers well for many years, but its use is questioned when students' performance is judged against established criteria.

Criterion-referenced scores cannot be averaged and combined mathematically, according to Woolfolk (1995, p. 577), since each test, performance task, or other assignment measures the attainment of particular objectives. She contends that nothing meaningful is communicated when an average is reported for a student's level of proficiency on different assignments. For example, what is communicated to a student and her parents on a report card when the average of a student's scores on a unit test, homework, and rubrics assessing problem solving and group collaboration are reported? Multiple interpretations of the average score are possible. The more sensible alternative when using criterion-referenced grading is to identify the objectives and describe each student's performance relative to the objectives. This approach would change what is communicated on report cards from As, Bs, and Cs to written statements of a student's attainment.

While a few middle and secondary schools use criterion-referenced report cards to indicate students' progress toward specific goals, the vast majority of schools require that students' grades be reported as numerical scores. Even if classroom assignments are criterion-based, the teacher is still expected to produce numerical scores that can be converted to letter grades for report cards. Student grades resulting from norm-referenced systems are typically reported as numerical scores, but simply computing an average from a group of norm-referenced scores can also produce misleading results. Students' performance on two or more assign-

ments can only be compared by converting the raw scores to standard scores such as Z scores (mean of 0 and standard deviation of 1.00), T scores (mean of 5 and standard deviation of 10), or Stanine scores (mean of 5 and standard deviation of 2). Unfortunately, few teachers make these conversions.

Woolfolk (1995) recommends two systems for combining grades from different assignments that conform to traditional grading practices and help address some of the problems we have mentioned—the point system and percentage grading. When using the point system, a total number of points is awarded for each assignment, determined by its value (Woolfolk, 1995, p. 578). For example, a maximum score of 15 points could be awarded for a performance task worth 15 percent of the term grade; a maximum score of 20 points could be awarded for a unit test worth 20 percent; and a maximum score of 30 points could be awarded for a portfolio worth 30 percent. A portfolio that meets all the criteria would be given a score of 30 points, whereas one that meets some but not all the criteria would be given less than 30 points. To calculate final grades using this system, the teacher would simply add up the points for each student. Letter grades could be given based on a normal distribution of scores, by grouping scores based on natural breaks of two or more points, or by using a previously established scale. An established scale might look something like this:

Term Grading Scale
Maximum possible points = 250

A	200–250 points
B	150–199 points
C	100–149 points
D	50–99 points
F	below 50 points

Percentage grading involves assigning grades based on the percentage of an assignment a student has accomplished or mastered. Applying this system, the teacher gives percentage scores for class tests, performance tasks, concept maps, and other assignments, then computes an average for these scores to arrive at a term grade. Suppose a student's test scores were 85 percent and 74 percent, her portfolio score was 93 percent, and her concept map score was 61 percent. Her average grade would be 78 percent. This score would be recorded as a C if the following percentage categories were applied:

A	90–100 percent
B	80–89 percent
C	70–79 percent

D   60–69 percent

F   below 60 percent

An often overlooked flaw in the percentage system of grading is the failure to communicate what was to be learned by students and what, say, 78 percent means in terms of what a student has actually learned (Woolfolk, 1995, p. 579). When using the percentage system teachers need to provide information to students, parents, and administrators so that a score can be meaningfully interpreted.

The Meaning of Grades

Historically, the purpose of grades has been to communicate information about students' achievement in a subject area. But in practice, grades are often a function of achievement in addition to other variables, including attitude, student ability, and effort (Pilcher, 1994). These variables are often used by teachers to make adjustments to achievement scores, adjustments that could either reward students or penalize them. For example, it is not uncommon for teachers to give extra credit points to students who have come after school for help on a difficult concept or to grade the paper of a low-ability student more leniently than the papers of more academically talented students.

The meaning of grades is also influenced by the ways in which they are used. According to Pilcher (1994, p. 85), grades are used by teachers and parents to extrinsically motivate students to complete their school work and to perform in class. He contends that students often view grades as tokens that are used to bribe and control them. For example, parents might tell

their high school-age son that they will buy him a new car if he makes good grades or a teacher might tell a star basketball player that she will not be able to compete if she makes lower than a C for the grading period. It is the use of grades in this way that "encourages students to learn for the purpose of receiving rewards or avoiding punishment" rather than learning for its intrinsic value (Pilcher, 1994, p. 86).

The meaning of grades is also affected when grades are assigned for group work. Arguments in favor of group grading include preparing students for the world of work, where functioning as a member of a team is important, cutting teacher workload, and encouraging students of different backgrounds to work together. But Kagan (1995, p. 68) urges teachers not to give group grades. He states that "giving the same grade to everyone on a team is not only patently unfair, it undermines the positive outcomes of cooperative learning." Kagan goes on to say that group grading stifles motivation, because slackers rely on the work of others and high achievers feel that their efforts will not be rewarded, and is not an effective way to teach students how to work with others.

Grading, regardless of the system used, is always a challenge for the teacher. Students are concerned about their grades and want to know how they will be graded. Students sometimes feel that they are treated unfairly when grades are assigned, so it is important that the teacher inform them of the system to be used and why the system is fair. Giving students one grade for achievement and separate grades for working cooperatively, effort, and attitude is one way of being fair to all students. TenBrink (1990, p. 339) states, "Assigning grades has forever been a task teachers dislike. There seems to be no 'fair' way to do it and grading systems seem to be subject to all kinds of interpretation problems."

ASSESSING AND REVIEWING

1. Define the terms *alternative, authentic,* and *performance* as they apply to assessment in science. Then describe a science assessment that is alternative, authentic, and performance based.

2. Construct or locate several examples of different types of measurement (including test items) that correspond with a set of instructional objectives for

a unit of study. Discuss the measurements with other members of your science methods class to determine how well they are constructed, focusing on clarity and the degree to which they correspond with the stated objectives.

3. Suppose a teacher told you that she does not have time for diagnostic and formative assessment in her

science classes. What would you say to try to convince her to include these forms of assessment in her teaching plans?

4. The developer of the open-ended question that follows claims that it is both reliable and valid. What questions would you ask the developer and what answers would you expect to hear in order to feel confident in the developer's claim?

   Suppose the sun stopped shining tomorrow. What effect would this have on the world?

5. Write five questions that could be used to interview students in a science class to determine their attitudes about a particular science subject. Describe the type of information that would likely be obtained using these questions. How would the information obtained by interviewing students compare with the information obtained from using a semantic differential instrument?

6. Examine multiple-choice, true-false, matching, or completion questions included on a test you took in one of your college science courses. Classify them using Bloom's taxonomy. If you find any knowledge-level questions, pick one and rewrite it so that it assesses a higher level of cognitive processing.

7. Develop a table to help you organize the information about the different alternative assessment methods presented in this chapter. Label the columns of the table: Method, Strengths, Limitations, Suggestions for Use, and Example(s).

8. The grading procedures addressed in the chapter include norm-referenced, criterion-referenced, point system, and percentage. Which one would you choose to use with your science classes? Provide reasons for your choice.

■

RESOURCES TO EXAMINE

Active Assessment for Active Science. 1994. Published by Heinemann, 361 Hanover Street, Portsmouth, NH 03801.

   A wealth of information about assessment in science applicable to middle and secondary school classes is provided in this book by George Hein and Sabra Price. Chapters are devoted to alternative forms of assessment, how to transition from traditional tests to alternative assessment practices, and systematic scoring procedures.

"An Alternative Final Evaluation." 1996, April, *Science Scope,* pp. 18–21.

   Lillian Gondree and Valerie Tundo tell how they and their colleagues redesigned their district-wide science exam from a test of general science knowledge to a critical-thinking and problem-solving experience. Their new exam makes use of videodisc technology and performance tasks and addresses a variety of student learning styles. Sample performance-based questions from the exam are presented in the article.

Assessing Student Outcomes: Performance Assessment Using the Dimensions of Learning Model. 1993. Association for Supervision and Curriculum Development, 1250 North Pitt Street, Alexandria, VA 22314.

   Robert Marzano, Debra Pickering, and Jay McTighe present an approach to assessment that illuminates its connections to teaching and learning. Central to the approach is the effective use of performance tasks and rubrics to assess performance. Included in the book are example performance tasks and generic rubrics from which task-specific rubrics can be developed.

"Changing Assessment Practices in Science and Mathematics." 1995, April, *School Science and Mathematics,* pp. 182–186.

   Incorporating alternative assessment practices into the science classroom can be a difficult task. Sarah Berenson and Glenda Carter describe and give examples of five alternative assessment practices, including journal writing, open-ended problems, portfolios, and interviews. Additionally, they provide hints for the successful use of the practices in middle and secondary classrooms.

■
─────────

REFERENCES

Baxter, G. P., Shavelson, R. J., Herman, S. J., Brown, K. A., & Valadez, J. R. (1993). Mathematics performance assessment: Technical quality and diverse student impact. *Journal of Research in Mathematics Education, 3*, 190–216.

Bell, B. (1995). Interviewing: A technique for assessing science knowledge. In S. M. Glynn & R. Duit (Eds.), *Learning science in the schools*. Mahwah, NJ: Erlbaum.

Berenson, S. B., & Carter, G. S. (1995). Changing assessment practices in science and mathematics. *School Science and Mathematics, 95*, 182–186.

Bloom, B. S. (Ed.) (1956). *Taxonomy of educational objectives, Handbook 1. Cognitive domain*. New York: David Mckay.

Borg, W. R., & Gall, M. D. (1983). *Educational research* (4th ed.). New York: Longman.

Carter, G., & Berenson, S. B. (1996). Authentic assessment: Vehicle for reform. In J. Rhoton & P. Bowers (Eds.), *Issues in science education*. Arlington, VA: National Science Teachers Association.

Chambers, D. W. (1983). Stereotypic images of the scientist: The draw-a-scientist test. *Science Education, 67*, 255–265.

Crawley, F. E., & Koballa, T. R. (1994). Attitude research in science education: Contemporary models and methods. *Science Education, 78*, 35–55.

Eiss, A. F., & Harbeck, M. B. (1969). *Behavioral objectives in the affective domain*. Washington, DC: National Education Publications.

Fishbein, M., & Ajzen, I. (1975). *Belief, attitude, intention, and behavior: An introduction to theory and research*. Reading, MA: Addison-Wesley.

Gitomer, D. H., & Duschl, R. A. (1995). Moving toward a portfolio culture in science education. In S. M. Glynn & R. Duit (Eds.), *Learning science in the schools*. Mahwah, NJ: Erlbaum.

Gronlund, N. E. (1973). *Preparing criterion-referenced tests for classroom instruction*. Upper Saddle River, NJ: Merrill/Prentice Hall.

Hein, G. E., & Price, S. (1994). *Active assessment for active science*. Portsmouth, NH: Heinemann.

Herman, J. L., Gearhart, M., Baker, E. L. (1993). Assessing writing portfolios: Issues in the validity and meaning of scores. *Educational Assessment, 1*(3), 201–224.

Kagan, S. (1995). Group grades miss the mark. *Educational Leadership, 52*(8), 68–71.

Khattri, N., Kane, M. B., Reeve, A. L. (1995). Research report: How performance assessments affect teaching and learning. *Educational Leadership, 53*(3), 80–83.

Klopfer, L. E. (1976). A structure for the affective domain in relation to science education. *Science Education, 69*, 299–312.

Krathwohl, D. R., Bloom, B. S., & Masia, B. B. (1964). *Taxonomy of educational objectives, Handbook II. Affective domain*. New York: David McKay.

Likert, R. (1932). A technique for the measurement of attitudes. *Archives of Psychology, 22*(140), 1–55.

Martin, D. J. (1996). *Elementary science methods: A constructivist approach*. Albany, NY: Delmar.

Marzano, R. J., Pickering, D., McTighe, J. (1993). *Assessing student outcomes*. Alexandria, VA: Association for Supervision and Curriculum Development.

Mason, C. L., Kahle, J. B., & Gardner, A. L. (1991). Draw-a-scientist test: Future implications. *School Science and Mathematics, 91*, 193–198.

Matthews, R. W., Koballa, T. R., Flage, L. R., & Pyle, E. J. (1996). *WOWBugs: New life for life science*. Athens, GA: Riverview Press.

National Research Council. (1996). *National science education standards*. Washington, DC: National Academy Press.

Nay, M. A., & Crocker, R. K. (1970). Science teaching and the affective attributes of scientists. *Science Education, 54*, 59–67.

Ochs, V. D. (1996). Assessing habits of mind through performance based assessment in science. In J. Rhoton & P. Bowers (Eds.), *Issues in science education*. Arlington, VA: National Science Teachers Association.

Oppewal, T. (1996). Science portfolios: Navigating uncharted waters. In J. Rhoton & P. Bowers (Eds.), *Issues in science education*. Arlington, VA: National Science Teachers Association.

Osgood, C. E., Succi, G., & Tannenbaum, P. (1967). *The measurement of meaning*. Urbana: University of Illinois Press.

Pilcher, J. K. (1994). The value-driven meaning of grades. *Educational Assessment, 2*(1), 69–88.

Rakow, S. J. (1992). Assessment: A driving force. *Science Scope, 15*(6), 3.

Rakow, S. J., & Gee, T. C. (1987). Test science, not reading. *The Science Teacher, 54*(2), 28–31.

Roth, W. M. (1992). Dynamic evaluation. *Science Scope, 15*(6), 37–40.

Schibeci, R. A., & Sorensen, I. (1983). Elementary school children's perceptions of scientists. *School Science and Mathematics, 83*, 14–20.

Shavelson, R. J., Baxter, G. P., Pine, J. (1991). *Alternative technology for assessing science understanding*. Paper presented at the annual meeting of the American Educational Research Association, Chicago.

Simpson, R. D., Koballa, T. R., Oliver, J. S., & Crawley, F. E. (1994). Research on the affective dimensions of science learning. In D. L. Gabel (Ed.), *Handbook of research on sci-*

ence teaching and learning. Upper Saddle River, NJ: Merrill/Prentice Hall.

Tamir, P. (1990). Evaluation of student work and its role in developing policy. In E. Hegarty-Hazel (Ed.), *The student laboratory and the science curriculum* (pp. 242–266). London: Routledge.

TenBrink, T. D. (1990). Evaluation. In J. M. Cooper (Ed.), *Classroom teaching skills* (4th ed.). Lexington, MA: D. C. Heath.

Tippins, D. J., & Dana, N. F. (1992). Culturally relevant alternative assessment. *Science Scope, 15*(6), 50–53.

Vargas, E. M., & Alvarez, H. J. (1992). Mapping out student's abilities. *Science Scope, 15*(6), 41–43.

Willis, S. (1996). On the cutting edge of assessment: Testing what students can do with knowledge. *ASCD Education Update, 38*(4), 1, 4–7.

Woolfolk, A. E. (1995). *Educational psychology* (6th ed.). Boston: Allyn and Bacon.

PART FIVE

PROFESSIONAL DEVELOPMENT

CHAPTER 15

Growing Professionally and Evaluating Teaching

■

GROWING PROFESSIONALLY AND EVALUATING TEACHING

Continuous professional development is the key to teaching effectiveness and long-term personal satisfaction.

Science teachers must keep up-to-date with new developments in their science discipline as well as with the new approaches, materials, and methods for the teaching of science. In order to be professionally active, science teachers should attend professional meetings in science education, participate in workshops and in inservice courses offered in and outside the school setting, and take graduate courses toward an advanced degree or for continued study to enrich their science background or to learn new techniques to improve their teaching competence. To keep abreast of recent developments in their science discipline, teachers should read books and periodicals in their field of science interest. It is also important that they read professional journals in science education to enrich themselves and to update their knowledge of new developments in the field of science teaching.

OBJECTIVES

This chapter is designed to help the reader meet the following objectives:

- Identify ways for middle school and secondary school science teachers to engage in professional activities in and outside the school setting, such as with inservice courses, graduate work, and professional organizations.

- Indicate how writing for professional journals will aid science teachers to grow professionally.

- Explain the importance of maintaining contact with other science teachers as well as engaging in research, hobbies, and professional leaves to help one grow professionally.

- Suggest some methods that can be used to evaluate teacher performance in the classroom.

THE IMPORTANCE OF PROFESSIONAL DEVELOPMENT

> Professional development for teachers should be analogous to professional development for other professionals. Becoming an effective science teacher is a continuous process that stretches from preservice experiences in undergraduate years to the end of a professional career. Science has a rapidly changing knowledge base and expanding relevance to societal issues, and teachers will need ongoing opportunities to build their understanding and ability. Teachers also must have opportunities to develop understanding of how students with diverse interests, abilities, and experiences make sense of scientific ideas and what a teacher does to support and guide all students. And teachers require the opportunity to study and engage in research on science teaching and learning, and to share with colleagues what they have learned. (National Research Council [NRC], 1996, pp. 55–56.)

As evident in the preceding quotation, science teachers must continually update their knowledge within many areas of their profession, from content knowledge to theories of learning. They must also keep informed of new methods and materials that will make their science instruction more stimulating and effective. They must be involved in promoting educational reform in their school systems if a science education reform is to take place in the United States. This involvement will require that teachers be well informed about what has taken place in the past in science education as well as what is currently taking place in the profession. It is not enough to earn one or two college degrees and acquire a science teacher certification.

In order to meet the challenge of helping our youth to become scientifically and technologically literate, science teachers must participate in inservice courses and workshops and graduate study. Further they must attend professional meetings of national, state, and local organizations for science teachers and read professional journals and books on science and science education. It is also beneficial for them to write, on occasion, an article for a professional journal. In addition, teachers must constantly evaluate their teaching to continue to improve their classroom performance and effectiveness.

A dedicated science teacher will devote a great deal of time and effort to being professionally active. Many of the activities are time-consuming and will necessarily be carried out after school hours. Committed teachers will always realize that they are not a finished product at any time during their professional teaching career and be stimulated to improve themselves on a continuous basis. As Showalter (1984, p. 21) stated many years ago, "Science teaching is such a complex, dynamic profession that it is difficult for a teacher to stay up-to-date. For a teacher to grow professionally, and become better as a teacher of science, a special continuous effort is required."

PROFESSIONAL DEVELOPMENT THROUGH INSERVICE COURSES, WORKSHOPS, AND GRADUATE WORK

Programs offered within the school setting can contribute significantly to the professional growth and development of both experienced and inexperienced teachers. These programs can take many forms, such as workshops, credit and noncredit graduate courses offered by university or college professors, and workshops and seminars conducted by science teachers themselves or by an expert in the field of interest. These activities are generally offered because the science teachers of a school or school system have indicated a need for them. For programs to be effective, they must have a purpose, they must be needed, and they must be well planned and implemented.

Inservice Courses and Workshops

Schools often require science teachers to participate in inservice programs about new instructional approaches or new scientific developments to update science instruction in a school or school system. The courses are usually underwritten by a school district and taught by science teachers, college instructors, or other experts to help improve or expand the science offerings in its schools. Some courses are offered to train teachers to implement new content in their courses or to implement a new curriculum. A case in point is the current interest to include science, technology and society (STS) in the science curriculum. Teachers must first learn new content and specific skills and techniques before they can introduce STS content in their courses. There are also the new initiatives to reform science education in the United States. These projects have been mentioned earlier. Project 2061; the Scope, Sequence, and Coordination Project; and the Science Education Reform Standards are expected to be driving forces to reform the teaching of science in our schools. Teachers can learn about these programs through inservice courses and workshops within the school setting.

The time schedule of inservice courses is usually contingent upon the amount of time required to accomplish the specified outcomes of the course. They can be offered biweekly, weekly, or monthly, after school hours, or on Saturdays. They can run for one month, one semester, or one academic year, depending on what must be accomplished.

Inservice courses taught by university or college professors on the school premises are often underwritten by the school district as part of its budget. Teachers generally have a need for the particular course and ask the school authorities to make arrangements to have the course offered. These courses may pertain to a specific science content area, methods of science instruction, or they may be organized around field trips to local areas of geological or biological significance.

Inservice workshops conducted by qualified science teachers or university or college professors are offered to address a particular need. Such workshops involve active participation on the part of the teachers who are enrolled. Workshops usually center around a specified project such as developing laboratory activities for a certain science course or developing new science units. In these workshops teachers generally work together in small groups to produce a particular product. Some workshops center around special projects that are relevant to the school's science program. Others focus on curriculum development, laboratory activities, teaching modules, and using the Internet to gather information and to communicate with other people.

Graduate Work

School systems usually require or encourage their teachers to pursue graduate work. An advanced degree is often required to qualify teachers for pay raises, tenure, or promotion. In many instances school systems will even pay for part or all of the tuition for graduate courses and workshops offered in the school setting or on college campuses by university or college professors.

Inservice courses and workshops taught by college professors in the school setting can usually be used toward a graduate degree. Beginning as well as experienced teachers should see the need for and realize the benefits of continued study to enrich their knowledge of science and improve their teaching competence.

Graduate programs leading to advanced degrees for science teachers vary considerably from institution to institution. Individual teachers should be careful to select the program that best suits their own needs. These programs can offer teachers an opportunity to extend their present knowledge within a science discipline and

expose them to areas with which they have had no previous experience. They can also provide opportunities to learn about new approaches and teaching strategies.

PROFESSIONAL ORGANIZATIONS FOR SCIENCE TEACHERS

National Professional Organizations

There are a number of national organizations for science teachers in the United States. Some of the larger organizations include the National Science Teachers Association, The American Association for the Advancement of Science, the National Association of Biology Teachers, the American Chemical Society, the American Association of Physics Teachers, and the National Association of Geology Teachers. The National Science Teachers Association is organized to represent all science teachers regardless of the grades they teach or the science discipline in which they are interested. It publishes journals for teachers interested in elementary, middle, and secondary school science teaching. The other organizations mentioned are for teachers who are interested in a specific science discipline, that is, biology, chemistry, geology (earth science), and physics. Each organization publishes a professional journal that contains up-to-date developments in a specific science area as well as methods and materials and new approaches in teaching a particular science discipline. There are other national organizations that are intended for those involved or interested in research in science education. Organizations such as the National Association for Research in Science Teaching and the Association of Teachers of Science publish professional journals that report the results of research in the area of science education. See Table 15.1 for an extensive list national organizations.

Statewide Professional Organizations

Most states, if not all, have organizations for science teachers that publish journals containing information about science and science education. Many publish newsletters informing science teachers about the availability of inservice courses and workshops that are offered by school districts in school settings or courses that are offered during the summer or academic year at statewide colleges and universities. They inform teachers about new classroom ideas, new resources for science

TABLE 15.1   Professional Organizations and Journals for Science Teachers

Some national organizations of importance to middle grade and secondary school science teachers are listed here. States and local areas have additional organizations. Names and addresses of these groups can be obtained from the state's science supervisor or a local science coordinator.

AAAS
American Association for the Advancement of Science
1333 H Street, NW
Washington, DC 20005
Publications: *Science, Science Books and Films, Science Education News*

AAPT
American Association of Physics Teachers
5110 Roanoke Place, Suite 101
College Park, MD 20740
Journal: *The Physics Teacher*

ACS
American Chemical Society
1155 16th Street, NW
Washington, DC 20036
Journals: *Journal of Chemical Education, Chem Matters, Chem Tech*
Also publishes a large number of publications useful for teaching chemistry.

AETS
Association for the Education of Teachers of Science
Joseph Peters, AETS Executive Secretary
The University of West Florida
11000 University Parkway
Pensacola, FL 32514
Journals: *Journal of Science Teacher Education, Science Education*

NABT
National Association of Biology Teachers
11250 Roger Bacon Drive #19
Reston, VA 22090-5202
Journal: *The American Biology Teacher*
Also publishes a large number of publications useful for teaching biology.

NARST
National Association for Research in Science Teaching
Arthur White, NARST Executive Secretary
The Ohio State University
1929 Kenny Road
Columbus, OH 43210
Journal: *Journal of Research in Science Teaching*

NAGT
National Association of Geology Teachers
P.O. Box 5443
Bellingham, Washington 90227-5443
Journal: *Journal of Geological Education*

NSTA
National Science Teachers Association
1840 Wilson Boulevard
Arlington, VA 22201-3000
Journals: *Science and Children, Science Scope, The Science Teacher, Journal of College Science Teaching*
Also publishes a large number of other publications for science teachers.

SSMA
School Science and Mathematics Association
Donald Pratt, Executive Secretary
Curriculum & Foundations
Bloomsburg University
Bloomsburg, PA 17815-1301
Journal: *School Science and Mathematics*

teachers, and events of current interests. The newsletters also contain new statewide policies regarding certification in science and changes in the science curriculum.

State organizations have statewide meetings that are as well organized as the meetings of national professional organizations. The meetings include guest speakers of note, forums, discussion sessions, workshops, book displays by publishing houses, and software and hardware displays by the companies that supply them. Science teachers can present papers regarding research in science teaching, new techniques, new ideas, and new approaches in teaching science.

Some state organizations feature local meetings that periodically meet during the school year. Usually teach-

ers in the local area plan programs that are centered around a particular theme or interest. Many state organizations are affiliated with the National Science Teachers Association.

Local Professional Organizations for Science Teachers

It is not uncommon for science teachers employed in urban settings to organize themselves into clubs or other types of organizations based on their interests or science discipline. Some school districts that employ a great number of science teachers may have a strong active organization that is highly respected by the administrators of the school district and consequently have an important voice in matters that concern the teaching of science in that district. Such organizations can help resolve problems, improve science curricula, improve science instruction, provide resources for teachers, and in general serve as a place where teachers can obtain feedback on individual ideas and interests. The inexperienced teacher is well advised to participate in the activities of such organizations as they present excellent opportunities to become acquainted and associated with more experienced science teachers.

Teachers from rural districts can also organize themselves into science teacher clubs or other types of organizations for science teachers. In order to provide a suitable critical mass to be effective, teachers from a number of rural districts located in close proximity to each other can organize themselves into active professional organizations that provide the same benefits as those in urban settings.

Local science teacher organizations should be encouraged. It is through such groups that coherent and effective secondary and middle science curricula can be developed and implemented. If an organization does not exist in an area or community in which beginning science teachers are employed, it is highly recommended that one be established.

Writing for Publication

Although national and regional meetings of professional organizations provide an excellent forum for exchanging teaching ideas, such meetings are not frequent enough during the year to provide continual contact with other science teachers. It is through the publications of professional organizations, therefore, that teachers are able to communicate.

Science teachers should be encouraged to write for professional journals. This activity can help teachers to improve their ability to communicate and express ideas through their written contributions to the various publications of science teacher organizations. In addition, such contributions are the most convenient way to exchange ideas with other science teachers.

Directions for submitting manuscripts to a professional journal can generally be found in any issue of the journal. Each journal has a specific format that must be followed, including special requirements for drawings, diagrams, and number and size of photographs. If specifics regarding format are not available in the journal, they can be obtained by requesting them from the editor of the journal.

OTHER ACTIVITIES FOR PROFESSIONAL GROWTH

Communication with Other Science Teachers

One of the most valuable sources of information and inspiration for beginning science teachers is the experienced teacher. Experienced teachers can be quite helpful in selecting objectives, methods, and materials and in brainstorming problems that the beginning teacher has encountered in the classroom. A great deal of help can be obtained by asking the experienced teacher to critique and evaluate the teaching performance of the inexperienced one in an actual class situation or during a peer teaching session without students.

Even well-qualified teachers can benefit from contacts with fellow teachers, including those who do not teach science. Often teachers who are not in the field of science can help science teachers see the relationships of science to other disciplines. These contacts serve to better coordinate the various offerings that are included in the school curriculum.

Science teachers should not restrict their professional contacts to teachers within their own school. They should interact with teachers in other schools in their district and other school districts through visitations, conferences, or special meetings. Just as with professional meetings, such contacts are excellent ways to exchange teaching ideas, and discuss mutual problems. A great deal of helpful information and insight can be gained through such contacts.

Travel

Science teachers can use travel to gather much information, experience, and material that will help them improve their teaching. A camera, preferably 35 mm, can be used to take photographs for use in the classroom. Advance planning is needed to obtain the greatest benefit from travel. Tourist bureaus, chambers of commerce, and travel agencies can provide information and literature about the places to be visited. Visits within the United States provide great opportunities to collect plant and animal specimens for biology teaching. Care must be taken, however, that no laws are broken when live materials are transported from state to state. Animals and plants can be studied in their natural habitats. Visits to museums give teachers many new ideas concerning exhibits and collections. Visits to local industries and places of geological importance and general scientific interest can be enhanced by taking photographs, obtain-

A great deal of helpful information can be gained by having a trusted colleague observe and critique your teaching performance.

ing samples, and collecting descriptive literature. Science teachers will acquire a great deal of information and material for enriching their teaching without detracting from personal enjoyment of the trip.

Summer Employment

Science teachers can contribute to their professional growth through science-related summer employment. Currently, industry is becoming quite cooperative in providing summer jobs that enable teachers to gain information concerning the applications of science in industry. Employment in laboratories, for example, can be fruitful in the development of skills and understandings of research methods for use in science instruction.

Science departments in colleges and universities often offer opportunities for science teachers to work as research assistants during the summer months. Working with university professors involved in research will help further develop a science teacher's laboratory and research skills. Such skills and the attitudes developed toward research can assist teachers in stimulating students enrolled in their science courses.

Hobbies

Teachers can enrich their science courses by having hobbies that relate to their teaching areas. For example,

some science teachers are ardent entomologists or ornithologists. Some are excellent water biologists. It is not uncommon to find a chemistry teacher who is an avid bird-watcher or a biology teacher who collects rocks. Physics teachers frequently are amateur astronomers or amateur radio operators. Such hobbies not only help these teachers enrich their courses, but also stimulate students to undertake science-related projects.

Research

Science.   Some science teachers have excellent in-depth knowledge in a science area that qualifies them to do research. They may have advanced degrees in a science area or a great deal of experience in research through previous employment. Teachers with such backgrounds should be involved in their own research if time permits.

Teachers who think they do not have the space, equipment, or materials to do research should solicit the help of a nearby university. University professors will often cooperate with teachers on a research project by providing space and equipment. Teachers should not overlook this source of aid if they are at all interested in pursuing a research project.

Students who know that teachers are actively engaged in a research project may be stimulated to work on projects of their own. By reporting their findings to the students, teachers may inspire many of the students to become interested in participating in the research project.

High school teachers who publish their research in recognized journals receive recognition from their colleagues as well as their students. These teachers are often regarded as specialists and authorities in their science area. Members of the community will also recognize them as outstanding teachers and scientists. They are recognized as the teachers under whom parents would like their children to study

Education.   The image that many teachers have of research in science education is that of an instructionally disruptive activity initiated and orchestrated by college or university professors. Teachers and their students serve as research subjects, usually with little understanding of the research questions and the experimental treatments in which they are asked to participate. The findings are presented at meetings that teachers do not attend and are published in journals teachers do not read. Often these results have little impact on classroom practice. Given this image, there is little wonder that teachers say they are unwilling to participate in educational research.

The truth is that teachers engage in some aspects of educational research every day. They think about their students' learning, make plans to implement new instructional techniques, compare one instructional method to another, change lessons to make them better, and share their findings with colleagues and school administrators. This type of research differs from that too often done by college and university researchers in that the focus is on questions and problems that are of immediate concern to teachers. The systematic investigation of questions and problems related to the day-to-day activities of teachers and their students is called **action research** (Sowell & Casey, 1982). In action research the teacher is the researcher and often an active participant in the study. As an active participant the teacher is able to bring an insider's perspective to the research (Veal & Tippins, 1996). The teacher's interest and classroom situation are the deciding factors in the question or problem investigated. The primary purpose of action research is to improve classroom practice. "Within the current science education reform environment, action research is being endorsed as a means to broaden the research base, expand the knowledge base, and strengthen the impact of research" (Berlin, 1996, p. 73).

Good action research is well planned and executed. Both qualitative and quantitative research methods can be applied in action research. According to Veal and Tippins (1996, pp. 84–85), the five phases involved in implementing action research are

1. deciding what to study
2. choosing what data to collect and how and when it should be collected
3. framing and organizing the data once collected
4. analyzing the data
5. implementing the results

When initiating action research, it is important to keep in mind that the question or problem must be manageable in a day-to-day work situation and that inferences from action research are typically not generalizable beyond the classroom studied, due to the absence of the full range of controls used in experimental studies.

Teachers are most likely to engage in action research when conditions are present that facilitate it. Conditions that facilitate action research are collaboration, communication, support, and recognition (Berlin, 1996, p. 77). Collaboration may involve colleagues who teach the same classes, building or district administrators, or college and university researchers. Communication between these people must be open and respectful of the perspective that each individual brings to the community. Support for action research, according to Berlin (1996), must include time and resources. In the absence of release time and special funds for action research, teachers should rely on colleagues for assistance and make use of school equipment, such as video cameras and computers, to collect and analyze data. Teachers committed to action research will find the time and resources needed to get the job done. Finally, the efforts of teachers to improve science teaching through research should be publicly recognized by school administrators and school board members and brought to the attention of the local community.

When teachers inquire into their own practice, they grow professionally and science teaching and learning is improved (NRC, 1996). Every science teacher should be an action researcher.

Leaves of Absence

Science teachers should take advantage of leaves of absence or sabbatical leaves if these options are available to them. They can use such extended leaves to update their science teaching methods and science content, or to work with a practicing scientist at a university on a research project, obtain an advanced degree to fulfill certification requirements, or acquire a background in a science area with which they have no previous experience. Generally leaves are for a specified period of time, such as one semester, one year, or longer, with full or half pay. The time period and pay must be negotiated with the school authorities approximately a year in advance of the leave so they can take into account the financial aspects of the leave when they plan the school budget. They also need this lead time to recruit a replacement for the teacher taking the leave.

Keeping Up-to-Date through Reading

A vast amount of valuable and pertinent literature is available to science teachers to keep abreast of new developments in science, technology, and science education. Teachers should devote time each week to reading for professional growth and development. This means that science teachers should either maintain a professional library or have one available to them in the school setting. Easy access to professional literature will encourage reading. Generally, if materials are not easily available, teachers will not read on a regular basis.

Science teachers need to have a professional library of science education journals and books on science teaching methods and content available to them. Books on the history and philosophy of science and books that contain collections of demonstrations and laboratory activities and other types of science activities can be very useful when planning units and courses of study. Curriculum materials including unit plans, courses of study, and syllabi prepared by state and local education departments and other science teachers should be collected for the professional library for future reference. Professional science education journals that are read on a regular basis can keep teachers up-to-date on recent developments in science teaching methods as well as provide suggestions for teaching activities. Articles in these journals are usually written by classroom science teachers and include many activities and suggestions for teaching science that have been tried in actual classrooms.

Periodicals that focus on recent developments in science and technology, such as *Scientific American, Science Digest, National Geographic, Discover, Science,* and *The New Scientist* can keep teachers current in various areas of science and technology. Newspapers such as the *New York Times* and periodicals such as *Time* and *Newsweek* have regular features on various scientific topics. These are valuable sources of information that help enrich science lessons and science instruction in general.

Publishers are currently increasing the number of books on science-related topics. Science teachers should take the opportunity to benefit from reading such books in order to update themselves and increase their science background. College textbooks are also excellent sources of information to help enrich the science background of teachers.

College science textbooks are revised periodically to keep the information current. College textbooks used during a teacher's college preparation are likely to be outdated and should not be used as a definitive source of science information. Maintaining an up-to-date library can be a very expensive enterprise for the science teacher to undertake. If cost is a problem, the school should be asked to maintain a professional library of books and journals that are useful in enriching and updating a science teacher's background in science and science education.

EVALUATING TEACHER PERFORMANCE IN THE CLASSROOM

Continuous evaluation of a teacher's classroom performance is essential for professional growth. The evaluation should consider teachers' performance in light of the goals they have set for themselves and the goals and instructional objectives that have been identified for a course of study.

Videotapes

Videotaping a science lesson is the simplest and most direct way to determine what is actually taking place in the classroom. Teachers can then assess their performance by viewing these tapes and asking themselves a number of questions such as:

- How much of the class time do I dominate?
- Do I interact with all students?
- How do I react to an unexpected question or answer?
- How do I respond to an incorrect answer from students?
- At what cognitive level is my lesson presented?
- Are my questions thought-provoking?
- Do the answers to my questions indicate the students are thinking?
- Are students constructing ideas in a manner that will make the subject matter meaningful to them?
- Are students constructing their own knowledge because I first determine what they know and begin instruction with their ideas?

These and other questions can be answered by analyzing a videotape recording subjectively.

The following statements concern the science teacher and what is happening during science class.
Circle only one number for each statement, using the following rating scale:

1 Almost always   2 Frequently   3 Sometimes   4 Once in a while   5 Not at all

1.	The teacher is interested in students.	1	2	3	4	5
2.	The teacher knows the subject matter well.	1	2	3	4	5
3.	The teacher is enthusiastic about the subject.	1	2	3	4	5
4.	The teacher uses several types of activities during a class period.	1	2	3	4	5
5.	The teacher often uses films, slides, and filmstrips with science lessons.	1	2	3	4	5
6.	The teacher uses examples from everyday living whenever possible.	1	2	3	4	5
7.	The teacher uses familiar objects to teach science lessons.	1	2	3	4	5
8.	Lessons are well prepared and organized.	1	2	3	4	5
9.	The teacher makes the objectives of a lesson clear.	1	2	3	4	5
10.	The lessons are presented so that they are interesting.	1	2	3	4	5
11.	The teacher makes the students think.	1	2	3	4	5
12.	The teacher can explain concepts and principles so that they can be understood.	1	2	3	4	5
13.	The teacher asks good questions.	1	2	3	4	5
14.	The teacher makes good use of class participation.	1	2	3	4	5
15.	The teacher writes all scientific words on the board as they are used.	1	2	3	4	5
16.	The teacher gives the students a chance to do projects outside the classroom.	1	2	3	4	5
17.	The teacher makes good homework assignments.	1	2	3	4	5
18.	The teacher writes good, clear tests.	1	2	3	4	5
19.	The tests are fair.	1	2	3	4	5
20.	The teacher uses the tests to help the students learn.	1	2	3	4	5
21.	The teacher is available for extra help.	1	2	3	4	5
22.	The laboratory is well organized.	1	2	3	4	5
23.	The laboratory exercises are stimulating.	1	2	3	4	5
24.	The laboratory exercises make students think.	1	2	3	4	5
25.	The laboratory gives students a chance to experiment.	1	2	3	4	5
26.	The students usually give full attention to what is taking place in the science class.	1	2	3	4	5
27.	The science class is usually exciting.	1	2	3	4	5
28.	The students in the class are generally interested in what is being taught.	1	2	3	4	5
29.	The science textbook for the course is written so that I can understand it.	1	2	3	4	5
30.	The science subject is interesting.	1	2	3	4	5
31.	The teachers and students in the class get along well.	1	2	3	4	5
32.	The teacher is well liked by students in the class.	1	2	3	4	5
33.	The teacher has good discipline.	1	2	3	4	5

FIGURE 15.1   Example of a Student Questionnaire to Assess Teacher Effectiveness

Who should analyze such recordings? Self-analysis of the tape may not be the best way to obtain information, because a teacher may overlook certain personal behaviors that, if pointed out, would improve teaching performance. Using other teachers to evaluate teaching performance will solicit feedback from a different perspective. This type of feedback can very often give rise to useful suggestions, which may help improve instruction. In short, the analysis of videotapes made by one's peers may point out important observations that might otherwise have gone unnoticed.

Questionnaires

Suggestions offered up to this point for analysis of classroom behavior contain little or no structure and therefore can give only a general subjective feeling about teacher performance in the classroom. Another way of obtaining information about teacher performance in a classroom is by asking students in a class to complete a questionnaire. The questionnaire is usually prepared by a teacher, a committee of teachers, or a committee of teachers and administrators. Typical questionnaires contain statements that are positively stated and associated with a scale (e.g., from one to five) that is used to rate

skill, performance, or personality traits. The students in the class are asked to complete the questionnaire with the assurance that their grades will not be affected by the results obtained. Students who complete the questionnaire are asked to remain anonymous. A sample student questionnaire that can be used to form an instrument for a particular teaching situation is presented in Figure 15.1. Figure 15.2 is an example of an instrument that a science supervisor might use to assess the professionalism of a science teacher. This instrument can provide science teachers with a greater awareness of some of the expectations that supervisors might have for them.

Information and feedback obtained through questionnaires are very useful for professional growth as well as for improving one's teaching. This process should be conducted periodically and the data examined for trends.

MAINTAINING A RESUME

It is advisable for science teachers to maintain a current record of professional activities that can be used for a resume or a curriculum vitae. This account of professional activities should include all aspects of a teacher's

---

The following statements concern the professional behavior of a science teacher.
Circle only one number for each statement, using the following rating scale:

1 Almost always	2 Frequently	3 Sometimes	4 Once in a while			5 Not at all	

	1	2	3	4	5
1. The science teacher works well with other teachers.	1	2	3	4	5
2. The science teacher is involved with the total science program.	1	2	3	4	5
3. The science teacher works with other teachers to improve the science curriculum.	1	2	3	4	5
4. The science teacher attends professional meetings.	1	2	3	4	5
5. The science teacher helps bring the community's attention to the school's science program.	1	2	3	4	5
6. The science teacher is a member of one or more professional organizations for science teachers.	1	2	3	4	5
7. The science teacher is involved in committee work associated with science curriculum improvement.	1	2	3	4	5
8. The science teacher reads professional journals, scientific publications, and current books on science to keep up-to-date.	1	2	3	4	5
9. The science teacher keeps up-to-date with advances in science education.	1	2	3	4	5

FIGURE 15.2 Example of an Instrument Used by a Science Supervisor or Administrator to Assess the Professionalism of a Science Teacher

active career, such as college degrees earned, dates degrees received, major and minor areas of study, a list of job positions, including place of employment, dates of employment, and the duties associated with the positions. A record of participation in inservice courses and workshops should also be included along with the titles and descriptions of the workshops and inservice courses. If the teacher is continuing graduate study toward an advanced degree, it is advisable to indicate the reason for pursuing the degree and the progress that has been made toward the degree. Additional activities should be mentioned, for example, attendance and participation at professional meetings with dates attended and reason for attendance, such as the presentation of a research paper or being a member of a panel. Membership in professional organizations and a description of the nature of participation in the professional organiza-

tions should also be mentioned. A list of publications that have been written and accepted for professional journals should be included. Committee memberships in and out of school along with duties associated with memberships should also be indicated. Special honors received, such as awards by NSTA and other professional organizations, are important to mention.

The list of items to include in a resume can be expanded or limited depending on the type and amount of information needed for a particular purpose. For example, those who request resumes often want to see an evaluation of classroom teaching. It is a good idea to keep summaries of teaching performance evaluations available in case they are needed. Further, resumes should be updated on a continuous basis. Often very important activities are forgotten if a continuous record is not maintained.

■

ASSESSING AND REVIEWING

1. Join the National Science Teachers Association. This is a very useful organization for you to become a member of, and if you are a full-time student there is a special rate. The address for this organization is given in Table 15.1 and at the end of this chapter in the Resources to Examine section.

2. Obtain a recent copy of *The Science Teacher* and review the various sections to determine what is generally emphasized. Do the same for another journal specific to your area of expertise and teaching interest, such as *The American Biology Teacher, Journal of Geological Education, Science Scope*, or *The Physics Teacher*. What types of articles are emphasized in the journals you have selected? Discuss the results of your reviews with the members of your methods class.

3. Examine several science periodicals such as *Scientific American, Discover, Natural History,* or *Science News*, which are often found in public and school libraries. Determine the types of articles that are emphasized. Identify one of these periodicals to which you might subscribe.

4. Visit two schools, each in a different school district in the immediate area, to determine what inservice programs they offer for professional growth. Also

determine other ways these schools foster professional growth (e.g., paying for graduate courses or by encouraging attendance of meetings of national organizations).

5. Identify the local and statewide science teacher organizations of the state in which you reside or the state in which your college or university is located. Obtain recent copies of their journals and newsletters. Determine how active the organizations are in the state by asking experienced science teachers about them. What are the advantages of being a member of the organizations?

6. Prepare a resume or curriculum vitae including some of the items indicated in these chapters. Show the resume to the instructor or a science teacher for his or her feedback. Revise it based on the feedback.

7. Assume you are applying for a position as a middle/junior or senior high school science teacher in a school in which you would like to teach. The position has not been advertised, but you know that one is available. Draft a letter of application to the principal of the school. Indicate the qualifications you have for the position and that you have just completed student teaching. Show the letter to other educators for feedback.

■

RESOURCES TO EXAMINE

Association for Supervision and Curriculum Development. 1250 N. Pitt Street, Alexandria, VA 22314-1453. Phone: (800)933-2723.

ASCD is a well-established professional organization that provides all teachers with many publications and activities to assist them in their work. Its journal *Educational Leadership* contains many ideas on teaching, learning, and schooling. In addition, the ASCD yearbooks and updates of current issues in education are useful for beginning as well as experienced teachers.

National Science Teachers Association. 1840 Wilson Boulevard, Arlington, VA 22201-3000. Phone: (703)243-7100.

The importance of joining this organization cannot be overstressed. NSTA provides many periodicals, such as *Science and Children*, *Science Scope*, *The Science Teacher*, *Journal of College Science Teaching,* and *NSTA Reports*. These journals are filled with useful information and teaching tips. Further, the organization holds a national convention each spring that

brings together some of the most outstanding scientists, science educators, and science teachers who contribute to a fabulous program. It also holds regional conventions each fall in various parts of the United States that feature many workshops and presentations on science teaching.

Taking Note: Improving Your Observational Note-taking. 1996. By Brenda Miller, New York: Stenhouse Publishers.

This small 88-page paperback is a practical guide for busy teachers. It provides suggestions on becoming a keen observer and notetaker regarding how students learn and what takes place in schools. The author gives tips on examining existing notes, breaking old habits, and managing time and materials so that observations are possible, which helps teachers to code notes for later use in assessment and research. The book can ease science teachers into action research, assisting them to uncover some of the complexities of the teaching and learning process.

■

REFERENCES

Berlin, D. F. (1996). Action research in the science classroom: Curriculum improvement and teacher professional development. In J. Rhoton & P. Bowers (Eds.), *Issues in science education* (pp. 73–80). Arlington, VA: National Science Teachers Association.

National Research Council. (1996). *National science education standards.* Washington, DC: National Academy Press.

Showalter, V. (Ed.). 1984. *Conditions for good science teaching.* Washington, DC: National Science Teachers Association.

Sowell, E. J., & Casey, R. J. (1982). *Research methods in education.* Belmont, CA: Wadsworth.

Veal, W. R., & Tippins, D. J. (1996). Action research: Creating a context for science teaching and learning. In J. Rhoton & P. Bowers (Eds.), *Issues in science education* (pp. 81–87). Arlington, VA: National Science Teachers Association.

LITTLE SCIENCE PUZZLERS

A DROP OF WATER

A Puzzling Situation

PURPOSE

Many aspects of science involve problem solving. Scientists often attempt to figure out how nature acts as it does or how things work. Further, they must explain what they find out. Water is an interesting substance that can stimulate curiosity, provide a context to learn more about fundamental science, and engage students in problem solving. For example, if you place a drop of water on a piece of wax paper and ask the question, Does the drop of water roll or slide across the paper? you will have a puzzle that needs to be resolved and explained.

MATERIALS

a piece of wax paper (approx. 8 cm × 8 cm) for every person

water and a dropper to distribute one drop to each person

a small amount of black pepper

liquid detergent and a toothpick for each person

PROCEDURE

1. Distribute a piece of wax paper to all participants and request that they place a drop of water on the paper.

2. Instruct participants to tilt their wax paper so that the drop of water moves across it. Pose the question:

   Does the drop of water roll or slide across the paper?

   Encourage participants to work on this puzzle by themselves to find a way to support their answer to the question and to determine for certain how the drop of water moves across the paper.

3. Circulate among the participants to observe how they are examining the movement of the drop of water across the wax paper. Ask them to give a statement regarding how the water moves—rolls or slides—and to demonstrate that in fact that is the way it occurs.

   HINT: By placing a speck of black pepper or chalk dust on the drop, one can readily see that the drop is rolling.

DISCUSSION

When most or all of the participants have solved the puzzle, ask them to explain the reason why the water rolls across the wax paper. Discuss the following concepts:

- **Adhesion:** the force of attraction between unlike molecules

- **Cohesion:** the force of attraction between like molecules

In this situation, we observe the cohesive effects of water molecules permitting a drop of liquid to form and maintain a spherical shape that will roll on a surface without breaking apart.

1. What happens when you place the tip of the toothpick into the detergent and then touch it to the drop of water?

2. How do you explain what happens to the drop of water?

   HINT: The one end of the detergent molecule bonds to the water molecule and disrupts the adhesion between water molecules at the surface of the drop, causing it to break apart.

HOT IS HOT!

A Little Puzzler

The Sun is a gigantic fireball approximately ninety-three million miles from Earth. This star produces enormous amounts of heat generated by its nuclear furnace where hydrogen fuses to form helium. These nuclear reactions produce high temperatures in the core of the Sun and a spectrum of radiation that spreads out into space. Humans can detect some of the Sun's radiation in the form of white light, which makes it possible to see during the daylight hours. We can also detect its heat, especially during the summer months.

If you could extract a pinhead-sized portion of the superheated material from the Sun's core, would a person feel this heat source on Earth from a distance of one mile, ten miles, or one hundred miles?

ANSWER: At one hundred miles, the heat would be so intense that it would kill a person.*

---

*Adapted from *The Cosmic Mind-boggling Book* by N. McAleer, 1982, New York: Warner Books.

HOW STRONG IS STRONG?

A Science Puzzler

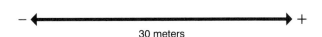

30 meters

Ask the participants to tell you what they know about the electromagnetic force. They should indicate that electromagnetism is one of the four fundamental forces that have been ascribed to nature by science. The four forces are called gravity, the weak nuclear force, the electromagnetic force, and the strong nuclear force. These ideas are used to describe the interactions that take place between the various types of matter: protons, neutrons, electrons, and so on.

Conduct a thought experiment whereby you ask the participants to visualize two bits of matter, each with a diameter of one millimeter. Imagine that you can transform all of the particles in one of these bits of matter into negative charges and all of the particles in the other bit into positive charges, as indicated in the diagram. Further, you separate the two bits of matter by a distance of thirty meters. Ask the following question:

At thirty meters will there be an attraction between the two bits of matter?

Solicit responses from many of the participants. Most individuals will say that there is a small attraction between the two bits of matter. However, they will indicate that the force of attraction is very small because of the distance. They may mention the relationship that holds for gravity and electrostatics, which says that the force of attraction is equal to a constant times the product of the masses of the two objects divided by the square of the distance between them. These are small pieces of matter and the distance of thirty meters is rather large.

The participants will be shocked when you tell them that the force of attraction between the two bits of matter, each with an opposite charge, is three million tons. Yes! Three million tons of force is pulling the bits of matter toward each other. Wow! Now do you believe that electromagnetic forces are STRONG?

THICK AND THIN LIGHT BULB FILAMENTS

A Little Science Puzzler

40 watts

75 watts

Have you ever wondered how light bulbs are constructed so that some give off more light than others?

The bulb on the left is rated at 40 watts and the one on the right is 75 watts.

Tell which bulb gives off more light and explain your answer.

ANSWER: The 75-watt light bulb produces more light. The main reason for this is the size of the filament inside the glass bulb. The 75-watt light bulb has a slightly thicker filament than the 40-watt light bulb. The larger size filament permits more electrical current to flow through it; thus it uses more energy and produces a brighter light than a lower wattage bulb. Examine the filaments inside light bulbs rated at different wattages and note the thickness of each filament.

THE EGGCITING EGG HUNT

A Puzzling Situation

CONTEXT

It was the week before Easter and Mrs. Barefoot and her five-year-old daughter, Caroline, were decorating eggs for the annual Easter egg hunt. They had just hard-boiled a dozen eggs and were preparing to boil a dozen more when the phone rang. Mrs. Barefoot went to answer the phone while Caroline stayed in the kitchen. Upon her return to the kitchen, Mrs. Barefoot saw that Caroline had mixed the hard-boiled eggs with the raw ones.

How can Mrs. Barefoot tell the difference between the hard-boiled eggs and the raw eggs?

MATERIALS

hard-boiled eggs
raw eggs

PROCEDURE

1. Spin each egg on a smooth flat surface.
2. Quickly stop each egg from spinning and then at once allow it to spin again.
3. Observe the behavior of each egg. Group the eggs into two piles based on their behavior.
4. Raw eggs spin when released, whereas hard-boiled eggs do not.

QUESTIONS & ANSWERS

How can you explain the different behavior of the raw and boiled eggs?

ANSWER: When the shell of the rotating raw egg is briefly stopped, its fluid will still be rotating.

RAISINS ON THE MOVE

A Puzzling Situation

CONTEXT

Its snack time and two friends, Jan and Mike, are enjoying their raisins and sparkling soda as they sit and talk. All of a sudden, they are bumped by a passer-by and some of Jan's raisins spill into Mike's cup of sparkling soda. Within a few minutes, they witness a strange occurrence. Raisins are moving up and down in the cup of sparkling soda. What causes the raisins to behave like this?

MATERIALS

raisins

clear plastic cup or drinking glass

sparkling soda (club soda, Sprite, or 7-Up)

PROCEDURE

1. Fill the plastic cup about two-thirds full of sparkling soda.

2. Gingerly add four to six raisins one at a time to the cup.

3. Watch the raisins and write down what you observe.

4. Come up with an explanation for the movement of the raisins.

DISCUSSION

When the raisins are first put into the cup, they sink to the bottom. While at the bottom of the cup, bubbles in the sparkling soda attach to the raisins. These are carbon dioxide bubbles. As the bubbles attach to a single raisin, they function like tiny life buoys, bringing the raisin to the surface. The carbon dioxide bubbles burst when they reach the surface, causing the raisin to sink. This process is repeated over and over until most of the carbon dioxide gas escapes from the sparkling soda and the soda becomes flat.

SCIENCE DEMONSTRATIONS

BERNOULLI'S PRINCIPLE

A Discrepant Event Science Demonstration

PURPOSE

Discrepant events create surprise and cause students to concentrate on what is taking place. Many science demonstrations present contradictions in our thinking, because they illustrate laws and principles that are not immediately understood by observation. Bernoulli's principle, which pertains to air pressure, is such an idea. Fortunately, there are many discrepant event demonstrations that can be conducted in the science classroom to help students learn about Bernoulli's principle and many other principles.

MATERIALS

two thick books of similar size and one sheet of 8$\frac{1}{2}$-by-11-inch paper (for "Blow under a Sheet of Paper")

one shoe box (or any container or bowl of similar size) and several playing cards (for "The Falling Card Trick")

a spoon and a water faucet (for "Squirting Water on the Spoon")

PROCEDURE FOR "BLOW UNDER A SHEET OF PAPER"

1. Set the two books on a table so they are approximately 5 inches apart.

2. Place one sheet of paper lengthwise so each end rests on one of the books. Center the paper between the two books (see illustration).

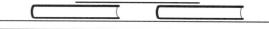

3. Ask the students to predict what they think will happen when someone blows hard between the two books and under the paper. Record their answers on the board.

4. Ask for a student volunteer to blow under the paper.

QUESTIONS & ANSWERS

1. **What happened when the air passed swiftly under the paper? Is this what you predicted?**

   ANSWER: The paper bent down toward the table. Many students will have predicted that the paper will rise up or it will be blown off the books.

2. **Why did the paper bend toward the table?**

ANSWER: When someone blows under the paper, that air is moving much faster than the air above the paper. The rapidly moving air moving across the underside of the paper produces less air pressure than the air above the paper, according to Bernoulli's principle. This action results in more air pressure above the paper, which forces the paper to bend down to the table. Bernoulli's principle states that the faster air moves across a surface, the less pressure it exerts on that surface.

3. **Predict what should happen if you hold a sheet of paper to your chin and blow across it. Why do you think so?**

ANSWER: The paper should rise. Let students try this out for themselves at their desks. The moving air on top of the paper has less air pressure than the air underneath the paper, thus the paper will lift.

PROCEDURE FOR "THE FALLING CARD TRICK"

1. Place a shoe box (or other container) on the floor directly in front of you.

2. Hold a playing card horizontally directly over the box and drop it into the box. Do not point out to the students the angle at which you release or hold the card.

3. Ask several students to come up and try to drop a card into the box.

QUESTIONS & ANSWERS

1. **Which cards fell into the box and which cards did not?**

ANSWER: The observant students should see that the cards that were initially held horizontally and dropped fell straight down into the box. The cards held vertically or at other angles drifted away from the box.

Some students might have trouble seeing this. You could make this a game where you predict whether each card dropped will fall in or not. After doing this a few times, through questioning, invite students to discover how you are holding each card as you drop it.

2. **Why do the cards that are held horizontally drop straight into the box?**

ANSWER: As the card falls, the air pressure above the card drops. Since the card is horizontal, the air pressure affects the card uniformly. This can be drawn on the board as follows:

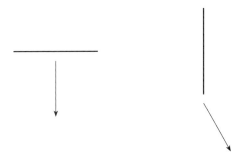

3. **Why do the cards dropped at an angle drift away?**

ANSWER: As in the example, when the card is released horizontally, the air pressure above the card decreases as it falls. However, when the card is at an angle, there is difference in air pressure around the card. The air pressure is the lightest over the lowest part of the card. The lighter pressure does not cause that end of the card to lift because it is still falling, but the lighter pressure does cause that end of the card to fall more slowly than the other end. The difference in the speed at which each end of the card falls causes it to drift away and often to tumble end over end. This too can be illustrated on the board.

PROCEDURE FOR "SQUIRTING WATER ON THE SPOON"

1. Turn on a water faucet to get a fast stream of water.

2. Loosely hold a spoon by its handle with the curved end 3 or 4 inches away from the stream of water. Ask the following question:

What will happen when I bring the curved underside of the spoon in contact with the fast-moving stream of water?

3. Let several of the students hold the spoon and feel it jump into the stream of water.

QUESTIONS & ANSWERS

1. **What caused the spoon to jump into the water?**

   ANSWER: The fast-moving water causes a decrease in the air pressure on the *bottom* of the spoon. Because the pressure on the bottom of the spoon is less than the air pressure on the top, the greater pressure pushes the spoon into the water.

2. **Can you think of examples of everyday things that demonstrate Bernoulli's principle?**

   EXAMPLE A. Airplane wing, hang gliders, and so on. The wings of an airplane are curved to form an airfoil. This shape creates an area of lighter pressure over the wing when the plane moves through the air. The greater pressure underneath forces the wing upward, creating lift for the airplane.

   EXAMPLE B. Baseball pitchers throw curve balls and drop balls by putting spin on the ball. When a great deal of spin is given to a baseball, it causes the air on one side of the ball to travel faster. This, in turn, causes a pressure change that pulls the ball to the side with the least pressure.

   EXAMPLE C. When a semitrailer rig travels down the highway, it creates an area behind its large cargo trailer that has a lower amount of air pressure than one normally experiences driving down the highway. When a vehicle travels at close proximity behind the trailer, the vehicle will be pulled along by the reduced air pressure that it experiences between it and the trailer.

   EXAMPLE D. Many internal combustion engines use a carburetor to mix air and gas together to facilitate combustion. The air traveling through the carburetor is channeled into a narrower passage, causing it to speed up. The reduced pressure in the air channels "pulls" the gas into the carburetor where it mixes with the air. Again, we observe Bernoulli's principle in effect.

THE NO-POP BALLOON

A Science Demonstration

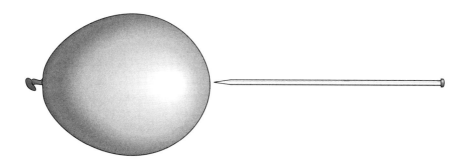

PURPOSE

You can demonstrate the property of a particular polymer by piercing a balloon with a sharp object and observing that the balloon does not pop. The rubberlike material that is used to manufacture balloons is composed of chains of carbon-based molecules. These polymers are very flexible and rather loosely structured, so a thin sharp object can slip between the sheets of polymer chains and not disrupt the material. By following the directions and with some practice you can present an attention-getting demonstration that will cause the audience to think more deeply about polymers and the wonders of man-made chemical products.

MATERIALS

several large, good quality balloons (i.e., balloons with heavy rubber walls)

a long, thin, sharp object to push into the balloon (an 8- or 10-inch length of coat hanger wire with one end sharpened or an upholstery needle)

some lubricant (cooking oil or liquid soap)

PROCEDURE

Remember, you should practice this demonstration a few times before you present it to the class.

1. Inflate the balloon to only about one-half its capacity and tie the end. You do *not* want the balloon to be filled to capacity with air so that the rubber walls are stretched tight, ready to burst at the touch of a sharp object.
2. Take the wire or needle and lubricate the sharp end that will be pushed into the end of the balloon. You want to slip the point between the polymer chains.
3. Locate the end of the balloon, opposite the tied-off end. You may notice that this region is not stretched as much as the middle area. Now gently push the needle into the balloon with a twisting motion until it penetrates far into the interior of the balloon.

QUESTIONS & ANSWERS

1. **Explain why the needle does not cause the balloon to pop or the air to rush out through the hole that the needle is making in its wall?**

   ANSWER: The needle is squeezing between the sheets of molecules that are held tightly against the needle. The air pressure in the half-filled balloon is not strong enough to disrupt this careful separation of rubber polymer.

2. **Do people bleed or feel the fine needles that are pushed into their skin when receiving acupuncture treatments?**

   ANSWER: Acupuncture is a similar process to inserting the needle into the balloon between the polymer chains. Skin is a polymer composed of protein-based tissue.

BRUISING FRUIT

A Science Demonstration

Have you ever wondered why an apple is sometimes brown on the inside when you bite into it or cut it open? If you examine the apple, in many instances you will notice that the skin has a slight indentation that indicates that the apple was hit or bruised, thus causing the meat under that area to turn brown and mushy. When an apple or other fruit is bruised, oxidative enzymes are activated that catalyze oxidation-reduction reactions. These enzymes are found in the cells of fruit. They react with oxygen to decompose the cells of the fruit, which causes the darkening of the fruit. You can retard this process and illustrate it with a demonstration* by adding a common chemical to fruit.

Vitamin C, also called ascorbic acid, is well known and is an important nutrient for humans. It is found in many citrus fruits and is used as a preservative and nutritional supplement. Vitamin C is a reducing agent. It belongs to the family of chemicals called antioxidants. As an antioxidant, vitamin C reacts with the oxidative enzymes in the fruit cell before they can destroy the fruit cell. The molecular formula for ascorbic acid is $C_6H_8O_6$.

PURPOSE

You can conduct the following demonstration to illustrate how to retard bruised fruit from browning.

---

* Adapted from "The Chemistry of Bruised Fruit" by T. Anthony, 1987, in E. L. Chiappetta (Ed.), *Ideas and Activities for Physical Science* (pp. 2-14–2-16), Houston: College of Education, University of Houston.

MATERIALS

vitamin C tablets

fruit juice

a few apples

six small beakers or cups

PROCEDURE

1. Prepare the following setup of equipment and materials to illustrate how to retard the browning of bruised fruit with the addition of vitamin C. Either place a copy of the table on a chalkboard or on an overhead transparency to summarize the results and observations (see chart below).

   Note that this is a set of experimental conditions that can be used for this demonstration. You can formulate other variables and conditions that may be even more illustrative of the ideas under study.

2. Slice an unpeeled apple (or pear) into six or more large pieces. Then bruise each piece of fruit by smashing it with your thumb. Place a bruised piece into each beaker and add the ingredients shown in the table. Then cover all of the beakers, except number 1.

3. Wait twenty-five minutes, then empty the beakers and make observations on the color of each piece of fruit.

QUESTIONS & ANSWERS

1. **How does the fruit slice in beaker 1 compare to the others?**

   ANSWER: It should be darker in color.

2. **How does the fruit slice in the fruit juice compare to that in the vitamin C solution?**

   ANSWER: It should be about the same color.

3. **How does mother nature protect her fruit from the oxidative enzymes?**

   ANSWER: Apples and pears have protective peels or skins.

4. **If you make a fruit salad, how does squirting it with lemon or lime juice help prevent browning?**

   ANSWER: Lemon and lime juice both contain vitamin C, an antioxidant that retards the chemical reactions that lead to browning of fruit.

Beaker	Observation of fruit	
	Beginning	End
1—no liquid, uncovered		
2—no liquid, covered		
3—filled with water, covered		
4—filled with boiled water, covered		
5—filled with vitamin C solution, covered		
6—filled with fruit juice, covered		

PULL IT OR YANK IT—WHAT IS THE DIFFERENCE?

A Science Demonstration

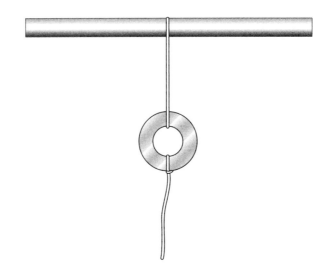

PURPOSE

Whether you pull or yank on a string that is attached to an object that you wish to move makes a big difference. In an attempt to move an object, you (the force) must overcome its **inertia**. According to Newton's first law of motion, or inertia, a body at rest tends to remain at rest and a body in motion tends to remain in motion unless acted on by a force. Certainly the mass of an object determines how easy or difficult it is to move the object or stop it if it is in motion. Here is a simple demonstration that illustrates the law of inertia.

SETUP

Obtain some light string or heavy thread for this demonstration. You need a line that can be snapped or broken by pulling on it. Get a small barbell weight (a two-and-one-half-pound weight works well). Tie the string to the weight in two places as shown in the illustration. The top end must be secured to something strong, such as the end of a desk or a broom handle.

PROCEDURE

1. Arrange the students so they are close to the apparatus and can see changes that will occur in the string.

2. Alert the students to observe the strings as you pull down slowly with an even force on the bottom string. The string will snap above the weight.

3. Alert the students to observe the strings as you yank down quickly and forcibly on the bottom string. The string will snap this time between the weight and your hand.

QUESTIONS & ANSWERS

1. **Why does a slow continuous downward force break the string *above* the weight?**

   ANSWER: When you pull down slowly the barbell weight actually moves down with this force and it adds to the stress placed on the upper string. Thus, the upper string has more force on it than the lower string and consequently it breaks first.

2. **Why does a sudden increase in the downward force break the string *below* the weight?**

   ANSWER: When you yank on the lower string, the barbell weight and the upper string are at rest and tend to remain at rest. Therefore, the lower string has to overcome both of their masses or inertia, according to Newton's first law. The lower string absorbs the full force of the downward motion of the hand.

Call on participants to repeat this demonstration to give them a feel for this inertial experience.

How Does a Weather Vane Work?

A Science Demonstration

Background

Knowledge of the direction from which winds are blowing is an important aspect of weather forecasting. In the Northern Hemisphere, winds move in a clockwise direction around centers of HIGH pressure and counterclockwise around centers of LOW pressure. Skies in a HIGH pressure area tend to be clear with generally fair weather, whereas skies in LOW pressure areas tend to be cloudy with stormy weather. By noting the direction from which the winds are blowing, the movements of HIGH and LOW pressure areas can be tracked and the next day's weather can be forecast.

Observations of wind direction can be made using a weather vane. Students are taught that a weather vane points in the direction from which the wind is blowing. This can lead to students forming a misconception about how a weather vane functions. Students tend to focus on the weather vane's pointing tip and neglect its size and shape. Which should be larger, the weather vane's tip or its tail? Does the shape of the weather vane affect its accuracy? These are the questions explored in this demonstration.

Materials

    five 3-by-5-inch index cards
    five plastic drinking straws
    five straight pins
    five pencils with erasers
    scissors
    cellophane tape
    a metric ruler
    a large fan or powerful hand-held hair dryer

Procedure

Weather Vane Construction

1. Cut one large and one small triangle out of an index card. The larger one should be about twice as large as the smaller one.

2. Cut two slits about 2 cm long at both ends of a plastic straw. Cut the slits so that the triangle index card pieces fit into the straw as shown in the illustration. Tape the index card pieces to the straw to hold them securely.

3. Find the weather vane's pivot point by balancing the straw on your index finger. Push a straight pin through the pivot point and into the eraser of a pencil. The weather vane should now spin freely on the pin and is ready to use.

4. Construct four more weather vanes that match the designs shown here. Mark the ends of each weather vane with the letters *a* and *b* as shown.

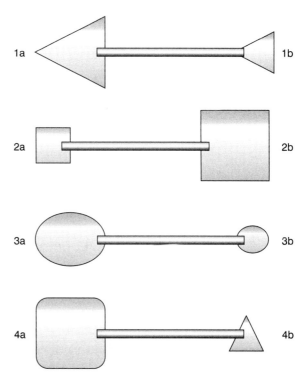

5. Copy the illustration of the four designs onto the chalkboard or prepare an overhead transparency of it.

Weather Vane Testing

6. Put the first weather vane constructed in front of a fan or hair dryer. Test it in the stream of moving air until its performance becomes predictable. Have students verify that the point of the weather vane is pointing in the direction from which the wind is blowing.

7. Show the students the other four weather vanes. Ask them to predict which of the following statements describes the performance of each in the stream of moving air. Tally the students' responses.

   - With respect to vane 1, is the wind coming from direction 1a or 1b?
   - With respect to vane 2, is the wind coming from direction 2a or 2b?
   - With respect to vane 3, is the wind coming from direction 3a or 3b?
   - With respect to vane 4, is the wind coming from direction 4a or 4b?

8. Put each of the four weather vanes one at a time in the stream of moving air and observe its performance. Compare the students' predictions with the observations for all four of the weather vane designs tested.

QUESTIONS & ANSWERS

1. **What happened when vane 1 was placed in the stream of moving air? Is this what students predicted?**

   ANSWER: End *b* pointed in the directions from which the wind is blowing. Many students will have predicted that the point of the weather vane, or end *a*, will point in the direction from which the wind is blowing.

2. **What happened when the three other weather vane designs shown in the figure were placed in the stream of moving air? Did the observations match the predictions?**

   ANSWER: For weather vane 2, the one with the squares, end *a* pointed in the direction from which the wind is blowing. For weather vanes 3 and 4, end *b* pointed in the direction from which the wind was blowing.

3. **Write a rule that fits the observations of the weather vane designs tested.**

   ANSWER: Examples of rules that fit the observations are:

   a. The small end of the weather vane points in the direction from which the wind is blowing, regardless of the shape of the tip and the tail.

   b. The point is not the critical variable; the critical variable is the surface area of the ends of the vane.

4. **Compare the rules written by the students.**

5. **Build and test a weather vane design not presented in this demonstration that fits the rule.**

MAKING A CLOUD

A Science Demonstration

BACKGROUND

Clouds form when moisture in the air condenses. But what causes the moisture in the air to condense, and what does the moisture condense on? These are questions for which too few students have answers. In this demonstration the contributions of air pressure, condensation nuclei, and moisture to the formation of clouds are examined.

MATERIALS

one clear two-liter plastic bottle with cap

water

matches

overhead projector (or other light source)

SAFETY

This demonstration requires the use of fire. Perform the demonstration away from flammable materials. Wear safety goggles.

PROCEDURE

1. Seal the bottle with its bottle cap and rest it on top of a lighted overhead projector. Direct the students to look into the bottle and not at the image projected by the overhead projector.

2. Repeatedly squeeze and release the bottle to change the pressure inside. (The air pressure inside is increased when force is applied by pressing on the outside of the bottle and decreased when the bottle is released.)

3. Add a couple of milliliters of water to the bottle, seal it again, and then repeatedly squeeze and release the bottle.

4. Put a lighted match inside the bottle and seal it. Then, repeatedly squeeze and release the bottle to change the air pressure inside.

QUESTIONS & ANSWERS

1. **What did you observe?**

   ANSWER: A cloud did not form when the empty bottle was squeezed or when it was squeezed with water inside. Only after the match was dropped inside the bottle containing water and the bottle was squeezed did the cloud form.

2. **Did the cloud form when the bottle was squeezed or when it was released? How do you explain your observation?**

   ANSWER: The cloud formed when the bottle was released. Releasing the bottle causes the air pressure inside to be reduced.

3. **Based on what you observed, what conditions are needed for a cloud to form?**

   ANSWER: Moisture, condensation nuclei, and pressure change. (In this demonstration, smoke served as the condensation nuclei. Dust particles are the most abundant condensation nuclei in the air.)

4. **Explain how a cloud might form in nature.**

   ANSWER: Water evaporating from a lake or the ocean puts water vapor or moisture into the air. Dust particles and smoke in the air provide the condensation nuclei necessary for the water to condense on. With moisture and condensation nuclei in the air, a cloud would form when air pressure is reduced, such as when air is heated and rises.

SCIENCE LABORATORY ACTIVITIES

THE COLORFUL WORLD OF ACID/BASE INDICATORS*
A Laboratory Exercise

BACKGROUND

The pH of solutions is important to their function in living systems as well as in the science laboratory. The acid and base concentrations in living tissues relate directly to the chemical reactions that take place in them, and these concentrations can mean life or death to the organism if they are not balanced. Many of the foods that we eat, especially fruits, have a certain concentration of acid in their cells that imparts just enough sourness to give them a characteristic savory taste. Acids are manufactured and used in large quantities in industry. Bases are also used in industrial processes as well as in household cleaners. How do we determine the concentration level of acid or base that is in a solution?

Fortunately, there are many acid/base indicators that give us clues as to the concentration of these important chemicals. These indicators change color according to the concentration or pH of the acid or base in the solution. Litmus paper is a common indicator. Red litmus turns blue in the presence of a base, and blue litmus turns red in the presence of an acid. There are many acid/base indicators that chemists use to determine pH, along with pH meters. You can even prepare acid/base indicators from tea, red cabbage, and flower petals.

PURPOSE

This laboratory exercise provides students with opportunities to engage in analytical procedures that center around acid/base indicators. It offers experiences with standard laboratory materials as well as some that can be found in the home. Further, the laboratory engages students in the use of many lab techniques that they should become familiar with in order to become capable inquirers.

MATERIALS

five test tubes per group
stirring rod
glass-marking pencil
50-ml graduated cylinder
test tube rack
distilled water
medicine dropper
litmus solution
phenolphthalein
Congo red solution
grape juice
tea solution

red cabbage juice

dilute hydrochloric acid

dilute sodium hydroxide

unknown solution

The science teacher should prepare a set of indicator solutions and dilute acid and base solutions for each lab group. Dropper bottles are ideal for dispensing the indicators. Eight bottles will be needed for each complete set. The solutions that you will need are listed in table C.1. You can improvise with this lab and alter it so that it is easy to prepare.

The preparation of solutions needed for this laboratory (indicators and acid and base solutions) follow.

a. *Litmus paper.* Obtain vials of red and blue litmus paper, which may be easier than finding litmus powder. In this instance, place the litmus paper in the solution to observe the color change.

b. *Phenolphthalein.* Dissolve 5 grams of powdered phenolphthalein in 250 milliliters of denatured alcohol. Add 250 milliliters of distilled water.

c. *Congo red.* Dissolve 5 grams of powdered Congo red dye in 500 milliliters of distilled water. It may be easier to find Congo red test paper.

d. *Grape juice.* Purchase bottled grape juice from the grocery store (e.g., Welch's). Dilute with an equal volume of distilled water.

e. *Tea.* Boil several tea bags in 500 milliliters of distilled water for several minutes to produce a strong tea solution.

f. *Red cabbage juice.* Chop up several red cabbage leaves and boil in 500 milliliters of distilled water until the leaves are colorless, then filter or decant the solution. This is a must as an indicator. Your students will enjoy the very vivid colors. This is also the best indicator to differentiate between the different concentrations of both acids and bases.

g. *Flower petals.* Find flowers with large petals. Grind or mash the petals and add distilled water.

h. *Dilute (2 molar) hydrochloric acid.* Mix 83 milliliters of concentrated (11.7 molar) HCl with 417 milliliters of distilled water to make one-half liter of solution. You must wear SAFETY GOGGLES to prepare acid/base solutions.

i. *Dilute (2 molar) sodium hydroxide solution.* Dissolve 40 grams of sodium hydroxide pellets in one-half liter of water.

Prelaboratory Discussion

Substances, such as litmus, that change color as the concentration of acid or base solution changes are called indicators. Litmus, phenolphthalein, and Congo red are commercially prepared indicator solutions. There are also several food extracts that change color as acidity of the solution changes. Tea, red cabbage juice, and grape juice have this property of changing color as the acidity of the solution changes.

Collect a few liquids found in the home, such as a cola beverage, lemon juice, liquid detergent, and ammonium cleaner. Illustrate their color effects with litmus paper. Give a brief explanation of pH.

Safety

Remember to exercise laboratory safety with this exercise because of the use of acids and bases. All people in the lab must wear safety goggles.

TABLE C.1   Color Reactions from Acid and Base Indicators

Indicator	Acidic solution (HCl)		Neutral solution	Basic solution (NaOH)	
	3 drops	1 drop		1 drop	3 drops
Litmus solution					
Phenolphthalein					
Congo red solution					
Grape juice					
Tea					
Red cabbage juice					
Flower petals					

PROCEDURE

1. Number five test tubes from 1 to 5 with a glass-marking pencil.

2. Place the five test tubes in numerical order in a test tube rack. Add 10 milliliters of distilled water to each of the five test tubes.

3. Add the acids and bases to the test tubes as follows. Stir after each addition.

    Test tube 1: Add three drops of dilute hydrochloric acid.

    Test tube 2: Add one drop of dilute hydrochloric acid.

    Test tube 3: Do not add anything. This is the control tube, because water is usually neutral—neither acidic nor basic.

    Test tube 4: Add one drop of dilute sodium hydroxide.

    Test tube 5: Add three drops of dilute sodium hydroxide.

4. Compare the five test tubes with each other and record on your data table the color of the liquid in each tube. You will use the same data table for all procedures in this lab.

5. Take a drop or two of liquid from each test tube and place the drops on the litmus paper. Note the color or color change and record it on the data table.

6. Discard the solutions in each test tube and rinse each tube.

7. Repeat steps 1–6 using three drops of phenolphthalein instead of litmus in each test tube. Add the acids and bases to each tube exactly as instructed above.

8. Record the color of the solution in each test tube on your data table.

9. Discard the solutions, rinse the test tubes, and repeat steps 1–6 using three drops of Congo red indicator or Congo red test paper.

10. With the tea, grape juice, and red cabbage juice, you may need to adjust their quantities, using a great deal or only a little so that you can readily see the color changes.

POSTLABORATORY DISCUSSION

Call on one group to place their data table and results on the board. Ask the participants to discuss the color reactions and their significance.

- Which indicators give a clear indication of pH?

- How does the pH of a solution affect the color of an indicator?

- Other than chemists and scientists, are there ordinary people who use pH indicators or other indicators in their everyday life?

THE DIFFUSION OF MOLECULES AND IONS

A Laboratory Exercise

PURPOSE

Diffusion is a fundamental principle that is present in our everyday world. It is the tendency of molecules or ions to move from areas of higher concentration to areas of lower concentration until the concentration is uniform throughout the system. Diffusion explains how gases in the air spread out when released from one location where the concentration of their molecules is higher than in the space surrounding their source. Diffusion also explains how ions and molecules in solutions spread out through the liquid in a container or how nutrients move across a cell membrane.

MATERIALS

bottle of perfume, cologne, or other odorous liquid

cornstarch solution (rather dilute solution)

Lugol's iodine solution

plastic sandwich bags (fold-over type, not zipper type), one for each group

beakers or large cups, one for each lab group

DEMONSTRATION

Take a bottle of any perfume or liquid that students will be able to smell when you remove the cap and pour some on a cotton ball. Ask participants the following questions:

1. How long did it take to detect the odor of the liquid once it was exposed to the air in the room?

2. How did the vapors of the liquid get from the cotton ball or the open container to your nose? How do the molecules of the liquid travel from the source to your nose, in a straight line or zigzag path or some other type of motion? Require the participants to draw a diagram of the phenomenon.

In the discussion that follows these questions, bring up the term **diffusion,** explain it, and list many situations in which diffusion occurs in everyday life.

PROCEDURE

Organize participants into lab groups in order for them to carry out the diffusion exercise whereby iodide ions move through a plastic membrane.

1. Pour about 50 milliliters of cornstarch solution in each plastic sandwich bag and tie the top with a rubber band or string.

2. Place the bag of cornstarch solution into a beaker half full of iodine solution (Lugol's solution).

3. It will take about fifteen to twenty minutes before you begin to see the cornstarch turn blue-black. If you wait one day, the reaction takes place to a greater extent and the color is more dramatic.

4. Ask the participants to devise tests to determine if other substances besides the ingredients that make up the iodine solution diffuse through the walls of the plastic sandwich bag.

QUESTIONS & ANSWERS

1. **What does the color change inside the bag signify?**

   ANSWER: A chemical passed through the walls of the plastic bag into the starch solution. The chemical was iodine. The iodide ions were small enough to pass through spaces in the plastic and interact with the starch, giving the characteristic blue-black color that shows the presence of starch.

2. **Were the water molecules able to diffuse through the plastic bag into the starch solution?**

   ANSWER: The water molecules are probably too large to diffuse through the plastic membrane.

OSMOSIS AND A CHICKEN EGG
A Laboratory Exercise

BACKGROUND

Life is maintained by an intricate balance of substances passing into and out of a cell through a membrane. Water, glucose, amino acids, carbon dioxide, and many other chemical elements and compounds pass through cellular membranes to maintain the proper nutrition that a cell must have in order to function. This dynamic process is partly explained by diffusion, which is the spreading of molecules from an area of greater concentration to an area of lower concentration. A type of diffusion associated with water is called osmosis. Osmosis is the diffusion of water through a selectively permeable membrane from an area of greater concentration to an area of lesser concentration. Osmosis is an essential process that takes place in all cells with water molecules moving through the cell membrane.

PURPOSE

This activity illustrates osmosis taking place through the membrane of a chicken egg. A chicken egg is ideal for this exercise because it is large and has a cell membrane that becomes visible when you remove the shell in a particular manner. Although you may not have noticed, there is a membrane between the shell and the yolk/white part of the egg. If you remove the shell of an egg, the membrane can be observed surrounding the liquid material on the inside. With only the membrane to keep an egg intact, the effects of osmosis can be observed when the egg is placed in water where the concentration of water is greater on the outside of the egg than on the inside.

PROCEDURE

This exercise takes approximately three days and can be conducted as a take-home laboratory exercise. During the first twenty-four-hour period, the shell of one egg is removed by placing it in vinegar, which dissolves the calcified shell.

1. Each participant should obtain two eggs of the same size and place each egg in a separate cup. In the first cup, pour in enough water to cover the egg. In the second cup, pour in enough white vinegar to cover the egg. The liquid level in both cups should be at least three centimeters above the egg. Let stand for twenty-four hours.

2. On the second day, make and record observations on both eggs. Remove the vinegar in the second cup and rinse the egg—carefully. Then pour in enough water to cover the membrane-exposed egg so that the water level is three centimeters above the egg. Leave for another day.

3. Make observations of the intact egg in the first cup with water and the egg with the shell removed in the second cup with water. What are the similarities and differences between the two eggs?

CONCLUSION

Write a few paragraphs describing what took place in this experiment and the science behind the events.

RADIOACTIVE HALF-LIFE

A Laboratory Simulation Exercise

PURPOSE

The purpose of this laboratory simulation is to illustrate some concepts related to radioactive half-life. Radioactivity is an important process that occurs all the time in nature. It is occurring among some of the elements in our bodies every second of our life. The laws of chance are also illustrated in this simulation401
 because radioactive decay is a random process similar to tossing a coin. This exercise is designed to review important background information that is necessary to understanding radioactivity and the atom.

MATERIALS

shallow square cardboard boxes with covers (approximately 5-by-5 inches), one for every two students. You can make square boxes from rectan-

gular ones by cutting off the long dimension and restoring the sides with tape.

unpopped popcorn, approximately one pound

felt-tip pens

graph paper, one sheet for every two students

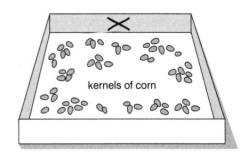

kernels of corn

Students will work in pairs. Each pair will be given one box, and 100 pieces of corn will be placed into each box. You can facilitate the preparation of this lab by asking a few students to help you count out the 100 pieces of corn for each box. A simple way to do this is to arrange the corn in rows and columns of ten, producing a ten-by-ten matrix, making it easy to see when you have 100 pieces of corn.

The boxes can be obtained at department stores, gift stores, or box stores. Mark an X on one of the inside walls of the box. Place a rubber band around each box to secure the cover so the corn does not spill.

PRELABORATORY DISCUSSION

Review some basic concepts related to radioactive decay with students by asking:

What happens when a radioactive element decays?

ANSWER: The nucleus of the element gives off rays or particles. In some instances this release of matter and energy changes the mass of the element by reducing the number of protons and neutrons in the nucleus, thus forming a new element with a lower atomic mass (equation A). In other instances it results in the transformation of a neutron into a proton, thereby increasing the atomic number by one (equation B) while maintaining the same atomic mass.

A. $^{226}_{88}\text{Ra} \rightarrow {}^{222}_{86}\text{Rn} + {}^{4}_{2}\text{He}$
      radium   radon   alpha particle

B. $^{210}_{83}\text{Bi} \rightarrow {}^{210}_{84}\text{Po} + {}^{0}_{-1}\text{e}$
      bismuth   polonium beta particle

When a neutron transforms, it forms a proton and an electron (or a beta particle). Yes, it is strange to have a situation where energy and matter are given off, yet you end up with an element that has a greater atomic number—another unusual facet of nature.

Why are some elements unstable and decay?

ANSWER: When elements have too many particles or neutrons versus protons in their nucleus, they have an abundance of energy in their nucleus. This excess energy causes the atom to be unstable and give up energy in the form of particles so that it can stabilize. Remember, everything in nature wants to become stable.

How can you tell if a substance is radioactive?

ANSWER: Radioactive substances give off particles, rays, or energy that can be detected and measured accurately.

What is half-life?

ANSWER: Since a radioactive isotope is constantly changing into something else, a very useful question is, How long will the isotope last before all the atoms in it have changed to something else? Half-life is the time it takes for one-half of the radioactivity to be given up. One way to tell how many atoms of a radioactive isotope are left is to use an instrument, such as a Geiger counter, that measures radioactivity by measuring the number of alpha, beta, or gamma rays emitted. Generally, the less radioactive material there is, the weaker the radioactivity will be.

Why do radioactive substances behave this way?

ANSWER: Whether an atom is going to decay or not in the next second is a matter of chance. It might decay now, or it might not decay for another million years. As with flipping a coin, there are only two possible outcomes, the atom either decays or it doesn't. The chances that an atom will decay in the next second are a lot greater with an isotope that has a short half-life than one with a long half-life.

How can you illustrate a fifty-fifty chance occurrence?

ANSWER: Flip a coin many times, each time recording whether a head or tail appears. What is the chance of getting a head or a tail? If you flip the coin only ten times what do you get? Flip the coin thirty or forty times and you will find that the fifty-fifty probability becomes more apparent. Radioactive decay is a similar process.

Tell the students that they are going to perform a half-life laboratory activity using kernels of corn. Each box has 100 kernels of corn. Go over the following procedure before you permit students to begin the activity.

PROCEDURE

1. Pass out the boxes, each containing 100 kernels of corn. Note that each kernel of corn has a pointed end. When the corn is in the box, the pointed end will point to one of the four sides of the box. What are the chances of a particular kernel pointing to the side marked X? (Answer: one in four).

2. With the cover securely on the box, shake it five or six times. Place the box on the table and remove the cover.

3. Remove the kernels that are pointing to the side with the X. Remember the kernels can be pointing to any part of the side with the X, not just directly at the X itself. If some of the kernels are pointing

exactly at the X-side's corners, take one-half of those out. Do not put any of the kernels back into the box.

4. Record the number of kernels taken out and the number left. Repeat this activity for ten trials.

Data table of half-life graph

Trial	Started with	Took out	Number left
1	100		
2			
3			
4			
5			
6			
7			
8			
9			
10			

5. After the ten trials, graph the results: number of kernels remaining versus trials. Ask the students to label axes of the graph; they need practice in this skill. Connect the points with a smooth line rather than using a ruler.

6. Use the figures from the class totals to construct a composite graph on the chalkboard from everyone's results.

POSTLABORATORY DISCUSSION

1. Call on many groups of students to hold up their half-life graphs and compare the curves. Discuss the variation in the graphs. Point out that this is not due to students' errors, but to the fact that the smaller the sample, the greater the variation. Note that the composite curve produced from everyone's results is generally smoother because the number of trials is greater on this curve than on any individual group's curve. In an experiment measuring the radioactivity

of actual materials, the curve would be very smooth because the sample of material would contain millions of atoms.

2. **Ask why a curved line was obtained instead of a straight line.**

ANSWER: When you take one-half of a quantity, you get something even though it may be very small. In other words, you do not just end up with nothing quickly.

3. **Define half life.**

ANSWER: Half-life is the time it takes for one-half of the radioactive atoms to disintegrate.

4. **During radioactive decay, when does an element decrease its atomic number? Increase it?**

ANSWER: When the nucleus of an element gives up an alpha particle, it loses four atomic mass units—two protons and two neutrons—and forms a lighter element. When one of the neutrons transforms into a proton and a beta particle, it forms a new element with a larger atomic number. (See the examples given earlier.)

5. **What is the significance of a long half-life versus a short half-life?**

ANSWER: An element with a long half-life gives off matter/energy slowly; therefore, its radioactivity is not very intense. Consequently, it is generally not very dangerous but will be around a long time as a radioactive element. An element with a short half-life gives off matter/energy very quickly; therefore, its radioactivity is intense. It will not be around as long, but it may be very dangerous because of the rate at which it gives off radioactivity.

6. **How many trials did it take to use up half the kernels?**

ANSWER: Usually two or three.

7. **How many trials did it take to use up half of the fifty kernels that were left?**

ANSWER: Usually four or five.

RESPIRATION IN YEAST

A Laboratory Exercise

BACKGROUND

Yeasts are single-celled fungi that form chains of cells. They belong to the class of fungi called Hemias-

comycetes, which contains more than thirty thousand species. The energy-releasing process that enables yeasts to live, grow, and reproduce is called cellular respiration. A principle source of energy used to carry on respiration is sugar ($C_6H_{12}O_6$), which may be derived from other multicarbon compounds.

Yeasts of the genus *Saccharomyces* are used to make alcohol in the production of cider, beer, and wine. Alcohol and carbon dioxide are produced when the yeast is grown in vats that contain little or no oxygen. Respiration under these conditions is called fermentation. A different strain of *Saccharomyces* is used in bread making. Here, the process is the same, but yields different results. As the sugar in the bread dough is used by the yeast cells, carbon dioxide is released, which makes the dough rise. Heat from the oven drives out the carbon dioxide gas and evaporates the alcohol, leaving the fluffy textured bread.

The equation for fermentation (anaerobic respiration) in yeast is

$$C_6H_{12}O_6 \longrightarrow 2C_2H_5OH + 2CO_2 + 2\sim P$$
$$\text{(2 phosphate groups)}$$

PURPOSE

In the experiment that follows, yeast will be grown in the presence of little oxygen. The purpose of the experiment is to determine the effect of different amounts of sugar on yeast respiration rate.

MATERIALS

six 250-milliliter clear glass or plastic bottles
six 200-milliliter clear glass or plastic cups
six pieces of aquarium hose, each about 30 cm long
two 6-ounce containers or bars of modeling clay
100 grams of table sugar
two packages of dry baker's yeast
600 milliliters of warm distilled water
$\frac{1}{2}$ and 1 teaspoon size measuring spoons
six graduated cylinders
50 milliliters Bromthymol blue (BTB) (*Caution:* BTB will stain clothes and skin.)

PROCEDURE

1. Write the question, What is the effect of different amounts of sugar on the respiration rate of yeast? on the chalkboard.

2. Have students construct hypotheses related to the question before beginning the investigation. Ask them to provide reasons for their hypotheses. Proceed with the investigation once two or three hypotheses have been generated and discussed. An example hypothesis is: As the amount of sugar is increased, the rate of respiration will decrease.

Assembling the Experimental Apparatus

3. Label the 250-milliliter bottles 1, 2, 3, 4, 5, or 6 to correspond with the treatment condition to which your group has been assigned. (Treatment groups are specified in the accompanying table. All treatment conditions should be represented in the class.)

4. Assemble the stopper apparatus for your bottle by rolling clay around the aquarium hose.

5. Pour 100 milliliters of warm distilled water into your bottle.

6. Add table sugar to your bottle in the amount indicated in the table. (5 grams = approximately 1 teaspoon)

7. Add 2 grams of yeast to your bottle. (2 grams = approximately $\frac{1}{2}$ teaspoon)

8. Using the stopper apparatus, seal the top of your bottle. Make sure that the tubing is *not* touching the sugar solution.

9. Place the other end of the tubing in a cup of tap water to which two to three drops of BTB has been added.

10. Swirl the sugar and yeast solution in the bottle, then allow the experimental apparatus (shown here) to set for ten minutes.

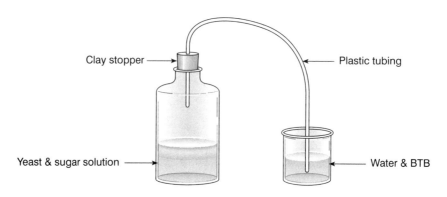

Clay stopper →   ← Plastic tubing

Yeast & sugar solution →   ← Water & BTB

Data Collection

11. Count the number of bubbles released into your cup of water in five minutes. (All groups should start and stop counting bubbles at the same time.)

12. Then calculate the number of bubbles released per minute from the bottle by dividing the number of bubbles that you counted by five.

13. Copy the table and graph (as illustrated) onto a sheet of paper.

14. Record the number of bubbles per minute released from your group's bottle and the bottles of other groups in the appropriate spaces in the table.

15. Complete the graph using your class data.

Table

Bottle	Amount of Sugar	Number of Bubbles per Minute
1	0 g	
3	5 g	
3	10 g	
4	15 g	
5	20 g	
6	25 g	

Graph

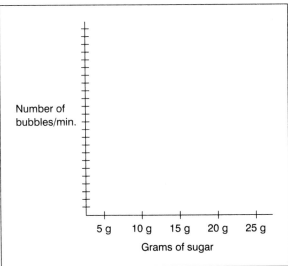

Number of bubbles/min.

5 g   10 g   15 g   20 g   25 g

Grams of sugar

QUESTIONS & ANSWERS

1. **What evidence do you have that a gas is produced in the bottles?**

   ANSWER: Bubbles are released into the cup of water.

2. **What is the gas being released from the bottles? What evidence supports your assumption?**

   ANSWER: The gas being released must be carbon dioxide because the BTB in the cup turned green or yellow, indicating that the water has become more acidic.

3. **How does the amount of sugar affect the amount of gas produced?**

   ANSWER: Answers will vary depending on results. The typical results show that more gas is produced when more sugar is added. A limit to the number of bubbles produced per minute is eventually seen when amounts in excess of 25 grams of sugar are added to the experimental apparatus. When the available sugar exceeds that which can be metabolized by the yeast in a fixed period of time, a leveling off of the respiration rate is seen.

4. **Do the results of the experiment support your hypothesis?**

   ANSWER: Answers will vary.

5. **What are the manipulated (independent) and responding (dependent) variables in this experiment? What variables were controlled?**

   ANSWER: Amount of sugar is the manipulated variable. Number of bubbles is the responding variable. Variables controlled include amount and temperature of water in the bottle, amount of yeast added to the bottle, and length of time bubbles were counted.

EXTENSIONS

1. Use the graph of class data to estimate the number of bubbles released per minute when 30 grams and 12 grams of sugar are added to the experimental apparatus. Check your estimates by repeating the experiment using these amounts of sugar.

   NOTE: Estimates beyond the range of available data are called **extrapolations** and estimates within the range of data are called **interpolations**.

2. Determine the approximate amount of sugar in grape or apple juice. Substitute 100 milliliters of juice for the sugar solution. After adding yeast and letting the apparatus set for ten minutes, count the bubbles for five minutes and then calculate the average bubble count per minute. Using the graph prepared from class data, estimate the amount of sugar in the juice.

MASS AND VOLUME RELATIONSHIPS

An Inductive Laboratory Exercise

BACKGROUND

Students learn some science concepts better by discovery than by being told about them. Density is one of those concepts. Density is the amount of matter in a given space and can be expressed as mass per unit volume. Regardless of the size of the samples, as long as they are composed of the same material, then their density will be the same.

In this laboratory students determine the mass and volume of rubber stoppers of different sizes. By graphing the mass and volume relationship for each stopper and calculating the slope of the resulting line, students discover, often for the first time, the meaning of a concept that they have worked with since middle school.

MATERIALS

five solid rubber stoppers of different sizes (*must be the same type*) per group

two or three graduated cylinders per group sized to contain the different stoppers

one balance per group

graph paper

tap water

PROCEDURES

1. Tell students that the purpose of the lab is to determine the relationship between mass and volume experimentally.

2. Instruct students to copy the table illustrated here onto a separate sheet of paper.

3. Give five different rubber stoppers to each group. Instruct the groups to determine the mass and volume of each stopper and then record their data in the table. (Mass may be determined using the balance and volume by the displacement method.)

4. Next instruct them to construct a graph like the one shown here on a sheet of graph paper, making sure that the scales on the *x* and *y* axes are appropriate for their data.

5. Then instruct students to plot their mass and volume data for each stopper on the graph and draw a **line of best fit** through the data points.

Table

Stopper No	Mass of Stopper	Volume of Stopper

Graph

QUESTIONS & ANSWERS

1. **Describe the relationship between mass and volume shown on your graph.**

    ANSWER: Answers will vary, but indicate that as mass increases, volume also increases.

2. **Calculate the slope of the line on your graph using two points on your line of best fit. Then calculate the slope a second and a third time using different combinations of points on your line of best fit. [Slope $= \Delta y/\Delta x$, or $(y_2 - y_1)/(x_2 - x_1)$]**

Answer: The slope of the line should be greater than 1 and all three calculations of slope should be the same, or nearly so.

3. **What science concept (physical property) does the slope represent? You may wish to consult your physical science, earth science, or chemistry text for help in answering this question.**

Hint: You are looking for something that shows the relationship between mass and volume.

Answer: Density.

4. **How do the data collected in this laboratory verify the definition of this concept?**

Answer: The data show that the density of the rubber stoppers is the same regardless of the size of the stopper.

INDEX